Primary Genreflecting

Genreflecting Advisory Series

Diana Tixier Herald, Series Editor

Encountering Enchantment: A Guide to Speculative Fiction for Teens
  Susan Fichtelberg

Fluent in Fantasy: The Next Generation
  Diana Tixier Herald and Bonnie Kunzel

Gay, Lesbian, Bisexual, and Transgendered Literature: A Genre Guide
  Ellen Bosman and John Bradford; Edited by Robert B. Ridinger

Reality Rules!: A Guide to Teen Nonfiction Reading Interests
  Elizabeth Fraser

Historical Fiction II: A Guide to the Genre
  Sarah L. Johnson

Hooked on Horror III
  Anthony J. Fonseca and June Michele Pulliam

Caught Up in Crime: A Reader's Guide to Crime Fiction and Nonfiction
  Gary Warren Niebuhr

Latino Literature: A Guide to Reading Interests
  Edited by Sara E. Martinez

Teen Chick Lit: A Guide to Reading Interests
  Christine Meloni

Now Read This III: A Guide to Mainstream Fiction
  Nancy Pearl and Sarah Statz Cords

Gay, Lesbian, Bisexual, Transgender and Questioning Teen Literature: A Guide to Reading Interests
  Carlisle K. Webber

This Is My Life: A Guide to Realistic Fiction for Teens
  Rachel L. Wadham

Primary Genreflecting

A Guide to Picture Books and Easy Readers

Susan Fichtelberg and Bridget Dealy Volz

Genreflecting Advisory Series
Diana Tixier Herald, Series Editor

LIBRARIES UNLIMITED

AN IMPRINT OF ABC-CLIO, LLC
Santa Barbara, California • Denver, Colorado • Oxford, England

WAUKESHA PUBLIC LIBRARY

IWPL0010411494

Copyright 2010 by ABC-CLIO, LLC

All rights reserved. No part of this publication may be reproduced, stored in a retrieval system, or transmitted, in any form or by any means, electronic, mechanical, photocopying, recording, or otherwise, except for the inclusion of brief quotations in a review, without prior permission in writing from the publisher.

Library of Congress Cataloging-in-Publication Data

Fichtelberg, Susan.
   Primary genreflecting : a guide to picture books and easy readers / Susan Fichtelberg
and Bridget Dealy Volz.
    p. cm. — (Genreflecting advisory series)
  Includes bibliographical references and index.
  ISBN 978-1-56308-907-7 (alk. paper)
1. Picture books for children—United States—Bibliography. 2. Children's literature,
American—Bibliography. 3. Children's literature, American—Stories, plots, etc. 4. Readers'
advisory services—United States. I. Volz, Bridget Dealy. II. Title.
Z1033.P52F53 2010
011.62—dc22   2010036578

ISBN: 978-1-56308-907-7

14 13 12 11 10   1 2 3 4 5

This book is also available on the World Wide Web as an eBook.
Visit www.abc-clio.com for details.

Libraries Unlimited
An Imprint of ABC-CLIO, LLC

ABC-CLIO, LLC
130 Cremona Drive, P.O. Box 1911
Santa Barbara, California 93116-1911

This book is printed on acid-free paper ∞
Manufactured in the United States of America

For Miriam, who befriended a nine-year-old girl and is still her friend today. SF

To my wonderful family: Barbara Dealy, Katy Dealy, Tony Gottlieb, and Aaron Gottlieb; and my dear friend, Mary Phillips. I want to thank you for making this possible. BDV

Contents

Preface

Bridget Dealy Volz

This is it! This is the most exciting time of children's early years, when knowledge is coming to them from every angle, almost crashing in upon them, and there they are, looking so innocent and peaceful while they're actually working overtime, absorbing information. As parents, caregivers, educators, and librarians, the best part about this time is that we get to be there. We are the lucky ones who get to be involved in this miracle. We get to watch them grow. We get to be part of their lives as they experience everything for the very first time, and we get to see them become separate individuals with their own thoughts and ideas. Though it's never too early to start reading to children, when the time is right, children begin to develop their own preferences in the kinds of stories and books they want to listen to and then read on their own. When this happens, and when children are figuring out the way things work and what their place in the world is, this book is filled with titles to read to them, or titles they can read themselves that just might have what they are looking for. They may want to hear a funny story, or you might be looking for a new bedtime story for them. When they're a little older, they might want to know if there are any Angelina Ballerina stories that they might have missed, or if there's a book out there where other kids are going to school. That's where this book comes in. *Primary Genreflecting* can be a lifesaver for adults when their young ones want to hear just one more story, about topics ranging from bedtime and birthdays to school and even the larger world around them.

This book was a delight for me to work on, even though I wanted to include "just one more title." Of course, there are other books that could be included under each genre and subject; this is merely a suggestion of all the wonderful titles that are available. There are so many books that give children imaginative adventures, a greater understanding of their world and the world around them, and a time to laugh and have fun. These are the children who will ask questions and want to learn more, and that is because you are presenting them with a smorgasbord of ideas in their early reading.

Good luck with all the excitement that lies ahead.

Acknowledgments

We would like to thank Barbara Ittner, our editor extraordinaire, who consistently showed an amazing amount of patience, and who guided us through this process with keen observations and great understanding.

Susan would like to thank the children's department of the Woodbridge Public library for all of their support, as well as Mary Pritting, a children's librarian, an assistant director, and a friend, who gave sound advice about organization and items of interest to librarians working with children. She also gave unparalleled assistance in checking titles.

Introduction

Childhood is the perfect time to forge a lifelong connection between young people and books. No child is too young to listen to stories. Even before children can comprehend the meaning of the story, listening is how they learn to speak, develop vocabulary, and share a time of bonding with a caring adult or older sibling. As they grow up and are read to on a regular basis, the wonder of words opening myriad worlds begins. In books children can meet other boys and girls going though the same things they are, such as losing a favorite toy or starting school, and they can encounter imaginative journeys that whisk them away to realms of mystery or magic. Books can teach them their ABCs and 123s, and they can introduce them to characters that have entertained generations, like Cinderella and Rumpelstiltskin. As they become more experienced with books, they will begin to develop their own tastes and preferences. They may want to hear a funny story, an adventure tale, or a book starring cats or dogs. *Primary Genreflecting* is designed to help librarians, teachers, parents, and caregivers find just the right books for their young listeners and readers by clustering together books with certain commonalities. Some of these commonalities are standard genres, such as fantasy or historical fiction, but others are unique to the picture book world, like concept books. All the categories included are grouped in ways that will help adults find the books that are just right.

Purpose and Audience

The purpose of *Primary Genreflecting* is threefold. First is to aid in readers' advisory services. By organizing picture books and easy readers by subject and/or genre, this volume provides a resource for adults who wish to read to children or recommend books to them or their caregivers. Adults working with and caring for children will have easy access to high-quality books. Second, *Primary Genreflecting* presents a way to introduce children, ages three to eight, to a variety of books, to see if they might have a strong interest in a particular genre. Then if children just want to hear some funny stories, or if they want to read about other children who are going to school or making new friends, they'll be able to find books on that specific subject. All titles are annotated, except those in an extensive series, in which case there is a series annotation. In series entries, titles are listed in chronological order by the date they were published, so the reader can follow the story arc that the episodes create.

The third purpose of this volume is to assist in collection development. Librarians will have the opportunity to build up specific areas of their collections, teachers will have suggestions for classroom libraries that can supplement the curriculum, and parents will have a resource that recommends books they might like to include in their home libraries.

The audience for *Primary Genreflecting* is librarians (public and school), teachers, parents, grandparents, adults working in homeschooling environments, day-care providers, and anyone who might wish to share a wealth of literature with young audiences.

Books Included

The books that are included fit the appropriate subject; have been positively reviewed in professional journals such as *School Library Journal*, *Kirkus*, and *Horn Book*; and have been deemed important according to the authors' professional judgment. Many are award-winning books, but not every worthwhile book wins an honor. Books that are popular, fun, and likely to stimulate interest in a particular subject or genre are present as well. This volume is not an exhaustive list of all picture books and easy readers published between 1999 and 2009, or even of all recommended picture books and easy readers. Rather, it is a selection of titles published over the past ten years (with some classics and 2010 titles added in) that just might encourage readers to look for more books in that category or genre. Readers might even find they like a genre that they were never interested in before. If a particular book is part of a series, the entire series is included, even if some of the books were published before 1999. If a book is a companion or sequel to another, both books are listed. Out-of-print books are included if they are part of an ongoing series in which the newest books are in print. Books released as original paperback series are not included.

If a book has received an award, it is marked with this symbol 🎗. The following awards are represented:

Amelia Frances Howard Gibbon Illustrator's Medal, given by the Canadian Association of Children's Librarians, a division of the Canadian Library Association

ALA Notable Books for Children (ALAN), given by the Association for Library Service to Children (ALSC), a division of the American Library Association (ALA)

The Boston Globe Award and Honors, given by *The Boston Globe* and *Horn Book Magazine*

Caldecott Medal and Honors, given by ALSC

The Coretta Scott King Award and Honors, given by the Social Responsibilities Round Table of ALA

The Charlotte Zolotow Award and Honors, given by the Cooperative Children's Book Center

The Ethel Turner Prize, given by the New South Wales Ministry for the Arts, Australia

The Golden Kite Award and Honors, given by the Society of Children's Book Writers and Illustrators

The Governor General's Literary Award, given by the Canada Council

The Jane Addams Book Award and Honors, given by the Women's International League for Peace and Freedom and the Jane Addams Peace Association

The Kate Greenaway Medal, given by the Youth Libraries Group of the British Library Association

New York Times Best Illustrated, given by *The New York Times*

Pura Belpre Award and Honors, given by ALSC and the National Association to Promote Library Services to the Spanish Speaking

The Sydney Taylor Award, given by the Association of Jewish Libraries

The Theodore Seuss Geisel Award, given by ALSC

All titles listed below an author's name are in publication date order. Full bibliographic information is provided for each title. Where no illustrator is given, the author is also the illustrator. The thirteen-digit ISBN that is listed refers to the hardcover edition unless stated otherwise. Library editions and paperbacks are only listed if there are no hardcover editions available at the time of compiling. Books go in and out of print quickly, so availability should be confirmed with a bookseller. If there aren't any page numbers in a book, which often happens in picture books, the word "unpaged" is used instead of the number of pages.

Easy reader sections are included when there are quality easy readers available in the subject. They are grouped together rather than being interfiled, because searching for books that are for children who are just learning to read or are practicing their reading skills is different than searching for a book to read aloud. Picture books are written for adults to read to children. They often have an adult vocabulary, because children can understand many more words than they can read, especially when they are first learning how to read. In other words, their listening vocabulary is greater than their reading vocabulary. Easy readers, on the other hand, are specifically written for children who are learning to read. They have simple words and phrases that are often repeated. The sentence structures are simple, and they deliberately use a limited vocabulary. A picture book for grades 1–3 is very different from an easy reader for grades 1–3. A first to third grader may enjoy listening to the picture book, but will be able to read the easy reader. Because the majority of holiday easy readers are part of long-running series, there is no easy reader section in chapter 6. Curriculum-related, leveled readers are not included.

Grade levels are taken from published reviews and are given at the end of the bibliographic information. They represent a range of possible interest and ability. Children can read above grade level when they have a keen interest in a subject. Grade level codes used are the following:

T-K toddler to kindergartener, ages 2–5

PreS-K preschooler to kindergartener, ages 3–5

PreS-1 preschooler to first grader, ages 3–6

PreS-2 preschooler to second grader, ages 3–7

PreS-3 preschooler to third grader, ages 3–8

Gr. K–2 kindergartener to second grader, ages 5–7

Gr. K–3 kindergartener to third grader, ages 5–8

Gr. 1–3 first grader to third grader, ages 6–8

Gr. 2 & up second grader and up, ages 7 and up

Gr. 3 & up third grader and up, ages 8 and up

All picture books are meant to be read aloud, but some work better as lap-sit books, and some are great for group sharing. **Titles the authors thought were especially good for storytimes are marked with an asterisk (*).** Titles available in Spanish at the time of this writing are labeled (SP). Books that are in English and Spanish in one volume are marked (Bilingual). Books that are particular favorites of the authors are listed at the end of each chapter. For the most part, wordless picture books are listed in chapter 15.

When dividing books into subject areas and genres, there frequently is overlap. If a book could be placed in more than one category, the authors used their professional judgment in placing it and cross-referenced it from the secondary category. Cross-category books can also be found in the extensive subject index.

Conclusion

This book has been written to help anyone trying to find books on a particular subject for the youngest readers and listeners. Selecting the titles to include was the best and worst part of the process. New books are coming out all the time, and there is always the temptation to keep adding titles. The love of story and of books can enrich the lives of children as it does adults, and this book exists to assist in creating and nurturing that love.

Chapter 1

Everyday Life—The World of the Child: Regular Activities of Childhood and Feelings and Self-Expression

Everyday life encompasses the vast array of books that describe today's world through stories. In other words, these are works of realistic fiction, even though some may feature animal characters. The books here describe real situations. Actual people (or animals who act like people)—not imaginary friends, animals, or stuffed toys—are the focus of the central narrative. As discussed in chapter 10, books in which animals act like people (thinking, talking, going to school, living in houses, etc.) are included here in their appropriate subject areas, because in these books the animal characters are substitutes for children and their friends, families, and neighbors. In these books, young children meet others who are grappling with the same developmental tasks they are. They are beginning to see themselves as individuals, realizing their own potential, beginning to separate themselves from their mothers, fathers, and caregivers. They are learning to do things by themselves—getting dressed, going to the bathroom, going to sleep—and they're developing feelings of satisfaction about their accomplishments. Encountering fictional characters who are going through the same things they are lets children know that they're not alone in these new experiences.

Because everyday life is such a large category, it has been divided into two chapters: "The World of the Child" (chapter 1), which includes the task of growing from preschooler to the elementary school-aged child, and "The World Surrounding the Child" (chapter 2), which includes friends, family, school, and challenging situations. The books are listed alphabetically under specific task categories, such as bath time, potty training, and bedtime. General living stories and series that overlap with other categories, such as friends, family, and school, are also included. Emotions are covered under "Feelings and Self-Expression," and this chapter's last topic section is "Everyday Life in General."

Regular Activities and Experiences of Childhood

Bath Time

Appelt, Kathi.

Bubba and Beau, Best Friends. See under "Friends" in chapter 2.

Arnold, Tedd.

No More Water in the Tub! New York: Dial, 1995. Unpaged. ISBN 9780803715813. **PreS–2**

William is taking his bath, but his older brother has forgotten to turn the water off, and the tub overflows. The water whisks William away on an adventure, told in a rollicking cumulative rhyme.

Gerver, Jane E.

Bath Time. Illustrated by Laura Ovresat. New York: Children's Press, 2004. 31pp. ISBN 9780516246772. **T–K**

A little boy delights in taking a bubble bath. He is thrilled with everything about bath time, especially with how clean he feels when he's finished.

Kay, Julia.

Gulliver Snip. New York: Holt, 2008. Unpaged. ISBN 9780805079920. **PreS–2**

A rhyming text with a catchy refrain relates the experiences of a young boy who imagines his bathtub is a clipper ship, which he sails away on all kinds of adventures.

Neubecker, Robert.

Beasty Bath. New York: Orchard, 2005. 32pp. ISBN 9780439640008. **T–K**

A mother snags her beloved child, who loves pretending to be one wild beast or another, and pops her progeny into the tub. The transformations continue until the child dries off, squeaky clean and ready for bed.

Wood, Audrey.

🏅*King Bidgood's in the Bathtub.* Illustrated by Don Wood. San Diego: Harcourt, 1985. 30pp. ISBN 9780152427306. **Gr. 1–3**

Despite the best efforts of his courtiers, King Bidgood insists on staying in the bathtub, engaged in more and more elaborate games, until his page devises a clever way to dislodge him. Sumptuously illustrated with Wood's oil paintings depicting shocked courtiers in Elizabethan attire and a king having a rollickingly good time. (ALAN, Caldecott Honor)

Bedtime

Bedtime books may focus on the daily routine of getting ready for bed or describe a nighttime adventure. Here are the books featuring the routine (for humans and sometimes for animals as well). The nighttime adventure books are listed in chapter 15 under "Fanciful Bedtime Stories."

Adler, David.

It's Time to Sleep, It's Time to Dream. **Illustrated by Kay Chorao. New York: Holiday House, 2009. Unpaged. ISBN 9780823419241. T–K**
> Parents get their son ready for bed, incorporating images of the seasons in their nighttime lullaby.

Anastas, Margaret.

Mommy's Best Kisses. **Illustrated by Susan Winter New York: HarperCollins, 2003. 32pp. ISBN 9780066236018. T–K**
> An array of animal mothers get their young ones ready for sleep, with an abundance of kisses, concluding with a human mother and child cuddling close.

Appelt, Kathi.

Bubba and Beau Go Night-Night. See under "Friends" in chapter 2.

Averbeck, Jim.

🌱**In a Blue Room.* **Illustrated by Tricia Tusa. Orlando, FL: Harcourt, 2008. 32pp. ISBN 9780152059927. PreS–1**
> An exuberant Alice is up past her bedtime, and her mother is trying to lure her into relaxing. She declares that she can only sleep if her room is blue. Her mother brings her flowers, tea, and an extra quilt. Each time Alice points out that the things are not blue, but she grows sleepier and sleepier as her mother tells her to be patient. When her mother turns out the light at last, moonlight washes the room in blue. The perfectly paced prose is complemented by a lullaby of color in the pen and watercolor illustrations. (Charlotte Zolotow Honor)

Banks, Kate.

🌱*And If the Moon Could Talk.* **Illustrated by Georg Hallensleben. New York: Frances Foster Books, 1998. Unpaged. ISBN 9780374302993. PreS–2**
> As a little girl gets ready for bed, twilight melts into night. In the sky, the moon not only watches over her, but also over all of the nighttime world as it settles into sleep as well. (ALAN, Boston Globe Award)

Bean, Jonathan.

🌺*At Night.* New York: Farrar, Straus & Giroux, 2007. 28pp. ISBN 9780374304461.
T–K

When a young city girl can't sleep, she collects her blanket, pillows, and cat and tramps up to the roof, with her mother following unobserved. The child makes a nest of bedclothes and falls asleep, caressed by the breeze and watched over by her mother. (Boston Globe Award, Charlotte Zolotow Honor)

Bradman, Tony.

Daddy's Lullaby. Illustrated by Jason Cockcroft. New York: Margaret K. McElderry Books, 2002. Unpaged. ISBN 9780689842955. **PreS–2**

When an exhausted father returns home from work late on Friday night, he thinks that only the cat is still stirring. He finds, however, that the baby is awake as well. He scoops up his child, checks on his wife, and then eases into a seat to sing his son a lullaby.

Butler, John.

*Hush Little Ones. Atlanta, GA: Peachtree, 2002. 32pp. ISBN 9781561452699. **T–K**

The rhyming text and gentle acrylic and colored-pencil illustrations present a variety of animal mothers and their young preparing for sleep.

Bedtime in the Jungle. Atlanta, GA: Peachtree, 2009. 32pp. ISBN 9781561454860. **T–K**

Following the pattern of "Over in the Meadow," this tale depicts a series of jungle animal mothers getting their young to close their eyes and sleep. The gorgeous illustrations bring the animals to life.

Daddo, Andrew.

Goodnight, Me. Illustrated by Emma Quay. New York: Bloomsbury, 2007. 29pp. ISBN 9781599901534. **T–K**

After Mama tucks him in for the night, a young orangutan bids goodnight to various body parts with thanks for what they have done for him during the day. He is grateful to his feet for running, to his legs for jumping, and so on, until he falls asleep at last.

Davies, Jacqueline.

The Night Is Singing. Illustrated by Kyrsten Brooker. New York: Dial, 2006. 32pp. ISBN 9780803730045. **PreS–1**

In the country, before her mama tucks her in, a little girl can hear all the special sounds of the night crooning a lullaby.

Demers, Dominique.

Every Single Night. Illustrated by Nicolas Debon. Toronto: Groundwood, 2006. 32pp. ISBN 9780888996992. **PreS–1**

In a sleep-inducing bedtime ritual, Dad gradually pulls up the covers for Simon, starting with his feet. As he does so, he describes how various animals of the world are also snuggling down to sleep.

Dewdney, Anna.

Llama, Llama, Red Pajama. See under "Families" in chapter 2.

DiPucchio, Kelly S.

Dinosnores. See under "Dinosaurs" in chapter 10.

Fleming, Denise.

Sleepy, Oh So Sleepy. New York: Holt, 2010. 32pp. ISBN 9780805081268. **PreS–1**

    A loving human mother lulls her little one to sleep, as animal babies throughout the world also snuggle into slumber.

Fox, Mem.

*Time for Bed. Illustrated by Jane Dyer. San Diego: Harcourt, 1993. Unpaged. ISBN 9780152881832. **PreS–1**

    With soothing sets of rhyming couplets, Fox describes pairs of parents and children, both human and animal, as they slip into slumber. Dyer's vivid watercolors show detailed animals surrounded by the dusky hues of approaching night.

Geisert, Arthur.

Lights Out. Boston: Houghton Mifflin, 2005. 32pp. ISBN 9780618478927. **Gr. 1–3**

    When his parents insist on lights out at eight o'clock, an ingenious piglet who is afraid of the dark invents an intricate contraption that winds its way through the house and turns off his light just after he has fallen asleep.

Henry, Rohan.

Good Night, Baby Ruby. New York: Abrams, 2009. 32pp. ISBN 978-0810983236. **T–K**

    Ruby, a toddler, does everything she can to avoid going to bed.

Hest, Amy.

Kiss Good Night. Illustrated by Anita Jeram. Cambridge, MA: Candlewick, 2001. Unpaged. ISBN 9780763607807. **T–K**

    On a dark and stormy night, a bear cub named Sam remains sleepless, even though his mother has performed all of their bedtime rituals. They've shared a story and arranged Sam's stuffed animals. Mama has even brought him a glass of warm milk, but each time she asks if he is ready for bed, he replies that he is waiting. Finally, Mama figures out why and gives him a kiss good night. A deeply satisfying story.

Hindley, Judy.

Sleepy Places. Illustrated by Tor Freeman. Cambridge, MA: Candlewick, 2006. 32pp. ISBN 9780763629830. `PreS-3`

Three young children, who are just about ready to go to sleep themselves, tell about all the different places that people and animals go when they want to fall asleep.

Inches, Alison.

The Stuffed Animals Get Ready for Bed. Illustrated by Bryan Langdo. Orlando: Harcourt, 2006. 32pp. ISBN 9780152164669. `PreS-1`

As bedtime nears, a girl gets her stuffed animals ready for bed so they can all go to sleep together.

Kanevsky, Polly.

Sleepy Boy. Illustrated by Stephanie Anderson. New York: Atheneum, 2006. 32pp. ISBN 9780689867354. `T-K`

A father lies down with his young son in an attempt to help him fall asleep. His child has spent the day at the zoo observing the lions and is far too excited to sleep. While safe in his father's arms, the boy remembers the lions. He drifts off to sleep to the remembered sound of the cubs' purring. Luscious watercolor and charcoal illustrations glow with life.

Katz, Alan.

Stalling. Illustrated by Elwood H. Smith. New York: Margaret K. McElderry Books, 2010. Unpaged. ISBN 9781416955672. `PreS-1`

This rhyming verse relates the many things a boy must get done before he thinks that he is indeed ready for bed.

Kono, Erin Eitter.

Hula Lullaby. New York: Little, Brown, 2005. 32pp. ISBN 9780316735919. `PreS-2`

In Hawaii, a little girl drifts off to sleep as hula dancers perform with a musical accompaniment.

Lewis, Kim.

Good Night, Harry. See under "Regular Activities and Experiences of Childhood: Toys" in this chapter.

Lillegard, Dee.

Who Will Sing a Lullaby. Illustrated by Dan Yaccarino. New York: Knopf, 2007. 32pp. ISBN 9780375815737. `T-K`

As a baby cries, various birds vie for the chance to sing him to sleep.

Lyon, George Ella.

Sleepsong. Illustrated by Peter Catalanotto. New York: Atheneum, 2008. 40pp. ISBN 9780689869730. **T–K**

A mother and father lovingly prepare their little daughter for bed, giving her a bath, reading her a story, and tucking her into bed. The gouache-and-watercolor paintings show the family and the parallel world of creatures also slowing down to sleep.

Markes, Julie.

Shhhhh! Everybody's Sleeping. Illustrated by David Parkins. New York: HarperCollins, 2005. 32pp. ISBN 9780060537906. **T–K**

A comforting rhyming text lists all the community helpers, such as a librarian, a fire fighter, and a police officer, who have already gone to bed.

Moore, Raina.

How Do You Say Goodnight? Illustrated by Robin Luebs. New York: HarperCollins, 2008. 32pp. ISBN 9780060831639. **T–K**

In gentle rhyme an array of animals and a little girl all ask the question in the title, with various responses.

Mora, Pat.

Dulces Sueños/Sweet Dreams. Illustrated by Maribel Suarez. New York: Rayo, 2008. 24pp. ISBN 9780060850418. **T–K** (Bilingual)

Abuelita tucks in her three grandchildren and lulls them to sleep by recounting all the different animals that are going to sleep as well.

Nakamura, Katherine Riley.

Song of Night: It's Time to Go to Bed. Illustrated by Linnea Asplind Riley. New York: Blue Sky Press, 2002. Unpaged. ISBN 9780439266789. **T–K**

A mother rabbit soothes her child to sleep by describing in lilting verse how all the other animals are also getting ready for bed.

Oppenheim, Joanne.

The Prince's Bedtime. Illustrated by Miriam Latimer. Cambridge, MA: Barefoot Books, 2006. 32pp. ISBN 9781841485973. **PreS–1**

The prince will not go to sleep, and the king and queen summon everyone in the kingdom who might succeed in sending him off to slumber. When dancers, magicians, and doctors fail, an old woman with a book succeeds.

Rockwell, Anne.

Here Comes the Night. New York: Holt, 2006. 32pp. ISBN 9780805076639. **T–K**

A mother gently gets her son ready for bed, with bath time, brushing teeth, a story, and a song.

Rosenthal, Amy Krouse.

Little Hoot. **Illustrated by Jen Corace. San Francisco: Chronicle, 2008. 36pp. ISBN 9780811860239.** `PreS-2`

Little Hoot likes going to owl school to learn pondering and staring, but he absolutely hates going to bed late. He begs his parents to let him go to bed early like all of his friends, but they force him to play for another hour, as all good owls should. Detailed ink and watercolor illustrations deftly convey Little Hoot's feelings.

Bedtime for Mommy. **Illustrated by Leuyen Pham. New York: Bloomsbury, 2010. 32pp. ISBN 9781599903415.** `PreS-2`

Parent and child switch roles in this tale of a daughter who helps her mother get ready for bed.

Saltzberg, Barney.

Cornelius P. Mud, Are You Ready for Bed? See under "Everyday Life in General" in this chapter.

Sartell, Debra.

Time for Bed, Baby Ted. **Illustrated by Kay Chorao. New York: Holiday House, 2010. Unpaged. ISBN 9780823419685.** `T-K`

Baby Ted does not want to go to bed and pretends to be various kinds of animals in an imaginative attempt to avoid his fate.

Shea, Bob.

Dinosaur vs. Bedtime. See under "Dinosaurs" in chapter 10.

Race You to Bed. **New York: Katherine Tegen Books, 2010. 32pp. ISBN 9780061704178.** `T-K`

This active rhyme involves readers in the rabbit's adventures as he does his best to skip going to bed.

Shields, Gillian.

When the World Is Ready for Bed. **Illustrated by Anna Currey. New York: Bloomsbury, 2009. 32pp. ISBN 9781599903392.** `PreS-1`

As dusk descends, a rabbit family has dinner and cleans up. Then the little ones brush their teeth, listen to a bedtime story, and slide into sleep.

Swanson, Susan Marie.

🎖*The House in the Night.* **Illustrated by Beth Krommes. Boston: Houghton Mifflin, 2008. 36pp. ISBN 9780618862443.** `PreS-1`

Cumulative verse weaves a story that leads children to a house with a light on that is filled with books, art, music, and most important, love. It concludes with a child tucked into bed, illuminated by the light of the moon. The succinct and poetic text is strikingly visualized by black-and-white scratchboard illustrations that are accented by a rich yellow light. (ALAN, Caldecott Medal)

Vail, Rachel.

Jibberwillies at Night. **Illustrated by Yumi Heo. New York: Scholastic,** 2008. 29pp. ISBN 9780439420709. **PreS-2**

Kate joyfully spins through her day, playing with friends and family members, but when her nighttime fears manifest as jibberwillies, she has some trouble. She tries to get rid of them by thinking good thoughts, but when that doesn't do the trick, she calls for mom. Mom helps her put all the jibberwillies in a bucket, and together they toss them out the window.

Whybrow, Ian.

The Noisy Way to Bed. **Illustrated by Tiphanie Beeke. New York: Arthur A.** Levine, 2004. 32pp. ISBN 9780439556897. **PreS-1**

A tired farm boy is trying to head to bed, but various animals keep interrupting him. They follow him home in a cacophonous parade, where he is finally able to go to bed.

Willems, Mo.

Don't Let the Pigeon Stay up Late. See in chapter 14.

Wing, Natasha.

Go to Bed, Monster! **Illustrated by Sylvie Kantorovitz. Orlando: Harcourt,** 2007. 29pp. ISBN 9780152057756. **PreS-1**

Lucy isn't ready to go to sleep yet, so she gets out her crayons and draws a monster for a playmate. She doesn't expect the monster to want to keep playing after she's ready for bed, though. Now she has to figure out how to get him to fall asleep.

Wright, Michael.

Jake Stays Awake. **New York: Feiwel & Friends, 2007. 32pp. ISBN 978-** 0312367978. **PreS-1**

Jake got used to sleeping with his parents when he was little, but now that he's bigger, they think it's time for him to be more independent. He is sure that he cannot sleep without them, so they agree to sleep in the same place, just not the same bed, but every place they try has a problem. At last Jake thinks he'll try his own bed, and it works wonderfully.

Yolen, Jane.

How Do Dinosaurs Say Goodnight? See under "Dinosaurs" in chapter 10.

Hush, Little Horsie. **Illustrated by Ruth Sanderson. New York: Random** House, 2010. 32pp. ISBN 9780375858536. **T-K**

Lilting rhyme recounts for foals how their mothers are always there, watching over them whether they are frolicking or sleeping.

Babysitters

Kromhout, Rindert.

Little Donkey and the Baby-Sitter. **Illustrated by Annemarie Von Haeringen. New York: North South, 2006. 32pp. ISBN 9780735820579.** `PreS-2`

When Mama goes out to the movies, Little Donkey misbehaves for the babysitter, but her kindness wins him over by the time Mama returns.

London, Jonathan.

Froggy's Best Babysitter. See under "Everyday Life in General" in this chapter.

Stewart, Amber.

No Babysitters Allowed. **Illustrated by Laura Rankin. New York: Bloomsbury, 2008. Unpaged. ISBN 9781599901541.** `PreS-1`

Hopscotch is a brave bunny until his parents leave him with Mrs. Honeybunch, the babysitter. He hides in his fort until Mrs. Honeybunch cleverly convinces him to come out.

Birthdays

De Groat, Diane.

Happy Birthday to You, You Belong in a Zoo. See under "Everyday Life in General" in this chapter.

Dokas, Dara.

Muriel's Red Sweater. **Illustrated by Bernadette Pons. New York: Dutton, 2009. 22pp. ISBN 9780525479628.** `PreS-1`

As Murial the duck delivers invitations to her birthday party, she snags her red sweater. Although she doesn't notice it, her sweater unravels as she goes, making it fun for readers to spot the red thread in the illustrations. Fortunately, she gets a warm replacement for her birthday.

Fleming, Candace.

Clever Jake Takes the Cake. **Illustrated by Brian G. Karas. New York: Schwartz & Wade Books, 2010. Unpaged. ISBN 9780375849794.** `Gr. 1-3`

This original fairy tale relates the adventures of resourceful Jake, who is bringing a birthday cake to the princess's tenth birthday party.

Graham, Bob.

Oscar's Half Birthday. **Cambridge, MA: Candlewick, 2005. 32pp. ISBN 978-0763626990.** `PreS-1` **(SP)**

A family can't wait for baby Oscar to reach his first birthday, so they celebrate his six-month birthday with a picnic in the park.

Horse, Harry.

Little Rabbit Lost. See under "Everyday Life in General" in this chapter.

Klise, Kate.

Why Do You Cry? Not a Sob Story. See under "Everyday Life in General" in this chapter.

Kromhout, Rindert.

Little Donkey and the Birthday Present. Illustrated by Annemarie Von Haeringen. New York: North South, 2007. 32pp. ISBN 9780735821323. `PreS-2`
> Mama and Little Donkey select a birthday present for his friend Jackie, but by the time they've made it back home, Little Donkey wants to keep the present. It's up to Mama to show him why it's better to give it away.

Lewis, Rose.

Every Year on Your Birthday. See under "Families: Adoption" in chapter 2.

McPhail, David.

Big Brown Bear's Birthday Surprise. See under "Friends" in chapter 2.

Rose, Deborah Lee.

Birthday Zoo. Illustrated by Lynn Munsinger. Morton Grove, IL: Albert Whitman, 2002. Unpaged. ISBN 9780807507766. `PreS-2`
> Rhyming text details how various zoo animals plan and carry out a birthday party for a young boy.

Schotter, Roni.

Mama, I'll Give You the World. Illustrated by Susan Saelig Gallagher. New York: Schwartz & Wade Books, 2006. 40pp. ISBN 9780375836121. `PreS-3`
> Every day after school, Luisa goes to the beauty salon where her mother works. She longs to see her mother smile again, so with the workers and customers at the salon, she throws her a surprise birthday party.

Schoenherr, Ian.

Pip & Squeak. New York: Greenwillow, 2007. 32pp. ISBN 9780060872533. `PreS-2`
> Pip and Squeak are mice pals on their way to a birthday party for their friend Gus. They have a package of cheese for Gus but get caught up in winter play and end up present-less. Spying a snowman with a carrot nose that they mistake for cheese, they arrive toting the vegetable. It turns out to be the perfect gift for Gus, who is a rabbit.

Thomas, Shelley Moore.

Happy Birthday, Good Knight. See under "Fantasy and Magic: in chapter 15.

Viorst, Judith.

Just in Case. See under "Everyday Life in General" in this chapter.

Williams, Vera B.

Something Special for Me. See under "Families: Families in General" in chapter 2.

Getting Dressed

Chodos-Irvine, Margaret.

🌳*Ella Sarah Gets Dressed.* San Diego: Harcourt, 2003. Unpaged. ISBN 9780152164133. **PreS–K**

Ella Sarah knows exactly what she wants to wear: her pink polka-dot pants, orange-and-green dress, purple-striped socks, yellow shoes, and red hat. Every member of her family tries to get her to tone down her outfit, but Ella Sarah cannot be swayed. When her friends arrive all dressed up in equally wild outfits, they enjoy a tea party as they wear the perfect clothes. (ALAN, Caldecott Honor)

Cuyler, Margery.

Princess Bess Gets Dressed. Illustrated by Heather Maione. New York: Simon & Schuster, 2009. Unpaged. ISBN 9781416938330. **PreS–3**

Princess Bess possesses an extensive wardrobe, and these rhyming couplets describe her vast supply of outfits, finishing with what Bess likes to wear best. A perfect choice for aspiring princesses.

Fleming, Candace.

This Is the Baby. Illustrated by Maggie Smith. New York: Melanie Kroupa Books, 2004. 40pp. ISBN 9780374374860. **T–K**

In playful, cumulative rhyme, Fleming shows mom's efforts to get her toddler dressed. Just as she succeeds, he undoes all of her hard work in a flash.

French, Vivian.

Polly's Pink Pajamas. Illustrated by Sue Heap. Somerville, MA: Candlewick, 2010. 32pp. ISBN 9780763648077. **PreS–1**

Polly wants to wear nothing but her pink pajamas whether she's awake or asleep. When she gets an invitation to a party, she accepts her friends' offers to borrow some clothes and ends up with an unusual outfit.

London, Jonathan.

Froggy Gets Dressed. See under "Everyday Life in General" in this chapter.

Reidy, Jean.

Too Purpley! Illustrated by Genevieve Leloup. New York: Bloomsbury, 2010. 32pp. ISBN 9781599903071. **T-K**

> A young girl is stuck in her underwear because she can't decide what to wear. Everything is too itchy, stripey, purpley, and so on. She finally settles on a comfortable outfit that is just right.

New Bed

Bergstein, Rita.

My Big Boy Bed. Illustrated by Maggie Smith. New York: Clarion, 2003. 32pp. ISBN 9780618177424. **T-K**

> Donny happily moves from his crib to his new bed. He makes himself comfortable with it by jumping on it, hiding under it, and tucking in his stuffed animals.

Your Own Big Bed. Illustrated by Susan Kathleen Hartung. New York: Viking, 2008. 28pp. ISBN 9780670060795. **T-K**

> This story compares the growth of animals on the farm and in nature to a child's growth, presenting the move to a big bed as a natural step in development.

Hines, Anna Grossnickle.

My Own Big Bed. Illustrated by Mary Watson. New York: Greenwillow, 1998. 24pp. ISBN 9780688155995. **T-K**

> In her new big bed, a little girl thinks about the scary things and the fun things about having a bed instead of a crib. Her mother reads her a bedtime story and tucks her in, and she feels cozy and safe.

McGhee, Alison.

Bye-Bye Crib. Illustrated by Ross MacDonald. New York: Simon &Schuster, 2008. 28pp. ISBN 9781416916215. **T-K**

> A young boy, together with Baby Kitty, Red Blankie, and Big Pillow, is reluctant to move from the secure crib to a big boy bed, until the boy tosses his beloved items to the bed and they assure him that it's safe.

Potty Training

Cole, Joanna.

My Big Boy Potty Book. Illustrated by Maxie Chambliss. New York: HarperCollins, 2000. Unpaged. ISBN 9780688170424. **T-K**

My Big Girl Potty Book. Illustrated by Maxie Chambliss. New York: HarperCollins, 2000. Unpaged. ISBN 9780688170417. **T-K**

> In these two books, the text is the same except for the gender of the child. They focus on helping toddlers through potty training. The illustrations are appropriately modified to show the gender differentiation.

Ford, Bernette.

No More Diapers for Ducky. **Illustrated by Sam Williams. New York: Boxer Books, 2006. 32pp. ISBN 9781905417087.** `T-K`

> Ducky visits Piggy, ready to play, but has to wait because Piggy is on the potty. As she waits, her diaper gets wet and then cold. She kicks it off, deciding not to wear diapers any more. Now Piggy has to wait for Ducky.

O'Connell, Rebecca.

Danny Is Done with Diapers: A Potty ABC. **Illustrated by Amanda Gulliver. Chicago: Albert Whitman, 2010. 32pp. ISBN 9780807514665.** `T-K`

> An alphabetic tour of potty training is conducted by matching alliterative young-sters.

Teeth

Bate, Lucy.

Little Rabbit's Loose Tooth. **Illustrated by Diane De Groat. New York: Random House, 2006. 32pp. ISBN 9780375832772.** `PreS-2`

> This reissue of a title first published in 1975 has a smaller trim size with a smaller font. Little Rabbit's tooth is loose, so she eats hard things (like carrots) with her other teeth and only soft things (like ice cream) with her loose tooth, until it falls out. All the while, she wonders what the Tooth Fairy will do with it.

Borden, Louise.

The Lost-and-Found Tooth. **Illustrated by Adam Gustavson. New York: Margaret K. McElderry Books, 2008. 40pp. ISBN 9781416918141.** `Gr. 1-3`

> In Lucy's second grade class, her teacher has posted a "Who's Lost a Tooth?" calendar. As one by one Lucy's classmates' baby teeth fall out, and they mark the calendar, Lucy worries that her teeth will never come out.

Diakite, Penda.

I Lost My Tooth in Africa. See in chapter 3.

Edwards, Pamela Duncan.

Dear Tooth Fairy. **Illustrated by Marie Louise Fitzpatrick. New York: HarperCollins, 2003. Unpaged. ISBN 9780066239729.** `PreS-2`

> Six-year-old Claire is worried because she hasn't had one loose tooth yet, so she writes letter after letter to the Tooth Fairy. The Tooth Fairy (Grandma) replies with sensible advice that she be patient and keep brushing her teeth. When the big day arrives at last, the Tooth Fairy promises to use her newest acquisition in a special way.

Elya, Susan Middleton.

Tooth on the Loose. Illustrated by Jennifer Mattheson. New York: Putnam, 2008. 30pp. ISBN 9780399244599. **PreS–1**

In rhyming text sprinkled with Spanish words, a Latina girl wishes her loose tooth would finally fall out. She is worried that it will hurt, but she wants to use the money from the Tooth Fairy to buy her father a birthday present.

McGhee, Alison.

Mrs. Watson Wants Your Teeth. See under "School" in chapter 2.

Palatini, Margie.

Sweet Tooth. Illustrated by Jack E. Davis. New York: Simon & Schuster, 2004. Unpaged. ISBN 9780689851599. **Gr. K–3**

Young Stewart's talking molar is constantly demanding sweets. When giving in to it causes trouble, he eats vegetables to keep it quiet. Crunching on a carrot causes it to fall out, and the trouble-making tooth is now in the custody of the Tooth Fairy.

Ruelle, Karen Gray.

Dear Tooth Fairy. See under "Families: Easy Readers" in chapter 2.

Vrombaut, An.

Clarabella's Teeth. New York: Clarion, 2003. Unpaged. ISBN 978-0618333790. **PreS–1**

Clarabella the crocodile starts each day by brushing her teeth, but she has so many that she never gets a chance to play with her friends. They are going to bed by the time her teeth are clean. Then her friends come up with a special surprise that helps them all.

Toys

Buell, Janet.

Sail Away, Little Boat. Illustrated by Jui Ishida. Minneapolis, MN: Carolrhoda, 2006. 32pp. ISBN 9781575058214. **PreS–3**

A boy and a girl place a sailboat named *Friendship* in the current of a flowing brook so that they can share their toy with other children. It travels through the country until it reaches the ocean. As it beaches on the shore, three children discover it with delight.

Kroll, Virginia L.

Everybody Has a Teddy. Illustrated by Sophie Allsop. New York: Sterling, 2007. 24pp. ISBN 9781402735806. **T–K**

Rhyming text describes a class full of teddy bears. When naptime rolls around, everyone snuggles up with their teddies, except the narrator, who cuddles his stuffed monkey.

Shannon, David.

Too Many Toys. New York: Blue Sky Press, 2008. 32pp. ISBN 9780439490290. **PreS–2**

Spencer has so many toys that they fill up the entire house. His mom insists that he sort through them to find some to give away. Even while he complies, Spencer is thinking up a way to save his beloved collection.

Willems, Mo.

The Knuffle Bunny Series. **PreS–2**

Willems, a master of humor and accompanying imaginative art, as well as a keen understanding of the experiences of childhood, recounts the adventures of young Trixie and her beloved stuffed toy, Knuffle Bunny.

Knuffle Bunny: A Cautionary Tale. New York: Hyperion, 2004. 37pp. ISBN 9781423102991. (SP)

Trixie, a toddler who is too young to speak but old enough to go on errands with dad, joyfully accompanies him to the laundromat. All is well until they are heading home and Trixie realizes she has a problem. Because gibberish is her only means of communication, she can't get dad to understand, even when she throws a tantrum, but when they return home, mom realizes immediately that she doesn't have her Knuffle Bunny. In this brilliantly designed book, colorful cartoon-style people are set against black-and-white photographs of a Brooklyn neighborhood. (ALAN, Caldecott Honor, Charlotte Zolotow Honor)

Knuffle Bunny Too: A Case of Mistaken Identity. New York: Hyperion, 2007. 37pp. ISBN 9781423102991.

An older Trixie heads off to preschool, eager to introduce her one-of-a-kind best friend, Knuffle Bunny, to her new friends. When she gets there, however, she finds that Sonja has a bunny just like hers. The two girls fight, and the teacher takes the bunnies away until the end of the day. Although each child thinks she has been reunited with her best friend, the girls find each has the wrong Knuffle Bunny. The dads arrange a nighttime exchange, which begins a friendship between Trixie and Sonja. (ALAN, Caldecott Honor)

Knuffle Bunny Free: An Unexpected Diversion. New York: Balzer & Bray, 2010. 48pp. ISBN 9780061929588.

Trixie and her family go on vacation to Holland, and though there is much excitement, there is also a great deal of distress when Knuffle Bunny gets misplaced once more.

Feelings and Self-Expression

Emotions

Bang, Molly.

🌺*When Sophie Gets Angry—Really, Really Angry.* **New York: Scholastic, 1999. Unpaged. ISBN 9780590189798.** `PreS–2`

> Sophie has to share her toy with her sister, stumbles over another, and gets no sympathy from her mother, so her anger erupts. First she kicks and screams and then runs out of the house to cry in the woods. As her tears ease, she notices the natural world around her. When she calms down she returns home. Bang's blazing artwork effectively depicts Sophie's emotions in this realistic tale. (ALAN, Caldecott Honor, Charlotte Zolotow Award)

Beaumont, Karen.

I Like Myself. **Illustrated by David Catrow. Orlando, FL: Harcourt, 2004. 32pp. ISBN 9780152020132.** `PreS–2`

> In rhyming verse, a young African American girl delightedly describes how she likes herself in all kinds of zany situations, in this celebration of self-affirmation.

Browne, Anthony.

Silly Billy. **Cambridge, MA: Candlewick, 2006. 32pp. ISBN 9780763631246.** `PreS–2`

> Even though his parents try to reassure him, Billy can't stop worrying about everything, until his grandmother teaches him how to use Guatemalan worry dolls.

Crum, Shutta.

Bravest of the Brave. **Illustrated by Tim Bowers. New York: Knopf, 2005. 40pp. ISBN 9780375826375.** `PreS–1`

> A skunk makes his way home through twilight woods and convinces himself to be brave as he faces one danger after another. The dangers turn out to be his friends, who take him to a party, but his courage is real.

Curtis, Jamie Lee.

Today I Feel Silly and Other Moods That Make My Day. **Illustrated by Laura Cornell. New York: HarperCollins, 1998. 32pp. ISBN 9780060245603.** `PreS–2`

> Curtis's rhyming text explores the many ups and downs of one little girl, from cranky to joyful and everything in between.

I'm Gonna Like Me. **Illustrated by Laura Cornell. New York: Joanna Cotler Books, 2002. Unpaged. ISBN 9780060287610.** `PreS–2`

> Jaunty rhymes reiterate all the ways a boy and girl will like themselves no matter what happens.

Frame, Jeron Ashford.

Yesterday I Had the Blues. **Illustrated by R. Gregory Christie. Berkley, CA: Tricycle Press, 2003. Unpaged. ISBN 9781582460840.** `Gr. 1-3`

> An African American boy recalls how blue he felt the day before and then goes on to describe the moods of the people in his family and the colors he associates with the emotions, concluding with the warm, golden feeling that being part of his family gives him.

Harris, Robie H.

The Day Leo Said I Hate You! **Illustrated by Molly Bang. New York: Little, Brown, 2008. 40pp. ISBN 9780316065801.** `PreS-1`

> When Leo is constantly thwarted by his mother, he gets so angry that he screams, "I hate you!" He regrets it instantly. His patient mother is upset but able to reassure him that she loves him and explain to him how words can hurt, as they restore their relationship. The vividly colored illustrations, including collages, accurately reveal the emotions of parent and child.

Hest, Amy.

Little Chick. **Illustrated by Anita Jeram. Somerville, MA: Candlewick, 2009. Unpaged. ISBN 9780763628901.** `PreS-1`

> Each time Little Chick feels frustration and impatience in these three episodes, Old-Auntie Hen helps him work through the situation.

hooks, bell.

Grump, Groan, Growl. **Illustrated by Christopher Raschka. New York: Hyperion, 2008. 30pp. ISBN 9780786808168.** `PreS-2`

> With a profound yet spare text, hooks describes the negative feelings of being in a bad mood and proposes letting the feelings slide away as a method of moving beyond them. Raschka's expressionistic watercolors exquisitely portray anger and frustration, and finally, calm.

Keller, Holly.

Nosy Rosie. **New York: Greenwillow, 2006. 22pp. ISBN 9780060787585.** `PreS-2`

> Rosie the fox likes using her exceptional sense of smell to help people find things, until she is teased about it. Her friends hurt her feelings, calling her, "Nosy Rosie," so she decides to stop helping them. When her nose helps her find her baby brother, she earns everyone's respect and the name calling stops.

Kurtz, Jane.

Rain Romp: Stomping Away a Grouchy Day. See under "Weather" in chapter 9.

Lester, Helen.

Something Might Happen. **Illustrated by Lynn Munsinger. Boston: Houghton Mifflin, 2003. 32pp. ISBN 9780618254064.** `PreS-2`

Twitchly Fidget, a young lemur, is afraid of doing anything because something frightening might happen. He won't roast marshmallows with his friends because he might get stuck to others with the gooey treat. He won't go to the parade because he thinks he might get sucked into a trombone. When his Aunt Bridget arrives for a visit, she convinces him that just because something might happen, doesn't mean it will.

Menchin, Scott.

Taking a Bath with the Dog and Other Things That Make Me Happy. **Cambridge, MA: Candlewick, 2007. 32pp. ISBN 9780763629199.** `PreS-1`

When a tearful little girl tries to figure out what would cheer her up, she asks those around her what makes them happy.

Parr, Todd.

The Feel Good Book. **Boston: Little, Brown, 2002. 32pp. ISBN 978-0316072069.** `T-K`

Employing his signature illustrations, Parr lists a number of things that make people happy, from sharing to reading to wearing new pajamas.

The I Love You Book. **New York: Little, Brown, 2009. 32pp. ISBN 978-0316019859.** `T-K`

Using a plethora of primary colors, Parr presents people in a variety of situations, declaring love even when children are feeling negative emotions.

Roenthal, Amy Krouse.

One of Those Days. **Illustrated by Rebecca Doughty. New York: Putnam, 2006. 32pp. ISBN 9780399243653.** `PreS-2`

It isn't the worst day, it's just one of those days—short pants day, left out day, annoying sibling day, and others—presented so readers can laugh and know that there's always a new dawn and a brand new day.

Seeger, Laura Vaccaro.

🎖*Walter Was Worried.* **New Milford, CT: Roaring Brook, 2005. 40pp. ISBN 9781596430686.** `PreS-2`

A group of children experience various emotions as a thunderstorm approaches, rumbles to life, and then passes. Seeger cleverly incorporates the letters of the words in the faces of the children, making this multifaceted book work on many levels. (ALAN)

Urban, Linda.

Mouse Was Mad. Illustrated by Henry Cole. Orlando, FL: Harcourt, 2009. 26pp. ISBN 9780152053376. **PreS–2**

A furious Mouse engages in a variety of activities to show how mad he is and finally calms down when he perfects standing still.

Viorst, Judith.

Alexander and the Terrible, Horrible, No Good, Very Bad Day. Illustrated by Ray Cruz. New York: Atheneum, 1972. 32pp. ISBN 9780689300721. **PreS–3** (SP)

When Alexander wakes up with gum in his hair, he knows it's going to be a very bad day. Things only get worse from there, and he thinks he'll move to Australia.

Watt, Melanie.

Scaredy Squirrel Series. Tonawanda, NY: Kids Can Press. **PreS–2**

Scaredy Squirrel is afraid of everything, and in each book faces a new situation that he finds frightening.

🏵*Scaredy Squirrel*. 2006. 34pp. ISBN 9781553379591.

Scaredy Squirrel feels safe in his tree until his emergency kit falls to the ground. He panics and leaps after it, discovering that he is actually a flying squirrel. (ALAN, Amelia Frances Howard Gibbon Illustrator's Medal)

Scaredy Squirrel Makes a Friend. 2007. 29pp. ISBN 9781554531813.

Scaredy Squirrel is lonely because he's too afraid to make a friend, but when he spots a goldfish, he thinks he may have found the perfect nonbiting, germ-free companion.

Scaredy Squirrel at the Beach. 2008. 32pp. ISBN 9781554532254.

Everything about the seashore, from jellyfish to sea monsters, makes Scaredy Squirrel tremble, so he stays home and constructs his own beachlike atmosphere. Deciding he really needs a seashell, he concocts a plan whereby he mails himself to the seaside and discovers he loves being there.

Scaredy Squirrel at Night. 2009. 32pp. ISBN 9781554532889.

Fear of bad dreams keeps Scaredy Squirrel from sleeping until he is able to face his feelings.

Whybrow, Ian.

Bella Gets Her Skates On. Illustrated by Rosie Reeve. New York: Abrams, 2007. 32pp. ISBN 9780810994164. **PreS–1**

Bella, a young rabbit, always feels anxious about new experiences, so when her father suggests the family go ice skating, Bella would rather frolic in the snow instead. Her father praises her as she succeeds in her snowy activities, until she feels confident enough to don her skates.

Wilson, Karma.

Bear Feels Scared. See under "Friends" in chapter 2.

Individuality

Jameison, Victoria.

Bea Rocks the Flock. New York: Bloomsbury, 2009. Unpaged. ISBN 9781599902609. `PreS–2`

Bea is a sheep who marches to the beat of her own drummer amid a flock that strives to all be the same. After being scolded one too many times for being different, Bea heads off for the big city, where she is sure her specialness will be appreciated. After experimenting with various jobs, she enters a dog contest and wins, "Most Unique Dog." Sure that all the sheep in her flock should be recognized for their individuality, she returns home to encourage them to fulfill their own dreams. Tongue-in-cheek acrylic illustrations add levity to the story.

Katz, Karen.

Princess Baby. New York: Schwartz & Wade, 2008. 32pp. ISBN 978-0375841194. `T–K`

This toddler is sick and tired of her parents calling her various pet names and makes clear to one and all that she is Princess Baby.

Princess Baby, Night-Night. New York: Schwartz & Wade, 2009. Unpaged. ISBN 9780375844621. Sequel. `T–K`

Princess Baby is getting ready for bed, but she is doing it her own way, by gathering all her toys on her bed and reading to them.

Keane, Dave.

Sloppy Joe. Illustrated by Denise Brunkus. New York: HarperCollins, 2009. Unpaged. ISBN 9780061710209. `Gr. K–2`

Joe revels in riotous levels of messiness and thwarts all adult attempts to get him to clean up his act, until his family comes down with the flu. He does his best to turn into Neat Joe to care for his ailing relatives. The results are both humorous and tender.

Lester, Helen.

Tacky the Penguin Series. Illustrated by Lynn Munsinger. Boston: Houghton, Mifflin. `PreS–2`

Tacky the Penguin delights in completely doing things his own way while all the other penguins perform identically. When Tacky's antics turn out to save the day, his fellow penguins begins to appreciate him.

Tacky the Penguin. 1988. 32pp. ISBN 9780395455364. (SP)

Three Cheers for Tacky. 1994. 32pp. ISBN 9780395668412.

Tacky in Trouble. 1998. 32pp. ISBN 9780395861134.

Tacky the Emperor. 2000. Unpaged. ISBN 9780395981207.

Tacky Locks and the Three Bears. 2002. 32pp. ISBN 9780618224906.

Tacky and the Winter Games. 2005. 32pp. ISBN 9780618556595.

Tacky Goes to Camp. 2009. Unpaged. ISBN 9780618988129.

Tacky's Christmas. 2010. 32pp. ISBN 9780547172088.

Meng, Cece.

Tough Chicks. Illustrated by Melissa Suber. New York: Clarion, 2009. 32pp. ISBN 9780618824151. PreS–2

Penny, Polly, and Molly are newly hatched chicks who don't do anything their fellow barnyard animals expect. They like to race bugs, rope roosters, and tinker with the farmer's tractor, rather than preen, cluck, and build nests. The animals and the farmer want their mother to make them behave, until the farmer's tractor crashes out of control, and it's Penny, Polly, and Molly who save the day.

O'Connor, Jane.

Fancy Nancy Series. Illustrated by Robin Preiss-Glasser. New York: HarperCollins. PreS–2

Young Nancy likes all things fancy and does everything she can think of to make her sense of style and panache part of everyday life. Preiss-Glasser's exuberant and intricate illustrations bring to life Nancy's inimitable fashions. Fancy Nancy is also featured in her own easy reader series, with illustrations in the style of Robin Preiss-Glasser.

Fancy Nancy. 2005. 32pp. ISBN 9780060542092.

Fancy Nancy and the Posh Puppy. 2007. 32pp. ISBN 9780060542139.

Fancy Nancy: Bonjour, Butterfly. 2008. Unpaged. ISBN 9780061235887.

Fancy Nancy's Favorite Fancy Words: From Accessories to Zany. 2008. 32pp. ISBN 9780061549236.

Fancy Nancy: Tea Parties. 2009. 27pp. ISBN 9780061801747.

Fancy Nancy: Splendiforous Christmas. 2009. 32pp. ISBN 9780061235900.

Fancy Nancy: Ooh La La! It's Beauty Day. 2010. 40pp. ISBN 9780061915253.

Parr, Todd.

It's Okay to Be Different. Boston: Little, Brown, 2001. Unpaged. ISBN 978-0316666039. PreS–2

Presenting a variety of differences with bright, childlike art, Parr encourages readers to accept the differences in others.

Sattler, Jennifer.

Sylvie. New York: Random House, 2009. 40pp. ISBN 9780375857089. `PreS-2`

Sylvie, a young flamingo, learns that she is pink because of the shrimp she eats, so she samples things of different colors and patterns. She transforms into a flamingo of a different color, but settles back on pink, with just a touch of rainbow.

Thompson, Kay.

The Eloise Series. **Illustrated by Hilary Knight. New York: Simon & Schuster.** `Gr. 1-3`

The precocious Eloise is a six-year-old girl who lives on the top floor of the Plaza Hotel in New York City. She is a resourceful young lady who has adventures in a variety of cities. These books were first published in the 1950s and have been reissued several times with some revisions. They are listed here in original publication order, but because there have been changes to the text, they have the copyright date of the most recent edition.

Eloise. 2009. 64pp. ISBN 9780689843112.

Kay Thompson's Eloise in Paris. 1999. Unpaged. ISBN 9780689827044.

Kay Thompson's Eloise at Christmas. 1999. Unpaged. ISBN 9780689830396.

Kay Thompson's Eloise in Moscow. 2000. Unpaged. ISBN 9780689832116.

Kay Thompson's Eloise Takes a Bawth. (With additional illustrations by Crowley, Mart.) 2002. 64pp. ISBN 9780689842887.

Kay Thompson's Eloise's What I Absolutely Love Love Love. 2004. 32pp. ISBN 9780689849657.

Eloise's Christmas Trinkles. 2007. 41pp. ISBN 9780689874253.

Willems, Mo.

Naked Mole Rat Gets Dressed. New York: Hyperion, 2009. Unpaged. ISBN 9781423114376. `PreS-2`

Wilbur is a naked mole rat who likes to wear clothes. His extensive wardrobe includes a tux and a space suit. Appalled, the rats call a meeting to discuss the distressing situation. To their amazement, the much revered Grand-pah attends, dressed in a good-looking suit and convinces everyone that for those who want to try them, clothes can be fun.

Everyday Life in General

Aliki.

All by Myself. New York: HarperCollins, 2000. Unpaged. ISBN 9780060289294. `PreS-1`

An enthusiastic preschooler delights in doing a variety of life's daily tasks, from getting dressed in the morning, through going to school and the library, all the way to bed, all on his own.

Asch, Frank.

The Sun Is My Favorite Star. San Diego: Harcourt, 2000. Unpaged. ISBN 9780152021276. **PreS–K**

A young child wakes when the morning sun shines through the window and goes through the day describing all the ways the sun is important.

Best, Cari.

Sally Jean, the Bicycle Queen. Illustrated by Christine Davenier. New York: Farrar, Straus & Giroux. 32pp. ISBN 9780374363864. **Gr. K–2**

Sally Jean absolutely adores riding her bike. When she outgrows her two-wheeler and her parents can't afford a new one, she becomes determined to earn enough money for a new one.

Brown, Marc.

Arthur Series. Boston: Little, Brown. Gr. K–3

Arthur the aardvark and his family live in a friendly neighborhood with other anthropomorphized animals. He goes to school, does his homework, and participates in family vacations and other activities of everyday life, in a series that has thrived for over thirty years. It has spawned several other series, including one about his little sister, D. W., an easy reader series, a chapter book series, and a television series. Brown is especially adept in capturing a child's feelings and perspectives and portraying them in a way children relate to both in text and illustrations. Except for the anniversary edition of *Arthur's Nose*, the early volumes are only available in paperback.

Arthur's Nose: 25th Anniversary Limited Edition. 2001. Unpaged. ISBN 978-0316118842.

Arthur's Nose was originally released in 1976. Brown was inspired to write the story after telling bedtime stories to his own son, Arthur. This anniversary edition includes illustrations showing how Arthur's nose changed over the years.

Arthur's Eyes. 1979. 27pp. ISBN 9780316110693 (pb).

Arthur's Valentine. 1980. 32pp. ISBN 9780316111874 (pb).

Arthur and the True Francine. 1981. Unpaged. ISBN 9780316109499 (pb).

Arthur Goes to Camp. 1982. 32pp. ISBN 9780316110587 (pb).

Arthur's Halloween. 1982. 32pp. ISBN 9780316110594 (pb).

Arthur's April Fool. 1983. 32pp. ISBN 9780316112345 (pb).

Arthur's Thanksgiving. 1983. 32pp. ISBN 9780316112321 (pb).

Arthur's Christmas. 1984. 31pp. ISBN 9780316109932 (pb).

Arthur's Tooth. 1985. 32pp. ISBN 9780316112468 (pb).

Arthur's Teacher Trouble. 1986. 32pp. ISBN 9780316111867 (pb). (SP)

Arthur's Baby. 1987. 32pp. ISBN 9780316111232.

Arthur's Birthday. 1989. 32pp. ISBN 9780316110730.

Arthur's Pet Business. 1990. 32pp. ISBN 9780316118637 (pb). (SP)

Arthur Meets the President. 1991. Unpaged. ISBN 9780316112918 (pb).

Arthur Babysits. 1992. Unpaged. ISBN 9780316114424 (pb).

Arthur's Family Vacation. 1993. Unpaged. ISBN 9780316109581 (pb). (SP)

Arthur's New Puppy. 1993. Unpaged. ISBN 9780316109215 (pb). (SP)

Arthur's First Sleepover. 1994. Unpaged. ISBN 9780316110495 (pb).

Arthur's Chicken Pox. 1994. Unpaged. ISBN 9780316110501 (pb).

Arthur's TV Trouble. 1995. Unpaged. ISBN 9780316110471 (pb).

Arthur Writes a Story. 1996. Unpaged. ISBN 9780316109161.

Arthur's Computer Disaster. 1997. Unpaged. ISBN 9780316110167.

Arthur Lost and Found. 1998. Unpaged. ISBN 9780316109123.

Arthur's Underwear. 1999. Unpaged. ISBN 9780316110129.

Arthur's Teacher Moves In. 2000. Unpaged. ISBN 9780316119795.

Arthur's Perfect Christmas. 2000. Unpaged. ISBN 9780316119689.

D. W. Series. Boston: Little, Brown. `PreS–2`

D. W. is Arthur's little sister who eventually got a series of her own. D. W. is self-assured and persistent and often vies with Arthur. Just as Brown brings readers into Arthur's world, here he escorts them into D. W.'s.

D. W. Flips! 1987. 20pp. ISBN 9780316112697 (pb).

D. W. All Wet. 1988. Unpaged. ISBN 9780316112680 (pb).

D. W. Rides Again. 1993. Unpaged. ISBN 9780316110488 (pb).

D. W. Thinks Big. 1993. Unpaged. ISBN 9780316109222 (pb).

D. W. the Picky Eater. 1995. Unpaged. ISBN 9780316110488 (pb).

D. W.'s Lost Blankie. 1998. Unpaged. ISBN 9780316109147 (o.p.).

D. W. Go to Your Room. 1999. Unpaged. ISBN 9780316109055.

D. W.'s Library Card. 2001. Unpaged. ISBN 9780316110136.

D. W.'s Guide to Preschool. 2003. Unpaged. ISBN 9780316120692.

D. W.'s Guide to Perfect Manners. 2006. 32pp. ISBN 9780316121064.

Bunting, Eve.

Our Library. **Illustrated by Maggie Smith. New York: Clarion, 2008. 32pp. ISBN 9780618494583.** `Gr. K–2`

Raccoon and his friends don't take the news that their library will be closing due to lack of funds lying down. They take out books that help them fix up the building and raise funds to keep it open.

Cole, Joanna.

My Friend the Doctor. **Illustrated by Maxie Chambliss. New York: HarperCollins, 2005. 32pp. ISBN 9780060505004.** **T-K**

This reassuring book follows a little girl through her checkup with the doctor.

De Groat, Diane.

The Gilbert Series. **PreS-2**

Gilbert, a porcupine who deals with typical family situations, is a student who goes to school with other critters and celebrates seasonal holidays. All titles are illustrated with watercolors that capture the emotions and experiences of the young characters.

Roses Are Pink, Your Feet Really Stink. New York: William Morrow, 1996. Unpaged. ISBN 9780688136048.

Trick or Treat, Smell My Feet. New York: William Morrow, 1998. Unpaged. ISBN 9780688170615 (pb).

Happy Birthday to You, You Belong in a Zoo. William Morrow, 1999. Unpaged. ISBN 9780060010294 (pb).

Jingle Bells, Homework Smells. William Morrow, 2000. Unpaged. ISBN 978-0688175450 (pb).

Good Night, Sleep Tight, Don't Let the Bedbugs Bite! New York: Seastar Books, 2002. Unpaged. ISBN 9781587171291.

Liar, Liar Pants on Fire. New York: Seastar Books, 2003. Unpaged. ISBN 9780811854535 (pb).

Brand-New Pencils, Brand-New Books. New York: HarperCollins, 2005. Unpaged. ISBN 9780060726157 (lb).

No More Pencils, No More Books, No More Teacher's Dirty Looks! New York: HarperCollins, 2006. Unpaged. ISBN 9780060791155 (lb).

Last One in Is a Rotten Egg! New York: HarperCollins, 2007. Unpaged. ISBN 9780060892944.

Mother, You're the Best! (But Sister, You're a Pest!). New York: HarperCollins, 2008. Unpaged. ISBN 9780061238994.

April Fool! Watch Out at School! New York: HarperCollins, 2009. ISBN 9780061430428.

Falconer, Ian.

Olivia Series. **New York: Atheneum.** **PreS-2** (SP)

Olivia is a little girl pig who exudes energy and delight no matter what she is doing. Humor comes shining through in the illustrations, which burst off the page in a droll counterpoint to the understated text. Interesting use of color, which begins with deftly designed charcoal and red, expands in subsequent titles and makes the books even more intriguing.

🌲 *Olivia.* 2000. Unpaged. ISBN 9780689829536.

> The exuberant Olivia twirls through her day, from sampling seventeen outfits to choose one to start the day, to bargaining about how many books to read at bedtime. (ALAN, Caldecott Honor)

🌲 *Olivia Saves the Circus.* 2001. Unpaged. ISBN 9780689829543.

> Olivia takes center stage as she entertains her classmates with her vacation visit to the circus. When all the performers get sick, Olivia fills in for every act, as a lion tamer, a juggler, a clown, and a trapeze artist. (ALAN, New York Times Best Illustrated)

Olivia . . . and the Missing Toy. 2003. 40pp. ISBN 9780689852916.

> When Olivia loses her favorite toy, she hunts for it everywhere on a dark and stormy night. To her horror, when she finds it, she discovers that her dog has chomped on it. Not one to be upset for long, Olivia repairs the damage and forgives her pup.

Olivia Forms a Band. 2006. 44pp. ISBN 9781416924548.

> Olivia and her family go out for some summer fireworks. Olivia, disappointed to learn that there is no band, declares her intention to form one. Her family scatters to avoid being drafted into service, so Olivia demonstrates that she can be a quite capable one-pig band.

*Olivia Helps with Christmas.*2007. 42pp. ISBN 9781416907862.

> Olivia and her family are preparing for Christmas. In between hanging stockings, baking cookies, and decorating the tree, Olivia is always waiting for Santa.

Olivia Goes to Venice. 2010. 50pp. ISBN 9781416996743.

> Olivia and her family journey to the legendary Italian city for a vacation they will never forget.

Fox, Mem.

*Ten Little Fingers, Ten Little Toes. **Illustrated by Helen Oxenbury. Orlando: Harcourt, 2008. Unpaged. ISBN 9780152060572.** `T-K`

> This lilting poem pairs babies from around the world, demonstrating in words and pictures that no matter how different they seem, there are many things that are the same, like ten little fingers and ten little toes.

Henkes, Kevin.

Mouse Books. **New York: Greenwillow.** `PreS-2` **(SP)**

> Award-winning Henkes has created a cluster of stories featuring mice as main characters. Some of the stories share characters. They all tap into the feelings of children and are accompanied by watercolor-and-ink illustrations that beautifully capture the emotions of the featured mice. The author groups these titles together on his Web site, so they are grouped together here.

A Weekend with Wendell. 1986. 32pp. ISBN 9780688063252.

Wendell is not the best house guest when he goes to visit Sophie. He insists they play games his way, messes up her toys, and snatches her dessert when she's distracted. At last, Sophie has had enough and plays a trick that teaches Wendell a lesson.

Sheila Rae, the Brave. 1987. 32pp. ISBN 9780688071554.

Fearless Sheila Rae faces every danger without backing down. Full of confidence, she takes a new way home, but when she gets lost, she cries out for help. Little sister Louise, who has been following her, bravely leads her back home.

🌳*Chester's Way.* 1988. 32pp. ISBN 9780688076078.

Chester is a very precise mouse. He likes everything just so, as does his friend Wilson. So the two don't quite know what to make of their new neighbor Lilly and her freewheeling ways. (ALAN)

Julius, the Baby of the World. 1990. 32pp. ISBN 9780688089436.

Lilly's parents think that Julius is the perfect baby, but Lilly knows he's not because she hates him. When she tries acting like a baby to get her parents' attention, she only earns their disapproval, but things turn around when a cousin criticizes Julius, and Lilly defends her baby brother.

🌳*Chrysanthemum.* 1991. Unpaged. ISBN 9780688096991.

Chrysanthemum loves her flower name, until she goes to kindergarten, where she is teased by those with shorter, simpler names. Her mother and father offer her hugs and kisses to cheer her, but it's her music teacher who helps relieve her distress, for her name is Delphinium, and she plans to name her new baby the most beautiful name she's ever heard: Chrysanthemum. (ALAN)

🌳*Owen.* 1993. Unpaged. ISBN 9780688114497.

Owen loves his blanket, Fuzzy, and carries it everywhere with him. Owen's parents patiently listen to tips from a neighbor about how to separate Owen and Fuzzy. When the time for school draws near, Owen's mother transforms the worn-out blanket into handkerchiefs so that Owen can continue to carry it with him. (ALAN, Boston Globe Honor, Caldecott Honor)

🌳*Lilly's Purple Plastic Purse.* 1996. Unpaged. ISBN 9780688128975.

Lilly adores everything about school until her teacher, Mr. Slinger, won't let her interrupt the lessons to show off her weekend treasures, which include her purple plastic purse. Suddenly he seems to be the meanest teacher in the world, and Lilly leaves, not expressing her feelings. When she finds his kind note in her purse, she feels terrible, and with the help of her parents, reconciles with her teacher. (ALAN)

🌳*Lilly's Big Day.* 2006. 32pp. ISBN 9780060742362.

Lilly's teacher Mr. Slinger announces that he and Ms. Shotwell will be getting married. Despite her parents' best efforts to convince her otherwise, Lilly is convinced that she will be their flower girl. Mr. Slinger breaks the news to her that his niece will fill that role, but he convinces Lilly to take on the role of assistant, a much-needed job, as it turns out. (ALAN)

hooks, bell.

Skin Again. **Illustrated by Christopher Raschka. New York: Hyperion, 2004. 32pp. ISBN 9780786808250.** `Gr. K-3`

Hooks has penned a text that emphasizes that skin is just a covering and that to know any person, readers must know them from the inside, not the outside. Raschka's bold illustrations show children reaching out of boxes to discover each other beyond ordinary barriers.

Horse, Harry.

<u>Little Rabbit Series</u>. Atlanta, GA: Peachtree. `PreS-1`

In these gentle stories, Little Rabbit lives with his family and goes through a number of typical childhood experiences. Illustrated with delicate pen-and-ink and watercolor paintings.

Little Rabbit Lost. 2002. 32pp. ISBN 9781561452736.

On Little Rabbit's birthday, excitement fills the air as the entire clan heads out to the Rabbit World amusement park. Sure that he is a big rabbit now, Little Rabbit isn't worried when he wanders away from his family, at first. When he realizes he can no longer see his mother, he begins to feel small again, but his red birthday balloon helps the family members find each other. Reunited, they enjoy a celebratory picnic.

Little Rabbit Goes to School. 2004. 32pp. ISBN 9781561453207.

The first day of school begins with Little Rabbit insisting he take his favorite toy with him. He blames the toy for all of his misdeeds, but he also makes new friends and wisely decides to leave the toy home the next day.

Little Rabbit Runaway. 2005. 32pp. ISBN 9781561453436.

After a scolding from his parents, Little Rabbit concludes that he does not want to be bossed about anymore, so he runs away. He meets fellow runaway Molly Mouse, and they build a house together, but he soon discovers that she can be just as bossy as his family members. When both of the mamas find them, they are ready to return home.

Little Rabbit's Christmas. 2007. 32pp. ISBN 9781561454198.

Little Rabbit wishes for a whooshing red sled for Christmas. When he gets just what he wants, he won't let any of his friends ride it, but he quickly gets in trouble as he ventures too far and the sled breaks. His friends help him fix the sled, and he sees how important they are. They finish the day sledding together.

Little Rabbit's New Baby. 2008. 32pp. ISBN 9781561454310.

Little Rabbit is anticipating the birth of his new sibling with joy, because he is convinced the baby will be his playmate. When triplets are born, he does his best to help care for them, but soon begins to feel neglected when his parents pay so much attention to the new arrivals. However, when he is the only one who can get the triplets to fall asleep, Little Rabbit feels like an important part of the family once again.

Howie, Betsy.

The Block Mess Monster. **Illustrated by C. B. Decker. New York: Holt, 2008. 32pp. ISBN 9780805079401.** PreS–2

Calpurnia's problem is that her mother wants her to clean her room, but the Block Mess Monster refuses to allow this. Her mother can't see the monster and begins to lose patience, but then concocts a plan that works for everyone.

Jenkins, Emily.

What Happens on Wednesdays. **Illustrated by Lauren Castillo. New York: Farrar, Straus & Giroux, 2007. 32pp. ISBN 9780374383039.** PreS–1

A preschooler in Brooklyn describes her routine with her with her parents on Wednesdays, from breakfast through bedtime, giving readers insight into her independent personality.

Klise, Kate.

The Little Rabbit Series. Illustrated by M. Sarah Klise. Gr. K–2

Little Rabbit is a kindhearted youngster with a patient mother, who experiences holidays, emotions, and an imaginary friend. Detailed acrylic illustrations add warmth and touches of humor.

Shall I Knit You a Hat? A Christmas Yarn. New York: Holt, 2005. 32pp. ISBN 9780805073188.

When a snowstorm is predicted to arrive on Christmas Eve, Mother Rabbit knits her son a special hat. Concerned for his friends, Little Rabbit suggests they make hats for all of his friends as Christmas presents. He designs them to be unique for each animal, and his mother knits them. At first his friends are a bit bewildered by their strangely shaped headgear, but when the snow swirls down, they realize what warm gifts they've been given.

Why Do You Cry? Not a Sob Story. New York: Holt, 2006. 32pp. ISBN 978-0805073195.

Since Little Rabbit is turning five, he decides that he will not be crying any more. Furthermore, no one who cries will be invited to his birthday party. Then he finds out that not only do all of his animal friends still cry sometimes, even his mother still cries, and sometimes it's when she's happy. Learning this, he decides to reinvite all of his friends to his party.

Imagine Harry. Orlando, FL: Harcourt, 2007. 32pp. ISBN 9780152057046.

Little Rabbit's best friend is his imaginary playmate Harry, who accompanies him on a variety of seasonal activities. Mother Rabbit even supplies cookies and lemonade for him, but she warns that Harry will not have a desk in school and will have to be very quiet. Harry is so quiet that Little Rabbit is able to make new friends, and Harry is able to disappear.

Little Rabbit and the Night Mare. Orlando, FL: Harcourt, 2008. Unpaged. ISBN 9780152057176.

Little Rabbit has to do a report for school, but he's not sure what topic he should choose. His mother makes several suggestions, but he rejects them all.

At night, his fears invade his dreams, as he worries about his report. Mother Rabbit explains he is having a nightmare and gives him some ideas about taming his anxiety. When he faces his fears, he is able to get a good night's sleep and to write a quality report.

Little Rabbit and the Meanest Mother on Earth. Orlando, FL: Harcourt, 2010. 32pp. ISBN 9780152062019.

Little Rabbit's mother will only let him go to the circus if he cleans his room. Thinking he will never finish, he imagines selling tickets to a new attraction, the Meanest Mother on Earth.

Kuskin, Karla.

I Am Me. **Illustrated by Dyanna Wolcott. New York: Simon & Schuster, 2000. Unpaged. ISBN 9780689814730.** `T–K`

During a day at the beach, a preschooler lists all the ways in which she is like various relatives.

Lamb, Albert.

Sam's Winter Hat. **Illustrated by David McPhail. New York: Scholastic, 2006. Unpaged. ISBN 9780439793049.** `T–K`

An absentminded bear cub is always misplacing his things. When he loses the brand new hat from Grandma, he becomes determined to change his ways.

Landry, Leo.

Eat Your Peas, Ivy Louise! **Boston: Houghton Mifflin, 2005. Unpaged. ISBN 9780618448869.** `T–K`

Toddler Ivy Louise has much more interesting things to do with her peas than eat them, for they are performing a variety of circus tricks just for her.

Lin, Grace.

Dim Sum for Everyone. **New York: Knopf, 2001. 32pp. ISBN 9780375810824.** `PreS–2`

A Chinese American family with three daughters goes to a restaurant in Chinatown for the narrator's favorite kind of meal, dim sum. The servers present a variety of small Chinese dishes, like pork buns and egg tarts, and each family member selects his or her own treats.

Fortune Cookie Fortunes. **New York: Knopf, 2004. Unpaged. ISBN 978-0375815218. Sequel.** `PreS–2`

In this follow-up to *Dim Sum for Everyone*, the family is once again eating in a Chinese restaurant. This time the narrator explains why fortune cookies are so much fun.

London, Jonathan.

Froggy Series. New York: Viking. Illustrated by Frank Remkiewicz. `PreS–3`

Froggy is a childlike amphibian with a mind of his own and a loving family. He celebrates various holidays, plays different sports, and encounters various experiences at school, with his family, and with his friends.

Froggy Gets Dressed. 1992. Unpaged. ISBN 9780670842490. (SP)

Let's Go Froggy. 1994. Unpaged. ISBN 9780670850556.

Froggy Learns to Swim. 1995. Unpaged. ISBN 9780670855513.

Froggy Goes to School. 1996. Unpaged. ISBN 9780670867264.

Froggy's First Kiss. 1998. Unpaged. ISBN 9780670870646.

Froggy Plays Soccer. 1999. Unpaged. ISBN 9780670882571. (SP)

Froggy's Halloween. 1999. Unpaged. ISBN 9780142300688 (pb).

Froggy Goes to Bed. 2000. Unpaged. ISBN 9780670888603.

Froggy's Best Christmas. 2000. 32pp. ISBN 9780140567359 (pb).

Froggy Eats Out. 2001. 28pp. ISBN 9780670896868.

Froggy Goes to the Doctor. 2002. 32pp. ISBN 9780670035786.

Froggy Plays in the Band. 2002. Unpaged. ISBN 9780142400517 (pb).

Froggy's Baby Sister. 2003. 32pp. ISBN 9780670036592.

Froggy's Day with Dad. 2004. 32pp. ISBN 9780670035960.

Froggy Sleepover. 2005. 32pp. ISBN 9780670060047.

Froggy Rides a Bike. 2006. 32pp. ISBN 9780670060993.

Froggy Plays T–Ball. 2007. 30pp. ISBN 9780670061877.

Froggy Goes to Camp. 2008. 32pp. ISBN 9780670010981.

Froggy's Best Babysitter. 2009. 28pp. ISBN 9780670011766.

Froggy Goes to Hawaii. 2011. 32pp. ISBN 9780670012213.

Mayhew, James.

Where's My Hug? Illustrated by Susan Hellard. New York: Bloomsbury, 2008. 32pp. ISBN 9781599902258. `PreS–2`

When Jake refuses a hug from his mom as she drops him off at school, she gives it to his dad, and he in turn passes his to the next person. Jake finds he wants a hug later, but has to go on a quest to find it.

McClements, George.

Night of the Veggie Monster. New York: Bloomsbury, 2008. Unpaged. ISBN 9781599900612. **PreS–3**

When it's time for a child to eat his peas, he transforms into a wiggling veggie monster, but when he actually swallows the vegetable, he finds he likes it.

Milgrim, David.

Time to Get up, Time to Go. New York: Clarion, 2006. 32pp. ISBN 9780618519989. **T–K**

A young boy zooms through his daily activities from waking up in the morning to bedtime, all the while taking good care of his stuffed blue doll.

Myers, Walter Dean.

Looking Like Me. Illustrated by Christopher Myers. New York: Random House, 2009. 32pp. ISBN 9781606840016. **Gr. 1–3**

With raplike rhyme and cadence, young Jeremy looks in the mirror and describes in positives the boy who looks back at him, and then he relates how he is a different person from the people in his life (a brother, a son, etc.). Illustrated with fluorescent collages that add to the verses' exuberance.

Park, Linda Sue.

Bee-Bim Bop! Illustrated by Ho Baek Lee. New York: Clarion, 2005. 31pp. ISBN 9780618265114. **PreS–2**

From the grocery shopping to the cooking, a Korean American girl helps her mother prepare the traditional Korean dish, bee-bim bop.

Parr, Todd.

Reading Makes You Feel Good. New York: Little, Brown, 2005. 32pp. ISBN 9780316160049. **PreS–2** (SP)

Parr uses his bright illustrations to show a selection of places that can be visited and fun things that can be learned through reading.

Pinkney, Sandra L.

Shades of Black: A Celebration of Our Children. Illustrated by Myles C. Pinkney. New York: Scholastic, 2000. Unpaged. ISBN 9780439148924. **PreS–1**

Striking, sharp color photographs of African American children illustrate an affirmative text that utilizes apt metaphors to describe differing skin tones, hair types, and eye color.

I Am Latino: The Beauty in Me. Illustrated by Myles C. Pinkney. New York: Little, Brown, 2007. 32pp. ISBN 9780316160094. **PreS–1** (Bilingual)

Clear color photographs of Latino children accompany a poetic text with a Spanish translation that invites readers to experience a culture's language, family, cuisine, and heritage.

Roosa, Karen.

Beach Day. **Illustrated by Maggie Smith. New York: Clarion, 2001. 32pp. ISBN 9780618029235.** `T-K`

A family spends a joyful day at the beach splashing in the waves and building a sand castle.

Rosenberry, Vera.

Vera Series. New York: Holt. `PreS–2`

Vera is a spunky heroine who is tackling a variety of life experiences, from a new baby in the family to starting in a new school. As she grows up, she relishes becoming independent.

When Vera Was Sick. 1998. Unpaged. ISBN 9780805068320 (pb).

Vera's First Day of School. 1999. Unpaged. ISBN 9780805072693 (pb).

Vera Runs Away. 2000. Unpaged. ISBN 9780805062670 (o.p.).

Vera Goes to the Dentist. 2002. Unpaged. ISBN 9780805066685.

Vera Rides a Bike. 2004. 32pp. ISBN 9780805071252.

Vera's Baby Sister. 2005. 32pp. ISBN 9780805071269.

Vera's New School. 2006. 32pp. ISBN 9780805076134.

Vera's Halloween. 2008. 32pp. ISBN 9780805081442.

Shannon, David.

The David Series. New York: Blue Sky Press. `PreS–2` (SP)

Bold and childlike acrylic illustrations depict David, a mischievous young boy who delights in getting into one scrape after another, in these books whose art and adventures come from the author's own childhood.

🔖 *No, David!* 1998. 32pp. ISBN 9780590930024.

David, a mischievous boy, creates havoc throughout the day, as his mother repeatedly admonishes him. After he stretches too far for the cookie jar, tramps mud all over the carpet, bangs on pots, dashes naked down the road, and destroys a vase, his mother puts him in time out, but affirms that she still loves him. (ALAN, Caldecott Honor, New York Times Best Illustrated)

David Goes to School. 1999. Unpaged. ISBN 9780590480871.

When David goes to school, he breaks as many rules there as he did at home. This time his teacher corrects him when he cuts in line, runs in the hall, and daydreams. Finally, when he draws on the desk, his teacher demands that he stay after school to clean all of the desks as punishment. He performs the task admirably and wins his teacher's praise at last.

David Gets in Trouble. 2002. Unpaged. ISBN 9780439050227.

David's high-energy escapades are still getting him in trouble, but this time he has an excuse for each episode. He accidentally throws a baseball through a window, pulls the cat's tail because she likes it, and denies eating the cake even though his face is covered with frosting. This spirited tale concludes with his confession of guilt to his mother and her acceptance of his apology.

Saltzberg, Barney.

The Cornelius P. Mud Series. Cambridge, MA: Candlewick. `PreS-1`

Cornelius is a cheerful young pig who is usually ready for almost anything, but the illustrations reveal that he does things his own way, creating a humorous series of stories.

Cornelius P. Mud, Are You Ready for Bed? 2005. 32pp. ISBN 9780763623999.

It's bedtime, and Cornelius's parents ask him all the traditional questions about getting ready for bed. Each time he answers in the affirmative, but the illustrations show the true story.

Cornelius P. Mud, Are You Ready for School? 2007. 32pp. ISBN 978 0763629137.

While his mother asks Cornelius several questions about his preparations for school and Cornelius answers in the affirmative, the illustrations show him holding balloons, eating cotton candy, and filling his backpack with toys, which all makes sense, because he is heading off to clown school.

Cornelius P. Mud, Are You Ready for Baby? 2009. Unpaged. ISBN 978-0763635961.

When Cornelius's mother brings home his new baby brother, Cornelius asks question after question, until his mother assures him that she can love them both.

Tafolla, Carmen.

🎗*What Can You Do with a Rebozo?* Illustrated by Amy Cordova. Berkeley, CA: Tricycle, 2008. 32pp. ISBN 9781582462707. `Gr. K-2` (SP)

A young girl describes all the things she can do with her rebozo, a brightly colored Mexican shawl, from using it as her superhero cape to cradling her baby brother in it. (ALA, Pura Belpre Honor)

Torrey, Richard.

Almost. New York: HarperCollins, 2009. 40pp. ISBN 9780061561665. `PreS-1`

Jack is almost six and is convinced that he is almost big enough for many things that he's not quite ready for, like making his own breakfast and wearing big boy clothes.

Viorst, Judith.

Just in Case. Illustrated by Diana Cain Bluthenthal. New York: Atheneum, 2006. Unpaged. ISBN 9780689871641. `Gr. 1-3`

Charlie, a boy with an overactive imagination, likes to be prepared, in case things don't go well. He digs a pit in the back yard in case a lion escapes from the zoo. He takes a net to the beach in case a mermaid grabs him. He stock-piles peanut butter sandwiches in case the stores run out of food. However, when he's not prepared for his surprise birthday party, he realizes that sometimes the unexpected can be fun.

Weston, Tamson.

Hey, Pancakes! **Illustrated by Stephen Gammell. San Diego: Harcourt, 2003. 32pp. ISBN 9780152165024.** `PreS-1`

Exuberant rhymes enumerate the steps three excited children execute as they make pancakes, creating a delicious mess in the kitchen at the same time. Gammell uses his signature paint-splattered artwork to convey delight and chaos.

Easy Readers

Brown, Marc.

Arthur Easy Reader Series. New York: Random House. `Gr. 1-3`

Arthur the aardvark, who first starred in a series of picture books and then in his own TV show, is featured here with his friends, in books designed for children who are striking out on their own reading adventures.

Arthur's Reading Race. 1996. 24pp. ISBN 9780679867388 (pb).

Arthur Tricks the Tooth Fairy. 1998. Unpaged. ISBN 9780679884644 (pb).

Arthur's Fire Drill. 2000. 21pp. ISBN 9780679984764 (lb).

Arthur's Lost Puppy.. 2000. 24pp. ISBN 9780679984665 (lb).

Arthur's Back-to-School Surprise. 2002. Unpaged. ISBN 9780375910005 (lb).

Arthur and the School Pet. 2003. 24pp. ISBN 9780375910012 (lb).

Arthur's Science Fair Trouble. 2003. 18pp. ISBN 9780375910036 (lb).

Arthur and the New Kid. 2004. 23pp. ISBN 9780375913815 (o.p.).

Arthur Breaks the Bank. 2004. 24pp. ISBN 9780375910029 (o.p.).

Arthur Lost in the Museum. 2005. 23pp. ISBN 9780375929731 (lb).

Arthur Loses a Friend. 2006. 24pp. ISBN 9780375929748 (lb).

Arthur in New York. 2008. 24pp. ISBN 9780375929762 (lb).

Arthur's Reading Trick. 2009. 24pp. ISBN 9780375929779 (lb).

Danziger, Paula.

A Is for Amber Series. Illustrated by Tony Ross. New York: Putnam. `Gr. 1-3`

The feisty character Amber Brown debuted in the transitional chapter book, *Amber Brown Is Not a Crayon*, and continued as the protagonist in many sequels. Here, she stars in a series of prequels for younger readers, featuring a younger Amber and her adventures at school, with friends, and at home. As always, Danziger perfectly captures the concerns of children as they navigate their world, portraying situations with empathy and humor. Ross's colorful and high-spirited illustrations highlight Amber's feelings and add amusing details to the stories.

It's Justin Time, Amber Brown. 2001. 48pp. ISBN 9780698119079 (pb).

What a Trip, Amber Brown. 2001. 48pp. ISBN 9780399234699.

It's a Fair Day, Amber Brown. 2002. 48pp. ISBN 9780399236068.

Get Ready for Second Grade, Amber Brown. 2002. 48pp. ISBN 9780399236075.

Second Grade Rules, Amber Brown. 2004. 48pp. ISBN 9780399234729.

Aren't You Glad It's Halloween, Amber Brown. 2005. 48pp. ISBN 978-0399234712.

O'Connor, Jane.

Fancy Nancy Series (I Can Read). Illustrated in the style of Robin Preiss-Glasser by Ted Enik. New York: HarperCollins. `Gr. 1-3`

Fancy Nancy, who started out as the protagonist of her own picture book series, here stars in her own set of easy to read books. Each adventure is graced with her unique style and includes a glossary of Nancy's "Fancy Words."

Fancy Nancy and the Boy from Paris. 2008. 32pp. ISBN 9780061236105.

Fancy Nancy at the Museum. 2008. 32pp. ISBN 9780061236082.

Fancy Nancy Sees Stars. 2008. 32pp. ISBN 9780061236129.

Fancy Nancy: Poison Ivy Expert. 32pp. ISBN 9780061236143.

Fancy Nancy: The Dazzling Book Report. 32pp. ISBN 9780061703690.

Fancy Nancy: Pajama Day. 2009. 32pp. ISBN 9780061703713.

Fancy Nancy: 100th Day of School. 2009. 32pp. ISBN 9780061703751.

Fancy Nancy: Every Day Is Earth Day. 2010. 32pp. ISBN 9780061873270.

Van Leeuwen, Jean.

The Tales of Amanda and Oliver Pig. New York: Dial. `Gr. 1-3`

Amanda and Oliver are sibling pigs who experience the typical trials and tribulations of growing up: sibling rivalry, starting school, making friends, and celebrating the holidays.

Van Leeuwen's deft touch provides characters reader's can readily identify with as they hone their reading skills.

Tales of Oliver Pig. Illustrated by Arthur Lobel. 1979. 64pp. ISBN 978-0140365498 (pb).

❦*More Tales of Oliver Pig.* Illustrated by Arthur Lobel. 1981. 64pp. ISBN 978-0140365542 (pb). (ALAN)

❦*Amanda Pig and Her Big Brother Oliver.* Illustrated by Ann Schweninger. 1982. Unpaged. ISBN 9780140370089 (pb). (ALAN)

❦*Tales of Amanda Pig.* Illustrated by Ann Schweninger. 1983. 56pp. ISBN 978-0140368406 (pb). (ALAN)

More Tales of Amanda Pig. Illustrated by Ann Schweninger. 1985. 56pp. ISBN 978- 0140376036 (pb).

Oliver, Amanda and Grandmother Pig. Illustrated by Ann Schweninger. 1987. 56pp. ISBN 9780140373868 (pb).

Oliver and Amanda's Christmas. Illustrated by Ann Schweninger. 1989. 56pp. ISBN 9780803706361 (o.p.).

Oliver Pig at School. Illustrated by Ann Schweninger. 1990. 48pp. ISBN 978-0803708129 (o.p.).

Amanda Pig on Her Own. Illustrated by Ann Schweninger. 1991. 48pp. ISBN 978-0140371444 (pb).

Oliver and Amanda's Halloween. Illustrated by Ann Schweninger. 1992. 48pp. ISBN 9780803712379 (o.p.).

Oliver and Amanda and the Big Snow. Illustrated by Ann Schweninger. 1995. 48pp. ISBN 9780140382501 (pb).

Amanda Pig, Schoolgirl. Illustrated by Ann Schweninger. 1997. 48pp. ISBN 978-0141303574 (pb).

Amanda and Her Best Friend Lollipop. Illustrated by Ann Schweninger. 1998. 48pp. ISBN 9780140379990 (pb).

Oliver and Albert, Friends Forever. Illustrated by Ann Schweninger. 2000. 48pp. ISBN 9780803725171 (o.p.).

Amanda Pig and the Awful, Scary Monster. Illustrated by Ann Schweninger. 2000. 48pp. ISBN 9780142402030 (pb).

Oliver the Mighty Pig. Illustrated by Ann Schweninger. 2004. 48pp. ISBN 978-0803728868.

❦*Amanda Pig and the Really Hot Day.* Illustrated by Ann Schweninger. 2005. 48pp. ISBN 9780803728875. (ALAN; Geisel Honor)

Oliver Pig and the Best Fort Ever. 2006. Illustrated by Ann Schweninger. 40pp. ISBN 9780803728882.

Amanda Pig, First Grader. Illustrated by Ann Schweninger. 2007. 40pp. ISBN 9780803731813.

Amanda Pig and the Wiggly Tooth. Illustrated by Ann Schweninger. 2008. 39pp. ISBN 9780803731042.

Favorites

In a Blue Room by Jim Averbeck

Big Bad Bunny by Franny Billingsley

The A Is for Amber Series by Paula Danziger

Time for Bed by Mem Fox

Tacky the Penguin by Helen Lester

Tough Chicks by Cece Meng

Knuffle Bunny by Mo Willems

King Bidgood's in the Bathtub by Audrey Wood

1

2

3

4

5

6

7

8

Chapter 2

Everyday Life—The World Surrounding the Child: Family, Friends, School, and Challenging Situations

The world surrounding the child includes the people and experiences that are closest to him or her, but encompassing a larger circle of people than the more task-oriented realistic fiction of the preceding chapter. As before, stories with animal characters in which the animals are stand-ins for humans are included. The topics here progress from specific to general.

Families

Families are central to the lives of children, and picture books abound that depict all kinds of families, family relationships, and family activities. They help young people explore different families and families like their own. They feature moms and dads, grandparents, brothers and sisters, and having a new baby in the family.

Parents and Children

Father and Child

Although many family stories center around the activities of children and their parents, the following titles emphasize the bond between parents and their children.

Banks, Kate.

🏵*Night Worker*. **Illustrated by Georg Hallensleben. New York: Farrar, Straus & Giroux, 2000. Unpaged. ISBN 9780374355203.** `PreS–2`
When Alex accompanies his engineer father to work on his night job, he is filled with awe of the exciting, powerful world of construction. (ALAN, Charlotte Zolotow Award)

That's Papa's Way. **Illustrated by Lauren Castillo. New York: Farrar, Straus & Giroux, 2009. Unpaged. ISBN 9780374374457.** `PreS-2`

> As dawn lightens to day, a father and daughter tramp through the woods to spend the day together fishing, each taking pleasure in being together.

Bennett, Kelly.

Dad and Pop: An Ode to Fathers & Step Fathers. **Illustrated by Paul Meisel. Somerville, MA: Candlewick, 2010. 40pp. ISBN 9780763633790.** `PreS-2`

> A chipper young girl presents her two fathers. One is her biological Dad and the other is her stepfather; she calls him Pop. Although they are very different men, they both love her dearly.

Browne, Anthony.

My Dad. **New York: Farrar, Straus & Giroux, 2001. Unpaged. ISBN 978-0374351014.** `PreS-3`

> A child who exudes love for his father lists all his admirable traits, while humorous illustrations depict dad demonstrating his prowess.

Bruchac, Joseph.

My Father Is Taller Than a Tree. **Illustrated by Wendy Halperin. New York: Dial, 2010. 32pp. ISBN 9780803731738.** `PreS-1`

> Brief rhymes present the loving relationships between thirteen pairs of fathers and sons. Delicate crayon-and-pencil drawings enhance the caring reiterated in the text.

Cusimano, Maryann K.

You Are My I Love You. **Illustrated by Satomi Ichikawa. New York: Philomel, 2001. Unpaged. ISBN 9780399233920.** `PreS-2`

> Through poetic metaphors and a rhyming text, a teddy bear father describes all the ways a parent can love a child.

Dorros, Arthur.

🐾*Papá and Me.* **Illustrated by Rudy Gutierrez. New York: HarperCollins, 2008. Unpaged. ISBN 9780060581565.** `PreS-3`

> A Latino boy and his Papá enjoy a day together, starting out with pancakes for breakfast, moving on to playing in the park, and concluding with a bus ride to grandma's. The father speaks Spanish, and his son translates his words into English. Gutierrez's dynamic illustrations are filled with swirls of color that vividly bring to life the love between this father and son. (Pura Belpre Honor)

Emmett, Jonathan.

Someone Bigger.* **Illustrated by Adrian Reynolds. New York: Clarion, 2004. Unpaged. ISBN 9780618443970. `PreS-1`

> In this cumulative tale, a father and son go out to fly a kite. It's such a windy day that the father gets whisked away, along with a succession of townspeople. It's up to his son to bring them all back to earth.

I Love You Always and Forever. **Illustrated by Daniel Howarth. New York: Scholastic, 2007. 32pp. ISBN 9780439916547. T-K**

> Littletail and Longtail, father and daughter field mice, play together in the forest. When Littletail grows discouraged, her father reassures her that even though she is small now, she will get bigger and one day will be faster than he is. He also reiterates that no matter what, he will always love her.

George, Kristine O'Connell.

Up! **Illustrated by Hiroe Nakata. New York: Clarion, 2005. 32pp. ISBN 9780618064892. T-K**

> A father and his toddler daughter share a day of fun at the park.

McBratney, Sam.

🎗*Guess How Much I Love You*. **Illustrated by Anita Jeram. Cambridge, MA: Candlewick, 1995. 32pp. ISBN 9780763641757. PreS-1 (SP)**

> Little Nutbrown Hare and his father engage in a game of one-upmanship to express how much they love each other. (ALAN)

Norac, Carl.

My Daddy Is a Giant. **Illustrated by Ingrid Godon. New York: Clarion, 2005. 29pp. ISBN 9780618443994. PreS-1**

> A young boy describes his father in larger-than-life terms—he's so tall clouds sit on his shoulders, when he sneezes he blows the sea away—but he's a giant who has time to play marbles with his son, who always feels safe with him.

Parr, Todd.

The Daddy Book. **Boston: Little, Brown, 2002. Unpaged. ISBN 978-0316607995. T-K**

> With childlike illustrations in bold, neon colors and a simple text, Parr describes various kinds of daddies who all love their children.

Pfister, Marcus.

Bertie: Just Like Daddy. **New York: North South, 2009. Unpaged. ISBN 9780735822245. T-K**

> Bertie is a little hippo who wants to be just like his loving father.

Plourde, Lynn.

Dad, Aren't You Glad? **Illustrated by Amy Wummer. New York: Dutton, 2005. 32pp. ISBN 9780525473626. PreS-2**

> A little boy does his best to help his dad with the household chores, never noticing that each time he does, he creates a small disaster.

Schaefer, Lola.

Toolbox Twins. Illustrated by Melissa Iwai. New York: Holt, 2006. 32pp. ISBN 9780805077339. **PreS-1**

Father and son use their own tools together to fix things up around the house.

Warnes, Tim.

Daddy Hug. Illustrated by Jane Chapman. New York: HarperCollins, 2008. Unpaged. ISBN 9780060589509. **T-K**

Rhyming text and vibrant illustrations portray a variety of animal fathers interacting with their young, demonstrating admirable fatherly characteristics.

Yaccarino, Dan.

�$Every Friday.* New York: Holt, 2007. 32pp. ISBN 9780805077247. **PreS-2**

Friday is a boy's favorite day because he and his father have a standing date to have breakfast together at a local diner. They enjoy each other's company as they walk through their city neighborhood, greeting friends and arriving at the diner, where the waitress knows just what they want to eat. (New York Times Best Illustrated)

Yolen, Jane.

🌟*Owl Moon.* Illustrated by John Schoenherr. New York: Philomel, 1987. 32pp. ISBN 9780399214578. **PreS-3**

A father and daughter go out on a snowy night to watch for the great horned owl. Lyrical prose is accompanied by glorious watercolors of the New England landscape. (ALAN, Caldecott Medal)

Mother and Child

Bang, Molly.

In My Heart. New York: Little, Brown, 2005. 32pp. ISBN 9780316796170. **T-K**

A loving mother reassures her child that even though she leaves her little one every day to go to work, she always carries her child in her heart.

Billingsley, Franny.

Big Bad Bunny. Illustrated by G. Brian Karas. New York: Atheneum, 2008. 32pp. ISBN 9781416906018. **PreS-2**

Big Bad Bunny has long sharp claws and pointy teeth and stops at nothing. While she roams through the forest, Mama Mouse is settling her babies down for a nap. When she realizes that Baby Boo-Boo is missing, she goes out searching for her, covering the same ground as Big Bad Bunny. Big Bad Bunny gets lost and begins to howl, which leads Mama Mouse right to her. The illustrations reveal that Big Bad Bunny and Baby Boo-Boo are in fact the same being.

Browne, Anthony.

My Mom. New York: Farrar, Straus & Giroux, 2005. 32pp. ISBN 978-0374350987. **Gr. K–3**

This salute to moms lists a variety of admirable qualities, accompanied by humorous illustrations.

Cruise, Robin.

Only You. Illustrated by Margaret Chodos-Irvine. Orlando, FL: Harcourt, 2007. Unpaged. ISBN 9780152166045. **T–K**

Rhyming verses and pastel prints present the ways parents love their children, focusing on three parent–child pairs: an Asian American mother and baby in the morning, an African American father and toddler at midday, and a European American mother and preschooler at bedtime.

Dewdney, Anna.

The Llama Llama Series. New York: Viking. **T–K**

Baby Llama experiences a range of typical preschooler's emotions at bedtime, when he gets angry with his mother, and when he misses his mother, all expressed through gentle rhymes. Colorful and endearing illustrations reveal the characters' emotions.

Llama Llama, Red Pajama. 2005. 40pp. ISBN 9780670059836.

Baby Llama is all tucked in but grows anxious when mama leaves the room. He calls for her, but when she doesn't return right away, he cries full throttle. Mama comes running and assures Baby Llama that even if it doesn't seem like it, she is always nearby.

Llama Llama, Mad at Mama. 2007. 40pp. ISBN 9780670062409.

Baby Llama's annoyance at having to stop playing and go grocery shopping with Mama Llama grows into a full-fledged temper tantrum in the store. Patient Mama is able to sooth her child and together, they clean up the mess, finish shopping, and then go out for ice-cream.

Llama Llama, Misses Mama. 2009. 40pp. ISBN 9780670061983.

Llama Llama is now old enough to start school, and on the first day he misses his mama very much. His gentle teacher and friendly animal classmates show him the fun things there are to do at school, and by the end of the day, he realizes he can love school and mama at the same time.

Llama Llama, Holiday Drama. 2010. 40pp. ISBN 9780670011612.

As Christmas approaches, Llama Llama gets caught up in all the things there are to do before the big day and begins to feel swamped, until Mama brings to mind the true importance of the holiday.

Downing, Julie.

No Hugs Till Saturday. **New York: Clarion, 2008. 31pp. ISBN 9780618910786.** `PreS–1`

Felix, a young mischief-making dragon, and his mom often share a variety of hugs, from soft and snuggly to monster mashes. When he throws his baseball in the house and his mom takes the ball away from him, he decides to deprive her of these special times by banning hugs for the week. As the day progresses and Felix misses hugs more than he thought he would, he progressively moves the deadline a day closer, until he relents at bedtime. The watercolor and colored-pencil illustrations add humorous and loving touches.

Elya, Susan Middleton.

Bebé Goes Shopping. **Illustrated by Steven Salerno. Orlando, FL: Harcourt, 2006. 40pp. ISBN 9780152054267.** `T–K`

The rhyming text, which scatters Spanish words throughout, describes an expedition to the grocery store.

Bebé Goes to the Beach. **Illustrated by Steven Salerno. Orlando, FL: Harcourt, 2008. 40pp. ISBN 9780152060008. Sequel.** `T–K`

Once again smoothly weaving Spanish words into the English rhymes, Elya describes a delightful day for mother and toddler at the beach.

Glenn, Sharlee.

Just What Mama Needs. **Illustrated by Amiko Hirao. Orlando, FL: Harcourt, 2008. 30pp. ISBN 9780152057596.** `PreS–2`

Abby, an enthusiastic young pup, dresses up in a different costume every day. For each outfit, Mom comes up with just the right way for Abby to help.

Goode, Diane.

The Most Perfect Spot. **New York: HarperCollins, 2006. 32pp. ISBN 978-0060726980.** `PreS–1`

A boy takes his mom to the park for a picnic lunch, but one thing after another disrupts them until they return home and discover a pup in need of a home. The watercolor illustrations, which place the story in the early twentieth century, show that the newly adopted dog was the source of their previous troubles.

Grambling, Lois.

My Mom Is a Firefighter. **Illustrated by Jane Manning. New York: HarperCollins, 2007. 28pp. ISBN 9780060586409.** `PreS–3`

Billy is very proud that his mom is a firefighter and delights in visiting her at the station.

Jenkins, Emily.

Love You When You Whine. Illustrated by Sergio Ruzzier. New York: Farrar, Straus & Giroux, 2006. 32pp. ISBN 9780374346522. **T–K**
> A patient mother cat assures her mischievous kitten that she will love her no matter what.

Keller, Holly.

Miranda's Beach Day. New York: Greenwillow, 2009. 32pp. ISBN 978-0061582981. **PreS–1**
> Miranda and her mother spend a day at the beach, and Miranda delights in building a sand castle for a hermit crab. When a wave washes the castle away and sends the crab scuttling, Miranda is upset. Her mother explains that the crab and the sand belong to the ocean, just the way Miranda belongs to her.

Norac, Carl.

My Mommy Is Magic. Illustrated by Ingrid Godon. New York: Clarion, 2007. 29pp. ISBN 9780618757664. **PreS–1** (SP)
> A little girl explains all the ways in which her mother is magic: she makes monsters disappear, heals boo-boos with a kiss, and can make flowers grow. When the little girl grows up, she wants to be magic, just like her mom.

Parr, Todd.

The Mommy Book. Boston: Little, Brown, 2002. Unpaged. ISBN 978-0316608275. **T–K**
> With his signature neon colors and childlike illustrations accompanying a straightforward text, Parr lists all kinds of things that mothers can do.

Ryder, Joanne.

My Mother's Voice. Illustrated by Peter Catalanotto. New York: HarperCollins, 2006. 32pp. ISBN 9780060295097. **Gr. 1–3**
> A daughter describes her close relationship with her mother by relating the tones in her mother's voice, from calling her to breakfast, to laughter, humming, and singing.

Wild, Margaret.

*Kiss, Kiss. Illustrated by Bridget Strevens-Marzo. New York: Simon & Schuster, 2003. Unpaged. ISBN 9780689862793. **T–K**
> Baby Hippo happily tromps through the jungle to play but forgets to give his mama a kiss good-bye. Along the way he sees several kinds of animals give their own mothers kisses, which reminds him of his own forgetfulness and causes him to turn around and rush back home.

Willis, Jeanne.

Mommy, Do You Love Me? Illustrated by Jan Fearnley. Cambridge, MA: Candlewick, 2008. 24pp. ISBN 9780763634704. **T–K**

A young chick seeks reassurance that his mother will always love him and tests her assertions with small acts of misbehavior. Mom is patient, until his constant cheeping makes her lose her cool. Her anger scares him, but provides another way for her to reassure him that she loves him, even when she gets mad.

New Baby

Welcoming

Aston, Dianna Hutts.

When You Were Born. Illustrated by E. B. Lewis. Cambridge, MA: Candlewick, 2004. 32pp. ISBN 9780763614386. **PreS–2**

In a poem full of love, a mother relates her impressions of her precious newborn and then describes the responses of friends and family.

McCormick, Wendy.

The Night You Were Born. Illustrated by Sophy Williams. Atlanta, GA: Peachtree, 2000. 32pp. ISBN 9781561452255. **PreS–2**

While James stays at home with his Aunt Isabel awaiting word from his parents about the birth of his sister, his aunt tells him about waiting for him on the night that he was born.

Peddicord, Jane Ann.

That Special Little Baby. Illustrated by Meilo So. Orlando, FL: Harcourt, 2007. Unpaged. ISBN 9780152054304. **PreS–1**

Joyous rhymes proclaim the achievements of the new baby, from infancy to toddlerhood, accompanied by vibrant watercolor illustrations.

Vamos, Samantha R.

Before You Were Here, Mi Amor. Illustrated by Santiago Cohen. New York: Viking, 2009. Unpaged. ISBN 9780670063017. **PreS–2**

A loving mother-to-be describes to her unborn child all the preparations the extended family has gone through to get ready for the baby's arrival, in an English text sprinkled with Spanish words and phrases.

Sibling Response

Appelt, Kathi.

Brand-New Baby Blues. Illustrated by Kelly Murphy. New York: HarperCollins, 2009. 32pp. ISBN 9780060532338. **PreS–1**

In rhyming stanzas, a young girl laments the arrival of her new baby brother, because she is no longer the center of attention. Comfort from her parents helps her gradually accept her new sibling.

Ashman, Linda.

When I Was King. Illustrated by David McPhail. New York: HarperCollins, 2008. Unpaged. ISBN 9780060290511. `PreS–2`

> With clever rhymes, an older brother details the ways in which he has been dethroned by the new baby. Mostly, he tolerates the changes in his life, until the baby chomps on his catcher's mitt. His mother calms him down by showing him how important it is to be a big brother. McPhail's lovely watercolor-and-ink illustrations perfectly match the story's humor and emotion.

Cole, Joanna.

I'm a Big Brother. Illustrated by Rosalinda Kightley. New York: HarperFestival, 2010. rev. ed. Unpaged. ISBN 9780061900655. `T–K` (SP)

> A young lad, who is delighted to be a big brother, describes the many things his new baby brother can do. Bright illustrations complement the upbeat tone of the story.

I'm a Big Sister. Illustrated by Rosalinda Kightley. New York: HarperFestival, 2010. rev. ed. Unpaged. ISBN 9780061900624. `T–K` (SP)

> A young girl is happy to be a big sister and happy about all the things she can do because she is big. Cheerful illustrations add lightness to this positive story.

Harper, Anita.

It's Not Fair! Illustrated by Mary McQuillan. New York: Holiday House, 2007. Unpaged. ISBN 9780823420940. `PreS–1`

> In this cat family, the older sister is distressed by all the things that her new baby brother is allowed to get away with, like screaming and making a mess. She sees their situations reverse when the new arrival is old enough to realize all the things that he can't do but his sister can.

Harris, Robie H.

Mail Harry to the Moon! Illustrated by Michael Emberley. New York: Little, Brown, 2008. 38pp. ISBN 9780316153768. `PreS–1`

> A big brother bemoans his displacement in the family by his new baby brother, Harry. After each annoying incident, the protagonist has suggestions about what the family can do to restore the former glory days, until big brother gets worried that his parents have actually sent Harry to the moon. He stages a daring rescue and bonds with his brother at the same time.

Henkes, Kevin.

Julius, the Baby of the World. See under "Everyday Life in General" in chapter 1.

Horse, Harry.

Little Rabbit's New Baby. See under "Everyday Life in General" in chapter 1.

Jenkins, Emily.

🏵*That New Animal.* **Illustrated by Pierre Pratt. New York: Farrar, Straus & Giroux, 2005. Unpaged. ISBN 9780374374433.** `PreS-1`

Dogs FudgeFudge and Marshmellow are exceedingly annoyed when their humans bring home a "new animal," which has a distinct and human odor. Instead of playing catch with them and rubbing their bellies, all the humans do is gaze with adoration at the baby. They try a variety of ways to get rid of it, but only get reprimanded for their trouble. Then, when Grandpa tries to pick up the baby, they growl protectively, beginning to realize that the baby is part of their family. Jenkins dog's-eye-view of a new sibling brings the warmth of humor to this common family phenomenon. (Boston Globe Honor)

Lobel, Gill.

Too Small for Honey Cake. **Illustrated by Sebastien Braun. Orlando: Harcourt, 2006. 32pp. ISBN 9780152060978.** `PreS-2`

Little Fox grows jealous of all the time his father is spending with the new baby, until Daddy offers to share some honey cake together, which the baby is not big enough to eat.

London, Jonathan.

Froggy's Baby Sister. See under "Everyday Life in General" in chapter 1.

Patz, Nancy.

Babies Can't Eat Kimchee! **Illustrated by Susan Roth. New York: Bloomsbury, 2006. 32pp. ISBN 9781599900179.** `PreS-2`

A Korean American big sister is a bit disappointed when there are a lot of things her new baby sister can't do, like eat the spicy Korean dish kimchee, play dress-up, or go to ballet class. She decides that what she must do is be patient, because eventually they will have lots of fun together.

Rosenberry, Vera.

Vera's Baby Sister. See under "Everyday Life in General" in chapter 1.

Saltzberg, Barney.

Cornelius P. Mud, Are You Ready for Baby? See under "Everyday Life in General" in chapter 1.

Schotter, Roni.

The House of Joyful Living. Illustrated by Terry Widener. New York: Farrar, Straus & Giroux, 2008. Unpaged. ISBN 9780374334291. **Gr. K-3**

> A young girl enjoys living in her Manhattan apartment building with her neighbors of various ethnicities. One of her favorite things is when they gather at the rooftop garden to share stories and cuisine. Her mother is pregnant, and she wonders if the community has enough love for two children.

Shipton, Jonathan.

Baby Baby Blah Blah Blah! Illustrated by Francesca Chessa. New York: Holiday House, 2009. 32pp. ISBN 9780823422135. **PreS-1**

> When Emily's parents tell her she's going to be a big sister, she makes a list of pros and cons. Her parents reassure her that they will love her no matter how the baby changes their lives, which is a good thing, because the final illustration reveals that mom has twins.

Sullivan, Sarah.

Dear Baby: Letters from Your Big Brother. Illustrated by Paul Meisel. Cambridge, MA: Candlewick, 2005. 40pp. ISBN 9780763621261. **Gr. K-2**

> Mike writes letters to his new little sister Erica even before she is born and keeps writing during her first year of life. He makes the letters into a scrapbook and gives them to her as she celebrates her first birthday.

Uegaki, Chieri.

Rosie and Buttercup. Illustrated by Stephanie Jorisch. Tonawanda, NY: Kids Can Press, 2008. 29pp. ISBN 9781553379973. **PreS-2**

> At first Rosie the rodent enjoys playing with her new baby sister, but as the baby becomes increasingly disruptive, Rosie decides the solution is to give her away. She gives the baby to a neighbor, who is also their babysitter. He cares for her, and when Rosie has a change of heart, he gives her back.

Wigersma, Tanneke.

Baby Brother. Illustrated by Nynke Mare Talsma. Asheville, NC: Front Street, 2005. 32pp. ISBN 9781932425550. **PreS-2**

> As Mia pens a letter to her grandmother, she concentrates on detailing the changes in the family as their cat prepares to have kittens, but the pen-and-ink and watercolor illustrations show that mom is pregnant.

Woodson, Jacqueline.

Pecan Pie Baby. Illustrated by Sophie Blackall. New York: Putnam, 2010. 32pp. ISBN 9780399239878. **PreS-2**

> Mama is pregnant, and Gia is worried that the special feelings she and Mama share will disappear when the new baby arrives.

Siblings

Baguley, Elizabeth.

A Long Way from Home. **Illustrated by Jane Chapman. Kansas City, MO: Tiger Tales, 2008. 32pp. ISBN 9781589250741.** `PreS-2`

Noah is the smallest bunny in a family with a bountiful number of brothers and sisters. Longing for some solitude, Noah gets a ride to the land of the North Star on the back of an accommodating albatross. He falls asleep as the solitary inhabitant of an ice cave, but when he wakes up, he realizes he's lonely. The albatross flies him home, and he nestles in with his siblings, content once again.

Birdsall, Jeanne.

Flora's Very Windy Day. **Illustrated by Matt Phelan. New York: Clarion, 2010. 32pp. ISBN 9780618986767.** `PreS-2`

Flora often finds her little brother Crispin annoying. So when a gusty wind blows him away, she is severely tempted to give him away to the many who offer to take him, but in the end decides he's worth keeping after all.

Blumenthal, Deborah.

Don't Let the Peas Touch! And Other Stories. **Illustrated by Timothy Basil Ering. New York: Arthur A. Levine, 2004. 48pp. ISBN 9780439297325.** `Gr. K-2`

Sisters Annie and Sophie like different things, as demonstrated in these three stories. Annie, a preteen, loves to cook, but preschooler Sophie is finicky, providing a challenge for the budding chef. Sophie is rambunctious, whereas Annie likes a bit of quiet time to read. Annie is old enough to take on the responsibility of caring for a pet, and Sophie thinks she is, too, but no one will listen to her. The girls clash and resolve their differences in endearing and realistic ways.

Browne, Anthony.

My Brother. **New York: Farrar, Straus & Giroux, 2007. 32pp. ISBN 9780374351205.** `Gr. K-3`

A younger brother sings the praises of his older brother, who is so cool that he can play school, skateboard, and stand up to bullies, among a long list of admirable skills. Lighthearted cartoon illustrations aptly extend the fun of the cheery text.

Child, Lauren.

The Charlie and Lola Series. Cambridge, MA: Candlewick. `PreS-1`

Charlie and Lola are a brother and sister team who not only star in a series of picture books but also in their own television show. Charlie, the patient older brother, narrates the escapades of his energetic and imaginative little sister. All are illustrated in Lauren's signature collage and cartoon style, which adds to the delight of the stories. Included here are the picture books written by Lauren Child, not the spin-off series based on the television show.

🎖 *I Will Never Not Ever Eat a Tomato.* 2000. Unpaged. ISBN 9780763611880. (SP)

Charlie is charged with giving his little sister Lola her supper, and she promptly lists all the foods she will not eat. Unwilling to give in to her, Charlie creates exotic names for each food, and soon Lola is munching on orange twiglets from Jupiter (carrots) and asking for her favorite moonsquirters (tomatoes). (Kate Greenaway Medal)

I Am Not Sleepy and Will Not Go to Bed. 2001. Unpaged. ISBN 9780763615703.

When Lola imaginatively puts off getting ready for bed because whales are filling up the bathtub, a lion is brushing his teeth, and she has to get pajamas from the dancing dogs, Charlie cajoles her into co-operating with the promise of strawberry milk before bed. Lola agrees to get ready, but only if her three tiger friends can share the treat with her.

I Am Too Absolutely Small for School. 2004. 32pp. ISBN 9780763624033.

Lola absolutely does not want to start school. No matter what reason Charlie gives her, she counters it, until he tells her that her invisible friend will be starting school also and will be lonely without her.

Fearnley, Jan.

Martha in the Middle. **Cambridge, MA: Candlewick, 2008. 40pp. ISBN 9780763638009.** PreS–2

Martha's the middle mouse in her family. Clara, her older sister, is praised for being sensible, and her baby brother Ben is cooed over by everyone, but Martha is so ordinary, she's hardly noticed. Fed up with this, Martha decides to run away. Reaching the far end of the garden, she encounters a frog, which kindly listens to her and then gives her many examples that prove that the middle is the best place to be. When her siblings find her, she realizes that the frog is exactly right.

Fisher, Valorie.

My Big Brother. **New York: Atheneum, 2002. Unpaged. ISBN 978-0689843273.** T–K

In the voice of a baby narrator, Fisher lists ways in which the child's big brother is wonderful and shows those positive attributes in full-color photographs.

My Big Sister. **New York: Atheneum, 2003. Unpaged. ISBN 9780689854798.** T–K

This time Fisher provides the baby's perspective on sisterhood, accompanying the straightforward text with color photographs that reveal their loving relationship.

Funke, Cornelia.

The Wildest Brother. Illustrated by Kerstin Meyer. New York: Chicken House, 2006. 32pp. ISBN 9780439828628. `Gr. K–3`

> Anna's little brother Ben is brave and strong and on the go all day, protecting her from monsters and creating quite a mess while he's at it. At night their roles reverse, for Ben is afraid of the creaks and squeaks in the night, and Anna soothes him to sleep.

Gary, Meredith.

Sometimes You Get What You Want. Illustrated by Lisa Brown. New York: HarperCollins, 2008. 32pp. ISBN 9780061140150. `PreS–1`

> As two preschool twins, brother and sister, go through their day at home and at school, they learn the balance between getting what you want and giving it up.

Gay, Marie-Louise.

The Stella and Sam Series. Toronto: Groundwood. `PreS–2`

> Imaginative and quirky Stella and her little brother Sam are companionable siblings who enjoy a variety of activities together in different seasons. Sam is full of questions, and Stella always supplies answers, some of which are accurate and some made up.

Stella the Star of the Sea. 1999. 32pp. ISBN 9780888993373.

Stella the Queen of the Snow. 2000. Unpaged. ISBN 9780888994042.

Stella the Fairy of the Forest. 2002. Unpaged. ISBN 9780888994486. (SP)

Good Morning Sam. 2003. Unpaged. ISBN 9780888995285.

Good Night Sam. 2003. Unpaged. ISBN 9780888995308. (SP)

Stella the Princess of the Sky. 2004. 32pp. ISBN 9780888996015.

What Are You Doing Sam? 2007. 32pp. ISBN 9780888997340.

When Stella Was Very, Very Small. 2009. 32pp. ISBN 9780888999061.

Guy, Ginger Foglesong.

🌸*Siesta.* Illustrated by René King Moreno. New York: Greenwillow, 2005. Unpaged. ISBN 9780060560614. `PreS–1` (Bilingual)

> In a text that alternates English and Spanish, a brother and sisters gather the things they need to take their siesta outside. (ALAN)

Kvasnosky, Laura McGee.

Zelda and Ivy Tales. Cambridge, MA: Candlewick. `Gr. K–3`

> Fox sisters Zelda and Ivy negotiate the ups and downs of life. Though older sister Zelda tends to be bossy, and younger sister Ivy tends to be gullible, the two love

each other very much. The first three books are picture books, and the rest are easy readers.

🎀 *Zelda and Ivy.* 1998. 34pp. ISBN 9780763632618 (pb).

> In three tales of sisterhood, Zelda and Ivy have adventures on a swing, dress up their tales, and play with a baton. (ALAN, Golden Kite Honor)

Zelda and Ivy and the Boy Next Door. 1999. 34pp. ISBN 9780763637996 (pb).

> When Eugene becomes their new fox neighbor, Zelda and Ivy make a new friend, who sometimes makes their life even more complicated. (Reissued in 2009 in easy reader format.)

Zelda and Ivy One Christmas. 2000. 33pp. ISBN 9780763630478 (pb).

> Zelda and Ivy each long for a special gift for Christmas, but when they find out that their neighbor, Mrs. Brownlie, is going to be alone on Christmas, they turn their thoughts to planning ways to help.

Kurtz, Jane.

In the Small, Small Night. **Illustrated by Rachel Isadora. New York: Greenwillow, 2005. Unpaged. ISBN 9780066238142.** **PreS–2**

> On their first night in America, big sister Abena comforts little brother Kofi by telling him tales from their homeland of Ghana.

Lewison, Wendy Cheyette.

Two Is for Twins. **Illustrated by Hiroe Nakata, Hiroe. New York: Viking, 2006. 32pp. ISBN 9780670061280.** **T–K**

> Simple and cheerful rhymes express the specialness of being a twin by listing several things that two can do together.

Madison, Alan.

Velma Gratch and the Way Cool Butterfly. **Illustrated by Kevin Hawkes. New York: Schwartz & Wade, 2007. 40pp. ISBN 9780375835971.** **Gr. K–3**

> First grader Velma Gratch is the youngest of three sisters and longs to find a way to prove that she is unique. She gets her wish when a science lesson on butterflies leads to her special bonding with the creatures.

Milgrim, David.

Amelia Makes a Movie. **New York: Putnam, 2008. 32pp. ISBN 978-0399246708.** **Gr. 1–3**

> Since her parents are busy, Amelia decides to write, direct, and film her own movie. Her little brother gets underfoot a lot, but once Amelia starts listening to him, she realizes he has some good ideas and enlists his aid as her assistant.

Nolen, Jerdine.

Pitching in for Eubie. **Illustrated by E. B. Lewis. New York: Amistad, 2007. 32pp. ISBN 9780688149178.** Gr. 1–3

Everyone in this African American family is delighted when oldest daughter Eubie gets a scholarship to college, and they all pitch in to raise money for her room and board. Youngest sister Lily wants to contribute as well, but nothing she tries works, until she gets a job keeping her neighbor's elderly mother company.

O'Hair, Margaret.

Twin to Twin. **Illustrated by Thierry Courtin. New York: Margaret K. McElderry, 2003. 32pp. ISBN 9780689844942.** T–K

Upbeat rhymes proclaim all the wonderful activities these brother and sister twins can do.

Polacco, Patricia.

🎗*My Rotten Red-Headed Older Brother.* **New York: Philomel, 1994. Unpaged. ISBN 9780671727512.** Gr. 1–3

In this autobiographical tale, Patricia resents her rotten red-headed older brother Ritchie, who always outdoes her every time they compete. When she stays on the carousel longer than he does, she's finally better at something. Her satisfaction turns to newfound respect, after her dizziness makes her fall and her brother carries her home. Illustrated with Polacco's signature style and told with her warmth and flair. (ALAN)

Rotten Richie and the Ultimate Dare. **New York: Philomel, 2006. 48pp. ISBN 9780399245312.** Gr. 1–3

When Tricia and Ritchie's family move to a new town and start at a new school, Ritchie is always embarrassing Tricia. They always fight about which is better, his hockey or her ballet. One day Tricia triple dares him to perform at her ballet recital. He agrees on the condition that she play a hockey game with his team. She ends up scoring the winning goal, and he succeeds in performing the dance when the lead gets hurt. Polacco portrays a realistic sibling relationship with humor and genuine affection.

Schneider, Josh.

You'll Be Sorry. **New York: Clarion, 2007. 32pp. ISBN 9780618819324.** PreS–1

In a mouse family, the parents tell Samantha not to hit her baby brother or she will be sorry, but Samantha does it anyway. Her brother cries so much he floods the entire neighborhood, but it's his expression of sadness that makes her relent and apologize.

Stewart, Amber.

Little by Little. **Illustrated by Layn Marlow. New York: Orchard, 2008. 24pp. ISBN 9780545061636.** T–K

Otto the otter is making a list of all the things he can do and all the things he can't. Unfortunately the can't list is longer than the can list. What he wants most to be able to do is swim, but he fails until his older sister gives him some wise advice. She tells him to start small and work his way up to the harder skills. With this in mind as well as encouragement from his mom, Otto succeeds at last.

Voake, Charlotte.

🎗*Hello Twins.* Cambridge, MA: Candlewick, 2006. 24pp. ISBN 978-0763630034. **T–K**

Fraternal twins Charlotte and Simon are nothing alike. Charlotte enjoys stacking blocks, and Simon loves knocking them down. Simon likes to look at pictures in books, and Charlotte likes to color her own. Despite their differences, in the end they like each other just the way they are. (New York Times Best Illustrated)

Wells, Rosemary.

The Max and Ruby Series. New York: Viking. **PreS–1**

Max and Ruby are sibling bunnies who first appeared in a series of board books, and then picture books. They now star in their own television show. Max is a mischievous preschooler who has a mind of his own, and Ruby is his bossy older sister. Their slice-of-life adventures are realistic and heartwarming. Listed here are the picture books.

🎗*Max's Dragon Shirt.* 1991. Unpaged. ISBN 9780140567274 (pb). (ALAN)

Bunny Cakes. 1997. Unpaged. ISBN 9780670886869.

Bunny Money. 1997. Unpaged. ISBN 9780670886883.

🎗*Max's Chocolate Chicken.* 1999. Unpaged. ISBN 9780670887132. (ALAN)

Max Cleans Up. 2000. Unpaged. ISBN 9780670892181.

Bunny Party. 2001. Unpaged. ISBN 9780670035014.

Bunny Mail. 2004. Unpaged. ISBN 9780670036301.

Max Bunny Business. 2008. Unpaged. ISBN 9780670011056.

Max and Ruby's Bedtime Book. 2010. Unpaged. ISBN 9780670011414.

Max's Christmas. 2010. Unpaged. ISBN 9780670887156.

Wilson, Sarah.

Friends and Pals and Brothers, Too. Illustrated by Leo Landry. New York: Holt, 2008. 32pp. ISBN 9780805076431. **PreS–1**

Through all the seasons, two brothers enjoy a variety of activities together.

Winthrop, Elizabeth.

🌲*Squashed in the Middle*. Illustrated by Pat Cummings. New York: Holt, 2005. 32pp. ISBN 9780805064971. PreS–2

Daisy is the middle child in this African-American family. She's frustrated because no one will listen to her, so she makes a plan to bring about the attention she needs. (ALAN)

Grandparents

Boelts, Maribeth.

Those Shoes. Illustrated by Noah Z. Jones. Cambridge, MA: Candlewick, 2007. 40pp. ISBN 9780763624996. Gr. K–3

Jeremy desperately wants a pair of the hottest new sneakers, but his grandmother reminds him that money is tight and they must use what they have to buy the boots he needs. She helps him search the thrift shops. Although they find a used pair, they're much too small. Jeremy buys them anyway, but in the end decides to give them to a friend who needs them more than he does.

Bowen, Anne.

I Loved You Before You Were Born. Illustrated by Greg Shed. New York: HarperCollins, 2001. Unpaged. ISBN 9780060287207. PreS–1

A loving grandmother describes for the infant in her arms how much she loved the child and looked forward to his arrival.

When You Visit Grandma & Grandpa. Illustrated by Tomek Bogacki. Minneapolis, MN: Carolrhoda, 2004. 32pp. ISBN 9781575056104. Gr. K–2

A big sister tells her baby brother the wonderful things to do each season when staying with grandma and grandpa.

Cruise, Robin.

Little Mamá Forgets. Illustrated by Stacey Dressen-McQueen. New York: Farrar, Straus & Giroux, 2006. 32pp. ISBN 9780374346133. Gr. K–3

In this close Mexican American family, Lucy shares a special bond with her grandma, Little Mamá. Even though Little Mamá is losing her memory, she always knows how much she loves Lucy. Bright illustrations inspired by Mexican folk art heighten the warmth of this heartfelt story that is sprinkled with Spanish words and phrases.

Dorros, Arthur.

🌲*Abuela*. Illustrated by Elisa Kleven. New York: Dutton, 1991. Unpaged. ISBN 9780525447504. PreS–3

Latina American Rosalba imagines what it would be like to soar over New York City with her Spanish-speaking grandmother. Spanish words and phrases are woven into the text. (ALAN)

Isla. Illustrated by Elisa Kleven. New York: Dutton, 1995. Unpaged. ISBN 9780140565058 (pb). Sequel. **PreS-3**

> Rosalba and her grandmother are soaring again. This time, buoyed by Abuela's stories of her home; they fly over the Caribbean island where her grandmother, mother, and uncle were raised.

England, Kathryn.

Grandfather's Wrinkles. Illustrated by Richard McFarland, Richard. Brooklyn, NY: Flashlight Press, 2007. 32pp. ISBN 9780972922593. **PreS-2**

> When Lucy asks her grandfather where the crinkles on his face came from, he explains that they are from especially big smiles and relates remembrances as she points to each one.

Guy, Ginger Foglesong.

My Grandma/Mi Abuelita. Illustrated by Vivi Escriva. New York: Rayo/HarperCollins, 2007. 24pp. ISBN 9780060790981. **PreS-2** (Bilingual)

> In this book in English and Spanish, a family leaves the city by plane and arrives for a visit with grandma in the country.

Hines, Anna Grossnickle.

My Grandma Is Coming to Town. Illustrated by Melissa Sweet. Cambridge, MA: Candlewick, 2003. ISBN 9780763612375. **PreS-2**

> Albert doesn't remember ever meeting his grandmother, since he was a baby at the time, but they talk to each other on the phone and send letters and pictures. When he learns that she is coming for a visit, he's excited, but when she arrives, he feels shy. Grandma wins him over with kindness and their traditional phone greeting.

Juster, Norton.

🌺*The Hello, Goodbye Window*. Illustrated by Christopher Raschka. New York: Hyperion, 2005. 32pp. ISBN 9780786809141. **PreS-2**

> When a little girl goes to visit her Nanna and Poppy, the kitchen window of their home in the middle of town is a place of special magic for them. Through the window they watch the night stars. Next to the window they play games together, and at the window they wave hello and good-bye. The bouncy text, which conveys multigenerational love, is vividly illustrated by Raschka's mixed-media paintings that combine color-rich watercolors with pastel crayons to create images that are both childlike and masterful. (ALAN, Boston Globe Honor, Caldecott Medal, New York Times Best Illustrated)

Sourpuss and Sweetie Pie. Illustrated by Christopher Raschka. New York: Michael di Capua Books, 2008. 30pp. ISBN 9780439929431. Sequel. **PreS-2**

> The star of *The Hello Goodbye Window* returns, and this time she describes how her loving grandparents respond to her mood swings. Sometimes she's Sourpuss and sometimes she's Sweetie Pie, and while her grandpar-

ents enjoy Sweetie Pie more, they love their granddaughter no matter how mercurial her moods.

Lindbergh, Reeve.

My Hippie Grandmother. **Illustrated by Abby Carter. Cambridge, MA: Candlewick, 2003. Unpaged. ISBN 9780763606718.** `PreS-3`

Rhyming text presents a grandma who wears love beads, grows her own vegetables, drives a purple van, pickets city hall, and has a granddaughter who wants to grow up to be just like her.

My Little Grandmother Often Forgets. **Illustrated by Kathryn Brown. Cambridge, MA: Candlewick, 2007. 32pp. ISBN 9780763619893.** `PreS-1`

Tom describes his relationship with his grandmother in moving rhyme that tells of her transition from independence to living with her son and his family. Even though she is confused by being in an unfamiliar home, she finds her grandson and declares that she will stay.

Lloyd-Jones, Sally.

The Ultimate Guide to Grandmas & Grandpas! **Illustrated by Michael Emberley. New York: HarperCollins, 2008. Unpaged. ISBN 9780060756871.** `PreS-3`

This tongue-in-cheek advice book instructs youngsters, both animal and human, on how to treat their grandparents. They should share their ice cream, teach them how to play football, let them win sometimes, and most important, give plenty of hugs and kisses.

Look, Lenore.

Love as Strong as Ginger. **Illustrated by Stephen T. Johnson. New York: Atheneum, 1999. Unpaged. ISBN 9780689812484.** `Gr. 1-3`

This poetic text conveys the deep love Katie and her grandmother share. When Katie visits GinnGinn in Chinatown on Saturdays, she loves watching her Chinese grandmother cook and expresses a wish to grow up to be just like her. Her grandmother, however, has other plans for her. She wants Katie to go to college. She takes Katie to work with her one day to the factory where she and the other workers wield mallets to shell mountains of crab. It's backbreaking labor for very little money, money that she is saving for Katie's education. Katie realizes that her grandmother's love for her is as strong as ginger.

Park, Frances, and Ginger Park.

The Have a Good Day Café. **Illustrated by Katherine Potter. New York: Lee & Low, 2005. 32pp. ISBN 9781584301714.** `Gr. 1-3`

Mike is worried about his grandmother, who has recently arrived from Korea and seems to spend most of her time missing home. He's also concerned about his parents' business. They run a food cart in the park, but they are losing out to the competition. He and his grandmother come up with a plan to change the menu from bagels and hot dogs to traditional Korean cuisine, which both transforms the business into a success and helps his grandmother find her place in her new world.

Parr, Todd.

The Grandma Book. New York: Little, Brown, 2006. 24pp. ISBN 978-0316058025. **T-K**

Parr extols the wonders of grandmas and their love, illustrating his straight-forward text with his signature neon, childlike pictures.

The Grandpa Book. New York: Little, Brown, 2006. 24pp. ISBN 978-0316058018. **T-K**

As he did with grandmas, here Parr lists the fabulous attributes of grandpas.

Ryan, Pam Muñoz.

Mice and Beans. Illustrated by Joe Cepeda. New York: Scholastic, 2001. Unpaged. ISBN 9780439183031. **PreS-2**

Rosa Maria is preparing a lavish birthday party for her granddaughter. Un-beknownst to her, a family of mice is helping themselves to her treats, but they help save her party just in the nick of time. (ALAN)

Saenz, Benjamin Alire.

A Perfect Season for Dreaming/Una Tiempo Perfecto Para Sonar. Illustrated by Esau Morales. El Paso, TX: Cinco Puntos Press, 2008. 40pp. ISBN 9781933693019. **Gr. 1-3** (Bilingual)

Seventy-eight-year-old Octavio Rivera is having a summer full of amazing dreams, which he shares with his six-year-old granddaughter in this English/Spanish bilingual tale.

Savadier, Elivia.

Will Sheila Share? New Milford, CT: Roaring Brook, 2008. 24pp. ISBN 9781596432895. **T-K**

Toddler Sheila most definitely does not like to share, but Nana knows just how to teach her to change her ways.

Say, Allen.

Grandfather's Journey. Boston: Houghton Mifflin, 1993. 32pp. ISBN 9780395570357. **Gr. 3 & up**

Say relates the travels of three generations of his family between the United States and Japan. His grandfather journeyed from Japan to America and set-tled in San Francisco, but when his daughter is almost grown, he moves his family back to Japan, where Say is born. He in turn moves to America at the age of sixteen. Exquisitely illustrated with Say's watercolor paintings. (ALAN, Boston Globe Award, Caldecott Medal)

Adoption

Bergren, Lisa Tawn.

God Found Us You. Illustrated by Laura J. Bryant. New York: HarperCollins, 2009. 32pp. ISBN 9780061131769. **PreS–1**

In this religious adoption story, Little Fox begs his mother to repeat the tale of the day he came home to her. She does and assures him that his birth mother had a big reason for giving him up. She tells him how she prayed that God would bring her a child of her own to love.

Bunting, Eve.

Jin Woo. Illustrated by Chris K. Soentpiet. New York: Clarion, 2001. 30pp. ISBN 9780395938720. **PreS–1**

David wants to feel happy when his new baby brother arrives from Korea, but instead he feels resentful, even though he is adopted also. Gradually his worry recedes as he begins to bond with the baby, and his mother reads him a letter that she has written to him in the voice of his new brother.

Cummings, Mary.

Three Names of Me. Illustrated by Lin Wang. Morton Grove, IL: Albert Whitman, 2006. 40pp. ISBN 9780807579039. **Gr. 2 & up**

A Chinese American girl ruminates on her adoption, explaining that although she does not know the name her birth mother could have given her, she knows the people at the orphanage called her Wang Bin, and her new American parents named her Ada.

Friedman, Darlene.

Star of the Week: A Story of Love, Adoption, and Brownies with Sprinkles. Illustrated by Roger Roth. New York: HarperCollins, 2009. 30pp. ISBN 978-0061141362. **Gr. K–3**

When kindergartener Cassidy-Li is selected to be the Star of the Week, she is invited to do a project that will share something special with the class. She creates a photo-collage poster that depicts the story of her adoption from China. While she puts this together, she thinks about her birth parents, the other children in the orphanage, and the love of her family.

Heo, Yumi.

Ten Days and Nine Nights. New York: Schwartz & Wade, 2009. 40pp. ISBN 9780375847189. **Gr. K–3**

A Korean American girl eagerly awaits her mother's return from Korea, for she will bring her new little sister with her.

Krishnaswami, Uma.

Bringing Asha Home. **Illustrated by Jamel Akib. New York: Lee & Low, 2006. 32pp. ISBN 9781584302599. `Gr. K–3`**

> In this biracial family, Arun eagerly anticipates the arrival of his new sister, who is being adopted from India. She arrives just in time for them to celebrate the Hindu holiday of Rakhi Day, which honors the bond of siblings.

Lears, Laurie.

Megan's Birthday Tree: A Story about Open Adoption. **Illustrated by Bill Farnsworth. Morton Grove, IL: Albert Whitman, 2005. 32pp. ISBN 9780807550366. `Gr. 1–3`**

> Megan has a loving relationship with both her adoptive parents and her birth mother, Kendra. Kendra planted a tree the year Megan was born, but now she is marrying and moving away, and Megan is worried that without the tree to remind her, Kendra will forget about her daughter. Her mother assures her that Kendra loved her very much but gave her up because she knew it would best for Megan. Megan is especially reassured when Kendra lets her know that even though she carries Megan in her heart, she transplanted her tree to the new family home.

Lewis, Rose.

I Love You Like Crazy Cakes. **Illustrated by Jane Dyer. Boston: Little, Brown, 2000. Unpaged. ISBN 9780316525381. `PreS–1` (SP)**

> The narrator, a single mother, describes to her newly adopted daughter how she traveled to China to adopt her and bring her home. The watercolor illustrations are brimming with as much love as the text, and together they make this title an outstanding contribution to the selection of adoption books.

Every Year on Your Birthday. **Illustrated by Jane Dyer. New York: Little Brown, 2007. 26pp. ISBN 9780316525527. Sequel. `PreS–1`**

> With the daughter she adopted from China now a school-aged child, the mother from *I Love You Like Crazy Cakes* relates her memories of all their birthday celebrations.

Lin, Grace.

The Red Thread: An Adoption Fairy Tale. **Morton Grove, IL: Albert Whitman, 2007. 28pp. ISBN 9780807569221. `PreS–3`**

> In this story within a story, a Chinese American girl with Caucasian parents asks for the fairy tale of the Red Thread. They tell the tale of a king and queen in China who could not identify the pain in their chests until it was revealed that a red thread was attached to each of them. When they followed the thread across land and sea to find the baby on the other end, they found the child who was waiting just for them and happily brought her home.

Lopez, Susana.

The Best Family in the World. **Illustrated by Ulises Wensell. Tulsa, OK: Kane Miller, 2010. 28pp. ISBN 9781935279471.** `PreS-3`

When Carlotta, who lives in an orphanage, learns that her new family is coming to adopt her, she imagines a variety of exotic families. It turns out that they are an everyday, loving family, and that's just what Carlotta wants most.

Okimoto, Jean Davies, and Elaine Mei Aoki.

The White Swan Express: A Story about Adoption. **Illustrated by Meilo So. New York: Clarion, 2002. 32pp. ISBN 9780618164530.** `Gr. K-3`

Four families from North America, three from the United States and one from Canada, journey to the Chinese city of Guangzhou to adopt baby girls. They meet each other at the White Swan Hotel, where they are all staying while they work their way through the paperwork to finalize the adoption process. They grow close during their wait and stay in touch after they return home to raise their children.

Parr, Todd.

We Belong Together: A Book about Adoption and Families. **New York: Little, Brown, 2007. 32pp. ISBN 9780316016681.** `PreS-1`

With an inclusive yet simple text, Parr reassures all adoptive children in all kinds of families that they are loved and wanted. Illustrated with his distinctive bold colors and black-outline pictures, depicting people in an array of neon colors.

Peacock, Carol.

Mommy Far, Mommy Near: An Adoption Story. **Illustrated by Shawn Costello Brownell. Morton Grove, IL: Albert Whitman, 2000. 32pp. ISBN 9780807552346.** `Gr. K-3`

A young Chinese girl learns why her American family chose to adopt her and her little sister.

Sugarman, Brynn Olenberg.

Rebecca's Journey Home. **Illustrated by Michelle Shapiro. Minneapolis, MN: Kar-Ben Publishing, 2006. 32pp. ISBN 9781580131575.** `Gr. K-3`

Jacob and Gabriel Stein, brothers in a Jewish family, are looking forward to having a little sister, as their mother journeys to Vietnam to adopt a little girl.

Young, Ed.

My Mei Mei. **New York: Philomel, 2006. 32pp. ISBN 9780399243394.** `PreS-2`

A tale of adoption told by Antonia, the first daughter adopted from China. As she grows up, Antonia longs for a little sister (Mei Mei in Chinese), but when her parents adopt another girl from China, Antonia discovers having a sibling isn't everything she thought it would be. The baby can't talk, walk, or play, and yet she gets all of the attention. As the baby grows, she and Antonia form a strong sibling bond, in this story that is lushly illustrated with Young's gouache, pastel, and collage that radiate emotion.

Parent in the Military

Brisson, Pat.

Sometimes We Were Brave. Illustrated by France Brassard. Honesdale, PA: Boyds Mills Press, 2010. 32pp. ISBN 9781590785867. **Gr. K-2**

> Jerome has a comfortable family life when his sailor mom's ship is in port; she comes home every night. But when her ship leaves port, Jerome experiences difficulties. Although sometimes he has fun, sometimes he is afraid and misses his mom. He acts up in school and has a bed wetting problem. His understanding father is always a strong support for him, and together they look forward to the time when Mom will come home.

Bunting, Eve.

My Red Balloon. Illustrated by Kay Life. Honesdale, PA: Boyds Mills Press, 2005. 32pp. ISBN 9781590782637. **PreS-3**

> On the day his father's ship is to arrive as he returns home from a tour of duty in the navy, Bobby and his mother go down to the dock to meet the ship. Bobby wears a red balloon tied around his wrist so that his father can find him. He's distraught when the balloon slips away, but his father is able to locate him anyway, resulting in a joyous reunion.

McElroy, Lisa.

Love, Lizzie: Letters to a Military Mom. Illustrated by Diane Paterson. Morton Grove, IL: Albert Whitman, 2005. 32pp. ISBN 9780807547779. **Gr. K-3**

> While her mom serves in the military overseas, Lizzie writes her a series of letters to keep her current with events at home and to express how much she misses her.

Norman, Geoffrey.

Stars above Us. Illustrated by E. B. Lewis. New York: Putnam, 2009. 32pp. ISBN 9780399247248. **Gr. K-3**

> Before Amanda's father is deployed, the family decorates her ceiling with cutout stars. Her father shows her the North Star in the sky and on the ceiling and tells her to think of him when she sees the star.

Pelton, Mindy L.

When Dad's at Sea. Illustrated by Robert Gantt Steele. Morton Grove, IL: Albert Whitman, 2005. 32pp. ISBN 9780807563397. **Gr. K-2**

> Emily misses her father, who is a navy pilot on deployment for six months. She stays in touch with e-mail and phone calls and makes a friend on her father's ship.

Families with Gay or Lesbian Relatives

Brannen, Sarah S.

Uncle Bobby's Wedding. New York: Putnam, 2008. Unpaged. ISBN 9780399247125. **Gr. 2 & up**

> In this guinea pig family, Chloe's favorite uncle, Uncle Bobby, is going to marry his significant other, Jamie. Jamie wins Chloe's affections and assures her that Uncle Bobby will always have time for her, and she will now have two uncles to spend time with her. Reassured, Chloe gladly participates in the wedding as a flower girl.

Garden, Nancy.

Molly's Family. **Illustrated by Sharon Wooding. New York: Farrar, Straus & Giroux, 2004. 32pp. ISBN 9780374350024.** **PreS–1**

> When Molly draws a family picture that includes both of her mommies, Tommy declares that that is not a family. While her teacher explains that there are all kinds of families, Molly feels distressed and turns to her mommies. They explain that they had so much love to share they wanted to share it with a baby, so Mommy is her birth mother and Mama Lu is her adopted mother.

Polacco, Patricia.

In Our Mothers' House. New York: Philomel, 2009. 48pp. ISBN 9780399250767. **Gr. 2 & up**

> The African American narrator describes her life with her adopted mothers, a female gay couple whom the girl calls Marmee and Meema, and her adopted Asian brother and red-headed sister. They grow up in a loving home amid a mostly supportive neighborhood and return to visit their mothers with children of their own.

Richardson, Justin, and Peter Parnell.

🐧*And Tango Makes Three.* **Illustrated by Henry Cole. New York: Simon & Schuster, 2005. Unpaged. ISBN 9780689878459.** **PreS–3**

> Based on the true story of a penguin family living in New York City's Central Park Zoo, this book tells of two male penguins who share a nest and adopt a baby girl penguin. (ALAN)

Families in General

Best, Cari.

🐧*Are You Going to Be Good?* **Illustrated by G. Brian Karas. New York: Farrar, Straus & Giroux, 2005. Unpaged. ISBN 9780374303945.** **Gr. K–2**

> As Robert and his parents drive to Great-Gran Sadie's 100th birthday party, they encourage Robert to be on his best behavior. Full of energy, Robert hears the oft repeated phrase, "Don't do that!" At last the dancing begins, and his great-grandmother tells him to do his moves again. (New York Times Best Illustrated)

What's So Bad About Being an Only Child? **Illustrated by Sophie Blackall. New York: Farrar, Straus & Giroux, 2007. 30pp. ISBN 9780374399436.** `Gr. K–2`

> Rosemary, an only child who longs for a family full of brothers and sisters to play with, tells her parents they need to have another child right away. Her parents, however, are happy to have just Rosemary as their child. So Rosemary begins collecting "only" things. When one of those things that she thought was a rock turns out to be a turtle, Rosemary begins collecting pets and at last has some of the companionship she craves.

Buehner, Caralyn.

Would I Ever Lie to You? **Illustrated by Jack E. Davis. New York: Dial, 2007. 32pp. ISBN 9780803727939.** `Gr. K–3`

> The narrator's cousin Ed is always teasing him by lying to him, to the point where he doesn't know whether to believe what Ed tells him or not. Eventually he turns the tables by telling his cousin the same kind of tall tale that fools him.

Elliott, Zetta.

Bird. **Illustrated by Shadra Strickland. New York: Lee & Low, 2008. Unpaged. ISBN 9781600602412.** `Gr. 3 & up`

> African American Mehkai, nicknamed Bird, adores his older brother Marcus. They share a love of art, but as they grow up, Marcus slides deeper and deeper into drug abuse. Bird's life is thrown into emotional turmoil when first his beloved grandfather dies, and then Marcus. (ALAN)

Ernst, Lisa Campbell.

This Is the Van That Dad Cleaned. **New York: Simon & Schuster, 2005. Unpaged. ISBN 9780689861901.** `PreS–2`

> This cumulative story that follows the format of "The House That Jack Built," describes the adventures of an active family as they go for a ride in the just-cleaned van.

Feiffer, Kate.

My Mom Is Trying to Ruin My Life. See in chapter 14.

Hoffman, Mary.

<u>**The Grace Series.**</u> **New York: Dial.** `Gr. K–3`

> Grace is an independent and imaginative African American girl with a loving mother and grandmother to help her when life becomes challenging.

> *Amazing Grace.* Illustrated by Caroline Binch. 1991. Unpaged. ISBN 978-0803710405.

> > Grace loves to act, so when her class learns they are going to do *Peter Pan*, Grace wants to play Peter. One classmate informs her that she can't because she's a girl, and another tells her that she can't because

she's black. Discouraged, Grace tells her mother and grandmother. They encourage her to be anything she wants to be. Grace puts her heart and soul into the audition and secures the role she's dreamed she'd win. (ALAN)

Boundless Grace. Illustrated by Caroline Binch. 1995. Unpaged. ISBN 978-0803717152.

Grace, a lover of stories, wants a storybook family. When her father, who moved to Gambia after the divorce, invites her to visit, she travels to Africa with her grandmother, hoping to find the family she has imagined. She's disappointed when she feels like she doesn't fit in, but her beloved Nana helps her understand that there are many kinds of families.

Princess Grace. Illustrated by Ying-Hwa Hu and Cornelius Van Wright. 32pp. ISBN 9780803732605.

Two girls from Grace's class will be chosen as the princesses for the class's float in the town parade, and Grace would like to be one of them. Her wise teacher introduces the class to historical princesses from around the world, who did much more than look pretty, inspiring all the girls in class to want to be princesses. In the end, Grace rides on the float as a Gambian princess, wearing the Kente cloth of her father's homeland, and with her are all her friends, as princes and princesses representing a variety of global cultures.

James, Simon.

The Baby Brains Series. Cambridge, MA: Candlewick. `PreS–1`

Mr. and Mrs. Brains have the smartest baby around. Though the infant genius has extraordinary adventures, he always comes home to his loving parents.

Baby Brains. 2004. Unpaged. ISBN 9780763625078.

Mr. and Mrs. Brains want to ensure they have a very smart baby, so they read to their unborn child, play music for him, and turn up the volume on the news. Baby Brains is so smart that he reads the paper as soon as they bring him home from the hospital. In two weeks he is practicing medicine. When a group of scientists invite him to journey into outer space with them, he joins them and takes a walk in space. Then he cries that he wants his mommy. Order is restored when he is rushed home to his doting parents.

Baby Brains Superstar. 2005. Unpaged. ISBN 9780763628949.

Baby Brains turns his prodigious abilities toward music. After mastering an array of instruments, the toddler wins a talent contest and is about to perform when he realizes he wants his mommy once again.

Baby Brains and Robomom. 2008. 25pp. ISBN 9780763634636.

Now Baby Brains is experimenting with his chemistry set and creating inventions to help his parents. When his new Robomom goes too far, he realizes the original model is best.

Lloyd-Jones, Sally.

How to Be a Baby . . . by Me, the Big Sister. Illustrated by Sue Heap. New York: Schwartz & Wade, 2007. 32pp. ISBN 9780375838439. Gr. K–3

A savvy big sister lists what it's like to be a baby for her brother, including lots of things that babies can't do but big sisters can, concluding on a positive note about the huggabilty of little ones. Humor comes from the cartoon acrylic, crayon, and felt-tip pen illustrations.

How to Get Married . . . by Me, the Bride. Illustrated by Sue Heap. New York: Schwartz & Wade, 2009. 32pp. ISBN 9780375841187. Sequel. Gr. K–3

The worldly-wise big sister is back, and this time her lists are full of advice for planning and having a wedding. Once again, the acrylic cartoons add humorous details that complement the comic text.

Look, Lenore.

🎋*Henry's First-Moon Birthday.* Illustrated by Yumi Heo. New York: Atheneum, 2001. Unpaged. ISBN 9780689822940. PreS–2

Chinese American Jenny is helping her grandmother get ready for baby brother Henry's first-moon birthday, even though she doesn't think the infant's done much to deserve a celebration. When the relatives arrive, Jenny creates a little good-natured havoc and enjoys the Chinese treats with her cousins, deciding that Henry's not so bad after all. (ALAN)

🎋*Uncle Peter's Amazing Chinese Wedding.* Illustrated by Yumi Heo. New York: Atheneum, 2006. Unpaged. ISBN 9780689844584. Sequel. Gr. K–3

Uncle Peter is getting married, and Jen describes Chinese American wedding traditions. She has mixed feelings about her uncle getting married. She feels she might be losing him, but in the end, her new aunt finds a way to make her feel included. (ALAN, Charlotte Zolotow Honor)

Manning, Maurie.

Kitchen Dance. New York: Clarion, 2008. 32pp. ISBN 9780618991105. PreS–1

In this Afro-Latino family, the children peek into the kitchen when they hear splashing and clanking sounds. They see that mom and dad are cleaning up, but they are singing and dancing as they do. Papa sings to Mama in Spanish and twirls her around. When they spy the children, they include them in their joyous activity.

McKissack, Patricia.

Stitchin' and Pullin' a Gee's Bend Quilt. Illustrated by Cozbi A. Cabrera. New York: Random House, 2008. Gr. 1–3

In this African American family in Gee's Bend, Alabama, Baby Girl is learning how to quilt from her mother, grandmother, aunts, and neighbors.

O'Hair, Margaret.

Star Baby. Illustrated by Erin Eitter Kono. New York: Clarion, 2005. 32pp. ISBN 9780618306688. `T–K`

Brief rhymes and vibrant illustrations depict a day with a loving mother and her baby, concluding with a bedtime snuggle with mommy and daddy.

Parr, Todd.

The Family Book. New York: Little, Brown, 2003. 32pp. ISBN 9780316738965. `PreS–2`

With his intensely hued and childlike illustrations and simple text, Parr introduces children to a variety of kinds of families including human, animal, and extraterrestrial.

Perkins, Lynne Rae.

🎗*Pictures from Our Vacation.* New York: Greenwillow, 2007. 32pp. ISBN 978-0060850975. `Gr. 2 & up`

The narrator, her brother, and their parents travel across the country on their summer vacation to meet with their extended family for a reunion at the now-unused farm that was their grandparents'. (ALAN, Charlotte Zolotow Honor)

Polacco, Patricia.

🎗*The Keeping Quilt.* New York: Simon & Schuster, 1998. 48pp. ISBN 978-0689820908. `Gr. K–3`

This tenth-anniversary edition of a book first released in 1988 is the story of Polacco's great-grandmother, who journeyed to America from Eastern Europe and used cloth from her dress and babushka in a quilt. The quilt was handed down generation after generation. The original edition ended with the birth of Polacco's daughter. The revised edition includes several new pages, which continue the story with Polacco's two children and the death of her mother and concludes with the idea of how the tradition will continue. A moving story that is illustrated in Polacco's folk-art style. (Sydney Taylor Award)

When Lightning Comes in a Jar. New York: Philomel, 2002. ISBN 9780399231643. `Gr. 1–3`

As adult Tricia is preparing for a family reunion in her home, she pauses to remember the reunions of her childhood, when they played baseball and croquet, and caught fireflies in a jar.

Something about Hensley's. New York: Philomel, 2006. 48pp. ISBN 9780399245381. `Gr. K–3`

When a single mother and her two daughters move to a small town with a general store and a kindly store owner, they find everything they need there, even the unexpected.

Ramos, Jorge.

I'm Just Like My Mom & I'm Just Like My Dad/Me Parezco Tanto a Mi Mama & Me Parezco Tanto a mi Papa. **Illustrated by Akemi Gutierrez. New York: Rayo, 2008. Unpaged. ISBN 9780061239687.** `PreS-1` (Bilingual)

In this flip book in Spanish and English, half the book describes how a girl is like her mother and grandmother, and the flipped half describes how the boy is like his father and grandfather.

Recorvits, Helen.

The Yoon Series. Illustrated by Gabi Swiatkowska. New York: Farrar, Straus & Giroux. `Gr. 1-3`

When Yoon emigrates with her family from Korea to the United States, she has a variety of challenges to deal with in her new country.

🖤*My Name Is Yoon.* **New York: Farrar, Straus & Giroux, 2003. 32pp. ISBN 9780374351144.**

Yoon moves with her family from Korea to America and is having trouble adjusting to her new life. Even though her father teaches her how to write her name in English, she hates the way it looks and refuses to put it on her papers at school. Instead, she writes the simple words she learns in school until she makes a friend and begins to feel more at home. (ALAN)

Yoon and the Christmas Mitten. **New York: Farrar, Straus & Giroux, 2006. 32pp. ISBN 9780374386887.**

Yoon, fascinated by the story of Santa that she has learned at school, convinces her parents to bring some Christmas traditions into their family celebrations.

Yoon and the Jade Bracelet. **New York: Farrar, Straus & Giroux, 2008. 32pp. ISBN 9780374386894.**

Yoon longs for a jump rope for her birthday so that she can join the girls who play with theirs at school. Instead she receives a book and a valued bracelet, a family heirloom. When an older girl at school offers to teach her how to jump rope in exchange for the bracelet, Yoon almost loses the treasure for good. Using what she learns from the Korean folktale in her new book, she is able to win back her birthday gift.

Rylant, Cynthia.

🖤*The Relatives Came.* **Illustrated by Stephen Gammell. New York: Bradbury, 1985. 32pp. ISBN 9780689845086.** `PreS-3`

A large extended family gathers from north and south to meet in Virginia for a joyous family reunion. Gammell's amusing illustrations add to the hilarity of the text. (ALAN, Caldecott Honor, New York Times Best Illustrated)

Schaefer, Carole Lexa.

Big Little Monkey. **Illustrated by Pierre Pratt. Cambridge, MA: Candlewick, 2008. 32pp. ISBN 9780763620066.** `PreS-2`

While Little Monkey's family is sleeping, he decides it's time to explore the jungle and make new friends. He meets Steady Sloth but thinks he's too quiet, Proud Parrot is too squawky, and Sly Boa is definitely too tricky. After these encounters, Little Monkey thinks it's time to return home to his mama.

Viorst, Judith.

Super-Completely and Totally the Messiest. **Illustrated by Robin Preiss-Glasser. New York: Atheneum, 2001. 32pp. ISBN 9781416942009.** `PreS-3`

Older sister Olivia emphatically presents a case for younger sister Sophie being the messiest person of all time as she describes all the activities Sophie pursues while creating her chaos. Although tidy Olivia is frustrated with her sister, she does report on the nice things her brother and parents say about her wayward but much-loved sister.

Nobody Here but Me. **Illustrated by Christine Davenier. New York: Farrar, Straus & Giroux, 2008. Unpaged. ISBN 9780374355401.** `PreS-2`

The narrator is frustrated because even though his whole family is home, no one is paying any attention to him. His mom is talking on the phone, while his dad answers his e-mail, and his sister just wants him to go away so that she can play with her friend. He becomes mischievous to try to draw their notice and finally succeeds when he goes to bed early.

Williams, Vera B.

Rosa and Her Family. **New York: Greenwillow.** `PreS-3`

Rosa lives with her mother and grandmother, and though the family goes through some tough times financially, it's always filled with love.

🏵*A Chair for My Mother.* 1982. 32pp. ISBN 9780688009144. (SP)

After a terrible fire burns up their furniture, Rosa and her mother save up all the tips she makes from her waitressing job. They pour the coins into a large jar and add the ones that Grandma donates as well. At last the jar is full, and it's time to pick out just the right chair for her mother. (ALAN, Boston Globe Award; Caldecott Honor)

Something Special for Me. 1983. 32pp. ISBN 9780688065263 (pb).

Once again Rosa and her family are saving coins in their jar, but this time it's Rosa who gets to pick out a treat for her birthday.

Music, Music for Everyone. 1984. 32pp. ISBN 9780688026035.

When Rosa's grandmother gets sick, all the money the family has saved in their jar of coins gets used up to pay for the medical expenses. Rosa and her friends make music to cheer up her grandmother, and that gives her a wonderful idea of how she can help her family.

A Chair for Always. 2009. 40pp. ISBN 9780061722790.

> Aunt Ida and Uncle Sandy now live with Rosa and her family. While a midwife is upstairs helping to deliver Aunt Ida's baby, Rosa sits curled in her favorite chair imagining what life with her new cousin will be like. Her mother and grandmother suggest that it might be time to replace or reupholster the chair, but Rosa reminds them how important the chair is because they bought it with the coins they saved in their special jar.

Winter, Jeanette.

Angelina's Island. New York: Farrar, Straus & Giroux, 2007. 32pp. ISBN 9780374303495. **PreS–2**

> Angelina and her family have recently moved from Jamaica to New York City, and Angelina longs for her tropical island life. Her understanding mother arranges for her to participate in a Carnival parade, and Angelina begins to feel at home at last.

Woodson, Jacqueline.

Visiting Day. Illustrated by James Ransome. New York: Scholastic, 2002. 32pp. ISBN 9780590400053. **Gr. 2 & up**

> An African American girl is excited by all the preparations she and her grandmother make for visiting day, including frying up some chicken and braiding her hair. They take a bus to the prison, and she gets to sit on her father's lap while she tells him everything that has happened in the last month. She is sad when they have to say good-bye and watch the guards lead him away, but at home she gets right to work drawing pictures for him.

Easy Readers

Banks, Kate.

Monkeys and Dog Days. Illustrated by Tomek Bogacki. New York: Farrar, Straus & Giroux, 2008. 48pp. ISBN 9780374350291. **Gr. 1–3**

> In this suburban monkey family, brothers Max and Pete want a dog. They assure their parents that they will both take care of their new pet Fudge, but soon Pete leaves everything to Max. When Fudge shows a preference for Max, Pete realizes he has to do his fair share.

Monkeys and the Universe. Illustrated by Tomek Bogacki. New York: Farrar, Straus & Giroux, 2009. 48pp. ISBN 9780374350284. Sequel. **Gr. 1–3**

> Pete loves everything he is learning about the universe, and so his younger brother Max, who wants to be just like him, does too. When Max feels left out by all that Pete knows before he does, their parents take them to an observatory so that they can learn together.

Delacre, Lulu.

Rafi and Rosi. New York: HarperCollins, 2004. 63pp. ISBN 9780060098971 (pb). **Gr. 2–3** (SP)

> Rafi and Rosi are sibling Puerto Rican tree frogs, and although Rafi loves to tease his little sister, they always end up as friends, in three episodes that cover magnetism, bioluminescence, and mangroves.

Rafi and Rosi: Carnival! New York: Rayo, 2006. 63pp. ISBN 9780060735975. Sequel. **Gr. 2–3** (SP)

> Brother and sister tree frogs Rafi and Rosi are back, and this time they are enjoying Puerto Rico's Carnival parade. The Spanish words used in the text are defined in the glossary.

Kvasnosky, Laura McGee.

🏵*Zelda and Ivy: The Runaways.* Cambridge, MA: Candlewick, 2006. 42pp. ISBN 9780763626891. **Gr. 1–3**

> Fox sisters Zelda and Ivy, who were first featured in picture books, transition here to easy reader format in three linked stories. In the first, the sisters run away to the backyard to avoid having to eat cucumber sandwiches. In the second, they put together their very own time capsule, and in the third, their friend Eugene helps Zelda overcome her writer's block. (ALAN, Geisel Award)

Zelda and Ivy: Keeping Secrets. Somerville, MA: Candlewick, 2009. 42pp. ISBN 9780763641795. Sequel. **Gr. 1–3**

> In three more stories of Zelda, Ivy, and neighbor Eugene, they encounter secrets and pranks, and put on their own production of Cleopatra.

Mills, Claudia.

Gus and Grandpa Series. Illustrated by Catherine Stock. New York: Farrar, Straus & Giroux. **Gr. 1–3**

> Gus and Grandpa have a close, loving relationship and enjoy a variety of activities together, including sports and holiday fun.
>
> *Gus and Grandpa.* 1997. 48pp. ISBN 9780374428471 (pb).
>
> *Gus and Grandpa and the Christmas Cookies.* 1997. 47pp. ISBN 9780374328238 (o.p.)
>
> *Gus and Grandpa Ride the Train.* 1998. 47pp. ISBN 9780374428136 (pb).
>
> *Gus and Grandpa at the Hospital.* 1998. 47pp. ISBN 9780374428129 (pb).
>
> *Gus and Grandpa and the Two-Wheeled Bike.* 1999. 47pp. ISBN 9780374428167 (pb).
>
> *Gus and Grandpa and Show-and-Tell.* 2000. 47pp. ISBN 9780374428488 (pb).
>
> 🏵*Gus and Grandpa at Basketball.* 2001. 47pp. ISBN 9780374328184. (o.p.). (ALAN)
>
> *Gus and Grandpa and the Halloween Costume.* 2002. 48pp. ISBN 9780374328160.
>
> *Gus and Grandpa Go Fishing.* 2003. 48pp. ISBN 9780374328153.
>
> *Gus and Grandpa and the Piano Lesson.* 2004. 46pp. ISBN 9780374328146.

Ormerod, Jan.

The Ballet Sisters. See under "Art" in chapter 7.

Ruelle, Karen Gray.

The Harry and Emily Adventures. New York: Holiday House. `Gr. 1-3`

Harry and Emily are cat siblings who celebrate holidays and seasons in typical childlike fashion.

The Monster in Harry's Backyard. 1999. 32pp. ISBN 9780823414178 (o.p.).

The Thanksgiving Beast Feast. 1999. 32pp. ISBN 9780823415113. (o.p.)

Snow Valentines. 2000. 32pp. ISBN 9780823415335.

Spookier Than a Ghost. 2001. 32pp. ISBN 9780823416677.

April Fool! 2002. 32pp. ISBN 9780823416868.

Easy as Apple Pie. 2002. 32pp. ISBN 9780823417599.

Mother's Day Mess. 2003. 32pp. ISBN 9780823417735.

The Crunchy, Munchy Christmas Tree. 2003. 32pp. ISBN 9780823417872.

Easter Egg Disaster. 2004. 32pp. ISBN 9780823418060.

Just in Time for New Year's! 2004. 31pp. ISBN 9780823418411.

Great Groundhogs! 2005. 32pp. ISBN 9780823419302.

Dear Tooth Fairy. 2006. 32pp. ISBN 9780823419296.

Rylant, Cynthia.

Henry and Mudge Series. See chapter 10.

Shore, Diane Z.

How to Drive Your Sister Crazy. Illustrated by Laura Rankin. New York: HarperCollins, 2008. 48pp. ISBN 9780060527624. `Gr. 1-3`

Little brother Bradley Harris Pinkerton plays pranks on his sister until his tricks cause too much trouble. He writes out an apology, but that doesn't stop him from planning his next ambush.

Van Leeuwen, Jean.

The Tales of Amanda and Oliver Pig. See under "Everyday Life in General" in chapter 1.

Friends

Friends in General

Alter, Anna.

Abigail Spells. **New York: Knopf, 2009. 30pp. ISBN 9780375856174.** `Gr. K-2`

Abigail and George are best friends. Abigail enters a spelling contest with George's encouragement, but stage fright strikes, and she makes a mistake. Devastated to be eliminated from the competition, she turns to George, who tells her a story about what a truly wonderful person she is, no matter how she did in the spelling bee.

Beaumont, Karen.

Being Friends. **Illustrated by Joy Allen. New York: Dial, 2002. Unpaged. ISBN 9780803725294.** `T-K`

This lively rhyming text presents the similarities and differences between two young girls who are very close friends.

Becker, Bonny.

A Visitor for Bear. **Illustrated by Kady MacDonald Denton. Cambridge, MA: Candlewick, 2008. Unpaged. ISBN 9780763628079.** `PreS-2`

Bear doesn't want any visitors at all, but no matter what he does to discourage him, a small, persistent mouse doesn't give up until they become friends. (Sequel: *Birthday for Bear*; see under "Friends: Easy Readers" in this chapter.)

Bloom, Suzanne.

Bear and Goose Stories. Honesdale, PA: Boyds Mills Press. `T-K`

Delightful characters Bear and Goose share a tender friendship.

🏵*A Splendid Friend Indeed*. 2005. 32pp. ISBN 9781590782866. `T-K`

Bear likes quiet activities like reading, writing, and thinking. Each time he tries one, curious Goose interrupts with questions. When thinking makes Goose hungry, he goes to the kitchen for a snack. While there, he writes Bear a note declaring that Bear is a splendid friend indeed, and Bear responds with a great big bear hug. (ALAN, Giesel Honor)

Treasure. 2007. Unpaged. ISBN 9781590784570. `T-K`

Goose mistakenly believes Bear has a treasure map. He's disappointed when he doesn't find any treasure, until Bear reminds him that their true treasure is their friendship.

What about Bear? 2010. 32pp. ISBN 9781590785287. `T-K`

Best friends Goose and Bear welcome Fox into their friendship, but then have to find a way to make sure no one feels left out.

Bottner, Barbara.

Raymond and Nelda. Illustrated by Nancy Hayashi. Atlanta, GA: Peachtree, 2007. 32pp. ISBN 9781561453948. `PreS-1`

Raymond, a squirrel, and Nelda, a rabbit, are the best of friends until Raymond laughs at Nelda. Feelings hurt, Nelda doesn't want to play together any more. Raymond tries to apologize in notes, but things only get worse. At last, their letter carrier comes up with a plan to help them repair their friendship.

Bottner, Barbara, and Gerald Kruglik.

Wallace's Lists. Illustrated by Olof Landström. New York: HarperCollins, 2004. Unpaged. ISBN 9780060002244. `PreS-2`

Wallace is a sincere mouse who lives his life according to the lists he makes. When spontaneous Albert moves in next door, he gradually wins Wallace over to a night of adventure. In the morning, Wallace makes a new list and puts the name of his best friend Albert at the top.

Browne, Anthony.

Little Beauty. Somerville, MA: Candlewick, 2008. 32pp. ISBN 978-0763639594. `PreS-3`

Inspired by the story of Koko the gorilla, who learned to communicate with sign language and befriended a kitten, Browne spins a story of just such a gorilla–kitten friendship. The unlikely pals have fun together until they watch the movie *King Kong* on TV. The gorilla, upset by the film, destroys the TV. When the caretakers want to remove Beauty, the kitten, she convinces them it was her doing, and they let the pair stay happily together.

Chodos-Irvine, Margaret.

❀*Best Best Friends*. Orlando, FL: Harcourt, 2006. 40pp. ISBN 978-0152056940. `PreS-1`

Preschoolers Mary and Clare are best friends who greet each other with a hug each morning and play together all day at preschool. Things change on Mary's birthday. When their teacher and classmates pay more attention to Mary than to Clare, Clare grows resentful. Her jealousy leads to a fight. They play with other children until after naptime, when Clare gives Mary her homemade birthday picture, and all is forgiven. (ALAN)

Cooper, Helen.

The Pumpkin Soup Stories. New York: Farrar, Straus & Giroux. `PreS-2`

Three friends, Squirrel, Cat, and Duck, are housemates who enjoy different activities. No matter what their differences are, they always stay friends to the end.

Pumpkin Soup. 1999. Unpaged. ISBN 9780374460310 (pb). (SP)

When Squirrel, Cat, and Duck make their favorite pumpkin soup, each one has a role, and Duck's is to add a pipkin of salt at the end. When he decides he wants to stir the soup instead, Squirrel won't let him. Duck storms off into the forest in a huff. His friends search for him and return home, worried, to find him there waiting. All three have learned they need to be flexible in how they do things.

A Pipkin of Pepper. 2005. Unpaged. ISBN 9780374400248 (pb).

The three animal friends are once again making luscious pumpkin soup when they realize they are out of salt. They journey to the city to replace their stores, but Duck gets distracted by a pepper store. He steps into that store while Squirrel and Cat are focused on getting salt. The directionally challenged Duck is quickly lost, and it's up to his friends to find him.

Delicious. 2007. Unpaged. ISBN 9780374317560.

Cat, Duck, and Squirrel can't find any ripe pumpkins in their garden, so they can't make pumpkin soup. Duck rejects all the other soups his friends come up with, until Cat combines ingredients so that the new soup looks like pumpkin. Duck announces that it's delicious.

Foley, Greg E.

The Bear and Mouse Series. New York: Viking. T-K

Bear and Mouse are good friends who help each other with a variety of situations. Foley, an award-winning graphic designer, has created watercolor animal figures outlined in black against a plain background to produce a smooth welding of words and pictures that will appeal to young listeners.

Thank You Bear. 2007. 32pp. ISBN 9780670061655.

Bear and Mouse are good friends, and when Bear finds a box, he is sure Mouse will find it a tremendous treasure. On his way to give the box to mouse, the other animals express their disdain for the gift, and Bear begins to doubt his first impression, but in the end, he knows his friend. Mouse thinks the box is fabulous. (Charlotte Zolotow Award)

Don't Worry Bear. 2008. 32pp. ISBN 9780670062454.

When Bear worries that he will never see caterpillar again because he's slipped inside his cocoon, Mouse reassures him. Mouse is proved right when caterpillar emerges as a butterfly.

Good Luck Bear. 2009. 32pp. ISBN 9780670062584.

When Bear finds a three-leaf clover, Mouse tells him that a four-leaf clover is especially lucky. Bear searches for one unsuccessfully, making Bear feel unlucky indeed, until Mouse shares his find of a five-leaf clover with his friend.

Frazee, Marla.

A Couple of Boys Have the Best Week Ever. **Orlando, FL: Harcourt, 2008. 40pp. ISBN 9780152060206.** PreS-3

In a humorous story that juxtaposes a straightforward text with contradictory and comic illustrations, Frazee depicts the escapades of two friends, James and

Eamon, who are spending the week at Eamon's grandparents' beach house to attend nature camp. While they do go to camp, they have the most fun at the beach house with each other, watching TV, playing video games, building a model Antarctic village complete with penguins, and just being together. (ALAN, Boston Globe Honor, Caldecott Honor)

Fucile, Tony.

Let's Do Nothing! Somerville, MA: Candlewick, 2009. 40pp. ISBN 978-0763634407. **PreS–1**

When best friends Sal and Frankie have exhausted all entertaining activities, Sal decides that they will do nothing, but Frankie's active imagination puts the kibosh on Sal's plans. Children will readily identify with the stars of this laugh-out-loud story.

Gretz, Susanna.

Riley and Rose in the Picture. Cambridge, MA: Candlewick, 2005. 32pp. ISBN 9780763626815. **PreS–2**

Riley the dog and Rose the cat need to find something to do inside because it's raining. They decide to draw pictures and are determined not to fight, but they each have very different imaginations. Despite their best efforts, a fight erupts. When they calm down, they decide to give creative expression another try and this time succeed in sharing each other's point of view.

Haas, Irene.

Bess and Bella. New York: Margaret K. McElderry Books, 2006. Unpaged. ISBN 9781416900139. **PreS–3**

When Bess wishes for a friend one lonely winter afternoon as she is having a solitary outdoor tea party, an amicable bird named Bella arrives bearing magical suitcases. From them Bella produces a feast, which draws a variety of guests. Girl and bird stay friends through spring, when Bella wings away as Bess finds a human friend.

Harper, Charise Mericle.

When Randolph Turned Rotten. New York: Knopf, 2007. Unpaged. ISBN 9780375840715. **PreS–2**

Best friends Randolph the Beaver and Ivy the Canada goose enjoy eating, playing, and reading together, but when Ivy gets invited to an all-girl sleepover party, Randolph's jealousy overwhelms him. He tries to sabotage the party, but his feelings of guilt lead him to apologize, and he ends up the hero, as their friendship's balance is restored.

Hills, Tad.

Duck and Goose. New York: Schwartz & Wade, 2006. 40pp. ISBN 9780375836114. **PreS–1**

In this story filled with childlike humor, Duck and Goose find a ball that they think is an egg. Each claims it and sits on it, waiting for it to hatch.

Eventually they realize their mistake and decide to become friends and play with the ball instead. The cheerfully bright, oil paintings make the expressions and emotions of the animals clear and draw children into the humor of the story. (ALAN)

Duck, Duck, Goose. **New York: Schwartz & Wade, 2006. 40pp. 2007. ISBN 9780375840685. Sequel.** `PreS-1`

Duck and Goose are now fast friends who enjoy running through the meadow and watching the clouds go by, but their leisure is disrupted by Thistle, a very competitive duck. Thistle turns every activity into a competition, which she naturally wins. At last Duck and Goose engage her in a napping contest so that they can have some time to play in peace.

Howe, James.

The Horace, Morris, and Dolores Series. Illustrated by Amy Walrod. New York: Atheneum. `Gr. K–3`

Horace, Morris, and Dolores are three mice friends who encounter different situations that prove to be a challenge to their friendship.

Horace and Morris but Mostly Dolores. 1999. Unpaged. ISBN 9780689856754 (pb).

Three mice children, Horace, Morris, and Dolores, have fun playing together until Horace and Morris decide to join the Mega-Mice Club, which is for boys only. Consequently, Dolores takes up with the Cheese Puffs, for girls only. Separated, none of the friends is especially happy, so when Dolores invites the boys to accompany her on an exploration adventure, they eagerly accept.

Horace and Morris Join the Chorus (But What about Dolores?). 2002. Unpaged. ISBN 9781416906162 (pb).

The three mice friends return and try out for chorus. Horace and Morris are accepted, but Dolores doesn't make it because she sings notes no one has ever heard before. Devastated, she pens a letter in rhyme begging to be given another chance. Moustro Provolone is so enchanted that he wants to turn it into a song. He lets Dolores join the chorus and gives her singing lessons.

Horace and Morris Say Cheese (Which Makes Dolores Sneeze). New York: Atheneum, 2009. 32pp. ISBN 9780689839405.

Dolores enjoys munching on all kinds of cheese with her pals Horace and Morris until she develops an allergy to cheese. Even though it makes her break out in hives, she dreams of cheese and sometimes samples some, but is saved by discovering her delight in creating her own cheeseless dishes.

Jeffers, Oliver.

Lost and Found. **New York: Philomel, 2005. 32pp. ISBN 9780399245039.** `PreS-2`

When a young boy discovers a penguin on his doorstep, he assumes that he's lost and rows him back home to the South Pole. Along the way he tells stories to fill the long hours of the voyage. After he drops the penguin off and heads for home, he realizes that the penguin wasn't lost, but lonely and searching for a friend. The boy turns around and picks him up, and they journey back together.

Joosse, Barbara M.

Friends (Mostly). **Illustrated by Tomaso Milian. New York: Greenwillow, 2010. 32pp. ISBN 9780060882211.** `PreS-2`

Henry and Ruby experience ups and downs in their relationship but remain best friends forever.

Keller, Holly.

Farfallina & Marcel. See under "Insects and Arachnids" in chapter 10.

Help! A Story of Friendship. **New York: Greenwillow, 2007. 32pp. ISBN 9780061239137.** `PreS-3`

Mouse is friends with many animals in the forest, including Snake, until Skunk warns him that snakes are dangerous to mice. Afraid, he tries to hide and accidentally falls in a hole, injuring his foot. His other friends can't help him out of such a deep and narrow spot, but Snake comes to the rescue.

Lin, Grace.

Lissy's Friends. **New York: Viking, 2007. 40pp. ISBN 9780670060726.** `Gr. K-2`

Lissy is starting at a new school and feeling shy. Alone at lunch she makes an origami crane to keep her company. Each day she makes more and more paper animals, who come alive in her imagination, until a strong wind on the playground blows them away. When Paige returns Lissy's crane and asks her to teach her to make them, a new friendship is born.

Marshall, James.

George and Martha: The Complete Stories of Two Best Friends. **Boston: Houghton Mifflin, 2008. 350pp. ISBN 9780618891955.** `Gr. K-3`

Hippo pals George and Martha are icons of friendship in children's literature. The seven George and Martha stories were released beginning in the 1970s and are collected here with reminiscences of prominent figures in the field of children's literature, including Susan Meddaugh, Jon Scieszka, and Anita Silvey. Through all their ups and downs, George and Martha were the best of friends in stories filled with wit and love.

McPhail, David.

Silvie & True. **New York: Farrar, Straus & Giroux, 2007. 31pp. ISBN 9780374373641.** `PreS-2`

Sylvie, a rabbit, and True, a giant water snake, live in an apartment together in the city and are the closest of friends, even though their tastes and activities are very different. McPhail's charming watercolors highlight the warmth of their friendship.

Mitton, Tony.

Playful Little Penguins. **Illustrated by Guy Parker-Rees. New York: Walker, 2007. 24pp. ISBN 9780802797100.** `PreS-1`

The rhyming text relates the adventures of a seal pup who becomes stranded on an ice floe. A group of exuberant penguins befriend him and entertain him until his mother arrives.

Paul, Ann Whitford.

Manana Iguana. **Illustrated by Ethan Long. New York: Holiday House, 2004. Unpaged. ISBN 9780823418084.** `PreS-3`

Iguana is getting ready for fiesta and when none of her friends, a rabbit, a turtle, and a snake, will help her, she tells them they cannot come to her party. Watching from afar, her friends realize how much work Iguana has done and how exhausted she is and decide to pitch in at the end. They clean up after the party, and Iguana shares the leftovers with them. Spanish words pepper the text, and vivid gouache artwork gives the flavor of the Southwestern desert.

Fiesta Fiasco. **New York: Holiday House, 2007. 32pp. ISBN 9780823420377. Sequel.** `PreS-3`

The four animal friends are back, and this time they are celebrating Snake's birthday. Rabbit suggests different kinds of presents for him, all of which would be better for Rabbit than for Snake. Spanish words and brightly colored artwork are integral elements of the story.

Robbins, Jacqui.

The New Girl and Me. **Illustrated by Matt Phelan. New York: Atheneum, 2006. 32pp. ISBN 9780689864681.** `Gr. K-3`

When a new girl, Shakeeta, joins Mia's class, all the girls cluster around her on the first day as she tells them she has an iguana. Mia is too shy to join in, but she does some research on iguanas. The next day both girls are left out of the soccer game, and Mia asks Shakeeta about her iguana. Sharing stories and laughter, the girls become fast friends.

Two of a Kind. **Illustrated by Matt Phelan. New York: Atheneum, 2009. Unpaged. ISBN 9781416924371.** `Gr. K-3`

Kayla and Melanie do everything together, including making fun of the other girls in their class. Julisa and Anna are best friends as well, but they include the others instead of teasing them. For a short time, Anna is lured into joining the mean girls, but she soon realizes who her true friends are.

Rodman, Mary.

🌱*My Best Friend.* **Illustrated by E. B. Lewis. New York: Viking, 2005. 32pp. ISBN 9780670059898.** `Gr. 1-3`

At the neighborhood pool, African American Lily, who is six years old, yearns to befriend seven-year-old Tamika. Mostly Tamika either ignores her or teases her, so eventually Lily gives up and turns her attention to six-year-old Keesha, who is eager to be her friend. Lewis's watercolor paintings are filled with summer light and aptly express the children's longing. (Charlotte Zolotow Award)

Rohmann, Eric

🎗*My Friend Rabbit*. Brookfield, CT: Roaring Brook, 2002. Unpaged. ISBN 9780761315353. **PreS–1**

In this nearly wordless story, Rabbit sends his friend Mouse soaring in his toy plane, which then gets stuck in a tree. Rabbit assures Mouse that he will find a way to get him down, which he accomplishes by creating a precarious stack of animals to reach the branches of the tree. The highlight of the story is Rohman's hand-colored relief prints, which deftly depict emotion and whimsy. (ALAN, Caldecott Medal)

Root, Phyllis.

Toot Toot Zoom! Illustrated by Matthew Cordell. Somerville, MA: Candlewick, 2009. 40pp. ISBN 9780763634520. **PreS–2**

Pierre, a red fox, lives by himself at the top of a very steep mountain. Lonely, he decides to go in search of a friend. He takes off in his little red car and toot toot zooms down the mountain. He stops frequently to pick up animals in need of a ride along the way and finds that he's made new friends without even realizing it.

Rosen, Michael.

Bear's Day Out. Illustrated by Adrian Reynolds. New York: Bloomsbury, 2007. 24pp. ISBN 9781599900070. **PreS–2**

A bear who's used to being on his own journeys to the city. He gets lost among all the busy people until a group of friendly children lead him back to his cave. Rosen's repetition of onomatopoetic sounds encourages audience participation.

Scieszka, Jon.

Cowboy & Octopus. Illustrated by Lane Smith. New York: Viking, 2007. Unpaged. ISBN 9780670910588. **Gr. 1–3**

Paper cutout characters Cowboy and Octopus show the ups and downs of friendship in seven short, humorous stories. The book begins with how the pals met when Cowboy tried to play on a seesaw by himself, and Octopus climbed on to demonstrate that it's better to do some things with a friend. After adventures with Halloween costumes, beans at dinner time, and an experience of the value of truthfulness, the book concludes with the friends contemplating a picture postcard sunset. Illustrated with Lane's zany mixed-media collage that heightens the humor of the tales.

Seeger, Laura Vaccaro.

The Dog and Bear Series. New Milford, CT: Roaring Brook. `PreS–1`

Dog, an energetic dachshund, and Bear, a multicolored teddy bear, are the best of friends who star in a series of gentle tales. The two friends are painted with black outlines and filled in with bold colors that make the books both childlike and charming.

Dog and Bear. 2007. Unpaged. ISBN 9781596430532.

> Three stories introduce best friends Dog and Bear. When Dog wants to go outside to play, he has to figure out a way to get Bear down from the chair so that they can play together. Next, Dog drags out a selection of toys, but Bear is too busy reading. Finally, Dog asks Bear to read to him. In the last story, Dog is searching for a new name, and they imagine what he would like with different traditional dog names. They settle on "My Best Friend Dog."

🏆*Dog and Bear: Two's Company.* 2008. Unpaged. ISBN 9781596432734.

> Dog and Bear return to take center stage in three episodes that explore the complications of friendship. First Dog is so angry with Bear that he's going to run away. Patient Bear helps him pack but then offers ice cream—a treat Dog cannot resist. Next Dog wants to help celebrate Bear's birthday. He bakes and decorates a cake, but eats it all up before Bear sees it. Last, Dog is not feeling well and wears Bear out as he tries to take care of his friend. (ALAN, Boston Globe Honor)

Dog and Bear: Three to Get Ready. 2009. ISBN 9781596433960.

> The friendship between Dog and Bear continues to grow in three more stories. First Bear has a bucket stuck on his head and needs Dog's help to get it off. Then, Dog creates scenes of silliness by bouncing on the bed, and finally, the two must locate Dog's sock monkey.

Simmons, Jane.

Together. New York: Knopf, 2007. 32pp. ISBN 9780375843396. `T–K`

> Mousse and Nut are two dogs who like completely different things. Though they become friends right away, it takes work to keep their relationship going.

Sones, Sonya, and Bennett Tramer.

Violet and Winston. Illustrated by Christopher Raschka. New York: Dial, 2009. 32pp. ISBN 9780803732346. `Gr. K–2`

> Violet the swan and Winston the duck have been friends for a long time. Sometimes they find each other's foibles exasperating, but their evident affection shines in three tales of their life together.

Wilson, Karma.

The Bear Tales. Illustrated by Jane Chapman. New York: Margaret K. McElderry. `PreS–1`

Bear and his animal friends from the forest have a variety of adventures in these smoothly rhyming stories that are perfectly cadenced for reading aloud, with repetition that begs for participation and illustrations that are lush and infused with light and the warmth of friendship.

Bear Snores On. 2002. Unpaged. ISBN 9780689831874.

> On a stormy winter night, Bear is sleeping soundly in his cave when one by one, his friends come by to warm up. As they party, Bear snores on until pepper wakes him and he joins the fun. (ALAN)

Bear Wants More. 2003. Unpaged. ISBN 9780689845093.

> Spring is greening the forest and a wide-awake Bear is hungry. His friends show him where to find food, but he always wants more. Meanwhile, they are preparing a party for him back at his cave.

Bear Stays up for Christmas. 2004. 32pp. ISBN 9780689852787.

> Bear is working hard to stay awake for Christmas while his friends find a tree, decorate it, and hang up their stockings. Each nods off, but Bear stays up wrapping presents. He's so busy that he does not notice a visit from Santa.

Bear's New Friend. 2006. Unpaged. ISBN 9780689859847.

> While playing outside on a summer morning, Bear hears a rustling sound. He tries to guess which of his friends it is, but it turns out to be a new friend, owl.

Bear Feels Sick. 2007. 32pp. ISBN 9780689859854.

> Although it's a lovely autumn day, Bear feels sick with a cold and is huddled in his cave. His friends come to comfort and take care of him with soft blankets and hot broth.

Bear Feels Scared. 2008. Unpaged. ISBN 9780689859861.

> Bear is out on a stormy night, seeking a snack, when he gets lost. Worried about him, his friends search for him. They find him close to home and lead him back to his comfy cave.

Easy Readers

Becker, Bonny.

Birthday for Bear. **Illustrated by Kady MacDonald Denton. Somerville, MA: Candlewick, 2009. ISBN 9780763637460.** `PreS-2`

> Bear and Mouse first became friends in the picture book *A Visitor for Bear*. In this easy to read sequel, Mouse insists on celebrating Bear's birthday, no matter how Bear tries to discourage him.

Chaconas, Dori.

The Cork and Fuzz Series. **Illustrated by Lisa McCue. New York: Viking.** `Gr. K-2`

> Cork and Fuzz are a muskrat and a possum who become best friends even though they have nothing in common. Illustrated with warmth and humor by McCue's endearing ink and watercolor paintings.

Cork and Fuzz. 2005. 32pp. ISBN 9780670036028.

> Cork the muskrat loves to eat leaves and other veggie stuff, while Fuzz the possum munches on beetles. Cork loves to swim, while Fuzz sinks in the water. But they both love rocks, and a new friendship is born.

🎗 *Cork and Fuzz: Short and Tall.* 2006. 32pp. ISBN 9780670059850.

> Realizing they are different sizes, Cork and Fuzz try various ways to remedy this situation, until they realize that friends don't have to be the same. (ALAN)

Cork and Fuzz: Good Sports. 2007. 32pp. ISBN 9780670061457.

> Cork and Fuzz like to play lots of games together, but when Fuzz always wins, Cork gets increasingly frustrated, especially when Fuzz brags about it. When they see that their friendship is in danger, they find a way to compromise.

Cork and Fuzz: The Collectors. 2008. 32pp. ISBN 9780670062867.

> Cork and Fuzz love collecting rocks, but when they think duck eggs are precious stones, they get caught in a case of mistaken identity with mother duck. She comes to collect her ducklings and mistakes the feather-toting Fuzz for one of her offspring. It's up to Cork to find a way to rescue his friend.

Cork and Fuzz: Finders Keepers. 2009. 32pp. ISBN 9780670011131.

> The two friends need to find a way to resolve their conflict when Cork loses his treasured green stone. Fuzz finds it and won't give it back, calling out, "Finders keepers!"

Cork and Fuzz: The Babysitters. 2010. 32pp. ISBN 9780670012008.

> Cork and Fuzz find babysitting a young porcupine a prickly situation.

Cutler, Jane.

Rose and Riley. **Illustrated by Thomas F. Yezerski. New York: Farrar, Straus & Giroux, 2005. 48pp. ISBN 9780374363406.** `Gr. K–2`

> Rose the vole is a worrier, while Riley the groundhog is a carefree soul. In three stories, Rose's worries continually increase until her friend Riley makes her a set of worry dolls and teaches her how to use them.

Rose and Riley Come and Go. **Illustrated by Thomas F. Yezerski. New York: Farrar, Straus & Giroux, 2005. 48pp. ISBN 9780374363413. Sequel.** `Gr. K–2`

> The two friends return for outdoor adventures as they visit the beach, embark on an expedition for wildflowers, and investigate a mocking bird.

Dotlich, Rebecca Kai.

Peanut and Pearl's Picnic Adventure. **Illustrated by R. W. Alley. New York: HarperCollins, 2007. 32pp. ISBN 9780060549206.** `PreS–1`

> Animal friends Peanut and Pearl set out for a picnic together, but they go in different directions and wind up lost. When they find each other again, they decide that next time they should plan their route.

Guest, Elissa Haden.

The Iris and Walter Series. Illustrated by Christine Davenier. San Diego: Harcourt. `Gr. 1-3`

Iris and Walter are inseparable friends. They met when Iris first moved to the country and was missing the city. Now, they are friends who share in life's everyday experiences at home and school. Energetic pen-and-ink illustrations complement the text.

🎗*Iris and Walter.* 2000. 43pp. ISBN 9780152021221. (ALAN)

Iris and Walter: True Friends. 2001. 44pp. ISBN 9780152056803 (pb).

Iris and Walter and Baby Rose. 2002. 44pp. ISBN 9780152056506 (pb).

Iris and Walter: The Sleepover. 2002. 44pp. ISBN 9780152056681 (pb).

Iris and Walter: The School Play. 2003. 44pp. ISBN 9780152056681 (pb).

Iris and Walter and Cousin Howie. 2003. 44pp. ISBN 9780152056568 (pb).

Iris and Walter Lost and Found. 2004. 44pp. ISBN 9780152056629 (pb).

Iris and Walter and the Substitute Teachers. 2004. 44pp. ISBN 9780152050139.

Iris and Walter and the Field Trip. 2005. 44pp. ISBN 9780152050146.

Iris and Walter and the Birthday Party. 2006. 43pp. ISBN 9780152050153.

Lobel, Arnold.

The Frog and Toad Books. New York: HarperCollins. `Gr. 1-3` (SP)

Frog and Toad are the quintessential best friends of children's literature. As they share experiences and affection throughout their adventures, they win the hearts of generation after generation of children.

🎗*Frog and Toad Are Friends.* 1970. 64pp. ISBN 9780060239572.

Five summer adventures of two best friends who each help the other in times of need. (Caldecott Honor)

🎗*Frog and Toad Together.* 1972. 64pp. ISBN 9780060239596.

Frog and Toad continue to do everything together, from gardening to finding a way to be brave together. (Newbery Honor)

🎗*Frog and Toad All Year.* 1976. 64pp. ISBN 9780060239503.

Each season of the year features an adventure for these animal pals. (ALAN)

🎗*Days with Frog and Toad.* 1979. 64pp. ISBN 9780060239633.

Frog and Toad enjoy each other's company every day, whether they are flying kites, celebrating birthdays, or whispering scary stories. (ALAN)

Silverman, Erica.

The Cowgirl Kate and Cocoa Series. Illustrated by Betsy Lewin. `Gr. K-2`

Cowgirl Kate and her talking horse Cocoa are devoted to each other and share a variety of adventures on the farm and at school. Lewin's fluid watercolors clearly show how much the girl and horse love each other.

🏵*Cowgirl Kate and Cocoa.* Orlando: Harcourt, 2005. 42pp. ISBN 9780152021245. (ALAN, Geisel Honor)

Cowgirl Kate and Cocoa: Partners. Orlando: Harcourt, 2006. 43pp. ISBN 978-0152021252.

Cowgirl Kate and Cocoa: School Days. Orlando: Harcourt, 2007. 48pp. ISBN 978-0152053789.

Cowgirl Kate and Cocoa: Rain or Shine. Orlando: Harcourt, 2008. 44pp. ISBN 978-0152053840.

Cowgirl Kate and Cocoa: Horse in the House. New York: Harcourt, 2009. Unpaged. ISBN 9780152053901.

Cowgirl Kate and Cocoa: Spring Babies. New York: Harcourt, 2010. Unpaged. ISBN 9780152053963.

Willems, Mo.

The Elephant & Piggie Books. New York: Hyperion. `Gr. K-3`

Two unlikely friends, serious Gerald the elephant and lighthearted Piggie, star in books that focus on everyday activities like cheering up a friend, playing outside, and getting a new toy. Willems's humorous cartoon illustrations make these two characters stars of delightful, laugh-out-loud stories.

My Friend Is Sad. 2007. 57pp. ISBN 9781423102977.

Today I Will Fly. 2007. 57pp. ISBN 9781423102953.

There Is a Bird on Your Head. 2007. 57pp. ISBN 9781423106869.

I Am Invited to a Party! 2007. 56pp. ISBN 9781423106876.

I Love My New Toy! 2008. 57pp. ISBN 9781423109617.

I Will Surprise My Friend. 2008. 57pp. ISBN 9781423109624.

🏵*Are You Ready to Play Outside?* 2008. 57pp. ISBN 9781423113478. (ALAN, Geisel Award)

Watch Me Throw the Ball! 2009. 57pp. ISBN 9781423113485.

Elephants Cannot Dance! 2009. 57pp. ISBN 9781423114109.

Pigs Make Me Sneeze! 2009. 56pp. ISBN 9781423114116.

Can I Play Too? 2010. 64pp. ISBN 9781423119913.

We Are in a Book! 2010. 64pp. ISBN 9781423133087.

Yee, Wong Herbert.

The Mouse and Mole Series. Boston: Houghton Mifflin. `Gr. K-3`

Mouse and Mole approach life from different points of view, but become fine friends nonetheless. Bamboo-pen and watercolor with colored-pencil illustrations show the details of their habitat as well as their expressions.

Upstairs Mouse, Downstairs Mole. 2005. 47pp. ISBN 9780618473137.

Mouse lives in a hole on the side of an oak tree, and Mole lives in a hole underneath. The neighbors discover that although they are very different, they can find compromises and be friends.

Abracadabra! Magic with Mouse and Mole. 2007. 48pp. ISBN 9780618759262.

Mole is very excited because the magician, Minkus the Magnificent, will be performing for the forest creatures. At first, Mole loves the show, but when the table falls, revealing the magician's tricks, Mole is bitterly disappointed. To help cheer him up, Mouse creates a show with the magic of nature.

A Brand New Day with Mouse and Mole. 2008. 48pp. ISBN 9780618966769.

When Mole discovers moth holes in his clothes, he and Mouse go shopping for some new ones.

Mouse and Mole, Fine Feathered Friends. 2009. 48pp. ISBN 9780547152226.

Spring brings many birds that the two friends are eager to watch. In an effort to watch them more closely without frightening them away, Mouse and Mole apply feathers to their bodies to see if that will do the trick.

Mouse and Mole, a Winter Wonderland. 2010. 48pp. ISBN 9780547341521.

Mouse and Mole enjoy a day full of snowy activities and make some new friends along the way.

Neighborhoods

Neighborhoods in General

Caseley, Judith.

On the Town: A Community Adventure. New York: Greenwillow, 2002. Unpaged. ISBN 9780060295844. `Gr. K-2`

Charlie has to explore his neighborhood for a homework assignment, so he and his mother run errands around town. Charlie draws pictures of the people who work at various establishments, such as the bank, fire station, and post office.

Cole, Henry.

On Meadowview Street. New York: Greenwillow, 2007. 32pp. ISBN 978-0060564810. `Gr. 1-3`

Caroline loves nature, so when her family moves to a subdivision where the houses are all the same, she heads out to search for a meadow, which seems to be missing from Meadowview Street. When she finds a wildflower growing in the backyard, she convinces her father not to mow the lawn and soon has her own nature preserve. Her success inspires the rest of the residents of her new neighborhood.

English, Karen.

Hot Day on Abbott Avenue. See under "Weather" in chapter 9.

Harshman, Marc.

Only One Neighborhood. Illustrated by Barbara Monfried. New York: Dutton, 2007. 30pp. ISBN 9780525474685. `Gr. K-3`

This book combines the concepts of one and many, counting, and communities. It presents one element of a neighborhood, such as a bakery or a pizzeria, and then shows the many different varieties of that item through collage art.

Hartland, Jessie.

Night Shift. New York: Bloomsbury, 2007. 30pp. ISBN 9781599900254. `Gr. K-3`

From a night-time street sweeper to an early-rising baker, Hartland reviews the various work that is done in towns at night.

Hudes, Quiara Alegria.

Welcome to My Neighborhood! A Barrio ABC. Illustrated by Shino Arihara. New York: Arthur A. Levine, 2010. 32pp. ISBN 9780545094245. `PreS-1` (SP)

A girl who lives in an urban neighborhood takes readers on an alphabetical journey through the city.

Isadora, Rachel.

Say Hello! New York: Putnam, 2010. 32pp. ISBN 9780399252303. `PreS-1`

As Carmelita and her mother travel through their multi-ethnic neighborhood on the way to visit Abuela Rosa, Carmelita enjoys greeting her neighbors in their various languages, including: Spanish, French, and Japanese.

Johnson, D. B.

Eddie's Kingdom. Boston: Houghton Mifflin, 2005. 32pp. ISBN 9780618562992. `PreS-3`

Eddie lives in an apartment building where all of his neighbors are quarrelling. Determined to change the negative environment, he visits each neighbor, carrying a rolled up piece of paper and a pencil. He draws as he listens to their complaints, and his final picture helps bring laughter to the community.

Lord, Janet.

Albert the Fix-It Man. **Illustrated by Julie Paschkis. Atlanta, GA: Peachtree, 2008. Unpaged. ISBN 9781561454334.** `PreS-1`

Albert the white-bearded, fix-it man enjoys strolling through his neighborhood fixing things in need of repair for his neighbors. When he's laid up with a cold, all the neighbors he has helped come to care for him.

Lozano, Jose.

Once Around the Block/Una Vuelta a La Manzana. **El Paso, TX: Cinco Puntos Press, 2009. Unpaged. ISBN 9781933693576.** `PreS-2` **(Bilingual)**

This presents a fun alphabetical romp through a Mexican American neighborhood.

Nielson, Laura F.

Mrs. Muddle's Holidays. **Illustrated by Thomas F. Yezerski. New York: Farrar, Straus & Giroux, 2008. 32pp. ISBN 9780374350949.** `Gr. K-2`

In Katie's multicultural neighborhood, all the holidays are celebrated. Katie is puzzled, however, when her neighbor Mrs. Muddle is decorating bushes in March. Mrs. Muddle explains that she is honoring "First Robin's Day." In fact, she celebrates a variety of nature holidays. Soon the whole neighborhood celebrates them as well, and Katie names a holiday of her own after Mrs. Muddle.

Schwartz, Amy.

A Glorious Day. **New York: Atheneum, 2004. Unpaged. ISBN 978-0689848025.** `PreS-1`

Henry lives in an apartment building and takes readers through the normal activities of the children in the building, morning, afternoon, and night.

Wellington, Monica.

Pizza at Sally's. **New York: Dutton, 2006. 32pp. ISBN 9780525477150.** `PreS-1`

Sally runs the neighborhood pizzeria. She picks her tomatoes from the community garden and makes all the pizza for her hungry customers.

Wyeth, Sharon Dennis.

Something Beautiful. **Illustrated by Chris K. Soentpiet. New York: Doubleday, 1998. 32pp. ISBN 9780385322393.** `Gr. 3 & up`

An African American girl is distressed by all the trash and graffiti in her inner city neighborhood and is searching for something beautiful. As she asks her neighbors for their thoughts, she is surprised to find beauty in unexpected places.

Zimmerman, Andrea, and David Clemesha.

🎗*Trashy Town*. **Illustrated by Dan Yaccarino. New York: HarperCollins, 1999. Unpaged. ISBN 9780060271398.** `PreS-2`

Mr. Gilly drives his garbage truck around town, making sure he keeps the town clean by picking up the trash at various locations, including the school, the park, and the doctor's office. (ALAN)

Community Helpers

Construction Workers

Roth, Susan L.

Hard Hat Area. **New York: Bloomsbury, 2004. 40pp. ISBN 9781582349466.** `Gr. 1-3`

Kristin, an apprentice iron worker, scales a skyscraper-in-the-making, talking to each worker along her way and taking orders for tools and snacks. Full-page spreads of collage illustrations show the workers and their tools while the text provides explanations.

Sutton, Sally.

Roadwork. **Illustrated by Brian Lovelock. Cambridge, MA: Candlewick, 2008. 29pp. ISBN 9780763639129.** `T-K`

With rhymes and onomatopoeia, this book presents every phase of road construction, from surveying through completion.

Zimmerman, Andrea, and David Clemesha.

Digger Man. **New York: Holt, 2003. 32pp. ISBN 9780805066289.** `PreS-1`

Playing in his sandbox with his baby brother, a preschooler imagines what it would be like to operate construction vehicles to build a playground.

Firefighters

Boelts, Maribeth.

The Firefighters' Thanksgiving. See under "Thanksgiving" in chapter 6.

Godwin, Laura.

This Is the Firefighter. **Illustrated by Julian Hector. New York: Hyperion, 2009. 32pp. ISBN 9781423108009.** `PreS-2`

Verse that follows a modified "House That Jack Built" format relates a day in the life of a firefighter, introducing his equipment and accompanying him to a fire. He and his fellow firefighters rescue a family and a pet and successfully put out the fire.

Grambling, Lois G.

My Mom Is a Firefighter. Illustrated by Jane Manning. New York: HarperCollins, 2007. 28pp. ISBN 9780060586409. `Gr. K-3`

> Billy wants to grow up to be just like his mom, the firefighter. He describes how she takes care of equipment, fights fires, and teaches his class safety tips.

Greene, Rhonda Gowler.

Firebears: The Rescue Team. Illustrated by Dan Andreasen. New York: Holt, 2005. 32pp. ISBN 9780805070101. `PreS-2`

> A team of firefighting bears from Fire Station Number Eight rush through town when the alarm sounds. First they rescue a cat that is stuck up a tree, but then they must put out a blaze in a store and move on to the next emergency, for there is a house on fire as well. This action-filled story is told in rhyme. Illustrations in 1950s style give the book an old-fashioned feel.

Hamilton, Kersten R.

Firefighters to the Rescue. Illustrated by Rich Davis. New York: Viking, 2005. 32pp. ISBN 9780670035038. `PreS-1`

> A firefighting story in rhyme set in the 1950s, this book begins with the firefighters in the station. They are doing regular chores like mopping and cooking, and they play pranks on their fellow firefighters. When the alarm rings, they don their gear and hurry to the rescue.

Hubbell, Patricia.

Firefighters: Speeding! Spraying! Saving! Illustrated by Viviana Garofoli. Tarrytown, NY: Marshall Cavendish, 2007. 32pp. ISBN 9780761453376. `PreS-1`

> Rhyming action follows a four-person team (three men and one woman) of firefighters. When the alarm clangs, they zoom to the fire, rescue the trapped people, and fight the blaze until it's extinguished. Back at the station, they relax with cookies and coffee.

Osborne, Mary Pope.

New York's Bravest. Illustrated by Steve Johnson and Lou Fancher. New York: Knopf, 2002. Unpaged. ISBN 9780375821967. `Gr. 1-3`

> In a story that is dedicated to the firefighters who gave their lives on 9/11 in New York City, Osborne retells the tall tale of Mose Humphreys, a legendary firefighter of the nineteenth century. Eight feet tall and so brave that he ran toward danger when others ran away, Mose could lift damaged trolleys, rescue babies, and fight fires with his fellows. When an especially vicious hotel fire traps a number of people, Mose returns to the burning building again and again until everyone is safe. After the fire is out, his team realizes that he's missing and not coming back, but they know that he will always be with them each time they face danger and stop the destruction caused by fire. Striking artwork reveals Mose's courage and caring.

Whiting, Sue.

The Firefighters. Illustrated by Donna Rawlins. Cambridge, MA: Candlewick, 2008. 24pp. ISBN 9780763640194. `PreS-2`

Mrs. Iverson and her students have fun pretending they are firefighters putting out a roaring fire, and then two real firefighters, a man and a woman, visit their class to explain how to stay safe in a fire.

Zimmerman, Andrea, and David Clemesha.

Fire Engine Man. New York: Holt, 2007. 32pp. ISBN 9780805079050. `PreS-1`

The brothers from *Digger Man* return. This time the older brother is imagining what it would be like to grow up to become a firefighter.

Librarians

Bottner, Barbara.

Miss Brooks Loves Books! (And I Don't). Illustrated by Michael Emberley. New York: Knopf, 2010. Unpaged. ISBN 9780375846823. `PreS-2`

Miss Brooks loves being a librarian, dressing in costume for storytime, and finding just the right book for each child. Only the narrator resists, until Miss Brooks presents her with *Shrek* and her conversion begins.

Sierra, Judy.

✿*Wild about Books.* Illustrated by Marc Brown. New York: Knopf, 2004. Unpaged. ISBN 9780375825385. `PreS-3` (SP)

In this tribute to Dr. Seuss, Sierra presents a story whose meter and rhyme resemble Seuss at his best. When Molly McGrew, the librarian, drives the bookmobile into the zoo, the animals fall in love with books, and Molly has just the right book for each. (ALAN)

Williams, Suzanne.

Library Lil. Illustrated by Steven Kellogg. New York: Dial, 1997. Unpaged. ISBN 9780803716988. `Gr. 2 & up`

In this tall-tale-style story, Library Lil grows tired of having no one come to her storytimes. When a power failure causes all the TVs to shut down, Lil pushes the book mobile around town and turns the townsfolk into book lovers.

Police Officers

Hamilton, Kersten R.

Police Officers on Patrol. Illustrated by R. W. Alley. New York: Viking, 2009. 32pp. ISBN 9780670063154. `PreS-1`

Rhyming text relates the activities that various police officers perform after their sergeant dispatches them. Officer Mike controls traffic when a light stops working. Officer Jan, on horseback, helps a child find his mother, and Officer Carl stops an ATM robbery.

Hubbell, Patricia.

Police: Hurrying! Helping! Saving! **Illustrated by Viviana Garofoli. Tarrytown, NY: Marshall Cavendish, 2007. Unpaged. ISBN 9780761454212.** `PreS-1`

Rhyming verse describes a day in the life of police officers who are both men and women and represent different ethnic backgrounds. They direct traffic, prevent crimes, and catch a burglar, utilizing various modes of transportation including horses, patrol cars, and motorcycles.

Niemann, Christoph.

The Police Cloud. **New York: Schwartz & Wade, 2007. 40pp. ISBN 978-0375839634.** `PreS-1`

Since he was small, this cloud has wanted to be a police officer so that he can help people. He dons the big blue hat, but it turns out he's too fluffy. Bank robbers walk right through him. He makes traffic worse because people can't see past his fog, and in the park he blocks out the sunlight. Distressed, he floats above the buildings, crying, and finds his true calling, fighting fires. Retro art gives this tale a whimsical feel.

Rathmann, Peggy.

Officer Buckle and Gloria. **New York: Putnam, 1995. Unpaged. ISBN 9780399226168.** `Gr. K-3`

Officer Buckle delivers safety lessons at Napville school, but the students fall asleep during his talks until the new police dog, Gloria, starts acting out the procedures behind his back. When Buckle discovers that Gloria is really the star of the show, he refuses to do any more. Gloria flops without him, and the two realize that they work best as a team. The energy-filled cartoons are stellar. (ALAN, Caldecott Medal)

School

From the anticipation regarding the start of school, to making friends, to learning how to interact with teachers, school is a major part of any child's life. Since the topic is so board, it is divided into the subtopics of starting school, the 100th day, teachers, and school in general.

Starting School

Borden, Louise.

Off to First Grade. **Illustrated by Joan Rankin.New York: Margaret K. McElderry Books, 2008. 31pp. ISBN 9780689873959.** `Gr. K-3`

In alphabetical order, a group of animal students and their teacher, principal, and bus driver describe the activities and feelings on their first day of first grade.

Carlson, Nancy.

First Grade, Here I Come. See under "School in General" in this chapter.

Look Out Kindergarten, Here I Come! See under "School in General" in this chapter.

Carlstrom, Nancy White.

***It's Your First Day of School, Annie Claire.* Illustrated by Margie Moore. New York: Abrams, 2009. 32pp. ISBN 9780810940574. PreS–1**
Pup Annie Claire has concerns about starting school, and as she shares each one with her mother, her mother provides reassuring answers.

Child, Lauren.

I Am Too Absolutely Small for School. See under "Families: Siblings" in this chapter.

Cocca-Leffler, Maryann.

***Jack's Talent.* New York: Farrar, Straus & Giroux, 2007. 29pp. ISBN 9780374336813. PreS–2**
On the first day of school, Jack's new teacher, Miss Lucinda, wants each child to share his or her special talent. It will help the children get to know each other and give Miss Lucinda something unique to add to their name tags. Jack thinks there isn't anything he can do that's extraordinary, but everyone discovers that that's not true.

Danneberg, Julie.

First Day Jitters. See under "School: Teachers" in this chapter.

Davis, Katie.

***Kindergarten Rocks!* Orlando, FL: Harcourt, 2005. Unpaged. ISBN 9780152049324. PreS–K**
Dexter isn't at all nervous about going to kindergarten, but Buster, Dexter's stuffed animal friend, doesn't feel the same way. Buster is very, very nervous!

De Groat, Diane.

Brand-New Pencils, Brand-New Books. See under "Everyday Life in General" in chapter 1.

Dewdney, Anna.

Llama Llama, Misses Mama. See under "Families: Parents and Children: Mother and Child" in this chapter.

Grindley, Sally.

It's My School. Illustrated by Margaret Chamberlain. New York: Walker, 2006. 32pp. ISBN 9780802780867. **Gr. K–2**
> Tom and his little sister Alice are starting school together for the first time. Even though Tom is not too sure he wants to share his school with kindergartener Alice, his parents tell him to keep an eye on her. When he spots her crying on the playground, he dashes to the rescue and realizes that maybe it's not so bad to have her in school after all.

Harper, Jamie.

Miss Mingo and the First Day of School. See under "School: Teachers" in this chapter.

Harris, Robie.

I'm Not Going to School Today. Illustrated by Jan Ormerod. New York: Margaret K. McElderry, 2003. Unpaged. ISBN 9780689839139. **PreS–2**
> A young boy gets ready for the first day of preschool by preparing his backpack and selecting his outfit for the next day, but as he tries to sleep, clinging to his stuffed monkey Hank, he decides that he's not going to go after all. His parents promise that he can take Hank with him, which finally convinces him to reconsider. When he arrives, he sees that many children are clutching their favorite stuffed animals as well.

Horse, Harry.

Little Rabbit Goes to School. See under "Everyday Life in General" in chapter 1.

Hays, Anna Jane.

Kindergarten Countdown. Illustrated by Linda Davick. New York: Knopf, 2007. 24pp. ISBN 9780375842528. **PreS–K**
> This little girl is very excited and happy as she runs and dances her way through the last seven days before kindergarten begins.

Henkes, Kevin.

Chrysanthemum. See under "Everyday Life in General" in chapter 1.

McAllister, Angela.

Take a Kiss to School. Illustrated by Susan Hellard. New York: Bloomsbury, 2006. 32pp. ISBN 9781582347028. **PreS–2**
> Digby, a young wombat, feels anxious about school after attending for only one day. His mother slips twelve kisses into his pocket and tells him to reach in and pull out a kiss whenever he needs to feel that she is there with him. Feeling loved and reassured, Digby's time at school goes smoothly.

London, Jonathan.

Froggy Goes to School. See under "Everyday Life in General" in chapter 1.

Pak, Soyung.

Sumi's First Day of School Ever. **Illustrated by Joung Kim. New York: Viking, 2003. 32pp. ISBN 9780670035229.** `Gr. K-3`

Sumi, a Korean child who is just starting school in America, worries because she does not speak English. Although one child does tease her, her kind teacher reprimands him, and another child befriends her, convincing Sumi that perhaps school is not as lonely or scary as she thought it would be.

Perez, L. King.

🎗*First Day in Grapes.* **Illustrated by Robert Casilla. New York: Lee & Low, 2002. 32pp. ISBN 9781584300458.** `Gr. 1-3`

Chico's family members are migrant farmworkers, so they move around the state of California regularly, following the crops. Each time they move, Chico has to start in a new school, and he finds it hard to always be the new kid. When he begins third grade at yet another new school, he stands up to two fourth grade bullies, and that gives him confidence to face the year. (Pura Belpre Honor)

Poydar, Nancy.

First Day, Hooray. **New York: Holiday House, 1999. Unpaged. ISBN 978-0823414376.** `Gr. K-3`

As young Ivy Green worries about the first day of school, so do her bus driver, teacher, and principal.

Rosenberry, Vera.

Vera's First Day of School. See under "Everyday Life in General" in chapter 1.

Rylant, Cynthia.

The Ticky-Tacky Doll. **Illustrated by Harvey Stevenson. San Diego: Harcourt, 2002. 32pp. ISBN 9780152010782.** `PreS-2`

A little girl who is about to start school becomes unhappy when she realizes she has to leave her beloved, handmade doll at home. Only her grandmother discerns the cause of her sadness. She makes a miniature doll that her granddaughter can carry to school in her book bag, and that cheers her up completely.

Slate, Joseph.

Miss Bindergarten Gets Ready for Kindergarten. See under "School: Teachers" in this chapter.

Thompson, Lauren.

Mouse's First Day of School. Illustrated by Buket Erdogan. New York: Simon & Schuster, 2003. Unpaged. ISBN 9780689847271. `PreS-K`

The mouse who has experienced various holiday adventures (see chapter 6) climbs into a backpack for his very first visit to school.

Zalben, Jane Breskin.

Don't Go. New York: Clarion, 2001. Unpaged. ISBN 9780618072507. `PreS-K`

Daniel the elephant is feeling a bit anxious about starting preschool, so his mother reassures him and explains step-by-step how the day will go.

100th Day

Cuyler, Margery.

100th Day Worries. See under "School: School in General" in this chapter.

Laminack, Lester L.

Jake's 100th Day of School. Illustrated by Judy Love. Atlanta, GA: Peachtree, 2006. 32pp. ISBN 9781561453559. `Gr. K-3`

Everyone in Jake's class has been working on 100th- day projects. Jake's is a scrapbook with 100 family photos, but he's so excited, he forgets to bring it to school. Luckily, his principal helps him devise another collection.

Slate, Joseph.

Miss Bindergarten Celebrates the 100th Day of Kindergarten. See under "School: Teachers" in this chapter.

Wells, Rosemary.

Emily's First 100 Days of School. New York: Hyperion, 2000. Unpaged. ISBN 9780786813544 (pb). (SP)

As Emily the bunny starts school, her teacher tells the class they will become acquainted with a new number each day until they reach 100. Each page honors a successive number, interwoven with elements from Emily's life.

Teachers

Allard, Harry.

The Miss Nelson Series. Illustrated by James Marshall. Boston: Houghton Mifflin. `Gr. K-3`

Miss Nelson is the nicest teacher in school, but sometimes her students misbehave so much, the stern ways of her counterpart, Miss Viola Swamp, are needed.

Miss Nelson Is Missing. 1977. 32pp. ISBN 9780395252963.

The kids in Miss Nelson's class act up all the time until Miss Nelson suddenly disappears and Miss Viola Swamp, the meanest teacher in school, takes over.

Miss Nelson Is Back. 1982. 32pp. ISBN 9780395329566.

When Miss Nelson has to leave her class for a week, the kids in room 207 plan all the ways they can have fun. Unfortunately for them, their substitute teacher is Miss Viola Swamp.

Miss Nelson Has a Field Day. 1985. 32pp. ISBN 9780395366905.

The football team for Horace B. Smedley School cannot win a football game no matter what they try, until Coach Swamp dons the whistle and whips the team into shape.

Bowen, Anne.

What Do Teachers Do (After You Leave School)? **Illustrated by Barry Gott. Minneapolis, MN: Carolrhoda, 2006. 32pp. ISBN 9781575059228.** `Gr. K–2`

The teachers in this school let loose once the students go home. They change into jeans and create a riotous kind of chaos. Rhyming text and cartoon illustrations bring the humor of the story to life.

I Know an Old Teacher. **Illustrated by Stephen Gammell. Minneapolis, MN: Carolrhoda, 2008. 32pp. ISBN 9780822579847.** `Gr. K–3`

This wild variation of "I Know an Old Lady Who Swallowed a Fly" shows a teacher who takes home all the class pets for the weekend. The unusual odyssey begins when she accidently swallows a flea. She progresses through all the class pets while her students watch through her windows. Fortunately she stops with the animals and doesn't move on to the children. Gammell's spatter art pictures are suitably bizarre.

Danneberg, Julie.

The School Year Books of Sarah Jane Hartwell. Illustrated by Judith DufourLove. Watertown, MA: Charlesbridge. `Gr. K–3`

Sarah Jane Hartwell goes through her first year of teaching, experiencing a variety of emotions.

First Day Jitters. 2000. Unpaged. ISBN 9781580890540. `Gr. K–3` (SP)

Sarah Jane Hartwell hides under her covers while Mr. Hartwell encourages her to come and go to school. She's worried about what it will be like starting in a new place, if she will like the school, if the children will be nice. When at last she braces herself to face the day, we discover that she's not a student, she's the teacher.

First Year Letters. 2003. Unpaged. ISBN 9781580890847.

Now that Sarah is actually teaching her class, she sets up a school post office. Through the letters that her students deposit there, readers learn about the adventures in Sarah's year teaching, including a class pet getting loose and a visit from the fire department that is not a drill. While the letters maintain a straightforward tone, the illustrations show the wild and humorous events of the classroom.

Last Day Blues. 2006. Unpaged. ISBN 9781580890465.

Sarah's students are sure that she will be sad at the end of school, so they make her a good-bye present. While the children plan their present, the illustrations show the teachers happily preparing for their summer vacation.

Finchler, Judy.

The Miss Malarkey Series. Illustrated by Kevin O'Malley. New York: Walker. Gr. 1-3

Miss Malarkey is an elementary school teacher who has a variety of adventures with her students including field trips, soccer coaching, and standardized testing. O'Malley's watercolor-and-pencil illustrations vividly depict humor in differing situations.

Miss Malarkey Doesn't Live in Room 10. 1995. Unpaged. ISBN 978-0802774989 (pb).

Miss Malarkey Won't Be in Today. 1998. Unpaged. ISBN 9780802775917 (pb).

Testing Miss Malarkey. 2000. 32pp. ISBN 9780802776242 (pb).

You're a Good Sport, Miss Malarkey. 2002. 32pp. ISBN 9780802788153.

Miss Malarkey's Field Trip. 2004. 32pp. ISBN 9780802789129.

Miss Malarkey Leaves No Reader Behind. 2006. 32pp. ISBN 9780802780843.

Congratulations, Miss Malarkey! 2009. 32pp. ISBN 9780802798350.

Harper, Jamie.

Miss Mingo and the First Day of School. Cambridge, MA: Candlewick, 2006. 26pp. ISBN 9780763624101. Gr. K-3

Miss Mingo the flamingo teaches a class full of creatures from the natural world, including an octopus, a hippo, and a centipede, among others. On the first day of school she asks each animal to share something unusual about themselves as a way to get to know each other.

Miss Mingo and the Fire Drill. Somerville, MA: Candlewick, 2009. Unpaged. ISBN 9780763635978. Sequel. Gr. K-3

Miss Mingo and her class of assorted creatures prepare for a fire drill.

Hennessy, B. G.

Mr. Ouchy's First Day. Illustrated by Paul Meisel. New York: Penguin, 2006. 32pp. ISBN 9780399242489. Gr. K-3

Mr. Ouchy is looking forward to his first day of teaching, but he's a bit nervous as well. He wonders if he will remember his students' names and find the bathroom. The day goes smoothly, and at night, he tells his mother all about it on the phone.

Pattou, Edith.

Mrs. Spitzer's Garden. **Illustrated by Tricia Tusa. San Diego: Harcourt, 2001. 32pp. ISBN 9780152019785. Gr. K–3**

In this story where flowers symbolize children, the teacher, Mrs. Spitzer, tends her garden with care throughout the year.

Rosen, Michael.

Totally Wonderful Miss Plumberry. **Illustrated by Chinlun Lee. Cambridge, MA: Candlewick, 2006. 40pp. ISBN 9780763627447. PreS–2**

Molly is having a totally wonderful day at school until the other kids start paying more attention to a classmate's toy than to her crystal. Her sensitive teacher, Miss Plumberry, handily turns their attention back to Molly, making it a wonderful day once more.

Slate, Joseph.

The Miss Bindergarten Series. Wolff, Ashley Illustrated by New York: Dutton.
PreS–K

Miss Bindergarten is a black-and-white dog who teaches a class full of alphabetically named animal students who have a variety of adventures throughout the school year. Rhyming text and brightly colored illustrations make these perfect books for kindergarteners.

Miss Bindergarten Gets Ready for Kindergarten. 1996. Unpaged. ISBN 978-0525454465.

Miss Bindergarten Celebrates the 100th Day of Kindergarten. 1998. 32pp. ISBN 9780525460008.

Miss Bindergarten Stays Home from Kindergarten. 2000. Unpaged. ISBN 9780142301272 (pb).

Miss Bindergarten Takes a Field Trip with Kindergarten. 2001. Unpaged. ISBN 9780142401392 (pb).

Miss Bindergarten Plans a Circus with Kindergarten. 2002. Unpaged. ISBN 978-0525468844.

Miss Bindergarten Has a Wild Day in Kindergarten. 2005. Unpaged. ISBN 978-0525470847.

Miss Bindergarten Celebrates the Last Day of Kindergarten. 2006. Unpaged. ISBN 9780525477440.

Winters, Kay.

My Teacher for President. Illustrated by Denise Brunkus. New York: Dutton, 2004. 32pp. ISBN 9780525471868. **Gr. K–3**

> Oliver writes a letter to a local TV channel explaining why his teacher would make a great president. While the text lists presidential qualifications, the illustrations show the teacher engaged in school activities.

Zemach, Kaethe.

Ms. McCaw Learns to Draw. New York: Arthur A. Levine Books, 2008. 32pp. ISBN 9780439829144. **Gr. 1–3**

> Dudley would rather daydream than pay attention in class, but his teacher, Ms. McCaw, patiently explains things to him until he understands. When she tries to draw on the blackboard, however, their roles are reversed. She admits to the class that she can't draw, and Dudley volunteers to show her how. He's good at drawing, and this time he is patient with her as he shows her how to draw.

School in General

Best, Cari.

Shrinking Violet. Illustrated by Giselle Potter. New York: Farrar, Straus & Giroux, 2001. Unpaged. ISBN 9780374368821. **Gr. K–2**

> Violet is very shy, and her teacher and friends all try to help her lessen her fear, except for Irwin, who teases her every day. When it comes time to put on a class play about the planets, her teacher comes up with the perfect part for her. She gives Violet an offstage speaking part, which bolsters her courage so much she can stand up to Irwin.

Borden, Louise.

The Day Eddie Met the Author. Illustrated by Adam Gustavson. New York: Margaret K. McElderry Books, 2001. 44pp. ISBN 9780689867200 (pb). **Gr. 1–3**

> Mrs. Morrow's third grade class is preparing for an author visit, and no one is more excited than Eddie. He is hoping that he will get to ask the author his very important question.

The A+ Custodian. Illustrated by Adam Gustavson. New York: Margaret K. McElderry Books, 2004. Unpaged. ISBN 9780689849954. **Gr. 1–3**

> Gracie and Zach always get to school early because their mother is a teacher, so they become the custodian's helpers. John Carillo takes meticulous care of Dublin Elementary and can fix anything. Gracie gets an idea to show him how much he is appreciated and enlists the aid of the principal and the entire school to carry out her plan.

The Last Day of School. Illustrated by Adam Gustavson. New York: Margaret K. McElderry Books, 2006. Unpaged. ISBN 9780689868696. **Gr. 1–3**

> All the kids of Chapman Elementary are excited that it's the last day of school. Matthew has a special gift for his teacher, but in the chaos, he almost misses the chance to give it to her.

The John Hancock Club. **Illustrated by Adam Gustavson. New York: Margaret K. McElderry Books, 2007. 36pp. ISBN 9781416918134.** `Gr. 1–3`

> Sean is starting third grade and is worried about learning to write in cursive. His teacher explains that as they master their new skill, they will become members of the John Hancock Club. Despite his concerns, Sean is able to learn the new writing style, as well as history about John Hancock along the way.

Bunting, Eve.

One Green Apple. **Illustrated by Ted Lewin. New York: Clarion, 2006. 32pp. ISBN 9780618434770.** `Gr. 1–3`

> Farah, a Muslim girl, goes with her new class to an apple orchard. She feels isolated because she doesn't speak English and because she wears the dupatta on her head. When each child selects an apple for the press to make cider, Farah picks one that is small and green. It's different, just as she is different. By the end of the day, she is befriended by two girls, who teacher her the word, "apple" as they share the cider made from mixing the juice from various apples.

Carlson, Nancy.

The Henry Series. New York: Viking. `PreS–1`

> Henry is a young mouse who starts kindergarten and has a variety of experiences in his school life, including homesickness on his first day of kindergarten, struggling with learning to read, and learning how to save money. Brightly colored illustrations highlight these realistic school situations.

> *Look Out Kindergarten, Here I Come!* 1999. 32pp. ISBN 9780670883783. (SP)

> *Henry's 100 Days of Kindergarten*. 2004. 32pp. ISBN 9780142407585 (pb).

> *Henry's Show and Tell*. 2004. 32pp. ISBN 9780670036950 (o.p.).

> *First Grade, Here I Come*. 2006. 32pp. ISBN 9780670061273.

> *I Don't Like to Read*. 2007. 30pp. ISBN 9780670061914.

> *Henry's Amazing Imagination*. 2008. 32pp. ISBN 9780670062966.

> *Henry and the Valentine Surprise*. 2008. 32pp. ISBN 9780670062676.

> *Start Saving, Henry*. 2009. 32pp. ISBN 9780670011476.

> *Henry and the Bully*. 2010. 32pp. ISBN 9780670011483.

Choldenko, Gennifer.

Louder, Lili. **Illustrated by S. D. Schindler. New York: Putnam, 2007. 32pp. ISBN 9780399242526.** `Gr. K–3`

> Lili, a girl who is so shy that she rarely speaks in school, finally speaks up when a classmate is about to be cruel the class guinea pig.

Cuyler, Margery.

The Jessica Stories. Illustrated by Arthur Howard. New York: Simon & Schuster. `PreS-2`

Jessica goes through the year of first grade learning how to cope with a variety of situations.

100th Day Worries. 2000. 32pp. ISBN 9780689829796.

The 100th day of first grade is approaching and everyone is supposed to bring in a collection of 100 things. Jessica is worried, because she doesn't have 100 of anything. With the help of her family, she comes up with a unique collection.

Stop Drop and Roll. 2001. Unpaged. ISBN 9780689843556.

Fire Safety Week is coming and everyone in Jessica's class will have to demonstrate one of the fire safety rules. Jessica is responsible for showing everyone how to stop, drop, and roll. She is concerned that her stage fright will cause her to mess up, but she makes it through just fine.

Hooray for Reading Day. 2008. 30pp. ISBN 9780689861888.

Jessica is feeling anxious about Reading Theater Day, because she has difficulty reading aloud. She practices at home with her dog and gets good enough, so that all goes smoothly.

Bullies Never Win. 2009. 32pp. ISBN 9780689861871.

Jessica's previous worries seem small compared to dealing with Brenda, who belittles her at every opportunity. In tears, Jessica tells her mother, who gives her two options. She says Jessica should either tell Brenda how she feels or tell the teacher. When Brenda bullies her next, Jessica at last stands up for herself.

I Repeat, Don't Cheat! 2010. 32pp. ISBN 9781416971672.

When Jessica's best friend Lizzie needs help with her schoolwork, Jessica is happy to pitch in, but she worries about what the right thing to do is when the help becomes cheating.

DiPucchio, Kelly S.

Grace for President. Illustrated by Leuyen Pham. New York: Hyperion, 2008. 32pp. ISBN 9780786839193. `Gr. 1-3`

Grace, an African American girl, is astonished to learn that there has never been a woman president. She declares that when she grows up, she will run for president, so her teacher suggests that she run for school president to get a taste of politics.

Fraser, Mary Ann.

The I. Q. Series. New York: Walker. `Gr. K-3`

The new class pet, I. Q., proves to be a far from ordinary mouse. The pencil, gouache, and pen-and-ink illustrations are colorful and charming.

I. Q. Goes to School. 2002. 32pp. ISBN 9780802776983 (pb).

I. Q. is not content to stay in his cage as the class's pet mouse. He does all the work with the students, aiming to win the coveted title of "Student of the Week."

I. Q. Goes to the Library. 2003. 32pp. ISBN 9780802788771.

I. Q. loves to learn, so he is delighted to join the class on their library trip, where he learns about the different resources available.

I. Q., It's Time. 2005. 32pp. ISBN 9780802789785.

The students in Mrs. Furber's class and I. Q. are very busy getting ready for Parents' Night and learning to tell time along the way.

I. Q. Gets Fit. 2007. 32pp. ISBN 9780802795588.

It's Health Month, and everyone in Mrs. Furber's class, including I. Q., is preparing for the Student Fitness Challenge.

Guy, Ginger Foglesong.

My School/Mi Escuela. **Illustrated by Vivi Escriva. New York: HarperFestival/ Rayo, 2006. 24pp. ISBN 9780060791018. T-K (Bilingual)**

Simple words and phrases in English and Spanish present a day at school.

Henkes, Kevin.

Lilly's Purple Plastic Purse. See under "Everyday Life in General" in chapter 1.

Krishnaswami, Uma.

The Happiest Tree: A Yoga Story. **Illustrated by Ruth Jeyaveeran. New York: Lee & Low, 2005. 32pp. ISBN 9781584302377. Gr. 1-3**

Meena, an Asian Indian American, is a bit clumsy and so doesn't want to be in the school play, even though she is playing a tree. She's afraid she will do something terribly embarrassing. However, after she takes some yoga classes and learns to move gracefully, she is able to participate in the play with confidence.

McGhee, Alison.

Countdown to Kindergarten. **Illustrated by Harry Bliss. San Diego: Harcourt, 2002. Unpaged. ISBN 9780152025168. PreS-K**

A soon-to-be kindergartener spends the ten days leading up to kindergarten worried about not being able to tie her shoes, because she's heard from a first grader that that is the first thing she must be able to do.

Mrs. Watson Wants Your Teeth. **Illustrated by Harry Bliss. Orlando, FL: Harcourt, 2004. 36pp. ISBN 9780152049317. Sequel. Gr. K-2**

Now entering first grade, the protagonist hears from a second grader that her new teacher, Mrs. Watson, is really an alien with a purple tongue who collects baby teeth.

Plourde, Lynn.

The Mrs. Shepherd's Class Series. **Illustrated by Thor Wickstrom. New York: Dutton.** `Gr. K-3`

Each book in the series focuses on special school events and highlights the actions of students who do things a little bit differently. Tongue-in-cheek humor and bright color cartoons make these amusing school tales.

School Picture Day. 2002. Unpaged. ISBN 9780142401507 (pb).

Everyone in Mrs. Shepherd's class arrives at school all dressed up for picture day except Josephina Caroleena Wattasheena the First. Josephina is much more interested in figuring out how things work, like the pencil sharpener and the sprinkler system. Unfortunately, her tinkering gets everyone messy. She redeems herself, though, when the photographer's camera doesn't work, and Josephina is able to fix it.

Teacher Appreciation Day. 2003. Unpaged. ISBN 9780142402832 (pb).

Mrs. Shepherd's students bring apples to show how much they value her on Teacher Appreciation Day, except for Maybella Jean Wishywashy. She is not sure what to give, because she has a wide variety to choose from. The trouble is, she just can't make up her mind.

Pajama Day. 2005. Unpaged. ISBN 9780525473558.

The day has arrived when everyone is supposed to go to school in their pajamas, but Drew A. Blank forgets, despite the notes he's left himself everywhere. Drew doesn't want to be left out, so he comes up with an imaginative solution.

Book Fair Day. 2006. 40pp. ISBN 9780525476962.

Dewey Booker loves to read and is super excited that it's book fair day. When he discovers that his class will be the last to go to the fair, he worries that there will be nothing good still available and angles all day to go earlier.

Science Fair Day. 2008. 40pp. ISBN 9780525478782.

It's the day when all of Mrs. Shepherd's students have brought their science fair projects to school. Ima Kindanozee pelts each student with questions and inadvertently ruins the projects in the process. Mrs. Shepherd patiently helps repair the damage in time for the principal's inspection. Then Ima questions the students in ways that perfectly display how much they have learned while making their projects.

Field Trip Day. 2010. 40pp. ISBN 9780525479949.

When Mrs. Shepherd takes her class on a field trip to an organic farm, the inquisitive Juan keeps them on their toes, both because of his questions and his tendency to keep running ahead to satisfy his curiosity.

Polacco, Patricia.

Thank You, Mr. Falker. **New York: Philomel, 1998. Unpaged. ISBN 9780399231667.** `Gr. 1-3` **(SP)**

Polacco based this story on her own childhood. Young Trisha loves stories and is looking forward to learning how to read, but when she starts school, she can't do it because the words seem to wiggle. Year after year, she gets by in school but constantly thinks she's stupid, until the family moves to California. Trisha's new teacher is Mr. Falker. He realizes that Trisha is dyslexic and gets her the help she needs to learn to read. This moving story is expertly told and illustrated with Polacco's gouache-and-pencil pictures that reveal the feelings of the characters.

Poydar, Nancy.

Bunny Business. New York: Holiday House, 2003. Unpaged. ISBN 978-0823417711. Gr. K–3

Harry has trouble paying attention and sitting still in class, so when he is cast as the Funny Bunny in the class play, he makes the wrong kind of ears. Another student complains that he will ruin the show, so he works extra hard at listening. All his efforts pay off, because he learns everyone's lines and can fill in when the lead freezes on stage.

Last Day, Hooray. New York: Holiday House, 2004. 32pp. ISBN 9780823418077. Gr. K–3

Students, teachers, and staff participate in last-day-of-school activities, like classroom parties and cleaning up, while they daydream about the things they'll do on summer vacation.

The Biggest Test in the Universe. New York: Holiday House, 2005. 32pp. ISBN 9780823419449. Gr. 1–3

Sam and his classmates dread the end of the year standardized tests, especially when the older kids tell them how hard it is, but their teacher prepares them well and all goes smoothly.

The Bad-News Report Card. New York: Holiday House, 2006. 32pp. ISBN 9780823419920. Gr. 1–3

Isabel eagerly anticipates getting her report card until she concentrates on all the areas where her teacher might write, "needs improvement." Worried, she deliberately leaves the report card on the bus and lies to her parents, telling them she lost it. In the end, she must face her misdeeds and show her parents her report card, which turns out to be a good one after all.

Zip, Zip . . . Homework. New York: Holiday House, 2008. Unpaged. ISBN 9780823420902. Gr. K–3

Violet adores her new backpack with all its zippers, snaps, and pockets, but when she fails to put her first homework assignment anywhere in the backpack and then lies about it, she learns that it's important to tell the truth.

Pulver, Robin.

The Punctuation Series. Illustrated by Lynn Rowe Reed. New York: Holiday House. Gr. 1–3

The punctuation, parts of speech, and letters in Mr. Wright's class take on a life of their own.

Punctuation Takes a Vacation. 2003. Unpaged. ISBN 9780823416875. **Gr. 1–3**

When the punctuation marks decide to take a vacation from Mr. Wright's classroom, the students soon discover that life is full of mix-ups without them and must find a way to get them to come back. Whimsical illustrations help make this a lighthearted exploration of grammar.

Nouns and Verbs Have a Field Day. 2006. 32pp. ISBN 9780823419821. **Gr. 1–3**

When the students in Mr. Wright's class go outside for Field Day, the nouns and verbs inside come to life and decide to have a contest of their own. The verbs team up, as do the nouns and pronouns, but they quickly see that in order to make sentences, they have to work together.

Silent Letters Loud and Clear. 2008. Unpaged. ISBN 9780823421275. **Gr. 1–3**

Mr. Wright's students are tired of silent letters. At their teacher's suggestion, they send an e-mail to the newspaper recommending banning all silent letters. The letters take offence and disappear from the e-mail, proving just how important they are.

Rockwell, Anne F.

My Preschool. **New York: Holt, 2008. 28pp. ISBN 9780805079555. PreS–K**

Chipper text follows a boy through his day at preschool, including playing at the sand and water tables, circle time, storytime, and snack time.

Scieszka, Jon.

🖋*Math Curse.* **Illustrated by Lane Smith. New York: Viking, 1995. Unpaged. ISBN 9780670861941. Gr. 3 & up**

When the narrator's teacher, Mrs. Fibonacci, tells the class most things in life can be viewed as a kind of math problem, suddenly everything is an arithmetic puzzle, which the narrator finds overwhelming. Smith's wild collages incorporate geometric shapes and add to the humor of the story. (ALAN, BBYA)

🖋*Science Verse.* **Illustrated by Lane Smith. New York: Viking, 2004. 40pp. ISBN 9780670910571. Gr. 3 & up**

Mr. Newton informs his class that by listening carefully, you can hear the poetry of science in everything, and immediately all sorts of scientific concepts are cast in the poetic forms of works by Edgar Allan Poe, Lewis Carroll, and Robert Frost, among others. Smith's zany artwork adds to the hilarity. (ALAN)

Scotton, Rob.

<u>**Splat the Cat Series.**</u> **New York: HarperCollins. Gr. K–2**

Splat the Cat has interesting adventures at school and celebrating holidays.

Splat the Cat. 2008. 32pp. ISBN 9780060831547.

Splat the Cat worries about starting school. Just as he thinks it might not be so bad, he learns that cats are supposed to chase mice. Splat doesn't chase mice. As a matter of fact, his best friend is his pet mouse, Seymour, whom he's brought with him to school. When Seymour does escape, the cats do chase him, but Seymour saves the day by being able to crawl into a very small hole and unlock the milk supply. Now Splat is convinced that school is indeed a fun place.

Love Splat. 2008. 32pp. ISBN 9780060831578.

Splat is back, and this time he is in love with the green-eyed Kitten. He's made a Valentine card for her, proclaiming his devotion, but tosses it in the trash when Spike assures him that he likes Kitten better. Kitten, who is more partial to Splat, finds his discarded Valentine and gives him one of her own, much to his delight.

Merry Christmas, Splat. 2009. Unpaged. ISBN 9780060831608.

On Christmas Eve, Splat has high hopes for a present from Santa. When his sister puts doubt in his mind about whether or not he deserves a present, he races about trying to do enough good deeds to please the jolly old elf, even if they don't need doing.

Scaredy-Cat, Splat! 40pp. 2010. ISBN 9780061177606.

As Halloween approaches, Splat unknowingly becomes the scariest cat in school.

Sierra, Judy.

Preschool to the Rescue. **Illustrated by Will Hillenbrand. San Diego: Harcourt, 2001. Unpaged. ISBN 9780152020354.** PreS–K

Outside of a preschool, a mud puddle comes to life and grabs hold of a series of vehicles, starting with the pizza delivery truck. A troop of raingear-clad, animal preschoolers arrive to dig out the trucks, which are actually toys. As the rain stops and the sun edges out, the children complete their destruction of the puddle by making mud pies and sculptures.

Shannon, David.

David Goes to School. See under "Everyday Life in General" in chapter 1.

Stuve-Bodeen, Stephanie.

Elizabeti's School. See in chapter 3.

Wells, Rosemary.

My Kindergarten. **New York: Hyperion, 2004. 90pp. ISBN 9780786808335. PreS–K**

Emily, from *Emily's First 100 Days*, returns to attend kindergarten in this book that follows her month by month as she learns, colors, numbers, letters, and so much more, in her lively first year of school.

Otto Runs for President. **New York: Scholastic, 2008. 40pp. ISBN 9780545037228.** Gr. K–3

In Barkadelphia School, where all the students are dogs, Tiffany the poodle and Charlie the bulldog are running for school president. When a student observes that they only seem to be thinking about themselves, Otto the Jack Russell decides to make it a three-way race, even though he doesn't think he has much of a chance of winning.

Easy Readers

Brown, Marc.

Arthur's Back to School Surprise. See under "Everyday Life in General" in chapter 1.

Danziger, Paula.

Get Ready for Second Grade, Amber Brown. See under "Everyday Life in General" in chapter 1.

De Groat, Diane.

Gilbert, the Surfer Dude. New York: HarperCollins, 2009. 31pp. ISBN 9780061252112. **Gr. K–2**
   Gilbert, whose first stories were in picture books, here migrates to the easy reader format. When Gilbert and his family go for a day at the beach, Gilbert forgets his bathing suit and must make do with one that is too big.

Kenah, Katharine.

The Best Seat in Second Grade. Illustrated by Abby Carter. New York: HarperCollins, 2005. 48pp. ISBN 9780060007348. **Gr. K–2**
   Sam thinks he has the best seat in second grade because he gets to sit next to George Washington the hamster. When he sneaks the class pet out for a field trip, he discovers the responsibilities involved in caring for an animal.

The Best Teacher in Second Grade. Illustrated by Abby Carter. New York: HarperCollins, 2006. 48pp. ISBN 9780060535643. **Gr. K–2**
   Luna, a new girl, proposes a midnight circus for Family Night because she loves the planets, but her classmates are carried away by the circus part of her idea. When they find out another class is planning a circus, their teacher is able to steer them back to Luna's idea, much to her delight.

The Best Chef in Second Grade. Illustrated by Abby Carter. New York: HarperCollins, 2007. 44pp. ISBN 9780060535612. **Gr. K–2**
   When a TV chef is going to visit their classroom, Mr. Hopper gives the class the assignment of cooking a family favorite. Ollie longs to be a great chef, but experiences some frustration along the way.

Van Leeuwen, Jean.

Amanda Pig, Schoolgirl. See under "Everyday Life in General" in chapter 1.

Challenging Situations in Life

All kinds of situations can arise in children's lives, and sometimes encountering stories where characters are going through similar situations helps children understand and/or cope with the things that are happening in their own lives. Listed here are some of the books dealing with just such circumstances. Not all of the issues are negative, but issues are central to all of the books.

Abuse

Aboff, Marcie.

Uncle Willy's Tickles: A Child's Right to Say No. **Illustrated by Kathleen Gartner. Washington, DC: Magination Press, 2003. 32pp. ISBN 9781557989987.** `Gr. 1-3`

Mark does not like the way his Uncle Willy "tickles" him. He tries to get him to stop, but he persists. When he turns to his mother, she reassures him and encourages him to remain firm with his uncle. Included is a chapter for parents with advice on how to explain to children the difference between good touching and bad touching.

Campbell, Bebe Moore.

Sometimes My Mommy Gets Angry. **Illustrated by E. B. Lewis. New York: Putnam, 2003. 32pp. ISBN 9780142403594.** `Gr. 1-3`

Annie's mother has an untreated mental illness that causes drastic mood swings. In the morning she cheerfully makes Annie breakfast, but when she arrives home from school her mother screams at her. Annie knows that she can call her grandmother for comfort and help, but instead she copes on her own. Waiting for her mother's mood to shift, she snuggles with her teddy bear and realizes that the darkness is not within her but in her mother.

Ledwon, Peter.

Mia's Secret. **Illustrated by Marilyn Mets. Toronto: Tundra, 2006. 24pp. ISBN 9780887768019 (pb).** `Gr. 1-3`

Mia is being sexually abused, but she promised not to tell. Then she realizes that her stuffed bear Tikki has seen everything, and Tikki hasn't made any promises. So she has Tikki tell her mother to make the man stop.

Riggs, Shannon.

Not in Room 204. **Illustrated by Jaime Zollars. Morton Grove, IL: Albert Whitman, 2007. 29pp. ISBN 9780807557648.** `Gr. 1-3`

Mrs. Salvador keeps a very orderly classroom, which helps her students feel secure. When she presents a unit on stranger danger, she also explains that strangers are not the only ones who can touch a child inappropriately. Quiet Regina comes to school early the next day and tells her teacher that her father has been touching her in a way that he shouldn't, and her teacher assures her that she knows just what to do to make sure that Regina is safe. A straightforward book about dealing with sexual abuse.

Tabor, Nancy Maria Grande.

Bottles Break. Watertown, MA: Charlesbridge, 1999. Unpaged. ISBN 9780881063172. `Gr. 1–3`

The young child of an alcoholic mother describes how it feels to cope with this difficult situation. The bottles in the pictures are both literally the mother's empty bottles and also, when they break, they are symbols for the child's feelings. A caring teacher gives the child help, but there are no pat solutions. Contact information for organizations that can offer aid to children of alcoholics concludes the volume.

Woodson, Jacqueline.

Our Gracie Aunt. Illustrated by Jon J. Muth. New York: Hyperion, 2001. 29pp. ISBN 9780786814428. `Gr. 1–3`

In this African American family, Beebee and her younger brother Johnson are frequently left alone for days at a time by their neglectful mother. Eventually a social worker places them with their Aunt Gracie, who provides a secure and loving home for the children.

Bullies

Alexander, Claire.

Lucy and the Bully. Morton Grove, IL: Albert Whitman, 2008. 32pp. ISBN 9780807547861. `Gr. K–3`

Lucy the lamb loves art. She is so good at drawing that everyone in class wants her to draw for them. Everyone except Tommy the bull. He does everything he can to ruin her work and threatens her so that she won't tell on him. Eventually, her mother gets her to tell the story, and she calls the teacher. A much chastened Tommy is sad the next day at school. Feeling sorry for him, Lucy compliments his drawing, and the two begin to start down the path to friendship.

Aston, Dianna Hutts.

Not So Tall for Six. Illustrated by Frank W. Dormer. Watertown, MA: Charlesbridge, 2008. 32pp. ISBN 9781570917059. `PreS–3`

With a Southwestern twang, Aston tells the tale of Kylie Bell, who is small for her age. Kylie is constantly picked on by Rusty Jacks, a new boy who delights in using his size to intimidate smaller children. Fed up, Kylie stands up to him, but later relents and invites him to join her reading circle. The kindness paves the way to friendship.

Bateman, Teresa.

The Bully Blockers Club. Illustrated by Jackie Urbanovic. Morton Grove, IL: Albert Whitman, 2004. Unpaged. ISBN 9780807509197 (pb). `Gr. K–3`

Lotty Raccoon is excited about starting school but distressed to find herself the target of Grant Grizzly, the class bully. She tries different solutions, including ignoring him, but nothing works until she forms a club of fellow students who are also tired of being bullied and are willing to stick up for each other.

Carlson, Nancy.

Henry and the Bully. See under "School: School in General" in this chapter.

Caseley, Judith.

Bully. New York: Greenwillow, 2001. Unpaged. ISBN 9780688178673. **Gr. K–3**
Mickey and Jack used to be friends, but now Jack is bullying him all the time. Mickey gets advice from his family, but his own solution of returning kindness even when Jack teases him works best.

Choldenko, Gennifer.

Louder, Lili. See under "School: School in General" in this chapter.

Cuyler, Margery.

Bullies Never Win. See under "School: School in General" in this chapter.

Kroll, Steven.

Jungle Bullies. Illustrated by Vincent Nguyen. New York: Marshall Cavendish, 2006. 30pp. ISBN 9780761452973. **PreS–1**
In this cumulative story, bigger jungle animals force the smaller ones out of the way, until baby Monkey takes a stand for himself and demands that Leopard share the space and be friendly. The turnaround attitude reverses all the way up the size chain, creating an environment of sharing instead of bullying.

Ludwig, Trudy.

My Secret Bully. Illustrated by Abigail Marble. Ashland, OR: RiverWood Books, 2003. Unpaged. ISBN 9781582461595. **Gr. 2 & up** (SP)
Monica and Katie, who have been friends since kindergarten, are having troubles. For reasons that elude Monica, Katie seems to be taking every opportunity to leave Monica out and embarrass her. Distraught, Monica turns to her mother for advice. Though her mother gives her wise counsel, there are no easy answers.

Just Kidding. Illustrated by Adam Gustavson. Berkeley, CA: Tricycle, 2005. 32pp. ISBN 9781582461632. **Gr. 1–3** (SP)
D. J. is tired of the mean things that Vince is always saying to him, using the excuse that he's just kidding. He tries several strategies, including walking away, to deal with the bullying. The most successful one, suggested by the school counselor, is for D. J. to spend time with friends who make D. J. feel good about himself.

McCain, Becky R.

Nobody Knew What to Do: A Story about Bullying. **Illustrated by Todd Leonardo. Morton Grove, IL: Albert Whitman, 2001. Unpaged. ISBN 9780807557112.** `Gr. K–3`

> The narrator describes the problem of a bully at school, whom no one stops until the protagonist learns that his friend is going to be attacked. Then he tells the teacher, who intercedes immediately.

O'Neill, Alexis.

The Recess Queen. **Illustrated by Laura Huliska-Beith. New York: Scholastic, 2002. Unpaged. ISBN 9780439206372.** `Gr. K–3`

> Mean Jean is the recess queen, and no one can play with anything until she does, until the new girl, Katie Sue, who doesn't know any better, has fun first. Jean is on the brink of exploding when Katie Sue invites her to break in her new jump rope with her. The offer is too good for Jean to pass up, and she discovers that she likes being friends better than being a bully.

Pearson, Tracey Campbell.

Myrtle. **New York: Farrar, Straus & Giroux, 2004. 32pp. ISBN 978-0374351571.** `Gr. K–2`

> Myrtle is a mouse who enjoys having fun until mean Frances moves in next door and makes a practice of tormenting Myrtle and her baby brother. Soon Myrtle refuses to go outside at all. When her beloved Aunt Tizzy returns from safari, Myrtle pours out her heart and gets some good advice from her about roaring back, which Myrtle follows with great success.

Death

Death of a Pet

Cochran, Bill.

The Forever Dog. **Illustrated by Dan Andreasen. New York: HarperCollins, 2007. 32pp. ISBN 9780060539399.** `PreS–3`

> Mike has raised his dog Corky from a puppy. They do everything together, and Mike makes a forever pact with him. Unfortunately, Corky dies unexpectedly. Sad and lonely, Mike feels that Corky has broken his promise, until his mother teaches him to view forever in a different way.

Disalvo-Ryan, Dyanne.

A Dog Like Jack. **New York: Holiday House, 1999. 32pp. ISBN 978-0823413690.** `PreS–3`

> Mike and his family adopt an eight-year-old dog from a shelter, and Mike quickly bonds with his canine pal, Jack. As the years pass, Jack doesn't have the energy to play the way he used to, and eventually the day comes when Jack dies. Mike and his parents experience realistic sadness, and although

Mike thinks someday they may adopt another dog, he is sure no dog will ever replace Jack in his heart.

Harris, Robie H.

Goodbye Mousie. **Illustrated by Jan Ormerod. New York: Margaret K. McElderry, 2001. 32pp. ISBN 9780689871344.** `PreS–2`

In this realistic portrayal of a young person's reaction to the death of a pet, the young narrator discovers his mouse won't wake up one morning. His father gently explains that the mouse has died. At first the boy refuses to believe it, then he grows angry, and finally sad. He decorates a shoebox to bury his friend, and after he sheds some tears, he thinks he might get a new mouse in the future, but not right now.

Parker, Marjorie Blain.

Jasper's Day. **Illustrated by Janet Wilson. Tonawanda, NY: Kids Can Press, 2002. Unpaged. ISBN 9781553377641 (pb).** `Gr. K–3`

The family dog, Jasper, is very ill with cancer. Riley knows that his dog is in a lot of pain and will not recover. He agrees that he should be put to sleep and understands that this means he will die. On Jasper's last day, the family visits places they had fun together. Riley and his mother wait at home while his father takes Jasper to the vet. When he comes home, they bury him in the backyard.

Partridge, Elizabeth.

Big Cat Pepper. **Illustrated by Lauren Castillo. New York: Bloomsbury, 2009. 32pp. ISBN 9781599900247.** `Gr. K–2`

A boy loves his cat Pepper, who's been part of the family his whole life, but the tabby is old now. When he dies, the boy grieves but eventually comes to accept that Pepper will always live in his heart.

Rylant, Cynthia.

Dog Heaven. **New York: Scholastic, 1995. Unpaged. ISBN 9780590417013.** `PreS–2`

For those dealing with the death of a pet dog, this book in rhyme offers an idyllic view of heaven where a dog can run and jump and play.

Cat Heaven. **New York: Scholastic, 1997. Unpaged. ISBN 9780590100540.** `PreS–2`

This rhyming book is designed to help children cope with the death of a beloved pet cat. Rylant describes how much fun a cat will have in heaven.

Viorst, Judith.

The Tenth Good Thing about Barney. **Illustrated by Erik Blegvad. New York: Atheneum, 1971. 25pp. ISBN 9780689206887.** `Gr. K–3`

When the boy's cat Barney dies, the family holds a funeral and buries him in the backyard. At the ceremony they list the things they remember about their beloved pet.

Death of a Friend or Family Member

Brisson, Pat.

I Remember Miss Perry. Illustrated by Stephane Jorisch. New York: Dial, 2006. 32pp. ISBN 9780803729810. **Gr. 1–3**

> Stevie is anxious on his first day of class, and his new teacher, Miss Perry, deftly puts him at ease. As the days go by, the class comes to love their teacher. Unfortunately, she is taken from them quite suddenly when she dies in a car accident. The counselor helps them through the tragedy as they share their memories of their teacher.

Burrowes, Adjoa J.

Grandma's Purple Flowers. New York: Lee & Low, 2000. 30pp. ISBN 9781880000731. **PreS–2**

> An African American girl shares a special bond with her beloved grandmother and through the seasons she looks forward to crossing the park to visit her. In the spring she picks the purple flowers that her grandmother loves so much. In the summer, she skips on the way to grandma's. In the fall, they discuss how the falling leaves die each year. By winter, her grandmother has died, but in the spring, the blooming of the purple flowers reminds her of the happy memories she still has of her grandmother.

Crowe, Carole.

Turtle Girl. Illustrated by Jim Postier. Honesdale, PA: Boyds Mills, 2008. 32pp. ISBN 9781590782620. **Gr. 1–3**

> Magdalena and her grandmother enjoy watching and protecting the nesting sea turtles that live on the beach of their island home. When her grandmother dies, Magdalena is too devastated to care for the hatchlings alone, until she hears the squawk of a hungry seagull. She knows the turtles need her. With her mother's company, she runs to help them and senses her grandmother's presence as she does so.

Doyle, Roddy.

Her Mother's Face. Illustrated by Freya Blackwood. New York: Arthur A. Levine Books, 2008. 40pp. ISBN 9780439815017. **Gr. 1–3**

> In Dublin, ten-year-old Siobhn, whose mother died seven years ago, struggles to remember what her mother looked like, because there are no photos in the house. When a mysterious woman in the park suggests she look in the mirror, she takes her advice and begins the healing process.

Durant, Alan.

Always and Forever. Illustrated by Debi Gliori. Orlando, FL: Harcourt, 2004. 32pp. ISBN 9780152166366. **PreS–3**

> Otter, Mole, Fox, and Hare live together in a house in the forest as the best of friends. Fox's unexpected death plunges the friends into grief, and it is only

when they can share their true and not idealized memories of him that they begin to emerge from their sorrow.

Fritts, Mary Bahr.

If Nathan Were Here. Illustrated by Karen A. Jerome. Grand Rapids, MI: Eerdmans , 2000. Unpaged. ISBN 9780802851871. **Gr. 1-3**

A boy grieves deeply at the death of his best friend, Nathan. He focuses on remembering all the good times they shared, selecting something to put in the class memory box, and reaching out to Nathan's sister in friendship and understanding.

Goldman, Judy.

Uncle Monarch and the Day of the Dead. Illustrated by René King Moreno. Honesdale, PA: Boyds Mills, 2008. 32pp. ISBN 9781590784259. **Gr. 1-3**

Lupita and Tio Urbano are very close. It is her uncle who explains that the monarch butterflies who return to Mexico each year represent the souls of the dead. This year, as they await the butterflies and make preparation for the Day of the Dead, her uncle is very ill. Lupita is distraught when he dies two days before the celebration, but finds comfort in the holiday and the presence of the butterflies.

Krishnaswami, Uma.

Remembering Grandpa. Illustrated by Layne Johnson. Honesdale, PA: Boyds Mills, 2007. 32pp. ISBN 9781590784242. **Gr. K-3**

Daysha the bunny rabbit is trying to make her grandmother feel better a year after her grandfather's death. She collects various items that remind them both of happier times. Her grandmother cries, and Daysha gives her a hug, realizing that's what she needs most.

Lobel, Gillian.

Moonshadow's Journey. Illustrated by Karin Littlewood. Morton Grove, IL: Albert Whitman, 2009. 32pp. ISBN 9780807552735. **Gr. 1-3**

A young cygnet makes his first migration flight. He experiences the wonders of nature along the way and is confident because his grandfather is leading the flock, as he has many times before. During a storm, the young one falters and his parents help him to safety. They learn that Grandfather did not make it. Now, his father must lead the swans the rest of the way, and he explains to his son that in time it will be his turn to lead.

Plourde, Lynn.

Thank You, Grandpa. Illustrated by Jason Cockcroft. New York: Dutton, 2003. 32pp. ISBN 9780525469926. **Gr. K-3**

A girl and her grandfather enjoy walking through the woods together. As she grows up, he teaches her about life and death in the forest. Eventually, he can only walk with her assistance, and then one year, she walks alone.

Raschka, Chris.

The Purple Balloon. New York: Schwartz & Wade, 2007. 22pp. ISBN 9780375841460. **Gr. 1-3**

This book discusses death in a simple, straightforward manner designed for families coping with terminally ill children. The illustrations of purple balloons floating away symbolize the death of a child.

Reagan, Jean.

Always My Brother. Illustrated by Phyllis Pollema-Cahill. Gardiner, ME: Tilbury House, 2009. Unpaged. ISBN 9780884483137. **Gr. 2 & up**

In this moving account, Becky relates her experiences regarding the death of her brother and her gradual passage through grief.

Rosen, Michael.

❀*Michael Rosen's Sad Book.* Illustrated by Quentin Blake. Cambridge, MA: Candlewick, 2005. Unpaged. ISBN 9780763625979. **Gr. 3 & up** (SP)

This personal account of the author's deep sadness after the death of his teenage son clearly relates the profound despair he experienced. It also moves to memories of happier times, which give the author and the reader hope. (Boston Globe Honor)

Smith, Patricia.

Janna and the Kings. Illustrated by Aaron Boyd. New York: Lee & Low, 2003. Unpaged. ISBN 9781584300885. **Gr. 2 & up**

African American Janna enjoys spending Saturdays with her grandfather as they stroll down the main street of town. They stop at various stores and end their trip at the barbershop, where all of her grandfather's friends greet her with delight and treat her like a princess. Her grandfather's death plunges her into sadness, and she doesn't begin to recover until she makes the journey down the street and finds the friends in the shop still there to welcome her.

Divorce

Adams, Eric J., and Kathleen Adams.

On the Day His Daddy Left. Illustrated by Layne Johnson. Morton Grove, IL: Albert Whitman, 2000. 24pp. ISBN 9780807560723. **Gr. K-2**

Danny's parents are getting a divorce, and when the day arrives for his father to move out, Danny writes down a secret question that is worrying him. He shows the question to a teacher and a friend, and finally to his parents. He is wondering if it's his fault that his father is leaving, and all assure him that it's not.

Bunting, Eve.

Days of Summer. Illustrated by William Low. San Diego: Harcourt, 2001. Unpaged. ISBN 9780152018405. `Gr. K–3`

Two sisters struggle to adjust to the announcement that their grandparents are getting divorced. They fear they may never see their grandfather again, but when they visit their grandmother, they talk to him on the phone and set up a time to visit.

My Mom's Wedding. Illustrated by Lisa Papp. Chelsea, MI: Sleeping Bear Press, 2006. 32pp. ISBN 9781585362882. `Gr. K–3`

Seven-year-old Pinky thinks she is used to her parents being divorced and likes her prospective stepfather, Jim. However, when she sees her father on the day of the wedding, she offers to give him the rings she is carrying if he will remarry her mother. He gently reminds her that they are just friends now, and the wedding proceeds with Pinky reconciling herself to her new family.

Clarke, Jane.

The Best of Both Nests. Illustrated by Anne Kennedy. Morton Grove, IL: Albert Whitman, 2007. 30pp. ISBN 9780807506684. `PreS–2`

Stanley the stork's parents have decided to separate because they are always fighting. At first Stanley is not sure how he will feel calling two nests home, but both parents work hard to make him feel loved.

Cochran, Bill.

My Parents Are Divorced, My Elbows Have Nicknames, and Other Facts about Me. Illustrated by Steve Bjorkman. New York: HarperCollins, 2009. 30pp. ISBN 9780060539429. `Gr. 1–3`

Ted knows that some people think him odd because he does things like giving nicknames to his elbows. His feelings about his parents' divorce, however, don't make him odd at all. As he gets used to shuttling between two homes and a new stepparent, he still wishes for family life the way it used to be. Gradually he comes to realize that his parents both love him even though things have changed.

Coffelt, Nancy.

🏺*Fred Stays with Me.* Illustrated by Tricia Tusa. New York: Little, Brown, 2007. 30pp. ISBN 9780316882699. `Gr. K–3`

In this book that is one of the stand-outs in the bevy of books about divorce, a young girl relates how she lives sometimes with her mom and sometimes with her dad, but wherever she goes, her dog Fred goes with her. Although the two homes are different, Fred misbehaves in both, driving her parents to distraction. When that happens, she reminds them that Fred stays with her, no matter what. With Fred as her faithful companion, she feels a sense of security. (ALAN, Boston Globe Honor)

Holmberg, Bo R.

A Day with Dad. Illustrated by Eva Eriksson. Cambridge, MA: Candlewick, 2008. 30pp. ISBN 9780763632212. `PreS-2`

> After the divorce, Tim and his mom have moved to a new town. Consequently, his dad takes the train to visit. Tim's mom takes him to the station where they meet his dad, and he and his dad spend the day together engaged in various activities. While the story clearly shows how loved Tim is, it shows his sadness as well.

Masurel, Claire.

Two Homes. Illustrated by Kady MacDonald Denton. Cambridge, MA: Candlewick, 2001. 28pp. ISBN 9780763619848 (pb). `PreS-1`

> BecauseAlex's parents are divorced, Alex splits his time between his mom's house and his dad's. He has his own room in each home, as well as a selection of his favorite things, and different friends in each location. The first person narration aptly portrays Alex's emotions.

Ormerod, Jan.

Molly and Her Dad. Illustrated by Carol Thompson. New York: Roaring Brook, 2008. 40pp. ISBN 9781596432857. `PreS-2`

> Because Molly's dad lives a plane ride away, she doesn't see him often and doesn't really know him very well. She creates stories about him to tell her friends at school, but when he comes to take care of her for the week that her mother is away, she learns that he is far zanier than she had imagined. At first she feels distant toward him, but love grows as they spend time together and she realizes how similar they are.

Ransom, Jeanie Franz.

I Don't Want to Talk about It. Illustrated by Kathryn Kunz Finney. Washington, D.C.: Magination Press, 2000. 28pp. ISBN 9781557986641. `Gr. K-3`

> When her parents tell her that they are getting a divorce, a young girl describes her feelings in terms of the animals that she would like to be.

Schmitz, Tamara.

Standing on My Own Two Feet: A Child's Affirmation of Love in the Midst of Divorce. New York: Price Stern Sloan, 2008. 32pp. ISBN 9780843132212. `PreS-2`

> When his parents get divorced, Addison has to adjust to having two homes. His parents make clear to him that the divorce is not his fault and that they love him very much.

Shreeve, Elizabeth.

Oliver at the Window. **Illustrated by Candice Hartsough McDonald. Honesdale, PA: Front Street, 2009. Unpaged. ISBN 9781590785485.** `PreS–1`

> Oliver is having a hard time adjusting as his parents are going through a divorce. Now he has two homes and a new school. Instead of joining in activities with his classmates, he waits by the window, as he wonders which parent will pick him up this day. Gradually he gains confidence and begins to participate in school. When a new girl arrives who is clearly unhappy, he befriends her.

Illness

Altman, Alexandra Jessup.

Waiting for Benjamin: A Story about Autism. **Illustrated by Susan Keeter. Morton Grove, IL: Albert Whitman, 2008. 32pp. ISBN 9780807573648.** `PreS–2`

> Alexander's two-year-old brother Benjamin has been diagnosed with autism, and when special teachers come to the house to work with Benjamin, Alexander resents the extra attention he gets. Gradually Benjamin begins to develop some language tools and is able to interact with Alexander, which helps bridge the gap between them.

Borden, Louise.

Good Luck, Mrs. K.! **Illustrated by Adam Gustavson. New York: Margaret K. McElderry Books, 1999. Unpaged. ISBN 9780689851193 (pb).** `Gr. 3 & up`

> Mrs. Kempczinski's third grade class loves the way she makes learning fun, especially the dance of delight she does when homework is turned in on time. Halfway through the year the principal explains that she is in the hospital being treated for cancer. Through the rest of the year, the students send her cards and reports on what they are studying with the substitute. A surprise visit from Mrs. K. at the end of the year cheers them, and the story concludes with her return to teaching the next year. The tenderly told story is based on a true story that did not have such a happy ending.

Golding, Theresa Martin.

Abby's Asthma and the Big Race. **Illustrated by Margeaux Lucus. Morton Grove, IL: Albert Whitman, 2009. 32pp. ISBN 9780807504659.** `Gr. K–2`

> Even though Abby has asthma, she is determined to enter the race at the fair this year. Despite being teased and feeling discouraged, she gets help from her doctor and the trainer at the gym, so that she can realize her dream.

Johnson, Mo.

Noah's Garden: When Someone You Love Is in the Hospital. **Josse, Annabelle Illustrated by Somerville, MA: Candlewick, 2010. 32pp. ISBN 9780763647827.** `Gr. K–3`

> When Noah's baby sister becomes so ill she has to be hospitalized, Noah and his family visit a nearby garden. Worry gnaws at them. Noah uses his imagination to help him deal with his anxiety.

Matthies, Janna.

Peter, the Knight with Asthma. Illustrated by Anthony Lewis. Morton Grove, IL: Albert Whitman, 2009. ISBN 9780807565179. **Gr. K–2**

> Peter, a young boy with asthma, imagines fighting a fire-breathing dragon, but is interrupted by an asthma attack. Mom brings him his inhaler but decides a visit to the doctor would be helpful. The doctor prescribes nebulizer treatment as well, and with it, Peter slays the dragon at last. Asthma treatment information is included at the end.

Peete, Holly Robinson, and Elizabeth Ryan Peete.

My Brother Charlie. Illustrated by Shane W. Evans. New York: Scholastic, 2010. 40pp. ISBN 9780545094665. **PreS–2**

> Callie and Charlie are twins, and although they have many things in common, there are significant differences as well. Charlie has autism. Callie shares with the readers the frustrations and rewards of having a brother with special needs.

Polacco, Patricia.

The Lemonade Club. New York: Philomel, 2007. 40pp. ISBN 9780399245404. **Gr. 2 & up**

> Traci and Marilyn are best friends having a grand time in fifth grade with their caring teacher, Miss Wichelman, whose motto is to make lemonade when life gives you lemons. Unfortunately, Marilynn is diagnosed with leukemia. Her family and Traci stand by her during the chemotherapy treatments and the side effects. In addition, Traci and Miss Wichelman form the lemonade club and plan a special surprise for Marilyn when she returns to school. This moving tale is relayed with Polacco's signature tenderness and compassion and is based on an event in her daughter's life.

Tinkham, Kelly.

Hair for Mama. Illustrated by Amy June Bates. New York: Dial, 2007. Unpaged. ISBN 9780803729551. **Gr. 2 & up**

> Eight-year-old African American Marcus is worried about his mom, who doesn't want to join in for the annual family photo because she's lost her hair due to chemotherapy treatments. He sets out to try to find his mother some hair and ends up discovering an unexpected solution.

Manners

Breznak, Irene.

Sneezy Louise. Illustrated by Janet Pedersen. New York: Random House, 2009. 40pp. ISBN 9780375851698. **PreS–2**

> Louise wakes up with a cold, and throughout the day whenever she sneezes, she is reminded to cover her mouth.

Dewdney, Anna.

Nobunny's Perfect. **New York: Viking, 2008. 30pp. ISBN 9780670062881.** `T-K`
    Bunnies who are good most of the time demonstrate how feeling mad or sad can
    sometimes lead to screaming, kicking, or fighting. Then they show what well-be-
    haved bunnies should do by following the rules and giving hugs, among other
    things.

DiPucchio, Kelly S.

What's the Magic Word? **Illustrated by Marsha Winborn. New York:
HarperCollins, 2005. Unpaged. ISBN 9780060005788.** `PreS–1`
    When a gusty wind blows a newly hatched baby from his nest, he seeks shelter
    with various farm animals, but they each want to hear the magic word first. When
    he finally arrives back at his own nest, his mother reveals that the magic word is
    "Please."

Keller, Laurie.

Do unto Otters: A Book about Manners. **New York: Holt, 2007. 40pp. ISBN
9780805079968.** `Gr. 1–3`
    Mr. Rabbit has new neighbors when a family of otter moves in, and he's worried
    that they might not get along. A wise owl advises that Mr. Rabbit "do unto otters,"
    by treating them the way he would want to be treated, being polite, honest, and
    considerate.

Sierra, Judy.

Mind Your Manners B. B. Wolf. **Illustrated by J. Otto Seibold. New York: Knopf,
2007. Unpaged. ISBN 9780375835322.** `PreS–1`
    B. B. (Big Bad) Wolf receives an invitation to a library storybook tea and practices
    polite behavior with his friend crocodile so he can go and make a good impression
    on the children and the librarian.

Stein, David Ezra.

The Nice Book. **New York: Putnam, 2008. 32pp. ISBN 9780399250507.** `T-K`
    Colorful animals demonstrate what it means to be polite and well-behaved.

Moving

Gleeson, Libby.

Half a World Away. **Illustrated by Freya Blackwood. New York: Arthur A. Levine, 2007. 40pp. ISBN 9780439889773.** `Gr. K-2`
    Amy and Louie are best friends and neighbors in Australia. They live so close that
    all they have to do is give a special call and their friend will dash over. That all
    changes when Amy's family moves to New York City, and the friends must find a
    new way to stay in touch.

Herman, Charlotte.

First Rain. Illustrated by Katherine Mitter. Chicago: Albert Whitman, 2010. Unpaged. ISBN 9780807524534. **Gr. 1–3**

Abby and her parents are moving to Israel, but Abby is sad to be leaving her grandmother. The rain aptly reflects her distress. The two maintain their close relationship through letters, phone calls, and e-mail.

Lobel, Anita.

Nini Here and There. New York: Greenwillow, 2007. 32pp. ISBN 978-0060787684 (pb). **PreS–2**

Nini the cat sees her family packing and worries about whether or not they will abandon her. When they coax her into her carrier, she dreams about traveling to different places, and when they arrive in their new home in the country, she realizes they did not leave without her after all.

Meltzer, Amy.

Mezuzah on the Door. Illustrated by Janice Fried. Minneapolis, MN: Kar-Ben, 2007. 32pp. ISBN 9781580132497. **Gr. K–3**

When his family moves from an apartment in the city to a house in the sub-urbs, Noah misses his old friends. They hold a Hanukkat Habayit to dedi-cate the house as a Jewish home and invite all of their old friends. After the mezuzahs are hung on the doors and Noah's friends have touched the one on his door, he feels the comfort of their love even after they return to their homes.

Rostoker-Gruber, Karen.

Bandit. Illustrated by Vincent Nguyen. New York: Marshall Cavendish, 2008. 32pp. ISBN 9780761453826. **PreS–2**

Bandit the cat is exceedingly annoyed to see that his bed, food, and toys have all been moved. His mood doesn't improve when he is shoved into his carrier, either. First he assumes they are going to the vet, but when the car ride goes on and on, he decides it must be a vacation. Unimpressed by the empty house, he saunters back across town to his old home to sun in his fa-vorite spot, only he finds it's not his home anymore. His owner fetches him back and shows him his bed, food, and toys in his new house.

Wong, Janet S.

Homegrown House. Illustrated by E. B. Lewis. New York: Margaret K. McElderry Books, 2009. 40pp. ISBN 9780689847189. **PreS–3**

A young girl whose family has moved three times in eight years and now is planning to move again just when she has five really good friends, worries about what their new home will be like. She wants a house with a home-grown feel like her grandmother's, so she borrows some ideas to make her new house feel like home.

Physically Challenged

Anderson, Peggy Perry.

We Go in a Circle. Boston: Houghton Mifflin, 2004. 31pp. ISBN 9780618447565.
PreS–2

When a racehorse's leg is injured, he is taken to a therapy center. After his leg heals, he's fitted with a special saddle and gives rides to wheelchair-bound children as part of their physical therapy treatments.

Chaconas, Dori.

Dancing with Katya. **Illustrated by Constance Rummel Bergum. Atlanta, GA: Peachtree, 2006. 32pp. ISBN 9781561453764.** **Gr. K–3**

Anna and her little sister Katya love to dance together and pretend that they are ballerinas, until Katya contracts polio. Her legs are so weak that she fears she will never dance again, especially when she can barely manage to walk with the heavy braces on her legs. Worried for her sister, Anna buys a pair of gloves, decorates them, and gives them to Katya so that she can dance with her hands.

Millman, Isaac.

The Moses Series. New York: Farrar, Straus & Giroux. **Gr. K–3**

Moses is deaf, as are his classmates. Together they go to school and embark on a variety of enlightening class trips. One adventure is with his family.

Moses Goes to a Concert. 1998. Unpaged. ISBN 9780374350673.

Moses and his classmates are given balloons at the concert so that they can feel the vibrations the music makes. Afterward they meet the percussionist, who is also deaf. She shows them how she plays in her stocking feet so that she can feel the vibrations, lets them try her instruments, and assures them that they can be anything they want to be if they are willing to work hard.

Moses Goes to School. 2000. Unpaged. ISBN 9780374350697.

Moses and his classmates return to their school for deaf and hard-of-hearing children. They tell each other about their summer vacations and start their traditional classes of reading, writing, computer, etc. Throughout they are communicating using American Sign Language.

Moses Goes to the Circus. 2003. 32pp. ISBN 9780374350642.

Moses and his family go to the Big Apple Circus's Circus of the Senses for vision- and hearing-impaired children. Moses and his family use American Sign Language, even his little sister Renee, who is too young to talk.

Moses Sees a Play. 2004. 32pp. ISBN 9780374350666.

Moses and his classmates attend a production of *Cinderella* put on by the Theater for the Deaf and decide that they would like to put on a play of their own.

Seeger, Pete, and Paul Dubois Jacobs.

The Deaf Musicians. Illustrated by R. Gregory Christie. New York: Putnam, 2006. Unpaged. ISBN 9780399243165. `Gr. K–3`

When a jazz musician loses his hearing, he takes a job teaching music at a local school for the deaf.

Shirley, Debra.

Best Friend on Wheels. Illustrated by Judy Stead. Morton Grove, IL: Albert Whitman, 2008. 30pp. ISBN 9780807588680. `Gr. K–3`

Shirley and Sarah, best friends, love reading, playing Frisbee, and eating pizza (as long as there are no peppers). Sarah's in a wheelchair, and when they first met Shirley felt uncomfortable, but they quickly found things in common and have been buddies ever since.

Favorites

A Visitor for Bear by Bonny Becker

A Splendid Friend Indeed by Suzanne Bloom

Fred Stays with Me by Nancy Coffelt

Amazing Grace by Mary Hoffman

Love as Strong as Ginger by Lenore Look

New York's Bravest by Mary Pope Osborne

Thank You, Mr. Falker by Patricia Polacco

Punctuation Takes a Vacation by Robin Pulver

Cat Heaven by Cynthia Rylant

Miss Bindergarten Gets Ready for Kindergarten by Joseph Slate

Chapter 3

Life Around the World: Africa, Asia, Australia, South America, and Europe

Life in countries around the world is represented in picture books, both contemporary and historical, as well as in folk and fairy tales. The majority of these titles are for older children because some understanding of the world is needed. For historical fiction see chapter 13, and for folk and fairy tales see chapter 15. A majority of picture books that take place in English-speaking countries are included in their subject areas.

Africa

Alalou, Elizabeth, and Ali Alalou.

The Butter Man. **Illustrated by Julie Klear Essakalli. Watertown, MA: Charlesbridge, 2008. 31pp. ISBN 9781580891271.** `Gr. K–3`

While a hungry Nora waits for her father to prepare the traditional Saturday afternoon meal of couscous and vegetables, he tells her a story from his childhood in Morocco. In a time of drought, when food was scarce, his mother sent him out to wait for the butter man with his piece of bread. Each day he would eat the bread before the butter man came. After the rains came, his father returned with food, and he no longer had to wait for the butter man.

Barasch, Lynne.

First Come the Zebra. **New York: Lee & Low, 2009. Unpaged. ISBN 978-1600603655.** `Gr. 2 & up`

In Kenya, the Maasai herd cattle and the Kikuyu farm the land. For generations the two groups have been at odds, but when two boys, one from each side, form a friendship, things begin to change.

Bynum, Eboni, and Roland Jackson.

Jamari's Drum. Illustrated by Baba Wagué Diakité. Toronto: Groundwood, 2004. 32pp. ISBN 9780888995315. `Gr. K-3`

As a boy living in an African village at the base of the Chafua mountain, Jamari loved listening to the elder Baba Mdogo play the drums. Baba tells him the drums must be played every day to keep the peace. Later Baba gives Jamari the responsibility of playing the drums, but as Jamari grows up and gets married, the distractions of life take him away from his drumming. When Chafue erupts into a volcano, Jamari remembers he must drum, and miraculously, the lava flows backward. After that Jamari never forgets to drum every day.

Cunnane, Kelly.

For You Are a Kenyan Child. Illustrated by Ana Juan. New York: Atheneum, 2006. 40pp. ISBN 9780689861949. `PreS-3`

In Kenya a boy is supposed to be watching over his grandfather's cows, but along the way he gets distracted, becoming engaged in a variety of activities until the sun begins to set. He runs toward the cows, but his forgiving grandfather is already bringing them in.

Daly, Niki.

Welcome to Zanibar Road. New York: Clarion, 2006. 31pp. ISBN 9780618649266. `PreS-2`

Mama Jumbo the elephant thunders down Zanibar Road in Africa and finds the perfect spot to build her new home. The local animals give her a hand, and she soon settles in. Realizing she is lonely, she adopts Little Chico the chicken, and then throws a birthday party for him, inviting all their neighbors.

Diakité, Penda.

🎵*I Lost My Tooth in Africa.* Illustrated by Baba Wagué Diakité. New York: Scholastic, 2006. 32pp. ISBN 9780439662260. `Gr. K-3`

A little girl goes to visit her father's family in Mali, with a loose tooth. She finds that when a tooth falls out in West Africa, the tooth fairy leaves a hen and a rooster. (ALAN)

Diouf, Sylviane A.

Bintou's Braids. Illustrated by Shane W. Evans. San Francisco: Chronicle, 2001. 40pp. ISBN 9780811846295 (pb). `Gr. K-3`

Bintou longs to have long, luxurious braids like the grown-up women in her West African village, but her grandmother explains that little girls can only have cornrows or tufts. When Bintou helps save her cousins from drowning during a baptism, she asks to have braids for her reward, and her grandmother has to come up with a creative solution.

Ichikawa, Satomi.

My Father's Shop. La Jolla, CA: Kane/Miller, 2006. 32pp. ISBN 978-1929132997. `Gr. K–2`

While his father wants him to learn how to sell carpets, Mustafa sneaks out for a day of fun in the Moroccan marketplace.

Javaherbin, Mina.

Goal! Illustrated by A. G. Ford. Somerville, MA: Candlewick, 2010. 40pp. ISBN 9780763645717. `Gr. 2 & up`

In a small town in South Africa, Ajani and his friends play soccer every day after their homework and chores are done. The area is dangerous, however, and they have to have a plan for keeping their prized federation-sized ball away from the bullies who would steal it.

Joosse, Barbara.

Papa, Do You Love Me? Illustrated by Barbara Lavallee. San Francisco: Chronicle Books, 2005. 32pp. ISBN 9780811842655. `PreS–2`

In a rural Maasai village on the Serengeti Plain, a father assures his son of his unconditional love.

Mollel, Tololwa M.

🌺*My Rows and Piles of Coins.* Illustrated by E. B. Lewis. New York: Clarion, 1999. 32pp. ISBN 9780395751862. `Gr. K–3`

In Tanzania in the 1960s, young Saruni saves money to buy a bike so that he can help his mother on market day. Although he never saves enough to buy one from the bike seller, his father sells him an old bike when he buys a scooter. Now, Saruni is saving for a cart. (ALAN, Coretta Scott King Honor)

Rumford, James.

🌺*Calabash Cat and His Amazing Journey.* Boston: Houghton Mifflin, 2004. Unpaged. ISBN 9780618224234. `PreS–3`

Inspired by an animal carving that the author purchased in Chad, he recounts the journey of the curious Calabash Cat, who wishes to see where the world ends. Each time he thinks he's reached the goal of his journey, he encounters another animal who conducts him through another part of the world, until at last he rides on the back of the eagle and sees a world without end. This story is written in English and Arabic. (Charlotte Zolotow Honor)

Stock, Catherine.

Gugu's House. New York: Clarion, 2001. 31pp. ISBN 9780618003891. `Gr. K–2`

Kukamba, who lives in a city in Zimbabwe, travels to her grandmother's village for a visit and marvels at her grandmother's artwork.

Stuve-Bodeen, Stephanie

Babu's Song. Illustrated by Aaron Boyd. New York: Lee & Low, 2003. Unpaged. ISBN 9781584300588. `Gr. K–2`

In Tanzania, Bernardi lives with his grandfather. Together they eke out a living selling the things his mute grandfather crafts out of scraps, but there is not enough money to pay for school for Bernardi. The boy loves to play soccer, so when a tourist offers a large sum of money for the special music box that his grandfather made just for him, Bernardi cannot resist temptation, for now he can buy the coveted soccer ball. Still, selling the music box fills him with sorrow, and he confesses to his grandfather as he gives him the money. His forgiving grandfather uses the funds to send him to school and makes him a soccer ball.

The Elizabeti Series. Illustrated by Christy Hale. New York: Lee & Low. `Gr. K–3`

Elizabeti lives with her family in Tanzania and must meet a variety of situations with resilience.

🌺*Elizabeti's Doll.* 1998. 32pp. ISBN 9781880000700. (SP)

In Tanzania, Elizabeti wishes to have a doll to care for the way her mother tends to her new baby brother. When she finds a doll-shaped rock, she adopts it, names it Eva, and lavishes it with affection. (ALAN)

Mama Elizabeti. 2000. Unpaged. ISBN 9781584300021.

As mama cares for the new baby, Flora, Elizabeti must take care of her brother Obedi. She is sure that nurturing her rock-doll, Eva, has prepared her, but quickly discovers how different a living child can be.

Elizabeti's School. 2002. 32pp. ISBN 9781584300434.

Dressed in her new school clothes, Elizabeti is initially excited about starting school, but when she sees how busy and crowded it is, she becomes shy and homesick. Returning to her family at the end of the day, she shares with them all the things she's learned and decides school might have its uses after all.

Asia

Baasansuren, Bolormaa.

My Little Round House. Adapted by Helen Mixter. Toronto: Groundwood, 2009. Unpaged. ISBN 9780888999344. `Gr. K–2`

A Mongolian child describes a year in his family's nomadic life, which centers around their special roundhouse. It is a building that can be taken apart and put back together, so that they have a home in each new location.

Bridges, Shirin Yim.

The Umbrella Queen. Illustrated by Taeeun Yoo. New York: Greenwillow, 2008. Unpaged. ISBN 9780060750404. `Gr. K–3`

Noot and her family live in the high hills of Thailand. Everyone in the village paints flowers and butterflies on the umbrellas that they sell, but when Noot starts painting, she chooses to decorate the umbrellas with elephants. The king inspects the artwork and declares her the Umbrella Queen, because she painted from her heart.

Choi, Yangsook.

Peach Heaven. See under "Seasons: Summer" in chapter 9.

Choung, Eun-hee.

Minji's Salon. La Jolla, CA: Kane/Miller, 2008. 28pp. ISBN 9781933605678. **PreS–2**
In Korea, a young girl decides to give her dog a beauty treatment while her mom is at the salon.

Gershator, Phillis.

Sky Sweeper. **Illustrated by Holly Meade. New York: Farrar, Straus & Giroux, 2007. 40pp. ISBN 9780374370077. Gr. 1-3**.
In Japan, young Takeboki takes a job as a Flower Keeper in a Buddhist monastery and discovers that caring for the flowers in the temple's garden is his life's work.

Gower, Catherine.

Long-Long's New Year: A Story about the Chinese Spring Festival. See under "Chinese New Year" in chapter 6.

Jeyaveeran, Ruth.

The Road to Mumbai. **Boston: Houghton Mifflin, 2004. Unpaged. ISBN 9780618434190. PreS–3**
Young Shoba and her stuffed monkey Fuzzy Patel need to attend a monkey wedding, so they fly on Shoba's bed around India until they reach their destination, after adventures with elephants, camels, and a snake charmer.

Krishnaswami, Uma.

Monsoon. See under "Weather" in chapter 9.

Mannis, Celeste Davidson.

One Leaf Rides the Wind: Counting in a Japanese Garden. See under "Counting" in chapter 4.

Rumford, James.

Silent Music: A Story of Baghdad. **New York: Roaring Brook, 2008. 32pp. ISBN 9781596432765. Gr. 2 & up**
Ali is a young boy who lives in contemporary Baghdad. He loves to play soccer and listen to loud music, but most of all he loves practicing the flow-

ing script of Arabic calligraphy, like his hero Yakut, a famous thirteenth-century calligrapher. When violence disrupts his world, he turns to calligraphy to help shut out the war, coping with destruction by creating beauty. (ALAN, Charlotte Zolotow Honor)

Say, Allen.

Erika-San. Boston: Houghton Mifflin, 2009. 30pp. ISBN 9780618889334. **Gr. 3 & up**

Erika grows up loving Japan, so after college, she moves there. Tokyo is too crowded for her. Even a small town is not what she is looking for. Finally, she settles on a mountainous island. This is gracefully illustrated with Say's stunning paintings.

Shea, Pegi Deitz.

Ten Mice for Tet. See under "Counting" in chapter 4.

Yi, Hu Yong.

Good Morning China. New Milford, CT: Roaring Brook, 2007. 32pp. ISBN 978-1596432406. **PreS–1**

A variety of people in China enjoy the early morning in the park.

Australia

Lester, Alison.

Are We There Yet? A Journey Around Australia. La Jolla, CA: Kane/Miller, 2005. 32pp. ISBN 9781929132737. **Gr. K–2**

Eight-year-old Grace and her family take a month's trip and travel around Australia.

Napoli, Donna Jo.

Ready to Dream. See under "Art" in chapter 7.

Ormerod, Jan.

Lizzie Nonsense. **Illustrated by Paul Ormerod. New York: Clarion, 2005. 32pp. ISBN 9780618574933.** **Gr. K–2**

In Australia's pioneer days, Lizzie and her family live in the bush country. When her father is gone for weeks at a time to sell their products in town, Lizzie uses her imagination to pass the time while waiting for him to return.

Mexico, Central and South America

Amado, Elisa.

Tricycle. Illustrated by Alfanso Ruana. Toronto: Groundwood, 2007. 32pp. ISBN 9780888996145. **Gr. 1-3** (SP)

> In an unnamed Latin American country, Margarita, whose family is wealthy, sees a less well-off classmate, Rosario, steal a bicycle. Feeling torn, Margarita must decide what to do.

Bootman, Colin.

Fish for the Grand Lady. New York: Holiday House, 2006. 32pp. ISBN 9780823418985. **Gr. 1–3**

> In Trinidad, two young brothers, set out to catch an abundance of fish so that they can make their grandmother proud, but things don't go quite the way they expected.

Fine, Edith Hope, and Judith Jacobson Josephson.

Armondo and the Blue Tarp School. Illustrated by Hernaìn Sosa. New York: Lee & Low, 2007. 32pp. ISBN 9781584302780. **Gr. 1-3**

> This is a fictionalized account of the work of David Lynch, who went to Mexico in the 1980s and began "open air" teaching. Armondo lives with his family near the Tijuana city dump. They barely manage to survive by combing the dump for items to sell. When Seor David lays out a blue tarp nearby and begins teaching children, Armondo's parents hesitate to send their son, but the relent when they realize that an education can bring him a better life.

Foreman, Michael.

Mia's Story: A Sketchbook of Hopes and Dreams. Cambridge, MA: Candlewick, 2006. 32pp. ISBN 9780763630638. **Gr. 1–3**

> Inspired by a family the author met in Chile, he tells the tale of Mia and her family, who live in poverty in a shanty and dream of being able to have a house of brick. They scavenge items to sell from the junkyard. When their new puppy disappears, Mia searches high into the mountains for it. Enjoying the clear, fresh air, she discovers a gorgeous patch of wildflowers. She transplants some of them, and they grow so well near her home that soon the family has a new business selling flowers and are just a bit closer to their dreams. Illustrated with small pencil drawings and larger watercolor landscapes; Foreman endows his art with both the sense of privation and the feeling of hope.

Geeslin, Campbell.

Elena's Serenade. Illustrated by Ana Juan. New York: Atheneum, 2004. Unpaged. ISBN 9780689849084. **Gr. K–3** (SP)

> In a small village in Mexico, young Elena longs to be a glassblower like her father, but he dismisses her dreams because she is a girl. Disguising herself

as a boy, she journeys to Monterrey to learn her trade. When she has mastered her art, she blows a glass swallow, which carries her home. The illustrations are striking acrylic and crayon done in a folk art style. Spanish words are woven into the text.

Ramirez, Antonio.

The Napi Series. Illustrated by Domi. Toronto: Groundwood. `Gr. K–3`

Napi, a Mazateca girl who lives beside a river in Oaxaca, Mexico, has imaginative, magical, and realistic adventures.

Napi. 2004. 32pp. ISBN 9780888996114. (SP)

> Napi is a Mazateca girl who lives beside a river in Oaxaca, Mexico. She describes life in her village throughout the day and at night dreams a special dream of being a heron flying over her village.

Napi Goes to the Mountain. 2006. 48pp. ISBN 9780888997135. (SP)

> When Napi's father doesn't come home from working in the fields, Napi and her brother Nici go to look for him. Their search up the river and into the jungle transforms into a magical quest, on which the siblings become different animal creatures. Finally the armadillo announces their father's return. They shift back to human form as they make their way back home.

Napí Funda un Pueblo/Napí Makes a Village. 2010. 48pp. ISBN 9780888999658. (Bilingual)

> This bilingual book is based on a true story and describes what happens to Napi's village when the government builds a dam, which forces Napi's entire village to find a new place to settle.

Shahan, Sherry.

Spicy Hot Colors/Colores Picantes. See under "Colors" in chapter 4.

Europe

Banks, Kate.

The Cat Who Walked across France. See in chapter 10.

Bunting, Eve.

Gleam and Glow. Illustrated by Peter Sylvada. San Diego: Harcourt, 2001. Unpaged. ISBN 9780152025960. `Gr. 2 & up`

> This book is inspired by a true story of a family in Bosnia-Herzegovina during the recent civil war. Eight-year-old Viktor lives with his family in a small village. First his father leaves to join the army, then streams of refugees pass through, seeking safety at the border. One man leaves golden fish with Viktor. When Viktor, his mother, and his sister must flee as well, Viktor releases the fish in the family pond. After weeks away, the family and father are reunited. Months pass, and at last

they return home. Much in the village has been destroyed, but to everyone's amazement, the fish, Gleam and Glow, have not only survived, they have produced many offspring. This book is a poignant story of hope in times of war.

Walking to School. **Illustrated by Michael Dooling. New York: Dutton, 2008. 32pp. ISBN 9780618261444.** `Gr. 2 & up`

During the "Troubles" in Northern Ireland, two girls, one Catholic and one Protestant, take the first steps toward friendship.

Fleming, Candace.

Gabriella's Song. **Illustrated by Giselle Potter. New York: Atheneum, 1997. Unpaged. ISBN 9780689841750 (pb).** `Gr. 1-3`

As young Gabriella does her errands in Venice, the various sounds of the city make music for her. She hums the tune and others pick it up, until a composer creates his greatest symphony with it.

Heide, Iris van der.

A Strange Day. **Illustrated by Marijke ten Cate. Honesdale, PA: Lemniscaat, 2007. 32pp. ISBN 9781932425949.** `Gr. K-2`

In this story translated from the Dutch, Jack is hoping to receive a positive letter about the drawing contest that he has entered. Unbeknownst to Jack, who thinks his letter has not arrived, the wind has whisked it away. As the postman tries to catch it, Jack meanders through the village, unaware of the good deeds he performs along the way.

Kimmelman, Leslie.

Everybody Bonjours! **Illustrated by Sarah McMenemy. New York: Knopf, 2008. 32pp. ISBN 9780375844430.** `PreS-3`

Rhyming text relates a family's visit to Paris, where everywhere people greet them with a glad cry of "Bonjour!"

Shulevitz, Uri.

Snow. See under "Weather" in chapter 9.

Spirin, Gennadii.

Martha. **New York: Philomel, 2005. 32pp. ISBN 9780399239809.** `Gr. K-2`

Ilya and his family live in Moscow. When he finds an injured crow, he brings her home and the family nurtures her back to health. Because she will never fly again, she becomes part of the family.

Young, Amy.

Belinda in Paris. See under "Dance" in chapter 7.

Favorites

Gleam and Glow by Eve Bunting

Everybody Bonjours! by Leslie Kimmelman

Silent Music: A Story of Baghdad by James Rumford

Elizabeti's Doll by Stephanie Stuve-Bodeen

Chapter 4

Concepts: Alphabet, Counting, Colors, Shapes, Opposites, and General Concepts

Concept books introduce children to the basics: numbers and counting, sights and sounds, colors, and more. Aiding children with identification and differentiation, these books give visual and verbal explanations for abstract ideas and include opposites, shapes, colors, letters, and numbers.

Alphabet

Ashman, Linda.

M Is for Mischief: An A to Z of Naughty Children. Illustrated by Nancy Carpenter, Nancy. New York: Dutton, 2008. 32pp. ISBN 9780525475644. `Gr. K–3`
From Angry Abby to Zany Zelda, this book lures children to the wild side with twenty-six examples of naughty behavior.

Aylesworth, Jim.

Naughty Little Monkeys. Illustrated by Henry Cole. New York: Dutton, 2003. 40pp. ISBN 9780525469407. `PreS–2`
When their human parents unwisely leave twenty-six little monkeys alone for the evening, chaos ensues, in alphabetical order.

Little Bitty Mousie. Illustrated by Michael Hague. New York: Walker, 2007. 28pp. ISBN 9780802796370. `PreS–1`
A little bitty mousie takes a nocturnal stroll around the house and discovers an alphabetical arrangement of luscious things to eat.

Azarian, Mary.

A Gardener's Alphabet. Boston: Houghton Mifflin, 2000. Unpaged. ISBN 9780618033805. `Gr. K-2`
> Full-page woodcuts with colorful watercolor washes depict an array of garden-related words in alphabetical order.

Bunting, Eve.

Girls A to Z. Illustrated by Suzanne Bloom. Honesdale, PA: Boyds Mills, 2002. Unpaged. ISBN 9781563971471. `PreS-2`
> From Aliki the astronaut to Zoe the zookeeper, Bunting's rhythmic verse provides rhymes for twenty-six young ladies, with occupations that alliteratively accompany their names.

Cronin, Doreen.

Click, Clack, Quackity-Quack: An Alphabetic Adventure. Illustrated by Betsy Lewin. New York: Atheneum, 2005. 24pp. ISBN 9780689877155. `T-K`
> Alphabetical alliteration leads readers through a picnic adventure with the farm animals from *Click, Clack Moo: Cows That Type*.

Demarest, Chris L.

Firefighters A to Z. New York: Margaret K. McElderry Books, 2000. Unpaged. ISBN 9780689837982. `Gr. K-2`
> One rhyming line per page takes readers through a dramatic day for firefighters, conveying lots of information for firefighter fans, as well as reinforcing letter recognition.

Ehlert, Lois.

Eating the Alphabet: Vegetables and Fruit from A to Z. San Diego: Harcourt, 1989. 34pp. ISBN 9780152244354. `PreS-1`
> Vivid watercolor collages depict a delectable assortment of fruits and vegetables.

Elting, Mary, and Michael Folsom.

Q Is for Duck: An Alphabet Guessing Game. Illustrated by Jack Kent. New York: Clarion, 2005. 64pp. ISBN 9780618573899. `T-K`
> This unusual alphabet book matches letters with animals in an unusual way. Q is for duck because ducks quack. Children will enjoy playing the game while they learn their letters.

Ernst, Lisa Campbell.

🐾 *The Turn-Around, Upside-Down Alphabet Book.* New York: Simon & Schuster, 2004. Unpaged. ISBN 9780689856853. `PreS-2`
> The bold graphic design of this book places each letter in a box and frames it with a sentence that asks readers to rotate the book and then observe what the letter becomes. (ALAN)

Fisher, Valorie.

Ellsworth's Extraordinary Electric Ears: And Other Amazing Alphabet Anecdotes. New York: Atheneum, 2003. Unpaged. ISBN 9780689850301. **PreS–3**

> Sharp color photographs filled with a variety of miniature toys, accompanied by an alliterative text, invite readers to search the pictures for items beginning with the letter of the page.

1

Fleming, Denise.

🌸*The Alphabet under Construction.* New York: Holt, 2002. 32pp. ISBN 9780805068481. **PreS–K**

> Using verbs that begin with the appropriate letter, a hard-working mouse constructs an alphabet. The outstanding illustrations were made from colored cotton fiber poured through hand-cut stencils. (ALAN)

2

3

Floca, Brian.

🌸*The Racecar Alphabet.* New York: Atheneum, 2003. Unpaged. ISBN 9780689850912. **PreS–2**

> This cruise through the alphabet begins with an old-fashioned race car and quickly and alliteratively careens to contemporary NASCAR racers. Floca captures the excitement and blur of racing while zooming through successive letters. (ALAN)

4

Haas, Jessie.

Appaloosa Zebra: A Horse Lover's Alphabet. Illustrated by Margot Apple. New York: Greenwill, 2002. Unpaged. ISBN 9780688178802. **Gr. K–3**

> A little girl longs for a horse, but she will have to make do with her figurines for now. She imagines all kinds of horses and how to care for them, beginning with Appaloosa and ending with Zebra. Young horse lovers will enjoy the colored pencil illustrations. Older horse lovers will also value the information.

5

6

Horowitz, Dave.

Twenty-Six Princesses. New York: Putnam, 2008. 32pp. ISBN 978-0399246074. **PreS–2**

> When a frog prince sends out an invitation, twenty-six princesses respond in order. Each princess is accompanied by a rhymed couplet and a cartoon illustration that both depicts the personality of the princess and reveals that everyone else in the castle is a frog of one kind or another.

7

Hudes, Quiara Alegria.

Welcome to My Neighborhood! A Barrio ABC. Illustrated by Shino Arihara. New York: Arthur A. Levine, 2010. 32pp. ISBN 9780545094245. **PreS–1**

> A young city girl takes readers on an alphabetical tour of her neighborhood.

8

Leopold, Nikia Speliakos Clark.

K Is for Kitten. Illustrated by Susan Jeffers. New York: Putnam, 2002. 32pp. ISBN 9780399235634. **T-K**

> Four lines of verse detail the rescue of a kitten by a little girl who finds the stray in the alley and gives her a new home. Successive letters are featured, one in each quatrain. Jeffers's gouache and colored-ink illustrations light up the story with warmth and life.

Leuck, Laura.

Jeepers Creepers: A Monstrous ABC. Illustrated by David Parkins. San Francisco: Chronicle Books, 2003. 32pp. ISBN 9780811835091. **PreS–1**

> Twenty-six odd monsters introduce each letter of the alphabet as they have a playful day at school. Parkins's acrylic-and-alkyd paintings provide a lively accompaniment to the text.

MacDonald, Suse.

🎋*Alphabatics.* New York: Simon & Schuster, 1986. Unpaged. ISBN 978-0027615203. **Gr. K–3**

> Upper- and lowercase letters sit in the upper left of each page, but they don't stay at rest, for MacDonald tumbles them acrobatically into new figures on the facing page. A becomes an ark, N a nest, etc. An innovative concept book that makes learning exhilarating. (Caldecott Honor, Golden Kite Award)

Martin, Bill, and John Archambault.

🎋*Chicka Chicka Boom Boom.* Illustrated by Lois Ehlert. New York: Simon & Schuster, 1989. 36pp. ISBN 9780671679491. **PreS–1**

> All the letters race up a coconut tree, until x, y, and z make the tree top heavy, and they all come tumbling down. Ehlert's bold colors aptly match the brightness of the verse. The companion book is *Chicka, Chicka, 1, 2, 3.* Board book versions have also been released. (ALAN, Boston Globe Honor)

Mayer, Bill.

All Aboard! A Traveling Alphabet. New York: Margaret K. McElderry Books, 2008. 27pp. ISBN 9780689852497. **Gr. K–2**

> The airbrush and digital art hides a capital letter as this book sequentially portrays different kinds of transportation.

McDonnell, Flora.

Flora McDonnell's ABC. Cambridge, MA: Candlewick, 1997. Unpaged. ISBN 9780763601188. **PreS–1**

> This alphabet book not only introduces things that begin with the appropriate letter, but also compares large and small items of the same letter, so that egg and elephant both appear on the E page. Intensely colored illustrations add to the effectiveness of the book.

McLeod, Bob.

Superhero ABC. New York: HarperCollins, 2006. 40pp. ISBN 978-0060745141. **PreS-2**

Twenty-six superheroes with letter-suitable powers appear in this comic-book lovers' dream of an alphabet book.

Mora, Pat.

Marimba: Animales from A to Z. Illustrated by Doug Cushman. New York: Clarion, 2006. 32pp. ISBN 9780618194537. **PreS-1**

As the zookeeper naps, the animals cavort through the alphabet, with their names presented in English and often in Spanish as well.

Most, Bernard.

ABC T-Rex. San Diego: Harcourt, 2000. Unpaged. ISBN 9780152020071. **PreS-3**

Brightly colored cartoon illustrations show a hungry T. rex munching on each letter of the alphabet.

Pearle, Ida.

A Child's Day: An Alphabet of Play. Orlando: Harcourt, 2008. 40pp. ISBN 9780152065522. **T-K**

Cut-paper collages show children at play in this alphabet of action words that ranges from Act to Zoom.

Pearson, Debora.

Alphabeep: A Zipping, Zooming ABC. Illustrated by Edward Miller. New York: Holiday House, 2003. Unpaged. ISBN 9780823417223. **PreS-1**

This jaunty text, which includes onomatopoeic words, regales readers with an alphabet full of vehicles.

Polacco, Patricia.

G Is for Goat. New York: Philomel, 2003. 32pp. ISBN 9780399240188. **T-K**

A young shepherd girl extols all the wonderful things about goats to coincide with the alphabet, accompanied by Polacco's trademark pencil and watercolor art.

Rose, Deborah Lee.

Into the A, B, Sea: An Ocean Alphabet. Illustrated by Steve Jenkins. New York: Scholastic, 2000. Unpaged. ISBN 9780439096966. **PreS-3**

Rhyming couplets invite readers to dive in and explore twenty-six different creatures of the sea. Jenkins's signature textured collages, created from layers of cut-paper, immerse the verse in aquatic beauty.

Schnur, Steven.

The Alphabet Acrostics. Illustrated by Leslie Evans. New York: Clarion. `PreS-3`

These books celebrate the seasons alphabetically with twenty-six acrostic poems that work on many levels. Each poem begins with its sequential letter. Also, the first letter of each line is highlighted so that the letters, read vertically, spell out a word related to the season. The poems are small gems, set in richly colored linoleum block illustrations that together make these books treasures.

Autumn: An Alphabet Acrostic. 1997. Unpaged. ISBN 9780395770436.

Spring: An Alphabet Acrostic. 1999. Unpaged. ISBN 9780395822692.

Summer: An Alphabet Acrostic. 2001. Unpaged. ISBN 9780618023721.

Winter: An Alphabet Acrostic. 2002. Unpaged. ISBN 9780618023745.

Sobel, June.

B Is for Bulldozer: A Construction ABC. **Illustrated by Melissa Iwai. San Diego: Harcourt, 2003. Unpaged. ISBN 9780152022501.** `T-K`

This simple rhyming text draws in lovers of heavy machinery as friends and family observe the construction of an amusement park from Asphalt to Zoom.

Shiver Me Letters: A Pirate Alphabet. **Illustrated by Henry Cole. Orlando: Harcourt, 2006. 32pp. ISBN 9780152167325.** `Gr. K-2`

A crew of animal pirates and their captain set off in search of more letters than just R in the hopes of pressing them into service aboard ship. The featured letters are highlighted in red within the text.

Spirin, Gennadii.

A: Apple Pie. **New York: Philomel, 2005. 32pp. ISBN 9780399239816.** `T-K`

Spirin has created whimsical watercolors filled with Victorian details to illustrate this seventeenth-century English alphabet rhyme.

Weill, Cynthia, and K. B. Basseches.

Abecedarios/Alphabets: Mexican Folk Art, ABCs in Spanish and English. **Illustrated by Moisés and Armando Jiménez. El Paso, TX: Cinco Puntos Press, 2007. 32pp. ISBN 9781933693132.** `Gr. 1-3`. **(Bilingual)**

Folk art sculpted by a family of artists in Oaxaca, Mexico, adorns each page of this alphabet book, showing an animal for every letter, with a text that names the animal in English and Spanish.

Wells, Rosemary.

Max's ABCs. **New York: Viking, 2006. 32pp. ISBN 9780670060740.** `T-K`

Rabbit siblings Max and Ruby, of picture book, board book, and TV fame, enter the alphabet book realm with a clever story about "Ants" escaping Max's ant farm searching for birthday cake. As Max and Ruby try to recapture the fleeing "Ants," the story wends through the alphabet while the illustrations highlight each letter in sequence.

Counting

Andreasen, Dan.

The Baker's Dozen. New York: Holt, 2007. 32pp. ISBN 9780805078091. **PreS–1**

The rhyming couplets tell of an early-rising baker who whips up a selection of tasty treats for numbers one to thirteen.

Baker, Keith.

Potato Joe. Orlando: Harcourt, 2008. 40pp. ISBN 9780152062309. **PreS–1**

Using the well-known "one potato, two," rhyme as a springboard, here ten potatoes pop out of the ground, bursting to life with new rhymes of their own.

Bang, Molly.

Ten, Nine, Eight. New York: Greenwillow, 1989. 24pp. ISBN 978-0688009069. **T–K**

This is the twentieth-anniversary edition of the classic tale of a father and daughter ,counting down from 10 to 1 as the little girl gets ready for bed. (ALAN, Caldecott Honor)

Bauer, Marion Dane.

One Brown Bunny. Illustrated by Ivan Bates. New York: Orchard, 2008. Unpaged. ISBN 9780439680103. **T–K**

On a beautiful sunny day in the forest, Bunny bounces out to find a playmate. He finds increasingly larger groups of animals, but none are interested in playing until the surprise ending.

Beaumont, Karen.

Doggone Dogs! Illustrated by David Catrow. New York: Dial, 2008. 40pp. ISBN 9780803731578. **T–K**

Ten rambunctious dogs romp through the park, leaving havoc in their wake, as their harried owner, wearing nothing but his pajamas, chases after them, leashes in hand. The countdown begins when they at last return home.

Blackstone, Stella.

My Granny Went to Market: A Round-the-World Counting Rhyme. **Illustrated by Christopher Corr. Cambridge, MA: Barefoot Books, 2005. 24pp. ISBN 9781841487922.** `Gr. K-3` **(SP)**

> Zooming from country to country on a magic carpet, Granny accumulates the items she needs.

Butler, John.

*Ten in the Den. **Atlanta, GA: Peachtree, 2005. 32pp. ISBN 9781561453443.** `T-K`

> In this fresh take on a traditional counting rhyme, Butler sets ten cuddly forest creatures in a cozy den. One by one they roll down a hill as the mouse calls, "Roll over, roll over." Perfect for a participatory read-aloud.

Ten in the Meadow. **Atlanta, GA: Peachtree, 2006. 32pp. ISBN 9781561453726.** `T-K`

> The ten adorable animal friends who all rolled over are back, and this time they are playing a game of hide-and-seek in a vibrant meadow.

Cabrera, Jane.

Ten in the Bed. **New York: Holiday House, 2006. 32pp. ISBN 9780823420278.** `PreS-1`

> Ten stuffed animals, wearing the costumes of various professions, such as ballerina and doctor, each fall out of bed in this rollover count down.

Carle, Eric.

Ten Little Rubber Ducks. **New York: HarperCollins, 2005. 28pp. ISBN 978-0060740757.** `PreS-1` **(SP)**

> Inspired by the true story of bathtub toys that fell off a container ship, Carle crafts a tale of ten rubber ducks that end up in the ocean. One by one they float away from each other, ending up with various animals, until the last one joins a family of ducks. Illustrated in Carle's signature style.

Cronin, Doreen.

Click, Clack, Splish, Splash: A Counting Adventure. **Illustrated by Betsy Lewin. New York: Atheneum, 2006. Unpaged. ISBN 9780689877162.** `T-K`

> The farm animals that starred in *Click, Clack Moo* go on an un-fishing trip as they take a numerical journey that leads to them releasing ten of Farmer Brown's goldfish into the pond.

Donaldson, Julia.

One Ted Falls out of Bed. **Illustrated by Anna Currey. New York: Holt, 2006. 32pp. ISBN 9780805077872.** `T-K`

> In soothingly rhythmic rhyme, Donaldson relates the numeric tale of one Teddy Bear who falls out of bed. He can't climb back in and is invited to play by increasing numbers of various toys.

Durango, Julia.

Cha-Cha Chimps. Illustrated by Eleanor Taylor. New York: Simon & Schuster, 2006. 32pp. ISBN 9780689864568. `PreS-2`

> In this upbeat countdown book, ten chimps sneak out to go dancing, and as they learn new dances, one by one their numbers diminish, until only one remains.

Edwards, Pamela Duncan.

Roar! A Noisy Counting Book. Illustrated by Henry Cole. New York: HarperCollins, 2000. Unpaged. ISBN 9780060283841. `PreS-1`

> A lion cub searches for playmates on the African savanna and encounters increasing numbers of animals, until she finds nine lions that ROAR!

Falwell, Cathryn.

🏵*Turtle Splash: Countdown at the Pond*. New York: Greenwillow, 2001. Unpaged. ISBN 9780060294625. `PreS-2`

> In this reverse counting book, various forest animals surprise ten Eastern painted turtles, who one by one splash back into the water. (ALAN)

Gayzagian, Doris A.

One White Wishing Stone: A Beach Day Counting Book. Illustrated by Kristina Swarner. Washington, DC: National Geographic, 2006. 32pp. ISBN 9780792255734. `T-K`

> Mother and daughter spend a delightful day at the beach. The little girl counts out her treasures as she adds them to her sandcastle.

Hoban, Tana.

Let's Count. New York: Greenwillow, 1999. Unpaged. ISBN 978-0688160081. `PreS-2`

> Crisp color photographs with the appropriate number of items face pages with the matching numeral, the word spelled out, and the exact number of dots in this counting book, which illustrates numbers 1 through 15, 20, 30, 40, 50, and 100.

Hutchins, Pat.

Ten Red Apples. New York: Greenwillow, 2000. Unpaged. ISBN 978-0688167974. `PreS-1`

> Ten ripe red apples dangle on the branches of a tree and are eaten one by one by nine farm animals and the farmer.

Jay, Alison.

1-2-3: A Child's First Counting Book. New York: Dutton, 2007. 30pp. ISBN 9780525478362. **PreS–2**

One little girl dreams that she is riding a golden goose and visiting increasing numbers of nursery rhyme and fairy tale characters. Beautifully illustrated in Jay's crackle-glaze style.

Katz, Karen.

Counting Christmas. New York: Margaret K. McElderry Books, 2003. Unpaged. ISBN 9780689849251. **T–K**

A family of five counts down from Christmas Eve to Christmas, going from ten to one.

Daddy Hugs 1 2 3. New York: Margaret K. McElderry Books, 2005. 32pp. ISBN 9780689877711. **T–K**

From morning to bedtime, a father counts off from one to ten the ways to hug his baby.

Ten Tiny Tickles. New York: Margaret K. McElderry Books, 2005. 24pp. ISBN 9780689859762. **T–K**

Family members tickle a baby awake and get the child ready for the day as each finds a different place to tickle.

Mommy Hugs. New York: Margaret K. McElderry Books, 2006. 32pp. ISBN 978-0689877728. Sequel. **T–K**

Mommy gets equal time in this follow-up counting book of hugs.

Ten Tiny Babies. York: Margaret K. McElderry Books, 2008. 32pp. ISBN 978-1416935469. **T–K**

One by one, tiny tots get new companions to play with, until they reach the number ten.

Kimmelman, Leslie.

How Do I Love You? Illustrated by Lisa McCue. New York: HarperCollins, 2005. Unpaged. ISBN 9780060012007. **PreS–1**

Counting from one to twenty, a crocodile parent lists the ways the child croc is loved.

Lessac, Frane.

Island Counting 1 2 3. Cambridge, MA: Candlewick, 2005. Unpaged. ISBN 9780763619602. **T–K**

A Caribbean island provides the counting items for this list of people, animals, and objects.

Long, Ethan.

One Drowsy Dragon. New York: Orchard, 2010. 32pp. ISBN 9780545165570. `PreS-1`

One tired dragon is trying to slip into sleep, but increasing numbers of fellow dragons are so noisy, his can't take his much-needed nap.

Lottridge, Celia Barker.

One Watermelon Seed. Illustrated by Karen Patkau. Markham, ON: Fitzhenry & Whiteside, 2008. 32pp. ISBN 9781554550340. `PreS-2`

Max and Josephine plant seeds for a variety of fruits and vegetables, and although they plant the seeds from one to ten, the produce grows to such abundance that the counting jumps to proceeding by tens.

MacDonald, Suse.

Fish, Swish! Splash, Dash! Counting Round and Round. New York: Little Simon, 2007. 30pp. ISBN 9781416936053. `PreS-1`

A beautifully designed book invites readers below the sea to count the die-cut fish. Readers proceed from one to ten and then follow the fish in reverse and find completely different species.

Mannis, Celeste Davidson.

One Leaf Rides the Wind: Counting in a Japanese Garden. Illustrated by Susan Kathleen Hartung. New York: Viking, 2002. 40pp. ISBN 9780142401958 (pb). `PreS-1`

This counting book accompanies a Japanese girl as she meanders through a traditional garden.

Martin, Bill, and Michael R. Sampson.

Chicka, Chicka 1, 2, 3. Illustrated by Lois Ehlert. New York: Simon & Schuster, 2004. Unpaged. ISBN 9780689858819. `PreS-2`

In this companion to *Chicka, Chicka, Boom, Boom*, numbers climb an apple tree. As numerals 1–20, followed by tens to 90, embark on their journey upward, lonely 0 waits at the bottom wondering, "Chicka chicka 1, 2, 3 . . . will there be a place for me?" When bees chase the numbers out of their tree, they all descend except for 10. Zero ascends and finds the perfect spot, making the number 100.

McFarland, Lyn Rossiter.

Mouse Went out to Get a Snack. Illustrated by Jim McFarland. New York: Farrar, Straus & Giroux. Unpaged. ISBN 9780374376727. `PreS-1`

This clever tale weaves counting into the story of a mouse who sneaks out for a snack and gets distracted by a feast.

Milich, Zoran.

City 123. Toronto: Kids Can Press, 2005. 32pp. ISBN 9781553375401. **T-K**
  Sharp color photographs of city scenes invite readers to count.

Mitton, Tony.

Spooky Hour. Illustrated by Guy Parker-Rees. New York: Orchard, 2004. 32pp.
ISBN 9780439603737. **PreS-2**
  As the clock strikes midnight, a cat and dog witness a parade of spine-tingling
  creatures go by, including eleven witches, ten ghosts, and on down to one gigantic
  pumpkin pie to feed everyone gathered for the Halloween party.

Olson, K. C.

Construction Countdown. Illustrated by David Gordon. New York: Holt, 2004.
21pp. ISBN 9780805069204. **T-K**
  Rhymed couplets count down from ten to one a variety of construction vehicles
  that turn out to be children's toys in a sandbox.

Parenteau, Shirley.

One Frog Sang. Illustrated by Cynthia Jabar. Cambridge, MA: Candlewick, 2007.
24pp. ISBN 9780763623944. **Gr. K–2**
  Gatherings of frogs from one to ten emit every sound a frog can, from ribbits to
  peeps to woomps. When a car whizzes by, the count goes back down as the frogs
  find places to hide.

Parker, Kim.

Counting in the Garden. New York: Orchard, 2005. 32pp. ISBN 9780439694520. **T-K**
  The pages of this book are bursting with beautiful blossoms while the counting focuses on finding the creatures lurking in the luscious garden.

Paul, Ann Whitford.

Count on Culebra: Go from 1 to 10 in Spanish. Illustrated by Ethan Long. New
York: Holiday House, 2008. 32pp. ISBN 9780823421244. **PreS-3**
  The friends from *Maana, Iguana* and *Fiesta Fiasco* distract Iguana from the pain of
  her stubbed toe by attaching kitchen utensils to her tail, all the while counting in
  Spanish.

Provost, Elizabeth.

Ten Little Sleepyheads. See under "Fanciful Bedtime Stories" in chapter 15.

Reiser, Lynn.

Hardworking Puppies. Orlando: Harcourt, 2006. 40pp. ISBN 9780152054045. **PreS-2**
  Ten puppies count down by finding jobs with humans.

Root, Phyllis.

*One Duck Stuck. Illustrated by Jane Chapman. Cambridge, MA: Candlewick, 1998. 40pp. ISBN 9780763603342. **PreS-1**

> A duck gets stuck in a swamp and calls for help. Increasing numbers of animals and insects come to assist, but they cannot budge the duck until they all work together. A great participatory read-aloud.

Rose, Deborah Lee.

One Nighttime Sea: An Ocean Counting Rhyme. Illustrated by Steve Jenkins. New York: Scholastic, 2003. Unpaged. ISBN 9780439339063. **PreS-2**

> This poetic and rhythmic text invites readers for a nighttime visit under the sea to count sea creatures busy with their nocturnal activities. Illustrated with vibrant cut-paper collages.

The Twelve Days of Kindergarten: A Counting Book. Illustrated by Carey Armstrong-Ellis. New York: Abrams, 2003. 32pp. ISBN 9780810945128. **PreS-1**

> Following the pattern of "The Twelve Days of Christmas," this book lists the fabulous things a teacher gives her new students. The text is deliberately straightforward, and the illustrations provide a humorous counterpoint.

The Twelve Days of Winter. Illustrated by Carey Armstrong-Ellis. New York: Abrams, 2006. 32pp. ISBN 9780810954724. **PreS-1**

> Those kindergarteners are back, and this time are engaged in a series of wintry activities to commemorate the beginning of the season. Again the amusing illustrations make this title stand out.

The Twelve Days of Springtime: A School Counting Book. Illustrated by Carey Armstrong-Ellis. New York: Abrams, 2009. 32pp. ISBN 978-0810983304. **PreS-1**

> More seasonal activities for those fun-loving kindergarteners and their increasingly worn-out teacher.

Schertle, Alice.

1, 2, I Love You. Illustrated by Emily Arnold McCully. San Francisco: Chronicle, 2004. 32pp. ISBN 9780811835183. **T-K**

> In rhyming verse, a mother elephant counts up to ten and then back down, enumerating all the things she and her child do together.

Schulman, Janet.

10 Trick-or-Treaters. See under "Halloween" in chapter 6.

Seeger, Laura Vaccaro.

One Boy. New York: Roaring Brook, 2008. 42pp. ISBN 9781596432741. **PreS-2**

> Seeger has created an intriguing concept book that works both as a counting book and a hidden word book. The die-cut pages first provide a window

that reveals the subject of the description, showing a numbered item, but with the page turn the reader sees three letters from the previous page becoming part of the next sentence. Intricate and satisfying on multiple levels.

Shea, Pegi Deitz, and Cynthia Weill.

Ten Mice for Tet. **Illustrated by Tô Ngoc Trang and PhạmViêt Đinh. San Francisco: Chronicle, 2003. 36pp. ISBN 9780811834964.** `Gr. K–2`

A series of mice from one to ten prepare for the Vietnamese New Year. Vibrant embroidered artwork complements the text.

Singer, Marilyn.

Quiet Night. **Illustrated by John Manders. New York: Clarion, 2002. 25pp. ISBN 9780618120444.** `PreS–1`

This cumulative counting book features a series of woodland creatures creating a cacophony.

City Lullaby. **Illustrated by Carll Cneut. New York: Clarion, 2007. 27pp. ISBN 9780618607037.** `PreS–2`

Starting with a traffic jam and ten car horns that are beeping, Singer counts down a variety of city sounds while a baby sleeps peacefully in a stroller.

Siy, Alexandra.

One Tractor: A Counting Book. **Illustrated by Jacqueline Rogers. New York: Holiday House, 2008. 32pp. ISBN 9780823419234.** `Gr. K–2`

A young boy sits in the grass and plays with his toy tractor, then imagines flying in a plane while a mouse flies another, making two. They are joined by three ships of pirates, who cavort among increasing numbers of toy vehicles as the boy falls asleep.

Slaughter, Tom.

1 2 3. **Tornoto: Tundra, 2003. 24pp. ISBN 9780887766640.** `T–K`

Cut-paper images of everyday objects provide counting practice in this book created by an artist whose prints have been displayed in the Museum of Modern Art.

Stevens, April.

Waking up Wendell. **Illustrated by Tad Hills. New York: Schwartz & Wade, 2007. 40pp. ISBN 9780375836213.** `PreS–2`

The pigs that live at successively numbered houses wake up one morning to an assortment of birdsongs.

Stiegemeyer, Julie.

Gobble Gobble Crash! A Barnyard Counting Bash: A Barnyard Counting Bash. **Illustrated by Valeri Gorbachev. New York: Dutton, 2008. Unpaged. ISBN 9780525479598.** `PreS-1`
> Rhyming couplets count from one to ten and back again as the barnyard animals settle in for the night and are disrupted by four wild turkeys.

Tafuri, Nancy.

The Big Storm: A Very Soggy Counting Book. **New York: Simon & Schuster, 2009. 29pp. ISBN 9781416967958.** `T-K`
> As a storm gathers, ten small forest animals scamper to a cave for shelter, in a story that includes both counting up to ten and back down again.

Thong, Roseanne.

One Is a Drummer: A Book of Numbers. **Illustrated by Grace Lin. San Francisco: Chronicle, 2004. 36pp. ISBN 9780811864824 (pb).** `PreS-1`
> Using upbeat verse, the Chinese-American girl from *Round Is a Mooncake* counts her favorite things.

Wadsworth, Olive.

Over in the Meadow. **Illustrated by Anna Vojtech. New York: North-South, 2002. Unpaged. ISBN 9780735815964.** `PreS-2` **(SP)**
> This nineteenth-century counting rhyme is given a fresh set of illustrations depicting a variety of meadow creatures.

Walsh, Ellen Stoll.

🐭*Mouse Count.* **San Diego: Harcourt, 1991. Unpaged. ISBN 978-0152560232.** `PreS-1`
> A sneaky snake thinks he's found his dinner when he comes across ten sleeping mice (from *Mouse Paint*) and slips them one by one into a jar, but the mice outwit him and the count goes back down as they each escape. (ALAN)

Wells, Rosemary.

Max Counts His Chickens. **New York: Viking, 2007. 22pp. ISBN 978-0670062225.** `T-K`
> Max and Ruby enter the concept book realm with this story of the sibling bunnies searching for the ten marshmallow chicks hidden for them by the Easter Bunny.

Williams, Suzanne.

Ten Naughty Little Monkeys. **Illustrated by Suzanne Watts. New York: HarperCollins, 2007. 32pp. ISBN 9780060599041.** `T-K`

> This variation on the familiar story of ten little monkeys jumping on the bed relates the escapades of ten active monkeys whose adventures lead to injuries and doctor's visits.

Wilson, Karma.

A Frog in the Bog. **Illustrated by Joan Rankin. New York: Margaret K. McElderry Books, 2003. Unpaged. ISBN 9780689840814.** `T-K`

> In amusing rhyme, this verse details the numbers of insects swallowed by a frog, whose mouth opens wide in a scream when he realizes he's perched on an alligator.

Wojtowycz, David.

Animal Antics from 1 to 10. **New York: Holiday House, 2000. Unpaged. ISBN 9780823415526.** `T-K`

> The guests in Hotel 1 2 3 are numerically aligned, flamboyantly costumed animals in rooms one through ten.

Colors

Crews, Donald.

🎋*Freight Train.* **New York: William Morrow, 1978. 22pp. ISBN 9780688801656.** `PreS-2` **(SP)**

> A train with cars painted each color of the rainbow zooms through the countryside, through tunnels, past cities, and over trestles. (ALAN, Caldecott Honor)

Ehlert, Lois.

🎋*Color Zoo.* **New York: HarperCollins, 1989. 32pp. ISBN 9780397322596.** `Gr. K-2`

> Layered die-cut pages in brilliant colors reveal a variety of zoo animals with each turn of the page. (ALAN, Caldecott Honor)

Color Farm. **New York: Lippincott, 1990. 34pp. ISBN 9780397324408.** `Gr. K-2`

> Using the same technique as *Color Zoo,* Ehlert uses her die-cut designs to create an assortment of farm animals.

Gonzalez, Maya Christina.

🎋*My Colors, My World/Mis Colores, Mi Mundo.* **San Francisco: Children's Book Press, 2007. 23pp. ISBN 9780892392216.** `PreS-2` **(Bilingual)**

> Young Maya lives in California's Mojave Desert and ventures out in search of the colors in her everyday and natural worlds. (Caldecott Honor, Pura Belpre Honor)

Hoban, Tana.

🖋️*Of Colors and Things.* New York: Greenwillow, 1989. 21pp. ISBN 9780688045852 (pb). `PreS–1`

Hoban's glorious color-saturated photos are grouped by colors to lead page turners through a multihued world. (ALAN)

Colors Everywhere. New York: Greenwillow, 1995. Unpaged. ISBN 9780688127626. `PreS–1`

In this wordless book, Hoban's brilliant photographs present vivid scenes from the natural worlds, such as a peacock feather set against an array of daffodils. On the facing page, rectangles of colors display the various hues in the photograph.

Hubbard, Patricia.

My Crayons Talk. Illustrated by G. Brian Karas. New York: Holt, 1996. Unpaged. ISBN 9780805035292. `PreS–1`

A rambunctious bunch of crayons shout, sing, and roar in rhyme about their activities.

Jay, Alison.

Red, Green, Blue: A First Book of Colors. New York: Dutton, 2010. 40pp. ISBN 9780525423034. `PreS–1`

Nursery rhyme characters focus on the colors that their traditional verses emphasize.

Jonas, Ann.

Color Dance. New York: Greenwillow, 1989. 32pp. ISBN 9780688059903. `PreS–2`

Young dancers swirling scarves of primary colors whirl them in various combinations to demonstrate how colors blend together to create different colors.

Lionni, Leo.

Little Blue and Little Yellow: A Story for Pippo and Ann and Other Children. New York: Knopf, 2009. Unpaged. ISBN 9780375860133. `PreS–1`

This is the fiftieth-anniversary edition of the classic tale of two circular splashes of color, blue and yellow, who are friends. When their colors meld together, and they turn green, the friends have to devise a method for returning to their original hues.

Martin, Bill.

*Brown Bear, Brown Bear, What Do You See? Illustrated by Eric Carle. New York: Holt, 1983. 27pp. ISBN 9780805002010. `PreS-2`

> One vividly colored animal after another spies the next animal. Some of the colors are realistic, some are fanciful, in this tale that makes a fun participatory read-aloud. Illustrated in Carle's signature style.

Milich, Zoran.

City Colors. Tonawanda, NY: Kids Can Press, 2004. 34pp. ISBN 9781553375425. `T-K`

> Focusing on colors in the city, this book presents a close-up of the item depicting the specified color, and the page turn reveals the object in its city scene.

Park, Linda Sue.

What Does Bunny See? A Book of Colors and Flowers. Illustrated by Maggie Smith. New York: Clarion, 2005. 32pp. ISBN 9780618234851. `T-K`

> As a bunny hops about a cottage garden, rhymes give readers clues to the upcoming colors.

Seeger, Laura Vaccaro.

🐟*Lemons Are Not Red.* Brookfield, CT: Roaring Brook, 2004. 32pp. ISBN 9781596430082. `PreS-2`

> In this brilliantly designed concept book, the text proclaims what color the item is not, while the die-cut pages show the same item in the wrong color. A page turn states and shows what is really that color while also showing the original item in its true color. Thus, the sequence that begins, "Lemons are NOT red," while showing a red lemon, with a page turn reveals the yellow lemon and the red apple, stating, "Apples are red." A delight! (ALAN)

Shahan, Sherry.

Spicy Hot Colors/Colores Picantes. Illustrated by Paula Barragan. Little Rock, AR: August House, 2004. 28pp. ISBN 9780874837414. `PreS-1`

> This book takes readers on a color-filled tour of Latin America while it also introduces the Spanish words for the colors.

Shannon, George.

🐟*White Is for Blueberry.* Illustrated by Laura Dronzek. New York: Greenwillow, 2005. 40pp. ISBN 9780060292751. `PreS-1`

> Both text and pictures turn the traditional color book on its ear. The opening sequence of each ten scenarios states that the item stands for a color other than the obvious one, and then the page turn reveals how that can be true. Thus pink is for crow (pictured as black), when the crow is first hatched (pictured pink). Ingenious. (ALAN)

Tafuri, Nancy.

Blue Goose. New York: Simon & Schuster, 2008. 32pp. ISBN 978-1416928348. **PreS–1**
> Blue Goose, Red Hen, Yellow Chick, and White Duck decide to make use of the time while Farmer Gray is away and paint their drab barnyard. They paint several things using the colors they are named for and then they pair up to create other colors.

Thong, Roseanne.

Red Is a Dragon: A Book of Colors. Illustrated by Grace Lin. San Francisco: Chronicle Books, 2001. 30pp. ISBN 9780811831772. **PreS–1**
> With a lyrical rhyming text, a Chinese American girl provides a list of items of each color. Accompanied by lush gouache paintings that make use of Chinese-style patterning.

Walsh, Ellen Stoll.

🏵*Mouse Paint.* San Diego: Harcourt, 1989. 32pp. ISBN 9780152560256. **PreS–1**
> Three white mice spy red, yellow, and blue paint and go for a dip. They play together and create a wide array of colors and hues. (ALAN)

Wood, Audrey.

The Deep Blue Sea: A Book of Colors. Illustrated by Robert Bruce Wood. New York: Blue Sky Press, 2005. 40pp. ISBN 9780439753821. **PreS–1**
> Digital, eye-popping art steers children through a sea journey full of colors.

Shapes

Hoban, Tana.

Shapes, Shapes, Shapes. New York: William Morrow, 1986. 32pp. ISBN 9780688058326. **PreS–2**
> In a wordless book filled with sharp color photographs, Hoban introduces various shapes, such as circles, hexagons, parallelograms, and stars, and challenges children to find the shapes in the cityscapes.

So Many Circles, So Many Squares. New York: Greenwillow, 1998. Unpaged. ISBN 9780688151652. **PreS–2**
> Twenty-nine intriguing photographs beg the audience to see circles and squares in the ordinary and the extraordinary.

MacDonald, Suse.

Shape by Shape. New York: Little Simon, 2009. Unpaged. ISBN 9781416971474. `PreS–1`

> Using die-cut shapes and bold colors, MacDonald makes readers aware of how different shapes can combine to become something surprising.

Thong, Roseanne.

Round Is a Mooncake: A Book of Shapes. Illustrated by Grace Lin. San Francisco: Chronicle, 2000. Unpaged. ISBN 9780811826761. `PreS–1`

> A Chinese American girl uses rhyming text to describe different shapes such as circles, squares, and rectangles in terms of the things that are familiar in her world. So, round is a mooncake and a rice bowl, giving readers a glimpse of Chinese culture.

Walsh, Ellen Stoll.

Mouse Shapes. Orlando: Harcourt, 2007. 40pp. ISBN 9780152060916. `PreS–1`

> Cut-paper collage mice have to hide from the cat, so they take cover in a pile of shapes. They make pictures with the shapes, and as they do they come up with a way to outwit the cat.

Opposites

Davis, Nancy.

A Garden of Opposites. New York: Schwartz & Wade Books, 2009. Unpaged. ISBN 9780375856662. `T–K`

> A redheaded girl in pigtails escorts readers through her garden, while clean graphic images present the pairs of opposites.

Guy, Ginger Foglesong.

Perros! Perros!/Dogs! Dogs! A Story in English and Spanish. Illustrated by Sharon Glick. New York: Greenwillow, 2006. 32pp. ISBN 9780060835743. `T–K` (Bilingual)

> In a text in both English and Spanish, a young girl dreams of dogs and when she wakes, she sees a variety of dogs that are opposites, including black and white, fast and slow, and wide and narrow.

Harper, Charise Mericle.

The Little Book of Not So. Boston: Houghton Mifflin, 2005. 32pp. ISBN 9780618473199. `T–K`

> This small book presents pairs of opposites through negation by showing things in relation to other things. So, an illustration of an ice cream cone is big when compared to a mouse, but not so big when compared to an elephant.

Hoban, Tana.

Exactly the Opposite. New York: Greenwillow, 1990. 32pp. ISBN 978-0688088613. **PreS–1**

Using sharp, color photographs featuring a variety of people, animals, and objects from the city and the country, Hoban wordlessly demonstrates concepts such as push/pull, left/right, etc.

Jocelyn, Marthe.

Over Under. Illustrated by Tom Slaughter. Tornoto: Tundra, 2005. 24pp. ISBN 9780887767081. **T–K**

Vibrant cut-paper animals and a spare text present opposites such as over/under, big/small, up/down, and so on.

Lewis, J. Patrick.

Big Is Big (and little, little): A Book of Contrasts. Illustrated by Bob Barner. New York: Holiday House, 2007. 32pp. ISBN 9780823419098. **PreS–1**

Lewis, a noted poet, turns his attention to versifying about contrasts, creating rhymes that reiterate the difference between things like day and night, old and young, and big and little. The bright collages of torn paper, pastels, and tempera help make the concepts clear.

Miller, Margaret.

Big and Little. New York: Greenwillow, 1998. Unpaged. ISBN 978-0688147488. **PreS–1**

Using a minimal text and clean color photographs of children and adults of various ages, Miller clearly shows scenes depicting big and little.

Pittau, Francisco.

Elephant Elephant: A Book of Opposites. Illustrated by Bernadette Gervais. New York: Abrams, 2001. Unpaged. ISBN 9780810936997. **PreS–2**

Elephants drawn with marker depict thirty-five pairs of words, ranging from the traditional, big/small, to the more unusual, plains/mountains.

Seeger, Laura Vaccaro.

❀*Black? White! Day? Night! A Book of Opposites.* New Milford, CT: Roaring Brook, 2006. 24pp. ISBN 9781596431850. **PreS–2**

Following a lift-the-flap format, Seeger cleverly introduces the pairs of opposites by presenting the first image on the outside flap and then artistically transforming it to its opposite in the picture underneath. Brilliant! (ALAN)

Weill, Cynthia.

Opuestos:—Mexican Folk Art Opposites in English and Spanish. **Illustrated by Quirino Santiago and Martin Santiago. El Paso, TX: Cinco Puntos Press, 2009. 32pp. ISBN 9781933693569.** `Gr. K–3` **(Bilingual)**
> Various pairs of opposites, such as high and low and outside and inside, are illustrated with Oaxacan folk art statues.

General Concepts

Some concepts books don't fit neatly into the previous categories, either because they include several concepts or because they cover different concepts.

Coffelt, Nancy.

Big, Bigger, Biggest! **New York: Holt, 2009. Unpaged. ISBN 9780805080896.** `T–K`
> Coffelt employs a variety of creatures to demonstrate superlative adjectives in this book that not only demonstrates comparisons but also increases vocabulary, providing both synonyms and antonyms.

Carle, Eric.

The Very Hungry Caterpillar. See under "Insects and Arachnids" in chapter 10.

Fleming, Denise.

The Everything Book. **New York: Holt, 2000. 64pp. ISBN 9780805062922.** `T–K`
> Beautiful and bright hand-cut stencils illustrate a plethora of concepts, including the alphabet, counting, shapes, seasons, traffic lights, trains, and more.

Gravett, Emily.

🐾*Orange Pear Apple Bear.* **New York: Simon & Schuster, 2007. Unpaged. ISBN 9781416939993.** `PreS–1`
> Using only five words, four of which appear in the title, Gravett cleverly whisks readers into a playful experience of shapes, colors, and sequence, as her cuddly bear interacts with the designated fresh produce. (ALAN)

Hoban, Tana.

26 Letters and 99 Cents. **New York: Greenwillow, 1987. 32pp. ISBN 978-0688063610.** `PreS–2`
> Hoban's signature clear, bright photographs highlight objects that represent each letter of the alphabet and numbers, presented singly through 30, by fives through 50, and by tens to 90, using money as the means to show counting.

More, Fewer, Less. New York: Greenwillow, 1998. 32pp. ISBN 978-0688156930. `PreS-2`

Hoban arranges her photographs of ordinary objects and familiar animals to illustrate the comparative concept of the title.

Jocelyn, Marthe.

Same Same. Illustrated by Tom Slaughter. Toronto: Tundra, 2009. 22pp. ISBN 9780887768859. `T-K`

Beautiful yet simple painted paper cut-outs cluster in groups of three on each page. The text states the one thing they have in common. One item also appears on the next page with two new entities as the text states the commonality of these three things. Everything a concept book should be.

Kuskin, Karla.

Green as a Bean. Illustrated by Melissa Iwai. New York: Laura Geringer Books, 2007. 32pp. ISBN 9780060753320. `PreS-2`

Kuskin's poetic text asks readers a series of whimsical questions that emphasize various concepts (colors, shapes, etc.) and inspire imaginative answers.

Milich, Zoran.

City Signs. Toronto: Kids Can Press, 2002. Unpaged. ISBN 9781553370031. `T-K`

Milich presents thirty artfully composed photographs that show various signs in the city scene context.

Miller, Margaret.

My Five Senses. New York: Simon & Schuster, 1994. Unpaged. ISBN 9780689820090 (pb). `T-K`

Five children of various ethnicities introduce sharp, color photographs that demonstrate the use of each one of the senses.

Pinto, Sara.

Apples & Oranges: Going Bananas with Pairs. New York: Bloomsbury, 2007. 32pp. ISBN 9781599901039. `Gr. K-3`

Pinto pairs two items that have obvious things in common and asks the reader to figure out how they are alike, but the page turn reveals the silly reasons that they are similar. So an apple and orange are alike because they don't wear glasses, and so on.

Seeger, Laura Vaccaro.

First the Egg. New Milford, CT: Roaring Brook, 2007. Unpaged. ISBN 9781596432727. `PreS-1`

Seeger pairs deceptively simple and yet playful sequencing tandems with luscious artwork to lead children through before and after scenarios like first the egg, then the chicken. (ALAN, Caldecott Honor, Geisel Honor, New York Times Best Illustrated)

Thornhill, Jan.

The Wildlife ABC & 123: A Nature Alphabet & Counting Book. **Toronto: Maple Tree Press, 2004. Unpaged. ISBN 9781897066096.** `PreS-2`
> Originally published as two separate volumes, here they are united into one book in which rhyming couplets celebrate nature.

Weeks, Sarah.

Counting Ovejas. **Illustrated by David Diaz. New York: Atheneum, 2006. 32pp. ISBN 9780689867507.** `PreS-1` **(Bilingual)**
> When a boy has trouble sleeping, he tries counting sheep, which appear in increasing numbers and different colors. The text works well in English and in Spanish and is beautifully enhanced by Diaz's acrylic-and-pencil illustrations.

Wells, Rosemary.

My Kindergarten. See under "School: School in General" in chapter 2.

Favorites

Freight Train by Donald Crews

Eating the Alphabet: Vegetables and Fruit A to Z by Lois Ehlert

The Turn-Around, Upside-down Alphabet Book by Lisa Campbell Ernst

Green as a Bean by Karla Kuskin

Little Blue and Little Yellow: A Story for Pippo and Ann and Other Children by Leo Lionni

Brown Bear, Brown Bear, What Do You See? by Bill Martin

Chicka Chicka Boom Boom by Bill Martin and John Archambault

One Duck Stuck by Phyllis Root

Lemons Are Not Red by Laura Vaccaro Seeger

White Is for Blueberries by George Shannon

Chapter 5

Mother Goose and Other Nursery Rhymes

Mother Goose rhymes have been part of English and American literature for children for nearly 300 years. The rhythm, rhyme, and play with language inherent in the rhymes lend themselves to developing emergent literacy. The sound and feel of the words is enough to bring delight to the youngest children, even before they can understand the meaning. Many of today's finest illustrators have selected rhymes from the traditional canon and imbued them with their own artistic vision.

Mother Goose

Crews, Nina.

The Neighborhood Mother Goose. New York: Greenwillow, 2003. 63pp. ISBN 9780060515737. PreS–3

Crews places the traditional rhymes in an urban setting. Using digital collage, she features a multiethnic group of children participating in the play of the language. (ALAN)

dePaola, Tomie.

Tomie dePaola's Mother Goose. New York: Putnam, 1985. 127pp. ISBN 9780399212581. PreS–2

DePaola employs his signature style to illustrate more than 200 classic rhymes with a cheerful, multiethnic cast of children. (ALAN)

Dillon, Leo, and Diane Dillon.

Mother Goose Numbers on the Loose. Orlando, FL: Harcourt, 2007. 47pp. ISBN 9780152056766. PreS–1

The Dillons have culled twenty-four traditional counting rhymes and illustrated them with vibrant pictures that are both detailed and whimsical. (ALAN)

Hines, Anna Grossnickle.

1, 2, Buckle My Shoe. Orlando, FL: Harcourt, 2008. 32pp. ISBN 9780152063054. **PreS–1**

This traditional counting rhyme is completely illustrated with decorated quilt patches. Included in the decorations are the number of buttons that the numeral of the verse indicates.

Long, Sylvia.

Sylvia Long's Mother Goose. San Francisco: Chronicle Books, 1999. 109pp. ISBN 9780811820882. **PreS–1**

Elegantly attired animals, reptiles, and insects illustrate eighty-two nursery rhymes, both well known and unfamiliar.

Moses, Will.

Mother Goose. New York: Philomel, 2003. 61pp. ISBN 9780399237447. **PreS–1**

Folk artist Will Moses has created a spectacular series of oil paintings for the double-page spreads, as well as spot art, to illustrate this collection of more than sixty rhymes.

Opie, Iona Archibald, ed.

🖋*My Very First Mother Goose.* Illustrated by Rosemary Wells. Cambridge, MA: Candlewick, 1996. 107pp. ISBN 9781564026200. **T–K**

Wells has illustrated more than sixty rhymes with a boldly colored assortment of animals, nicely placed on the pages with large text and plenty of white space that make this collection perfect for sharing with the youngest listeners. (ALAN)

Here Comes Mother Goose. Illustrated by Rosemary Wells. Cambridge, MA: Candlewick, 1999. Unpaged. ISBN 9780763606831. **T–K**

This companion volume continues with the format begun in *Here Comes Mother Goose*, with whimsical illustrations accompanying fifty more rhymes.

Mother Goose's Little Treasures. Illustrated by Rosemary Wells. Cambridge, MA: Candlewick, 2007. 52pp. ISBN 9780763636555. Sequel. **PreS–2**

For this collection, Opie and Wells have selected twenty-two lesser-known nursery rhymes and placed them in a smaller volume. Wells has illustrated these with pastel-colored depictions of her signature creatures.

Sanderson, Ruth.

Mother Goose and Friends. Boston: Little, Brown, 2008. 64pp. ISBN 978-0316777186. **Gr. K–3**

Sanderson has selected sixty-seven rhymes, most well-known traditional rhymes and some from the early twentieth century, and illustrated them with lush oil paintings filled with Victorian elves, fairies, and flowers.

Schefler, Axel.

Mother Goose's Storytime Nursery Rhymes. New York: Arthur A. Levine, 2007. 128pp. ISBN 9780439903066. `PreS–1`

A mother goose shares little rhymes with her three goslings throughout the day. Soon other geese are doing this as well. One of them writes them down, and Mother Goose's nursery rhymes are created. The activities of the geese are interspersed among the well-known rhymes. Illustrated with cartoon-style pictures.

Scieszka, Jon.

Truckery Rhymes. See under "Trucks" in chapter 8.

Sierra, Judy.

Monster Goose. Illustrated by Jack E. Davis. San Diego: Harcourt, 2001. Unpaged. ISBN 9780152020347. `Gr. 3 & up`

These rhymes follow the format of Mother Goose, but substitute trolls, mummies, ghouls, and other creatures to give readers the shivers. The acrylic and colored-pencil illustrations add to the humor and the gross-out factor.

Wright, Blanche Fisher.

The Real Mother Goose. New York: Scholastic, 2006. 143pp. ISBN 978-0439858755. `PreS–1`

This is an anniversary edition, illustrated with old-fashioned illustrations.

Other Nursery Rhymes

Nursery rhymes extend beyond Mother Goose to those traditional rhymes from other countries and English rhymes not part of the Mother Goose canon.

Ada, Alma Flor, and F. Isabel Campoy.

Pio Peep! Traditional Spanish Nursery Rhymes. Illustrated by Vivi Escriva. New York: HarperCollins, 2003. 64pp. ISBN 9780688160197. `PreS–1` (Bilingual)

Ada and Campoy present twenty-nine rhymes from Latin American and the American Southwestern tradition in the original Spanish and in English. The rhymes cover a variety of everyday activities and are accompanied by lively watercolor illustrations.

Muu, Moo! Rimas De Animales/Animal Nursery Rhymes. Illustrated by Vivi Escriva. New York: Rayo, 2010. 48pp. ISBN 9780061346132. `PreS–1` (Bilingual)

This creative team presents rhymes featuring animals from the Spanish tradition, as well as verses written by the compilers. The English translations emphasize language rhythm and flow rather than exact translations.

Chorao, Kay.

Rhymes Round the World. New York: Dutton, 2009. 40p. ISBN 9780525478751. **PreS-1**

Poems and rhymes from traditions in many countries are accompanied by Charo's signature vivid paintings.

Collins, Heather.

Out Came the Sun: A Day in Nursery Rhymes. Tonawanda, NY: Kids Can Press, 2007. 91pp. ISBN 9781553378815. **PreS-1**

Collins arranges traditional rhymes in a loose narrative format so that they follow the course of a day from sunup to bedtime. Watercolor illustrations bring brightness to the volume.

Siomades, Lorianne.

*The Three Little Kittens. Honesdale, PA: Boyds Mills, 2000. Unpaged. ISBN 9781563978456. **T-K**

This version sports brightly colored illustrations that make this a lovely edition for storytimes.

Taback, Simms.

This Is the House That Jack Built. New York: Putnam, 2002. Unpaged. ISBN 9780399234880. **PreS-2**

Taback has created a plethora of zany illustrations to give new life to an old rhyme.

Favorites

Mother Goose Numbers on the Loose by Leo Dillon and Diane Dillon

My Very First Mother Goose edited by Iona Archibald Opie and illustrated by Rosemary Wells

My Very First Mother Goose by Ruth Sanderson

Chapter 6

Holidays

Holidays of all sorts, religious and secular, are a significant part of children's lives. There are many picture books, fanciful and straightforward, related to all of the major holidays. Listed here are the stories (and some poems) that focus on the holidays, which are arranged in chronological order through the year.

New Year's Day

Piernas-Davenport, Gail.

Shanté Keys and the New Year's Peas. **Illustrated by Marion Eldridge. Morton Grove, IL: Albert Whitman, 2007. 27pp. ISBN 9780807573303.** `Gr. K-2`

Shante, an African American girl, lives in a family with a New Year tradition of gathering for a feast featuring black-eyed peas for luck. Her grandma is a cooking up a storm when she realizes she has forgotten an essential ingredient. She sends Shante to the neighbors to see if she can find some. As she visits she learns about traditions from China, Scotland, Mexico, and India, and she invites her neighbors home to sample her family's traditional foods.

Rylant, Cynthia.

The Stars Will Still Shine. **Illustrated by Tiphanie Beeke. New York: HarperCollins, 2005. 40pp. ISBN 9780060546397.** `T-K`

In this lyrical poem, Rylant welcomes the new year and celebrates all the good things to come.

Chinese New Year

Chen, Yong.

A Gift. **Honesdale, PA: Boyds Mills Press, 2009. Unpaged. ISBN 9781590786109.** `Gr. K-2`

Amy, a Chinese American girl, receives a precious gift from her aunt in China, as she and her family are in the midst of preparing to celebrate the Chinese New Year.

Gower, Catherine.

Long-Long's New Year: A Story about the Chinese Spring Festival. **Illustrated by He Zhihong. Boston: Tuttle, 2005. 32pp. ISBN 9780804836661.** `Gr. K-2`

> Long-Long and his grandfather, who live in rural China, journey to market to sell cabbages and raise money to purchase what they need to celebrate the New Year.

Katz, Karen.

My First Chinese New Year. **New York: Holt, 2005. 32pp. ISBN 9780805070767.** `T-K`

> A Chinese American girl and her family celebrate the New Year, from sweeping away the bad luck of the previous year to decorating the home, enjoying a special dinner, and watching the parade in Chinatown.

Lin, Grace.

Bringing in the New Year. **New York: Knopf, 2008. 32pp. ISBN 9780375837456.** `PreS-2`

> Three Chinese American sisters and their parents prepare for the Lunar New Year festivities by sweeping out the old year, hanging happiness poems, and making get-rich dumplings. All the activities culminate in fireworks and the lucky dragon parade.

Groundhog Day

Cox, Judy.

Go to Sleep, Groundhog! **Illustrated by Paul Meisel. New York: Holiday House, 2003. Unpaged. ISBN 9780823416455.** `PreS-2`

> On Columbus Day, Groundhog sets his alarm clock for February 2 and settles in for his winter nap, but he has trouble sleeping. Each time he wakes up early a different holiday character tucks him back into bed. By February he's sleeping soundly, but wakes up long enough to look for his shadow.

Cuyler, Margery.

Groundhog Stays up Late. **Illustrated by Jean Cassels. New York: Walker, 2005. 32pp. ISBN 9780802789396.** `Gr. K-3`

> Even though winter has arrived, Groundhog would rather play than sleep. His plan backfires when he runs out of food, and he declares spring has come early so his friends will wake up and share their stores. When they realize the trick he's played on them, his friends play a trick of their own.

Freeman, Don.

Gregory's Shadow. **New York: Viking, 2000. Unpaged. ISBN 9780670893287.** `PreS-2`

> Gregory the groundhog and his shadow help each other feel brave. When he loses his shadow shortly before the big day, Gregory searches frantically. The two are

reunited at last and now must devise a way to stay together without alarming the farmers about the length of time it will take spring to arrive.

Hill, Susanna Leonard.

Punxsutawney Phyllis. Illustrated by Jeffrey Ebbeler. New York: Holiday House, 2005. 32pp. ISBN 9780823418725. **Gr. K-3**

> Phyllis the groundhog is an expert in recognizing coming weather changes and longs to take over Uncle Punxsutawney Phil's spring predicting duties when he retires. Everyone says that she can't because she's a girl; she proves them wrong by doing a better job than her uncle.

Holub, Joan.

Groundhog Weather School. Illustrated by Kristin Sorra. New York: Putnam, 2009. Unpaged. ISBN 9780399246593. **Gr. K-3**

> A group of groundhogs gather to garner some tips for their big day as they study weather, dig burrows, and make shadows in Professor Groundhog's class.

Miller, Pat.

Substitute Groundhog. Illustrated by Kathi Ember. Morton Grove, IL: Albert Whitman, 2006. 30pp. ISBN 9780807576434. **Gr. K-3**

> When Groundhog comes down with the flu just before his big day, he has to hold auditions for his replacement.

Valentine's Day

Brown, Marc.

Arthur's Valentine. See under "Everyday Life in General" in chapter 1.

Carlson, Nancy.

Henry and the Valentine Surprise. See under "Everyday Life in General" in chapter 1.

Carr, Jan.

Sweet Hearts. Illustrated by Dorothy Donohue. New York: Holiday House, 2002. 32pp. ISBN 9780823417322. **PreS-1**

> A peppy panda makes Valentines for his parents and hides them all over the house.

1

2

3

4

5

6

7

8

Demas, Corinne.

Valentine Surprise. **Illustrated by R. W. Alley. New York: Walker, 2007. 42pp. ISBN 9780802796646.** `PreS–1`

For the entire week before Valentine's Day, Lily tries to make the perfect heart for her mother, but each day something is wrong with her creations. Her mother assures her that it doesn't matter if they are imperfect because the heart inside Lily is just right.

Friedman, Laurie.

Love, Ruby Valentine. **Illustrated by Lynne Avril Cravath. Minneapolis: Carolrhoda, 2006. 32pp. ISBN 9781575058993.** `Gr. K–3`

Ruby Valentine works for days making valentines for everyone in town, but she is so exhausted that she sleeps through the big day and distributes her creations the following day.

Jackson, Alison.

The Ballad of Valentine. **Illustrated by Tricia Tusa. New York: Dutton, 2002. 32pp. ISBN 9780525467205.** `Gr. K–3`

In a story that follows the pattern of the song, "My Darling, Clementine," a gentleman tries every means at his disposal to send his neighbor a valentine declaring his love.

Novak, Matt.

My Froggy Valentine. **New Milford, CT: Roaring Brook, 2008. 32pp. ISBN 9781596432048.** `Gr. 1–3`

In this twist on the *Frog Prince* tale, four frogs wait their turn to be kissed by the princess, but the transformations are not what any of them expect.

Poydar, Nancy.

Rhyme Time Valentine. **New York: Holiday House, 2002. 32pp. ISBN 978-0823416844.** `Gr. K–3`

Valentine's Day is Ruby's favorite holiday, and red is the best color in the world to her. On the way to school on February 14, a gust of wind whips her homemade valentines out of her hands. The day is saved when she remembers the box of chocolates from her parents and gives them out to her friends.

Rylant, Cynthia.

If You'll Be My Valentine. **Illustrated by Fumi Kosaka. New York: HarperCollins, 2004. 32pp. ISBN 9780060092702.** `PreS–2`

A little boy creates valentines for his friends, family, and pets. Each handmade card includes a personal, rhyming message.

Scotton, Rob.

Love Splat. See under "School: School in General" in chapter 2.

St. Patrick's Day

Bunting, Eve.

That's What Leprechauns Do. See under "Fantasy and Magic" in chapter 15.

Callahan, Sean.

Shannon and the World's Tallest Leprechaun. **Illustrated by Kathleen Kemly. Morton Grove, IL: Albert Whitman, 2008. 30pp. ISBN 9780807573266.** `Gr. 1–3`

> Shannon is practicing her step dancing for St. Patrick's Day when the heel breaks on her shoe. Knowing her parents can't afford to buy her new shoes, she recalls a family tradition and counts backward in Gaelic. A six-foot-tall leprechaun appears. He grants her three wishes in a most unusual way.

Edwards, Pamela Duncan.

The Leprechaun's Gold. See under "Folk and Fairy Tales" in chapter 15.

Krensky, Stephen.

Too Many Leprechauns: Or How That Pot O' Gold Got to the End of the Rainbow. **Illustrated by Dan Andreasen. New York: Simon & Schuster, 2007. 32pp. ISBN 9780689851124.** `Gr. K–3`

> Finn O'Finnegan returns home from Dublin to find his village in an uproar. They are all sleep deprived because of the noise of all the leprechauns making shoes. It's up to Finn to come up with a way to set things to rights.

Wojciechowski, Susan.

A Fine St. Patrick's Day. **Illustrated by Tom Curry. New York: Random House, 2004. 40pp. ISBN 9780385736404 (pb).** `Gr. K–3`

> The people of two rival towns in Ireland, Tralee and Tralah, have a decorating competition every year for St. Patrick's Day. Every year Tralah wins, until the people of Tralee help a leprechaun, even though it means they can't finish their preparations. In the night the leprechaun finishes their work. They win for the first time and then decide that there are things more important than competition.

Easter

Brett, Jan.

The Easter Egg. **New York: Putnam, 2010. Unpaged. ISBN 9780399252389.** `PreS–2`
> Hoppi the bunny longs to give out the decorated eggs with the Easter Bunny, so he plans to win the egg-decorating contest. When he finds a robin's egg that has fallen from its nest, however, he gives up his hopes and spends his time guarding the egg instead.

Burg, Sarah Emanuelle.

One More Egg. **New York: North South, 2006. 32pp. ISBN 9780735820012.** `PreS–1`
> The Easter Bunny needs just one more egg and asks a young chick for help.

Friedrich, Priscilla, and Otto Friedrich.

The Easter Bunny That Overslept. **Illustrated by Donald Saaf. New York: HarperCollins, 2002. Unpaged. ISBN 9780060296452.** `PreS–3`
> In this revised and newly illustrated edition of a book first released in 1957, the Easter Bunny sleeps through a rainy Easter day and tries to deliver his eggs on other holidays.

Grambling, Lois G.

Here Comes T. Rex Cottontail. **Illustrated by Jack E. Davis. New York: Katherine Tegen Books, 2007. 32pp. ISBN 9780060531294.** `PreS–2`
> When Peter Cottontail gets sick, T. Rex volunteers to take his place. His plans go awry when he accidentally smashes all the eggs, and he needs his friends to help him fix the mess he's made.

Hulme, Joy N.

Easter Babies: A Springtime Counting Book. **Illustrated by Dan Andreasen. New York: Sterling, 2010. 24pp. ISBN 9781402763526.** `T–K`
> As animals welcome spring with their new young ones, eleven children have fun in the park looking for Easter eggs.

Mortimer, Anne.

Bunny's Easter Egg. **New York: Katherine Tegen Books, 2010. 32pp. ISBN 9780061366642.** `PreS–2`
> When Bunny grows too tired to deliver her last Easter egg, she decides to settle down for a nap. Just as she is drifting off, the egg starts to crack. Bunny searches everywhere for a quiet place to sleep, but ends up back at her basket, where she befriends the newly hatched duckling.

Stoeke, Janet.

Minerva Louise and the Colored Eggs. See in chapter 14.

Wells, Rosemary.

Max Counts His Chickens. See under "Counting" in chapter 4.

Max's Chocolate Chicken. See under "Families: Siblings" in chapter 2.

Passover

Howland, Naomi.

The Matzah Man: A Passover Story. **New York: Clarion, 2002. 32pp. ISBN 9780618117505.** PreS-2

In this version of "The Gingerbread Man," a baker shapes the last bit of matzah into a man, who runs away as soon as he pops out of the oven. He outruns everyone until he meets Mendel Fox, who hides him under a matzah cover, where he meets his end as part of the Seder service.

Portnoy, Mindy Avra.

A Tale of Two Seders. **Illustrated by Valeria Cis. Minneapolis: Kar-Ben 2010. 32pp. ISBN 9780822599074.** PreS-2

A young girl now has two Passover seders to celebrate, because her parents have gotten divorced.

Shulman, Lisa.

The Matzo Ball Boy. **Illustrated by Rosanne Litzinger. New York: Dutton, 2005. Unpaged. ISBN 9780525471691.** Gr. K-3

This Passover version of "The Gingerbread Man" features a savory story spiced with Yiddish words and phrases. Bubbe is a lonely old woman with no one to celebrate Passover with. So she makes a matzo ball boy to keep her company, but as soon as she removes the lid from the pot, he jumps out, and the traditional chase ensues.

Mother's Day

Ashman, Linda.

Mama's Day. **Illustrated by Jan Ormerod. New York: Simon & Schuster, 2006. Unpaged. ISBN 9780689834752.** PreS-2

Rhyming text and soft illustrations celebrate the special bond between mother and child.

Grambling, Lois G.

T. Rex and the Mother's Day Hug. **Illustrated by Jack E. Davis. New York: Katherine Tegen Books, 2008. 32pp. ISBN 9780060531263.** `Gr. K-2`

> Instead of giving his mother a present on Mother's Day, T. Rex likes to do something special for her. Mama says that all she wants is a great big hug, but when T. Rex glimpses her car, he decides to fix it up for her. Mama receives her hug and is grateful that Mother's Day comes only once a year.

Krensky, Stephen.

Mother's Day Surprise. **Illustrated by Kathi Ember. New York: Marshall Cavendish, 2010. 32pp. ISBN 9780761456339.** `PreS-2`

> Violet the snake sees all the other animals making Mother's Day presents. She would like to make a present too, but has trouble coming up with something she can make since she has no arms, legs, or teeth.

Father's Day

Callahan, Sean.

A Wild Father's Day. **Illustrated by Daniel Howarth. Morton Grove, IL: Albert Whitman, 2009. 32pp. ISBN 9780807522936.** `PreS-K`

> When his children wish him a wild Father's Day, he proposes they spend the day acting like animals. They pretend they are kangaroos, cats, cheetahs, and so on.

Nolan, Janet.

A Father's Day Thank You. **Illustrated by Kathi Ember. Morton Grove, IL: Albert Whitman, 2007. 32pp. ISBN 9780807522912.** `PreS-2`

> Harvey the bear is trying to come up with the perfect Father's Day present. His siblings give the same things every year, and Harvey wants his gift to be different. At last he alights on the idea that the best gift is spending the day together.

Independence Day

Ketteman, Helen.

The Great Cake Bake. **Illustrated by Matt Collins. New York: Walker, 2005. 32pp. ISBN 9780802789501.** `Gr. 1-3`

> Donna Rae, who is extremely competitive, is determined to win the Fourth of July cake-baking contest and tries out more and more outrageous kinds of cake creations.

Priceman, Marjorie.

How to Make a Cherry Pie and See the U.S.A. New York: Knopf, 2008. 40pp. ISBN 9780375812552. `Gr. 1-3`

An intrepid baker travels the United States gathering the ingredients she needs to make a cherry pie for the Fourth of July.

Wong, Janet S.

Apple Pie Fourth of July. Illustrated by Margaret Chodos-Irvine. San Diego: Harcourt, 2002. Unpaged. ISBN 9780152025434. `Gr. K-2`

A Chinese American girl who helps her parents in their market, which is open every day, even on the Fourth of July, tries to explain that no one will want Chinese food on this most American holiday. A rush of customers between the end of the parade and the beginning of the fireworks proves her wrong.

Rosh Hashanah and Yom Kippur

Cohen, Deborah Bodin.

Engineer Ari and the Rosh Hashanah Ride. Illustrated by Sharar Cober. Minneapolis, MN: Kar-Ben, 2008. 32pp. ISBN 9780822586487. `PreS-2`

In 1892, Ari is excited about being the first engineer on the train running between Jaffa and Jerusalem. He boasts about his selection to his friends, but he forgets to say good-bye to them. When he makes a stop, he gathers what he needs to celebrate the Jewish New Year. In considering the meaning of the holiday, he realizes that he has neglected his friends and promises to do better.

Kimmelman, Leslie.

Sound the Shofar: A Story for Rosh Hashanah and Yom Kippur. Illustrated by John Himmelman. New York: HarperCollins, 1998. 32pp. ISBN 9780060275013. `PreS-1`

An extended family gathers to celebrate the Jewish High Holy days, the New Year and the Day of Atonement. It is a time of good food, family fun, and heartfelt prayer.

Wayland, April Halprin.

New Year at the Pier: A Rosh Hashanah Story. Illustrated by Stephane Jorisch. New York: Dial, 2009. 32pp. ISBN 9780803732797. `Gr. K-3`

Izzy, his sister Miriam, and their mother, along with those in their community, are participating in the New Year ceremony of Tashlich. They consider their misdeeds of the past year, apologize to those they have wronged, and give forgiveness to those who ask it of them. Then they toss bread crumbs into the water to symbolize casting off their sins.

Ramadan and Eid

Addasi, Maha.

The White Nights of Ramadan. **Illustrated by Ned Gannon. Honesdale, PA: Boyds Mills, 2008. 32pp. ISBN 9781590785232.** `Gr. 1–3`

In Kuwait, Noor and her family celebrate Girgian, a Muslim tradition observed in the middle of Ramadan. The family make candy, prays, and after sunset, walk under the full moon to share the treats they have made. Noor and her grandfather also deliver a basket of food to those in need.

Mobin-Uddin, Asma.

The Best Eid Holiday Ever. **Illustrated by Laura Jacobsen. Honesdale, PA: Boyds Mills, 2007. 32pp. ISBN 9781590784310.** `Gr. 1–3`

Aneesa is staying with her grandmother for the Muslim holiday of Eid al-Adha because her parents have traveled from their home in America to Saudia Arabia to perform the Hajj pilgrimage. Aneesa misses them, so her grandmother involves her in cooking and a visit to the mosque. When Aneesa sees some refugee children, she forms a plan to make their holiday special as well.

A Party in Ramadon. **Illustrated by Laura Jacobsen. Honesdale, PA: Boyds Mills, 2009. 32pp. ISBN 9781590786048.** `Gr. 2 & up`

Leena Ahmad is fasting for Ramadan, so when she receives an invitation to a pony party, she feels torn. She decides to attend the party but not eat anything. It proves to be harder than she thinks, but she is able to hold fast to her decision.

Halloween

Auch, Mary Jane.

Poultrygeist. **Illustrated by Herm Auch. New York: Holiday House, 2003. Unpaged. ISBN 9780823417568.** `Gr. 1–3`

Roosters Rudy and Ralph relish creating a cacophony to the dismay of some of their fellow barnyard inhabitants. As the animals prepare their costumes for the Halloween parade, the roosts are haunted by a "poultrygeist," awakened by their racket.

Brenner, Tom.

And Then Comes Halloween. **Illustrated by Holly Meade. Somerville, MA: Candlewick, 2009. 30pp. ISBN 9780763636593.** `Gr. K–2`

A group of neighborhood families experience the activities of fall, including raking leaves, carving pumpkins, and going trick-or-treating.

Brown, Marc.

Arthur's Halloween. See under "Everyday Life in General" in chapter 1.

Brown, Margaret Wise.

The Fierce Yellow Pumpkin. **Illustrated by Richard Egielski. New York: HarperCollins, 2003. 32pp. ISBN 9780060244798.** `PreS-3`

> A fat, round pumpkin who longs to be as frightening as a scarecrow and hot as the sun, has his wish come true as a group of children first select him and then transform him into a jack-o-lantern.

Cazet, Denys.

The Perfect Pumpkin Pie. **New York: Atheneum, 2005. Unpaged. ISBN 9780689864674.** `Gr. K–3`

> When Jack's grandmother makes a delicious pumpkin pie for Halloween, a cranky ghost haunts the pair searching for the perfect pumpkin pie.

Choi, Yangsook.

Behind the Mask. **New York: Farrar, Straus & Giroux, 2006. 40pp. ISBN 9780374305222.** `Gr. K–2`

> Korean American Kimin, who was once afraid of his grandfather's traditional Korean dancing masks, now wears one proudly for Halloween.

Cuyler, Margery.

The Bumpy Little Pumpkin. **Illustrated by Will Hillenbrand. New York: Scholastic, 2005. 32pp. ISBN 9780439528351.** `PreS-2`

> Little Nell, Big Mama, Big Sarah, and Big Lizzie all live in a house in the country and help each other tend their pumpkin patch all summer. Nell's big sisters have no trouble selecting big, smooth, round pumpkins for their jack-o'-lanterns, but Nell takes her time and picks a small pumpkin. Even though it's a little bit bumpy, the animals of the forest help her carve a jack-o'-lantern that's just right.

De Groat, Diane.

Trick or Treat, Smell My Feet. See under "Everyday Life in General" in chapter 1.

Duval, Kathy

The Three Bears' Halloween. **Illustrated by Paul Meisel. New York: Holiday House, 2007. 32pp. ISBN 9780823420322.** `PreS-1`

> The three bears don their Halloween costumes and go trick-or-treating in the forest. When they come upon a haunted house, they enter and sample the treats, unaware that Goldilocks is supplying them.

Ehlert, Lois.

Boo to You. New York: Beach Lane Books, 2009. 42pp. ISBN 9781416986256. `PreS–2`

A pair of mice and their friends are putting together an autumn feast, and at the same time do their best to avoid the black cat who might like to make them into a feast. Illustrated with complex collages utilizing autumn items.

Evans, Cambria.

Bone Soup. Boston: Houghton Mifflin, 2008. 32pp. ISBN 9780618809080. `Gr. K–3`

Finnigin the skeleton has a reputation for being ravenous. When he enters a town populated with witches, mummies, and zombies on Halloween night, they all hide their tasty stewed eyeballs and batwings. Finnigin doesn't give up easily, so he begins to brew soup with his magic bone and gradually convinces everyone to contribute.

Fleming, Denise.

*Pumpkin Eye. New York: Holt, 2001. Unpaged. ISBN 9780805066814. `T–K`

This rhyming ode to Halloween celebrates the scary fun of trick-or-treating. The simple text is accompanied by Fleming's stunning, signature illustrations.

Galbraith, Kathryn Osebold.

Boo, Bunny! Illustrated by Jeff Mack. Orlando: Harcourt, 2008. 40pp. ISBN 9780152162467. `T–K`

Two bunnies, who are both a little leery about trick-or-treating, bump into each other. They continue on together, each bolstering the other's courage.

Goodhart, Pippa.

Three Little Ghosties. Illustrated by Annalaura Cantone. New York: Bloomsbury, 2007. 32pp. ISBN 9781582347110. `PreS–2`

Amusing verse tells of three ghost friends who have fun boasting to each other. They run into more trouble than they bargain for, however, when they try to scare a little boy.

Holabird, Katharine.

Angelina's Halloween. See under "Dance" in chapter 7.

Kohara, Kazuno.

🏮*Ghosts in the House!* New York: Roaring Brook, 2008. 32pp. ISBN 978-1596434271. `PreS–1`

A young witch moves into a house that turns out to be haunted. Luckily, she knows just the course of action to take. She rounds them all up, puts them through the laundry, and transforms them into useful household items. Dynamically illustrated with block prints in black and orange. (New York Times Best Illustrated)

Krosoczka, Jarrett.

Annie Was Warned. New York: Knopf, 2003. 24pp. ISBN 9780375815676. `PreS-3`

Annie's birthday is on Halloween, and when a friend dares her to visit a haunted mansion, she takes up the challenge even though her parents and other friends warn her not to go. Flashlight in hand, she braves the spooky approach to the house and enters, discovering a surprise birthday party.

Lewis, Kevin.

The Runaway Pumpkin. Illustrated by S. D. Schindler. New York: Orchard, 2003. 32pp. ISBN 9780439439749. `PreS-2`

On Halloween night, the two Baxter brothers and their little sister Lil come upon a humongous pumpkin. They snip it free from the vine and it careens away from them. It tumbles past various family members, who imagine the delicious things Granny could make from the pumpkin. Finally Poppa is able to stop the pumpkin, and Granny prepares a feast.

London, Jonathan.

Froggy's Halloween. See under "Everyday Life in General" in chapter 1.

MacDonald, Maryann.

The Costume Copycat. Illustrated by Anne Wilsdorf. New York: Dial, 2006. 32pp. ISBN 9780803729292. `PreS-2`

Youngest sister, Angela, is tired of wearing hand-me-down costumes for Halloween, so she creates an outstandingly original costume of her very own.

Martin, Bill.

A Beasty Story. Illustrated by Steven Kellogg. San Diego: Harcourt, 1999. Unpaged. ISBN 9780152016838. `PreS-1`

Four mice venture into a dark, dark wood and find a dark, dark house. Undeterred, they keep exploring and end up discovering a surprise.

McCourt, Lisa.

Happy Halloween, Stinky Face. See under "Families" in chapter 2.

McGhee, Alison.

A Very Brave Witch. Illustrated by Harry Bliss. New York: Simon & Schuster, 2006. 32pp. ISBN 9780689867309. `Gr. K-2`

A young witch lives in a haunted house, as do most witches. Most witches are also afraid of humans, but this brave witch decides to investigate what humans are really like for herself on Halloween night.

Only a Witch Can Fly. **Illustrated by Taeeun Yoo. New York: Feiwel & Friends, 2009. 32pp. ISBN 9780312375034.** `Gr. K–2`

This lyrical tale, which takes the form of a sestina, relates the longing of a young trick-or-treater to fly. She mounts the broom, but takes a tumble in the pumpkin patch. Persistent, she at last soars toward the moon, her black cat perched behind her.

Michelson, Richard.

Oh No, Not Ghosts! **Illustrated by Adam McCauley. Orlando, FL: Harcourt, 2006. 44pp. ISBN 9780152051860.** `Gr. 1–3`

A big brother tries to quell his younger sister's nighttime fears, but each thing he says escalates her anxiety.

Montes, Marisa.

Los Gatos Black on Halloween. **Illustrated by Yuyi Morales. New York: Holt, 2006. 32pp. ISBN 9780805074291.** `Gr. 1–3`

This poem whirls readers into a spooky Halloween ball where the dancers are skeletons, ghosts, ghouls, and zombies. Spanish words are defined by their context and in a glossary. (ALAN, Pura Belpre Honor)

Murray, Marjorie Dennis.

Halloween Night. **Illustrated by Brandon Dorman. New York: Greenwillow, 2008. 32pp. ISBN 9780061351860.** `Gr. K–3`

This Halloween poem follows the form of *The Night Before Christmas* and describes the activities of bats, spiders, witches, ogres, ghosts, and banshees as they prepare a feast for young trick-or-treaters.

Rosenberry, Vera.

Vera's Halloween. See under "Everyday Life in General" in chapter 1.

Rylant, Cynthia.

Moonlight: The Halloween Cat. **Illustrated by Melissa Sweet. New York: HarperCollins, 2003. Unpaged. ISBN 9780060297114.** `PreS–2`

Moonlight, a green-eyed black cat, loves to prowl at night. Her favorite night for exploring is Halloween, because she adores the smiling pumpkins, scarecrows with laps, trick-or-treaters, and especially, a piece or two of candy.

Schulman, Janet.

10 Trick-or-Treaters. **Illustrated by Linda Davick. New York: Knopf, 2005. 34pp. ISBN 9780375832253.** `PreS–K`

Ten costumed trick-or-treaters leave their apartment building for a night of parties and Halloween fun in this countdown book.

Sierra, Judy.

The House That Drac Built. Illustrated by Will Hillenbrand. San Diego: Harcourt, 1995. 32pp. ISBN 9780152018795 (pb). **PreS-2**

> This cumulative rhyme in "The House That Jack Built" format begins with a mummy rising from his coffin and adds more and more spooky creatures until a band of trick-or-treaters arrive at the door.

Stoeke, Janet.

Minerva Louise on Halloween. See in chapter 14.

Thompson, Lauren.

Mouse's First Halloween. Illustrated by Buket Erdogan. New York: Simon & Schuster, 2000. Unpaged. ISBN 9780689831768. **T-K**

> On a dark and spooky night, the ever-curious Mouse ventures out for a walk to investigate a series of unusual sounds.

Williams, Linda.

The Little Old Lady Who Was Not Afraid of Anything. Illustrated by Megan Lloyd. New York: Crowell, 1986. 32pp. ISBN 9780690045840. **PreS-2**

> A fearless elderly woman enters the forest to gather items she wants to bring home, and as she journeys back, she has some strange encounters. Two shoes, a pair of pants, a shirt, two gloves, and a tall black hat approach her successively on the way home, each making a unique sound or motion. The little old lady refuses to be scared and continues on until a pumpkin head appears. She quickens her pace, but once she's home safe, the entire ensemble knocks on her door, trying to frighten her. But she has a better idea. The repetition of sounds and motions makes this a great participatory read-aloud.

Thanksgiving

Auch, Mary Jane.

Beauty and the Beaks: A Turkey's Cautionary Tale. Illustrated by Herm Auch. New York: Holiday House, 2007. 32pp. ISBN 9780823419906. **Gr. 1-3**

> In this eggstremely punny tale, when Lance the turkey discovers that he is going to be the main course for dinner, he relies on help from Beauty and her fellow hens, who all work in a beauty shop, to provide him with a convincing disguise.

Bildner, Phil.

Turkey Bowl. Illustrated by C. F. Payne. New York: Simon & Schuster, 2008. 30pp. ISBN 9780689878961. **PreS–2**

Until now, Ethan has not been old enough to join his family's annual football game, but this Thanksgiving, his turn has come. Unfortunately, a blizzard closes the roads and prevents the relatives from getting through. Ethan and his friends slog through the snow to the school, dispirited, until they realize they can play their own game.

Boelts, Maribeth.

The Firefighters' Thanksgiving. Illustrated by Terry Widener. New York: Putnam, 2004. 32pp. ISBN 9780399236006. **PreS–2**

It's Thanksgiving Day, and all the firefighters of Station 1 are busy preparing their Thanksgiving dinner, but they get so many calls throughout the day, their turkey never gets cooked. All is not lost, however, for when they return to the firehouse at last, they find a feast.

Brown, Marc.

Arthur's Thanksgiving. See under "Everyday Life in General" in chapter 1.

Cox, Judy.

One Is a Feast for Mouse: A Thanksgiving Tale. Illustrated by Jeffrey Ebbeler. New York: Holiday House, 2008. 32pp. ISBN 9780823419777. **PreS–2**

A hungry mouse slips out of his hole, drawn to the leftovers of a Thanksgiving dinner. He starts out with one small pea but can't resist sampling every dish. When the cat wakes up, the mouse realizes he might be in trouble.

Goode, Diane.

Thanksgiving Is Here! New York: HarperCollins, 2003. Unpaged. ISBN 978-0060515881. **Gr. K–3**

Family members begin to arrive as Grandma and Grandpa prepare a traditional Thanksgiving meal.

Markes, Julie.

Thanks for Thanksgiving. Illustrated by Doris Barrette. New York: HarperCollins, 2004. Unpaged. ISBN 9780060510961. **PreS–3**

As a family sits down to Thanksgiving dinner, they take turns sharing their gratitude for a variety of things in their lives.

Mayr, Diane.

Run, Turkey, Run! Illustrated by Laura Rader. New York: Walker, 2007. 32pp. ISBN 9780802796301. **PreS–2**

Thanksgiving time has arrived on the farm and that means the turkey has to run for his life. With his fellow animals urging him on, he eludes the farmer in the forest, and the family settles for grilled cheese sandwiches.

Reed, Rowena.

Thelonius Turkey Lives! **Illustrated by Reed, Lynn Rowe Reed. New York: Knopf, 2005. 40pp. ISBN 9780375831263.** `PreS-2`

Thelonius, a turkey, tries one scheme after another to escape a future as the main course for Thanksgiving, to no avail. Just as he reconciles himself to his fate, he learns that his owner is interested in his feathers, not his drumsticks.

Stiegemeyer, Julie.

Gobble-Gobble Crash! **Illustrated by Valeri Gorbachev. New York: Dutton, 2008. Unpaged. ISBN 9780525479598.** `PreS-1`

The catchy rhyme details how the farm animals, who have just settled into sleep, help four wild turkeys that urgently need to escape the farmer.

Christmas

Allen, Jonathan.

I'm Not Santa. See in chapter 14.

Alsenas, Linas.

Mrs. Claus Takes a Vacation. **New York: Scholastic, 2006. 32pp. ISBN 9780439779784.** `Gr. 1-3`

Promising to return by Christmas Eve, Mrs. Claus takes the sleigh and embarks on a round-the-world tour while Santa stays home and bakes cookies.

Appelt, Kathi.

Merry Christmas, Merry Crow. **Illustrated by Jon Goodell. Orlando, FL: Harcourt, 2005. 32pp. ISBN 9780152026516.** `PreS-2`

Rhyming verse details the excursions of a determined crow that soars about a snowy city full of Christmas revelers. He's collecting a strange assortment of items, which turn out to be decorations for his very own Christmas tree.

Auch, Mary Jane.

The Nutquacker. **New York: Holiday House, 1999. 32pp. ISBN 978-0823415243.** `Gr. 1-3`

Clara, a young duck, sets out to discover the true meaning of Christmas. She encounters a tractor, a deer, and a fox, but it isn't until the fox chases her back to her own barnyard that she realizes that the most important thing about Christmas is being with her friends.

Banks, Kate.

What's Coming for Christmas? Illustrated by Georg Hallensleben. New York: Farrar, Straus & Giroux, 2009. 40pp. ISBN 9780374399481. **PreS–2**

> On the farm, the humans and the animals all await the holiday with great anticipation.

Bauer, Marion Dane.

The Christmas Baby. Illustrated by Richard Cowdrey. New York: Simon & Schuster, 2009. Unpaged. ISBN 9781416978855. **T–K**

> In simple prose, Bauer retells the Christmas story. After Mary and Joseph find a place in the manger and the shepherds and Wise Men visit the Baby Jesus, Bauer explains that all babies are celebrated and the illustrations switch to welcoming a baby in contemporary times.

Bowen, Anne.

Christmas Is Coming. Illustrated by Tomek Bogacki. Minneapolis, MN: Carolrhoda, 2007. 32pp. ISBN 9781575059341. **PreS–1**

> It's her baby brother's first Christmas, so Anna tells him all about how to get ready for the holiday.

Brett, Jan.

Christmas Trolls. New York: Putnam, 1993. 32pp. ISBN 9780399225079. **Gr. K–3**

> Treva, a Scandinavian girl, shows two greedy trolls how to celebrate Christmas. They clean, decorate, and play games. She gives them a gift, to show them the most important aspect of Christmas is sharing, and they reciprocate on Christmas morning. Illustrated with Brett's finely detailed art.

Who's That Knocking on Christmas Eve? New York: Putnam, 2002. 30pp. ISBN 9780399238734. **Gr. K–2**

> In this story inspired by a Norwegian folktale, Kyri invites a boy traveling with his pet polar bear into her hut for Christmas Eve. When trolls disrupt the feast, the boy and his bear help her fend them off.

Brown, Marc.

Arthur's Christmas. See under "Everyday Life in General" in chapter 1.

Arthur's Perfect Christmas. See under "Everyday Life in General" in chapter 1.

Chaconas, Dori.

Christmas Mouseling. Illustrated by Susan Kathleen Hartung. New York: Viking, 2005. 32pp. ISBN 9780670059843. **PreS–2**

> Mother Mouse's brand new baby can't stop sneezing, so she seeks a warm, safe place for him and settles on a stable where her mouseling can snuggle next to an infant in a manger.

Climo, Shirley.

Cobweb Christmas. **Illustrated by Jane K. Manning. New York: HarperCollins, 2001. Unpaged. ISBN 9780060290337.** `PreS-1`

Originally released in 1982, this revised edition has all new illustrations. Based on a folktale, Climo relates the tale of a Bavarian woman who welcomes children and animals to her home to see her beautifully decorated Christmas tree and share treats. No spiders are allowed in until Kris Kringle opens the way for them. They leave the tree covered in cobwebs, which are transformed into strands of silver and gold, the first tinsel.

Cotten, Cynthia.

This Is the Stable. **Illustrated by Delana Bettoli. New York: Holt, 2006. 32pp. ISBN 9780805075564.** `PreS-1`

Cotten relates the tale of the activity in cumulative verse, patterned after "The House That Jack Built."

De Groat, Diane.

Jingle Bells, Homework Smells. See under "Everyday Life in General" in chapter 1.

dePaola, Tomie.

Merry Christmas Strega Nona. See under "Fantasy and Magic" in chapter 15.

The Legend of the Poinsettia. **New York: Putnam, 1994. 32pp. ISBN 9780399216923.** `Gr. 1-3`

DePaola retells a Mexican legend, relating the story of Lucida. Her mother is weaving a new blanket for the Baby Jesus in the Church's Christmas procession. When her mother falls ill, Lucida tries to finish the work, but makes a mess of it. Repentant, she offers weeds to the Christ Child and they burst into beautiful red blooms.

Four Friends at Christmas. **New York: Simon & Schuster, 2009. 32pp. ISBN 9781416991755.** `PreS-3`

Mister Frog is feeling a bit lonely on Christmas Eve, until his friends, Missy Cat, Master Dog, and Mistress Pig, surprise him with a special celebration.

DiCamillo, Kate.

Great Joy. **Illustrated by Bagram Ibatoulline. Cambridge, MA: Candlewick, 2007. 32pp. ISBN 9780763629205.** `Gr. K-3`

Frances lives with her mother in an apartment in the 1940s. Although she should be preparing for her role in the Christmas pageant, she is worried about the lonely organ grinder, whom she watches from her window. She invites him to church, and it is only when he arrives that she can say her line, "Behold! I bring you tidings of Great Joy!" This compassionate story is illustrated with Ibatoulline's luminous paintings.

Duval, Kathy.

The Three Bears' Christmas. **Illustrated by Paul Meisel. New York: Holiday House, 2005. 32pp. ISBN 9780823418718.** `PreS-1`

In this takeoff on the well-known tale, Santa is cast as Goldilocks, who visits the house of the three bears when they go out to let the gingerbread cookies cool.

Falconer, Ian.

Olivia Helps with Christmas. See under "Everyday Life in General" in chapter 1.

Hillenbrand, Will.

Cock-a-Doodle Christmas. **New York: Marshall Cavendish, 2007. 31pp. ISBN 9780761453543.** `PreS-1`

In the stable in Bethlehem, Harold the rooster can't crow loudly enough to wake anyone, until he is inspired by the Christ Child.

Hodges, Margaret.

The Wee Christmas Cabin. **Illustrated by Kimberly Bulcken Root. New York: Holiday House, 2009. Unpaged. ISBN 9780823415281.** `Gr. 1–3`

In this retelling of Ruth Sawyer's 1941 "The Wee Christmas Cabin of Carn-na-Ween," Oona, a poor daughter of tinkers living in Ireland, wishes for a home of her own. She spends her life doing good deeds and caring for others, but during a time of famine when no one will take her in, she lays down under a black-thorn tree to sleep on Christmas Eve. The fairies spy her, and wanting to honor her giving spirit, they build her a cabin of her own and stock it with food. In gratitude, Oona opens her home to those in need every Christmas.

Holabird, Katharine.

Angelina's Christmas. See under "Dance" in chapter 7.

Horacek, Petr.

Suzy Goose and the Christmas Star. See in chapter 14.

Horse, Harry.

Little Rabbit's Christmas. See under "Everyday Life in General" in chapter 1.

Jeffers, Susan.

The Nutcracker. **New York: HarperCollins, 2007. 40pp. ISBN 9780060743864.** `PreS-2`

Jeffers retells the classic ballet story of young Marie who finds a way to break the spell on her beloved nutcracker. Jeffers's lush and detailed illustrations bring a shimmering quality to the tale.

Katz, Karen.

Counting Christmas. See under "Counting" in chapter 4.

Kelley, True.

The Dog Who Saved Santa. New York: Holiday House, 2008. Unpaged. ISBN 9780823421206. **PreS–2**

In this humorous holiday tale, young Santa is a lazy fellow who delivers Christmas presents in a haphazard manner even though his dog Rodney and the elves have worked frantically to get everything just right. After Christmas Rodney, determined to reform Santa, orders a self-help video and whips Santa into shape, until he becomes the loveable and hardworking chap that he is today. The droll humor is aptly depicted in the cartoon illustrations done in acrylics, watercolor, and colored pencils.

Kladstrup, Kristin.

The Gingerbread Pirates. Illustrated by Matt Tavares. Cambridge, MA: Candlewick, 2009. 32pp. ISBN 9780763632236. **PreS–3**

Jim and his mom bake a buccaneer batch of gingerbread and decorate the cookies as pirates. They leave the cookies for Santa on Christmas Eve. One brave treat, Captain Cookie, does his best to save his fellows from being munched.

Klise, Kate.

Shall I Knit You a Hat? A Christmas Yarn. See under "Family in General" in chapter 1.

Kroll, Virginia.

Uno, Dos, Tres, Posada! Let's Celebrate Christmas. Illustrated by Loretta Lopez. New York: Viking, 2006. 32pp. ISBN 9780670059324. **PreS–2**

Using rhyme that includes both English and Spanish words, this counting book provides information on the preparation for and celebration of Posadas, a Latin American celebration that takes place nine days before Christmas.

Kvasnosky, Laura McGee.

Zelda and Ivy One Christmas. See under "Families: Siblings" in chapter 2.

Lawler, Janet.

Tyrannoclaus. Illustrated by John Schroades. New York: HarperCollins, 2009. 32pp. ISBN 9780061170546. **PreS–1**

In this dinosaur version of "The Night Before Christmas," Tyrannoclaus and his dinosaur assistants must escape a volcano before they can soar in the sleigh and deliver presents to all the good little dinosaur boys and girls.

London, Jonathan.

Froggy's Best Christmas. See under "Everyday Life in General" in chapter 1.

Long, Loren.

Drummer Boy. New York: Philomel, 2008. Unpaged. ISBN 9780399251740. `PreS–3`

When a little boy receives a package shortly before Christmas containing a toy soldier with a drum, it quickly becomes his favorite toy. Unfortunately, he loses it accidentally and the toy must make his own way in the world, braving dangerous situations as he searches for his owner. Everywhere he goes his plays his drum, which calms all those who hear it. At last the boy finds him on Christmas morning, brings him home, and sets him in his family's Christmas crèche, so that he can play for the Christ Child. Striking acrylic paintings illustrate this moving tale.

McAllister, Angela.

Santa's Little Helper. Illustrated by Daniel Howarth. New York: Orchard, 2008. 26pp. ISBN 9780545094443. `PreS–1`

While playing hide-and-seek on Christmas Eve, Snowball the bunny secrets himself in among Santa's toys and falls asleep. When Santa discovers him there, he enlists his aid in delivering presents.

McCourt, Frank.

Angela and the Baby Jesus. Illustrated by Raúl Colón. New York: Simon & Schuster, 2007. 29pp. ISBN 9781416937890. `Gr. 2 & up`

In an Ireland of a past generation, six-year-old Angela is worried about the Baby Jesus in the crèche at her church. He has no blanket, so she is afraid that he is too cold. Secretly, Angela brings the baby home with her and places him in her bed for warmth. Then she must wrestle with her conscience as to what to do next. Colon's watercolor and lithograph pencil illustrations imbue the story with light and warmth.

McCourt, Lisa.

Merry Christmas, Stinky Face. See under "Families" in chapter 2.

McKissack, Patricia.

🌸*The All-I'll-Ever-Want Christmas Doll.* Illustrated by Jerry Pinkney. New York: Schwartz & Wade, 2007. 32pp. ISBN 9780375837593. `Gr. K–3`

Growing up during the Great Depression, three African American sisters know that while Christmas always comes, Santa doesn't necessarily arrive with gifts. Still, the middle sister, Nella, writes him a letter to ask for a Baby Betty doll. Her sisters scoff, but on Christmas morning the doll awaits her new owner. Nella claims ownership and shoos her sisters away but soon sees that playing alone is not as fun and invites her sisters to a tea party to celebrate Baby Betty together. Pinkney's watercolors masterfully depict the sisters' emotions and the historical setting. (ALAN)

Milgrim, David.

Santa Duck. New York: Penguin, 2008. 32pp. ISBN 9780399250187. `PreS–1`
When Nicholas Duck dons the red coat and hat he finds on his doorstep on Christmas Eve, all the other animals insist on listing their Christmas wishes for him. At last he finds Santa and shares with him everything he's learned, forgetting to give Santa his own list. Dialog balloons impart portions of the story, which is accompanied by digital ink and oil pastel illustrations.

Moore, Clement Clarke.

The Night before Christmas. `PreS–3`
Various illustrators have created a vast array of versions of the classic poem recounting the visit of the "jolly old elf".

Illustrated by Jan Brett. New York: Putnam, 2008. 32pp. ISBN 9780399251931. This tenth-anniversary edition features Brett's signature full-page illustrations and detailed borders as she sets the action in a Victorian house in a New England village.

Illustrated by Will Moses. New York: Philomel, 2006. 33pp. ISBN 9780399237454. Employing the folk-art style similar to his great-grandmother's, Grandma Moses, Will Moses sets the poem in 1800s New England with spot vignettes and full-page oil paintings.

Illustrated by Jessica Smith. Boston: Houghton Mifflin, 2005. 32pp. ISBN 9780618616824. Smith, one of America's premier female illustrators of the late nineteenth and early twentieth centuries, used spare pen-and-ink illustrations as well as full-color paintings, which give this edition a nostalgic feel.

Illustrated by Gennadii Spirin. New York: Marshall Cavendish, 2006. 29pp. ISBN 9780761452980. Spirin's ornate colored-pencil and watercolor illustrations and meticulous book design give the poem the look of illuminated manuscript.

Illustrated by Matt Tavares. Cambridge, MA: Candlewick, 2002. Unpaged. ISBN 9780763615857. Tavares provides graceful black-and-white drawings for the classic poem, presented with the original spelling and grammar of the poem published in 1823 anonymously.

Illustrated by Richard Watson. New York: HarperCollins, 2006. 40pp. ISBN 9780060757410. Watson brings Santa up to date by giving him aviator goggles, a GPS to find his way, a rocket style sleigh, and a cast of multicultural elves.

Moulton, Mark Kimball.

Reindeer Christmas. **Illustrated by Karen Hillard Good. New York: Simon & Schuster, 2008. 40pp. ISBN 9781416961086.** `PreS–3`
As snow gently falls, while walking in the forest two siblings and their grandmother discover a hungry and exhausted deer, which they bring

home to nurture back to health. Doing so, they unwittingly save Christmas, as they learn on Christmas morning that the deer was one of Santa's reindeer.

Noble, Trinka Hakes.

Apple Tree Christmas. Chelsea, MI: Sleeping Bear Press, 2005. 32pp. ISBN 9781585362707. `Gr. 1-3`

This reissue of a book first released in 1984 relates a family story of two sisters and a beloved apple tree. In the 1880s the girls enjoy playing on and around their apple tree and are heartbroken when a blizzard topples the old tree. To their surprise, their father creates a special gift for them from the tree.

O'Connor, Jane.

Fancy Nancy Splendiferous Christmas. See under "Everyday Life in General" in chapter 1.

Oppenheim, Joanne.

The Miracle of the First Poinsettia: A Mexican Christmas Story. Illustrated by Fabian Negrin. Cambridge, MA: Barefoot Books, 2003. 32pp. ISBN 9781841482453. `Gr. K-2`

Papa is out of work, so Juanita has no gift to leave the Baby Jesus. As an angel directs her, Juanita gathers weeds and leaves them as her present. Miraculously they bloom with lovely red blossoms.

Palatini, Margie.

Three French Hens: A Holiday Tale. Illustrated by Richard Egielski. New York: Hyperion, 2005. 32pp. ISBN 9780786851676. `Gr. K-3`

Three feisty French hens, intended as gifts for Monsieur Philippe Renard along with a pear tree and two turtle doves, get separated from the other presents and end up with a down-and-out Phil Fox in the Bronx. He thinks dinner has arrived, but when the hens give his home a makeover and prepare a fowl-free feast, he realizes they're friends, not entrees. Egielski's fine watercolor and charcoal line illustrations give this winsome tale an added dollop of humor.

Polacco, Patricia.

Welcome Comfort. New York: Philomel, 1999. 32pp. ISBN 9780399231698. `Gr. 1-3`

Overweight and a foster child, Welcome Comfort is teased unmercifully by his classmates. Care comes into his life through the attention of the kindly school custodian, Quentin Hamp. Mr. Hamp and his wife take a trip every Christmas Eve, and by the time Welcome grows up and has a wife of his own, he finds that he has been groomed to take Mr. Hamp's place at school and on Christmas Eve.

Christmas Tapestry. New York: Philomel, 2002. 40pp. ISBN 9780399239557. `Gr. 1-3`

Jonathan resents it when his father, a Baptist minister, is transferred from Memphis to Detroit. Even so, he works hard to help restore the rundown church and is dismayed when a leak ruins a newly painted wall. When he and his father find a secondhand tapestry to cover the wall during the Christmas Eve service, it miraculously brings together a Jewish couple separated years earlier by the Holocaust.

An Orange for Frankie. New York: Philomel, 2004. 48pp. ISBN 978-0399243028. **Gr. 1-3**

Based on an incident in the childhood of Polacco's great-uncle, Frankie is one of ten children growing up on a family farm in rural Michigan. On the Christmas of his tenth year, he and his siblings eagerly await his father's return through a blizzard with the traditional oranges.

Poydar, Nancy.

Brave Santa. New York: Holiday House, 2004. ISBN 9780823418213. **PreS-1**

Jack feels shy about meeting Santa in the mall, so his parents help him practice with role-playing. Then, when they go, Jack discovers that Santa isn't feeling brave either, so Jack gives him some pointers about facing all those children.

Purmell, Ann.

Christmas Tree Farm. Illustrated by Jill Weber. New York: Holiday House, 2006. 32pp. ISBN 9780823418862. **PreS-2**

A boy helps his grandfather care for the family Christmas tree farm, from planting, to weeding, to cutting.

Rader, Laura.

When Santa Lost His Ho! Ho! Ho! New York: HarperCollins, 2008. Unpaged. ISBN 9780061141393. **PreS-2**

When word gets out that Santa's ability to laugh has slipped away, children all over the world send him funny pictures. Holly's self-portrait showing what she looks like on a bad day restores Santa's contagious chuckle.

Ray, Mary Lyn.

Christmas Farm. Illustrated by Barry Root. Orlando, FL: Harcourt, 2008. 40pp. ISBN 9780152162900. **Gr. 1-3**

Tired of growing flowers on her farm in New England, Wilma decides to start a Christmas tree farm. With the help of her five-year-old neighbor Parker, Wilma plants hundreds of balsam trees and tends them for five years. Finally, after all that hard work, they have trees to sell.

Santiago, Esmeralda.

A Doll for Navidades. Illustrated by Enrique O. Sánchez. New York: Scholastic, 2005. 32pp. ISBN 9780439553988. **PreS-3**

Set in sunny Puerto Rico, this semiautobiographical story describes the tradition of Dia de Los Tres Reyes Magos (Three King's Day) and goes on to tell of Esmerelda's longing for a doll. She leaves a note for the Magi, but it is her sister who receives the doll. Disappointed, she eventually masters her feelings and becomes the doll's godmother. The text is sprinkled with Spanish words and phrases, which are defined in a concluding glossary.

Scotton, Rob.

Merry Christmas, Splat. See under "School: School in General" in chapter 2.

Seuss, Dr.

How the Grinch Stole Christmas: A 50th Anniversary Retrospective. **New York: Random House, 2007. 85pp. ISBN 9780375838477.** `PreS-3`
In this fiftieth-anniversary edition of the classic tale of the grouchy Grinch who tried to steal Christmas from all those Whos down in Whoville, readers can learn the changes that various forms of media have brought to the story and see covers from editions from around the world.

Soto, Gary.

Too Many Tamales. **Illustrated by Ed Martinez. New York: Putnam, 1993. Unpaged. ISBN 9780399221460.** `PreS-3`
Maria is helping her mother make tamales because their relatives are coming. Later she realizes she is no longer wearing her mother's diamond ring, which she tried on secretly. Convinced it must be in the tamales, she and her cousins eat them all in an effort to find the ring, which turns out to be on her mother's finger after all.

Spinner, Stephanie.

The Nutcracker. **Illustrated by Peter Malone. New York: Knopf, 2008. Unpaged. ISBN 9780375844645.** `Gr. 1-3`
Spinner retells the story of the New York City Ballet version of Hoffman's tale of the bespelled nutcracker. An orchestral CD accompanies the book.

Stainton, Sue.

Christmas Magic. **Illustrated by Eva Melhuish. New York: Katherine Tegen Books, 2007. 29pp. ISBN 9780060785710.** `PreS-1`
In this light holiday tale, an elf named Little Santa borrows bells from the reindeer, hides them in the forest, and challenges his animal friends to find them.

Terrill, Beth.

The Barnyard Night before Christmas. **Illustrated by Greg Newbold. New York: Random House, 2007. 40pp. ISBN 9780375836824.** `Gr. 1-3`
When his reindeer cannot complete their appointed rounds, Santa recruits some bickering barnyard animals to help him out.

Thompson, Kay.

Eloise's Christmas Trinkles. See under "Everyday Life in General" in chapter 1.

Kay Thompson's Eloise at Christmas. See under "Everyday Life in General" in chapter 1.

Thompson, Lauren.

The Christmas Magic. **Illustrated by John J. Muth. New York: Scholastic, 2009. 40pp. ISBN 9780439774970.** `Gr. K-3`

Readers peek in on Santa on Christmas Eve day as he goes through all the preparations for the time of the "Christmas Magic," when he soars away in his sleigh.

Van Allsburg, Chris.

🏃*The Polar Express.* **Boston: Houghton Mifflin, 1985. 32pp. ISBN 978-0395389492.** `Gr. K-3`

A young boy rides a steam-powered train to the North Pole to witness Santa in action. Van Allsburg accompanies his text with muted yet glowing illustrations. (ALAN, Boston Globe Honor, Caldecott Medal)

Waddell, Martin.

Room for a Little One: A Christmas Tale. **Illustrated by Jason Crockcroft. New York: Margaret K. McElderry Books, 2004. Unpaged. ISBN 978-0689868412.** `PreS-1`

A kindhearted ox invites one animal after another into the stable for shelter and rest. When an old donkey brings in Mary and Joseph, the animals extend the welcome to them as well.

Walton, Rick.

Bunny Christmas. See under "Families" in chapter 2.

Wheeler, Lisa.

Where, Oh Where, Is Santa Claus? **Illustrated by Ivan Bates. Orlando: Harcourt, 2007. 26pp. ISBN 9780152164089.** `PreS-1`

Rhyming couplets chronicle the search for Santa by several Arctic animals.

Willey, Margaret.

A Clever Beatrice Christmas. See under "Folk and Fairy Tales" in chapter 15.

Wilson, Karma

Bear Stays up for Christmas. See under "Friends" in chapter 2.

Hanukkah

Cleary, Brian P.

Eight Wild Nights: A Family Hanukkah Tale. **Illustrated by David Udovic. Minneapolis, MN: Kar-Ben, 2006. 24pp. ISBN 9781580131520.** `Gr. K-3`

An extended family gathers to celebrate the eight nights of Hanukkah, but they have a strange and unusual way of enjoying each other's company.

Da Costa, Deborah.

Hanukkah Moon. **Illustrated by Gosia Mosz. Minneapolis, MN: Kar-Ben, 2007. 32pp. ISBN 9781580132442.** `Gr. 1-3`

Isobel goes to Mexico to spend Hanukkah with her Aunt Luisa and enjoys discovering some Spanish Jewish traditions.

Edwards, Michelle.

Papa's Latkes. **Illustrated by Stacey Schuett. Cambridge, MA: Candlewick, 2004. 32pp. ISBN 9780763607791.** `Gr. K-3`.

Sisters Selma and Dora prepare for their first Hanukkah since their mother's death by closely following her traditions. They even try to help Papa make latkes the way Mama used to make them. When they don't turn out right, Selma breaks down and cries. Papa comforts the sisters, and they light the candles, remembering Mama.

Glaser, Linda.

Hoppy Hanukkah. **Illustrated by Daniel Howarth. Morton Grove, IL: Albert Whitman, 2009. 24pp. ISBN 9780807533789.** `T-K`

An enthusiastic family, including several young bunnies, celebrate Hanukkah by lighting the candles on the menorah, munching on latkes, and playing dreidel.

Goldin, Barbara Diamond.

The Best Hanukkah Ever. **Illustrated by Avi Katz. New York: Marshall Cavendish, 2007. 32pp. ISBN 9780761453550.** `Gr. K-2`

The numbskull Knoodle family try to follow the rabbi's advice to give treasured gifts, but they get each other gifts they want for themselves rather than what's appropriate for the other person. Only when they turn to the rabbi for more advice does each person end up with the right gift.

Howland, Naomi.

Latkes, Latkes Good to Eat: A Chanukah Story. New York: Clarion, 1999. 31pp. ISBN 9780395899038. `Gr. K–2`

> When Sadie gives her firewood to an elderly woman, she is rewarded with a magic frying pan that will make latkes until she says the Hanukkah phrase, "A great miracle happened here." Although she warns her brothers not to use the pan, as soon as she leaves them alone, they start making latkes, but they don't know how to make it stop.

Kimmel, Eric.

🏹*Hershel and the Hanukkah Goblins.* Illustrated by Trina Chart Hyman. New York: Holiday House, 1989. 32pp. ISBN 9780823407699. `Gr. K–3`

> When Hershel enters a village that is too afraid of the goblins to celebrate Hanukkah, he forms a plan to outwit even the fiercest of them. Gorgeous illustrations highlight this clever tale. (ALAN, Caldecott Honor)

Zigazak: A Magical Hanukkah Night. Illustrated by Jon Goodell. New York: Double Day, 2001. 32pp. ISBN 9780385326520. `PreS–2`

> When two chaos-creating devils disrupt the Hanukkah festivities with their antics, the townspeople turn to the rabbi for help. Amused rather than afraid, he outsmarts the two and restores order.

Krensky, Stephen.

🏹*Hanukkah at Valley Forge.* Illustrated by Greg Harlin. New York: Dutton, 2006. 32pp. ISBN 9780525477389. `Gr. 2 & up`

> Based on a true story of a Polish immigrant celebrating Hanukkah at Valley Forge, Krensky constructs a tale of his encounter with a dispirited General Washington. He explains the history of the traditional menorah lighting, and General Washington sees the parallels between the struggles for freedom. Both come away from the event with renewed hope in miracles. (Sydney Taylor Award)

Kroll, Steven.

The Hanukkah Mice. Illustrated by Michelle Shapiro. New York: Marshall Cavendish, 2008. Unpaged. ISBN 9780761454281. `PreS–2`

> On the first night of Hanukkah, Rachel receives a dollhouse that is just the right size for a family of mice to explore.

Kropf, Latifa Berry.

It's Hanukkah Time! Illustrated by Tod Cohen. Minneapolis, MN: Kar-Ben, 2004. 24pp. ISBN 9781580131209. `T–K`

> A class of preschool students is busily preparing for their Hanukkah party. When their grandparents arrive, they sing, dance, light the Hanukkah candles, and eat the treats the children have made. The fun is highlighted by sharp color photographs.

Lamstein, Sarah Marwil.

Letter on the Wind. **Illustrated by Neil Waldman. Honesdale, PA: Boyds Mills Press, 2007. Unpaged. ISBN 9781932425741.** `Gr. 2 & up`

> In a poor village, the harvest is so scarce that there is not enough oil to light the menorahs. Hayim writes a letter to the Almighty for help and tosses it to the wind. The wind carries it to a rich merchant, who sends not only oil but food as well.

Lanton, Sandy.

Lots of Latkes: A Hanukkah Story. **Illustrated by Vicki Jo Redenbaugh. New York: Kar-Ben, 2003. 32pp. ISBN 9781580130912.** `Gr. K–3`

> When an old woman invites her friends for a Hanukkah dinner, she asks them to bring side dishes, for she will make the latkes. One mishap after another causes her friends to bring latkes instead. They sing, they dance, and they have lots of latkes. A recipe is included.

Levine, Abby.

This Is the Dreidel. **Illustrated by Paige Billin-Frye. Morton Grove, IL: Albert Whitman, 2003. 32pp. ISBN 9780807578841.** `PreS–2`

> This "House That Jack Built" rhyme details the activities of siblings Max and Ruth, who are playing dreidel, singing songs, eating latkes, and listening to the story of Hanukkah.

Ofanansky, Allison.

Harvest of Light. **Illustrated by Eliyahu Alpern. Minneapolis, MN: Kar-Ben, 2008. 29pp. ISBN 9780822573890.** `Gr. 1–3`

> In Israel a little girl explains how her family grows and harvests the olives that will be pressed into the oil used in their menorah. Color photographs show the process.

Penn, Audrey.

The Miracle Jar: A Hanukkah Story. **Illustrated by Lea Lyon. Terre Haute, IN: Tanglewood Press, 2008. 32pp. ISBN 9781933718163.** `Gr. K–2`

> In the Old Country, eight-year-old Sophie and her family are getting ready for Hanukkah. When a snowstorm keeps them in their cozy cottage for all eight days, they must find ways to make their cooking oil last.

Schotter, Roni.

Hanukkah! **Illustrated by Marylin Hafner. Boston: Little Brown, 2008. 28pp. ISBN 9780316034777.** `Gr. K–3`

> Originally published in 1990, this story describes how Nora and her family prepare for and celebrate the holiday.

Spinner, Stephanie.

It's a Miracle! A Hanukkah Storybook. **Illustrated by Jill McElmurry. New York: Atheneum, 2003. Unpaged. ISBN 9780689844935.** `Gr. 2 & up`
> On each night of Hanukkah, Grandma Karen tells her grandson Owen a story about a different family member.

Kwanzaa

Katz, Karen.

My First Kwanzaa. **New York: Holt, 2003. 32pp. ISBN 9780805070774.** `PreS–1`
> An African American girl explains Kwanzaa and how her family celebrates it.

Medearis, Angela Shelf.

Seven Spools of Thread: A Kwanzaa Story. **Illustrated by Daniel Minter.** Morton Grove, IL: Albert Whitman, 2000. 40pp. ISBN 9780807573150. `Gr. 1–3`
> This story illustrates the seven principles of Kwanzaa. The father of seven sons who argue all the time is very disappointed in them. When he dies, he leaves them a task that can only be accomplished if they all work together. Vivid linoleum block prints illustrate the rhythmic text.

Favorites

> *Pumpkin Eye* by Denise Fleming
>
> *Hershel and the Hanukkah Goblins* by Eric Kimmel
>
> *Apple Tree Christmas* by Trinka Hakes Noble
>
> *How the Grinch Stole Christmas* by Dr. Seuss
>
> *The House That Drac Built* by Judy Sierra
>
> *Gobble-Gobble Crash!* by Julie Stiegemeyer
>
> *The Little Old Lady Who Was Not Afraid of Anything* by Linda Williams
>
> *The Polar Express* by Chris Van Allsburg

Chapter 7

Arts and Activities:
Art, Dance, Music, Theater,
Writing, and Sports

Activities that involve artistic and/or athletic expression can be significant experiences in children's lives and so appear in an interesting array of titles.

Art

Ahlberg, Allan.

The Pencil. **Illustrated by Bruce Ingman. Cambridge, MA: Candlewick, 2008. Unpaged. ISBN 9780763638948.** `Gr. K–2`

When a pencil begins drawing, it creates a whole world, but is soon threatened by an eraser that wants to wipe out everything.

Beaumont, Karen.

🎗*I Ain't Gonna Paint No More!* **Illustrated by David Catrow. Orlando, FL: Harcourt, 2005. Unpaged. ISBN 9780152024888.** `PreS–2`

Following the format of "It Ain't Gonna Rain No More," the rhyming text and lively artwork portray a child going wild with paint. When his mother finds he has painted everything, she plops him into the bath tub and forbids further painting. The boy is not all dissuaded, however. As soon as he is clean, he reclaims his supplies and begins painting himself. (ALAN)

Bridges, Shirin Yim.

The Umbrella Queen. See under "Asia" in chapter 3.

dePaola, Tomie.

The Art Lesson. **New York: Putnam, 1989. 32pp. ISBN 9780399216886.** `Gr. K–3`

Young Tommy loves to draw. He treasures his box of sixty-four colors of crayons and always heeds the advice of his artist aunts: never copy. Although he's looking forward to the day the art teacher comes to school, he's severely disappointed when she wants the class to copy her drawing. Tommy refuses. With some help from his classroom teacher, they reach a compromise. Tommy will copy the art teacher's drawing and then get another piece of paper to make his own picture.

Ericsson, Jennifer A.

A Piece of Chalk. **Illustrated by Michelle Shapiro. New Milford, CT: Roaring Brook, 2007. 26pp. ISBN 9781596430570.** `PreS–2`

When a little girl gets a brand new box of colorful sidewalk chalk, she creates a masterpiece in her driveway.

Falwell, Cathryn.

David's Drawings. **New York: Lee & Low, 2001. Unpaged. ISBN 9781584300311.** `PreS–3`

David, a shy African American boy, spots a leafless winter tree on his way to school. It captures his imagination, so before school starts, he draws a picture of it. Soon classmates offer suggestions, which he adds, transforming the scene and making it a group picture, which he hangs on the class bulletin board. At home he draws the solitary tree once again and hangs it over his bed. He makes friends and retains his artistic integrity, all in a day. Illustrated with cut-paper and fabric collages.

Freedman, Deborah.

Scribble. **New York: Knopf, 2007. 40pp. ISBN 9780375839665.** `Gr. K–2`

When big sister Emma insults little sister Lucie by calling her drawing of a cat scribble, Lucie pays her back by scribbling all over Emma's drawing of a sleeping princess. Then Lucie's cat drawing comes to life and enters the picture of the princess, seeking to wake her up and live happily ever after.

Heap, Sue.

Danny's Drawing Book. **Cambridge, MA: Candlewick, 2008. 32pp. ISBN 978-0763636548.** `Gr. K–2`

When friends Danny and Ettie visit the zoo on a snowy day, they are captivated by the elephants and aardvarks. They decide to create a story about them and write and draw their tale of adventure inside Danny's yellow drawing book, which becomes the book in the reader's hand.

Johnson, Angela.

Lily Brown's Painting. **Illustrated by E. B. Lewis. New York: Orchard, 2007. 32pp. ISBN 9780439782258.** `Gr. K–2`

Lily, an African American girl, loves her life with her mother, father, and baby brother, and she loves to paint. With paintbrush in hand, she transforms the real world into an imaginary realm bursting with flights of fancy.

Johnson, Crockett.

Harold and the Purple Crayon. New York: HarperCollins, 1955. 54pp. ISBN 9780060229351. **PreS–1**

> Imaginative Harold wants to go for a walk in the moonlight. There isn't any moon, so he picks up his trusty purple crayon and draws one, thus embarking on a classic drawing adventure.

Lasky, Kathryn.

Georgia Rises: A Day in the Life of Georgia O'Keeffe. Illustrated by Ora Eitan. New York: Farrar, Straus & Giroux, 2009. 40pp. ISBN 9780374325299. **Gr. 2 & up**

> Lasky creates what a day could have been like in artist Georgia O'Keefe's later life in her adobe home on Ghost Ranch, in New Mexico. In this story inspired by her life, Georgia rises early to catch the lavender desert light of the morning and while walking in the desert, she finds a piece of bone that is just the white she wants to paint. She becomes so involved in her painting that she forgets her aches and pains, and at night she dreams of colors.

MacLachlan, Patricia, and Emily MacLachlan.

Painting the Wind. Illustrated by Katy Schneider. New York: Joanna Cotler, 2003. 40pp. ISBN 9780060297985. Gr. 1-3.

> A young artist lives on an island that harbors a variety of painters in the summer. He spends time with each one, learning how to paint flowers, portraits, and still-life forms.

McCarty, Peter.

Jeremy Draws a Monster. See under "Monsters" in chapter 15.

McDonnell, Patrick.

Art. New York: Little, Brown, 2006. 48pp. ISBN 9780316114912. **PreS–3** (SP)

> Art is a boy who loves experimenting with all kinds of art. His creations splash and swirl across the page in bright colors, using both paint and colored pencil, until tuckered at last, he falls asleep. When he wakes, he finds his mother has put his picture on the refrigerator because she loves his artwork. This is a stunning celebration of visual inspiration.

Mills, Claudia.

Ziggy's Blue-Ribbon Day. Illustrated by R. W. Alley. New York: Farrar, Straus & Giroux, 2005. Unpaged. ISBN 9780374323523. **Gr. K–2**

> Ziggy dreads track-and-field day at school. He's sure he will come in last in every event, because he's not athletic. He wishes they would give out blue ribbons for drawing instead, because he's great at that. Although he's right that he doesn't win one event, he does get some blue ribbons after all. A classmate spies the drawing he's done on the outside of his envelope and

trades one of her ribbons so that he will draw on hers. Soon a bevy of classmates want to trade for his artwork as well.

Napoli, Donna Jo, and Elena Furrow.

Ready to Dream. **Illustrated by Bronwyn Bancroft. New York: Bloomsbury, 2009. 32pp. ISBN 9781599900490.** Gr. 1-3

When Ally, a young artist, visits Australia with her mother, she meets Pauline, an aboriginal painter who encourages her to look with an artist's eye beyond appearance and into essence. By the end of the month, Pauline pronounces her an artist who is ready to dream. Bancroft, an aboriginal artist, uses the naïf in style in her acrylic paintings that present a book filled with indigenous Australian art.

Pinkwater, Daniel.

Bear's Picture. **Illustrated by B. D. Johnson. Boston: Houghton Mifflin, 2008. 32pp. ISBN 9780618759231.** Gr. K-3

In this newly illustrated edition of a book first released in 1972, a bear painting a picture continues with his art even when two gentlemen level harsh criticism.

Reynolds, Peter H.

The Dot. **Cambridge, MA: Candlewick, 2003. 32pp. ISBN 9780763619619.** Gr. K-3

Vashti is convinced that she can't draw and angrily gives her teacher a picture with one dot to prove it. When her teacher frames the picture, Vashti sets out to demonstrate that at least she can do better than that. In the process, she creates an array of paintings with brightly colored blotches that convince her she's an artist after all.

Ish. **Cambridge, MA: Candlewick, 2004. 32pp. ISBN 9780763623449.** Gr. K-3

Ramon adores drawing and does it constantly until his older brother hurts his feelings by announcing that his picture doesn't look the like the real item. Ramon crumples up his work, but later discovers that his younger sister has saved his pictures. She assures him that a picture doesn't have to be exact. Inspired, he picks up his pencil once again.

Rusch, Elizabeth.

A Day with No Crayons. **Illustrated by Chad Cameron. Flagstaff, AZ: Rising Moon, 2007. Unpaged. ISBN 9780873589109.** PreS-2

Liza loves drawing with her crayons, and when she runs out of paper, she draws on the walls. This does not please her mother, so she takes her crayons away. Undaunted, Liza discovers all the colors in nature and proceeds to create her art outdoors.

Weitzman, Jacqueline Preiss.

You Can't Take a Balloon into the Metropolitan Museum. See under "Wordless" in chapter 15.

Wiesner, David.

Art and Max. **New York: Clarion, 2010. Unpaged. ISBN 9780618756636.** `PreS-3`

Wiesner, who has won the Caldecott Medal three times, presents a story of art and friendship that will whisk readers away into the creative world of the artist. Max and Art are friends who both love to paint. Though Art has a great deal of experience, Max is only just beginning to learn. When Max first wields a paintbrush, the two friends are swept away into an adventurous exploration of various media, and it's Max's courage that brings their journey to a successful conclusion.

Wing, Natasha.

Go to Bed, Monster. See under "Fanciful Bedtime Stories" in chapter 15.

Dance

Ackerman, Karen.

🏆*Song and Dance Man.* **Illustrated by Stephen Gammell. New York: Random House, 1988. 30pp. ISBN 9780394893303.** `PreS-2`

Grandpa demonstrates his moves as a vaudeville song-and-dance man for his visiting grandchildren. Gammell's colored pencil line drawings bring the story to brilliant life. (ALAN; Caldecott Medal)

Allen, Debby.

Dancing in the Wings. **Illustrated by Kadir Nelson. New York: Dial, 2000. Unpaged. ISBN 9780803725010.** `Gr. K-2`

Sassy, an African American girl, loves ballet, even though she is taller than everyone in her class and has big feet. Some of the girls tease her, but Sassy is dedicated to her dream and is chosen to perform in a summer dance program.

Bradley, Kimberly Brubaker.

Ballerino Nate. **Illustrated by R. W. Alley. New York: Dial, 2006. 32pp. ISBN 9780803729544.** `PreS-2`

Nate, a first grader, wants to be a ballet dancer, but has second thoughts when his brother teases him, and his class is full of girls. When his mother takes him to a professional production, he sees that men can be dancers, too. Meeting one of them afterward convinces him to pursue his dream to become a ballerino.

Brisson, Pat.

Tap-Dance Fever. **Illustrated by Nancy Cote. Honesdale, PA: Boyds Mills, 2005. 32pp. ISBN 9781590782903.** `Gr. K-2`

Annabelle Applegate tap dances everywhere in town, until the townspeople get fed up with it. One day she comes across a passel of rattlesnakes. She dances them to the fairgrounds, and they dance along with her. On stage, they become famous and draw tourists to town, which helps win appreciation for Annabelle's talent.

DePalma, Mary Newell.

The Nutcracker Doll. **New York: Arthur A. Levine, 2007. Unpaged. ISBN 9780439802420.** `Gr. K-2`

After Kepley sees a production of the *Nutcracker* ballet for the first time, she becomes determined to be in the show the next year. She works hard and tries out. Even though she is cast as the doll, a nondancing part, she goes to all the rehearsals and relishes being in her first production.

Dillon, Leo, and Diane Dillon.

🐾*Rap a Tap Tap: Here's Bojangles—Think of That.* **New York: Blue Sky Press, 2002. Unpaged. ISBN 9780590478830.** `PreS-2`

In rhyming text, the Dillons pay tribute to African American tap dancer Bill "Bojangles" Robinson (1878–1949). They present the man who danced all over the city, creating art with his feet. The lively tale is accompanied by gouache paintings that are inspired by Harlem Renaissance artist Aaron Douglas. (ALAN, Coretta Scott King Honor)

French, Jackie.

Josephine Wants to Dance. **Illustrated by Bruce Whatley. New York: Abrams, 2007. 28pp. ISBN 9780810994317.** `PreS-1`

Josephine, the kangaroo who loves to dance, dreams of being a ballerina. Even when other kangaroos are doubtful, Josephine persists in practicing, and when the prima ballerina is injured, Josephine saves the show.

Geras, Adele.

Time for Ballet. **Illustrated by Shelagh McNicholas. New York: Dial, 2004. Unpaged. ISBN 9780803729780.** `PreS-2`

Tilly loves Tuesdays because she gets to go to ballet class. She describes the moves she learns as well as her role as a cat in the school recital.

Little Ballet Star. **Illustrated by Shelagh McNicholas. New York: Dial, 2008. Unpaged. ISBN 9780803732377. Sequel.** `PreS-2`

Tilly has the night of her life when she and her mother attend a performance of *Sleeping Beauty.* Her aunt is the prima ballerina, and at the end of the show she calls Tilly up to the stage for a twirl of her own.

Holabird, Katharine.

The Angelina Ballerina Series. Illustrated by Helen Craig. New York: Viking. `PreS-2`

Angelina, a mouse who adores ballet, begins her adventurous life by becoming a prima ballerina. The first book was published in 1982. The series has gone through various editions and has been the basis for a TV series. Listed here by original release date, but with the most recent publication information.

Angelina Ballerina. 2008. 25th anniversary edition. Unpaged. ISBN 9780670011179.

Angelina and the Princess. 2006. Unpaged. ISBN 9780670060856.

Angelina's Christmas. 2006. Unpaged. ISBN 9780670061037.

Angelina at the Fair. 2007. 32pp. ISBN 9780670062348.

Angelina on Stage. 2006. 32pp. ISBN 9780670060580.

Angelina and Alice. 2006. 24pp. ISBN 9780670061259.

Angelina's Birthday Surprise. 1989. 25pp. ISBN 9780517573259 (o.p.).

Angelina's Baby Sister. 2006. 32pp. ISBN 9780670061464.

Angelina Ice Skates. 2007. 24pp. ISBN 9780670062379.

Angelina's Halloween. 2006. 32pp. ISBN 9780142406212 (pb).

Angelina's Birthday. 2006. 24pp. ISBN 9780670060573.

Angelina and Henry. 2006. Unpaged. ISBN 9780142405901 (pb).

Angelina Star of the Show. 2008. 32pp. ISBN 9780670011087.

Angelina at the Palace. 2005. 32pp. ISBN 9780670060481.

Howe, James.

Brontorina. Illustrated by Randy Cecil. Somerville, MA: Candlewick, 2010. 32pp. ISBN 9780763644376. `Gr. K–3`

Although she is very large, this dinosaur is determined to make her dream of becoming a ballerina come true.

Isadora, Rachel.

On Your Toes: A Ballet ABC. New York: Greenwillow, 2003. Unpaged. ISBN 9780060502386. `Gr. K–2`

Lovely, richly hued pastels illustrate this alphabetical tour through ballet terms.

Lord, Michelle.

Little Sap and Monsieur Rodin. See under "Around the World: Asia" in chapter 13.

Roberts, Brenda C.

🏵*Jazzy Miz Mozetta.* **Illustrated by Frank Morrison. New York: Farrar, Straus & Giroux, 2004. 32pp. ISBN 9780374336745.** `Gr. K–3`

Miz Mozetta, a gray-haired African American woman, feels like dancing. She dons a snazzy red dress and goes in search of a dance partner, but no one will join her. She returns home, discouraged, but her friends have reconsidered and show up to jitterbug with her. The bouncy rhythm of the text is matched by the dynamic illustrations. (John Steptoe Award)

Wilson, Karma.

Hilda Must Be Dancing. **Illustrated by Suzanne Watts. New York: Margaret K. McElderry Books, 2004. Unpaged. ISBN 9780689847882.** `PreS–2`

Hilda the hippopotamus dances through the jungle, to the dismay of her neighbors, who think she is loud and clumsy. She tries quieter pastimes, but she just can't resist dancing. When she discovers water ballet, both she and her fellow creatures are happy at last. This rhyming tale is illustrated with bright cartoon pictures.

Young, Amy.

The Belinda Series. **New York: Viking.** `PreS–3`

Belinda is a young woman who simply wants to dance, but her overly large feet make things challenging.

Belinda the Ballerina. 2003. 32pp. ISBN 9780670035496.

When the dance judges ban Belinda from the ballet competition because of her big feet, she takes a job as a waitress. A band passes by, and Belinda can't help but dance. A crowd gathers and delights in her performance. Observing her dance, the maestro hires her on the spot, making her the star she's always longed to be.

Belinda in Paris. New York: Viking, 2005. 32pp. ISBN 9780670036936.

Belinda travels to Paris to perform, but her ballet shoes go astray, and she must find a way to cover her overly large feet by curtain time or the show will not go on.

Belinda and the Glass Slipper. 2006. 32pp. ISBN 9780670060825.

Belinda and a nasty girl named Lola both compete for the role of Cinderella in a professional ballet production. Belinda wins the role, but on opening night Lola locks her in the closet. When the fairy godmother dancer frees her, Belinda must win back her rightful place.

Belinda Begins Ballet. 2008. Unpaged. ISBN 9780670062447.

A young Belinda is forced into being a clown for the school talent show, but her true love is dancing, even though she's had big feet since babyhood. On the night of the performance, she follows her heart and wins over the audience when her clown is transformed into a ballet dancer, in this book that shows how Belinda got her start.

Music

Anderson, Peggy Perry.

Chuck's Band. See under "Farms: Talking Farm Animals" in chapter 10.

Busse, Sarah Martin, and Jacqueline Briggs Martin.

Banjo Granny. **Illustrated by Barry Root. Boston: Houghton Mifflin, 2006. 32pp. ISBN 9780618336036.** `PreS–2`

Granny's new grandbaby lives far away. When she hears that the child responds to bluegrass music, she picks up her banjo and sets off for a visit. For every obstacle that arises, she uses music to overcome it and at last arrive at her grandson's.

Calmenson, Stephanie.

Jazzmatazz! **Illustrated by Bruce Degan. New York: HarperCollins, 2008. 28pp. ISBN 9780060772895.** `T–K`

When a mouse escaping the cold dashes across a piano, he begins a musical chain of events that brings out each creature's inner musicality.

Cox, Judy.

✿*My Family Plays Music.* **Illustrated by Elbrite Brown. New York: Holiday House, 2003. Unpaged. ISBN 9780823415915.** `PreS–3`

This African American girl comes from a very musical family. She introduces each family member, the instruments they each play, and the kinds of music they like best. (John Steptoe Award)

Crow, Kristyn.

Cool Daddy Rat. **Illustrated by Mike Lester. New York: Putnam, 2008. 30pp. ISBN 9780399243752.** `Gr. K–2`

Cool Daddy Rat is a bass-playing rodent who has gigs all over New York City. When he discovers his son Ace has stowed away in his case, he takes him around with him, and Ace gets to demonstrate his own aptitude for jazz.

Daly, Niki.

Ruby Sings the Blues. New York: Bloomsbury, 2005. 32pp. ISBN 9781582349954.
Gr. K–3

> Ruby is a small girl with a big voice. Despite her parents' best efforts, Ruby's loudness annoys all those around her. Fortunately, they have neighbors who are jazz musicians, and they teach Ruby how to control her voice and then how to sing. Soon the whole neighborhood is bopping to her jazzy beat.

Ehrhardt, Karen.

This Jazz Man. **Illustrated by Robert Roth. Orlando, FL: Harcourt, 2006. 32pp. ISBN 9780152053079. PreS–2**

> Ehrhardt recasts the "This Old Man" man rhyme into an introduction of nine jazz greats such as Louis Armstrong and Dizzy Gillespie.

Hopkinson, Deborah.

Girl Wonder: A Baseball Story in Nine Innings. See under "American History" in chapter 13.

Isadora, Rachel.

Bring on That Beat. New York: Putnam, 2002. Unpaged. ISBN 9780399232329. **Gr. 1-3**

> Isadora's rhyming text and vivid watercolors introduce readers to the rhythmic sounds of the jazz of 1930s Harlem.

Johnson, Angela.

Violet's Music. **Illustrated by Laura Huliska-Beith. New York: Dial, 2007. Unpaged. ISBN 9780803727403. Gr. K–3**

> Violet is an African American girl who has loved making music since she was a baby. As she grows up, she searches for like-minded souls and finally meets Angel, Randy, and Juan. They form a band, fulfilling each others' dreams.

Krosoczka, Jarrett.

Punk Farm. See under "Farms: Talking Farm Animals" in chapter 10.

Lefrak, Karen.

Jake the Philharmonic Dog. **Illustrated by Marcin Baranski. New York: Walker, 2003. 32pp. ISBN 9780802795526. Gr. 1-3**.

> When Richie, a stagehand for the Philharmonic Orchestra, adopts Jake, he's fortunate that his new dog loves music, since they spend a lot of time at rehearsals together. Jake learns about the various instruments and eventually becomes the Philharmonic mascot.

McGhee, Alison.

The Song of Middle C. Illustrated by Scott Menchin. Somerville, MA: Candlewick, 2009. 30pp. ISBN 9780763630133. **Gr. 1-3**

1

> When a confident, young piano student gets struck with stage fright during her piano recital, she bravely plunges forward, even though the only note she manages is middle C.

McPhail, David.

Mole Music. New York: Holt, 1999. Unpaged. ISBN 9780805028195. **PreS-2**

2

> Mole digs all day and spends lonely nights eating his supper in front of the television. When he hears a violinist one night, he decides that he would like to learn to play as well. He orders an instrument of his own and begins practicing as soon as it arrives. With hard work, he progresses from unbearable to beautiful, and unbeknownst to him, he is creating music that draws creatures and people near and far and bestows upon them moments of tranquility. The effect of Mole's music is deftly conveyed in McPhail's pen-and-ink and watercolor illustrations.

3

Moss, Lloyd.

🏆*Zin! Zin! Zin!: A Violin*. Illustrated by Marjorie Priceman. New York: Simon & Schuster, 1995. ISBN 9780671882396. Unpaged. **Gr. K-3**

4

> Alliterative rhyming couplets present the sound of ten orchestra instruments as musicians gather on stage for a concert. Gouache illustrations in bright hues add whimsy to this celebration of sound. (ALAN, Caldecott Honor)

5

Schotter, Roni.

Doo-Wop Popp. Illustrated by Bryan Collier. New York: Amistad, 2008. 32pp. ISBN 9780060579685. **Gr. 1-3**

> Elijah Earl, an African American boy, is shy, but when the school janitor, Mr. Searles, who used to be a singer, taps him to join with other bashful students after school, things change. Mr. Searles teaches them how to find music in the sounds around them. As they practice for their show, they find friendship as well. Collier's collaged watercolors aptly depict both the students' musical discoveries and the doo-wop bands of the past.

6

Taylor, Debbie A.

7

Sweet Music in Harlem. Illustrated by Frank Morrison. New York: Lee & Low, 2004. Unpaged. ISBN 9781584301653. **Gr. 1-3**

> Inspired by Art Kane's 1958 photograph of fifty-seven celebrated jazz musicians in front of a brownstone in Harlem, Taylor spins a tale of C. J. sent to find his jazz-musician uncle's hat. As he searches, he finds various things his uncle has left behind, and when he returns, he finds the bevy of musicians gathered for the photo. In the evening, his uncle gives him an early

8

birthday present of his own clarinet, and they discover the missing hat nestled in the box.

Weaver, Tess.

Opera Cat. Illustrated by Andrea Wesson. New York: Clarion, 2002. 32pp. ISBN 9780618096350. `PreS–2`

Alma the cat has a mistress who is the star of the opera, and every day when Madame practices, Alma does as well. When Madam gets laryngitis, Alma hides in her mistress's tower of curls and sings exquisitely. Now she attends every show in case her talents are needed again.

Encore, Opera Cat. Illustrated by Andrea Wesson. New York: Clarion, 2009. 31pp. ISBN 9780547146478. Sequel. `PreS–2`

Alma the cat longs to display her vocal prowess on stage, and when her singing breaks one of Madame SoSo's glasses, the cat's mistress realizes it's time to bring her cat to the stage.

Wheeler, Lisa.

Jazz Baby. Illustrated by R. Gregory Christie. Orlando, FL: Harcourt, 2007. 29pp. ISBN 9780152025229. `PreS–1`

An extended family with a love of jazzy music engage a new baby in be-bop and hip-hop until the little one is tuckered out and lulled to sleep.

Theater

Aliki.

A Play's the Thing. New York: HarperCollins, 2005. 32pp. ISBN 9780060743567. `Gr. 1-3`

An enthusiastic Miss Brilliant gets her entire class excited about putting on a play, from writing the script, to making the costumes and scenery, to finally putting on the show for their parents. Even the discontented Jose and the shy Cameron eventually enjoy the activity.

dePaola, Tomie.

Stagestruck. New York: Putnam, 2005. 32pp. ISBN 9780399243387. `PreS–3`

Based on an event from his childhood first recounted in *Here We All Are*, dePaola recounts the episode of his part in the kindergarten's production of *Peter Rabbit*. Young Tommy wants to play Peter in the show, but the teacher casts him as Mopsy. Tommy is disappointed, and on the night of the show makes the most of his role, stealing the limelight. Although he earns lots of laughs, his mother and teacher are disappointed in him, and he has to apologize to the teacher and the boy who played Peter. Nevertheless, he is already anticipating the next time he'll be able to be in a show.

LaChanze.

Little Diva. **Illustrated by Brian Pinkney. New York: Feiwel & Friends, 2010. 32pp. ISBN 9780312370107.** `Gr. K–3`

Nena longs to be a Broadway star like her mother and is ready to work, learning to sing and dance to achieve her dream.

1

Schwartz, Amy.

Starring Miss Darlene. **New Milford, CT: Roaring Brook, 2007. Unpaged. ISBN 9781596432307.** `Gr. K–3`

Darlene the hippo takes acting classes, then wins larger and larger roles in theatrical productions. Although she unintentionally creates havoc, the critics love her, and a star is born.

2

Writing

3

Kirk, Daniel.

Library Mouse. **New York: Abrams, 2007. Unpaged. ISBN 9780810993464.** `Gr. K–3`

Sam the mouse lives in the library, right behind the wall where the children's reference books are shelved. He sleeps during the day and at night loves to read. When he writes his own stories and places them in the collection, the children love them, and the librarian invites him to come for an author day. Instead of appearing, he puts out writing supplies and invites the children to become authors themselves.

4

Library Mouse: A Friend's Tale. **New York: Abrams, 2009. Unpaged. ISBN 9780810989276. Sequel.** `Gr. K–3`

Sam the mouse befriends Tom, a member of the Writers and Illustrators Club, and the two begin collaborating on their literary creations. Tom writes the stories, and Sam draws the pictures.

5

McNaughton, Colin.

Once upon an Ordinary School Day. **Illustrated by Satoshi Kitamura. New York: Farrar, Straus & Giroux, 2005. 32pp. ISBN 9780374356347.** `Gr. K–3`

A boy begins an ordinary day, but when he arrives at school, he discovers he has a new teacher, Mr. Gee. Instead of an everyday lesson, he plays music for the class and instructs them to record what the music leads them to imagine. Soon the boy is delighting in the possibilities his words create. The illustrations begin as monochromatic and then burst into color, emphasizing the transition from ordinary to creative.

6

7

8

Spinelli, Eileen.

The Best Story. **Illustrated by Anne Wilsdorf. New York: Dial, 2008. Unpaged. ISBN 9780803730557.** `Gr. 1-3`

> Anne longs to win the writing contest, so she solicits advice from various family members. They each tell her to write a different kind of story. Only when her mother tells her to write from the heart does she finally create a story that satisfies her.

Sports

Berry, Lynne.

The Duck Family Series. **Illustrated by Hiroe Nakata. New York: Holt.** `PreS-K`

> Five duck siblings enjoy a variety of activities together.

> *Duck Skates.* 2005. 32pp. ISBN 9780805072198.
>> When cold grips the forest and snow piles high, five duck siblings don their winter gear and skate, have a snowball fight, and skate some more. They top off their day of winter delight with a warming mug of hot cocoa. The rhyming couplets illustrated with watercolor-and-ink pictures successfully portray the family fun.

> *Duck Dunks.* 2008. 32pp. ISBN 9780805081282.
>> This time the ducks are attired in their swimming gear and are heading off for a day of summer swimming and splashing at the beach.

> *Duck Tents.* 2009. 32pp. ISBN 9780805086966.
>> Five ducks carrying camping equipment, pitch their tent, fish, roast marshmallows, and have to find a way to overcome their fear of the nighttime noises.

Egan, Tim.

Roasted Peanuts. **Boston: Houghton Mifflin, 2006. 32pp. ISBN 9780618337187.** `Gr. K-3`

> Sam the horse and Jackson the cat are best friends who love to watch and play baseball. When they try out for the town team, only Sam makes it. Jackson has a great pitching arm, but he's slow at everything else. Separated, neither one does well until Jackson takes a job selling peanuts in the stands. With his friend there to support him, Sam starts hitting home runs once again.

Holabird, Katharine.

Angelina Ice Skates. See under "Dance" in this chapter.

Hopkinson, Deborah.

Girl Wonder: A Baseball Story in Nine Innings. Illustrated by Terry Widener. New York: Atheneum, 2003. Unpaged. ISBN 9780689833007. Gr. 1-3.

Inspired by the life of Alta Weiss, this fictionalized account details how Alta was the first woman to pitch for an all-male, semipro baseball team, the Vermilion Independents, whom she played for in 1907.

Keller, Holly.

Pearl's New Skates. New York: Greenwillow, 2005. 24pp. ISBN 978-0060562809. Gr. K-2

When Pearl receives a pair of skates for her birthday, she dashes out to the frozen pond to try them out, only to find that she can barely stand up in them, let alone skate. At first she refuses to try again, but with encouragement from Uncle Jack, she perseveres until she can glide across the ice.

Kolar, Bob.

Big Kicks. Cambridge, MA: Candlewick, 2008. 32pp. ISBN 9780763633905. Gr. K-2

Biggie Bear is big but not athletically inclined. He loves jazz and stamp collecting, but when the Mighty Giants, an all-animal soccer team, beg him to join their team, he agrees. They all discover that talent and interest are more important than size.

Lorbiecki, Marybeth.

Jackie's Bat. Illustrated by Brian J. Pinkney. New York: Simon & Schuster, 2008. 32pp. ISBN 9780689841026. Gr. 2 & up

Joey, a fictional batboy for the 1947 Dodgers, describes his year on the team with Jackie Robinson. At first he doesn't know how to treat Jackie, since he is white and Jackie is black. Joey ignores Jackie's requests until he and the team see the kind of player and man Jackie is.

Maloney, Peter.

The Magic Hockey Stick. Illustrated by Felicia Zekauskas. New York, Dial, 1999. Unpaged. ISBN 9780803724761. Gr. 1-3

When a young girl is given Wayne Gretzky's hockey stick, purchased at a charity auction, she becomes her team's top scorer, but Gretzky loses his scoring touch. Determined to save her hero, she returns the stick to him.

Nevius, Carol.

Baseball Hour. Illustrated by Bill Thomson. New York: Marshall Cavendish, 2008. 32pp. ISBN 9780761453802. Gr. K-2

Rhyming text presents a Little League practice session from warm-up through the finish of the game.

Noble, Trinka Hakes.

Jimmy's Boa and the Bungee Jump Slam Dunk. See chapter 14.

O'Malley, Kevin.

Mount Olympus Basketball. New York: Walker, 2003. Unpaged. ISBN 978-0802788443. **Gr. 2 & up**

> In a humorous story that uses paneled art and balloon dialog, two sportscasters provide a play-by-play account of a momentous basketball game between the Greek Gods and a team of mortal heroes.

Rappaport, Doreen, and Lyndall Callan.

Dirt on Their Skirts. Illustrated by E. B. Lewis. New York: Dial, 2000. Unpaged. ISBN 9780803720428. **Gr. 1-3**

> Margaret and her family cheer on the Wisconsin's Racine Belles as they play in the 1946 All-American Girls Professional Baseball League Championship.

Rodriguez, Edel.

Sergio Makes a Splash. New York: Little, Brown, 2008. 40pp. ISBN 978-0316066167. **PreS–2**

> Sergio the penguin loves to play in the water, except when it's the ocean. That's just too deep for him. When his class takes a trip there, he's afraid because he can't swim, but when he plunges in, he discovers just how much fun it is.

Sergio Saves the Game. New York: Little, Brown, 2009. Unpaged. ISBN 978-0316066174. Sequel. **PreS–2**

> Sergio dreams of being a superstar penguin soccer player but in real life is very clumsy on the field. He's always picked last for the team, until he begins playing goalie and with hard work, becomes an asset to the team.

Spradlin, Michael P.

Baseball from A to Z. Illustrated by Macky Pamintuan. New York: HarperCollins, 2010. 32pp. ISBN 9780061240812. **Gr. K-3**

> Action-packed illustrations and a zippy text explain an alphabetically arranged array of baseball terms.

Tavares, Matt.

Mudball. See under "American History" in chapter 13.

Wheeler, Lisa.

Dino-Hockey. Illustrated by Barry Gott. Minneapolis, MN: Carolrhoda, 2007. 32pp. ISBN 9780822561910. **PreS–3**

> Two wild teams of hockey-loving dinosaurs play a bone-jarring game of hockey to determine the winner of the cup. Snappy rhymes relate the moves of the Meat-Eaters vs. the Veggiesaurs.

Dino-Soccer. **Illustrated by Barry Gott. Minneapolis, MN: Carolrhoda, 2009. Unpaged. ISBN 9780822590286. Sequel.** `PreS-3`

New teams of dinosaurs, the Grazers and the Biters, compete in this soccer match. The score swings back and forth until the Biters win the day.

Dino-Baseball. **Illustrated by Barry Gott. Minneapolis, MN: Carolrhoda, 2010. 32pp. ISBN 9780761344292. Sequel.** `PreS-3`

More opposing dinosaurs get into the game, and this time, it's America's favorite pastime: baseball. The plant-eating Green Sox meet up with the meat-eating Rib-Eye Reds.

Easy Readers

Ormerod, Jan.

The Ballet Sisters: The Duckling and the Swan. **New York: Scholastic, 2007. 32pp. ISBN 9780439822817.** `Gr. 1-3`

Two sisters, Bonnie and Sylvie, love to dance together, but sometimes Sylvie gets annoyed with Bonnie thinking she can boss her around because Bonnie goes to ballet classes.

The Ballet Sisters: The Newest Dancer. **New York: Scholastic, 2008. 32pp. ISBN 9780439822824. Sequel.** `Gr. 1-3`

In this outing, Sylvie gets to visit ballet class with big sister Bonnie, and then have her own first ballet class.

Pierce, Terry.

Tae Kwon Do. **Illustrated by Todd Bonita. New York: Random House, 2006. 32pp. ISBN 9780375934483.** `Gr. K-2`

This beginning reader for those just starting out follows a brother and sister through all their moves in their tae kwon do class.

Favorites

Rap a Tap Tap: Here's Bojangles-Think of That by Leo Dillon and Diane Dillon

On Your Toes: A Ballet ABC by Rachel Isadora

Library Mouse by Daniel Kirk

The Magic Hockey Stick by Peter Maloney

Art by Patrick McDonnell

Zin! Zin! Zin! A Violin by Lloyd Moss

Chapter **8**

Transportation: Airplanes, Boats, Buses, Cars, Construction Vehicles, and Trucks

Vehicles of all kinds hold a vast appeal for many children, from the kind they can ride in themselves, like cars, boats, and planes, to the kind that they might like to run when they grow up, like constructions vehicles.

Airplanes

Breen, Steve.

Violet the Pilot. See in chapter 11.

Hubbell, Patricia.

My First Airplane Ride. **Illustrated by Nancy Speir. New York: Marshall Cavendish, 2008. 40pp. ISBN 9780761454366.** `PreS–1`

A boy recounts in rhyme how he and his parents prepare for and take a plane to visit his grandmother.

McCarty, Peter.

Moon Plane. See under "Regular Activities and Experiences of Childhood: Bedtime" in chapter 1.

Sturges, Philemon.

I Love Planes. **Illustrated by Shari Halpern. New York: HarperCollins, 2003. 32pp. ISBN 9780060288983.** `T–K`

A young boy creates a paper airplane and then imagines flying in every airborne device he can think of.

Boats

Crews, Donald.

Sail Away. New York: Greenwillow, 1995. Unpaged. ISBN 9780688110536. **PreS–2**

A family goes sailing on what starts out as a sunny day but turns into a stormy one. All return home safely as the sun sets, in this story that is illustrated with vivid watercolors.

de Seìve, Randall.

Toy Boat. **Illustrated by Loren Long. New York: Philomel, 2007. 40pp. ISBN 9780399243745.** **PreS–1**

When a boy creates a boat from a can, a cork, a pencil, and a scrap of cloth, he delights in sailing it on the lake until the day the string slips out of his hand. Then his boat embarks on his own adventure, encountering a variety of other vessels. It spends a lonely night on the water, wishing to be back with its boy. Finally a friendly breeze blows it back to shore. Lush acrylic illustrations filled with aquatic hues bring brilliance to the tale.

Gramatky, Hardie.

Little Toot. New York: Putnam, 2007. 86pp. ISBN 9780399247132. **PreS–3**

This reissue of the 1939 classic story of the brave tugboat who ventures out into the ocean to bring in his ship features newly restored illustrations and previously unpublished sketches.

Hubbell, Patricia.

Boats: Speeding! Sailing! Cruising! **Illustrated by Megan Halsey and Sean Addy.** New York: Marshall Cavendish, 2009. 32pp. ISBN 9780761455240. **PreS–1**

Lively rhymes describe all manner of water vehicles, from tugboats to ocean liners.

Lewis, Kevin.

Tugga Tugga Tug Boat. **Illustrated by Daniel Kirk. New York: Hyperion, 2006.** 32pp. ISBN 9780786856152. **T–K**

Exuberant rhymes bring the activities of a spunky little tugboat to life as it guides big ships safely into harbor. By the end of the story, the illustrations reveal that the tugboat carries out its missions in the bathtub.

Lund, Deb.

Dinosailors. See under "Dinosaurs" in chapter 10.

McMullan, Kate, and Jim McMullan.

I'm Mighty! New York: Joanna Cotler Books, 2002. Unpaged. ISBN 978-0060092900. **PreS-2**

> A supremely confident tugboat with a brash personality tells readers how he uses a variety of methods to steer ships of all sizes to safety because he is mighty.

Parker, Neal Evans.

Captain Annabel. Illustrated by Emily Harris Camden, ME: Down East Books, 2004. 32pp. ISBN 9780892726530. **PreS-3**

> Annabel began her seafaring career as a little girl who built a sailboat with her father. She travels the world on various vessels and returns home as captain of her own tugboat.

Soto, Gary.

Chato Goes Cruisin'. See under "Talking Animals" in chapter 10.

Winter, Jonah.

Here Comes the Garbage Barge! Illustrated by Red Nose Studio. New York: Schwartz & Wade, 2010. 40pp. ISBN 9780375852183. **Gr. K–3**

> This is a fictionalized version of the 1987 garbage barge from Long Island, New York, that traveled the world looking for a place to dump its garbage. No one would take it, and it ended up right back in New York.

Buses

Bloom, Suzanne.

The Bus for Us. Honesdale, PA: Boyds Mills Press, 2001. Unpaged. ISBN 9781563979323. **PreS-1** (SP)

> Tess is unsure which is her school bus, so each time any kind of vehicle comes by, she asks an older child, Gus, "Is this the bus for us?" Gus eventually grows impatient, so it's good that their school bus finally arrives.

Pulver, Robin.

Axle Annie. Illustrated by Tedd Arnold. New York: Dial, 1999. Unpaged. ISBN 9780803720961. **PreS-3**

> Axle Annie is a fun-loving school bus driver who is so good at her job that she always gets the kids to school, even in the worst wintry weather, until Shifty Rhodes, who hates driving a school bus and longs for a snow day, plots against her.

Axle Annie and the Speed Grumpp. **Illustrated by Tedd Arnold. New York: Dial, 2005. 32pp. ISBN 9780803727878. Sequel. `PreS–3`**

> The expert bus driver Annie returns, and this time she must keep her kids safe from the speed demons on the road, especially the notorious Rush Hotfoot.

Singer, Marilyn.

I'm Your Bus. **Illustrated by Evan Polenghi. New York: Scholastic, 2009. 30pp. ISBN 9780545089180. `PreS–2`**

> A cheerful school bus picks up its new students and describes in rhyme the morning and afternoon routine.

Cars

Aroner, Miriam.

Clink, Clank, Clunk. **Illustrated by Dominic Catalano. Honesdale, PA: Boyds Mills, 2006. 32pp. ISBN 9781590782705. `PreS–1`**

> Rabbit's purple convertible is the personification of clunker, but he decides to drive to town nonetheless. Along the way, he picks up a succession of animal friends. They almost make it, but in the end the passengers have to get out and push. Rabbit trades the vehicle in for a shiny new red car and gives his helpful companions a lift home.

Barton, Byron.

🏵*My Car.* **New York: Greenwillow, 2001. Unpaged. ISBN 9780060296247. `T–K`**

> Sam shows listeners how he takes care of his bright red car by cleaning it, getting gas, and driving carefully. Simple pictures with bold colors ably illustrate the text. (ALAN)

Bell, Babs.

Sputter, Sputter, Sput! **Illustrated by Bob Staake. New York: HarperCollins, 2008. 32pp. ISBN 9780060562229. `T–K`**

> This simple yet gleeful rhyming text follows a young driver as he zooms around the countryside until he runs out of gas. Illustrated with computer-created geometric graphics.

Drummond, Alan.

Tin Lizzie. **New York: Farrar, Straus & Giroux, 2008. Unpaged. ISBN 978-0374320003. `Gr. K–3`**

> Eliza has grown up with her grandpa, restoring his precious Tin Lizzie. When the car is finally ready, they go for a ride. Though they have fun, they realize all the problems automobiles have caused, from traffic to pollution, and begin to discuss possible solutions.

Hubbell, Patricia.

Cars: Rushing! Honking! Zooming! **Illustrated by Megan Halsey and Sean Addy. New York: Marshall Cavendish, 2006. 32pp. ISBN 9780761452966.** `PreS-1`

> Utilizing zippy rhymes, Hubbell reviews a variety of vehicles and their movement, from race cars to limousines.

1

Lord, Cynthia.

Hot Rod Hamster! **Illustrated by Derek Anderson. New York: Scholastic, 2010. 40pp. ISBN 9780545035309.** `PreS-2`

> This rhyming romp chronicles the exploits of a hamster who builds a race car in a junkyard so that he can enter the hot rod race.

2

Rex, Michael.

My Race Car. **New York: Holt, 2000. Unpaged. ISBN 9780805061017.** `Gr. K-2`

> As a child daydreams about being a race car driver, he describes what it's like to participate in a stock car race.

3

Steggall, Susan.

The Life of a Car. **New York: Holt, 2008. 24pp. ISBN 9780805087475.** `T-K`

> With a simple text and richly colored collage illustrations, Steggall takes his audience on a tour of the phases of a car's existence, from manufacturing to recycling.

4

Zane, Alexander.

The Wheels on the Race Car. **Illustrated by James Warhola. New York: Orchard, 2005. 32pp. ISBN 9780439590808.** `PreS-2`

> In this race car version of the song "The Wheels on the Bus," a variety of animals race their cars around the track.

5

6

Construction Vehicles

Barton, Byron.

Machines at Work. **New York: Crowell, 1987. 32pp. ISBN 9780694001903.** `T-K`

> Employing his signature style with boldly colored yet simple illustrations, Barton presents a typical day at a construction site, featuring a variety of big machines.

7

8

Hines, Anna Grossnickle.

I Am a Backhoe. Berkeley, CA: Tricycle Press, 2010. 40pp. ISBN 9781582463063. **T-K**
A creative young boy pretends he is a succession of construction vehicles, beginning with a backhoe. When Dad comes home, he joins his son's imaginative play.

Lund, Deb.

Monsters on Machines. **Illustrated by Robert Neubecker. Orlando, FL: Harcourt, 2008. 31pp. ISBN 9780152053659.** **PreS-1**
A quartet of wild things climb aboard their assigned vehicles and set to work until Mom arrives with lunch. They take a nap and then resume their construction activity.

McMullan, Kate, and Jim McMullan.

I'm Dirty! **New York: Joanna Cotler Books, 2006. 40pp. ISBN 9780060092931.** **PreS-2**
A backhoe, who relishes his job, enjoys clearing out the junk in an abandoned lot while counting down from 10 to 1 and getting dirty at the same time.

Nakagawa, Chihiro.

Who Made This Cake? **Illustrated by Junji Koyose. Asheville, NC: Front Street, 2008. 32pp. ISBN 9781590785959.** **PreS-2**
A crew of miniature workers create a birthday cake using a variety of construction vehicles to accomplish their task.

Nevius, Carol.

Building with Dad. **Illustrated by Bill Thomson. New York: Marshall Cavendish, 2006. Unpaged. ISBN 9780761453123.** **PreS-2**
Rhyming text relates the experiences of a construction-worker father who brings his son to the job site where a new school is being built. Big machines are used throughout, for breaking of the ground and cement pouring, among other things. At the completion of the project, the son decides he wants to have a job just like his dad's. The detailed and realistic paintings make this title stand out.

Trains

Bee, William.

And the Train Goes . . . Cambridge, MA: Candlewick, 2007. 32pp. ISBN 978-0763632489. **T-K**
In a British train station, an assortment of characters gather and take their places in different cars on the train, which eventually goes clickety-clack down the tracks.

Brown, Margaret Wise.

Two Little Trains. **Illustrated by Leo Dillon and Diane Dillon. New York: HarperCollins, 2001. Unpaged. ISBN 9780060283766.** `PreS-K`

> The Dillons have created new illustrations for a poem first published in 1949. One sleek, silver train travels west, and another, a toy, shadows its journey while remaining at home.

Crews, Donald.

Freight Train. See under "Colors" in chapter 4.

Hubbell, Patricia.

Trains: Steaming! Pulling! Huffing! **Illustrated by Megan Halsey and Sean** Addy. New York: Marshall Cavendish, 2005. 32pp. ISBN 9780761451945. `PreS-1`

> Energetic rhymes introduce an array of trains, from old-fashioned steam engines to modern electric trains.

Lewis, Kevin.

Chugga-Chugga Choo-Choo. **Illustrated by Daniel Kirk. New York: Hyperion, 1999. Unpaged. ISBN 9780786804290.** `PreS-1`

> While a young boy sleeps, his toy train and engineer come to life and chug around the tracks, moving their freight from one place to the next.

London, Jonathan.

A Train Goes Clickety-Clack. **Illustrated by Denis Roche. New York: Holt, 2007. 28pp. ISBN 9780805079722.** `PreS-K`

> Lively rhymes describe a variety of trains, from speedy giants to chugging freight trains.

Lund, Deb.

All Aboard the Dinotrain. See under "Dinosaurs" in chapter 10.

Newman, Patricia.

Jingle the Brass. **Illustrated by Michael Chesworth. New York: Melanie Kroupa Books, 2004. 32pp. ISBN 9780374336790.** `Gr. K-3`

> In 1926 an elderly engineer takes a young boy on a tour of his coal-powered train.

Rex, Michael.

My Freight Train. **New York: Holt, 2002. 32pp. ISBN 9780805066821.** `PreS-1`

> As a boy imagines that he is an engineer, he relays everything he knows about trains.

Sturges, Philemon.

I Love Trains. **Illustrated by Shari Halpern. New York: HarperCollins, 2001. Unpaged. ISBN 9780060289003.** `T-K`
> As a train passes by his window, a boy who displays his love for trains, from his overalls to his engineer's cap, describes in rhyme the different kinds of cars and what they carry.

Suen, Anastasia.

Subway. **Illustrated by Karen Katz. New York: Viking, 2004. Unpaged. ISBN 9780670036226.** `PreS-1`
> An African American girl and her mother go for a ride on the subway. They push through the turnstiles, head down for the platform, board the train, transfer, and happily arrive at their destination.

Van Allsburg, Chris.

The Polar Express. See under "Christmas" in chapter 6.

Watty, Piper.

The Little Engine That Could. See under "Toy Fantasy" in chapter 15.

Wickberg, Susan.

Hey, Mr. Choo-choo, Where Are You Going? **Illustrated by Yumi Heo. New York: Putnam, 2008. 32pp. ISBN 9780399239939.** `PreS-K`
> Incorporating the beat of a traveling train into her rhyme, Wickberg's train answers its passengers' curious questions.

Trucks

Hamilton, Kersten.

Red Truck. **Illustrated by Valeria Petrone. New York: Viking, 2008. 32pp. ISBN 9780670062751.** `PreS-2`
> On a rain-sodden day, a school bus full of children gets stuck in the muck, and a red tow truck, with a determined driver, arrives to rescue them.

Hubbell, Patricia.

Trucks: Whizz! Zoom! Rumble! **Illustrated by Megan Halsey. New York: Marshall Cavendish, 2003. Unpaged. ISBN 9780761451242.** `PreS-1`
> Revved up rhymes present a plethora of trucks.

Lewis, Kevin.

My Truck Is Stuck. Illustrated by Daniel Kirk. New York: Hyperion, 2002. 40pp. ISBN 9780786805341. **T-K**

> Two dogs are hauling a load of bones in their dump truck when they get stuck. Although many try to help them out, nothing works until a tow truck frees them from their predicament.

London, Jonathan.

A Truck Goes Rattley-Bumpa. Illustrated by Denis Roche. New York: Holt, 2005. 32pp. ISBN 9780805072334. **PreS-K**

> As his family's new house is being built, an observant boy notes all the different trucks involved in the process.

Lyon, George Ella.

Trucks Roll. Illustrated by Craig Frazier. New York: Atheneum, 2007. 40pp. ISBN 9781416924357. **PreS-1**

> Enthusiastic verse and vivid paintings present different kinds of trucks and their cargo, both realistic and imaginary.

McMullan, Kate, and Jim McMullan.

I Stink! New York: Joanna Cotler Books, 2002. Unpaged. ISBN 978-0060298487. **PreS-2**

> A gleeful garbage truck describes his job collecting trash, reveling in his task.

Moore, Patrick.

The Mighty Street Sweeper. New York: Holt, 2006. 32pp. ISBN 978-0805077896. **PreS-1**

> The street sweeper gets compared to a variety of other vehicles and shines as the mightiest, since nothing else keeps the streets clean.

Scieszka, Jon.

The Trucktown Series. Illustrated by David Shannon, Loren Long, and David Gordon. New York: Simon & Schuster. **PreS-1**

> Scieszka, the ambassador of children's literature, has partnered with these three prominent illustrators to collaboratively create the world of Trucktown, where all kinds of trucks have a life of their own. The world of personified vehicles has also spawned a series of easy readers.

Smash! Crash! 2008. 42pp. ISBN 9781416941330. **PreS-1**

> Jack Truck and Dump Truck Dan are in the mood to smash and crash, so they invite their friends to join them. When everyone else is busy, they help their friends with their tasks. In the end, Wrecking Crane Rosie needs their help as well, and this time it's just what they love

most: she needs them to smash and crash. Every child who loves to smash and crash will relish the refrain.

Melvin Might? 2008. Unpaged. ISBN 9781416941347.

Cement Mixer Melvin worries so much that his fear stops him from doing almost everything until his friend, the ambulance Rescue Rita, is in danger and only he can save her.

Truckery Rhymes. 2009. 57pp. ISBN 9781416941354.

Scieszka and his team have refashioned a selection of nursery rhymes to fit in Trucktown.

Wellington, Monica.

Truck Driver Tom. New York: Dutton, 2007. Unpaged. ISBN 9780525478317. PreS–1

In the morning, Tom fills his truck with fresh produce, and with his canine companion, he drives from the country to the city to deliver the fruit and vegetables.

Easy Readers

Scieszka, Jon.

The Trucktown Easy Readers. Illustrated by David Shannon, Loren Long, and David Gordon. New York: Simon & Schuster. Gr. K–2

The personified truck characters introduced in *Smash! Crash!* continue their adventures in books for beginning readers.

Pete's Party. 2008. Unpaged. ISBN 9781416941491 (lb).

Zoom! Boom! Bully! 2008. Unpaged. ISBN 9781416941507 (lb).

Snow Trucking. 2008. Unpaged. ISBN 9781416941514 (lb).

Uh-Oh, Max. 2009. Unpaged. ISBN 9781416941521 (lb).

The Spooky Tire. 2009. Unpaged. ISBN 9781416941538 (lb).

Kat's Mystery Gift. 2009. Unpaged. ISBN 9781416941545 (lb).

Trucksgiving. 2010. Unpaged. ISBN 9781416941576 (lb).

Favorites

Machines at Work by Byron Barton

Sail Away by Donald Crews

Hot Rod Hamster! by Cynthia Lord

I Stink! by Kate and Jim McMullan

Smash! Crash! by Jon Scieszka

Chapter 9

The Natural World: Seasons, Nature, Gardens, and Weather

Whether they live in the city, the suburbs, or the country, nature plays a major role in the lives of children. Here are books about both the full cycle of the seasons and individual seasons, about gardens, and about weather.

Seasons

Most of the books in which the season of the year is central to the story include the changes in nature as well as typical seasonal activities for children. Here the books are listed by season unless there are sets of all four seasons by one author or the book goes through multiple seasons. Those are listed under "Seasons in General."

Fall

dePaola, Tomie.

Four Friends in Autumn. New York: Simon & Schuster, 2004. Unpaged. ISBN 9780689859809. `PreS–2`

This story from the collection *Four Stories for Four Seasons*, originally released in 1980, features Mrs. Pig, who invites her friends over for dinner. She suggests they enjoy the fall while she puts the finishing touches on the meal. Unfortunately she ends up finishing the meal instead. Her friends are true friends, and they all go to a restaurant instead.

Ehlert, Lois.

Red Leaf, Yellow Leaf. San Diego: Harcourt, 1991. Unpaged. ISBN 978-0152661977. `PreS–3`

Striking illustrations that combine collage and water-colored paper beautifully illuminate the simple narrative of a child watching a sugar maple tree grow and change through the seasons and the year. (Boston Globe Honor)

🐾*Leaf Man.* Orlando, FL: Harcourt, 2005. 40pp. ISBN 9780152053048. `PreS–3`

Dazzling illustrations created from color photocopies of leaves work with die-cut pages to reveal the wind-whisked wonderings of Leaf Man. (ALAN, Boston Globe Honor)

Fleming, Denise.

Time to Sleep. New York: Holt, 1997. Unpaged. ISBN 9780805037623. `PreS–1`

Leaves go golden, frost tips the grass, and Bear knows his time to sleep is coming. He gives the message to his fellow forest dwellers and hunkers down to hibernate. Illustrated with Fleming's signature pulp painting style that produces textured pictures rich in autumnal colors.

Glaser, Linda.

It's Fall. See under "Seasons in General" in this chapter.

Raczka, Bob.

Who Loves the Fall? See under "Seasons in General" in this chapter.

Rawlinson, Julia.

*Fletcher and the Falling Leaves. Illustrated by Tiphanie Beeke. New York: Greenwillow, 2006. 24pp. ISBN 9780061134012. `PreS–2`

Fletcher, a young fox, grows concerned about his favorite tree when it starts losing its leaves. Even though his mother explains it's only the changing seasons, Fletcher does everything he can to catch the leaves and reattach them, to no avail. The day after the last leaf descends, Fletcher witnesses the tree's wintry transformation and feels satisfied. Glowing illustrations that deftly display the season's changing light accompany the lyrical text.

Rockwell, Anne.

Apples and Pumpkins. Illustrated by Lizzy Rockwell. New York: Simon & Schuster, 1989. 24pp. ISBN 9780027772708. `T–K`

In a fun-filled celebration of fall, a family takes a trip to a farm to pick apples and pumpkins.

Rylant, Cynthia.

In November. Illustrated by Jill Kastner. San Diego: Harcourt, 2000. Unpaged. ISBN 9780152010768. `PreS–2`

In this ode to autumn, Rylant's poetic text describes the preparations for winter, from the changes in the landscape to the activities of the animals, and finishes with the comings and goings of people, who are celebrating Thanksgiving.

Schnur, Steven.

Autumn: An Alphabet Acrostic. See under "Alphabet" in chapter 4.

Shannon, George.

Rabbit's Gift. Illustrated by Laura Dronzek. Orlando, FL: Harcourt, 2007. 26pp. ISBN 9780152060732. **T-K**

> As he gets ready for the coming of winter, Rabbit finds an extra turnip. Knowing that the one turnip he already has is enough for him, he rolls the root to Donkey. Donkey in turn gives it away as well, until it is unwittingly returned to Rabbit, who then invites all his friends to join him in a feast.

Spinelli, Eileen.

I Know It's Autumn. Illustrated by Nancy Hayashi. New York: HarperCollins, 2004. Unpaged. ISBN 9780060294229. **PreS-1**

> With a gentle rhyming text, a young girl lists the signs of fall, from collecting acorns to watching geese fly south and taking hay rides.

Tafuri, Nancy.

The Busy Little Squirrel. New York: Simon & Schuster, 2007. 28pp. ISBN 9780689873416. **T-K**

> As autumn leaves drift down, Squirrel is busy getting ready for winter by gathering berries and acorns. Although Mouse, Cat, and Frog all want him to pause to play, Squirrel cannot be distracted from his task, which he completes just as the first snow begins to fall.

Thompson, Lauren.

Mouse's First Fall. See under "Seasons in General" in this chapter.

Winter

Ehlert, Lois.

Snowballs. San Diego: Harcourt, 1995. Unpaged. ISBN 9780152000745. **PreS-3**
> With dynamic collage illustrations, Ehlert depicts the creation of an entire snow family including the dog, all decorated with unique items in this celebration of winter.

Fleming, Denise.

The First Day of Winter. New York: Holt, 2005. 32pp. ISBN 9780805073843. **PreS-1**
> Following the pattern of "The Twelve Days of Christmas," an African American boy divulges how he uses all his winter gifts to create a snowman.

Ford, Bernette.

First Snow. Illustrated by Sebastien Braun. New York: Holiday House, 2005. 32pp. ISBN 9780823419371. **PreS–2**
 A family of bunnies explore a world of winter white for the first time.

George, Kristine O'Connell.

One Mitten. Illustrated by Maggie Smith. New York: Clarion, 2004. 31pp. ISBN 9780618117567. **T–K**
 In winter, a girl loses a mitten and finds many things to do with the solo accessory.

Glaser, Linda.

It's Winter. See under "Seasons in General" in this chapter.

Hayes, Karel.

The Winter Visitors. Camden, Me.: Down East Books, 2007. 30pp. ISBN 978-0892727506. **PreS–3**
 As summer wanes, a family tidies up their lakeside home, packs the car, and zooms out of sight. As soon as they disappear, a family of bears moves in and cavorts through the first part of winter. After hibernating, the bears prepare the home for the human visitors.

Hubbell, Patricia.

Snow Happy. Illustrated by Hiroe Nakata. Berkeley, CA: Tricycle Press, 2010. 32pp. ISBN 9781582463292. **PreS–1**
 Several youngsters delight in all the activities a plentiful snowfall provides.

Johnson, David.

Snow Sounds: An Onomatopoeic Story. Boston: Houghton Mifflin, 2006. 32pp. ISBN 9780618473106. **PreS–2**
 In a story told in the sounds of snow, plows, and shovels, a young boy wakes up the day before Christmas vacation to a world washed in snow. After helping shovel, he boards the school bus for one last day of school. Ink-and-watercolor illustrations create shimmering snowscapes that are as evocative as the whooshing text.

Landry, Leo.

The Snow Ghosts. Boston: Houghton Mifflin, 2003. Unpaged. ISBN 978-0618196555. **T–K**
 In the far frozen north lives a fun-loving group of ghosts who have snowman-building contests, conduct ice-floe races, and delight in dancing in the moonlight.

Lewis, J. Patrick.

The Snowflake Sisters. Illustrated by Lisa Desimini. New York: Atheneum, 2003. Unpaged. ISBN 9780689850295. `Gr. K–2`
> In smoothly flowing verse, Lewis tells of snowflake sisters Crystal and Ivory, who hitch a ride on Santa's sleigh, watch the ball drop in Times Square on New Year's Eve, and then swirl down into Central Park.

Raczka, Bob.

Snowy, Blowy Winter. See under "Seasons in General" in this chapter.

Rose, Deborah Lee.

The Twelve Days of Winter. See under "Counting" in chapter 4.

Schnur, Steven.

Winter: An Alphabet Acrostic. See under "Alphabet" in chapter 4.

Spinelli, Eileen.

Now It Is Winter. Illustrated by Mary Newell Depalma. Grand Rapids, MI: Eerdmans, 2004. 32pp. ISBN 9780802852441. `PreS–1`
> In the heart of winter, while his brothers and sisters enjoy playing in the snow, a young mouse pesters his mother with worries about the return of spring.

Stringer, Lauren.

Winter Is the Warmest Season. Orlando, FL: Harcourt, 2006. 40pp. ISBN 9780152049676. `PreS–3`
> A child explains that winter is the warmest season because it is filled with puffy jackets, hot soup, and crackling fire in the fireplace. Luminous acrylics on watercolor paper heat up with the story.

Thomas, Patricia.

Red Sled. Illustrated by Chris Demarest. Honesdale, PA: Boyds Mills Press, 2008. 32pp. ISBN 9781590785591. `PreS–1`
> Rhyming pairs of words describe a father and son's night of sledding.

Thompson, Lauren.

Mouse's First Snow. See under "Seasons in General" in this chapter.

Yolen, Jane, and Heidi E. Y. Stemple.

Sleep, Black Bear, Sleep. Illustrated by Brooke Dyer. New York: HarperCollins, 2007. 32pp. ISBN 9780060815608. `PreS-1`

The soothing rhyming text describes twelve hibernating animals and concludes by informing the reader it's time for sleep.

Ziefert, Harriet.

Snow Party. Illustrated by Mark Jones. Maplewood, NJ: Blue Apple Books, 2008. 40pp. ISBN 9781934706282. `PreS-2`

When the first snow of winter falls on the winter solstice, snowmen and snowwomen come to life to celebrate.

Spring

Carr, Jan.

Splish, Splash Spring. Illustrated by Dorothy Donohue. New York: Holiday House, 2001. Unpaged. ISBN 9780823415786. `T-K`

The three friends are back, with their puppy. This time they slip outside during a spring shower to enjoy the wonders of the season.

Gershator, Phillis, and Mim Green.

Who's Awake in Springtime? Illustrated by Emilie Chollat. New York: Holt, 2010. 32pp. ISBN 9780805063905. `PreS-1`

In this rhymed, cumulative tale, baby animals frolic while their parents sleep soundly.

Glaser, Linda.

It's Spring. See under "Seasons in General" in this chapter.

Gomi, Taro.

Spring Is Here/Llego La Primavera. San Francisco: Chronicle, 2006. 40pp. ISBN 9780811847599. `T-K` (Bilingual)

This is a bilingual edition of a book first published in English in 1989. Snows melt, the brown earth is revealed, sprouts of green burst through, and spring has arrived.

Hubbell, Patricia.

Hooray for Spring. Illustrated by Taia Morley. Minnetonka, MN: NorthWord Press, 2005. 32pp. ISBN 9781559719131. `PreS-1`

A young boy enthusiastically engages in the activities of spring, from puddle jumping to seed planting.

Peters, Lisa Westberg.

🎗*Cold Little Duck, Duck, Duck.* Illustrated by Sam Williams. New York: Greenwillow, 2000. Unpaged. ISBN 9780688161781. `PreS-1`

> When a little duck arrives at her pond while winter still has the area in its grip, the duck thinks warm thoughts and the balmy of breezes of spring begin to stir. (ALAN)

Raczka, Bob.

Spring Things. See under "Seasons in General" in this chapter.

Rawlinson, Julia.

Fletcher and the Springtime Blossoms. Illustrated by Tiphanie Beeke. New York: Greenwillow, 2009. Unpaged. ISBN 9780061688553. `PreS-2`

> Winter has melted into spring, and Fletcher the fox is enjoying the sights and sounds of the new season as he wanders through the woods. When blossoms fall in the orchard, he believes winter has returned and quickly warns the other animals. Wiser than he, they realize his mistake, but soon all are reveling in the delight of a world bursting with new life. Beeke's light-drenched paintings illuminate the seasonal fun.

Rose, Deborah Lee.

The Twelve Days of Springtime: A School Counting Book. See under "School: School in General" in chapter 2.

Schnur, Steven.

Spring: An Acrostic Alphabet. See under "Alphabet" in chapter 4.

Thompson, Lauren.

Mouse's First Spring. See under "Seasons in General" in this chapter.

Summer

English, Karen.

Hot Day on Abbott Avenue. See under "Weather" in this chapter.

Gershator, Phillis, and David Gershator.

Summer Is Summer. Illustrated by Sophie Blackall. New York: Holt, 2006. 32pp. ISBN 9780805074444. `PreS-2`

> Four friends luxuriate in the summer sun, enjoying the activities of the season.

Glaser, Linda.

It's Summer. See under "Seasons in General" in this chapter.

Hakala, Marjorie Rose.

Mermaid Dance. **Illustrated by Mark Jones. Maplewood, NJ: Blue Apple Books, 2009. 32pp. ISBN 9781934706473.** `PreS–2`
> On the first night of summer a school of mermaids swims to shore to celebrate the summer solstice.

Koller, Jackie French.

Peter Spit a Seed at Sue. **Illustrated by John Manders. New York: Viking, 2008. 32pp. ISBN 9780670063093.** `PreS–3`
> Amusing rhymes recount the escapades of four friends who are bored on a summer's day, and liven things up by pelting each other with watermelon seeds.

Raczka, Bob.

Summer Wonders. See under "Seasons in General" in this chapter.

Schnur, Steven.

Summer: An Alphabet Acrostic. See under "Alphabet" in chapter 4.

Thompson, Lauren.

Mouse's First Summer. See under "Seasons in General" in this chapter.

Seasons in General

Gershator, Phillis.

Listen, Listen! **Illustrated by Alison Jay. Cambridge, MA: Barefoot Books, 2007. 32pp. ISBN 9781846860843.** `PreS–3`
> With a rhyming, onomatopoeic text and detail-filled crackled-paint surface illustrations, this book beautifully evokes the changing seasons.

Glaser, Linda.

Seasons Quartet. Illustrated by Susan Swan. Brookfield CT: Millbrook. `PreS–1`
> With lovely cut-paper artwork and a loosely rhyming text, these books celebrate the seasons.

> *It's Fall.* 2001. 32pp. ISBN 9780761313427 (pb).

> *It's Winter.* 2002. 32pp. ISBN 9780761317593 (lb).

> *It's Spring.* 2002. Unpaged. ISBN 9780761317609 (lb).

> *It's Summer.* 2003. 32pp. ISBN 9780761317579 (lb).

Henkes, Kevin.

🏆 *Old Bear*. New York: Greenwillow, 2008. 32pp. ISBN 9780061552052. **T–K**

Amid red leaves and falling snow, an old bear settles down for his extended winter's nap and dreams of his youth and of the changing seasons. When he wakes, he emerges from his cave to be greeted by the sight of spring flowers sprinkling the landscape. The glorious, richly colored illustrations, meticulous book design, and subtle text combine to create an incredible picture book. (ALAN)

Kleven, Elisa.

The Apple Doll. New York: Farrar, Straus & Giroux, 2007. 29pp. ISBN 9780374303808. **Gr. K–2**

Lizzy enjoys the apple tree in her family's yard all through the year, but especially in the fall when the apples ripen. She makes an apple doll to keep her company in school, but learns that toys are not allowed, so she leaves her home. The doll does not hold up well over time, until Lizzy's mother helps transform her into a dried apple doll.

Krauss, Ruth.

The Growing Story. Illustrated by Helen Oxenbury. New York: HarperCollins, 2007. 32pp. ISBN 9780060247164. **PreS–1**

New illustrations accompany a story first published in 1947. A young boy finds it hard to believe that he is growing, even though he observes pups and chicks growing through the changing seasons.

Raczka, Bob.

Seasons Quartet. Illustrated by Judy Stead. Morton Grove, IL: Albert Whitman. **PreS–2**

A variety of children celebrate each season with traditional activities. Bright and colorful illustrations add to the charm of these titles.

Spring Things. 2007. 28pp. ISBN 9780807575963.

Who Loves the Fall? 2007. 28pp. ISBN 9780807590379.

Snowy, Blowy Winter. 2008. 32pp. ISBN 9780807575260.

Summer Wonders. 2009. 32pp. ISBN 9780807576533.

Rohmann, Eric.

*A Kitten Tale. New York: Knopf, 2008. 32pp. ISBN 9780517709153. **PreS–1**

Four young kittens are experiencing seasons for the first time. They frolic through spring, summer, and fall, but three of them dread the arrival of winter, while the fourth can't wait. When snow finally fills the air with winter white, the fourth kitten is the first to dash out and play. Seeing how much fun he's having, the other three nip out to join him.

Rylant, Cynthia.

Long Night Moon. Illustrated by Mark Siegel. New York: Simon & Schuster, 2004. Unpaged. ISBN 9780689854262. `PreS–1`

> Inspired by the Native American tradition of naming each full moon, Rylant's lyrical poem both names the moon each month and provides evocative images of the season. Siegel's charcoal, pencil, and pastel illustrations almost seem to shimmer with the light of the moon.

Schertle, Alice.

Very Hairy Bear. Illustrated by Matt Phelan. Orlando, FL: Harcourt, 2007. 28pp. ISBN 9780152165680. `PreS–1`

> A large bear with hair everywhere except his nose enjoys sticking his nose in a splashing brook in the spring searching for salmon, in a bee tree in the summer, and in blueberry bushes in the fall. When winter arrives, however, it's time to lumber off to the cave to hibernate, with his nose safe from the cold.

Schnur, Steven.

The Acrostic Alphabet Quartet. See under "Alphabet" in chapter 4.

Schulman, Janet.

A Bunny for All Seasons. Illustrated by Meilo So. New York: Knopf, 2008. Unpaged. ISBN 9780375822568. `PreS–1`

> A brown bunny enjoys the various garden offerings as the seasons change, from sweet strawberries to yellow beans to radishes. She weathers the winter with her new friend, the grey bunny, and in the spring they return to the garden with their three little bunnies.

Stein, David Ezra.

Leaves. New York: Putnam, 2007. 29pp. ISBN 9780399246364. `PreS–2`

> When a young bear watches leaves change colors for the first time, he appreciates their beauty but worries as more and more leaves fall. He gathers them up, filling his cave with them, making a comfortable place for his winter's hibernation. He emerges in the spring and is flooded with relief to see new leaves on the trees.

Thompson, Lauren.

Mouse's First Seasons Quartet. Illustrated by Buket Erdogan. New York: Simon & Shuster. `T–K`

> Mouse experiences seasonal activities for the first time. For Mouse's holiday adventures, see chapter 6.

> *Mouse's First Summer.* 2004. 32pp. ISBN 9780689858352.

> *Mouse's First Spring.* 2005. Unpaged. ISBN 9780689858383.

> *Mouse's First Snow.* 2005. 32pp. ISBN 9780689858369.

> *Mouse's First Fall.* 2006. 32pp. ISBN 9780689858376.

Gardens

Aliki.

Quiet in the Garden. New York: Greenwillow, 2009. 32pp. ISBN 978-0061552076. `PreS-1`

A child enters a garden and stays still, observing the wildlife, from the bounty of blossoms to critters and insects at home in the quiet.

Ayres, Katherine.

Up, Down, and Around. Illustrated by Nadine Westcott. Cambridge, MA: Candlewick, 2007. 32pp. ISBN 9780763623784. `PreS-1`

Two children assist when the time comes to plant the garden, and they see firsthand which grow up, down, and around.

Brenner, Barbara.

Good Morning, Garden. Illustrated by Denise Ortakales. Chanhassen, MN: NorthWord Press, 2004. 32pp. ISBN 9781559718882. `Gr. K–3`

A joyful young girl welcomes the new day in her garden by giving greetings to flowers, berries, birds, and bugs.

Brown, Peter.

The Curious Garden. New York: Little Brown, 2009. 32pp. ISBN 978-0316015479. `Gr. 1–3`

In a city with no gardens, Liam spies wildflowers attempting to grow up through abandoned train tracks. Learning about gardening, he does what he can to encourage the plants to grow. Other residents begin nurturing growth as well, and soon the entire city, rooftops and all, is bursting with green and glorious life.

Ehlert, Lois.

Growing Vegetable Soup. San Diego: Harcourt, 1987. 32pp. ISBN 978-0152325756. `PreS-2` (SP)

Accompanied by richly colored illustrations, this book takes readers through every step of growing and cooking vegetables, from preparing the tools and the ground to planting and tending the garden. It concludes with harvesting the vegetables and plopping them in the soup.

Planting a Rainbow. San Diego: Harcourt, 1988. 22pp. ISBN 978-0152626099. `PreS-2` (SP)

A child and her mother plant a rainbow every year. In the fall they plant bulbs, in the winter they order seeds from a catalog. By spring the seedlings sprout, and in the summer the flowers are in full bloom. Gorgeous illustrations brimming with intense color bring brilliance to the book.

Henkes, Kevin.

My Garden. New York: Greenwillow, 2010. Unpaged. ISBN 9780061715174. `PreS-2`

A young girl who helps her grandmother tend the garden imagines growing her own garden, filled with unusual items such as polka-dotted flowers and jelly bean plants. Illustrated with bright spring colors that bring the tale to full bloom.

Hoberman, Mary Ann.

Whose Garden Is It? Illustrated by Jane Dyer. Orlando, FL: Harcourt, 2004. 40pp. ISBN 9780152026318. `PreS-1`

Mrs. McGee and her toddler are out for a stroll when they discover a garden and she wonders whose garden it is. The gardener and several creatures all claim it is their garden.

Lin, Grace.

Ugly Vegetables. Watertown, MA: Charlesbridge, 1999. Unpaged. ISBN 978-0881063363. `Gr. K–3`

A young Chinese American girl wishes that instead of growing ugly vegetables in her family's garden, they would grow beautiful flowers, the way everyone else does. Her mother assures her that she will soon be happy that they have the vegetables, and when her mother makes delicious soup from the vegetables, her daughter sees that she's right.

Swanson, Susan Marie.

To Be Like the Sun. Illustrated by Margaret Chodos-Irvine. Orlando, FL: Harcourt, 2008. 40pp. ISBN 9780152057961. `Gr. K–3`

A young girl carries on a one-sided conversation with her sunflower as she plants and tends it. Finally, as winter covers all in cold, she remembers the glories of her lovely flower.

Nature

Cole, Henry.

On Meadowview Street. See under "Neighborhoods" in chapter 2.

Jackson, Ellen.

Earth Mother. Illustrated by Leo Dillon and Diane Dillon. New York: Walker, 2005. 32pp. ISBN 9780802789921. `Gr. 1–3`

Earth Mother, imagined here as a lovely African American woman, arises with the morning and tends to the world and its creatures.

Locker, Thomas.

Water Dance. San Diego: Harcourt, 1997. Unpaged. ISBN 9780152012847. `Gr. K-3`
    With gorgeous landscape and seascape paintings and a haiku-like text, Locker presents water in various forms, seasons, and weather.

Cloud Dance. San Diego: Harcourt, 2000. Unpaged. ISBN 9780152022310. `Gr. K-3`
    Oil paintings and poetic text depict an array of clouds in different seasons and times of day.

Mountain Dance. San Diego: Harcourt, 2001. Unpaged. ISBN 978-0152026226. `Gr. K-3`
    This time, Locker uses his poetic lines combined with stunning mountain paintings to show the geology of a mountain through time.

McCarthy, Mary.

A Closer Look. New York: Greenwillow, 2007. 29pp. ISBN 9780061240737. `PreS-2`
    Striking handmade papers and collage illustrations lead readers from a close-up view through a step-by-step backward progression, until they reveal different objects from nature.

Schaefer, Lola M.

This Is the Sunflower. Illustrated by Donald Crews. New York: Greenwillow, 2000. Unpaged. ISBN 9780688164133. `PreS-2`
    Utilizing the cumulative pattern of, "The House That Jack Built," Schaefer presents the life cycle of a sunflower.

This Is the Rain. Illustrated by Jane Wattenberg. New York: Greenwillow, 2001. Unpaged. ISBN 9780688170394. `PreS-2`
    Following the same cumulative pattern as *This Is the Sunflower*, Schaefer's rhyming text explains the hydraulic cycle from the oceans to mist, to clouds, finally finishing with rain.

An Island Grows. Illustrated by Cathie Felstead. New York: Greenwillow, 2006. 40pp. ISBN 9780066239309. `PreS-2`
    With accurate yet simple rhyming phrases, Schaefer re-creates the stages of the formation of an island, from an underwater volcanic eruption; to an emerging land mass; to a home for flora, fauna, and eventually humans.

St. Pierre, Stephanie.

What the Sea Saw. Illustrated by Beverly Doyle. Atlanta, GA: Peachtree, 2006. 48pp. ISBN 9781561453597. `PreS-3`
    The poetic prose gives a voice to the perceptions of the sea and other forms of life connected to it, describing the sights, sounds, and creatures of the ecosystem.

Weather

Bauer, Marion Dane.

If Frogs Made the Weather. Illustrated by Dorothy Donohue. New York: Holiday House, 2005. 32pp. ISBN 9780823416226. **PreS–2**

This whimsical and lyrical text proposes several speculations on the kind of weather different animals would prefer.

Carlstrom, Nancy White.

Mama Will It Snow Tonight? Illustrated by Paul Tong. Honesdale, PA: Boyds Mills Press, 2009. 32pp. ISBN 9781590785621. **T–K**

Three youngsters, a girl, a fox, and a rabbit, ask their mothers if snow is coming, and their mothers answer with clues to the approaching winter.

Chessa, Francesca.

Holly's Red Boots. New York: Holiday House, 2005. 32pp. ISBN 9780823421589. **PreS–1**

When Holly sees the freshly fallen snow, she is ready to dash out and play, but her mother insists that she find her red boots first.

Choi, Yangsook.

Peach Heaven. New York: Farrar, Straus & Giroux, 2005. Unpaged. ISBN 9780374357610. **Gr. K–2**

In Puchon, South Korea, in the summer of 1976, young Yangsook wishes she could taste some of the delicious peaches that grow in the orchards covering the mountain that looms behind her home. The fruit is so expensive that she never gets a bite until a massive rainstorm loosens them from the trees and sends them hurtling down. Yangsook and her family feast on the sumptuous fruit, but when she considers the farmers who've lost their crop, she and her friends gather as many peaches as they can and return them.

Cotten, Cynthia.

Rain Play. Illustrated by Javaka Steptoe. New York: Holt, 2008. Unpaged. ISBN 9780805067958. **PreS–2**

A group of children continue to play even when a rainstorm drenches them. They only rush for cover when thunder and lightning crackle in the sky.

Derby, Sarah.

Whoosh Went the Wind! Illustrated by Vincent Nguyen. New York: Marshall Cavendish, 2006. 32pp. ISBN 9780761453093. **Gr. K–2**

When a young boy is late for school, he claims it's all the wind's fault. His teacher doesn't believe him until she opens the door to the outside herself.

Emmett, Jonathan.

Diamond in the Snow. Illustrated by Vanessa Cabban. Cambridge, MA: Candlewick, 2006. 32pp. ISBN 9780763631178. `PreS-2`

> When Mole explores the newly winter white world, he finds a glistening icicle. Mistaking it for a diamond, he totes it home, only to despair when it melts away. Fortunately his friends explain, and together they experience the thrill of a winter sunset.

English, Karen.

🏵*Hot Day on Abbott Avenue*. Illustrated by Javaka Steptoe. New York: Clarion, 2004. 32pp. ISBN 9780395985274. `PreS-3`

> On a sunny summer day, best friends Kishi and Renee refuse to speak to each other. As the temperature climbs, neighbors try to reconcile the girls, but nothing helps until the testy friends join a game of double-dutch and then share an ice pop. (ALAN, Jane Addams Honor)

Griessman, Annette.

Like a Hundred Drums. Illustrated by Julie Monks. Boston: Houghton Mifflin, 2006. 32pp. ISBN 9780618558780. `PreS-2`

> The human and animal residents of a farm anticipate and then experience an intense summer thunderstorm.

Hesse, Karen.

Come on, Rain! Illustrated by Jon J. Muth. New York: Scholastic, 1999. Unpaged. ISBN 9780590331258. `Gr. K-2`

> This elegant text evokes Tessie's longing for rain in the drought-plagued city.

Joosse, Barbara.

Hot City. Illustrated by Christie Gregory. New York: Philomel, 2004. 32pp. ISBN 9780399236402. `Gr. K-3`

> An African American brother and sister decide to visit the public library on a blisteringly hot summer day. Escaping the heat, they imagine themselves participating in the stories they've chosen.

Keats, Ezra Jack.

🏵*The Snowy Day*. New York: Viking, 1962. 32pp. ISBN 9780670654000. `PreS-3`

> In this classic story, an African American boy revels in his snow-covered world as he makes tracks and angels in the snow, goes sledding, watches a snowball fight, and slips some snow into his pocket in an attempt to save it for later. (Caldecott Medal)

Krishnaswami, Uma.

Monsoon. **Illustrated by Jamel Akib. New York: Farrar, Straus & Giroux, 2003. 32pp. ISBN 9780374350154.** `Gr. K–3`

The poetic prose evokes the feelings of a young girl as she and her mother run their errands in a bustling city in India, just before the beginning of monsoon season. They feel the atmospheric pressure build and long for the rains to fall to cool them and water the crops, while at the same time they worry about how much rain there will be.

Kurtz, Jane.

Rain Romp: Stomping away a Grouchy Day. **Illustrated by Dyanna Wolcott. New York: Greenwillow, 2002. Unpaged. ISBN 9780060298050.** `PreS–1`

A little girl feels as gloomy as the gray day, until her parents take her outside and join her in a rain romp.

Lakin, Patricia.

Snow Day! **Illustrated by Scott Nash. New York: Dial, 2002. 32pp. ISBN 978-0803726420.** `PreS–2`

Waking up to snowfall, four crocodiles don their winter garb and head out for a day of sledding. Thoughts of school interrupt them, and they reveal their true identities as principals when they call in the closing of their schools.

Beach Day! **Illustrated by Scott Nash. New York: Dial, 2004. 32pp. ISBN 978-0803728943. Sequel.** `PreS–2`

On a sweltering, sunny day, the four crocodile friends decide to spend the day at the beach.

Rainy Day! **Illustrated by Scott Nash. New York: Dial, 2007. 40pp. ISBN 978-0803730922. Sequel.** `PreS–2`

Bored inside while it's raining outside, the four crocodile friends grab their raingear and head out for some fun in the water-drenched world.

Lee, Harper.

Snow! Snow! Snow! **New York: Simon & Schuster, 2009. 40pp. ISBN 978-1416984542.** `T–K`

After a night of snow, a pair of pups and their fun-loving dad don their winter garb and enjoy a day of sledding.

London, Jonathan.

Hurricane! **Illustrated by Henri Sorenson. New York: Lothrop, Lee & Shepard, 1998. 32pp. ISBN 9780688129774.** `PreS–3`

On a beautiful, sunny day in Puerto Rico, a boy and his brother enjoy snorkeling in the blue-green waves. When the feel in the air and the look of the sky shift suddenly, the boys rush home with a warning. Hurriedly, the family pack and nervously take shelter from the storm.

Perkins, Lynne Rae.

🏅 *Snow Music*. New York: Greenwillow, 2003. Unpaged. ISBN 978-0066239569. `PreS–2`

Emphasizing an assortment of winter sounds, the story whooshes through the experiences of a boy who awakens to a winter wonderland of white and embarks on a mission to track down his disobedient dog, who escaped when he first opened the door to admire the snow. (Boston Globe Honor)

Perry, Elizabeth.

Think Cool Thoughts. Illustrated by Linda Bronson. New York: Clarion, 2005. 32pp. ISBN 9780618234936. `Gr. K–3`

The oppressive heat gives Angel's mom and Aunt Lucy the idea of camping out on the roof to cool off, the way they did as children. Angel slides into sleep counting imaginary ice cubes and is swept up in her magical dreams.

Polacco, Patricia.

Thunder Cake. New York: Philomel, 1990. 32pp. ISBN 9780399222313. `PreS–3`

Thunder growls, and Grandma helps her granddaughter overcome her fear by engaging her in the many steps required to make a special cake. The storm has passed by the time they finish the cake. A recipe is included in this charming book, illustrated with Polacco's signature vivid colors and Russian folk-art patterns.

Rylant, Cynthia.

Snow. Illustrated by Lauren Stringer. Orlando, FL: Harcourt, 2008. Unpaged. ISBN 9780152053031. `PreS–1`

This lyrical text extols the virtues of all different kinds of snow and the fun that can be had sledding, making snow angels, and building snowmen.

Sakai, Komako.

The Snow Day. New York: Arthur A. Levine, 2009. 32pp. ISBN 978-0545013215. `PreS–K`

When a little rabbit wakes up in the morning, he finds the city draped in snow. School is canceled, and he wants to go out and play, but his mother worries he'll catch cold. He spends a quiet day stuck inside, but ventures out onto the balcony of his apartment to make snowballs.

Sheth, Kashmira.

Monsoon Afternoon. Illustrated by Yoshiko Jaeggi. Atlanta: Peachtree, 2008. Unpaged. ISBN 9781561454556. `Gr. K–3`

Although the rainclouds are gathering during monsoon season in India, a young boy is longing for someone to play with him outside. Everyone in his family turns him down except his grandfather, who joins him in sailing paper boats in a washtub, taking a walk in the rain, and swinging on a banyan tree.

Shulevitz, Uri.

🐦*Snow*. New York: Farrar, Straus & Giroux, 1998. Unpaged. ISBN 978-0374370923. `PreS-2`

In a small European town in December, a young boy spies the first few snowflakes of the season and predicts an abundance of white. Despite the adults who dismiss his idea and contrary to the weather forecast, swirls of snow soon settle on the town, admirably fulfilling the boy's hopes. The spare text melds perfectly with the watercolor and pen-and-ink illustrations. (ALAN, Caldecott Honor, Charlotte Zolotow Award, Golden Kite Award)

Spinelli, Eileen.

Heat Wave. Illustrated by Betsy Lewin. Orlando, FL: Harcourt, 2007. 30pp. ISBN 9780152167790. `Gr. K-3`

In the bygone era of no air-conditioning, the human and canine residents of the town of Lumberville experiment with different methods of keeping cool. All congregate by the banks of the river, imagining the moment when the heat will dissipate.

Stojic, Manya.

🐦*Rain*. New York: Crown, 2000. Unpaged. ISBN 9780517800850. `PreS-2`

This cumulative tale details what the animals of the African savanna see and hear as they wait for the rain and then rejoice in its arrival. (New York Times Best Illustrated)

Trotter, Deborah W.

How Do You Know? Illustrated by Julie Downing. New York: Clarion, 2006. 30pp. ISBN 9780618463435. `PreS-2`

When a little girls wakes to find all the familiar things in her world hidden by fog, she goes on a walk with her mom to see if they are still there.

Winter, Jeanette.

Elsina's Clouds. New York: Frances Foster Books, 2004. 40pp. ISBN 978-0374321185. `PreS-3`

Elsina yearns to paint bright pictures on the family home in the Basotha tradition, whereby women of this southern Africa area paint their houses as a prayer to their ancestors to bring rain. Her wish is granted when her father builds an additional room for the new baby. Elsina paints and paints, hoping the drought will end. Each day the sky stays blue, until at last the rain clouds gather.

Yee, Wong Herbert

Tracks in the Snow. New York: Holt, 2003. 32pp. ISBN 9780805067712. `PreS-2`

When snow fills the woods outside her home, a young girl bundles up and journeys out, seeking to discover who made the tracks that pique her curiosity.

Who Likes Rain? **New York: Holt, 2007. 30pp. ISBN 9780805077346. PreS–2**
An Asian girl ventures outside to partake of the delights of a rainy day in the spring.

Favorites

Red Leaf, Yellow Leaf by Lois Ehlert

Come on, Rain! by Karen Hesse

Cold Little Duck, Duck, Duck by Lisa Westberg Peters

Fletcher and the Falling Leaves by Julia Rawlinson

Long Night Moon by Cynthia Rylant

Winter Is the Warmest Season by Lauren Stringer

Chapter **10**

Animals: Realistic, Talking, Farm Animals, Insects, and Dinosaurs

Animals star in a large number of picture books. Often they are replacements for people. If this is the case, the books are listed with the subject of the book rather than in this chapter. Since this book groups stories by genre, the animal stories that are left are divided into essentially realistic animal stories and talking animal stories (which can also be considered animal fantasy). The talking animal stories feature animals doing animal activities or imaginary activities that are animal-like, but they have the capacity to talk and/or think. The categories are further broken down into animal groups, domestic animals that are pets (dogs and cats being the most popular), animals in nature, and farm animals.

Realistic

Domestic

Cats

Banks, Kate.

The Cat Who Walked Across France. **Illustrated by Georg Hallensleben. New York: Frances Foster Books, 2004. 40pp. ISBN 9780374399689.** `Gr. K-3`
> A small gray cat lives in a house by the sea in France with his elderly owner, but when she dies, he's shipped north with her possessions. Remembering the salty sea air and the comforts of home, the determined cat makes his way through the cities and countryside until he arrives back home, where the new family adopts him.

Brown, Margaret Wise.

Sneakers, the Seaside Cat. Illustrated by Anne Mortimer. New York: HarperCollins, 2003. Unpaged. ISBN 9780060286927. **PreS–1**

> Adapted from a collection of stories released in 1955, *Sneakers: Seven Stories about a Cat*, this picture book version follows the escapades of a cat's first visit to the ocean. Illustrated with Mortimer's gorgeous cat paintings that bring Sneakers vividly to life.

Bruel, Nick.

Bad Kitty. New Milford, CT: Roaring Brook, 2005. 40pp. ISBN 9781596430693. **PreS–2**

> When kitty is forced to choose from an alphabetical list of vegetables because her owners have run out of cat food, she transforms into a bad kitty. She engages in bad behavior from A to Z until she can partake of delicious goodies again and redeems herself by performing virtuous acts, once more in alphabetical order. (See the sequel, *Poor Puppy*, under "Domestic: Dogs" in this chapter.)

Dodd, Emma.

I Don't Want a Cool Cat! New York: Little, Brown, 2010. 32pp. ISBN 978-0316036740. **PreS–2**

> In this companion to *I Don't Want a Posh Dog*, the young girl explores her options in feline friendship, as she searches for the cat that would be just right for her.

Fleming, Denise.

🐾*Mama Cat Has Three Kittens.* New York: Holt, 1998. 32pp. ISBN 978-0805057454. **T–K**

> Mama cat has three kittens, but only two of them follow her lead as she takes them on a garden journey, walking atop a stone wall, cleaning her paws, and chasing leaves. Boris, her rebellious offspring, naps until his family finally curls up for a snooze, too. Now Boris is ready to play. Illustrated with Fleming's signature color-saturated, paper-pulp artwork that makes the purring pets pounce off the page. (ALAN)

Henkes, Kevin.

🐾*Kitten's First Full Moon.* New York: Greenwillow, 2004. Unpaged. ISBN 9780060588281. **T–K** (SP)

> When a kitten spots her very first full moon, she mistakes it for a bowl of milk and does her best to find it. The rhythmic text is perfect for reading aloud, and the expressive black, white, and gray illustrations deftly depict the kitten's emotions. (ALAN, Caldecott Medal, Charlotte Zolotow Award, New York Times Best Illustrated)

Lazo, Caroline.

Someday When My Cat Can Talk. Illustrated by Kyrsten Brooker. New York: Schwartz & Wade, 2008. 32pp. ISBN 9780375837548. **Gr. K–2**

> In rhyming text, a young girl relates all the locales that she imagines her secretive cat has visited.

Meyers, Susan.

Kittens! Kittens! Kittens! Illustrated by David Walker. New York: Abrams, 2007. 32pp. ISBN 9780810912182. **Gr. K–2**

> Exuberant rhymes and charming illustrations portray the antics of newborn kittens as they explore their world and begin to grow up.

Myers, Christopher.

🌸*Black Cat.* New York: Scholastic, 1999. 40pp. ISBN 9780590033756. **Gr. 1–3**

> Rhythmic prose follows a streetwise black cat as he rambles through an urban landscape, depicted using striking photo collages. (ALAN, Coretta Scott King Honor)

Nodset, Joan.

Come Back, Cat. Illustrated by Steven Kellogg. New York: HarperCollins, 2008. 40pp. ISBN 9780060280819. **PreS–2**

> This reissue of a book first published in 1973 has been newly illustrated by Kellogg and features the experiences of a young girl befriending a ginger cat, who is shy at first but gradually grows content in the girl's arms.

Peters, Stephanie True.

Rumble Tum. Illustrated by Robert Papp. New York: Dutton, 2009. 32pp. ISBN 9780525421566. **PreS–2**

> Beth falls in love with her new kitten, Rumble Tum, from the first moment that she holds the purring ball of fluff in her hands. Rumble Tum gets into some kitty mischief, and when a thunderstorm strikes, the feline flees. Beth worries, but Rumble Tum returns home safely. Papp's illustrations glow with life and mutual affection.

Polacco, Patricia.

For the Love of Autumn. New York: Philomel, 2008. 40pp. ISBN 978-0399245411. **Gr. 1–3**

> Danielle, a student teacher, adopts a lost kitten. When she gets a teaching job in Washington State, she and Autumn move to their new home. They haven't been there long before Autumn gets hurt. Then she gets lost during a thunderstorm. Danielle and her class search for the kitten, but no one finds her. Six weeks later, Autumn appears at her own memorial service, and Danielle befriends Stephen, the man who has been caring for the injured Autumn.

Schachner, Judith.

The Grannyman. New York: Dutton, 1999. Unpaged. ISBN 9780525461227. **Gr. K–3**

Simon is an elderly Siamese on the brink of his demise when the family brings home a new kitten. Rejuvenated, Simon perks up and teaches the kitten all about life with his new family.

Smith, Linda.

🐾*Mrs. Crump's Cat.* Illustrated by David Roberts. New York: HarperCollins, 2006. 32pp. ISBN 9780060283025. **PreS–3**

One rainy morning Mrs. Crump discovers a bedraggled stray cat on her porch, and although she is determined not to keep him, the cat gradually purrs his way into her heart. (Charlotte Zolotow Honor)

Stainton, Sue.

The Lighthouse Cat. Illustrated by Anne Mortimer. New York: HarperCollins, 2004. 32pp. ISBN 9780060096045. **Gr. K–3**

A lonely lighthouse keeper adopts a stowaway cat and names him Mackerel. Not only does Mackerel keep him company, but when he gets sick, the cat and his friends come to the rescue by lighting the way with the reflection of light on their eyes.

Thompson, Lauren.

How Many Cats? Illustrated by Robin Eley. New York: Hyperion, 2009. 32pp. ISBN 9781423108016. **PreS–2**

When nineteen cats follow a kitten home, they create kitty chaos before departing in various-sized groups. This provides opportunities for addition, subtraction, and oodles of feline fun.

Weaver, Tess.

Cat Jumped In. Illustrated by Emily Arnold McCully. New York: Clarion, 2007. 32pp. ISBN 9780618614882. **PreS–2**

A curious cat creates havoc at home as he wanders from room to room and ends up leaving paw prints in the artist's studio.

Cats: Easy Readers

Rylant, Cynthia.

Mr. Putter & Tabby Series. Illustrated by Arthur Howard. **Gr. 1–3**

Mr. Putter, a senior citizen, is looking for some companionship, so he goes to the shelter and adopts an older tabby cat. Thus begins their successive cozy series of episodes that are both endearing and easy to read.

Mr. Putter & Tabby Pour the Tea. San Diego: Harcourt, 1994. Unpaged. ISBN 9780152562557.

Mr. Putter & Tabby Walk the Dog. San Diego: Harcourt, 1994. Unpaged. ISBN 9780152562595.

Mr. Putter & Tabby Bake the Cake. San Diego: Harcourt, 1994. Unpaged. ISBN 9780152002053.

Mr. Putter & Tabby Pick the Pears. San Diego: Harcourt, 1995. Unpaged. ISBN 9780152002459.

Mr. Putter & Tabby Fly the Plane. San Diego: Harcourt, 1997. Unpaged. ISBN 9780152562533.

Mr. Putter & Tabby Row the Boat. San Diego: Harcourt, 1997. Unpaged. ISBN 9780152562571 (pb).

Mr. Putter & Tabby Toot the Horn. San Diego: Harcourt, 1998. Unpaged. ISBN 9780152002442.

Mr. Putter & Tabby Take the Train. San Diego: Harcourt, 1998. 44pp. ISBN 9780152017866.

Mr. Putter & Tabby Paint the Porch. San Diego: Harcourt, 2000. Unpaged. ISBN 9780152017873.

Mr. Putter & Tabby Feed the Fish. San Diego: Harcourt, 2001. Unpaged. ISBN 9780152024086.

Mr. Putter & Tabby Catch the Cold. San Diego: Harcourt, 2002. 44pp. ISBN 9780152024147.

Mr. Putter & Tabby Stir the Soup. San Diego: Harcourt, 2003. 44pp. ISBN 9780152026370.

Mr. Putter & Tabby Write the Book. Orlando, FL: Harcourt, 2004. 44pp. ISBN 9780152002411.

Mr. Putter & Tabby Make a Wish. Orlando, FL: Harcourt, 2005. 44pp. ISBN 9780152024260.

Mr. Putter & Tabby Spin the Yarn. Orlando, FL: Harcourt, 2005. 44pp. ISBN 9780152050672.

Mr. Putter & Tabby See the Stars. Orlando, FL: Harcourt, 2007. 42pp. ISBN 9780152060756.

Mr. Putter & Tabby Run the Race. Orlando, FL: Harcourt, 2008. 40pp. ISBN 9780152060695.

Mr. Putter & Tabby Spill the Beans. Orlando, FL: Harcourt, 2009. 44pp. ISBN 9780152050702.

Mr. Putter & Tabby Drop the Ball. Orlando, FL: Harcourt, 2010. 44pp. ISBN 9780152050726.

Mr. Putter & Tabby Clear the Decks. Orlando, FL: Harcourt, 2010. 44pp. ISBN 9780152067151.

Schaefer, Lola.

The Mittens Series. Illustrated by Susan Kathleen Hartung. New York: HarperCollins. `Gr. K-2`

Simple language that is just right for beginning readers describes the experiences Nick has with his new kitten.

Mittens. 2006. 25pp. ISBN 9780060546595.

> Nick's new kitten Mittens is feeling skittish in his new home and searches for a safe place to hide until Nick convinces him everything is all right.

Follow Me, Mittens. 2007. 25pp. ISBN 9780060546656.

> When Mittens ventures outside, he wanders away from Nick and gets lost until he hears Nick calling for him.

What's That, Mittens? 2008. 32pp. ISBN 9780060546625.

> Mittens hears sounds on the other side of the backyard fence and digs through until he meets the dog on the other side.

Happy Halloween, Mittens. 2010. 32pp. ISBN 9780061702228.

> Mittens experiences the costumed holiday for the first time.

Dogs

Appelt, Kathi.

The Bubba and Beau Series. Illustrated by Arthur Howard. San Diego: Harcourt. `PreS-2`

Baby Bubba and his puppy Beau are the best of friends who enjoy doing everything together.

Bubba and Beau, Best Friends. 2002. Unpaged. ISBN 9780152020606.

> Bubba, a new baby, and Beau, a newborn puppy, adore each other and their favorite shared blankie, until Mama Pearl decides it's time to wash, not only the blanket, but also Bubba and Beau. Although the experience is traumatic, the fresh friends are soon reunited. The Texas drawl of the story, combined with the comic illustrations, makes this a humorous friendship tale.

Bubba and Beau Go Night-Night. 2003. 32pp. ISBN 9780152045937.

> Big Bubba takes Bubba and Beau out for a day of running errands, but when nighttime arrives, the youngsters aren't yet tuckered out. They need one more ride in the pickup truck before they slip into sleep.

Bubba and Beau Meet the Relatives. 2003. 32pp. ISBN 9780152166304.

> Bubba's family zips here and there, cleaning up the house for a visit from the kinfolk. When they arrive, Bubba and Beau discover they have more in common with their dressed-up cousin Arlene and her dog Bitsy than they thought.

Beaumont, Karen.

Doggone Dogs! Illustrated by David Catrow. New York: Dial, 2008. 40pp. ISBN 9780803731578. **PreS–1**

> Ten frenetic pups bark their owner awake at dawn and then dash out the door. Still wearing his pajamas, their owner chases them all the way to Central Bark.

Blake, Robert J.

Swift. New York: Philomel, 2007. 48pp. ISBN 9780399233838. **Gr. 2 & up**

> Johnnie and his dad head out on Johnnie's first bear hunt in Alaska with their dog Swift. Trouble arises when a grizzly bear attacks and Johnnie's father breaks his leg. He sends Johnnie and Swift for help, but they get lost, and it's only because of Swift that they are able to survive.

Boelts, Maribeth.

Before You Were Mine. Illustrated by David Walker. New York: Putnam, 2007. 28pp. ISBN 9780399245268. **PreS–2**

> When a boy adopts a dog from a shelter, he wonders what the animal's life was like before he came to his new home.

Bruel, Nick.

Poor Puppy. New Milford, CN: Roaring Brook, 2007. Unpaged. ISBN 9781596432703. **PreS–2**

> When Kitty from *Bad Kitty* won't play, Puppy goes in search of other activities and ends up playing with a numerically increasing number of toys, which also happen to be in alphabetical order.

Casanova, Mary.

Some Dog. Illustrated by Ard Hoyt. New York: Farrar, Straus & Giroux, 2007. 32pp. ISBN 9780374371333. **PreS–2**

> George, an affectionate basset hound, enjoys his happy home with his humans until they take in a stray pup with excessive amounts of energy. Zippity dashes about and dominates the home until a thunderstorm scares him and he disappears. George tracks him down, frees him from the muck, and leads him home.

Chichester Clark, Emma.

Piper. Grand Rapids, MI: Eerdmans, 2007. Unpaged. ISBN 9780802853141. **Gr. K–2**

> Piper's owner is nasty, so he runs away to the city. When he saves a woman's life, she adopts him.

9

10

11

12

13

14

15

Cowen-Fletcher, Jane.

Hello Puppy! Somerville, MA: Candlewick, 2010. Unpaged. ISBN 978-0763643034. **T–K**

When a young girl gets a new puppy, she enjoys playing with him and learning how to take care of him.

Demas, Corinne.

Always in Trouble. Illustrated by Noah Z. Jones. New York: Scholastic, 2009. 40pp. ISBN 9780545024532. **PreS–2**

Emma loves her dog Toby, but her family grows exasperated with him as he gets into trouble each day of the week. When one stint at obedience school doesn't help, they send him back. This time he returns home as a helpful housekeeping dog, until they take him to the park, where he reverts back to his old habits.

Dodd, Emma.

I Don't Want a Posh Dog. Little, Brown, 2009. 24pp. ISBN 9780316033909. **PreS–2**

A young girl imagines what life would be like with different kinds of dogs, until she finds one that's just right.

Goldfinger, Jennifer P.

My Dog Lyle. New York: Clarion, 2008. 29pp. ISBN 9780618639830. **PreS–2**

A little girl lists all the reasons her dog is far beyond ordinary.

Hest, Amy.

The Dog Who Belonged to No One. Illustrated by Amy Bates. New York: Abrams, 2008. 29pp. ISBN 9780810994836. **Gr. 1–3**

Lia, a hard-working girl who delivers baked goods from her family's business on her bicycle, is lonely. At the same time, a crooked-eared dog is searching for a home. When a storm strikes, they both end up in the bakery together, and from then on each has a new friend.

Lewis, Kim.

A Puppy for Annie. Cambridge, MA: Candlewick, 2006. 32pp. ISBN 978-0763632007. **T–K**

Annie brings home her new border collie, and her mother helps her interpret what Bess means when she rattles her bowl, scratches at the door, and wags her tail.

London, Jonathan.

Sled Dogs Run. Illustrated by Jon Van Zyle. New York: Walker. 32pp. ISBN 978-0802789570. **Gr. 1–3**

A young girl who lives in Alaska trains three Siberian huskies to be sled dogs.

Meister, Cari.

Tiny on the Farm. Illustrated by Rich Davis. New York: Viking, 2008. 30pp. ISBN 9780670062461. **PreS–2**

Tiny, a gigantic dog first featured in an easy reader series, here visits Uncle John's farm and helps his owner Eliot search for a missing cat and her kittens.

Pitzer, Susanna.

🎗*Not Afraid of Dogs.* Illustrated by Larry Day. New York: Walker, 2006. 32pp. ISBN 9780802780676. **PreS–2**

Daniel is very brave when it comes to facing spiders, snakes, and thunderstorms, but he isn't fond of dogs. He tries to stay in his room when his family is taking care of his aunt's dog, Bandit. In the middle of a thunderstorm he has to go to the bathroom and finds the dog cowering in a corner. As he comforts the pup, he overcomes his fear. (Golden Kite Award)

Radunsky, Vladimir.

You? Orlando, FL: Harcourt, 2009. Unpaged. ISBN 9780152051778. **PreS–2**

A dog and a girl, separated by a hedge in a park, are each lonely. The dog wishes for an owner and the girl wishes for a dog. They find each other when they breech the hedge, much to their mutual delight.

Ruelle, Karen Gray.

Bark Park. Atlanta, GA: Peachtree, 2008. 28pp. ISBN 9781561454341. **PreS–1**

Spritely rhymes present a diversity of dogs all headed for a romp in the park.

Rylant, Cynthia.

The Great Gracie Chase: Stop That Dog. Illustrated by Mark Teague. New York: Blue Sky Press, 2001. Unpaged. 9780590100410. **PreS–1**

Gracie, a brown-and-white dog, loves her quiet life at home, but things change drastically when painters come and disturb her peace. She barks at the cause of her distress and gets put outside, where she decides to go for a walk on her own. This venture leads to a bevy of folks chasing the wandering canine.

Sayre, April Pulley.

Hush, Little Puppy. Illustrated by Susan Winter. New York: Holt, 2007. 32pp. ISBN 9780805071023. **T–K**

In rhyme that follows the pattern of "Hush Little Baby," a young boy helps his puppy calm down for the night by recounting their activities.

Shannon, David.

Good Boy, Fergus! New York: Blue Sky Press, 2006. 40pp. ISBN 9780439490276. `PreS-3` (SP)

> Fergus, an energetic West Highland terrier with a mischievous streak, enjoys doing exactly what he wants no matter what commands his master gives him.

Simont, Marc.

🎗*The Stray Dog: From a True Story by Reiko Sassa.* New York: HarperCollins, 2001. Unpaged. ISBN 9780060289331. `PreS-2` (SP)

> On a family picnic, a brother and sister play with a friendly stray dog. Their parents won't allow them to bring him home, sure that he belongs to someone. When they return the next week, the siblings rescue the dog from the dog catcher, and their parents agree to adopt him. (ALAN, Boston Globe Honor, New York Times Best Illustrated)

Stuve-Bodeen, Stephanie.

A Small Brown Dog with a Wet Pink Nose. Illustrated by Linzie Hunter. New York: Little, Brown, 2010. 32pp. ISBN 9780316058308. `Gr. K-3`

> When Amelia's parents repeatedly tell her that she cannot have a dog, Amelia pretends that she has an imaginary dog named "Bones." She insists that Bones is lost, and her parents must help her find him, which leads them to a shelter, and the adoption that Amelia has wanted all along.

Swaim, Jessica.

The Hound from the Pound. Illustrated by Jill McElmurry. Cambridge, MA: Candlewick, 2007. 24pp. ISBN 9780763623302. `PreS-3`

> When Miss Mary Lynn MacIntosh decides to alleviate her loneliness by adopting a dog, she brings home Blue, a basset hound who has the habit of creating a mess. He also howls long and loud. So much so, that his canine companions from the shelter hear his crying and escape to keep him company. With the help of a dog trainer, Mary trains the new visitors and decides to adopt them all. Along the way, she and the trainer fall in love.

Wolff, Ashley.

When Lucy Goes Out Walking: A Puppy's First Year. New York: Holt, 2009. 32pp. ISBN 9780805081688. `PreS-2`

> Rhymes relay how a puppy grows into a dog while the seasons change.

Dogs: Easy Readers

Capucilli, Alyssa Satin.

The Biscuit Series. Illustrated by Pat Schories. New York: HarperCollins. `Gr. K-2`

> Biscuit, an adorable puppy, frolics at home and makes friends with other animals as well as having adventures at school, on a farm, and in a city. The simple text fea-

tures repetition and provides contextual clues to help beginning readers, and the clear, bright illustrations aid in understanding and convey Biscuit's liveliness. Listed here are only the Biscuit easy readers. There are also Biscuit paperback picture books and board books.

Biscuit. 1996. 25pp. ISBN 9780060261979.

Biscuit Finds a Friend. 1997. 24pp. ISBN 9780060274122.

Bathtime for Biscuit. 1998. 28pp. ISBN 9780060279387 (lb).

Biscuit's New Trick. 2000. Unpaged. ISBN 9780060280680.

Biscuit Wants to Play. 2001. 23pp. ISBN 9780060280697.

Biscuit Goes to School. 2002. 21pp. ISBN 9780060286828.

Biscuit's Big Friend. 2003. 25pp. ISBN 9780060291679.

Biscuit Wins a Prize. 2004. 24pp. ISBN 9780060094553.

Biscuit and the Baby. 2005. 23pp. ISBN 9780060094591.

Biscuit Visits the Big City. 2006. 28pp. ISBN 9780060741648.

Biscuit's Day at the Farm. 2007. 28pp. ISBN 9780060741679.

Biscuit and the Little Pup. 2008. 29pp. ISBN 9780060741709.

Biscuit Takes a Walk. 2009. 24pp. ISBN 9780061177453.

Biscuit Meets the Class Pet. 2009. 32pp. ISBN 9780061177477.

Meister, Cari.

The Tiny Series. Illustrated by Rich Davis. New York: Viking. Gr. K–2

Tiny, a dog who is larger than a bike, a chair, and even the boy who is his owner, embarks on canine adventures at home, at school, on a camping trip, and on a visit to the library. Simple text of one sentence per page makes this a good choice for pet-lovers who are just beginning to read. In 2008 the newest Tiny book was released as a picture book.

Tiny's Bath. 1999. Unpaged. ISBN 9780141302676 (pb).

When Tiny Was Tiny. 1999. Unpaged. ISBN 9780141304199 (pb).

Tiny Goes to the Library. 2000. Unpaged. ISBN 9780141304885 (pb).

Tiny the Snow Dog. 2001. Unpaged. ISBN 9780140567083 (pb).

Tiny Goes Camping. 2006. Unpaged. ISBN 9780670892501.

Rylant, Cynthia.

The Henry and Mudge Series. Gr. 1–3

Henry and his big, drooling dog Mudge are the best of friends and have an array of adventures in their everyday life. Text and illustrations work perfectly together to provide stories that are both confidence builders for beginning readers as they hone their skills, as well as books that are endearing tales of human–animal companionship. They are the quintessential boy and his dog easy readers. Henry and Mudge make guest appearances in Cousin Annie's series, <u>Annie and Snowball</u>.

Henry and Mudge. Illustrated by Sucie Stevenson. New York: Bradbury, 1987. 39pp. ISBN 9780689810046.

Henry and Mudge in Puddle Trouble. Illustrated by Sucie Stevenson. New York: Bradbury, 1987. 46pp. ISBN 9780689810022.

Henry and Mudge in the Green Time. Illustrated by Sucie Stevenson. New York: Bradbury, 1987. 48pp. ISBN 9780689810015 (pb).

Henry and Mudge under the Yellow Moon. Illustrated by Sucie Stevenson. New York: Bradbury, 1987. 48pp. ISBN 9780689810213 (pb).

Henry and Mudge in the Sparkle Days. Illustrated by Sucie Stevenson. New York: Bradbury, 1988. 45pp. ISBN 9780689810183.

Henry and Mudge and the Forever Sea. Illustrated by Sucie Stevenson. New York: Bradbury, 1989. 46pp. ISBN 9780689810176 (pb).

Henry and Mudge Get the Cold Shivers. Illustrated by Sucie Stevenson. New York: Bradbury, 1989. 48pp. ISBN 9780689810152.

Henry and Mudge and the Happy Cat. Illustrated by Sucie Stevenson. New York: Bradbury, 1990. 47pp. ISBN 9780689810138 (pb).

Henry and Mudge and the Bedtime Thumps. Illustrated by Sucie Stevenson. New York: Bradbury, 1991. 40pp. ISBN 9780689801624 (pb).

Henry and Mudge Take the Big Test. Illustrated by Sucie Stevenson. New York: Bradbury, 1991. 40pp. ISBN 9780689808869 (pb).

Henry and Mudge and the Long Weekend. Illustrated by Sucie Stevenson. New York: Bradbury, 1992. 40pp. ISBN 9780689808852 (pb).

Henry and Mudge and the Wild Wind. Illustrated by Sucie Stevenson. New York: Bradbury, 1992. 40pp. ISBN 9780689808388 (pb).

Henry and Mudge and the Careful Cousin. Illustrated by Sucie Stevenson. New York: Simon & Schuster, 1994. 47pp. ISBN 9780689810077.

Henry and Mudge and the Best Day of All. Illustrated by Sucie Stevenson. New York: Simon & Schuster, 1995. 40pp. ISBN 9780689813856 (pb).

Henry and Mudge in the Family Trees. Illustrated by Sucie Stevenson. New York: Simon & Schuster, 1997. 40pp. ISBN 9780689823176 (pb).

Henry and Mudge and the Sneaky Crackers. Illustrated by Sucie Stevenson. New York: Simon & Schuster, 1998. 40pp. ISBN 9780689825255 (pb).

Henry and Mudge and the Starry Night. Illustrated by Sucie Stevenson. New York: Simon & Schuster, 1998. 40pp. ISBN 9780689825866 (pb).

Henry and Mudge and Annie's Good Move. Illustrated by Sucie Stevenson. New York: Simon & Schuster, 1998. 40pp. ISBN 9780689811746.

Henry and Mudge and the Snowman Plan. Illustrated by Sucie Stevenson. New York: Simon & Schuster, 1999. 40pp. ISBN 9780689834493 (pb).

Henry and Mudge and Annie's Perfect Pet. Illustrated by Sucie Stevenson. New York: Simon & Schuster, 2000. 40pp. ISBN 9780689834431 (pb).

Henry and Mudge and the Tall Tree House. Illustrated by Carolyn Bracken in the style of Sucie Stevenson. New York: Simon & Schuster, 2002. 40pp. ISBN 9780689834455 (pb).

Henry and Mudge and Mrs. Hopper's House. Illustrated by Carolyn Bracken in the style of Sucie Stevenson. New York: Simon & Schuster, 2002. 40pp. ISBN 9780689834462 (pb).

Henry and Mudge and the Wild Goose Chase. Illustrated by Carolyn Bracken in the style of Sucie Stevenson. New York: Simon & Schuster, 2003. 40pp. ISBN 9780689811722.

Henry and Mudge and the Funny Lunch. Illustrated by Carolyn Bracken in the style of Sucie Stevenson. New York: Simon & Schuster, 2004. 40pp. ISBN 9780689811784.

Henry and Mudge and a Very Merry Christmas. Illustrated by Sucie Stevenson. New York: Simon & Schuster, 2005. 40pp. ISBN 9780689811685.

Henry and Mudge and the Great Grandpas. Illustrated by Sucie Stevenson. New York: Simon & Schuster, 2004. 40pp. ISBN 9780689811708.

Henry and Mudge and the Tumbling Trip. Illustrated by Carolyn Bracken in the style of Sucie Stevenson. New York: Simon & Schuster, 2005. 40pp. ISBN 9780689811807.

Henry and Mudge and the Big Sleepover. Illustrated by Sucie Stevenson. New York: Simon & Schuster, 2006. 40pp. ISBN 9780689811715.

Cats and Dogs

Himmelman, John.

Katie Loves the Kittens. New York: Holt, 2008. 32pp. ISBN 9780805086829. `PreS-2`

When Katie the dog's owner, Sara Ann, brings home three new kittens, Katie is so excited that she scares the kittens away. The next day she eats their food, and when Sara Ann scolds her, she slips away in sadness. She falls asleep and wakes up to find the kittens curled on her tummy. Quivering with delight, she nonetheless holds herself still so as not to disturb her new friends. Watercolor-and-ink illustrations add to the charm of this enjoyable tale.

McCarty, Peter.

🐾 *Hondo & Fabian.* New York: Holt, 2002. Unpaged. ISBN 9780805063523. `PreS–1`

Hondo the dog enjoys a day playing with his puppy friend at the beach, while Fabian the cat spends the time at home escaping a toddler eager to catch him. The parallel stories are presented with detailed colored-pencil illustrations. (ALAN, Caldecott Honor, New York Times Best Illustrated)

Fabian Escapes. New York: Holt, 2007. 32pp. ISBN 9780805077131. Sequel. `PreS–1`

The dog and cat pets return for another parallel story. This time Fabian leaps out of the window just as Hondo returns from his walk, and Fabian explores the great outdoors while Hondo encounters the toddler.

McFarland, Lyn.

Widget. Illustrated by Jim McFarland. New York: Farrar, Straus & Giroux, 2001. Unpaged. ISBN 9780374384289. `PreS–2`

Widget, a stray terrier who's cold and hungry, finds his way to the home of Mrs. Dodd, who owns six cats. Widget acts like a cat to earn acceptance, but when Mrs. Dodd gets hurt, it's Widget's barking that brings help.

Widget and the Puppy. Illustrated by Jim McFarland. New York: Farrar, Straus & Giroux, 2004. 32pp. ISBN 9780374384296. Sequel. `PreS–2`

A large puppy wanders into Mrs. Dodd's yard, and Widget is charged with watching over the rambunctious canine while his mistress searches for the owner. Widget gets so worn out keeping up with the energetic visitor that it's the girls—the cats—who actually keep track of him.

Different Pets and Multiple Pets

Although books about dogs and cats dominate the pet story field, there are books that feature other kinds of pets, either singly or together, with an array of different animals.

Bruel, Nick.

Little Red Bird. New York: Roaring Brook, 2008. 29pp. ISBN 9781596433397. `Gr. K–3`

This rhyming tale relates the quandary of a pet bird who one day finds both her cage door and a window open. With trepidation, she eases out of her cage and then flies free, but she wonders if she should stay in the park or return to her cage. This thought-provoking tale leaves the decision up to the reader.

Dodd, Emma.

What Pet to Get? New York: Scholastic, 2008. 28pp. ISBN 9780545035705. `PreS–2`

Jack longs for a pet and proposes a variety of animals to his mother, from an elephant to a polar bear. His patient mom replies with reasons why each animal would not be appropriate for their home. At last he settles on a dog, but the dog that he envisions is very different from the one his mother has in mind.

Henderson, Kathy.

Dog Story. Illustrated by Brita Granstrom. New York: Bloomsbury, 2004. 32pp. ISBN 9780747550716. **PreS–2**

Although Jo wants a dog more than anything, her parents are reluctant. They agree to let her get something smaller. Starting with a mouse, she eventually acquires a rabbit, guinea pig, and cat. When her parents announce that a new baby will be arriving, Jo still wants a dog, and eventually Grandma comes through with a pet puppy for the siblings.

Hughes, Ted.

My Brother Bert. Illustrated by Tracey Campbell Pearson. New York: Farrar, Straus & Giroux, 2009. Unpaged. ISBN 9780374399825. **PreS–3**

In light verse, Bert's sister reveals his secret collection of outrageous pets, including: a gorilla, grizzly bear, and lion, among others.

Javernick, Ellens.

The Birthday Pet. Illustrated by Kevin O'Malley. New York: Marshall Cavendish, 2009. 32pp. ISBN 9780761455226. **PreS–2**

Rhyming verse describes Danny's desire for a box turtle for his birthday. His family members, however, each give him a different kind of animal, until he convinces them that he really does want a turtle.

Orloff, Karin.

I Wanna Iguana. Illustrated by David Catrow. New York: Putnam, 2004. 32pp. ISBN 9780399237171. **PreS–3**

Alex and his mother exchange a series of letters. Alex is trying to convince his mother that he should adopt his friend's baby iguana, and his mother answers with all the reasons why it's not a good idea.

Poydar, Nancy.

Fish School. New York: Holiday House, 2009. Unpaged. ISBN 978-0823421404. **PreS–3**

When Charlie's class goes on a trip to the aquarium, Charlie brings his pet goldfish in a plastic bag filled with water so that he can teach his fish everything he learns.

Richards, Chuck.

Critter Sitter. New York: Walker, 2008. 32pp. ISBN 9780802795953. **Gr. 1–3**

Henry is confident that he can handle any situation when he embarks on his first critter sitting job, but he finds the Maloneys' menagerie almost too much to deal with.

Different Pets and Multiple Pets: Easy Readers

Rylant, Cynthia.

The Annie and Snowball Series. Illustrated by Sucie Stevenson. New York: Simon & Schuster. `Gr. 1-3`

Annie, Henry's cousin (from the Henry and Mudge series), and her pet bunny Snowball experience a variety of life's everyday events, from birthdays to tea parties. Rylant aptly portrays the feelings and episodes of childhood, deftly accompanied by Stevenson's warm pen-and-ink and watercolor illustrations.

Annie and Snowball and the Dress-up Birthday. 2007. 40pp. ISBN 9781416939436.

Annie and Snowball and the Prettiest House. 2007. 40pp. ISBN 9781416909392.

Annie and Snowball and the Teacup Club. 2008. 40pp. ISBN 9781416909408.

Annie and Snowball and the Pink Surprise. 2008. 40pp. ISBN 9781416909415.

Annie and Snowball and the Cozy Nest. 2009. 39pp. ISBN 9781416939436.

Annie and Snowball and the Shining Star. 2009. ISBN 9781416939467.

Annie and Snowball and the Magical House. 2010. ISBN 9781416939450.

Annie and Snowball and the Wintry Freeze. 2010. ISBN 9781416972051.

Wild Animals

Children in any environment, country, city, or suburbs, can see animals all around them that are not pets, such as squirrels and birds, so these animals also make their way into children's books.

Neighborhood Wildlife

Ehlert, Lois.

Nuts to You. **San Diego: Harcourt, 1993. Unpaged. ISBN 9780152576479.** `PreS-2`

An inquisitive city squirrel investigates a birdhouse, window boxes of flowers, and an apartment. The rhyming text is complemented by Ehlert's sumptuous signature illustrations.

Graham, Bob.

How to Heal a Broken Wing. **Cambridge, MA: Candlewick, 2008. Unpaged. ISBN 9780763639037.** `Gr. K-2`

In a city, a wounded pigeon tumbles to the sidewalk. No one notices until a young boy convinces his mother to bring the bird home, where the family nurses it with care until it can fly free once more. (ALAN, Charlotte Zolotow Award)

Henkes, Kevin.

🕊*Birds*. Illustrated by Laura Dronzek. New York: Greenwillow, 2009. 32pp. ISBN 9780061363047. **PreS–1**

> When a young girl hears birdsong through her window in the early morning, she begins to think about different kinds of birds in different seasons. (ALAN)

McPhail, David.

The Searcher and Old Tree. Watertown, MA: Charlesbridge, 2008. 32pp. ISBN 9781580892230. **PreS–1**

> After foraging for food all night, a raccoon returns to his tree home. Snuggled securely in its branches, he sleeps safely through a tremendous thunderstorm.

Wildlife

Arnosky, Jim.

Turtle in the Sea. New York: Putnam, 2002. Unpaged. ISBN 9780399227578. **Gr. K–3**

> Through the years a female sea turtle has faced dangers from man and nature, and now she works her way to the shore to lay her eggs.

Grandfather Buffalo. New York: Putnam, 2006. 32pp. ISBN 9780399241697. **Gr. 1–3**

> An old buffalo can no longer keep up with the herd. When he discovers another buffalo also lagging behind, he becomes her protector as she has her calf and then cares for the newborn.

Dolphins on the Sand. New York: Penguin, 2008. Unpaged. ISBN 978-0399246067. **Gr. K–3**

> When frolicking dolphins get stuck on a sandbar, a group of volunteers helps them back into the ocean. Gorgeous ocean images bring immediacy to this moving story.

Bunting, Eve.

Whales Passing. Illustrated by Lambert Davis. New York: Blue Sky Press, 2003. Unpaged. ISBN 9780590603584. **PreS–2**

> From a cliff overlooking the ocean, a father and son watch a pod of orca whales swimming by. The father provides informative answers to his son's questions.

Dowson, Nick.

🐾*Tracks of a Panda.* **Illustrated by Yu Rong. Cambridge, MA: Candlewick, 2007. 32pp. ISBN 9780763631468.** `PreS-2`

This lyrical text follows the life of a panda in China from birth through the conclusion of his first year. Watercolor illustrations that make use of traditional Chinese techniques effectively illuminate the life of the cub and his mother. (ALAN)

Ehlert, Lois.

Oodles of Animals. **Orlando, FL: Harcourt, 2008. 56pp. ISBN 9780152062743.** `PreS-2`

Different animals are presented through brightly colored cut-paper collages while a text of verse imparts a bit of information about each creature.

Elliot, David.

And Here's to You. **Illustrated by Randy Cecil. Cambridge, MA: Candlewick, 2004. Unpaged. ISBN 9780763614270.** `PreS-2`

This energetic rhyming text celebrates a variety of nature's creatures, illustrated with bold cartoon illustrations.

Falwell, Cathryn.

Scoot! **New York: Greenwillow, 2008. 32pp. ISBN 9780061288821.** `PreS-2`

Rhyming couplets describe the antics of an assortment of creatures that live down by the pond, including turtles, tadpoles, and salamanders. Brilliantly illustrated with paper collages.

Fox, Mem.

*Hello Baby! **Illustrated by Steve Jenkins. New York: Beach Lane Books, 2009. Unpaged. ISBN 9781416985136.** `T-K`

This smoothly cadenced rhyming story asks a baby, "Who are you?" and proposes different animals, such as zebras, lions, and elephants, as the possible responses. Beautifully accompanied by Jenkins's stunning cut-paper collages.

Kurtz, Jane, and Christopher Kurtz.

Water Hole Waiting. **Illustrated by Lee Christiansen. New York: Greenwillow, 2002. Unpaged. ISBN 9780060298500.** `PreS-3`

On an African savanna a vervet monkey and his mother wait their turn at a watering hole while a succession of animals take their turns.

Mayo, Margaret.

Roar! **Illustrated by Alex Ayliffe. Minneapolis: Carolrhoda, 2007. 24pp. ISBN 9780761394730.** `PreS-1`

A poetic text describes the traits of a variety of wild animals, including lions, zebras, elephants, and leopards.

Purmell, Ann.

Where Wild Babies Sleep. **Illustrated by Lorianne Siomades. Honesdale, PA: Boyds Mills, 2003. 24pp. ISBN 9781590780497.** `T-K`

Cut-paper collages and a simple text depict a variety of wild animals asleep with their mothers watching over them, including a kangaroo, a skunk, and a stingray.

Ryder, Joanne.

Each Living Thing. **Illustrated by Ashley Wolff. San Diego: Harcourt, 2000. Unpaged. ISBN 9780152018986.** `Gr. K-3`

In a book that promotes respect for all creatures, the elegant text and luscious illustrations combine to present a variety of wildlife in their natural habitats.

Talking Animals

These animal fantasies feature stories in which the animals engage in animal activities, but they talk and or share their thoughts in an anthropomorphic manner. They also participate in imaginative activities, but retain their essential animal natures. Talking animal stories in which the animals are more like humans than animals have been placed in their subject areas.

Domestic

Cats

Burningham, John.

It's a Secret! **Somerville, MA: Candlewick, 2009. 42pp. ISBN 978-0763642754.** `PreS-1`

Marie Elaine wonders where her cat, who sleeps all day, goes at night. When she spies him dressed in finery in the kitchen late one night, he confesses that he is going to a party. She begs to attend and he agrees to take her once she shrinks down to the appropriate size. She follows him to a rooftop gala, which includes dancing and a banquet with the Queen of Cats.

Kuskin, Karla.

*What's It Like to Be a Cat? **Illustrated by Betsy Lewin. New York: Atheneum, 2005. Unpaged. ISBN 9780689847332.** `PreS-3`

A curious boy interviews his cat to uncover the mysteries of what it's like to be a feline, in this story relayed in rhyming dialogue and accompanied by illustrations that capture the playful essence of cats.

Reibstein, Mark.

🐾*Wabi Sabi.* Illustrated by Ed Young. New York: Little, Brown, 2008. 40pp. ISBN 9780316118255. `Gr. 2 & up`

Kyoto the cat lived in Japan with her master. Curious about the meaning of her name, she travels about the country searching for information that will satisfy her yen to know. (New York Times Best Illustrated)

Rohmann, Eric.

A Kitten Tale. See under "Seasons" in chapter 9.

Rymond, Lynda Gene.

Oscar and the Mooncats. Illustrated by Nicoletta Ceccoli. Boston: Houghton Mifflin, 2007. 32pp. ISBN 9780618563166. `Gr. K–3`

When Oscar the cat takes a mighty leap from the roof, he soars all the way to the moon where he encounters the mooncats. He has such fun frolicking with them, he ignores the calls of his boy. He is about to drink the cream left by the cow who jumped over the moon when he receives a warning that if he does so he will become a mooncat himself and never be able to return home. While he's had fun on the moon, he loves his boy, so with another powerful leap, he arrives back home.

Schachner, Judith.

The Skippyjon Jones Series. See in chapter 11.

Soto, Gary.

The Chato Series. Illustrated by Susan Guevara. New York: Putnam. `Gr. 1-3` (SP)

Chato is quite convinced that he is the hippest cat in all of East Los Angeles, and he has a grand time on his adventures.

🐾*Chato's Kitchen.* 1995. Unpaged. ISBN 9780698116009 (pb).

Chato, a cool cat of East Los Angeles, invites the new family of mice over for dinner, with plans that are less than healthy for the mice. The crafty rodents turn the tables on him when they bring their dog friend with them. (ALAN, Pura Belpre Award)

🐾*Chato and the Party Animals.* 2000. Unpaged. ISBN 9780399231599.

Chato decides to throw a birthday party for his pal Novio Boy, but forgets to invite the guest of honor. When a search of the barrio yields nothing, Chato and his friends fear the worst, but Novio Boy soon turns up, bringing his new friends with him. The rollicking text is sprinkled with Spanish words. (ALAN, Pura Belpre Award)

🐾*Chato Goes Cruisin'.* 2005. 32pp. ISBN 9780142408100 (pb).

Chato and Novio Boy are delighted to win a trip on a cruise, but are dismayed when they arrive aboard ship to find that the rest of the passengers are all dogs. (New York Times Best Illustrated)

Talking Cats: Easy Readers

Seuss, Dr.

9

The Cat in the Hat. New York: Random House, 1957. 61pp. ISBN 978-0394800011. **Gr. K–3**

> This is the classic tale of the mischief-making cat that visits a brother and sister while their mother is out and wreaks fun-filled havoc.

The Cat in the Hat Comes Back. New York: Random House, 1958. 61pp. ISBN 9780394800028. Sequel. **Gr. K–3**

10

> The outrageous cat returns on a snowy day to entertain once again.

Willems, Mo.

The Cat the Cat Series. New York: Balzer & Bray. **Gr. K–2**

11

> With his characteristic cartoon illustrations and trademark sense of humor, Willems introduces the youngest readers to the world of Cat.

> *Cat the Cat, Who Is That?* 2010. 32pp. ISBN 9780061728402.

> *Let's Say Hi to Friends Who Fly.* 2010. 32pp. ISBN 9780061728464.

> *What's Your Sound, Hound the Hound?* 2010. 32pp. ISBN 9780061728457.

12

> *Time to Sleep, Sheep the Sheep.* 2010. 32pp. ISBN 9780061728471.

Dogs

Brown, Peter.

13

Chowder. New York: Little, Brown, 2006. 32pp. ISBN 9780316011808. **Gr. 1–3**

> Chowder is an English bulldog who likes reading the newspaper and using the computer, which makes all the other dogs in the neighborhood think that he's just plain weird. Lonely, he searches for friends in the newly discovered petting zoo.

14

The Fabulous Bouncing Chowder. New York: Little, Brown, 2007. 29pp. ISBN 9780316011792. Sequel. **Gr. 1–3**

> Chowder tries again to make friends with other dogs when he attends the Fabu Pooch Boot Camp, a sleepaway camp for well-behaved canines.

Christelow, Eileen.

15

Letters from a Desperate Dog. New York: Clarion, 2006. 32pp. ISBN 978-0618510030. **PreS–3**

> Emma, an unappreciated beagle-like dog, lives with her owner George, an artist, and his cat. When she spies an advice column in the *Weekly Bone*, she e-mails Queenie for advice on how to improve her situation.

The Desperate Dog Writes Again. Boston: Clarion, 2010. 32pp. ISBN 978-0547242057. Sequel. `PreS-3`

Emma is having troubles once again. This time she e-mails the advice columnist for help figuring out how to handle her owner's new girlfriend.

Ehlert, Lois.

Wag a Tail. Orlando, FL: Harcourt, 2007. 40pp. ISBN 9780152058432. `PreS-2`

A variety of playful city dogs accompany their owners, first to a farmer's market and then to the park. The rhyming text is conveyed in speech balloons and is accompanied by distinctive collage in bold colors.

Fleming, Denise.

Buster. New York: Holt, 2003. 40pp. ISBN 9780805062793. `PreS-3`

Buster's idyllic life is turned topsy-turvy when his owner brings home a small white cat.

Buster Goes to Cowboy Camp. New York: Holt, 2008. 40pp. ISBN 978-0805078923. Sequel. `PreS-3`

Buster is not at all happy that his owner drops him off at cowboy camp while he takes a weekend off, but the disgruntled canine soon changes his mind as he has a blast learning how to catch a ball, build a fire, and sing cowboy songs. (ALAN)

Gravett, Emily.

Dogs. New York: Simon & Schuster, 2010. Unpaged. ISBN 9781416987031. `PreS-1`

A narrator, who is unseen until the surprise ending, uses simple rhymes to present a variety of dogs who demonstrate why they make great pets.

Huneck, Stephen.

The Sally Series. New York: Abrams. `PreS-2`

This series chronicles the adventures of Sally, a black Labrador retriever. It is based on the life of Sally, who is a real dog, trained as a seeing-eye dog and later adopted by the author and his wife. The simple text relays Sally's experiences from the dog's point of view and is accompanied by striking woodcuts.

Sally Goes to the Beach. 2000. Unpaged. ISBN 9780810941861.

Sally Goes to the Mountains. 2001. Unpaged. ISBN 9780810944855.

Sally Goes to the Farm. 2002. Unpaged. ISBN 9780810944985.

Sally Goes to the Vet. 2004. Unpaged. ISBN 9780810948136.

Sally's Snow Adventure. 2006. 32pp. ISBN 9780810970618.

Sally Gets a Job. 2008. 31pp. ISBN 9780810994935.

Sally's Great Balloon Adventure. 2010. Unpaged. ISBN 9780810983311.

Kasza, Keiko.

The Dog Who Cried Wolf. New York: Putnam, 2005. 32pp. ISBN 978-0399242472. `PreS-1`

Moka the dog is happy with his owner Michelle until he learns about how real wolves live from a book. He decides he wants to live wild and free, until he encounters real wolves and hightails it back home.

McDonnell, Christine.

Dog Wants to Play. Illustrated by Jeff Mack. New York: Viking, 2009. 32pp. ISBN 9780670011261. `T-K`

Dog asks each animal on the farm to play with him, but they all have reasons why they can't. Dog feels forlorn until his boy arrives and can play with him all day. Endearing acrylic illustrations are the perfect match for this charming story.

Meddaugh, Susan.

The Martha Series. Boston: Houghton Mifflin. `PreS-3`

Martha is a mutt who learns to speak when she eats alphabet soup. Ink-line-and-watercolor cartoons add to the humor of the adventures of this talkative pup, who now stars in her own TV series. Listed here is the original series, not the books generated by the TV series based on Meddaugh's characters.

🎀*Martha Speaks.* 1992. 30pp. ISBN 9780395633137. (SP)
   (New York Times Best Illustrated)

Martha Calling. 1994. Unpaged. ISBN 9780395698259.

Martha Blah, Blah, Blah. 1996. 32pp. ISBN 9780395797556.

Martha Walks the Dog. 1998. 32pp. ISBN 9780395904947.

Perfectly Martha. 2004. 32pp. ISBN 9780618378579.

Oppel, Kenneth.

The King's Tester. Illustrated by Lou Fancher and Steve Johnson. New York: HarperCollins, 2009. 30pp. ISBN 9780060753726. `Gr. K-3`

Max the beagle is the king's taster and the cook's dog. He loves tasting all the dishes for the king, even though he is making sure there is no poison. When a young boy becomes king, he rejects all the cook's tried and true dishes. The cook and his dog set out to find new delicacies, but none of them please the king, until Max discovers the king is snacking on sweets, which is why he won't eat anything else. In the end the king changes his eating habits, and the cook and Max open their own restaurant.

Stevens, Janet.

Help Me, Mr. Mutt. See in chapter 14.

Walton, Rick.

Bertie Was a Watchdog. See in chapter 14.

Wood, Audrey.

A Dog Needs a Bone. New York: Blue Sky Press, 2007. 40pp. ISBN 9780545000055. `PreS-1`

> In chipper rhyme, a cartoonlike dog makes his mistress a plethora of promises if she will only give him a bone.

Multiple Animals, Domestic and Wild

Many talking animal books are filled with a variety of kinds of animals, both domestic and wild, all interacting with each other.

Bauer, Marion Dane.

The Longest Night. Illustrated by Ted Lewin. New York: Holiday House, 2009. Unpaged. ISBN 9780823420544. `Gr. 2 & up`

> Poetic prose swirls through the life of a series of wild animals on the longest night of the year. As the winter solstice progresses, they anxiously anticipate the arrival of dawn. Sumptuous watercolors give the night a stunning glow.

Beaumont, Karen.

*Move Over, Rover! Illustrated by Jane Dyer. Orlando, FL: Harcourt, 2006. 40pp. ISBN 9780152019792. `PreS-2`

> In this cumulative tale, when a rainstorm hits, Rover shares his doghouse with a variety of animals. They shelter there until a skunk arrives, sending the animals scurrying. (ALAN, Geisel Honor)

Chen, Chih-Yuan.

Guji, Guji. La Jolla, CA: Kane Miller, 2004. 32pp. ISBN 9781929132676. `PreS-3`

> Guji Guji, the crocodile is raised as a duck because his egg rolled into Mother Duck's nest. When he encounters three crocodiles who want duck for dinner, he has to choose between joining them in the hunt or saving the ducks. (ALAN)

Fraser, Mary Ann.

Pet Shop Lullaby. Honesdale, PA: Boyds Mills, 2009. ISBN 9781590786185. `PreS-1`.

> In a pet shop at night, all the animals are ready for sleep except for hamster, who is all set to exercise. When the creatures can't quiet the cacophony, they concoct a way to lull the hamster to sleep.

Kasza, Keiko.

The Mightiest. New York: Putnam, 2001. Unpaged. ISBN 9780399235863. `PreS-1`

A lion, an elephant, and a bear want to prove their strength to win the right to wear the golden crown, so they each attempt to frighten an old woman. Their plan is thwarted when a giant arrives and claims the crown for himself, but his mother, the little old woman, admonishes him for frightening the animals, and they declare that she is the mightiest of them all.

Larochelle, David.

The Best Pet of All. See under "Fantasy and Magic" in chapter 15.

Martin, Bill.

Brown Bear, Brown Bear, What Do You See? See under "Colors" in chapter 4.

Polar Bear, Polar Bear, What Do You Hear? Illustrated by Eric Carle. New York: Holt, 1991. 25pp. ISBN 9780805017595. `PreS-1` (SP)

Following the same format as *Brown Bear*, this book asks animals what sound they hear, and the sound with its appropriate animal appears on each succeeding page.

Panda Bear, Panda Bear, What Do You See? Illustrated by Eric Carle. New York: Holt, 2003. 32pp. ISBN 9780805017588. `PreS-1` (SP)

Martin and Carle return to their pattern and present a series of endangered animals, including a water buffalo, a whooping crane, and a sea turtle, among others. The book is strikingly illustrated with Carle's signature collages.

Baby Bear, Baby Bear, What Do You See? Illustrated by Eric Carle. New York: Holt, 2007. 32pp. ISBN 9780805083361. `PreS-1`

In their final collaboration, Martin and Carle present ten animals native to North America, including a blue heron, a red fox, and a screech owl.

Martin, David M.

We've All Got Bellybuttons! Illustrated by Randy Cecil. Cambridge, MA: Candlewick, 2005. 32pp. ISBN 9780763617752. `T-K`

Different animals, including cartoon-colored lions, giraffes, and zebras, point out the various body parts that are similar to those that humans have. Rhythmic text and bright illustrations make this a fun anatomical story.

Rex, Adam.

Pssst! Orlando, FL: Harcourt, 2007. 28pp. ISBN 9780152058173. `Gr. K-3`

When a girl visits a zoo, an array of animals makes requests for an odd assortment of items.

Sierra, Judy.

🎗*Wild about Books.* See under "Community Helpers: Librarians" in chapter 2.

Stein, David Ezra.

Pouch! New York: Putnam, 2009. Unpaged. ISBN 9780399250514. `PreS–1`

When a joey hops from his mother's pouch, he asks each animal he meets to identify himself. They answer, but the baby kangaroo always bounds back to his mother, until he meets another joey.

Wild Animals

Sea Creatures

Carle, Eric.

A House for Hermit Crab. New York: Simon & Schuster, 1991. 27pp. ISBN 9780887080562. `PreS–2`

Each year, as Hermit Crab grows too big for his shell, he sets off in search of a larger shell to call home, and along the way makes new friends.

Mister Seahorse. New York: Philomel, 2004. 32pp. ISBN 9780399242694. `PreS–2`

After Mrs. Seahorse lays her eggs in Mr. Seahorse's pouch, she leaves while he promises to take good care of them. He floats in the sea, encountering different sea fathers until his own young hatch, and he sends them out into the world on their own.

Pfister, Marcus.

The Rainbow Fish Series. New York: North South. `Gr. K–3`

A very shimmery fish helps his fellow ocean creatures in a variety of ways. Rainbow Fish also stars in a board book series.

Rainbow Fish. 1991. 32pp. ISBN 9781558580091. (SP)

Rainbow Fish to the Rescue. 1995. 32pp. ISBN 9781558584860.

Rainbow Fish and the Big Blue Whale. 1998. Unpaged. ISBN 9780735810099.

Rainbow Fish and the Sea Monster's Cave. 2001. 32pp. ISBN 9780735815377.

Rainbow Fish Finds His Way. 2006. 32pp. ISBN 9780735820845.

Lionni, Leo.

🎗*Swimmy.* New York: Pantheon, 1963. Reissued in 1991 by Knopf. 32pp. ISBN 9780394817132. `PreS–2`

When one small, black fish is the only one of his school to survive a tuna attack, he convinces a small school of red fish to join him in frightening the enemy away by working together. (Caldecott Honor, New York Times Best Illustrated)

Many Kinds of Creatures

Banks, Kate.

Fox. Illustrated by Georg Hallensleben. New York: Farrar, Straus & Giroux, 2007. 40pp. ISBN 9780374399672. **PreS–1**

> On a spring day, a baby fox is born. As his parents care for him, they teach him how to survive.

Carle, Eric.

Slowly, Slowly, Slowly, Said the Sloth. New York: Philomel, 2002. 32pp. ISBN 9780399239540. **Gr. K–3**

> As the sloth makes his unhurried way through his day in the Amazon rain forest, he defends his way of life to the inquisitive speedy animals around him.

Knudsen, Michelle.

Library Lion. Illustrated by Kevin Hawkes. Cambridge, MA: Candlewick, 2006. 48pp. ISBN 9780763622626. **PreS–3**

> A lion who loves stories agrees to Miss Merriweather's rule of no noise in the library so that he can come to storytime. He becomes a regular in the library until he lets out a mighty roar and is banned, but an act of heroism wins his place back for him.

Lies, Brian.

<u>**The Bats' Adventures.**</u> **Boston: Houghton Mifflin. PreS–3**

> A colony of bats enjoy various nighttime escapades.

Bats at the Beach. 2006. 32pp. ISBN 9780618557448.

> Lively rhymes recount a colony of bats' visit to the beach for a night of picnicking, games, and playing in the waves.

Bats at the Library. 2008. 32pp. ISBN 9780618999231.

> This time the bats pay a call on the local library by moonlight.

Bats at the Ballgame. 2010. 32pp. ISBN 9780547249704.

> Now, those ever-active bats are playing a game of baseball in the moonlight.

Rubin, Adam.

Those Darn Squirrels. Illustrated by Daniel Salmieri. New York: Clarion, 2009. 32pp. ISBN 9780547007038. **Gr. K–3**

> In this humorous tale, a grumpy old man, who only likes birds, engages in a war of wits with a gang of squirrels who are constantly raiding his bird feeder.

Shields, Carol Diggory.

Wombat Walkabout. Illustrated by Sophie Blackall. New York: Dutton, 2009. 28pp. ISBN 9780525478652. **Gr. K–2**

Six wombats Down Under go for a walkabout and almost end up as dinner for a dingo, but some quick thinking saves the day.

Wild, Margaret.

Puffling. Illustrated by Julie Vivas. New York: Feiwel and Friends, 2009. 32pp. ISBN 9780312565701. **T–K**

A baby puffin is eager to explore the ocean and begs his parents to let him go out on his own, but they insist that he must wait until he is big enough and strong enough.

Farms

Life on the Farm

Whether children live on or near a farm or even if they live far from the country in cities and suburbs, they all learn the sounds farm animals make and can experience the life of a farm and its animals through these titles. Once again, the books have been divided into realistic fiction and talking animal fantasy.

Carter, Don.

Old MacDonald Drives a Tractor. New Milford, CN: Roaring Brook, 2007. 24pp. ISBN 9781596430235. **T–K**

In this sprightly version of the traditional song, Old MacDonald takes out a tractor and clears a field.

Cooper, Elisha.

Farm. New York: Orchard, 2010. 48pp. ISBN 9780545070751. **PreS–1**

A farm family takes care of their land and animals throughout the seasons.

Lee, Huy Voun.

In the Leaves. New York: Holt, 2005. 32pp. ISBN 9780805067644. **Gr. 1–3**

One autumn day Xiao Ming and his friends visit a farm. Xiao writes the Chinese symbols for ten different things that they see in the dirt, explaining that Chinese characters are like pictures. A Mandarin Chinese pronunciation guide is appended.

Ransom, Candice F.

Tractor Day. Illustrated by Laura J. Bryant. New York: Walker, 2007. 32pp. ISBN 9780802780904. **T–K**

Short, rhyming phrases describe the day a father and his daughter spend on their tractor getting the fields ready for planting.

Rylant, Cynthia.

All in a Day. Illustrated by Nikki McClure. New York: Abrams, 2009. 32pp. ISBN 9780810983212. `PreS-2`

A boy spends a day on the family farm, planting seeds and gathering eggs, and then settles down for a nap. The cut-paper illustrations give the story a retro feel.

Realistic Farm Animals

Cole, Henry.

Trudy. New York: Greenwillow, 2009. 30pp. ISBN 9780061542671. `PreS-2`

At the country auction, Esme picks a goat as the animal that's just right to live in the small barn on her grandparents' property. She names her Trudy and soon discovers that Trudy stays in the barn whenever it's going to snow. One day Trudy stays in and there is no snow, which worries Esme, but when she enters the barn, she sees that Trudy has had a kid.

Cordsen, Carol Foskett.

Market Day. Illustrated by Douglas B. Jones. New York: Dutton, 2008. 30pp. ISBN 9780525478836. `PreS-2`

The Benson family (from *The Milkman*) is so busy packing their truck with produce to sell at the farmer's market that they forget to feed their cow. The hungry animal follows them and creates quite a ruckus.

Doyle, Malachy.

Horse. Illustrated by Angelo Rinaldi. New York: Margaret K. McElderry, 2008. 24pp. ISBN 9781416924678. `PreS-2`

Simple text describes the first year of a foal's life from birth to bridle, accompanied by gorgeous equine oil paintings.

Fleming, Denise.

🎖**Barnyard Banter.* New York: Holt, 1994. Unpaged. ISBN 9780805019575. `T-K`

As a goose chases a butterfly through the barnyard, a variety of farm animals create an onomatopoeic cacophony. The rhythmic rhyming text begs to be read aloud and encourages audience participation, both in chanting the animal sounds and in locating the goose hidden in each spread. Fleming's signature vivid pulp-painting pictures are stunning. (ALAN)

Gray, Rita.

The Wild Little Horse. Illustrated by Ashley Wolff. New York: Dutton, 2005. 32pp. ISBN 9780525474555. `PreS-2`

A curious colt first explores the farm where he lives and then the nearby seashore, before his parents arrive to lead him home.

Harrington, Janice N.

🔖*The Chicken-Chasing Queen of Lamar County*. **Illustrated by Shelley Jackson.
New York: Farrar, Straus & Giroux, 2007. 40pp. ISBN 9780374312510.** `Gr. K-2`

An African American girl who lives on a farm delights in chasing the chickens
even though her mother has repeatedly told her to leave them be. One bird, however, Miss Hen, always eludes her. She tries everything she can think of to catch
that hen and eventually finds her hidden away in the tall grass cuddling her
newly hatched chicks. The chicken-chasing queen decides to leave the happy family in peace at last. (ALAN)

Hutchins, Pat.

Ten Red Apples. See under "Counting" in chapter 4.

Jeffers, Susan.

My Chincoteague Pony. **New York: Hyperion, 2008. 27pp. ISBN 9781423100232.** `Gr. K-2`

Julie lives on a farm with her family and dreams of having a Chincoteague pony of
her own. The family travels to Chincoteague Island for Pony Penning Day. Julie
loses auction after auction and realizes that she does not have enough money
saved, but generous strangers make contributions so that her dream can come
true. Based on an incident from the author's childhood.

Lobel, Anita.

Hello Day! **New York: Greenwillow, 2008. 30pp. ISBN 9780060787653.** `T-K`

As dawn brightens the morning sky, the farm animals greet the rising sun with
their singular sounds.

Lujan, Jorge.

Rooster/Gallo. **Illustrated by Manuel Monroy. Toronto: Groundwood, 2004.
Unpaged. ISBN 9780888995582.** `PreS-2` **(Bilingual)**

This poem in Spanish and English portrays the rooster's call as the power that
brings the world into existence each day.

Rand, Gloria.

Mary Was a Little Lamb. **Illustrated by Ted Rand. New York: Holt, 2004.
Unpaged. ISBN 9780805068160.** `PreS-1`

When a newborn lamb is forgotten by her mother, Mrs. Paradise of Cranberry Island adopts her and names her Mary. As Mary grows, she becomes too much for
the island residents to handle, and she is donated to a petting zoo on the main-
land, in this episode that is based on a true story.

Spinelli, Eileen.

Best Time of Day. Illustrated by Bryan Langdo. Orlando, FL: Harcourt, 2005. Unpaged. ISBN 9780152050511. `PreS-3`

> This story in rhyme relates the best time of day for both the people and the animals who live on the farm.

Talking Farm Animals

These farm animal fantasies are set on a farm where the animals engage in animal activities but talk and or share their thoughts in an anthropomorphic manner. They also participate in imaginative activities, but retain their essential animal natures. Talking farm animal stories in which the animals are more like humans than animals have been placed in their subject area.

Anderson, Peggy Perry.

Chuck's Truck. Boston: Houghton Mifflin, 2006. Unpaged. ISBN 9780618668366. `PreS-2`

> As farmer Chuck starts up his old truck about to head for town, all of his animals decide they want to accompany him. The rhyming adventure escorts the crowd to town, where the truck breaks down, and they need the help of Handyman Hugh and his crew to get back to the farm.

Chuck's Band. Boston: Houghton Mifflin, 2008. 32pp. ISBN 9780618965069. Sequel. `PreS-2`

> Chuck and his farm animals return for another episode in rhyme. This time they each demonstrate their expertise on different instruments purchased for them by Chuck, who began the hoedown by playing his banjo.

Auch, Mary Jane.

Souperchicken. Illustrated by Herm Auch. New York: Holiday House, 2003. Unpaged. ISBN 9780823417049. `Gr. 1-3`

> Henrietta is a chicken who loves to read, a skill that ends up saving the lives of some of her fellow chickens. When some of her fellow hens are not laying as many eggs as they used to, the farmer tells them he is sending them on vacation, but Henrietta reads the name of the company on the truck, Souper Soup. Immediately she embarks on a mission to rescue them from this dire fate.

The Plot Chickens. Illustrated by Herm Auch. New York: Holiday House, 2009. Unpaged. ISBN 9780823420872. Sequel. `Gr. 1-3`

> Henrietta decides that since she loves to read so much, she will write a story of her own, but has trouble getting it published.

Beaumont, Karen.

Duck, Duck, Goose: A Coyote's on the Loose. **Illustrated by Jose Aruego and Ariane Dewey. New York: HarperCollins, 2004. Unpaged. ISBN 9780060508029.** `PreS-1`

Employing a lively rhyme, Beaumont versifies about a group of farm animals who fear a coyote is after them, when in reality, it's rabbit, who wants to play.

Bunting, Eve.

Hurry, Hurry. **Illustrated by Jeff Mack. Orlando, FL: Harcourt, 2007. Unpaged. ISBN 9780152054106.** `PreS-1`

A bevy of farm animals, including a rooster, a duck family, pigs, and a sheepdog, all gather at the barnyard entrance to watch the hatching of the newest chick.

Buzzeo, Toni.

Dawdle Duckling. **Illustrated by Margaret Spengler. New York: Dial, 2003. Unpaged. ISBN 9780803727311.** `PreS-2`

Three of Mama Duck's ducklings obediently swim close behind her, but her fourth duckling is having too much fun on his own, so she is always calling him. When he at last follows his mother's instructions, it's just in time to escape the jaws of a hungry alligator.

Ready or Not, Dawdle Duckling. **Illustrated by Margaret Spengler. New York: Dial, 2005. Unpaged. ISBN 9780803729599. Sequel.** `PreS-2`

Mama Duck is playing hide-and-seek with her four ducklings. Three scurry off quickly and find hiding places, but Dawdle Duckling gets distracted and is easy to find, until his animal friends help him locate a place of safety.

Cronin, Doreen.

The Animals of Farmer Brown's Farm Series. **Illustrated by Betsy Lewin. New York: Simon & Schuster.** `PreS-3`

The animals on Farmer Brown's farm are determined and demanding, and Duck is one of the foremost animal leaders. Expressive cartoon illustrations accent the innate humor of the stories.

🏵*Click Clack Moo: Cows That Type.* 2000. Unpaged. ISBN 9780689832130. (SP)

The cows in Farmer Brown's barn are cold, and they have an old-fashioned typewriter. They send him a note demanding electric blankets. When he's not forthcoming, they refuse to give milk until their needs are met. Next, the hens refuse to lay eggs. Finally, with Duck as an intermediary, the farmer agrees to the blankets in exchange for the typewriter. The cows get their blankets, but Duck gets the typewriter and new demands are issued. Throughout the story the refrain of "Click, clack, moo. Click, clack, moo. Clickety, clack, moo," is repeated, begging for audience participation. (ALAN, Caldecott Honor)

Giggle, Giggle, Quack. 2002. Unpaged. ISBN 9780689845062.

When Farmer Brown goes on vacation, he leaves his brother Bob in charge and warns him to watch out for Duck, who can be sly. Each day Bob follows the written instructions that he thinks come from his brother. He orders pizza for the cows and gives the pigs bubble baths, never noticing that Duck has a pencil clamped in his beak everywhere he goes.

🎗️*Duck for President.* 2004. Unpaged. ISBN 9780689863776. (SP)

Duck is tired of all the chores he has to do on the farm, so he organizes an election and ousts Farmer Brown. Quickly he realizes that running a farm is hard work and decides to run for governor and then for president. Those jobs too, are arduous, so he returns to the farm to write his memoirs. (New York Times Best Illustrated)

Dooby, Dooby Moo. 2006. Unpaged. ISBN 9780689845079.

Duck spies an ad in the paper for a talent show and organizes all the animals into groups for practicing their singing and dancing routines.

Thump, Quack, Moo: A Whacky Adventure. 2008. Unpaged. ISBN 978-1416916307. (SP)

Farmer Brown puts all of his animals to work constructing a Statue of Liberty maze for the annual festival, but Duck has other ideas. Making use of night-vision goggles and a glow-in-the-dark ruler, Duck creates his own version of the maze.

DiCamillo, Kate.

Louise, the Adventures of a Chicken. See in chapter 11.

Edwards, Pamela Duncan.

The Mixed-Up Rooster. **Illustrated by Megan Lloyd. New York: Katherine Tegen Books, 2006. Unpaged. ISBN 9780060290009.** `PreS-1`

Ned the rooster stays up too late at night to wake up early enough to crow and wake up the hens, so Daisy Mae fires him. When his nighttime alarm warns the hens of a dangerous snake, Daisy admits there's a place for him after all.

Fleming, Denise.

*The Cow Who Clucked. **New York: Holt, 2006. Unpaged. ISBN 978-0805072655.** `PreS-1`

A cow dreams of being a chicken and wakes up clucking instead of mooing. She approaches each animal on the farm to see if she can find her missing moo. The animals answer with the appropriate sound until she reaches Hen, who moos. They swap sounds and all is right in the barnyard once again.

Himmelman, John.

Chickens to the Rescue. New York: Holt, 2006. 32pp. ISBN 9780805079517. `PreS-2`

No matter what goes wrong throughout the week on Greenstalk farm, the chickens race to the rescue, except on Sunday, when they collapse in exhaustion.

Hutchins, Pat.

We're Going on a Picnic. New York: Greenwillow, 2002. Unpaged. ISBN 978-0688167998. `T–K`

> The weather is so lovely that Hen, Duck, and Goose decide to go for a picnic, but they get so involved in finding just the right place to eat that they don't notice the critters hopping in and out of their basket. They're completely puzzled when they return home and find all their food missing.

Kinerk, Robert.

Clorinda. Illustrated by Steven Kellogg. New York: Simon & Schuster, 2003. Unpaged. ISBN 9780689864490. `PreS–2`

> Clorinda the cow enjoys life on the farm until she sees a ballet and decides to journey to New York City to become a ballerina.

Clorinda Takes Flight. Illustrated by Steven Kellogg. New York: Simon & Schuster, 2007. Unpaged. ISBN 9780689868641. Sequel. `PreS–2`

> Clorinda returns, and this time she wants to take flight. With the help of friends from the farm, she soars aloft in a hot air balloon.

Krosoczka, Jarrett.

Punk Farm. New York: Knopf, 2005. Unpaged. ISBN 9780375824296. `PreS–2`

> Farmer Joe completes his chores and heads to bed, completely unaware that once he's gone his animals don their shades and tune up their instruments for a night of performing punk rock music for their fellow farm animals.

Punk Farm on Tour. New York: Knopf, 2007. Unpaged. ISBN 9780375833434. Sequel. `PreS–2`

> When Farmer Joe travels to a tractor conference, his band of animals takes their rock group on the road for a tour.

Lawrence, John.

🌑 *This Little Chick.* Cambridge, MA: Candlewick, 2002. Unpaged. ISBN 978-0763617165. `T–K`

> A friendly little chick visits the various animals in the barnyard and greets them with their own animal sounds. (New York Times Best Illustrated)

Meng, Cece.

Tough Chicks. See under "Feelings and Self-Expression: Individuality" in chapter 1.

Mitton, Tony.

Down by the Cool of the Pool. Illustrated by Guy Parker-Rees. New York: Orchard, 2006. Unpaged. ISBN 9780439309158. `PreS–2`

> On a farm with a pond, a fun-loving frog invites the animals to dance down by the cool of the pool, and the barnyard creatures shimmy on down.

Reynolds, Aaron.

Chicks and Salsa. Illustrated by Paulette Bogan. New York: Bloomsbury, 2005. Unpaged. ISBN 9781582349725. **Gr. K–2**

> When a savvy rooster starts cooking Southwestern-style meals for the chickens, the other animals soon want a taste.

Buffalo Wings. Illustrated by Paulette Bogan. New York: Bloomsbury, 2007. Unpaged. ISBN 9781599900629. Sequel. **Gr. K–2**

> The animals are settling down to watch a big football game with lots of snacks, but the rooster thinks that something is missing and goes off in search of buffalo so he can make some buffalo wings.

10

Schertle, Alice.

Little Blue Truck. Illustrated by Jill McElmurry. Orlando, FL: Harcourt, 2008. Unpaged. ISBN 9780152056612. **T–K**

> Blue, the little truck, jounces joyfully down the road in this rhyming jaunt. He greets each animal with a beep, and the animals respond with their signature sounds.

11

Little Blue Truck Leads the Way. Illustrated by Jill McElmurry. Orlando, FL: Harcourt, 2009. Unpaged. ISBN 9780152063894. Sequel. **T–K**

> Little Blue Truck returns to take a trip to the city, delivering produce to the market. As tall buildings surround Little Blue and traffic snarls, his advice helps all the vehicles get through.

12

Shannon, David.

🌑*Duck on a Bike.* New York: Blue Sky Press, 2002. Unpaged. ISBN 9780439050234. **PreS–2** (SP)

13

> Duck teaches himself to ride a bike and peddles past each animal on the farm, greeting them as he goes. The animals respond with moos, neighs, and barks, respectively, but think something positive or negative about Duck's exploits. When a group of children leave their bikes unattended, all of the animals get to ride and discover how much fun Duck has been having. Storytime audiences will delight in identifying the animals and join in chanting their sounds. (ALAN)

14

Shannon, George.

🌑*Tippy-Toe Chick, Go!* Illustrated by Laura Dronzek. New York: Greenwillow, 2003. Unpaged. ISBN 9780060298234. **PreS–2**

15

> When Hen takes her chicks to the garden to look for bugs, a loud dog deters her, but her young ones are sure they can find a way past him. (Charlotte Zolotow Honor)

Stiegemeyer, Julie.

Gobble-Gobble Crash! See under "Thanksgiving" in chapter 6.

Stoeke, Janet.

<u>The Minerva Louise Series.</u> See in chapter 14.

Tafuri, Nancy.

Five Little Chicks. New York: Simon & Schuster, 2006. Unpaged. ISBN 978-0689873423. `T–K`

Five just-hatched chicks search for food, but they don't find the right thing until Mama takes them to a corn field.

Whose Chick Are You? New York: Greenwillow, 2007. Unpaged. ISBN 978-0060825140. `T–K`

When mother and father swan swim away from their egg at dawn to find food, hen, duck, sparrow, and goose each wonder who the egg belongs to, until Mother Swan returns to claim it.

Van Leeuwen, Jean.

Chicken Soup. Illustrated by David Gavril. New York: Abrams, 2009. Unpaged. ISBN 9780810983267. `PreS–2`

When Mrs. Farmer hauls out the big soup pot, all the chickens hide. Little Chickie tries to take cover, but his cold gives him away every time. Mr. Farmer finally catches him, but Chickie learns she's not going into the soup, the soup is going into her.

Farm Life: Easy Readers

George, Jean Craighead.

🐾*Goose and Duck.* Illustrated by Priscilla Lamont. New York: Laura Geringer Books, 2008. 48pp. ISBN 9780061170768. `Gr. K–2`

When a boy finds a goose egg, the gosling hatches and thinks the boy is its mother. Then the goose finds a duck egg, and the duckling thinks the goose is its mother. The three stick together until the birds are old enough to rejoin their flocks. (ALAN)

Grant, Judyann Ackerman.

🐾*Chicken Said, "Cluck!"* Illustrated by Sue Truesdell. New York: HarperCollins, 2008. 32pp. ISBN 9780060287238. `Gr. K–2`

Earl and Pearl want to grow pumpkins, but they always have to shoo pesky Chicken away. When grasshoppers arrive, Chicken proves that she can be useful after all. (ALAN, Geisel Honor)

Shaw, Nancy.

The Sheep Series. Illustrated by Margot Apple. Boston: Houghton Mifflin. `PreS-2`

A flock of active sheep have a variety of unsheep-like adventures in stories that make apt use of simple sentences for the youngest readers.

Sheep in a Jeep. 1986. 32pp. ISBN 9780395411056.

Sheep on a Ship. 1989. 32pp. ISBN 9780395481608.

Sheep in a Shop. 1991. 32pp. ISBN 9780395536810.

Sheep out to Eat. 1992. 31pp. ISBN 9780395611289.

Sheep Take a Hike. 1994. Unpaged. ISBN 9780395683941.

Sheep Trick or Treat. 1997. Unpaged. ISBN 9780395841686.

Sheep Blast Off. 2008. Unpaged. ISBN 9780618131686.

Dinosaurs

Dinosaurs are perpetually popular. Virtually all dinosaur picture books are technically fantasy, for either they are set in contemporary times or they involve talking/thinking creatures. Both would make them imaginative rather than realistic.

Broach, Elise.

🌸*When Dinosaurs Came with Everything.* **Illustrated by David Small. New York: Atheneum, 2007. Unpaged. ISBN 9780689869228.** `PreS-2`

As a boy and his mother do the day's errands, the boy collects a dinosaur with every transaction, to his delight and his mother's dismay. (ALAN)

Buzzeo, Toni.

No T. Rex in the Library. **Illustrated by Sachiko Yoshikawa. New York: Margaret K. McElderry, 2010. 32pp. ISBN 9781416939276.** `T-K`

When the T. rex that Tess is reading about in the library suddenly springs to life, and the two go on a wild ride together.

DiPucchio, Kelly S.

Dinosnores. **Illustrated by Ponder Goembel. New York: HarperCollins, 2005. Unpaged. ISBN 9780060515775.** `Gr. K-3`

Various kinds of dinosaurs get ready for bed, fall asleep, and snore such great snores that the continent splits into two parts.

Donaldson, Julia.

Tyrannosaurus Drip. **Illustrated by David Roberts. New York: Feiwel & Friends, 2008. ISBN 9780312377472.** `Gr. K-3`

In this rhyming tale, the plant-eating, duck-billed dinosaurs live on one side of the river and the tyrannosaurs on the other side. Since they don't swim, there is no way for the tyrannosaurs to make a meal of the duck-bills. When a duck-billed egg ends up on the tyrannosaur side, he's raised as a tyrannosaur, but he shows his true colors at the most important moment.

Foreman, Michael.

The Littlest Dinosaur. **New York: Walker, 2008. Unpaged. ISBN 9780802797599.** `PreS-2`

A young dinosaur is the smallest of all his siblings, and the only safe place is for him is on top of a hill. That proves to be just the right spot, for he can see the long-necked dinosaur from his perch and knows just where to go to ask for his help when his family gets stuck in the muck.

The Littlest Dinosaur's Big Adventure. **New York: Walker, 2009. Unpaged. ISBN 9780802795458. Sequel.** `PreS-2`

The little dinosaur returns, and this time he chases frogs and butterflies until he ends up lost in the forest. There, he discovers an equally bewildered pterodactyl, whom he leads out of the woods.

French, Vivian.

T. Rex. **Illustrated by Alison Bartlett. Cambridge, MA: Candlewick, 2004. 29pp. ISBN 9780763621841.** `PreS-2`

Grandfather and grandson visit a dinosaur exhibit at a natural history museum, and the grandson peppers his grandfather with questions. His grandfather shares everything he knows about the king of dinosaurs.

Grambling, Lois G.

T. Rex and the Mother's Day Hug. See under "Mother's Day" in chapter 6.

Lewis, Kevin.

Dinosaur, Dinosaur. **Illustrated by Daniel Kirk. New York: Orchard, 2006. Unpaged. ISBN 9780439603713.** `T-K`

Following the pattern of the rhyme "Teddy Bear, Teddy Bear," this book presents a dinosaur's day, from waking up, through playing, getting ready for bed, and going to sleep.

Lund, Deb.

Dinosaur Series. Illustrated by Howard Fine. `PreS-2`

These adventurous dinosaurs love to travel using different modes of transportation. All are painted in vivid hues that bring the stories brilliantly to life.

Dinosailors. San Diego: Harcourt, 2003. Unpaged. ISBN 9780152046095.

> This story in rhyme relates the seafaring adventures of six dinosaurs that enjoy sailing, until a storm comes up and they all succumb to seasickness.

All Aboard the Dinotrain. Orlando, FL: Harcourt, 2006. Unpaged. ISBN 9780152052379.

> The intrepid dinosaurs return, and this time they delight in traveling by train, until they whiz over a bridge that isn't there and end up in a lake.

Dinosoaring. Orlando, FL: Harcourt, 2010. ISBN 9780152060169.

> Continuing their adventurous tradition, this time the brave creatures experience the wonders of flight.

McCarty, Peter.

T Is for Terrible. **New York: Holt, 2004. Unpaged. ISBN 9780805074048.** T–K

> Tyrannosaurus rex explains what it's like to be such a feared dinosaur and wonders why he is considered to be so terrible.

McClements, George.

Ridin' Dinos with Buck Bronco. **Orlando, FL: Harcourt, 2007. ISBN 9780152059897.** PreS–2

> Buck Bronco discovers some unusual eggs and brings them back to the ranch, only to discover that he has to raise a clutch of dinosaurs.

McMullan, Kate, and Jim McMullan.

I'm Bad! **New York: Joanna Cotler Books, 2008. Unpaged. ISBN 978-0061229718.** PreS–2

> A vocal T. rex proves just how bad he really is.

Mitton, Tony.

Dinorumpus. **Illustrated by Guy Parker-Rees. New York: Orchard, 2003. Unpaged. ISBN 9780439395144.** PreS–2

> All kinds of dinosaurs gather for a grand dinosaur dance.

Most, Bernard.

*If the Dinosaurs Came Back. **New York: Harcourt, 1978. 32pp. ISBN 9780152380205.** PreS–2

> A boy who loves dinosaurs imagines all the amazing things they could do if they came back.

Plourde, Lynn.

*Dino Pets. Illustrated by Gideon Kendall. New York: Dutton, 2007. Unpaged. ISBN 9780525477785. `PreS-2`

In this tale in rhyme, a boy makes repeated visits to a dinosaur pet store, attempting to find just the right dinosaur.

Rennert, Laura Joy.

Buying, Training, and Caring for Your Dinosaur. Illustrated by Marc Brown. New York: Knopf, 2009. Unpaged. ISBN 9780375836794. `Gr. K-3`

This humorous guide describes the various qualities of dinosaurs that can make them great pets.

Shea, Bob.

Dinosaur vs. Bedtime. New York: Hyperion, 2008. Unpaged. ISBN 978-1423113355. `T-K`

An on-the-go dinosaur, who loves to roar, absolutely does not want to go to bed.

Waddell, Martin.

Super Hungry Dinosaur. Illustrated by Leoni Lord. New York: Dial, 2009. Unpaged. ISBN 9780803734463. `PreS-2`

When a T. rex wants to devour Hal, the clever youngster captures the beast instead, but relents and feeds him a spaghetti supper because he knows he's hungry.

Wheeler, Lisa.

Dino-Hockey. See under "Sports" in chapter 7.

Willems, Mo.

Edwina the Dinosaur Who Didn't Know She Was Extinct. New York: Hyperion, 2006. Unpaged. ISBN 9780786837489. `Gr. K-3`

Know-it-all Reginald Von Hoobie-Doobie does his best to convince Edwina, the kind dinosaur who makes fabulous chocolate cookies, that she is extinct.

Yolen, Jane.

The How Do Dinosaurs . . . Series. Illustrated by Mark Teague. New York: Scholastic. `PreS-2`

In this inventive series, different types of dinosaurs (all identified) are portrayed as the children of the family, while the parents are human beings. Playful rhymes describe a variety of childhood activities, and bold, colorful illustrations depict dinosaurs engaged in those activities. There is also a spin-off board book series by the same team.

🎗**How Do Dinosaurs Say Goodnight?* 2000. Unpaged. ISBN 9780590316811. (ALAN)

How Do Dinosaurs Get Well Soon? 2003. Unpaged. ISBN 9780439241007.

How Do Dinosaurs Eat Their Food? 2005. Unpaged. ISBN 9780439241021.

How Do Dinosaurs Go to School? 2007. Unpaged. ISBN 9780439020817.

How Do Dinosaurs Say I Love You? 2009. Unpaged. ISBN 9780545143141.

Insects and Arachnids

Insects and spiders also hold a high level of fascination for young readers and listeners. As with the dinosaur books, the realistic and fanciful are listed together.

Carle, Eric.

*The Very Hungry Caterpillar. **New York: Philomel, 1983. Unpaged. ISBN 9780399208539.** PreS-1 **(SP)**

This classic concept book illustrated with Carle's signature collage depicts a tiny caterpillar that eats through an increasing variety of items on each day of the week, until he builds a cocoon and emerges as a beautiful butterfly. Young listeners enjoy participating through counting and naming the days of the week, as well as by guessing what the caterpillar will become.

🎗️**The Very Busy Spider.* **New York: Philomel, 1985. 22pp. ISBN 978-0399211669.** PreS-1 **(SP)**

In this classic concept book, the master artist and storyteller relates the work of a spider who is very busy spinning her web. She is so busy that she does not have time to answer any creature that queries her. She succeeds in catching a fly and in the end sleeps contentedly. The web is raised, providing a tactile experience for lap-sitters, but the story works just as well as a group read-aloud where participants can join in the repeated refrain, "But she was very busy." (ALAN)

*The Very Quiet Cricket. **New York: Philomel, 1990. 28pp. ISBN 978-0399218859.** PreS-1

From morning till night, various insects greet the newly hatched cricket. The cricket tries to answer as he rubs his wings together, but he can produce no sound until a lady cricket captures his attention. The final page turn activates a microchip that produces a cricket's sound. Listeners will delight in repeating the refrain and hearing the cricket chirp at last.

The Very Lonely Firefly. **New York: Philomel, 1995. Unpaged. ISBN 978-0399227745.** PreS-1

A solitary firefly, born just as the sun is setting, seeks others of his kind, following light sources from a candle to a cat's eyes, until at last it discovers its fellows. As in previous books, the last page turn contains a surprise: the cloud of fireflies have tails that truly light up.

The Very Clumsy Click Beetle. **New York: Philomel, 1999. Unpaged. ISBN 9780399232015.** PreS-1

When a click beetle gets stuck on his back, a variety of animals offer advice and encouraging words to help him flip over. Everything he attempts fails, until fear of a human boy motivates him to click correctly and escape capture. The last page turn emits the beetle's clicking sound.

Cronin, Doreen.

Diary of a Worm. **Illustrated by Harry Bliss. New York: Joanna Cotler Books, 2003. Unpaged. ISBN 9780060001506.** `Gr. K–3`

A worm fond of wearing his baseball cap and coiling himself around a pencil so that he can write records the misadventures of his life at home and at school, in this humorous tale made even more amusing by Bliss's whimsical illustrations.

Diary of a Spider. **Illustrated by Harry Bliss. New York: Joanna Cotler Books, 2005. Unpaged. ISBN 9780060001537.** `Gr. K–3`

Continuing the humorous thread begun in his pal Worm's diary, Spider keeps a journal of his own. He recounts tales of his life at home and school, where he brings his molted shell for show and tell and practices escaping in vacuum cleaner drills.

Diary of a Fly. **Illustrated by Harry Bliss. New York: Joanna Cotler Books, 2007. Unpaged. ISBN 9780060001568.** `Gr. K–3`

Fly reveals what her life at school is like, where she learns to fly and worries about whether anyone else will eat regurgitated food. She enjoys playing with her 327 brothers and sisters and longs to be a superhero.

Durango, Julia.

Pest Fest. **Illustrated by Kurt Cyrus. New York: Simon & Schuster, 2007. ISBN 9780689855696.** `PreS–K`

Lively rhymes relay the events of the pest talent competition as a variety of insects vie for the coveted title "Best Pest."

Ehlert, Lois.

🏵*Waiting for Wings.* **San Diego: Harcourt, 2001. Unpaged. ISBN 9780152026080.** `PreS–2`

This artfully designed book springs to life with Ehlert's brilliant color collage illustrations and uses pages of different sizes to add dimension to the story, which presents information about gardens, caterpillars, and butterflies while it follows the life cycle of a caterpillar. (ALAN)

Fleming, Denise.

Beetle Bop. **Orlando, FL: Harcourt, 2007. Unpaged. ISBN 9780152059361.** `PreS–2`

Fleming's brightly colored pressed-paper collages and jaunty verse present an assortment of beetles as they go about their daily lives, from laying eggs to escaping harm.

Gran, Julia.

Big Bug Surprise. New York: Scholastic, 2006. Unpaged. ISBN 978-0439676090. **Gr. K–3**

Prunella knows oodles about bugs of all kinds and loves to tell anyone who will listen. Her friends and family are not keen on listening to all her information, but when she rescues her class from a swarm of bees by conducting them to a new hive, they pay more attention to what she says.

Hanson, Warren.

Bugtown Boogie. Illustrated by Steve Johnson and Lou Fancher. New York: Laura Geringer Books, 2008. Unpaged. ISBN 9780060599379. **PreS–2**

Rhyming verse, with a beat to dance to, relates the discoveries of a boy who goes for a walk in the woods and finds a gathering of insects dancing up a storm.

Horacek, Petr.

Butterfly, Butterfly. Cambridge, MA: Candlewick, 2007. Unpaged. ISBN 9780763633431. **PreS–K**

Lucy scampers after a beautifully colored butterfly and ends up in a garden. When she returns to the garden the next day, she cannot spot the butterfly but finds a variety of other insects instead. Bright, acrylic paintings burst off the page, bringing the simple story to life.

Jarrett, Clare.

Arabella Miller's Tiny Caterpillar. Cambridge, MA: Candlewick, 2008. ISBN 9780763636609. **Gr. K–3**

Arabella Miller builds a home for the tiny caterpillar that she finds outside and watches it munch through leaves, spin a chrysalis, and emerge as a beautiful butterfly.

Keller, Holly.

Farfallina & Marcel. New York: Greenwillow, 2002. Unpaged. ISBN 9780066239323. **PreS–1**

Farfallina the caterpillar and Marcel the gosling encounter one another during a rain shower and quickly become friends. They enjoy each other's company until Farfallina climbs a tree. Listeners will guess she's in her cocoon, but Marcel waits and worries. When the two are reunited at last, they have changed so much that they don't recognize each other. Finally, the qualities they know and love shine through, and the friends find each other again. (Charlotte Zolotow Award)

10

11

12

13

14

15

Wheeler, Lisa.

Old Cricket. **Illustrated by Ponder Goembel. New York: Atheneum, 2003. Unpaged. ISBN 9780689845109.** `PreS–2`

Old Cricket finds excuses not to do the tasks his wife sets out for him, until Old Crow swoops down to munch on him for lunch. Then he swiftly returns home and complies with his wife's wishes.

Favorites

Move Over, Rover! by Karen Beaumont

The Very Hungry Caterpillar by Eric Carle

Click Clack Moo: Cows That Type by Doreen Cronin

Mama Cat Has Three Kittens by Denise Fleming

Hello Baby by Mem Fox

Kitten's First Full Moon by Kevin Henkes

Martha Speaks by Susan Meddaugh

The Henry and Mudge Series by Cynthia Rylant

Duck on a Bike by David Shannon

How Do Dinosaurs Say Goodnight? by Jane Yolen

Chapter 11

Adventure

Stories filled with excitement, a dash of suspense, and a dollop of daring-do engage young readers and listeners in real and imaginary experiences through which they can share the experiences of heroes who save the day.

Breen, Steve.

Violet the Pilot. **New York: Dial, 2008. 32pp. ISBN 9780803731257.** `Gr. K–3`

Violet Van Winkle, who can fix most anything, has an uncanny knack for invention, but not for making friends. She designs and builds her own airplane and plans on entering the air show to win acceptance, but as she is flying over a river, she spies several Boy Scouts in need of assistance. She rescues them from the rapids, giving up her hopes for the air show, but the mayor declares her a hero, bringing her the recognition she craves. The cartoon illustrations of watercolor, acrylic, and pencil add vivid details.

Broach, Elise.

Gumption! **Illustrated by Richard Egielski. New York: Atheneum, 2010. 40pp. ISBN 9781416916284.** `PreS–2`

Peter accompanies his explorer uncle on a trek through Africa, searching for a rare kind of mountain gorilla. As they encounter a variety of wild animals, his uncle assures Peter that all they need is gumption.

Buehner, Caralyn.

Superdog: The Heart of a Hero. **Illustrated by Mark Buehner. New York: HarperCollins, 2004. Unpaged. ISBN 9780066236209.** `PreS–3`

Dexter the dachshund dreams of being a superhero despite his small size and the merciless teasing of Cleevis the tomcat. He begins with a visit to the library to gather information and then embarks on an exercise regime to build body strength. Donning a superdog suit, he uses his powers for good for all in the neighborhood. When he saves Cleevis, the two team up to perform good deeds together.

DiCamillo, Kate.

Louise, the Adventures of a Chicken. Illustrated by Harry Bliss. New York: Joanna Cotler Books, 2008. 48pp. ISNB: 9780060755546. **PreS–3**

Louise the chicken, not content to remain in the henhouse, strikes out for adventure. In the course of four chapters, she gets captured by pirates, almost eaten by a lion in the circus, and kidnapped in a bazaar, where she devises a way to free herself and her fellow fowl prisoners. After each episode, she returns home to regale her fellow chickens with tales of her adventures. Bliss's sweeping watercolors dramatically depict Louise's exploits.

Dodds, Dayle Ann.

Where's Pup? Illustrated by Pierre Pratt. New York: Dial, 2003. 32pp. ISBN 9780803727441. **PreS–1**

A tiny clown encounters one circus performer after another as he searches for his missing pup.

Funke, Cornelia.

Pirate Girl. Illustrated by Kerstin Meyer. New York: Scholastic, 2005. 32pp. ISBN 9780439716727. **Gr. K–3**

When Molly sets sail to visit her grandmother, she is captured by Captain Firebeard and his dastardly crew. They intend to hold her for ransom, but despite all the chores they force her to do, she refuses to divulge her parents' address. Instead, she drops messages overboard in bottles and is rescued just in time by her mother.

Goodhart, Pippa.

Three Little Ghosties. Illustrated by Annalaura Cantone. New York: Bloomsbury, 2007. 32pp. ISBN 9781582347110. **PreS–3**

Three ghosts brag to each other of their escapades and then get a fright of their own.

Grossmann-Hensel, Katherina.

Papa Is a Pirate. New York: North South, 2009. 32pp. ISBN 9780735822375. **Gr. K–3**

Although his young son does not believe him at first, Papa vividly describes his life as a pirate.

Gutierrez, Akemi.

The Mummy and Other Adventures of Sam & Alice. Boston: Houghton Mifflin, 2005. 64pp. ISBN 9780618507610. **Gr. K–2**

Siblings Sam and Alice imagine adventures on a pirate ship, in a swamp, and on a rocket ship.

The Pirate and Other Adventures of Sam & Alice. **Boston: Houghton Mifflin, 2007. 52pp. ISBN 9780618737376. Sequel.** `Gr. K-2`

> Sam and Alice are back for more imaginary adventures. This time they blast off in a rocket ship, invent a genius crocodile, and locate a pirate's treasure.

9

Harley, Bill.

Dirty Joe, the Pirate: A True Story. **Illustrated by Jack E. Davis. New York: HarperCollins, 2008. 32pp. ISBN 9780066237800.** `PreS-2`

> Ahoy mateys, beware Dirty Joe and his ragged band of pirates, for they search high and low for dirty socks of all kinds. They meet their match when they come across Stinky Annie of the seven seas, who nabs undergarments and turns out to be Joe's sister.

10

Helakoski, Leslie.

The Big Chickens Series. Illustrated by Henry Cole. New York: Dutton. PreS–2

11

> Four flighty chickens have a variety of humorous misadventures.

> *Big Chickens.* 2006. 32pp. ISBN 9780525475750. `PreS-2`
>
>> Four flighty chickens flee the henhouse when they catch sight of a wolf and get themselves into scarier and scarier situations until they succeed in turning the tables on the wolf.

12

> *Big Chickens Fly the Coop.* 2008. 32pp. ISBN 9780525479154. `PreS-2`
>
>> The featherbrained fowl return to wander out of the henhouse in search of the farmhouse. Instead they stumble upon a doghouse, causing a fresh batch of chaos and a scrambling rush home.

13

> *Big Chickens Go to Town.* 2010. 32pp. ISBN 9780525421627. `PreS-2`
>
>> When the four fowl friends peck at seed in the back of their farmer's truck, they get whisked away for an unexpected adventure in town.

Joosse, Barbara.

14

Roawr! **Illustrated by Jan Jutte. New York: Philomel, 2009. 40pp. ISBN 9780399247774.** `PreS-1`

> At bedtime, when small Liam's father is away and his mother is asleep, a forest grows in his room. He hears ominous noises in the forest and so packs his supplies, including cake, and sets out to protect his mother. Bravely, he outwits a hungry bear, keeping his home and family safe.

15

Kelly, Ellen A.

My Life as a Chicken. **Illustrated by Michael Slack. Orlando, FL: Harcourt, 2007. 40pp. ISBN 9780152053062.** `Gr. K-3`

> Pauline Poulet, a chicken, escapes the farm to avoid becoming the key ingredient in chicken pot pie. The plucky poultry propels herself from one dangerous situation to the next, from a pirate ship to a hot air balloon and

more, until she finds a safe haven at a petting zoo. The vivacious rhymes and digital mixed-media illustrations are a perfect match for this breathless adventure.

Kitamura, Satoshi.

Stone Age Boy. Cambridge, MA: Candlewick, 2007. 32pp. ISBN 9780763634742. `Gr. 1-3` (SP)

When a boy falls, he travels through time and wakes up in the Stone Age. He learns to live there until another fall sends him back to the modern era.

Lester, Julius.

The Hungry Ghosts. Illustrated by Geraldo Valério. New York: Dial, 2009. 34pp. ISBN 9780803725133. `Gr. K–3`

When Malcolm David investigates what's waking him up in the middle of the night, he finds three ghosts who are exceedingly hungry. He cleans his room and discovers that the ghosts of leftovers he is getting rid of are just the right food for ghosts.

Leuck, Laura.

I Love My Pirate Papa. Illustrated by Kyle M. Stone. Orlando, FL: Harcourt, 2007. 21pp. ISBN 9780152056643. `PreS–2`

Using rollicking rhyme, a young boy enumerates all the wonderful things about having a pirate-captain dad, from raising the Jolly Roger in the morning to listening to stories about Captain Hook at bedtime.

Lionni, Leo.

Nicolas, Where Have You Been? New York: Knopf, 2007. 32pp. ISBN 978-0375844508. `PreS–2`

In this reissue of a book originally published in 1987, young Nicolas mouse sets out on his own across the field to find ripe berries. His adventure begins when a bird swoops down and grabs him.

Long, Melinda.

🌟*How I Became a Pirate.* Illustrated by David Shannon. San Diego: Harcourt, 2003. 44pp. ISBN 9780152018481. `PreS–3` (SP)

Jeremy Jacob is creating a sand castle when a band of pirates recruits him to join their escapades on the high seas. Jeremy loves the seafaring life for a little while, but soon misses the comforts of home and convinces his shipmates to bury their treasure in his backyard so that he can arrive home in time for soccer practice. Shannon's lively acrylics people his pictures with pop-eyed pirates. (ALAN)

Pirates Don't Change Diapers. Illustrated by David Shannon. Orlando, FL: Harcourt, 2007. 44pp. ISBN 9780152053536. Sequel. `PreS–3`

Jeremy Jacob is babysitting his little sister Bonney Anne when Captain Braid Beard and his crew arrive in search of their booty. Jeremy agrees to help them, if they in turn will help watch his sister. The trouble is, the pirates don't know anything about taking care of babies.

Martin, Bill.

The Ghost-Eye Tree. Illustrated by John Archambault. New York: Holt, 1985. 32pp. ISBN 9780805002089. `Gr. K-3`

> When a brother and sister are sent across town to fetch a bucket of milk after dark, they argue over who is most afraid of the Ghost-Eye Tree.

Mayer, Mercer.

The Bravest Knight. New York: Dial, 2007. 28pp. ISBN 9780803732063. `Gr. K-2`

> A little boy wishes he could have been born a thousand years ago to serve as a squire to the bravest knight in all the land, so that he could have adventures with dragons and trolls and meet with kings and queens.

Nolen, Jerdine.

🏵*Thunder Rose*. Illustrated by Kadir Nelson. San Diego: Harcourt, 2003. 32pp. ISBN 9780152164720. `Gr. K-3`

> In this original tall tale, Thunder Rose is born on a wild and stormy night to an African American couple living free in the frontier lands of the Old West. From the moment she is born, they know she is special, for she can roll lightning into balls and speak in full sentences. Her prowess grows as she gets older. She settles stampedes, hushes windstorms, and tames tornadoes. Nelson's artwork in oil, watercolor, and pencil is stunning. (Coretta Scott King Honor)

Reynolds, Aaron.

Superhero School. Illustrated by Andy Rash. New York: Bloomsbury, 2009. Unpaged. ISBN 9781599901664. `Gr. K-3`

> Leonard is excited to be attending superhero school but quickly becomes frustrated studying boring math instead of leaping tall buildings. Suddenly the superhero teachers are kidnapped and Leonard and his classmates must use their new math skills to save their teachers.

Rohmann, Eric.

Pumpkinhead. New York: Knopf, 2003. Unpaged. ISBN 9780375824166. `PreS-3`

> In this surreal tale, Otho is a boy born with a jack-o'-lantern head. While playing outside one day, a bat spies it, and thinking that it would be a good place for a home, snatches the head off Otho's body. He drops it in the sea, where a fish swallows it and eventually ends up in a fish market, where his mother buys it and returns the head to its body.

Rosenthal, Marc.

Archie and the Pirates. New York: HarperCollins, 2009. 30pp. ISBN 978-0061441646. `PreS-3`

> Although Archie the monkey has just washed ashore on a tropical island, he is not dismayed. He quickly builds a shelter and befriends local animals. When pirates kidnap one of his new pals, Archie's clever plan saves her.

Schachner, Judith.

The Skippyjon Jones Series. New York: Dutton. `Gr. K–3`

Skippyjon Jones, an extremely active Siamese kitten whose head and ears are too big for his body, enjoys imagining that he is a Chihuahua Zorro. Real and made-up Spanish phrases are sprinkled throughout the stories.

Skippyjon Jones. 2003. 32pp. ISBN 9780525471349.

> When his mother sends him to his room to contemplate what it means to be a cat, Skippyjon Jones slips into his Zorro disguise and dashes into the closet for an adventure as Skippito Friskito instead.

Skippyjon Jones in the Dog House. 2005. 32pp. ISBN 9780525472971.

> The impish Siamese who thinks he's a Chihuahua is sent to his room for coloring on the walls. Although his mother tells him he'll be in the doghouse if he escapes to his closet, he does just that, this time helping his friends, Los Chimichangos, make their home safe from the Bobble-ito monster.

Skippyjon Jones in Mummy Trouble. 2006. 32pp. ISBN 9780525477549.

> Skippyjon Jones, as El Skippito Friskito, meets up with his friends again, but this time they are in Ancient Egypt, where Skippyjon Jones must find the answer to the riddle of the Sphinx.

Skippyjon Jones, Lost in Spice. 2009. 32pp. ISBN 9780525479659.

> When Skippyjon Jones imagines a snowsuit in the closet is a space suit, he embarks on an imaginary journey to Mars.

Schwarz, Viviane.

Timothy and the Strong Pajamas. New York: Arthur A. Levine Books, 2008. 30pp. ISBN 9780545033299. `Gr. K–2`

> Tiny Timothy wishes with all his might that he could be strong as a superhero. He exercises and thinks strong thoughts, but it's not until his mother mends his favorite pajamas that he is endowed with super strength, through the patches of power and buttons of braveness. He embarks on a series of adventures with his friend Monkey, but his power disappears when his pajamas rip. Fortunately, those he's recently saved return the favor and rescue him.

Segal, John.

Alistair and Kip's Great Adventure! New York: Margaret K. McElderry Books, 2008. 29pp. ISBN 9781416902805. `PreS–2`

> Alistair the orange cat is bored, so he convinces his friend Kip the Beagle to build a boat with him. Although Kip is hesitant, they sail out to sea together, only to be capsized by a giant wave. When they head toward a nearby island, it turns out to be a friendly whale, who gives them a lift home. Although Kip is relieved to be back on solid ground, Alistair is dreaming about future expeditions.

Waddell, Martin.

Tiny's Big Adventure. **Illustrated by John Lawrence. Cambridge, MA: Candlewick, 2004. 27pp. ISBN 9780763621704.** `PreS-2`

9

Tiny the mouse thinks that his big sister Katy is brave and adventurous, so he asks her to take him to the wheat field for the first time. She introduces him to a variety of critters, as they play games together. She finds him quickly when they get separated, and as they make their way home, Tiny is already thinking about their next outing.

Wheeler, Lisa.

10

Castaway Cats. **Illustrated by Ponder Goembel. New York: Atheneum, 2006. 32pp. ISBN 9780689862328.** `PreS-2`

Eight cats and seven kittens swim for island safety after their boat capsizes. They set to work constructing a new one, but in the end they decide they would like to stay right where they are. Goembel's acrylic and ink illustrations complement Wheeler's finely honed verse.

11

Favorites

12

Superdog: The Heart of a Hero by Caralyn Buehner

Louise, the Adventures of a Chicken by Kate DiCamillo

Stone Age Boy by Satoshi Kitamura

Skippyjon Jones by Judith Schachner

13

Castaway Cats by Lisa Wheeler

14

15

Chapter 12

Mysteries and Puzzles

Although young children may not yet have the deductive reasoning abilities so often used to solve fictional mysteries, older children are just learning those skills. There are some picture books that utilize the clue-gathering and mystery-solving formula, but there are several easy reader series that successfully engage the reader in the process of solving the puzzle. These series help readers solve both the linguistic puzzle of honing their reading skills and the reasoning puzzle of connecting bits of information along with the fictional detective to solve cases along with the protagonists. While puzzle picture books also use observational skills, they are concentrating on stimulating the reader to interact with the visual clues in the pictures to work out the puzzle presented.

Mysteries

Biedrzycki, David.

Ace Lacewing: Bug Detective. Watertown, MA: Charlesbridge, 2005. 40pp. ISBN 9781570915697. **Gr. 2 & up**

> In the insect metropolis of Motham City, when Hive Rise Honey Company's Queenie Bee is kidnapped, Ace Lacewing and his companions track down the culprits.

Ace Lacewing Bug Detective: Bad Bugs Are My Business. Watertown, MA: Charlesbridge, 2009. 40pp. ISBN 9781570916922. Sequel. **Gr. 2 & up**

> When Ace sets out to investigate for his new client, a flea named Scratch Murphy, he discovers hoards of enemies who could be guilty of stealing from the aggrieved insect.

Cushman, Doug.

Mystery at the Club Sandwich. New York: Clarion, 2004. 30pp. ISBN 978-0618419692. **Gr. 1–3**

> Elephant Nick Trunk, who works for peanuts, is hired to locate Lola Gale's missing lucky marbles.

Kellogg, Steven.

The Missing Mitten Mystery. New York: Dial, 2000. Unpaged. ISBN 978-0803725669. **Gr. K–3**

> After playing all day in the snow, Annie suddenly realizes that she is missing one of her mittens and retraces her steps to discover the whereabouts of her stray garment.

Wisniewski, David.

Tough Cookie. New York: Lothrop Lee & Shepherd, 1999. Unpaged. ISBN 978-0688153373. **Gr. 1–3**.

> Tough Cookie rolls out a tale of life in the cookie jar, where he and his partner, Chips, solve crimes. Now his ex-girl friend, Pecan Sandy, warns him of his biggest challenge yet: Fingers is after him.

Yee, Wong Herbert.

Detective Small in the Amazing Banana Caper. Boston: Houghton Mifflin, 2007. 30pp. ISBN 9780618472857. **Gr. K–2**

> When all of the bananas in town disappear, the stumped police department calls on the sleuthing skills of Detective Small.

Mystery: Easy Readers

Adler, David.

The Young Cam Jansen Series. Illustrated by Susanna Natti. New York: Viking/Puffin. **Gr. 1–3**.

> This spin-off of the transitional chapter book Cam Jansen Series follows the cases of Cam Jansen, a young lady with a photographic memory.

> *Young Cam Jansen and the Dinosaur Game.* 1996. 32pp. ISBN 9780670863990.

> *Young Cam Jansen and the Missing Cookie.* 1996. 32pp. ISBN 9780140380507 (pb).

> *Young Cam Jansen and the Lost Tooth.* 1997. 32pp. ISBN 9780141302737 (pb).

> *Young Cam Jansen and the Ice Skate Mystery.* 1998. 31pp. ISBN 9780141300122 (pb).

> *Young Cam Jansen and the Baseball Mystery.* 1999. 31pp. ISBN 9780670884810.

> *Young Cam Jansen and the Pizza Shop Mystery.* 2000. 32pp. ISBN 9780142300206 (pb).

> *Young Cam Jansen and the Library Mystery.* 2001. 30pp. ISBN 9780670892815.

> *Young Cam Jansen and the Double Beach Mystery.* 2002. 30pp. ISBN 9780670035311.

Young Cam Jansen and the Zoo Note Mystery. 2003. 30pp. ISBN 978-0670036264.

Young Cam Jansen and the New Girl Mystery. 2004. 30pp. ISBN 978-0670059157.

Young Cam Jansen and the Substitute Mystery. 2005. 30pp. ISBN 978-0670059881.

Young Cam Jansen and the Spotted Cat Mystery. 2006. 31pp. ISBN 978-0670060948.

Young Cam Jansen and the Lions' Lunch Mystery. 2007. 30pp. ISBN 978-0670061716.

Young Cam Jansen and the Molly Shoe Mystery. 2008. 31pp. ISBN 978-0670061426.

Young Cam Jansen and the 100th Day of School. 2009. 32pp. ISBN 978-0670061723.

Young Cam Jansen and the Speedy Car Mystery. 2010. 32pp. ISBN 978-0670061433.

Cushman, Doug.

Dirk Bones and the Mystery of the Haunted House. New York: HarperCollins, 2006. 31pp. ISBN 9780060737641. Gr. K–2

Dirk Bones, a skeleton sleuth, is summoned to discover the cause of the ghoulish sounds emanating from the town of Ghostly's graveyard.

Dirk Bones and the Mystery of the Missing Books. New York: HarperCollins, 2009. ISBN 9780060737689. Sequel. Gr. K–2

When a book goes missing from the library, crack bony detective Dirk Bones sets out to track down the culprit.

Rylant, Cynthia.

The High-Rise Private Eyes Series. Illustrated by G. Brian Karas. New York: Greenwillow. Gr. 1–3

Bunny Brown and raccoon Jack Jones are best friends and super sleuths who solve cases brought to them by their friends and neighbors.

The Case of the Climbing Cat. 2000. 48pp. ISBN 9780064443074 (pb).

The Case of the Missing Monkey. 2000. 48pp. ISBN 9780064443067 (pb).

The Case of the Puzzling Possum. 2001. 48pp. ISBN 9780064443166 (pb).

The Case of the Troublesome Turtle. 2001. 48pp. ISBN 9780060013233 (pb).

The Case of the Sleepy Sloth. 2002. 48pp. ISBN 9780060090982 (o.p.).

The Case of the Fidgety Fox. 2003. 48pp. ISBN 9780060091019 (o.p.).

The Case of the Baffled Bear. 2004. 48pp. ISBN 9780060534486.

The Case of the Desperate Duck. 2005. 48pp. ISBN 9780060534530 (pb).

Sharmat, Marjorie Weinman.

The Nate the Great Series. New York: Coward McCan/Delacorte/Yearling. `Gr. 1–3`.

Young Nate loves eating pancakes and solving the mysteries of friends and family.

Nate the Great: 30th Anniversary Edition. Illustrated by Marc Simont. 2002. 60pp. ISBN 9780385730174.

Nate the Great Goes Undercover. Illustrated by Marc Simont. 1974. 47pp. ISBN 9780440463023 (pb).

Nate the Great and the Lost List. Illustrated by Marc Simont. 1975. 48pp. ISBN 9780440462828 (pb).

Nate the Great and the Phony Clue. Illustrated by Marc Simont. 1977. 48pp. ISBN 9780440463009 (pb).

Nate the Great and the Sticky Case. Illustrated by Marc Simont. 1978. 44pp. ISBN 9780440462897 (pb).

Nate the Great and the Missing Key. Illustrated by Marc Simont. 1981. 47pp. ISBN 9780440461913 (pb).

Nate the Great and the Snowy Trail. Illustrated by Marc Simont. 1982. 47pp. ISBN 9780440462767 (pb).

Nate the Great and the Fishy Prize. Illustrated by Marc Simont. 1985. 46pp. ISBN 9780440400394 (pb).

Nate the Great Stalks Stupidweed. Illustrated by Marc Simont. 1986. 47pp. ISBN 9780440401506 (pb).

Nate the Great and the Boring Beach Bag. Illustrated by Marc Simont. 1987. 46pp. ISBN 9780440401681 (pb).

Nate the Great and the Halloween Hunt. Illustrated by Marc Simont. 1989. 48pp. ISBN 9780440403418 (pb).

Nate the Great Down in the Dumps. Illustrated by Marc Simont. 1989. 48pp. ISBN 9780440404385 (pb).

Nate the Great and the Musical Note. Illustrated by Marc Simont. 1990. 46pp. ISBN 9780440404668 (pb).

Nate the Great and the Stolen Base. Illustrated by Marc Simont. 1992. 47pp. ISBN 9780440409328 (pb).

Nate the Great and the Pillowcase. Illustrated by Marc Simont. 1993. 47pp. ISBN 9780440410157 (pb).

Nate the Great and the Mushy Valentine. Illustrated by Marc Simont. 1994. 43pp. ISBN 9780440410133 (pb).

Nate the Great and the Tardy Tortoise. Coauthored with Craig Sharmat. Illustrated by Marc Simont. 1995. 41pp. ISBN 9780440412694 (pb).

Nate the Great and the Crunchy Christmas. Coauthored with Craig Sharmat. Illustrated by Marc Simont. 1996. 41pp. ISBN 9780440412991 (pb).

Nate the Great Saves the King of Sweden. Illustrated by Marc Simont. 1997. 40pp. ISBN 9780440413028 (pb).

Nate the Great and Me: The Case of the Fleeing Fang. Illustrated by Marc Simont. 1998. 63pp. ISBN 9780440413813 (pb).

Nate the Great and the Monster Mess. Weston, Martha (illus.). 1999. 45pp. ISBN 9780440416623 (pb).

Nate the Great, San Francisco Detective. Coauthored with Mitchell Sharmat. Illustrated by Martha Weston. 2000. 47pp. ISBN 9780440418214 (pb).

Nate the Great and the Big Sniff. Coauthored with Mitchell Sharmat. Illustrated by Martha Weston. 2001. 47pp. ISBN 9780440415022 (pb).

Nate the Great and the Owl Express. Coauthored with Mitchell Sharmat. Illustrated by Martha Weston. 2003. 45pp. ISBN 9780440419273 (pb).

Nate the Great Talks Turkey. Coauthored with Mitchell Sharmat. Illustrated by Judy Wheeler. 2006. 79pp. ISBN 9780440421269 (pb).

Nate the Great and the Hungry Book Club. Coauthored with Mitchell Sharmat. Illustrated by Judy Wheeler. 2009. 64pp. ISBN 9780385736954.

Puzzles

Handford, Martin.

The Where's Waldo Series. PreS-3

This series, originally released in England as Where's Wally, depicts the small character, Waldo, amid a sea of other figures, in various locations. The fun is in the finding of the diminutive protagonist. In the United States this series was originally published by Little, Brown. More recently, several of the titles have been reissued by Candlewick. Listed in original release order.

Where's Waldo? Cambridge, MA: Candlewick, 1997. 27pp. ISBN 978-0763603106. (SP)

Where's Waldo Now? Cambridge, MA: Candlewick, 2002. Unpaged. ISBN 9780763619213.

Find Waldo Now. Boston: Little, Brown, 1988. 26pp. ISBN 9780316342926 (o.p.).

The Great Waldo Search. Boston: Little, Brown, 1989. 24pp. ISBN 978-0316342827 (o.p.).

Where's Waldo? In Hollywood. Cambridge, MA: Candlewick, 2002. Unpaged. ISBN 9780763619190.

Where's Waldo? The Wonder Book. Cambridge, MA: Candlewick, 1997. Unpaged. ISBN 9780763603120.

Where's Waldo? The Fantastic Journey. Cambridge, MA: Candlewick, 1997. Unpaged. ISBN 9780763603090.

Where's Waldo? The Great Picture Hunt. Cambridge, MA: Candlewick, 2006. Unpaged. ISBN 9780763630430.

Where's Waldo? The Incredible Paper Chase. Cambridge, MA: Candlewick, 2009. Unpaged. ISBN 9780763646899.

Marzollo, Jean.

The I Spy Series. Illustrated by Walter Wick. New York: Scholastic. `PreS–3`

This seek-and-find series matches clue-giving riddles with sharp color photographs of various objects to give audiences hours of picture-searching entertainment.

I Spy. 1992. 33pp. ISBN 9780590450874.

I Spy Christmas. 1992. 33pp. ISBN 9780590458467.

I Spy Mystery. 1993. 37pp. ISBN 9780590462945.

I Spy Fun House. 1993. 33pp. ISBN 9780590462938.

I Spy Fantasy. 1994. 37pp. ISBN 9780590462952.

I Spy School Days. 1995. 33pp. ISBN 9780590481359.

I Spy Spooky Night. 1996. 31pp. ISBN 9780590481373.

I Spy Super Challenger. 1997. Unpaged. ISBN 9780590341288.

I Spy Gold Challenger. 1998. 31pp. ISBN 9780590042963.

I Spy Treasure Hunt. 1999. 36pp. ISBN 9780439042444.

I Spy Extreme Challenger. 2000. 31pp. ISBN 9780439199001.

I Spy Year-Round Challenger. 2001. Unpaged. ISBN 9780439316347.

I Spy Ultimate Challenger. 2003. 31pp. ISBN 9780439454018.

I Spy A to Z. 2009. Unpaged. ISBN 9780545107822.

I Spy a Christmas Tree. 2010. Unpaged. ISBN 9780545220927.

Micklethwait, Lucy.

<u>The I Spy Art Series.</u> **New York: Greenwillow.** `Gr. 2 & up`

Micklethwait uses selected masterpieces of artwork and matches them with concepts to create books in which children search for specified items or colors while at the same time exploring great works of art.

I Spy: An Alphabet in Art. 1992. Unpaged. ISBN 9780688116798.

I Spy Two Eyes: Numbers in Art. 1993. Unpaged. ISBN 9780688126407 (o.p.).

I Spy Shapes in Art. 2004. Unpaged. ISBN 9780060731939.

I Spy Colors in Art. 2007. 28pp. ISBN 9780061348372.

Thomson, Sarah L.

🌷*Imagine a Night.* **Illustrated by Rob Gonsalves. New York: Atheneum, 2003. Unpaged. ISBN 9780689852183.** `Gr. 2 & up`

A lyrical and whimsical text invites readers to imagine an amazing night accompanied by oil paintings to pore over depicting subtle and surreal transformations. (Governor General's Literary Award)

Imagine a Day. **Illustrated by Rob Gonsalves. New York: Atheneum, 2005. Unpaged. ISBN 9780689852190.** `Gr. 2 & up`

Here readers are welcomed into the light of day and the myriad images of daylight delight.

Imagine a Place. **Illustrated by Rob Gonsalves. New York: Atheneum, 2008. 40pp. ISBN 9781416968023.** `Gr. 2 & up`

Once again Thomas gives poetic guidance for imagination stretching, focusing on the painterly interior scenes and landscapes of Gonsalves.

Steiner, Joan.

<u>The Look-Alikes Series.</u> **Boston: Little Brown.** `Gr. 1-3`.

In this series, Steiner artfully arranges ordinary objects so they look like other things at first glance. Only close examination reveals what items create the scene. (Originally released in the late 1990s.)

Look-Alikes. Illustrated by Thomas Lindley. 2003. Unpaged. ISBN 978-0316713481.

Look-Alikes Jr. Illustrated by Thomas Lindley. 2003. Unpaged. ISBN 978-0316713474.

Look-Alikes Christmas. Illustrated by Ogden Gigli. 2003. Unpaged. ISBN 9780316811873.

Look-Alikes Around the World. Illustrated by Ogden Gigli. 2007. 32pp. ISBN 9780316811729.

Wick, Walter.

Can You See What I See? Series. New York: Scholastic. `Gr. 1 & up`

Wick presents a series of superbly photographed layouts teeming with objects that challenge children to find the items listed in the rhymes.

Can You See What I See? Picture Puzzles to Search and Solve. 2002. 35pp. ISBN 9780439163910.

Can You See What I See? Dream Machine. 2003. 35pp. ISBN 9780439399500.

Can You See What I See? Cool Collections. 2004. 35pp. ISBN 9780439617727.

Can You See What I See? Seymour and the Juice Box Boat. 2004. 29pp. ISBN 9780439617789.

Can You See What I See? The Night before Christmas. 2005. 35pp. ISBN 978-0439769273.

Can You See What I See? Once upon a Time. 2006. 35pp. ISBN 9780439617772.

Can You See What I See? On a Scary Night. 2008. 35pp. ISBN 9780439708708.

Can You See What I See? Treasure Ship. 2010. 40pp. ISBN 9780439026437.

Favorites

The High-Rise Private Eyes Series by Cynthia Rylant

The Nate the Great Series by Marjorie Sharmat

Imagine a Night by Sarah Thomson

Tough Cookie by David Wisniewski

Chapter 13

Historical Fiction: American History, European History, History Around the World

Historical fiction is any story that the author sets in the past. It can be an imaginary event in a real time period and/or a fictionalization of a real person's life. Generally a story must be set fifty years in the past to be considered historical fiction. Although there are not many historical fiction picture books for preschoolers, because readers need a certain amount of background knowledge to understand historical fiction, there are several books for the older picture book audience. Even though a majority of the books available in the United States are set there, there are several set in various European countries and some in countries around the world. The books set in the United States and Europe are divided by century, followed by books that take place in different countries.

American History

Fifteenth to Eighteenth Centuries

Atkins, Jeannine.

Anne Hutchinson's Way. **Illustrated by Michael Dooling. New York: Farrar, Straus & Giroux, 2007. 30pp. ISBN 9780374303655.** `Gr. 2 & up`

In this fictionalized episode from history, Anne Hutchinson's youngest daughter, Susannah, tells about the family's journey in 1634 from England to the Massachusetts Bay Colony. Trouble comes when Anne, who believes in a loving and forgiving God, not the stern and punishing God the preacher speaks of, begins having religious meetings in her home.

Borden, Louise.

Sleds on Boston Common: A Story from the American Revolution. **Illustrated by Robert Andrew Parker. New York: Margaret K. McElderry, 2000. Unpaged. ISBN 9780689828126.** `Gr. 2 & up`

> During the difficult winter of 1774 the citizens of Boston had to put up with their harbor being closed by the British and with British troops being quartered in their city. Nine-year-old Henry Price gets a new sled for his birthday, but he can't try it out on Boston Common because the British troops are occupying it. Screwing up his courage, he approaches General Gage himself for a solution.

Kay, Verla.

Tattered Sails. **Illustrated by Dan Andreasen. New York: Putnam, 2001. Unpaged. ISBN 9780399233456.** `Gr. K–3`

> In 1635 a Pilgrim family sails from London to the Massachusetts Bay Colony. The journey is told in rhythmic prose from the point of view of the three children.

Krensky, Stephen.

Dangerous Crossing: The Revolutionary Voyage of John and John Quincy Adams. **Illustrated by Greg Harlin. New York: Dutton, 2004. 30pp. ISBN 9780525469667.** `Gr. 2 & up`

> Krensky regales readers with a taut tale of a hazardous sea voyage across the Atlantic undertaken by John Adams and his ten-year-old son in 1778, while the Revolutionary War still raged. As they sailed to France to enlist the aid of the French, they were chased by British frigates, struck by lightning, and fired upon by a merchant vessel.

McDonald, Megan.

Saving the Liberty Bell. **Illustrated by Marsha Gray Carrington. New York: Atheneum, 2005. 32pp. ISBN 9780689851674.** `Gr. 1–3`

> During the British siege of 1777, eleven-year-old John Jacob and his father agree to help hide the Great Bell from the British. As the two arrive in Philadelphia, warnings circulate that the Red Coats are coming, and Colonel Benjamin Flower convinces them to smuggle the bell to safety.

McGill, Alice

🎗*Molly Bannaky.* **Illustrated by Chris K. Soentpiet. Boston: Houghton Mifflin, 1999. Unpaged. ISBN 9780395722879.** `Gr. 2 & up`

> In this fictionalized biography, when Molly is accused of stealing his lordship's milk in 1638 in England, she is sentenced to serve seven years as an indentured servant in America. She does her service in Maryland, and when she is free at last, she buys land of her own to raise tobacco. Vowing to free him as soon as she can, she purchases a slave, Bannaky. While working the farm, they fall in love. Molly frees him so they can be married. Years later she teaches her grandson, Benjamin Banneker, how to read and write and be proud of his heritage. (ALAN, Jane Addams Award)

Noble, Trinka Hakes.

Scarlet Stockings Spy. **Illustrated by Robert Papp. Chelsea, MI: Sleeping Bear Press, 2004. 48pp. ISBN 9781585362301.** `Gr. 3 & up`

In 1777 in Philadelphia, tense residents are waiting for an attack from the British. Young Maddy Rose does her best to help by hanging signals on her clothesline indicating suspicious ships in the harbor. She hopes that her brother, who is serving in General Washington's army, can interpret her messages.

Peacock, Carol.

Pilgrim Cat. **Illustrated by Doris Ettlinger. Morton Grove, IL: Albert Whitman, 2004. 32pp. ISBN 9780807565322.** `Gr. K–3`

When a tabby cat jumps onto the *Mayflower*, she journeys with the Pilgrims to the New World and provides the first litter of kittens for the colony of Plymouth.

Smith, Lane.

John, Paul, George & Ben. **New York: Hyperion, 2006. 40pp. ISBN 9780786848935.** `Gr. 2 & up`

With a wink at history, Smith combines facts and fiction as he introduces five founding fathers: John Hancock, Paul Revere, George Washington, Ben Franklin, and Tom Jefferson. The "Taking Liberties" page at the end separates fact from fiction. All in all, a book that makes history humorous and fun.

Yolen, Jane.

Encounter. **Illustrated by David Shannon. San Diego: Harcourt, 1992. Unpaged. ISBN 9780152259624.** `Gr. 2 & up`

In this poignant imagining of the first meeting between Columbus and native peoples, a young Taino boy recounts the welcome Columbus received. The graciousness of the boy's people was repaid with cruelty, as he and several other boys were subsequently kidnapped. The boy escapes and tries to warn others as he makes his way home, but sadly, no one will listen to him.

Elsie's Bird. **Illustrated by David Small. New York: Philomel, 2010. 32pp. ISBN 9780399252921.** `Gr. 1–3`

Elsie and her father enjoy their life in Boston. Nonetheless, they journey west to make a new home on the Nebraska prairie.

Nineteenth Century

Applegate, Katherine.

The Buffalo Storm. **Illustrated by Jan Ormerod. New York: Clarion, 2009. 32pp. ISBN 9780618535972.** `Gr. 3 & up`

Hallie does not want to leave the family farm or her beloved grandmother, but her parents have decided to follow the Oregon Trail and head west.

Braving floods, thunderstorms, rough terrain, and other Trail hardships, the family finally arrive in Oregon and make their new home.

Broyles, Anne.

Priscilla and the Hollyhocks. **Illustrated by Anna Alter. Watertown, MA: Charlesbridge, 2008. 32pp. ISBN 9781570916755.** `Gr. 2 & up`

Priscilla is born into slavery on a plantation in Georgia. When her mother is sold away, the hollyhocks are the only things that Priscilla has to remember her by. Feeling compassion, Old Sylvia teaches her how to make dolls out of the hollyhocks. Later she works in the big house and meets a kind white man, Basil Silkwood. After the master dies and Priscilla is sold to the Cherokee, Silkwood rescues her from the Trail of Tears by purchasing her freedom.

Carbone, Elisa.

Night Running: How James Escaped with the Help of His Faithful Dog. **Illustrated by E. B. Lewis. New York: Knopf, 2008. Unpaged. ISBN 9780375822476.** `Gr. 3 & up`

Based on a true story, this narrative recounts the experiences of James, a slave in Virginia in 1838. He escapes with the help of the dog Zeus. Reluctantly he lets the dog come with him on his journey north, and Zeus saves his life repeatedly.

Connor, Leslie.

Miss Bridie Chose a Shovel. **Illustrated by Mary Azarian. Boston: Houghton Mifflin, 2004. Unpaged. ISBN 9780618305643.** `Gr. K–3`

In 1856, when Miss Bridie immigrates to America, she decides to take her trusty shovel with her. She settles in New York City and uses the shovel for various tasks throughout her life in her new homeland.

Cotten, Cynthia.

Abbie in Stitches. **Illustrated by Beth Peck. New York: Farrar, Straus & Giroux, 2006. 32pp. ISBN 9780374300043.** `Gr. 1–3`

Abbie would much rather be reading than doing needlework, but in the early nineteenth century in upstate New York, it is mandatory for young ladies to embroider a sampler. Always wishing she were reading instead, Abbie stitches diligently through the fall and winter and finally finishes a work that pleases her parents and her teacher and earns her a special reward.

Esbaum, Jill.

Ste-E-E-Eamboat A-Comin'! **Illustrated by Adam Rex. New York: Farrar, Straus & Giroux, 2005. 32pp. ISBN 9780374372361.** `Gr. 1–3`

Inspired by a passage from Mark Twain's *Life on the Mississippi*, Esbaum has created a bouncy rhyme that conveys all the hustle and bustle a small river town experienced when the steamboat arrived.

Evans, Freddi Williams.

Hush Harbor: Praying in Secret. Illustrated by Erin Bennett Banks. Minneapolis, MN: Carolrhoda, 2009. Unpaged. ISBN 9780822579656. **Gr. 2 & up**

Even though slaves were not allowed to hold gatherings for fear of what they would plan, they held secret meetings anyway, called "hush harbors." On this night, Simmy serves as a lookout while the older slaves pray, sing, and dance. When Simmy hears the ominous sound of footsteps, he calls out a warning, and the slaves scatter, arriving safely back in their quarters, hoping to meet again and again until freedom comes.

Fern, Tracey E.

Buffalo Music. Illustrated by Lauren Castillo. New York: Clarion, 2008. 31pp. ISBN 9780618723416. **Gr. K–3**

When Molly and her husband first came to Texas, the ground would rumble and shake when the herds of buffalo roared past. Six years later, the buffalo were almost gone. Molly begins caring for young orphaned buffalos, and when she hears that Yellowstone National Park would like to rebuild their herd, she sends them four of her young charges. This is based on the life of Mary Ann Goodnight, who helped saved the buffalo from extinction in the late 1800s.

Fletcher, Susan.

Dadblamed Union Army Cow. Illustrated by Kimberly Bulcken Root. Cambridge, MA: Candlewick, 2007. 32pp. ISBN 9780763622633. **Gr. 2 & up**

This book was inspired by the true story of a cow who became famous traveling with the 59th Regiment of Indiana Volunteers during the Civil War. When a young man enlists in the army, his cow follows him throughout the war. As frustrated and embarrassed as the soldier is by the humorous bovine, the cow turns out to be helpful, swatting away flies with her tail and sharing her warmth in the winter and her milk in the times when food was hard to come by.

Gerstein, Mordicai.

Sparrow Jack. New York: Farrar, Straus & Giroux, 2007. 32pp. ISBN 9780374371395. **Gr. K–3**

In 1868 in Philadelphia, inchworms are a recurring plague that annually annoys the residents. John Bardsley, who grew up in England, returns to his native land and brings home a flock of sparrows, knowing they will eat the bothersome inchworms.

Grifalconi, Ann.

Ain't Nobody a Stranger to Me. Illustrated by Jerry Pinkney. New York: Jump at the Sun, 2007. 28pp. ISBN 9780786818570. **Gr. K–3**

Inspired by a true story, here an elderly grandfather explains to his granddaughter how he escaped from slavery with only a few appleseeds in his pocket. Helped by people on the Underground Railroad, he now walks in his own apple orchard, one that grew from the seeds that came north with him.

Hall, Donald.

🌳*The Ox-Cart Man.* **Illustrated by Barbara Cooney. New York: Viking, 1979. 40pp. ISBN 9780670533282.** `Gr. 2 & up`

A New England farmer and his family perform the seasonal chores that keep the farm going and provide the hustle and bustle of their daily lives. (ALAN, Caldecott Medal, New York Times Best Illustrated Book)

Hegamin, Tonya Cherie.

Most Loved in All the World. **Illustrated by Cozbi A. Cabrera. Boston: Houghton Mifflin, 2009. 26pp. ISBN 9780618419036.** `Gr. 3 & up`

Although the mother of the story labors as a slave in the cotton fields all day, every night she works tirelessly on a quilt that will map out the road to freedom for her young daughter, who is most loved in all the world. When the quilt is finished, she leads her daughter to the Underground Railroad and sends her north. Cabrera's acrylic paintings and textile collage not only deftly depict the action of the story, but also beautifully envision the quilt as the central image of the narrative.

Hopkinson, Deborah.

🌳*Apples to Oregon.* **Illustrated by Nancy Carpenter. New York: Atheneum, 2004. Unpaged. ISBN 9780689847691.** `Gr. K–3`

In a folksy tone, giving the story the feel of a tall tale, Delicious, the oldest of eight children, narrates the account of her family's journey from Iowa to Oregon in the mid-1800s. Her daddy longs to travel west, but he can't bear to leave his beloved apple trees behind, so he constructs a special wagon for them and relies on his wife and children to help them survive river crossings, hail, and frost. (ALAN, Golden Kite Award)

Howard, Elizabeth Fitzgerald.

🌳*Virgie Goes to School with Us Boys.* **Illustrated by E. B. Lewis. New York: Simon & Schuster. 2000. 32 pp. ISBN 9780689800764.** `Gr. 1 & up`

In post–Civil War Tennessee, Virgie, the youngest of six siblings and the only girl, longs to go to school with her brothers, but her parents fear that the seven-mile trek will be too much for her. A persistent Virgie perseveres and eventually wins permission to attend the Quaker school, despite the hazards. Lewis's engaging watercolor paintings illustrate both the warmth of Virgie's family and Virgie's determination. (Boston Globe Award, Coretta Scott King Award)

Hughes, Pat.

Seeing the Elephant: A Story of the Civil War. **Illustrated by Ken Stark. New York: Farrar, Straus & Giroux, 2007. 40pp. ISBN 9780374380243.** `Gr. 2 & up`

Ten-year-old Izzy chafes at being too young to be a soldier in the Union Army, so his aunt, who is a nurse, brings him to Washington, D.C., with her. He meets

Abraham Lincoln, goes to a the hospital where his aunt works tending wounded soldiers from both sides, and talks with a Rebel. His experiences dramatically change his perspective on the war.

Hurst, Carol Otis.

Terrible Storm. **Illustrated by S. D. Schindler. New York: Greenwillow, 2007. 32pp. ISBN 9780060090012.** `Gr. K–3`

Two grandpas recall that the Massachusetts blizzard of 1888 was the worst storm ever, but they believe this for very different reasons. Grandpa Walt, a friendly fellow, got stuck in a barn all alone, and Grandpa Fred, who was on the shy side, waited out the raging wind and snow in a tavern full of people.

Kerby, Mona.

Owney, the Mail-Pouch Pooch. **Illustrated by Lynne Barasch. New York: Farrar, Straus & Giroux, 2008. Unpaged. ISBN 9780374356859.** `Gr. 1–3`

Inspired by the actual stray terrier who first found a home in an Albany post office and then became a mascot of the U.S. Postal Service in the 1890s, Kerby regales readers with the adventures of Owney, who traveled far and wide, guarding the mail from town to town and country to country.

Krensky, Stephen.

Sisters of Scituate Light. **Illustrated by Stacey Schutt. New York: Dutton, 2008. 32pp. ISBN 9780525477921.** `Gr. K–3`

Based on the actual account of sisters Rebecca and Abigail Bates, Krensky provides a fictionalized version of their adventures. The daughters of a lighthouse keeper, they spot a British warship approaching during the war of 1812 and are able to fool the sailors into thinking that American troops are nearby.

Levine, Ellen.

🏃*Henry's Freedom Box.* **Illustrated by Kadir Nelson. New York: Scholastic, 2007. 40pp. ISBN 9780439777339.** `Gr. 2 & up`

Basing her story on historical events, Levine relates the experience of Henry "Box" Brown. He was born and raised a slave and worked in a tobacco factory. When his beloved wife and three children are sold, Henry is devastated and has no way to recover them. With nothing left to lose, he turns to a compassionate white man at the factory and convinces him to mail him in a crate to Philadelphia and freedom. Nelson's pencil, watercolor, and oil illustrations are brimming with beauty, despair, and hope. (ALAN, Caldecott Honor)

Lowell, Susan.

The Elephant Quilt: Stitch by Stitch to California! **Illustrated by Stacey Dressen-McQueen. New York: Farrar, Straus & Giroux, 2008. 40pp. ISBN 9780374382230.** `Gr. K–3`

> Inspired by an actual quilt, this account of an 1859 journey along the Santa Fe Trail relates the journey of Lily Rose and her family, who are on their way to California. Grandmother, mother, and Lily Rose stitch their adventures into a quilt, as they cross mountains, weather storms, and welcome a new baby.

McCully, Emily Arnold.

The Escape of Oney Judge: Martha Washington's Slave Finds Freedom. **New York: Farrar, Strauss & Giroux, 2007. 32pp. ISBN 9780374322250.** `Gr. 2 & up`

> Ten-year-old Oney is a slave for Martha Washington, and although Martha treats her well, as Oney grows up, she longs to be free. When the Washington family moves to Philadelphia, Oney sees free black people for the first time in her life. Realizing that freedom is possible and not just a dream, she first plans and then executes her escape. Based on a true story. (Jane Addams Book Award)

Morrow, Barbara Olenyik.

A Good Night for Freedom. **Illustrated by Leonard Jenkins. New York: Holiday House, 2007. Unpaged. ISBN 9780823417094.** `Gr. 1–3`

> Inspired by the lives of Quaker abolitionists Catharine and Levi Coffin, who lived in Indiana in the early 1800s, Morrow creates the story of Hallie, who stumbles upon two runaway slaves hiding in the Coffins' basement. Unsure what to do, she races home. Although her father advises her not to meddle, Hallie wrestles with her conscience, and when the slave catchers come hunting, she provides directions she hopes will lead them away from the runaways.

Moser, Lisa.

Kisses on the Wind. **Illustrated by Kathryn Brown. Somerville, MA: Candlewick, 2009. 32pp. ISBN 9780763631109.** `PreS–3`

> As Lydia's parents finish packing their covered wagon, Lydia expresses her sadness about leaving to her beloved grandmother. Rather than recommend Lydia bottle up her grief, her grandmother comforts her and gives Lydia a memory book filled with her stories, so that Lydia can still feel her grandmother's presence on the journey.

Noble, Trinka Hakes.

The Last Brother: A Civil War Tale. **Illustrated by Robert Papp. Chelsea, MI: Sleeping Bear Press, 2004. 48pp. ISBN 9781585362530.** `Gr. 3 & up`

> Just before the Battle of Gettysburg, Gabe, an eleven-year-old bugler, returns to the forest to practice the commands he must blow to let the soldiers know their commander's orders. As he plays, he hears answering notes, and then Orlee, a confederate bugler, emerges from the bushes. The two spend a companionable day by the stream. When the battle is joined the next day, Gabe feels torn between

his desire to keep his new friend safe and his loyalty to his brother, who is serving in the same troop.

Osborne, Mary Pope.

New York's Bravest. See under "Community Helpers: Firefighters" in chapter 2.

Polacco, Patricia.

🎗*Pink and Say.* New York: Philomel, 1994. Unpaged.
ISBN 9780399226717. **Gr. 2 & up** (SP)
> Two young Union soldiers—Say, a white youth from Ohio, and Pink, a black youth from Georgia—have a profound impact on each other's lives during the Civil War. After a fierce battle in Georgia, Pink comes upon the wounded Say. He brings him home to his mother to be nursed back to health. While they are able to forget about the war for a short time, when marauders murder Pink's mother, both boys know it's time to go back and fight. The Confederates capture them, and they are sent to Andersonville prison camp. Although Say is eventually released, Pink is hung for being black. A deeply moving story, illustrated with Polacco's dramatic and evocative artwork. (ALAN)

Prince, April Jones.

Twenty-One Elephants: And Still Standing. Illustrated by François Roca. Boston: Houghton Mifflin, 2005. 32pp. ISBN 9780618448876. **Gr. 1-3**
> When the Brooklyn Bridge opened, there was some concern about its safety throughout New York City. So the ever-resourceful P. T. Barnum organized the 1884 elephant parade to cross the newly opened Brooklyn Bridge, proving to all the sturdiness of the structure.

Rappaport, Doreen.

Freedom Ship. Illustrated by Curtis James. New York: Hyperion, 2006. 40pp. ISBN 9780786806454. **Gr. 3 & up**
> The historic event of May 13, 1862, when Robert Smalls and his crew of enslaved men took over the Confederate ship *Planter* and delivered it to the Union side, is told from the fictional point of view of a young boy whose family is rescued by Smalls and taken to freedom with the ship.

Raven, Margot Theis.

🎗*Night Boat to Freedom.* Illustrated by E. B. Lewis. New York: Farrar, Straus & Giroux, 2006. 40pp. ISBN 9780374312664. **Gr. 3 & up**
> Stitching together histories recorded in the Federal Writers' Project's Slave Narrative Collection, Raven creates a narrative of Granny Judith and twelve-year-old Christmas John, who share a cabin at the river border between Kentucky and Ohio. Christmas John rows slaves across the river until it becomes too dangerous to continue. Granny Judith encourages him to

escape himself, but he will not leave without her, and so they escape to freedom together. Lewis's moody watercolors bring both the environment and the emotions of the protagonists to life. (Jane Addams Honor Book)

Russell, Barbara T.

Maggie's Amerikay. **Illustrated by Jim Burke. New York: Farrar, Straus & Giroux, 2006. 40pp. ISBN 9780374347222.** `Gr. 2 & up`

In 1898 Maggie McCrary and her family move from Ireland to New Orleans and struggle to earn a living. Her father becomes a peddler, hoping to save enough to buy some land. That doesn't stop him from giving a used coronet to Nathan, a young black boy who longs to become a musician. Nathan does them a kindness in turn when Maggie needs a job. He sends her to Daddy Clements, a former slave, who pays her for writing down his history. As he relates his hardships, Maggie shares some of her own past with him.

Schroeder, Alan.

Minty: A Story of Young Harriet Tubman. **Illustrated by Jerry Pinkney. New York: Dial, 1996. Unpaged. ISBN 9780803718883.** `Gr. K–3`

Using rhythmic prose and colloquial dialogue, Schroeder spins a tale of Harriet Tubman's childhood based on the few incidents recorded in the 1869 biography *Harriet Tubman: The Moses of Her People*. Harriet Tubman's "cradle name" was Araminta, but people called her Minty from an early age. She was born around 1820 on the Brodas Plantation on Maryland's eastern shore, and as a child she displayed more independence than her mistress approved of. When Minty displeases Mrs. Brodas, she burns Minty's beloved ragdoll and banishes her to the fields. Minty's father sees her determination to be free and teaches her the skills she will need to survive and find her way north. (ALAN, Coretta Scott King Award, Golden Kite Honor)

Tingle, Tim.

Crossing Bok Chitto: A Choctaw Tale of Friendship & Freedom. **Illustrated by Jeanne Rorex Bridges. El Paso, TX: Cinco Puntos Press, 2006. 40pp. ISBN 9780938317777.** `Gr. 2 & up`

In the Mississippi of the 1800s, before the Civil War, the Bok Chitto River separates the tribes of the Choctaw from the plantations. Ignoring her mother's instructions, young Martha Tom crosses the river in search of blackberries. When she becomes lost in the woods on the plantation side, a slave boy named Little Mo guides her back to the river. The two become friends. When his mother is going to be sold away, Martha constructs a plan and helps spirit the family away to freedom.

Van Leeuwen, Jean.

Papa and the Pioneer Quilt. **Illustrated by Rebecca Bond. New York: Dial, 2007. 30pp. ISBN 9780803730281.** `Gr. K–3`

Rebecca's father has the urge to wander, and so the family is off again, this time traveling west from Missouri to Oregon. As they brave the hazards along the way,

Rebecca collects scraps of cloth and stitches a quilt with them for the family's new home.

Winter, Jeanette.

Follow the Drinking Gourd. New York: Knopf, 1988. 48pp. ISBN 978-0394896946. Gr. K-3

Before the Civil War, an old white sailor, Joe Peg Leg, traveled from plantation to plantation teaching slaves his folksongs, which contained hidden directions for following the Underground Railroad to freedom. Here, five slaves escape to Canada guided by the stars, with help from Quakers and Joe Peg Leg himself.

Woodson, Jacqueline.

Show Way. Illustrated by Hudson Talbott. New York: Putnam, 2005. 48pp. ISBN 9780399237492. Gr. 2 & up

This poetic narrative traces eight generations of Woodson's family, from Soonie's great-grandmother, who was sold away from her family at the age of seven, to Soonie's great-great-granddaughter, Woodson's own daughter Toshi. The story follows the lives of the women and incorporates the tradition of creating Show Ways, quilts that were embroidered with secret messages to help show the way to freedom. Striking multimedia art includes watercolors, chalk and fabric, and photographs incorporated into original art, producing a pictorial quilt of its own. (ALAN, Newbery Honor)

Yin.

Coolies. Illustrated by Chris K. Soentpiet. New York: Philomel, 2001. Unpaged. ISBN 9780399232275. Gr. 2 & up

Shek and his younger brother Wong make the arduous journey from China to America in 1865 and immediately join the workforce constructing the transcontinental railroad for the Central Pacific Railroad Company. The mistreated Chinese workers were paid less than the Europeans, required to perform the most dangerous tasks, and forced to labor on in the worst weather. Surviving a brutal four years, the brothers take their earnings, open a store in San Francisco, and bring the rest of the family across the Pacific to join them. Their experiences are illuminated by Soentpiet's glowing paintings. (ALAN)

Brothers. Illustrated by Chris K. Soentpiet. New York: Philomel, 2006. 40pp. ISBN 9780399234064. Sequel. Gr. 2 & up

Shek and Wong's brother Ming comes to work in the store in Chinatown. Times are hard, so Wong is left to mind the store while his brothers take other jobs. Bored, Ming takes to wandering past the borders of Chinatown and discovers a school that he longs to go to, but learns that the Chinese are not welcome there. Things take a turn for the better when he befriends Patrick, who begins teaching him to speak English. Together the friends devise a plan to help save the store.

Yolen, Jane.

My Uncle Emily. **Illustrated by Nancy Carpenter. New York: Philomel, 2009. 27pp. ISBN 9780399240058.** `Gr. 2 & up`

Yolen weaves a story around Emily Dickinson's relationship with her young nephew, Gib. Gib tells of their closeness, their shared experiences, and their connection through poetry.

Twentieth Century

Adler, David.

🎗️*The Babe and I.* **Illustrated by Terry Widener. San Diego: Harcourt, 1999. Unpaged. ISBN 9780152013783.** `Gr. 1–3`

In 1932, in the midst of the Great Depression, a boy spots his father selling apples. Realizing his father has lost his job like so many others, the boy begins to sell papers in front of Yankee Stadium. He even sells one to Babe Ruth! (Golden Kite Honor)

Armstrong, Jennifer.

Magnus at the Fire. **Illustrated by Owen Smith. New York: Simon & Schuster, 2005. Unpaged. ISBN 9780689839221.** `Gr. 2 & up`

In the early 1900s, strong horses were used to pull the fire trucks in New York City, and Magnus is a well-trained horse who responds immediately to the clang of the fire alarm. When a motorized engine replaces the horses, Magnus still wants to rush to the fire. He saves the day one last time when the new engine breaks down, and then is retired to a farm in the country.

Aston, Dianna Hutts.

🎗️*The Moon over Star.* **Illustrated by Jerry Pinkney. New York: Dial, 2008. 32pp. ISBN 9780803731073.** `Gr. K–3`

Mae Jemison, who grew up to be the first African American astronaut, remembers 1969, when she was nine years-old and watched men walk on the moon for the first time. Pinkney's extraordinary illustrations vividly depict the experience. (Coretta Scott King Honor)

Avi.

🎗️*Silent Movie.* **Illustrated by C. B. Mordan. New York: Atheneum, 2003. Unpaged. ISBN 9780689841453.** `Gr. K–3`

Presented in the format of an old-fashioned silent movie with black-and-white pictures and title cards, this book chronicles the story of a Swedish family that immigrates to New York City in 1909. They become separated, but are reunited when Gustav is cast in a silent movie. (ALAN)

Birtha, Becky.

Grandmama's Pride. **Illustrated by Colin Bootman. Morton Grove, IL: Albert Whitman, 2005. 32pp. ISBN 9780807530283.** `Gr. 2 & up`

> Sarah-Marie and her sister love to journey south every summer to visit their grandmother, but in the summer of 1956, after she has learned to read, Sarah-Marie begins to realize the effects of segregation.

Blue, Rose, and Corinne J. Naden.

Ron's Big Mission. **Illustrated by Don Tate. New York: Dutton, 2009. 32pp. ISBN 9780525478492.** `Gr. 1-3`

> Ron loves to read library books; the trouble is, he's not allowed to borrow any because in this 1950s South Carolina town, black people are not allowed to take home library books. He is the library's best customer, and finally, in the face of Ron's determination, the librarian gives Ron his own library card.

Bunting, Eve.

Pop's Bridge. **Illustrated by C. F. Payne. Orlando, FL: Harcourt, 2006. 28pp. ISBN 9780152047733.** `Gr. 1-3`

> Robert and his friend Charlie spend one afternoon after another watching their fathers build the Golden Gate Bridge in San Francisco. When ten men die in an accident, Robert comes to realize that every job on the bridge is important, as is every man's life.

Cooper, Floyd.

Willie and the All-Stars. **New York: Philomel, 2008. Unpaged. ISBN 9780399233401.** `Gr. 1-3`

> In 1942 on Chicago's North Side, young Willie, an African American boy, listens to every Major League Baseball game on the radio and dreams of becoming a star player himself. He's devastated when he learns that he's the "wrong color" for the Major League, but when he sees a game between the greats of the Negro League, like Satchel Paige and Josh Gibson, his hope is restored. Lusciously illustrated in golden earth tones.

Chaconas, Doris.

Dancing with Katya. See under "Challenging Situations in Life: Physically Challenged" in chapter 2.

Cordsen, Carol Foskett.

The Milkman. **Illustrated by Douglas B. Jones. New York: Dutton, 2005. 32pp. ISBN 9780525472087.** `PreS-2`

> This story provides a glimpse back to the days when milkmen delivered fresh milk each morning, as it follows one such professional through town on his rounds, delivering his products and helping out his customers whenever he can.

Corey, Shana.

Players in Pigtails. **Illustrated by Rebecca Gibbon. New York: Scholastic, 2003. 40pp. ISBN 9780439183055. Gr. K–3**

Inspired by a little-known verse in "Take Me out to the Ball Game," Corey creates the character of Katie Casey, who eschews ladylike ways in favor of playing baseball. She joins the All-American Girls Professional Baseball League of the 1940s and loves every minute of it.

Esbaum, Jill.

To the Big Top. **Illustrated by David Gordon. New York: Farrar, Straus & Giroux, 2008. 30p ISBN 9780374399344. Gr. K–3**

In the early twentieth century, when the circus comes to town, shivers of excitement delight the residents of the small town of Willow Grove. Sam and Benny enjoy every moment, and when they are asked to help, their circus experience becomes a treasure they'll remember forever.

Friedrich, Elizabeth.

Leah's Pony. **Illustrated by Michael Garland. Honesdale, PA: Boyds Mills Press, 1996. Unpaged. ISBN 9781563971891. Gr. K–3**

In the 1930s, Leah's family lives on a farm the Great Plains, but between locusts and drought, the bank is about to foreclose. Leah sells her beloved pony so that she will have money to bid at the mandated farm auction. She wins her father's tractor for the incredibly low sum of one dollar. Their sympathetic neighbors also bid low sums for all of the items and return them to the family so that they can stay on the farm. (Golden Kite Honor)

Gourley, Robbin.

Bring Me Some Apples and I'll Make You a Pie: A Story about Edna Lewis. **New York: Clarion, 2009. 45pp. ISBN 9780618158362. Gr. 1–3**

Based on the childhood of Edna Lewis, an African American girl who grew up to become a chef in New York City in the first half of the century, this story focuses on celebrating a year in her childhood that is a season of growing for the farming communities of Virginia.

Hall, Bruce Edward.

Henry and the Kite Dragon. **Illustrated by William Low. New York: Philomel, 2004. 40pp. ISBN 9780399237270. Gr. K–3**

Henry Chu lives in New York City's Chinatown in the 1920s, and he loves to help Grandfather Chin create his stunning kites. He also relishes flying the kites, but Tony Guglione and his friends from Little Italy keep throwing rocks at the kites, destroying the beautiful creations. When Henry confronts Tony, he learns that the kites scare Tony's homing pigeons, and the boys work out a compromise that pleases both sides. (Jane Addams Honor Book)

Harrington, Janice.

Going North. Illustrated by Jerome Lagarrigue. New York: Melanie Kroupa Books, 2004. 40pp. ISBN 9780374326814. **Gr. 3 & up**

> Lyrical prose recounts the journey of an African American family from Alabama to Nebraska in 1964. The young narrator is reluctant to leave, and segregation makes their travel difficult, but the closer they get to the North, the more hope they have that things will be better in their new life.

Henson, Heather.

Angel Coming. Illustrated by Susan Gaber. New York: Atheneum, 2005. Unpaged. ISBN 9780689855313. **PreS-2**

> Henson's poetic prose captures the cadence of Appalachia in the early part of the century, as the narrator awaits the arrival of a new sibling.

That Book Woman. Illustrated by David Small. New York: Atheneum, 2008. 40pp. ISBN 9781416908128. **Gr. 2 & up**

> Cal and his family live high in the Appalachian hills. Cal is proud of the hard work he does all day and has no patience for his sister Lark's love of reading. When the horseback riding librarian, one of the many WPA Pack Horse Librarians of the 1930s who brought books to people in isolated areas, brings Lark books, Cal wants nothing to do with her. However, when she delivers them in a snowstorm, he realizes how brave she is and asks his sister to teach him to read so that he can see what's so very important.

Hesse, Karen.

Spuds. Illustrated by Wendy Watson. New York: Scholastic, 2008. 32pp. ISBN 9780439879934. **Gr. 1-3**

> Watson's pencil, ink, watercolor, and gouache paintings place this story in the time of the Great Depression. Food is scarce in narrator Jack's home, even when Ma works hard on the night shift. One night, Jack and his siblings venture to their neighbor's farm to pick the potatoes that have been left behind. They dream of how delicious the potatoes will be when Ma cooks them up. Even though they've harvested more stones than potatoes, Ma makes them return their ill-gotten gains to the farmer. He lets them keep them, for the service of getting rid of the stones in his field. Ma cooks up the potatoes, and Jack realizes they are being cooked with love.

High, Linda Oatman.

Tenth Avenue Cowboy. Illustrated by Bill Farnsworth. Grand Rapids, MI: Eerdmans, 2008. 32pp. ISBN 9780802853301. **Gr. K-3**

> In 1910, Ben and his family move from the West to New York City. Ben is having trouble adjusting to city life and still nurtures dreams of being a cowboy. When he learns that there are actual cowboys in New York, he investigates. He finds that cowboys gallop down Tenth Avenue to warn pedestrians when a train is coming. Befriending the men and their horses, he begins to feel at home in the city.

Hopkinson, Deborah.

🎗*Girl Wonder: A Baseball Story in Nine Innings.* **Illustrated by Terry Widener. New York: Atheneum, 2003. Unpaged. ISBN 9780689833007.** `Gr. 1-3`

Hopkinson pitches a tale inspired by the life of female baseball player Alta Weiss, who played for the Vermilion Independents in 1907. Growing up, Alta loved baseball and practiced pitching at every opportunity. As a teen, she gets her chance to pitch for the all male, semi-pro team because she convinces the coach that people will buy tickets just to see a girl play. When she finishes her season in baseball, she tackles another unusual profession for a woman: medical school.

Saving Strawberry Farm. **Illustrated by Rachel Isadora. New York: Greenwillow, 2005. Unpaged. ISBN 9780688174002.** `PreS-2`

Times are hard for everyone in this Midwestern town in 1933 as the Great Depression takes its toll, but when young Davey learns that Miss Elsie is going to lose her beloved Strawberry farm to the bank, he gladly helps spread the word of Mr. Russell's plan to make the auction for the farm a penny auction. They keep the bidding low, and Miss Elsie is able to buy back her farm.

Sky Boys: How They Built the Empire State Building. **Illustrated by James E. Ransome. New York: Schwartz & Wade, 2006. 48pp. ISBN 9780375836107.** `Gr. 1-3`

Using second person narration, a young boy chronicles the construction of the Empire State Building in New York City during the grim days of the Great Depression. (ALAN, Boston Globe Honor)

Stage Coach Sal: Inspired by a True Tale. **Illustrated by Carson Ellis. New York: Hyperion, 2009. 26pp. ISBN 9781423111498.** `Gr. 1-3`

Sal, petite but perky, loves to sing, especially when riding shotgun with her father on the stagecoach. When she sets out on her first solo journey to deliver the mail, the famous robber Poetic Pete tries to relieve her of her cargo, but she is able to lull him to sleep with her singing and arrives with the bandit cuffed and the mail safe.

Johnson, Angela.

🎗*I Dream of Trains.* **Illustrated by Loren Long. New York: Simon & Schuster, 2003. Unpaged. ISBN 9780689826092.** `Gr. 3 & up`

In 1900 the son of a sharecropper watches the famous Casey Jones's train whoosh by and wishes he could whir across the landscape with him. When Casey is killed in a train wreck on April 30, 1900, the boy's dreams are shattered, until his father convinces him that his dreams can still come true. (Golden Kite Award)

A Sweet Smell of Roses. **Illustrated by Eric Velasquez. New York: Simon & Schuster, 2004. 32pp. ISBN 9780689832529.** `Gr. K-3`

During the days of the civil rights struggle in the South, two sisters sneak out of the house to participate in a freedom march led by Dr. Martin Luther King Jr. Johnson's poetic text and Velasquez's charcoal illustrations illuminate a pivotal period in the quest for racial equality.

Wind Flyers. **Illustrated by Loren Long. New York: Simon & Schuster, 2007. 32pp. ISBN 9780689848797.** `Gr. 2 & up`

An African American boy recounts the escapades of his great-uncle, who always wanted to fly, from the time he jumped off the chicken coop roof, to his service as one of the Tuskegee Airmen.

Kinsey-Warnock, Natalie.

Nora's Ark. Illustrated by Emily Arnold McCully. New York: HarperCollins, 2005. Unpaged. ISBN 9780688172442. `Gr. K–3`

Fortuitously Grandpa is building a new house for his wife high on a hill on their Vermont farm, when on November 2, 1927, the heavens open and seemingly unending streams of rain pour down. Grandma shelters in the new house and welcomes in neighbors and livestock. They weather the storm, but must go out in a rowboat to search for Grandpa, who has passed a wet night in a tree.

Lee, Milly.

Landed. Illustrated by Yangsook Choi. New York: Farrar, Straus & Giroux, 2006. 32pp. ISBN 9780374343149. `Gr. 3 & up`

The Chinese Exclusion Act of 1882 made it very difficult for the Chinese to emigrate to the United States, so when twelve-year-old Sun is preparing to leave China to join his father in San Francisco to work in his store, he must first study with a special tutor. Upon arrival on Angel Island, he is grilled to determine if his father truly works in the United States, because many Chinese families would send "paper sons," in the hope that they would make it into the country. Although Sun is terrified he'll make a mistake, he passes the test and is reunited with his father and brothers.

Lindsey, Kathleen D.

Sweet Potato Pie. Illustrated by Charlotte Riley-Webb. New York: Lee & Low, 2003. Unpaged. ISBN 9781584300618. `Gr. K–3`

Eight-year-old Sadie lives on a farm with her African American family in the early 1900s. Their crops are in danger of failing from the exceedingly dry weather, but the rain arrives just in time to save the sweet potato crop. When a letter of foreclosure comes from the bank, the family pitches in to make oodles of sweet potato pies. They sell enough at the Harvest Festival to pay off the bank.

Littlesugar, Amy.

Freedom School, Yes! Illustrated by Floyd Cooper. New York: Philomel, 2001. Unpaged. ISBN 9780399230066. `Gr. 2 & up`

Jolie, a young girl who lives in Mississippi, feels some trepidation about their new house guest, Annie, who has come to teach Freedom School during the 1964 Mississippi Summer Project organized by civil rights leaders to register African American voters in that state. When the school comes under threat from those who are opposed to it, Jolie realizes that learning is the best way to fight back.

Martin, Jacqueline Briggs.

🦃 *On Sand Island*. **Illustrated by David A. Johnson. Boston: Houghton Mifflin, 2003. Unpaged. ISBN 9780618231515.** `Gr. 1–3`

In 1916, ten-year-old Carl lives on Sand Island in Lake Superior, and what he wants most in the world is his own boat. When he finds some jetsam boards, he combines hard work with help from his neighbors to make his dream come true. (Golden Kite Honor)

McClintock, Barbara.

Adele and Simon in America. **New York: Farrar, Straus & Giroux, 2008. 40pp. ISBN 9780374399245.** `Gr. K–3`

In this sequel to *Adele and Simon*, which takes place in Paris, the siblings journey to America with their Aunt Cecile in the early 1900s and embark on a train trip across the country.

McKissack, Patricia.

🦃 *Goin' Someplace Special*. **Illustrated by Jerry Pinkney. New York: Atheneum, 2001. Unpaged. ISBN 9780689818851.** `Gr. K–3`

In the early 1950s, young Tricia Ann heads to town on her own for the first time, headed "someplace special." In the bustling city of Nashville, the cruelty of Jim Crow segregation accosts her on all sides, from the bus ride in, to restaurants and even the Grand Ol' Opry, but she feels triumphant when she at last reaches her destination, the Nashville Public Library. There the sign proclaims, "All Are Welcome!" This moving story, based on the author's childhood, is sumptuously illustrated by the award-winning Pinkney. (ALAN, Coretta Scott King Award)

Michelson, Richard.

Happy Feet: The Savoy Ballroom Lindy Hoppers and Me. **Illustrated by E. B. Lewis. Orlando, FL: Harcourt, 2005. 32pp. ISBN 9780152050573.** `Gr. 2 & up`

Young Happy Feet loves to hear the story of the night he was born, March 12, 1926—the same day his father opened his shoeshine shop across the street from the Savoy Ballroom, which also opened that night.

Across the Alley. **Illustrated by E. B. Lewis. New York: Putnam, 2006. 32pp. ISBN 9780399239700.** `Gr. K–3`

In post–World War II Brooklyn, Jewish Abe and African American Willie are best friends, but only at night when they can talk to each other across the alley, since their bedroom windows face each other. Abe helps Willie with his violin playing, and Willie gives Abe baseball tips. When Abe's grandfather realizes it's Willie that he hears playing so beautifully at night, he invites him to play at temple. Even though the neighborhood residents are scandalized when they walk to temple together and no one in the temple will sit next to Willie and his father, Willie wins them over with his recital. Now the boys are free to be friends in the daytime, too.

Miller, William.

The Piano. Illustrated by Susan Keeter. New York: Lee & Low, 2000. Unpaged. ISBN 9781880000984. **Gr. 2 & up**

In the early 1900s, Tia likes to wander the streets, secure in her African American neighborhood, but when she hears the strains of beautiful piano music, she follows the sound to a mansion. Entranced by the music, she takes a job as a maid and befriends the elderly resident. They grow fond of each other, and the mistress of the house agrees to teach Tia how to play the piano.

Mochizuki, Ken.

Baseball Saved Us. Illustrated by Dom Lee. New York: Lee & Low, 1993. Unpaged. ISBN 9781880000014. **Gr. 3 & up**

In 1942 "Shorty" and his family are forced to move into Japanese internment camps. The thing that helps him through the extreme hardship is playing baseball.

Paterson, Katherine, and John Paterson.

Blueberries for the Queen. Illustrated by Susan Jeffers. New York: HarperCollins, 2004. Unpaged. ISBN 9780066239422. **Gr. K–3**

In the summer of 1942, all of William's family is busy doing war work, but William is too little. He daydreams about being a knight and using magic to defeat Hitler. When he learns that Queen Wilhelmina of the Netherlands is temporarily living in Massachusetts because of the war, he longs to serve her. He and his father pick blueberries one day, and William hopes that this is war work, but his father calls it "peace work." Nonetheless, William takes a box of blueberries for the queen and is granted his wish for a royal audience.

Pinkney, Andrea Davis.

Fishing Day. Illustrated by Shane W. Evans. New York: Jump at the Sun, 2003. 32pp. ISBN 9780786807666. **Gr. K–3**

In the days of segregation, a black mother and daughter and a white father and son fish on opposite sides of a river called Jim Crow. Although the children might become friends, their parents keep them apart. Peter and his father have trouble catching fish, and in a moment when the children are on their own, Reenie helps, and the next time they see each other, they wave.

Boycott Blues: How Rosa Parks Inspired a Nation. Illustrated by Brian J. Pinkney. New York: Greenwillow, 2008. Unpaged. ISBN 9780060821180. **Gr. 3 & up**

Steeped in the events of the 1955 Montgomery bus boycott, this story swirls together fact and fiction in a bluesy rhythm to tell the tale of Rosa Parks's fight against Jim Crow segregation. The riveting artwork perfectly complements the text.

Reynolds, Aaron.

Back of the Bus. Illustrated by Floyd Cooper. New York: Philomel, 2009. 32pp. ISBN 9780399250910. `Gr. 1–3`

> A young African American boy who is sitting at the back of the bus with his mother in 1955 in Montgomery, Alabama, describes the famous events of the day Rosa Parks refused to give up her seat, in what became a crucial event in the civil rights movement.

Ryan, Pam Muñoz.

🌑*Amelia and Eleanor Go for a Ride: Based on a True Story.* Illustrated by Brian Selznick. New York: Scholastic, 1999. Unpaged. ISBN 9780590960755. `Gr. 1–3`

> On April 20, 1933, Amelia Earhart dined at the White House with her friend Eleanor Roosevelt, and her description of flying at night so intrigued the first lady that the two zipped off for a quick flight to Baltimore and were back just in time for dessert. Selznick's graphite and wash illustrations beautifully render their adventures. (ALAN)

Sandin, Joan.

Coyote School News. New York: Holt, 2003. 45pp. ISBN 9780805065589. `Gr. 2 & up`

> Mexican American Monchi Ram'rez regales readers with stories of life on a southern Arizona ranch from 1938 to 1939.

Say, Allen.

Music for Alice. Boston: Houghton Mifflin, 2004. 32pp. ISBN 9780618311187. `Gr. 3 & up`

> Even as a little girl, Alice loved to dance, but there is precious little dancing when she and her husband are forced from their home during World War II because they are Japanese Americans. They choose to work as farm laborers rather than go to the internment camp. After the war, they become the biggest sellers of gladiola bulbs in the country, but it isn't until after the death of her husband that Alice realizes she is free to dance again.

Stewart, Sarah.

🌑*The Gardener.* Illustrated by David Small. New York: Farrar, Straus & Giroux, 1997. Unpaged. ISBN 9780374325176. `PreS–2`

> In 1935, the tough times of the Depression mean that ten-year-old Lydia Grace is sent to live with dour Uncle Jim, who runs a bakery. In her suitcase, the irrepressible Lydia Grace has stowed a selection of seeds, and with them she transforms a rooftop into a garden, bringing a rare smile to her uncle's face and customers to his bakery. (ALAN, Caldecott Honor)

Tavares, Matt.

Mudball. Cambridge, MA: Candlewick, 2005. 32pp. ISBN 9780763623876. `Gr. 1–3`

> It's 1903, and Andy Oyler, the shortest player in the league, can't seem to get himself out of a batting slump. It's the ninth inning, with two outs and bases loaded,

and Oyler is up. Suddenly rain pours down. Oyler hits the ball, but no one can find it in the mud, and Oyler has his first, and only, grand slam.

Vander Zee, Ruth.

Mississippi Morning. Illustrated by Floyd Cooper. Grand Rapids, MI: Eerdmans, 2004. Unpaged. ISBN 9780802852113. **Gr. 3 & up**

Twelve-year-old James lives in Mississippi in 1933. He hangs out at his father's store and goes fishing with his African American friend. Life seems simple to him, until he learns that his father is a member of the Klu Klux Klan.

Weatherford, Carol.

🎗*Dear Mr. Rosenwald.* Illustrated by R. Gregory Christie. New York: Scholastic, 2006. 32pp. ISBN 9780439495226. **Gr. 2 & up**

Using free verse, a ten-year-old African American who lives in the rural south in 1921 tells how her town pitched in together to build a new school with start-up money from the Rosenwald Fund—money donated by the head of Sears, Roebuck & Company for the purpose of building decent schools for the children of sharecroppers. (Golden Kite Honor)

Weinstein, Muriel.

When Louis Armstrong Taught Me Scat. Illustrated by R. Gregory Christie. San Francisco: Chronicle, 2008. 32pp. ISBN 9780811851312. **PreS-3**

When an African American girl and her mother listen to Louis Armstrong on the radio, they can't help but do a dance just before bedtime. Once she's asleep, the girl dreams that Armstrong teaches her how to sing scat. The illustrations and story are as rhythmic and free-wheeling as the style of music they present.

Winter, Jonah.

Steel Town. Illustrated by Terry Widener. New York: Atheneum, 2008. 37pp. ISBN 9781416940814. **Gr. 3 & up**

This story introduces the gritty reality of 1930s U.S. steel mill factories in Pittsburgh, Pennsylvania, by following the workers through their daily routines.

Woodson, Jacqueline.

🎗*Coming on Home Soon.* Illustrated by E. B. Lewis. New York: Putnam, 2004. Unpaged. ISBN 9780399237485. **Gr. K-3**

Ada Ruth must live with her Grandma during World War II while her Mama works in Chicago, because there's work in the Windy City for African American women while the men are at war. Ada Ruth gets desperately lonely while her mother is gone, but a letter promising her return cheers her. (ALAN, Caldecott Honor, Charlotte Zolotow Honor)

European History

Thirteenth to Eighteenth Centuries

Costanza, Stephen.

Mozart Finds a Melody. New York: Holt, 2004. 40pp. ISBN 9780805066272. **Gr. K–3**

Young Mozart needs to compose a concerto but is suffering from writer's block. When his pet starling sings a fragment of a melody, Mozart feels inspired. The bird soars out the window, and Mozart chases her through the streets of Vienna, hearing more sounds that he eventually incorporates into Piano Concerto no. 17.

Cormora, Madeleine.

Rembrandt and Titus: Artist and Son. Illustrated by Thomas Locker. Golden, CO: Fulcrum, 2005. 32pp. ISBN 9781555914905. **Gr. 2 & up**

In this fictionalization of the great artist's life, his son tells readers how Rembrandt became an artist, the ups and downs of his life, and how he came to see light and shadow and incorporate that vision in his work. Illustrated with gorgeous paintings based on specific works of Rembrandt.

Freeman, Don.

Will's Quill, or, How a Goose Saved Shakespeare. New York: Viking, 2004. 32pp. ISBN 9780670036868. **Gr. 2 & up**

In this reissue of a book first published in 1975, Willoughby Waddle, an affable goose, travels around England. When young Will Shakespeare is kind to him, he takes to following him around and ends up giving him a feather, with which he pens his first play.

Gibfried, Diane Friemoth.

Brother Juniper. Illustrated by Meilo So. New York: Clarion, 2006. 32pp. ISBN 9780618543618. **Gr. K–3**

Brother Juniper, one of Father Francis of Assisi's friars, is so generous that he ends up giving everything away, down to his very own robe. His brother friars despair of him, but Father Francis wishes all of his friars would be like him.

Jacobson, Rick.

The Master's Apprentice. Illustrated by Laura Fernandez. Plattsburgh, NY: Tundra, 2008. 32pp. ISBN 9780887767838. **Gr. 3 & up**

Marco travels from Venice to Florence, where he is apprenticed to Michelangelo. He mixes paints using a secret family formula. Some of his colors please the master and some do not, but whatever he does, the jealous second apprentice, Ridolfo, tries to thwart him. Despite this, it is Marco the master selects to go to Rome with him.

Marcellino, Fred.

I, Crocodile. New York: Holiday House, 1999. Unpaged. ISBN 978-0062051684. `Gr. 1-3`

While a content crocodile is dining on the banks of the Nile, Napoleon and his troops invade Egypt. They capture the croc and cart him back to Paris. When the croc learns that he is to be the main ingredient in a pie, he makes his escape through the city's sewers.

Noyes, Deborah.

Hana in the Time of the Tulips. Illustrated by Bagram Ibatoulline. Cambridge, MA: Candlewick, 2004. 28pp. ISBN 9780763618759. `Gr. 2 & up`

In seventeenth-century Holland, tulip farmers so overproduced that the market for their products disappeared. Hana's father is one such tulip trader, and she misses his love and attention when his obsession with tulips occupies all of his time. When she sees his sadness, she asks one and all how to cheer him, and family friend, Rembrandt, suggests she paint her father a picture of a tulip, which she does. Ibatoulline's paintings glow in the style of Rembrandt and the Dutch masters.

Pettenati, Jean K.

Galileo's Journal, 1609–1610. Illustrated by Paolo Rui. Watertown, MA: Charlesbridge, 2006. 30pp. ISBN 9781570918797. `Gr. 2 & up`

Based on source materials, Pettenati has created an imaginary journal of Galileo as he records his thoughts about his observations of the planets, which led him to conclude that the earth revolved around the sun.

Rogers, Gregory.

The Boy, the Bear, the Baron, the Bard. Brookfield, CT: Roaring Brook , 2004. 32pp. ISBN 9781596430099. `Gr. 2 & up`

In this wordless book that uses various sized frames for the pictures, a boy chases his soccer ball into an abandoned theater in London and finds himself transported back in time to the sixteenth century, where he encounters the Bard himself and has assorted adventures.

Wilson, Sarah.

The Day We Danced in Underpants. Illustrated by Catherine Stock. Berkeley, CA: Tricycle, 2008. 32pp. ISBN 9781582462059. `PreS-1`

The family receives an invitation to attend a picnic with the king and queen of France. There is much excitement, but at the momentous event, Papa's pants split, revealing his underwear to all. Amused, the king declares that it's so hot, all must strip down to their skivvies as well.

Nineteenth Century

Ahlberg, Allan.

The Baby in the Hat. Illustrated by André Amstutz. Cambridge, MA: Candlewick, 2008. 32pp. ISBN 9780763639587. `Gr. 1–3`

As a young man goes walking in early nineteenth-century England, a baby girl falls from a second story window, and he catches her in his hat. With his reward money, he heads to London, where he eventually ends up serving in the king's navy. When he returns home years later, he looks up at the same window from which the baby fell and spies her all grown up, a lovely young woman, who becomes his wife.

Castaldo, Nancy F.

Pizza for the Queen. Illustrated by Melisande Potter. New York: Holiday House, 2005. 32pp. ISBN 9780823418657. `Gr. K–3`

Based on a true story, this book recounts the events of June 11, 1889, in Napoli, Italy, where Raffaele Esposito has a reputation for making the best pizza in the city. When Queen Margherita's emissary places an order for her, Raffaele gathers the freshest ingredients. He makes two pies, but when he is about to make the third he discovers his cat has eaten all the anchovies. So he decides to make a pizza reflecting the colors of the Italian flag, red, white, and green, using tomato, mozzarella, and basil. The queen adores the pizza, and Raffaele names it after her, in this charming anecdote.

Hopkinson, Deborah.

The Humblebee Hunter: Inspired by the Life & Experiments of Charles Darwin and His Children. Illustrated by Jen Corace. New York: Hyperion, 2010. 32pp. ISBN 9781423113560. `Gr. 2 & up`

Hopkinson relates a story from the childhood of Darwin's children. One day, while in their home in England, Darwin recruits some of his children to help him study humblebees, otherwise known as honey bees.

Woodruff, Elvira.

The Memory Coat. Illustrated by Michael Dooling. New York: Scholastic, 1999. Unpaged. ISBN 9780590677172. `Gr. 2 & up`

Grisha, an orphan, lives with his cousin Rachel's family in a shtetl in Russia. He mourns his lost parents and wears the last coat his mother made for him until it is practically in tatters, but Rachel is his best friend, and they find ways to have fun together. After the Cossacks attack their village, Rachel's family decides to flee to America. Grisha is almost turned back at Ellis Island, but Rachel's quick thinking enables him to enter New York City with them.

Yolen, Jane.

Naming Liberty. Illustrated by Jim Burke. New York: Philomel, 2008. Unpaged. ISBN 9780399242502. **Gr. 1–3**

Telling two stories simultaneously, Yolen pairs the tale of Gitl, the youngest in her Jewish family, who with her family escapes the pogroms and persecution of Czarist Russia, with that of Frédéric Auguste Bartholdi as he creates the Statue of Liberty. When at last Gitl sails into New York harbor, welcomed by the gracious Lady, she decides her new name will be Libby, in honor of Lady Liberty.

Twentieth Century

Fleming, Candace.

Boxes for Katje. Illustrated by Stacey Dressen-McQueen. New York: Farrar, Straus & Giroux, 2003. 40pp. ISBN 9780374309220. **Gr. 1–3**

In post–World War II Holland, Katje and her family struggle to get by in their war-torn country. When the postman unexpectedly delivers a box for Katje, she finds that Rosie, an American girl, has sent her a bar of soap, a pair of wool socks, some chocolate, and a letter. The two become pen pals, and Rosie's town rallies to donate more much-needed supplies. As the situation improve for the Dutch, Katje's family and neighbors send a box of tulip bulbs in thanks.

Hesse, Karen.

The Cats in Krasinski Square. Illustrated by Wendy Watson. New York: Scholastic, 2004. 32pp. ISBN 9780439435406. **Gr. 3 & up**

A young Jewish girl and her sister in Warsaw, Poland, in 1942 have succeeded in staying out of the Ghetto and plan to smuggle food to those starving beyond the fence. Somehow the Gestapo has heard whispers of the plan and bring dogs to Krasinski Square to sniff out the food. But the resisters are ready for them. They have smuggled in a plethora of cats and let them loose in the square. The dogs chase the cats, and the sisters and their friends are able to smuggle in the food. The text and illustrations combine to present a poignant combination of sorrow and hope. Based on actual events.

Johnston, Tony.

The Harmonica. Illustrated by Ron Mazellan. Watertown, MA: Charlesbridge, 2004. 32pp. ISBN 9781570915475. **Gr. 3 & up**

This story is based on a Holocaust survivor's experiences. A young Jewish boy lives happily with his parents and is learning how to play the harmonica from his father. When they are arrested, they are sent to separate camps, and the boy finds himself alone, enduring cold, hunger, and forced labor, with only his harmonica for comfort. When the commandant orders him to play, he complies with Schubert, in anguish because his enemy loves the same music that reminds him of his beloved parents. One night a fellow prisoner lets him know that the whole camp can hear him and his music helps them all. A poignant and dramatic story enhanced with dark illustrations.

Littlesugar, Amy.

Willy and Max: A Holocaust Story. **Illustrated by William Low. New York: Putnam, 2006. 40pp. ISBN 9780399234835.** `Gr. 3 & up`

In Belgium during World War II, Willy, a Christian boy, and Max, a Jewish boy, become "forever friends." When the Germans invade, Max and his family must flee, and Max's father asks Willy's father to keep a precious painting safe from the Nazis. Although he tries to honor his promise, the storm troopers confiscate the painting. After the war both Willy and Max end up in America, but they are never reunited. The painting, however, is returned to Willy, and he brings it to Max's surviving family members.

McClintock, Barbara.

Adele and Simon. **New York: Farrar, Straus & Giroux, 2006. 33pp. ISBN 9780374380441.** `Gr. K–3`

In early twentieth-century Paris, Adele picks her brother up from school each day, but the task is not as simple as it seems, for they must wend their way through the city searching for the things that Simon has lost. (See *Adele and Simon in America* under "American History: Twentieth Century" in this chapter.)

Polacco, Patricia.

The Butterfly. **New York: Philomel, 2000. Unpaged. ISBN 9780399231704.** `Gr. 2 & up`

Based on Polacco's family history, this moving story relates events occurring in a small village in France during the Nazi occupation of World War II. Monique does not know that her mother is sheltering a Jewish family, until one night she meets Serine, who is living in their basement. The two girls quickly become friends, and Monique brings Serine small presents, including a living butterfly. When a neighbor spots two girls in the bedroom window, she reports them, and Serine and her family are forced to flee.

Rappaport, Doreen.

The Secret Seder. **Illustrated by Emily Arnold McCully. New York: Hyperion, 2005. 40pp. ISBN 9780786807772.** `Gr. 2 & up`

Jacques and his parents live in a small village in France and are adept at appearing to be Catholic. Although he fears the Nazis, Jacques has practiced the answers to the Four Questions asked at Passover, so that he will be ready when his father takes him to the secret Seder in the mountains.

Shulevitz, Uri.

How I Learned Geography. **New York: Farrar, Straus & Giroux, 2008. 32pp. ISBN 9780374334994.** `Gr. 2 & up` **(SP)**

In this fictionalized, autobiographical tale, a young boy and his family flee Poland in 1939 and make their way on foot to Kazakhstan. They live in a dreary apartment with several other families and are always hungry. When the father comes home one day with a map instead of bread, at first the mother and son are furious. However, soon the boy studies the map and embarks on imaginary journeys around the world, realizing that his father was right to buy the map after all. Shulevitz's emotionally evocative art contrasts the grim trek to Kazakhstan with the brilliance of the boy's visions, creating a book with a profound impact on the reader. (ALAN)

U'Ren, Andrea.

Mary Smith. **New York: Farrar, Straus & Giroux, 2003. 32pp. ISBN 9780374348427.** `PreS–3`

In England in the days before alarm clocks, people would be paid to wake up the town folks each morning. Mary Smith used a peashooter to rattle the windows of the laundry maids, fishmonger, and mayor, prompting the mayor to proclaim that without Mary the entire town would still be sleeping.

History Around the World

Africa

Grifalconi, Ann

🎗*The Village That Vanished.* **Illustrated by Kadir Nelson. New York: Dial, 2002. 40pp. ISBN 9780803726239.** `Gr. 3 & up`

Abikanile, her mother, and her grandmother help the people of her Yao village in Africa escape the menacing slave traders. (Jane Addams Book Honor)

Mollel, Tololwa M.

🎗*My Rows and Piles of Coins.* **Illustrated by E. B. Lewis. New York: Clarion, 1999. 32pp. ISBN 9780395751862.** `PreS–3`

Saruni lives in Tanzania in the 1960s and helps his family raise fruits and vegetables to sell at the market. He dreams of having a bicycle of his own to ride for fun and to help his mother, but accumulating enough funds takes longer than he thought it would. (ALAN, Coretta Scott King Honor)

Asia

Bridges, Shirin Yim.

Ruby's Wish. **Illustrated by Sophie Blackall. San Francisco: Chronicle, 2002. Unpaged. ISBN 9780811834902.** `Gr. 2 & up` **(SP)**

Ruby loves to learn and is lucky that her grandfather, who earned his wealth in the California gold rush and then returned home to China, employs a teacher to educate the boys and girls in his household. As she grows up, her grandfather recognizes her gifts and in return gives her a special gift in celebration of the New Year: admission to university.

Lord, Michelle.

Little Sap and Monsieur Rodin. **Illustrated by Felicia Hoshino. New York: Lee & Low, 2006. 32pp. ISBN 9781584302483.** `Gr. 2 & up`

In early 1900s Cambodia, Little Sap, the daughter of poor rice farmers, longs to be a dancer for the royal dance company. When the princess selects her to join the troop, Sap works hard to master her nerves as well as the dance steps, transforming herself into a graceful performer. When the king takes a group of dancers to France, Sap journeys with them, and she and her fellow dancers capture the attention and imagination of Auguste Rodin. This is based on the true story that led to Rodin's *Danseuse Cambodgienne* sketches.

Park, Linda Sue.

The Firekeeper's Son. **Illustrated by Julie Downing. New York: Clarion, 2004. 37pp. ISBN 9780618133376.** `PreS–3`

In nineteenth-century Korea a series of signal fires alerted the king that the country remained safe from enemies. Every night Sang-Hee's father scans the ocean for a sign of any enemy and then hikes up the mountain to fire the signal. When he breaks his ankle, it is up to his son to carry the bucket of burning coals up the mountain alone.

Pennypacker, Sara.

Sparrow Girl. **Illustrated by Yoko Tanaka. New York: Hyperion, 2009. 26pp. ISBN 9781423111870.** `Gr. K–3`

In 1958 Mao Zedong issued an edict aimed at eradicating China's sparrow population in order prevent crop damage. This story imagines a possible response by a brave little girl. Ming-li loves the sparrows and secretly nurtures a few in her family's barn. When crops all around are threatened by locusts, Ming-Li reveals her sparrows, which help save the village.

Preus, Margi.

The Peace Bell. **Illustrated by Hideko Takahashi. New York: Holt, 2008. Unpaged. ISBN 9780805078008.** `Gr. K–3`

Yuko and her grandmother live in a small village in Japan, and when Katie visits from America, she tells them the story of the Peace Bell. The bell used to chime in the temple, but when metal became scarce during World War II, the bell was donated as scrap. American soldiers found it and sent it to Minnesota. Years later, it was sent back to Japan as a symbol of goodwill.

Say, Allen.

🔖*Kamishibai Man.* Boston: Houghton Mifflin, 2005. 32pp. ISBN 978-0618479542. `Gr. 1–3`

> In 1930s Japan, kamishibai ("paper theater") performers were storytellers who illustrated their tales with picture cards in small wooden theaters perched on their bicycles. Decades later a grandfather journeys to the city to nostalgically re-create his past art, drawing a crowd of adults who remember and applaud his stories. (ALAN)

Whelan, Gloria.

Yuki and the One Thousand Carriers. Illustrated by Yan Nascimbene. Chelsea, MI: Sleeping Bear Press, 2008. 32pp. ISBN 9781585363520. `Gr. 1–3`

> In seventeenth- and eighteenth-century Japan, provincial governors could be called to journey to the capital at the will of the emperor. When Yuki's father is called by his Shogun to Edo (modern Tokyo), she and her mother and family retainers embark on the 300-mile trek.

Canada

Cutler, Jane.

Guttersnipe. Illustrated by Emily Arnold McCully. New York: Farrar, Straus & Giroux, 2009. Unpaged. ISBN 9780374328139. `Gr. 1–3`

> After Ben's father dies, Ben wants to help his family, who are Jewish immigrants, by finding a job and making some money. He gets a job delivering hat linings, but on his first day he ends up in the gutter, his bike wrecked and the circles of silk ruined. Looking at the beautiful bright colors, Ben realizes that even though he has failed at this, he will be able to find another job.

Koldofsky, Eleanor.

Clip-Clop. Illustrated by David Parkins. Toronto: Tundra, 2005. 24pp. ISBN 9780887766817. `Gr. K–3`

> In Canada at the turn of the twentieth century, goods are delivered house to house by horse-drawn vehicles, and Consuela can recognize each one by the clip-clop of the different horses.

Taylor, Joanne.

Making Room. Illustrated by Peter Rankin. Toronto: Tundra, 2004. 23pp. ISBN 9780887766510. `Gr. 1–3`

> In Nova Scotia in the 1800s, John Williams builds a one-room house for himself, but after he marries and has children, he finds that he needs more and more room.

The Middle East

Farmer, Nancy.

Clever Ali. **Illustrated by Gail De Marcken. New York: Orchard, 2006. 40pp. ISBN 9780439370141.** `Gr. K-3`

In twelfth-century Egypt, Ali helps his father care for the messenger pigeons. When one pigeon steals cherries from the Sultan of Cairo, the Sultan gives Ali three days to replace 600 cherries or he will have his father put to death.

Hawes, Louise.

Muti's Necklace: The Oldest Story in the World. **Illustrated by Rebecca Guay-Mitchell. Boston: Houghton Mifflin, 2006. 32pp. ISBN 9780618535835.** `Gr. 1-3`

Inspired by a tale from ancient Egypt, Hawes crafts an original fairy tale centering on the beautiful Muti, who always wears a necklace given to her by her father. She attracts Pharaoh's attention as a servant, and he orders her to be the head rower for his all female team of rowers on his pleasure boat. When her precious necklace falls into the water, she has the audacity to stop paddling, and the royal magician parts the waves for her to find her lost treasure.

Favorites

Magnus at the Fire by Jennifer Armstrong

The Cats in Krasinski Square by Karen Hesse

Apples to Oregon by Deborah Hopkinson

Sweet Smell of Roses by Angela Johnson

Henry's Freedom Box by Ellen Levine

Goin' Someplace Special by Patricia McKissack

Pink and Say by Patricia Polacco

Amelia and Eleanor Go for a Ride: Based on a True Story by Pam Muñoz Ryan

Show Way by Jacqueline Woodson

When Louis Armstrong Taught Me Scat by Muriel Weinstein

Chapter 14

Humor

A good sense of humor keeps people going through the good times and the bad. Laughter lightens life, and funny stories abound both for preschoolers and older children. Children love direct humor and enjoy being able to figure out the joke by themselves. From a smile of recognition to understanding subtle nuances in clever stories, children appreciate a good dose of giggles and guffaws.

Agee, Jon.

🏵*Nothing*. New York: Hyperion, 2007. 32pp. ISBN 9780786836949. **Gr. K-3**

Otis, the antique dealer, sells everything in his shop. When Suzy Gump comes to buy something, he sells her a lot of "nothing." (ALAN)

Ahlberg, Allan.

The Runaway Dinner. Illustrated by Bruce Ingman. Cambridge, MA: Candlewick, 2006. 36pp. ISBN 9780763631420. **PreS-3**

In this rollicking adventure, Melvin the sausage jumps off the dinner plate in an attempt to elude his fate and is followed by the boy Banjo, his parents, and a plethora of cutlery, food, and an assortment of neighbors.

Armstrong, Jennifer.

🏵*Once upon a Banana*. Illustrated by David Small. New York: Simon & Schuster, 2006. 32pp. ISBN 9780689842511. **PreS-3**

When the monkey runs away from the juggler, the laughs begin. The subtle text appears only on the street signs, letting the visual humor of the clever illustrations spark the laughter for readers as they observe the banana getting in everyone's way. (ALAN)

Bachelet, Gilles.

🏵*My Cat, the Silliest Cat in the World*. New York: Abrams, 2006. 24pp. ISBN 9780810949133. **PreS-2** (SP)

The narrator relates the activities of his special cat, while the pictures depict an elephant engaged in feline behavior. (ALAN)

When the Silliest Cat Was Small. New York: Abrams, 2007. 26pp. ISBN 9780810994157. Sequel. `PreS-2` (SP)

> The narrator brings his cat (elephant) to his apartment, where he does the cutest kitten things, or so the narrator thinks.

Barrett, Judi.

*Animals Should Definitely Not Wear Clothing. Illustrated by Ron Barrett. New York: Atheneum, 1970. 32pp. ISBN 9780689205927. `PreS-1` (SP)

> The deadpan text explains why particular animals should not wear specific items of clothing, while colorful illustrations show the laugh-out-loud reasons why not.

🐟*Cloudy with a Chance of Meatballs.* Illustrated by Ron Barrett. New York: Atheneum, 1978. 32pp. ISBN 9780689306471. `Gr. K–3`

> Life is delicious for the residents of Chewandswallow, because the weather carries with it scrumptious things to eat and drink, until the day something goes awry. (New York Times Best Illustrated)

Pickles to Pittsburgh. Illustrated by Ron Barrett. New York: Atheneum, 1997. Unpaged. ISBN 9780689801044. `Gr. K–3`

> When the people of Chewandswallow return to their town, they begin operation clean-up. Finding an abundance of food, they distribute it worldwide.

Never Take a Shark to the Dentist: And Other Things Not to Do. Illustrated by John Nickle. New York: Atheneum, 2008. 28pp. ISBN 9781416907244. `PreS-2`

> Barrett presents a series of amusing rules to live by, accompanied by droll artwork that demonstrates the sense and the humor of the advice.

Black, Michael Ian.

Chicken Cheeks. Illustrated by Kevin Hawkes. New York: Simon & Schuster, 2009. 35pp. ISBN 9781416948643. `PreS-1`

> Animal backsides abound in this riotous story of creatures that create a living tower of themselves in an attempt to reach some honey.

Bluemle, Elizabeth.

My Father the Dog. Illustrated by Randy Cecil. Cambridge, MA: Candlewick, 2006. 22pp. ISBN 9780763622220. `PreS-3`

> A sincere, young narrator explains why she believes her father is really a dog: he scratches when he wakes up, likes to ride in the car with the window down, and growls if his nap is interrupted, among many more canine characteristics.

Bottner, Barbara.

Miss Brooks Loves Books (And I Don't). Illustrated by Michael Emberley. New York: Knopf, 2010. 32pp. ISBN 9780375846823. `PreS-2`

> Miss Brooks is a librarian who loves to entertain her audiences in costume and with puppets, but one youngster refuses to be captivated. She remains unim-

pressed until Miss Brooks introduces her to Shrek. Amusing watercolor illustrations add to the deadpan humor of the story.

Buehner, Caralyn.

The Queen of Style. **Illustrated by Mark Buehner. New York: Dial, 2008. 32pp. ISBN 9780803728783.** `Gr. K-3`

This playful story relates the escapades of a bored Queen Sophie, who takes a beauty correspondence course and practices on all her subjects, until her well-coifed farmers and their animals protest that they have no time left for their work.

The Snowmen Series. Illustrated by Mark Buehner. New York: Dial. `PreS-1`

A young boy imagines a variety of adventures for his snowmen

Snowmen at Night. 2002. 32pp. ISBN 9780803725508.

A young boy notices that the snowmen he built the day before look a bit droopy the next morning and imagines the fun they must have had: a busy night of sledding, skating, and having a snowball fight. Mark Buehner's oil-and-acrylic paintings excel in portraying the glee of these winter creations.

Snowmen at Christmas. 2005. 24pp. ISBN 9780803729957.

This time the narrator imagines what the free-spirited snowmen might do on Christmas Eve: trimming trees, playing games, and singing as they await a visit from Kris Kringle.

Snowmen All Year. 2010. 32pp. ISBN 9780803733831.

A young boy's imagination once more powers a story filled with the antics of snowmen. This time he imagines what would happen if a snowman could play with him all year long.

Christelow, Eileen.

Five Little Monkeys Series. New York: Clarion. `PreS-1`

This series, which chronicles the antic shenanigans of five funny monkeys, begins with the traditional action rhyme and then proceeds to relate several frantic adventures.

Five Little Monkeys Jumping on the Bed. 1989. 32pp. ISBN 9780899197692. (SP)

Five Little Monkeys Sitting in a Tree. 1991. 32pp. ISBN 9780395544341.

Five Little Monkeys with Nothing to Do. 1996. 36pp. ISBN 9780395758304. (SP)

Five Little Monkeys Wash the Car. 2000. 33pp. ISBN 9780395925669.

Five Little Monkeys Play Hide and Seek. 2004. 33pp. ISBN 9780618409495.

Five Little Monkeys Bake a Birthday Cake. 2005. Unpaged. ISBN 9780618496471. (SP)

Five Little Monkeys Go Shopping. 2007. 33pp. ISBN 9780618821617.

Coleen, Salley.

The Epossumondas Series. See under "Folk and Fairy Tales" in chapter 15.

Cronin, Doreen.

The Movement Series. Illustrated by Scott Menchin. New York: Simon & Schuster. T–K

> A puppy with oodles of energy demonstrates toddler-centered activities.

> *Wiggle.* 2005. 32pp. ISBN 9780689863752.
>> The playful pup leads toddlers through a day of wiggling.

> *Bounce.* 2007. 32pp. ISBN 9781416916277.
>> Cronin's energetic canine returns, and this time invites his audience to hop, jump, leap, and bounce.

> *Stretch.* 2009. Unpaged. ISBN 9781416953418.
>> The peppy pup returns and encourages listeners to stretch in a variety of ways.

Cuyler, Margery.

*Skeleton Hiccups. **Illustrated by S. D. Schindler. New York: Margaret K. McElderry Books, 2002. 32pp. ISBN 9780689847707.** `PreS–1`

> For children who like their humor on the dark side, here they can follow Skeleton through his day as he tries to get rid of his hiccups, with hilarious results. All his efforts are in vain, until Ghost comes up with the perfect solution.

Dorros, Alex, and Arthur Dorros.

Numero Uno/Number One. **Illustrated by Susan Guevara. New York: Abrams, 2007. Unpaged. ISBN 9780810957640.** `Gr. K–3`

> Brains and brawn vie for supremacy as both the architect Socrates Rivera and the builder Hercules Hernandez are engaged to build a bridge for their village in Mexico. Using some Spanish dialogue, each man makes his case to the villagers, and they continue arguing even when they are banished to the mountain to allow the villagers to complete the work. Much of the humor comes through in the details of the expressive illustrations.

Feiffer, Jules.

*Bark, George. **New York: HarperCollins, 1999. 30pp. ISBN 9780062051851.** `PreS–2`

> Each time George's mother tells her pup to bark, he tries to comply, but a different animal sound emerges instead. Frantic, she takes him to the vet, who extracts one animal after another. An excellent, participatory read-aloud. (ALAN, Charlotte Zolotow Honor)

Feiffer, Kate.

President Pennybaker. Illustrated by Diane Goode. New York: Simon & Schuster, 2008. 30pp. ISBN 9781416913542. `Gr. K–3`

> With deftly understated humor in text and illustration, this book articulates the rise to power of Luke Pennybaker. A regular kid, he grows tired of being told "no" and runs on a platform including the freedom to have a messy room and to eat ice cream any time. He wins in a landslide, but finds he can't please all the people all the time and leaves the job to his running mate, his dog Lily.

My Mom Is Trying to Ruin My Life. Illustrated by Diane Goode. New York: Simon & Schuster, 2009. 32pp. ISBN 9781416941002. `PreS–3`

> With sly humor, Feiffer gives her young narrator exactly what she wishes for: her parents incarcerated for reckless parenting (such as giving kisses good-bye in front of friends and enforcing bedtime). At first she is filled with glee, but when she envisions what life on her own might be, she decides a future without her parents might not be what she wants after all.

Fleming, Candace.

🏵*Muncha! Muncha! Muncha!* Illustrated by G. Brian Karas. New York: Atheneum, 2002. Unpaged. ISBN 9780689831522. `PreS–3`

> Using onomatopoeic refrains, Fleming relates the experiences of Mr. McGreely, who does everything he can to keep a trio of mischievous rabbits out of his garden, to no avail. (ALAN)

Tippy-Tippy-Tippy, Hide! Illustrated by G. Brian Karas. New York: Atheneum, 2007. 40pp. ISBN 9780689874796. Sequel. `PreS–3`

> Those three pesky bunnies are back, and this time they will stop at nothing until they are snuggled safe and sound in the warmth of Mr. McGreely's home, safe from the winter winds.

Frazee, Marla.

🏵*Roller Coaster*. San Diego: Harcourt, 2003. 32pp. ISBN 9780152045548. `PreS–1`

> A young girl waits in line for her very first roller coaster ride. The swirling text and illustrations plunge the reader into a dipping, zooming, wild ride, right along with the little girl. (ALAN)

French, Jackie.

🏵*Diary of a Wombat*. Illustrated by Bruce Whatley. New York: Clarion, 2003. Unpaged. ISBN 9780618381364. `Gr. K–2`

> This tongue-in-cheek tale relates the exploits of a wombat in Australia who mostly eats and sleeps until her human neighbors move in. Then she finds treats in their garden, creates a new scratching post, and does battle with a mighty enemy—the doormat. Whatley's acrylic scenes revel in the hilarious antics that are understated in the text. (ALAN)

Gaiman, Neil.

Crazy Hair. Illustrated by Dave McKean. New York: HarperCollins, 2009. 32pp. ISBN 9780060579081. **PreS–3**

> When Bonnie comments on a man's crazy hair, he describes all the unusual creatures, like lions and gorillas, who make their home in his unfettered hair.

Gravett, Emily.

The Odd Egg. New York: Simon & Schuster, 2009. 32pp. ISBN 9781416968726. **PreS–2**

> All the birds have laid their eggs. Duck. who is a male of the species, wants one, too. He goes out and finds an egg of his own. It's enormous, and all the other birds make fun of him, especially when their eggs hatch and his does not. Undisturbed, he keeps on knitting until, at last, his egg hatches into an alligator, who frightens the others away and wears his knitted booties with aplomb. The clever book design and pencil and watercolor illustrations make this book a gem.

Grossman, Bill.

*My Little Sister Ate One Hare. Illustrated by Kevin Hawkes. New York: Crown, 1996. Unpaged. ISBN 9780517596005. **Gr. K–3**

> This cumulative tale, accompanied by zany artwork, counts off an unusual assortment of items ingested by the narrator's sister, including bats and lizards, as well as ants and underpants.

My Little Sister Hugged an Ape. Illustrated by Kevin Hawkes. New York: Knopf, 2004. 32pp. ISBN 9780517800171. Sequel. **Gr. K–3**

> Employing rollicking rhymed couplets, the narrator records the alphabetically arranged animals that his adventurous sister hugs one after the other, with various degrees of success.

Hamilton, Richard.

If I Were You. Illustrated by Babette Cole. New York: Bloomsbury, 2008. 32pp. ISBN 9781599902890. **PreS–3**

> In this funny tale, father and daughter each imagine what it would be like if they switched places.

Haseley, Dennis.

The Invisible Moose. Illustrated by Steven Kellogg. New York: Dial, 2006. 40pp. ISBN 9780803728929. **PreS–3**

> A Canadian he-moose falls in love with a she-moose, only to lose her to a trapper, who carts her off to New York City. After partaking of an invisibility potion, the he-moose makes his way to the Big Apple to rescue her. His madcap adventures are portrayed with hilarious detail in the vibrant illustrations.

Hest, Amy.

When You Meet a Bear on Broadway. **Illustrated by Elivia Savadier. New York: Farrar, Straus & Giroux, 2009. Unpaged. ISBN 9780374400156. PreS-1**

> When a young New Yorker finds a lost bear cub on Broadway, she confidently helps him locate his mother.

Horacek, Petr.

<u>**The Suzy Goose Series.**</u> **Cambridge, MA: Candlewick. T-K**

> Suzy is a silly goose, whose misadventures somehow manage to turn out all right in the end.

Silly Suzy Goose. 2006. 40pp. ISBN 9780763630409. (SP)

> Suzy Goose wishes that she could be different from her fellow geese and tries to be like each animal she encounters, until she angers a lion and must use her new skills to return to the safety of her flock.

Look Out, Suzy Goose. 2008. 32pp. ISBN 9780763638030.

> Suzy Goose is still silly. This time she wanders into the forest alone in search of some peace and quiet, completely unaware that she is being stalked by a famished fox, a wolf, and a bear. Her honk of contentment and an owl's screech save the day.

Suzy Goose and the Christmas Star. Somerville, MA, 2009. Unpaged. ISBN 9780763644871.

> Suzy Goose wants a star for the top of the Christmas tree that she and her fellow farm animals have decorated, so she tries her best to fetch one down from the sky.

Jackson, Alison.

Thea's Tree. **Illustrated by Janet Pedersen. New York: Dutton, 2008. 32pp. ISBN 9780525474432. Gr. K-3**

> When Thea plants a purple bean in her yard for her science project, things go awry immediately. The ground becomes bubbly and purple, and the tree quickly grows to gigantic proportions. Desperately, Thea writes to one expert after another for help identifying her tree. Although the scientists are clueless, readers will recognize the golden egg, singing harp, and gold coins and know exactly what kind of "tree" Thea has planted.

Kasza, Keiko.

🏵*Don't Laugh, Joe!* **New York: Putnam, 1997. Unpaged. ISBN 978-0399230363. PreS-3**

> Giddy Joe the possum is trying to learn from his mother how to play dead, but his irrepressible giggles keep foiling her efforts. (Charlotte Zolotow Honor)

My Lucky Day. New York: Putnam, 2003. 32pp. ISBN 9780399238741. `PreS–2`

Mr. Fox thinks it's his lucky day when a piglet knocks on his door, but the clever piglet outfoxes him, so to speak.

Badger's Fancy Meal. New York: Putnam, 2007. 30pp. ISBN 9780399246036. `PreS–2`

Badger leaves his den in search of more sumptuous fare, but each animal he tries to catch for dinner eludes him and ends up dining on Badger's stores, in an ironic twist of fate.

Keller, Laurie.

The Scrambled States of America. New York: Holt, 1998. 40pp. ISBN 978-0805058024. `Gr. 3 & up`

The states are tired of being stuck in the same spot all the time, so they decide to trade places, but their new neighbors prove to be more of a challenge than anticipated.

The Scrambled States of America Talent Show. New York: Holt, 2008. 40pp. ISBN 9780805079975. Sequel. `Gr. 3 & up`

The states are moving around again, but this time it's to put on a talent show.

Koller, Jackie French.

*One Monkey Too Many. Illustrated by Lynn Munsinger. San Diego: Harcourt, 1999. 32pp. ISBN 9780152047641 (pb). `PreS–2`

Seven mischief-making monkeys leave chaos in their wake every time they add just one monkey more to whatever vehicle they happen to be riding at the time.

Seven Spunky Monkeys. Illustrated by Lynn Munsinger. Orlando, FL: Harcourt, 2005. 32pp. ISBN 9780152025199. Sequel. `Gr. K–2`

The high-spirited band of monkeys is back. On each day of the week, one departs to find a mate. Then the seven original friends reunite for a romp in the park with their spouses and little ones.

Kontis, Alethea.

Alpha Oops! The Day the Z Went First. Illustrated by Bob Kolar. Cambridge, MA: Candlewick, 2006. 48pp. ISBN 9780763627287. `Gr. K–2`

"A" tries to start the show, but "Z," tired of being last, bursts on stage and expresses his distress. The letters decide to mix things up a bit, with hilarious results.

Mahy, Margaret.

Down the Back of the Chair. Illustrated by Polly Dunbar. New York: Clarion, 2006. 29pp. ISBN 9780618693955. `Gr. K–3`

With exuberant wordplay, little Mary describes the amazing things dad finds when he looks down the back of the chair for his missing car keys. The cash-strapped family's fortunes are totally transformed by the amazing discoveries.

Bubble Trouble. Illustrated by Polly Dunbar. New York: Clarion, 2009. 37pp. ISBN 9780547074214. **Gr. K–3**

> When Mabel blows a bubble, it mysteriously envelopes her baby brother and gently bounces him around the village, gathering more and more villagers intent on rescuing him.

9

Nedwidek, John.

Ducks Don't Wear Socks. Illustrated by Lee White. New York: Viking, 2008. 32pp. ISBN 9780670061365. **PreS–2**

> Emily is an exceedingly serious girl who keeps encountering a silly duck, who wears amusing items of clothing. Emily does not crack a smile until she spots him sporting underpants.

10

Noble, Trinka Hakes

The Jimmy's Boa Series. Illustrated by Steven Kellogg. New York: Dial. **Gr. K–3**

> Jimmy's boa is always getting into mischief of one kind or another, and the narrator always tells the story starting from the end.

11

The Day Jimmy's Boa Ate the Wash. 1980. 32pp. ISBN 9780803717237.

> The narrator recounts the uproarious results of Jimmy's boa being let loose.

12

Jimmy's Boa Bounces Back. 1984. Unpaged. ISBN 9780140546545 (pb).

> Following the same reverse sequence as the first book, this book tells of the time the pet boa arrives at a garden party and stirs things up.

Jimmy's Boa and the Bungee Jump Slam Dunk. 2003. 32pp. ISBN 9780803726000.

> Jimmy's boa returns and slides into Miss Peachtree's dance class. Out of the chaos in the gym, they discover that basketball is the perfect game for a boa.

13

Numeroff, Laura.

14

If You Give a . . . Series. Illustrated by Felicia Bond. New York: HarperCollins. **PreS–2**

> Numeroff is the master of the circular story. In each case the initial action leads directly to the next, until the events come full circle.

If You Give a Mouse a Cookie. 1985. 32pp. ISBN 9780060245863. (SP)

15

If You Give a Moose a Muffin. 1991. 32pp. ISBN 9780060244057. (SP)

If You Give a Pig a Pancake. 1998. 32pp. ISBN 9780060266868. (SP)

If You Take a Mouse to the Movies. 2000. 32pp. ISBN 9780060278670. (SP)

If You Take a Mouse to School. 2002. 32pp. ISBN 9780060283285. (SP)

If You Give a Pig a Party. 2005. Unpaged. ISBN 9780060283261. (SP)

If You Give a Cat a Cupcake. 2008. 32pp. ISBN 9780060283247. (SP)

O'Malley, Kevin.

Gimme Cracked Corn & I Will Share. **New York: Walker, 2005. 32pp. ISBN 9780802796844.** `Gr. 1-3`

This egg-ceptional story full of punny yolks humorously relates the corny quest of two chickens that embark on a search for the treasure of all the corn any chicken could wish to eat.

Once upon a Cool Motorcycle Dude. **Illustrated by Scott Goto and Carol Heyer. New York: Walker, 2005. 32pp. ISBN 9780802789471.** `Gr. 1-3`

A boy and a girl share an assignment to write a fairy tale together, but she wants a princess to be the main character and he wants a cool motorcycle dude. Consequently, they create a most unusual tale.

Palatini, Margie.

Moo Who? **Illustrated by Keith Graves. New York: HarperCollins, 2004. Unpaged. ISBN 9780060001056.** `PreS-3`

Hilda Mae Heifer loves to sing, but her fellow barnyard creatures don't appreciate being serenaded. After she gets knocked on the noggin', she forgets how to moo and needs her friends to help her remember.

Boo-Hoo Moo. **Illustrated by Keith Graves. New York: HarperCollins, 2009. 32pp. ISBN 9780061143755. Sequel.** `PreS-3`

When Hilda Mae Heifer's moos take a turn toward melancholy, the rest of the farm animals decide to pitch in and help cheer her up.

Plourde, Lynn.

Grandpappy Snippy Snappies. **Illustrated by Christopher Santoro. New York: HarperCollins, 2009. 30pp. ISBN 9780060280505.** `Gr. K-2`

In a rhyming tale filled with alliteration, Grandpappy wields magic when he snaps his suspenders. With them he frees cows from mud and rights a derailed train. When his beloved Grandmammy needs rescuing, his suspenders lose their snap, and he resorts to his lightning-decorated undies.

Ransom, Jeanie Franz.

What Do Parents Do? (When You're Not Home). **Illustrated by Cyd Moore. Atlanta: Peachtree, 2007. Unpaged. ISBN 9781561454099.** `Gr. K-2`

When a brother and sister spend the night with their grandparents, the brother imagines all the trouble their parents could be getting into while their children are away, like jumping on the bed, sliding down the banister, and munching on pizza in front of the TV.

Rash, Andy.

Are You a Horse? New York: Arthur A. Levine, 2009. 30pp.Unpaged. ISBN 9780439724173. `Gr. K-2`

> Roy is a silly cowboy who doesn't know what to do with the saddle he receives for his birthday. He wanders through the desert, trying to find a horse so he can enjoy a ride.

Rathmann, Peggy.

The Day the Babies Crawled Away. New York: Putnam, 2003. 32pp. ISBN 9780399231964. `Gr. K-2`

> While all the parents are absorbed in eating their pie at the carnival, all the babies crawl away, and it's up to a lone toddler attired as a firefighter to save the day.

Rumford, James.

Don't Touch My Hat. New York: Knopf, 2007. 32pp. ISBN 9780375837821. `PreS-2`

> In this tale of the Wild West, Sheriff John is sure his ability to keep the peace is due to his ten-gallon hat. In a hurry one night, he grabs his wife's bonnet instead and is forced to fight crime in an unaccustomed chapeau.

Scieszka, Jon.

The Stinky Cheese Man and Other Fairly Stupid Tales. See under "Fractured Fairy Tales and Nursery Rhymes" in chapter 15.

Shields, Carol Diggory.

Food Fight! Illustrated by Doreen Gay-Kassel. Brooklyn, NY: Handprint Books, 2002. Unpaged. ISBN 9781929766291. `PreS-2`

> While all the people in the house are sleeping, the foodstuffs in the kitchen decide to toss up a party of their own.

Sierra, Judy.

Born to Read. Illustrated by Marc Brown. New York: Knopf, 2008. Unpaged. ISBN 9780375846878. `PreS-1`

> In amusing rhyming couplets, Sierra relates the experience of young Sam, who reads from the moment he is born.

Smith, Lane.

Madam President. New York: Hyperion, 2008. Unpaged. ISBN 978-1423108467. `Gr. K-3`

> A ponytailed girl in pinstripes describes her typical day at Eleanor Roosevelt Elementary School while she imagines being president.

Stanley, Diane.

🎗*Saving Sweetness*. Illustrated by G. Brian Karas. New York: Putnam, 1996. Unpaged. ISBN 9780698117679 (pb). `Gr. K–3`

This Texas tale details the exploits of Sweetness, an orphan who runs away from mean Mrs. Sump in the desert. The sheriff heads out to rescue her, but it's Sweetness who ends up saving him. (Golden Kite Award)

🎗*Raising Sweetness*. Illustrated by G. Brian Karas. New York: Putnam, 1999. Unpaged. ISBN 9780399232251. Sequel. `Gr. K–3`

The sheriff has adopted Sweetness and a whole passel of orphans and clearly has his hands full. When a letter arrives for him that he doesn't know how to read, Sweetness decides to learn so she can help her new pa. (ALAN)

Steffensmeier, Alexander.

Millie Waits for the Mail. New York: Walker, 2007. 24pp. ISBN 9780802796622. `PreS–1`

Millie the cow has a favorite time of day. It's right after she's been milked, because that's when the mailman comes. She loves to scare him and every day finds a new place to hide to spring upon him unawares.

Millie in the Snow. New York: Walker, 2008. 32pp. ISBN 9780802798008. Sequel. `PreS–1`

Millie is back, but this time she is helping the mail carrier deliver packages on Christmas Eve. When she gets lost in the snow, she slips and slides her way home.

Stevens, Janet.

The Great Fuzz Frenzy. Illustrated by Susan Stevens Crummel. Orlando, FL: Harcourt, 2005. Unpaged. ISBN 9780152046262. `PreS–2`

When Violet the dog drops a green tennis ball down a hole where prairie dogs live, the prairie dogs pick off all the fuzz for a variety of fashion creations. Big Bark warns them of danger, but when they fall asleep, he scoops up all the fuzz, which makes him the perfect target for a swooping eagle. Now the fuzzless prairie dogs must find a way to save him.

Help Me, Mr. Mutt. Illustrated by Susan Stevens Crummel. Orlando, FL: Harcourt, 2008. Unpaged. ISBN 9780152046286. `Gr. 1–3`

Dogs in difficulty across the country write to "Canine Counselor" Mr. Mutt for advice on their people problems, and the insightful pooch dishes out suggestions galore.

Stevenson, James.

Don't Make Me Laugh. New York: Farrar, Straus & Giroux, 1999. Unpaged. ISBN 9780374318277. (o.p.). `PreS–3`

Mr. Frimdimpny, a tyrannical crocodile, commands readers not to laugh or even smile as they read three slapstick animal stories, but even Mr. Frimdimpyny cannot follow his own orders.

No Laughing, No Smiling, No Giggling. New York: Farrar, Straus & Giroux, 2004. 32pp. ISBN 9780374318291. Sequel. **PreS-3**

> Mr. Frimdimpny, the grumpy crocodile, is back and still banning laughing, smiling, and giggling, but the pig Freddy Fafnaffer finds a way to outwit Mr. Frimdimpny.

9

Stoeke, Janet.

The Minerva Louise Series. New York: Dutton. **PreS-1**

> Minerva Louise, an endearing but truly bird-brained hen, experiences life on the farm in a dimwitted way that will make readers laugh out loud.

10

> *Minerva Louise.* 1988. 24pp. ISBN 9780525443742 (o.p.).

> 🏵*A Hat for Minerva Louise.* 1994. 32pp. ISBN 9780140556667 (pb). (ALAN)

> *Minerva Louise at School.* 1996. Unpaged. ISBN 9780525454946 (o.p.).

11

> *A Friend for Minerva Louise.* 1997. Unpaged. ISBN 9780525458692 (o.p.).

> *Minerva Louise at the Fair.* 2000. Unpaged. ISBN 9780525464396 (o.p.).

> *Minerva Louise and the Red Truck.* 2002. 32pp. ISBN 9780525469094.

> *Minerva Louise and the Colorful Eggs.* 2006. 24pp. ISBN 9780525476337.

12

> *Minerva Louise on Christmas Eve.* 2007. 24pp. ISBN 9780525478577.

> *Minerva Louise on Halloween.* 2009. Unpaged. ISBN 9780525421498.

Tankard, Jeremy.

13

Me Hungry. Cambridge, MA: Candlewick, 2008. 32pp. ISBN 978-0763633608. **PreS-1**

> In prehistoric times, a hungry boy is ignored by his parents, so he sets off to find his own food. His humorous attempts fail until he finds a friend.

Teague, Mark.

14

Funny Farm. New York: Orchard, 2009. 32pp. ISBN 9780439914994. **Gr. K-3**

> When Edward, a sophisticated city bulldog, visits his Uncle Earl's farm, he performs a variety of everyday chores, which the illustrations reveal are far from ordinary.

Urbanovic, Jackie.

15

The Duck Series. New York: HarperCollins. **Gr. K-3**

> A duck that stays put for the winter ends up joining a house full of animals and making new friends.

> *Duck at the Door.* 2007. 32pp. ISBN 9780061214387.

>> Max the Duck decides to skip the journey south for the winter, and the kindhearted Irene shares her pet-filled home with him. When he starts

taking over everything, especially the TV and the kitchen, everyone is wishing for spring, but once he's gone they realize how much they miss him.

Duck Soup. 2008. Unpaged. ISBN 9780061214417.

Max the Duck gets so engrossed in making soup that he must go into the garden to find the one ingredient that is missing. His friends think he's in danger of becoming dinner and don't realize that their rescue attempts are ruining his soup.

Duck and Cover. 2009. 30pp. ISBN 9780061214448.

When an alligator, an escapee from the zoo, shows up at Irene's door, Duck convinces his friends to shelter him. The animals are wary of the gator because of his appetite, but they whip up culinary delights for him and learn to appreciate his good side.

Sitting Duck. 2010. Unpaged. ISBN 9780061765834.

When Max the Duck agrees to babysit for a puppy named Anabel, he has no clue how much trouble a pup can create.

Walton, Rick.

Bertie Was a Watchdog. **Illustrated by Arthur Robins. Cambridge, MA : Candlewick Press, 2002. Unpaged. ISBN 9780763613853.** `PreS-1`

Bertie is such a tiny dog that he looks like he couldn't be a threat to anyone, but a burglar learns differently when Bertie challenges him to a series of bets that lead to the bad guy's arrest. Amusing watercolor illustrations add warmth to this comic tale.

Weeks, Sarah.

The Mrs. McNosh Series. Illustrated by Nadine Westcott. New York: HarperCollins. `T-K`

Mrs. McNosh does her daily chores in such unusual ways that she gives readers a rollicking good time.

*Mrs. McNosh Hangs up Her Wash. 1998. Unpaged. ISBN 9780694010769.

Mrs. McNosh gives new meaning to hanging out the wash! The regular clothes are fine, but soon there are shoes, the dog, a Christmas wreath, and so on. A snappy poem with repetition that will have any group laughing.

Mrs. McNosh and the Great Big Squash. 2000. Unpaged. ISBN 9780694012022 (o.p.).

The minute the seed for this squash gets in the ground, it takes off like an ambulance! The only way Mrs. McNosh can stop it is to hollow it out and make it her home.

Oh My Gosh, Mrs. McNosh! 2002. Unpaged. ISBN 9780694012046.

When Mrs. McNosh is walking her dog in the park and he gets away, a laugh-out-loud chase of a lifetime begins, through a ball game, a wedding, and even a boating party.

Wilcox, Leah.

Falling for Rapunzel. See under "Fantasy and Magic" in chapter 15.

Willems, Mo.

The Pigeon Series. New York: Hyperion. `PreS-2`

Willems's endearing cartoon pigeon insists on having his way in various humorous situations, which young readers and listeners readily understand.

🎗*Don't Let the Pigeon Drive the Bus.* 2003. Unpaged. ISBN 9780786819881. (SP)

> The pigeon longs to drive the bus, but the savvy bus driver addresses his audience directly and asks them not to let the pigeon drive the bus while he's away. The determined pigeon uses every trick in the book to win his chance to drive the bus. (ALAN, Caldecott Honor)

The Pigeon Finds a Hot Dog. 2004. Unpaged. ISBN 9780786818693.

> The pigeon returns, and much to his delight finds a hot dog, but a young duckling wants to share, and the pigeon must decide whether or not he is willing to give up part of his treat.

Don't Let the Pigeon Stay Up Late. 2006. 32pp. 9780786837465.

> The pigeon and the bus driver are back. Now it's bedtime, and a pajama-clad driver begs readers not to let the pigeon stay up late. The pigeon, of course, has no intention of going to bed.

The Pigeon Wants a Puppy. 2008. 32pp. ISBN 9781423109600.

> The pigeon has his heart set on getting a puppy, until he realizes just how big his new canine pal is.

Easy Readers

Arnold, Tedd.

The Fly Guy Series. New York: Scholastic. `Gr. K-2`

The boy, Buzz, and his insect pet, Fly Guy, embark on several silly adventures. This series is filled with slapstick humor, puns, and jokes that are perfect for the audience. Exaggerated cartoon illustrations accentuate the humor inherent in the situations.

🎗*Hi, Fly Guy.* 2005. 30pp. ISBN 9780439639033. (SP). (ALAN, Geisel Honor)

Super Fly Guy. 2006. 30pp. ISBN 9780439639040.

Shoo, Fly Guy. 2006. 30pp. ISBN 9780439639057. (SP).

There Was an Old Lady Who Swallowed Fly Guy. 30pp. ISBN 9780439639064.

Hooray, Fly Guy. 2008. 30pp. ISBN 9780545007245.

Fly High, Fly Guy. 2008. 30pp. ISBN 9780545007221. (SP).

I Spy Fly Guy. 2009. 30pp. ISBN 9780545110280.

Fly Guy Meets Fly Girl. 2010. 30pp. ISBN 9780545110297.

Parish, Herman.

The New Amelia Bedelia Series. Illustrated by Lynn Sweat. New York: Greenwillow. `Gr. 1-3`

Herman Parish continues the series begun by his aunt, Peggy Parish, in 1963, about the flighty maid, Amelia Bedelia, who takes things very literally, providing endless amusement for young readers.

Good Driving, Amelia Bedelia. 1995. 40pp. ISBN 9780688133580.

Bravo, Amelia Bedelia. 1997. 40pp. ISBN 9780688151546.

Amelia Bedelia 4 Mayer. 1999. 48pp. ISBN 9780688167219.

Calling Doctor Amelia Bedelia. 2002. 64pp. ISBN 9780060014216.

Amelia Bedelia, Bookworm. 2003. 64pp. ISBN 9780060518905.

Happy Haunting, Amelia Bedelia. 2004. 64pp. ISBN 9780060518936.

Amelia Bedelia, Rocket Scientist? 2005. 64pp. ISBN 9780060518882.

Amelia Bedelia under Construction. 2006. 64pp. ISBN 9780060843441.

Amelia Bedelia's Masterpiece. 2007. 64pp. ISBN 9780060843557.

Amelia Bedelia Talks Turkey. 2008. 64pp. ISBN 9780060843526.

Amelia Bedelia and the Cat. 2008. 48pp. ISBN 9780060843496.

Amelia Bedelia Bakes Off. 2010. 48pp. ISBN 9780060843588.

Willems, Mo.

The Elephant and Piggie Series. See under "Friends" in chapter 2.

Favorites

Once upon a Banana by Jennifer Armstrong

Animals Should Definitely Not Wear Clothing by Judi Barrett

Bark, George by Jules Fieffer

The Odd Egg by Emily Gravett

The Scrambled States of America by Laurie Keller

The Day Jimmy's Boa Ate the Wash by Trinka Hakes Noble

If You Give a Mouse a Cookie by Laura Numeroff

The Great Fuzz Frenzy by Janet Stevens

Don't Let the Pigeon Drive the Bus by Mo Willems

Chapter 15

Imagination: Fanciful Bedtime Stories, Monsters, Toy Fantasy, Fantasy and Magic, Fractured Fairy Tales, Folk and Fairy Tales, and Science Fiction

Albert Einstein said, "If you want your children to be intelligent, read them fairy tales. If you want them to be more intelligent, read them more fairy tales." Books that give wings to a child's imagination are extremely important both developmentally and for sheer pleasure. The enormous success of the <u>Harry Potter</u> books has demonstrated the popularity of fantasy for older children, but the literature of magic, imaginary realms, and daring deeds has deep roots in books for younger children as well. From the stories of oral tradition that have become the folk and fairy tales of today, to the original fairy tales of Hans Christian Andersen, to contemporary tales of magic and mischief, fantasy is as important for the picture book audience as it is for the chapter book crowd. From stories that actively engage a child's imagination at bedtime to tales of monsters, as well as tales with traditional fantasy elements, picture books brim with imaginary exploits. To cluster similar flights of fancy together, this chapter is divided into the following categories: "Fanciful Bedtime Stories," "Imagine," "Monsters," "Toy Fantasy," "Wordless Picture Books," "Fantasy and Magic," "Fractured Fairy Tales and Nursery Rhymes," "Folk and Fairy Tales," and "Science Fiction."

Fanciful Bedtime Stories

Although these stories often conclude with the main character going to bed, they also feature imaginative adventures.

Ashman, Linda.

Starry Safari. **Illustrated by Jeff Mack. Orlando, FL: Harcourt, 2005. Unpaged. ISBN 9780152047665.** `T–K`

A child, who from the illustrations could be a boy or a girl, embarks on a wild, imaginary jungle adventure until Dad comes to tuck her into bed.

Bergman, Mara.

Oliver Who Would Not Sleep. **Illustrated by Nick Maland. New York: Arthur A. Levine, 2007. 29pp. ISBN 9780439928267.** `PreS–1`

Oliver's active imagination leads him to paint, read, and even soar off into space and back. He will do anything but sleep, until at last he curls up in bed ready to lay down his head.

Butler, John.

Can You Growl Like a Bear? **Atlanta, GA: Peachtree, 2007. 32pp. ISBN 9781561453962.** `T–K`

Gentle rhymes invite listeners to imagine themselves as various creatures in the wild by making their sounds until it's time for all the critters to fall asleep.

Crimi, Carolyn.

Where's My Mummy? **Illustrated by John Manders. Cambridge, MA: Candlewick, 2008. 32pp. ISBN 9780763631963.** `PreS–1`

Little Baby Mummy wants to play Hide and Shriek in the graveyard instead of going to bed, but when he dashes out, Mama Mummy doesn't follow him. He searches through the scary woods for her, asking various creepy creatures if they are his Mummy, only to discover a blob, a skeleton, and a vampire, all getting ready for bed. When a tiny mouse terrifies him, he calls for Mama Mummy. She rescues him and tucks him into bed. Gouache paintings bring both humor and eeriness to the tale.

Crow, Kristyn.

Bedtime at the Swamp. **Illustrated by Macky Pamintuan. New York: HarperCollins, 2008. 32pp. ISBN 9780060839512.** `PreS–1`

When a boy hears scary sounds in the swamp, he races for refuge and hides among the branches of a willow tree. His sister comes to fetch him, but she hears the noise as well and joins him in the tree. Family member after family member joins him there. Even the monster climbs up. At last Ma arrives and shuttles them off home and into bed.

Dunbar, Joyce.

The Monster Who Ate Darkness. **Illustrated by Jimmy Liao. Somerville, MA: Candlewick, 2008. 48pp. ISBN 9780763638597.** `PreS–2`

The monster that lives under Jo-Jo's bed has a voracious appetite, and what he likes to eat is darkness. Eventually he consumes so much that all the world is light, and Jo-Jo cannot sleep. Contrite, the monster calms him with a lullaby as darkness descends once again.

Fore, S. J.

Tiger Can't Sleep. **Illustrated by R. W. Alley. New York: Viking, 2006. Unpaged. ISBN 9780670060788.** `PreS–2`

> A boy can't get to sleep because there is a tiger in his closet making too much noise. The tired boy takes away one noisemaker after another until he realizes that Tiger is afraid and invites the creature to snuggle into bed with him.

Fox, Mem.

Where the Giant Sleeps. **Illustrated by Vladimir Radunsky. Orlando, FL: Harcourt, 2007. 32pp. ISBN 9780152057855.** `PreS–2`

> In this gently rhyming tale, a child dreams of a fairy tale world where everyone is sleeping, including dragons, ogres, fairies, and wizards.

Harris, Robie H.

Maybe a Bear Ate It! **Illustrated by Michael Emberley. New York: Orchard, 2008. Unpaged. ISBN 9780439929615.** `PreS–1`

> When a small creature climbs into bed with an array of stuffed animals and his beloved book, he yawns and without realizing it, knocks the book under the bed. He searches frantically for it, imagining that one kind of animal after another has made a meal of his treasure, until he finds it at last.

Hennessy, B. G.

Claire and the Unicorn: Happy Ever After. **Illustrated by Susan Mitchell. New York: Simon & Schuster, 2005. 32pp. ISBN 9781416908159.** `Gr. K–3`

> Claire falls asleep holding her stuffed unicorn, after listening to her father read her a fairy tale. She dreams that the unicorn comes to life, and together the two of them search for what truly makes people live happily ever after.

Hicks, Barbara Jean.

Jitterbug Jam. **Illustrated by Alexis Deacon. New York: Farrar, Straus & Giroux, 2005. 32pp. ISBN 9780374336851.** `Gr. K–3`

> Little Bobo, a monster, is afraid of the boy under his bed, but his grandfather gives him some tips for dealing with the menace, and when the boy appears, Little Bobo befriends him.

Joosse, Barbara.

In the Night Garden. **Illustrated by Elizabeth Sayles. New York: Holt, 2008. 32pp. ISBN 9780805066715.** `PreS–1`

> Three girls, playing in their garden, imagine that they are animals, each choosing a favorite. They stay in character as they get ready for bed and snuggle down to sleep.

Le Guin, Ursula K.

Cat Dreams. Illustrated by S. D. Schindler. New York: Scholastic, 2009. 32pp. ISBN 9780545042161. PreS–1

> After chasing a chipmunk, a cat curls up for a nap and dreams of lapping cream from a fountain and finding a catnip tree.

Mack, Jeff.

Hush Little Polar Bear. New York: Roaring Brook Press, 2008. 40pp. ISBN 9781596433687. T–K

> Following the rhyme and meter of "Hush Little Baby," in this story a young girl and her stuffed polar slip off to sleep. As they dream, the polar bear comes to life and embarks on a nighttime journey through various habitats. Illustrations show the girl watching his adventures. At last he returns to the arms of the sleeping girl.

Massie, Diane Redfield.

*The Baby Beebee Bird. Illustrated by Steven Kellogg. New York: HarperCollins, 2000. Unpaged. ISBN 9780060280833. PreS–2

> This story, first published in 1963, has been reissued with new illustrations. When a newly arrived baby beebee bird creates a cacophony all night long at the zoo, none of the animals can sleep. They, in turn, hatch a scheme to keep the bird awake all day, so they all can snooze when the sun goes down. Children will take equal delight in chanting the "beebeebobbi," refrain and enjoying the sumptuously detailed illustrations.

Mayer, Mercer.

*There's a Nightmare in My Closet. New York: Dial, 1968. Unpaged. ISBN 9780803786820. PreS–2

> A young boy knows that there's a nightmare in his closet that will emerge after his parents go to bed. He's ready to conquer it, but he discovers that it's not weapons that win the day, it's friendship.

McCarty, Peter.

Moon Plane. New York: Holt, 2006. 32pp. ISBN 9780805079432. T–K

> When a boys spots a prop plane in the sky, he imagines himself in it, soaring past a train, over the ocean, into outer space, and to the moon. He climbs out for a walk across the moon and flies home just in time for his mother to tuck him into bed. Black, white, and gray pencil-on-watercolor paper illustrations give the book a perfect nighttime ambiance.

Morales, Yuyi.

Little Night: Nochecita. New Milford, CT: Roaring Brook, 2007. 32pp. ISBN 9781596430884. PreS–1 (SP)

> In a story firmly rooted in folktale tradition, Mother Sky gets her playful daughter, Little Night, ready for nighttime. Little Night plays a game of hide-and-seek

throughout the evening routine as her mother helps her bathe in starlight, don a gown of crocheted clouds, and drink milk from the Milky Way. Unlike a human child, though, when the routines are completed and the sky darkened, Little Night does not go to sleep, but plays with the moon instead.

Newman, Leslea.

Daddy's Song. Illustrated by Karen Ritz. New York: Holt, 2007. 32pp. ISBN 9780805069754. **PreS-1**

Softly strumming his guitar, a father sings his daughter to sleep by making up a whimsical song full of impossibilities, like ice cream cones falling from the sky and rabbits leaping in the stars. He concludes with a tender assurance of his love.

Numeroff, Laura.

When Sheep Sleep. Illustrated by David McPhail. New York: Abrams, 2006. 32pp. ISBN 9780810954694. **PreS-2**

When a little girl can't sleep, she thinks she'll count sheep, but discovers they are already asleep. She turns her attention to cows, but they're snoozing, too. Each group of animals she turns to has drifted off before her, until at last she drops into dreamland as well.

Paul, Ann Whitford.

Little Monkey Says Good Night. Illustrated by David Walker. New York: Farrar, Straus & Giroux, 2003. 32pp. ISBN 9780374346096. **PreS-2**

Although his father has called him to bed, Little Monkey must first bid goodnight to all the performers in the circus.

If Animals Kissed Good Night. Illustrated by David Walker. New York: Farrar, Straus & Giroux, 2008. Unpaged. ISBN 9780374380519. **T-K**

Gentle rhymes portray the imagined scenarios of pairs of parent–child animals giving goodnight kisses.

Pinkney, Andrea Davis.

Sleeping Cutie. Illustrated by Brian J. Pinkney. Orlando, FL: Harcourt, 2004. 32pp. ISBN 9780152025441. **PreS-1**

Cutie LaRue never wants to go to sleep, so her parents give her the magical toy Night Owl. Night Owl comes to life after dark and escorts Cutie to the Dreamland nightclub, where folk like the Slumber Brothers and the Sandman try to tucker her out.

Provost, Elizabeth.

Ten Little Sleepyheads. Illustrated by Donald Saaf. New York: Bloomsbury, 2005. 32pp. ISBN 9781582348384. **PreS-1**

In this rhyming countdown book, ten pajama-wearing insects drop off to sleep one by one.

Rex, Michael.

Goodnight Goon: A Petrifying Parody. New York: Putnam, 2008. 32pp. ISBN 9780399245343. `Gr. 1-3`

> In this parody of Margaret Wise Brown's *Goodnight Moon,* a werewolf's nighttime ritual is disrupted by a Goon who makes a mess of everything.

Robbins, Maria Polushkin.

*Mother, Mother, I Want Another. Illustrated by Jon Goodell. New York: Knopf, 2005. 24pp. ISBN 9780375825880. `PreS-1`

> This reissue of a book first published in 1976 features new illustrations. When Mother Mouse gives her son a goodnight kiss, he cries out that he wants another. Misunderstanding him, she thinks he wants another mother and does her best to find one, proposing one animal mother after another, until she discovers that what he wants is another kiss.

Rohmann, Eric.

Clara and Asha. New Milford, CT: Roaring Brook Press, 2005. Unpaged. ISBN 9781596430310. `PreS-1`

> Clara's mother calls out that it's time for bed, but instead of sleeping, Clara opens the window for her friend Asha, the giant fish, who takes her out for nighttime adventures.

Ryder, Joanne.

Won't You Be My Hugaroo? Illustrated by Melissa Sweet. Orlando, FL: Harcourt, 2004. 40pp. ISBN 9780152057787. `T-K`

> Whimsical rhymes display the affection shown through hugging as a young zebra and his friends spend a day at an amusement park.

Won't You Be My Kissaroo? Illustrated by Melissa Sweetn. Orlando, FL: Harcourt, 2004. 32pp. ISBN 9780152026417. `T-K`

> Smooth rhymes carry a lamb through a day that begins with a morning kiss and ends with a goodnight kiss. In between, all the young animals of the neighborhood and their parents exchange kisses as well.

Serfozo, Mary.

Whooo's There? Illustrated by Jeffrey Scherer. New York: Random House, 2007. 40pp. ISBN 9780375840500. `PreS-1`

> An owl soars through a darkened forest, questioning the nighttime creatures and keeping his home safe.

Shulevitz, Uri.

The So Sleepy Story. New York: Farrar, Straus & Giroux, 2006. 32pp. ISBN 9780374370312. **PreS–1**

9

> A young boy is sound asleep, as are all the personified objects in his home. When a melody drifts by, the household wakes up, dances to the snappy tune, and then returns to the state of slumber. The subdued watercolor and ink illustrations imbue the story with the feel of night.

Shulman, Lisa.

10

The Moon Might Be Milk. Illustrated by Will Hillenbrand. New York: Dutton, 2007. 32pp. ISBN 9780525476474. **PreS–1**

> As Rosie and her cat watch the moon, she wonders what it is made of. Her cat suggests a saucer of milk, but Rosie's not sure. Together, they ask a variety of animals and finish with Gran, who provides the most unique answer of all.

11

Sierra, Judy.

The Sleepy Little Alphabet: A Bedtime Story from Alphabet Town. Illustrated by Melissa Sweet. New York: Knopf, 2009. 40pp. ISBN 9780375840029. **PreS–2**

12

> A pleasing rhyming text relates how capital-letter parents calm down the active lowercase children and get them tucked into bed, in this endearing bedtime tale that doubles as an alphabet book.

Slater, Dashka.

Firefighters in the Dark. Illustrated by Nicoletta Ceccoli. Boston: Houghton Mifflin, 2006. 32pp. ISBN 9780618554591. **PreS–1**

13

> As a young girl slips into bed, she hears the wail of a siren and imagines a series of firefighting scenarios, including firefighters saving the royal family when a dragon accidentally sets it on fire. Acrylic and pastel paintings present pictures using unusual angles, contributing to the dreamlike quality of the book.

14

Sobel, June.

The Goodnight Train. Illustrated by Laura Huliska-Beith. Orlando, FL: Harcourt, 2006. 32pp. ISBN 9780152054366. **T–K**

> A boldly colored train rattles down the tracks, pulling a line of beds, each with a child all tucked in and ready to sleep. By the end of their journey, they all arrive in Dreamland.

15

Thompson, Lauren.

🎗*Polar Bear Night*. Illustrated by Stephen Savage. New York: Scholastic, 2004. 32pp. ISBN 9780439495240. **PreS–1**

> When a little polar bear cub is awakened during the night, she wanders outside to see a beautiful star shower. It's quite a sight, but when it ends the

place she wants to be is back inside, curled up right next to her mama, where it's warm and safe. The muted illustrations will dazzle children, and they'll be ready to snuggle up, too. (ALAN, Charlotte Zolotow Honor, New York Times Best Illustrated)

Wilson, Karma.

Sleepyhead. **Illustrated by John Segal. New York: Margaret K. McElderry, 2006. 32pp. ISBN 9781416912415.** `PreS–1`

In this story in rhyme, a cat mother tries to get her living teddy bear child, Sleepyhead, to go to sleep. While Sleepyhead employs several stalling techniques, like asking for one more story or a glass of water, he imagines a series of adventures that eventually lead to dreamland.

Wing, Natasha.

*Go to Bed, Monster! **Illustrated by Sylvie Kantorovitz. Orlando, FL: Harcourt, 2007. 29pp. ISBN 9780152057756.** `PreS–1`

When Lucy can't sleep, she draws a friendly monster to play with her. The two create crayon adventures and together explore a castle, fly an airplane, and march in a parade, but Lucy gets tired before her monster does. Finally, Lucy draws her monster a comfortable bed to sleep in, and the two settle into slumber. Oil paints and pastels are used to look like a child's crayon drawings and perfectly complement the text.

Imagination

Though imagination is required for any reader or listener to vicariously enter the world of the story, these books center around the imaginative experience.

Gorbachev, Valeri.

Turtle's Penguin Day. **New York: Knopf, 2008. Unpaged. ISBN 9780375843747.** `PreS–1`

When Little Turtle listens to a bedtime story about penguins, he dreams about them and in the morning goes to school pretending that he is one. His teacher encourages his classmates to join the fun, and they spend the day playing as penguins would.

Horse, Harry

Imagine Harry. See under "Everyday Life in General" in chapter 1.

Kvasnosky, Laura McGee.

Really Truly Bingo. **Cambridge, MA: Candlewick, 2008. 32pp. ISBN 978-0763632106.** `PreS–1`

When a bored Bea wants her mother to play princess with her, she is told to and use her imagination. When a large talking dog appears and encourages her to make mischief, Bea has the time of her life. By the end of the tale the audience knows that the dog is imaginary, and Bea has done exactly as her mother told her.

Lazo, Caroline.

Someday When My Cat Can Talk. Illustrated by Kyrsten Brooker. New York: Schwartz & Wade, 2008. 32pp. ISBN 9780375837548. Gr. K–2

This rhyming tale tells what a girl imagines her cat will tell her about his travels around the world.

Merz, Jennifer J.

Playground Day. New York: Clarion, 2007. 29pp. ISBN 9780618816965. T–K

A little girl pulls a wagon full of stuffed animals to the playground with her, and she, her mother, and her dog spend the day in play. With delight, she pretends to be each of the animals in her wagon.

Portis, Antoinette.

*Not a Box. New York: HarperCollins, 2006. 32pp. ISBN 9780061123221. PreS–1

When the offstage narrator asks the bunny, drawn with bold black lines, why he is sitting in a box, the bunny insists it's not a box, and each succeeding illustration shows what item the bunny's imagination has turned the box into, including a boat, a race car, and a mountain. Children will identify with the activity and enjoy naming each item the box has become.

*Not a Stick. New York: HarperCollins, 2008. 32pp. ISBN 9780061123252. PreS–1

This time a black-outlined pig has a stick, and the unseen narrator warns him to be careful with it. Each time, the pig insists it's not a stick and the illustrations show the transformations, as the stick becomes several different things, including a fishing pole, a paintbrush, and a sword.

Seuss, Dr.

And to Think That I Saw It on Mulberry Street. New York: Random House, 1988. 38pp. ISBN 9780394844947. PreS–3

This reissue of the classic, first published in 1939, relays in rhyme all the amazing sights a young boy imagines seeing on his way home from school.

Shea, Bob.

Big Plans. Illustrated by Lane Smith. New York: Hyperion, 2008. 48pp. ISBN 9781423111009. Gr. K–3

When a boy is forced to sit in the corner by himself for misbehaving, he imagines all the things that he will do, because he has big plans for his life, from running his own company to becoming the president of the United States.

Shulevitz, Uri.

When I Wore My Sailor Suit. New York: Farrar, Straus & Giroux, 2009. 32pp. ISBN 9780374347499. `PreS-3`

When a young boy visits a neighbor's apartment wearing his sailor suit, he embarks on an imaginary seafaring journey.

Sis, Peter.

Madlenka Series. `Pre S-3`

Madelenka lives in a multi-ethnic neighborhood and is a child with a rich imaginative life who is also good friends with her neighbors, all illustrated with detailed ink-and-watercolor paintings.

Madlenka. New York: Frances Foster Books, 2000. Unpaged. ISBN 978-0374399696.

> An excited Madlenka shares the news of her loose tooth with her neighbors, who are each from different parts of the world. As she makes her way from place to place, illustrations show the country she imagines for each of her neighbors, including France, Italy, and India.

Madlenka's Dog. New York: Frances Foster Books, 2002. Unpaged. ISBN 978-0374346997.

> Once again Madlenka tours her neighborhood, this time with her imaginary dog. As she meets her neighbors, they reminisce about their own childhood dogs, and a flap-lift reveals each person in his or her youth with the accompanying pooch. In the end she meets up with her best friend Cleopatra, who has an imaginary horse.

Madlenka's Music. New York: Random House, 2010. Unpaged. ISBN 978-0375828553.

> This time Madlenka serenades her neighbors by playing her violin. While they recall how they played different musical instruments when they were children, Madlenka imagines them all in one large orchestra.

Madlenka's Soccer Ball. New York: Random House, 2010. Unpaged. ISBN 978-0375828522.

> Madlenka loves soccer, and when she gets a new ball, she plays in an imaginary championship.

Soman, David.

The Ladybug Girl Series. Illustrated by Jacky Davis. New York: Dial, 2008. `PreS-2`

Lulu discovers the wonders of imaginative play when she finds a ladybug costume.

Ladybug Girl. 2008. Unpaged. ISBN 9780803731950.

> When Lulu's mother tells her to amuse herself for the morning, Lulu finds that none of her toys seem very interesting. Discovering a ladybug costume, she transforms herself into a superhero and rushes outside to aid those in need.

Ladybug Girl and the Bumble Bee. 2009. 40pp. ISBN 9780803733398.

> When Lulu, attired as Ladybug Girl, meets her friend Sam at the playground, he agrees to join her superhero adventures as Bumble Bee Boy.

Ladybug Girl at the Beach. 2010. 32pp. ISBN 9780803734166.

> Lulu dons her Ladybug Girl costume and spends the day at the beach, where she builds a sand castle, flies a kite, and overcomes her fear of the ocean by remembering that as Ladybug Girl, she can do anything.

Spinelli, Eileen.

Someday. **Illustrated by Rosie Winstead. New York: Dial, 2007. 30pp. ISBN 9780803729414.** `Gr. K-2`

> Goldie imagines all the things that she will be able to do someday, like ride a dolphin, win an Olympic medal, and be invited to the White House, while explaining the everyday things that she is doing today.

Spinelli, Jerry.

I Can Be Anything. **Illustrated by Jimmy Liao. New York: Little, Brown, 2010. 32pp. ISBN 9780316162265.** `PreS-1`

> With playful rhymes, Spinelli presents a young boy who is imagining all the different things he can be when he grows up, including a puddle jumper and an apple chomper.

Thomas, Sarah L.

Imagine a Night. See under "Puzzles" in chapter 12.

Monsters

From monsters under the bed to monsters in the forest, children's books often feature the creatures that can be frightening or friendly.

Case, Chris.

Sophie and the Next-Door Monsters. **New York: Walker, 2008. 32pp. ISBN 9780802797568.** `PreS-2`

> Sophie's new neighbors are literally monsters, and she's terrified of them. Despite her fear, her mother invites them to dinner, and Sophie discovers the child of the family, Charlie, can be a great friend.

Cuyler, Margery.

Monster Mess! **Illustrated by S. D. Schindler. New York: Margaret K. McElderry, 2008. 40pp. ISBN 9780689864056.** `PreS-K`

> While the family sleeps, a many-legged monster makes its way to the boy's room. Finding it a mess, the monster spends the night cleaning, and in the morning the two have a grand time playing together.

Hazen, Barbara Shook.

Who Is Your Favorite Monster, Mama? **Illustrated by Maryann Kovalski. New York: Hyperion, 2006. 32pp. ISBN 9780786818105.** `PreS–1`

> In this monster family, Harry is the middle child. He demands to know which monster is his mother's favorite, but she counters by asking him to choose his favorite pet.

Leuck, Laura.

My Monster Mama Loves Me So. **Illustrated by Mark Buehner. New York: Lothrop, Lee & Shepard, 1999. Unpaged. ISBN 9780688168667.** `PreS–K`

> This story in rhyme details all the ways a little monster's mother loves him. She combs cobwebs out of his eyes, attends all his beastball games, and bakes cookies with lots of bugs inside.

Lund, Deb.

Monsters on Machines. See under "Construction Vehicles" in chapter 8.

Mayer, Mercer.

There's a Nightmare in My Closet. See under "Fanciful Bedtime Stories" in this chapter.

McCarty, Peter.

Jeremy Draws a Monster. **New York: Holt, 2009. 32pp. ISBN 9780805069341.** `PreS–1`

> Jeremy, who doesn't like to leave his room, uses his blue pen to draw himself a monster companion. The monster makes one demand after another, until Jeremy draws a bus to trundle the monster away.

Sendak, Maurice.

🌸*Where the Wild Things Are.* **New York: HarperCollins, 1988. 32pp. ISBN 9780060254926.** `PreS–2`

> This anniversary edition of the classic tale first published in 1963 is printed from new engravings using the original artwork. When the mischievous Max creates a ruckus, his mother banishes him to his room. He sails away to the place where the Wild Things are and joins them for their wild rumpus. The stunning illustrations still captivate after all these years. (Caldecott Medal)

Sierra, Judy.

Thelonius Monster's Sky-High Fly-Pie. **Illustrated by Edward Koren. New York: Random House, 2006. 40pp. ISBN 9780375832185.** `Gr. K–3`

> In this rhyming text that begs to be read aloud, Thelonius Monster e-mails a spider for tips on catching flies and sets about making a stupendous pie for all his monster friends.

Stein, David E. S.

Monster Hug! New York: Putnam, 2007. 40pp. ISBN 9780399246371. **PreS-1**

Two exuberant monsters spend a day playing together, ending with a great, big monster hug.

9

Stewart, Joel.

Dexter Bexley and the Big Blue Beastie. New York: Holiday House, 2007. 30pp. ISBN 9780823420681. **PreS-2**

When Dexter Bexley is threatened by the Big Blue Beastie, he diverts the monster's attention with assorted activities, and the two end up becoming friends.

10

Taylor, Sean.

*When a Monster Is Born. Illustrated by Nick Sharratt. New Milford, CN: Roaring Brook, 2007. 32pp. ISBN 9781596432543. **PreS-1** (SP)

Beginning with the birth of a monster, this book presents two possibilities for each subsequent event. One option leads to the end and the other continues the story. Bold illustrations highlight the deadpan humor of the tale.

11

Wheeler, Lisa.

Boogie Knights. Illustrated by Mark Siegel. New York: Atheneum, 2008. 40pp. ISBN 9780689876394. **Gr. 1-3**

While seven knights are sleeping, a young prince watches a parade of zombies, werewolves, and mummies arrive at the castle to take part in the Madcap Monster Ball. The jazzy rhyme conveys the ways in which all the creepy creatures dance as the knights and the prince join the cavorting fun.

12

13

Willems, Mo.

Leonardo the Terrible Monster. New York: Hyperion, 2005. 48pp. ISBN 9780786852949. **PreS-1**

Leonardo is distressed because he just can't scare anyone. Loathe to give up, he tries to scare Sam, who is afraid of anything. He makes Sam cry, but it's because Sam is having a bad day, and Leonardo decides it's more important to be a good friend than a good monster. (ALAN)

14

Yaccarino, Dan.

The Lima Bean Monster. Illustrated by Adam McCauley. New York: Walker, 2001. 32pp. ISBN 9780802787767. **PreS-1**

Sammy hates lima beans, so he hides them in socks and buries them in a vacant lot. The neighborhood children catch on and follow suit. One night during a thunderstorm, a lightning strike creates the Lima Bean Monster from all the discarded vegetables. The monster captures all the adults, and the only way for the children to free them is to eat the monster.

15

Toy Fantasy

Since children can spend a lot of time playing with toys, it's not unusual to find fantasies featuring toys with a life of their own.

Cooper, Helen.

Tatty Ratty. New York: Farrar, Straus & Giroux, 2002. Unpaged. ISBN 9780374373863. `PreS-2`

When Molly loses her favorites stuffed rabbit on the bus, she is desperate to find him. Her parents help her to imagine his adventures until they find a toy in the store that Molly recognizes as Tatty Ratty.

Crews, Nina.

Below. New York: Holt, 2006. Unpaged. ISBN 9780805077285. `PreS-2`

When Jack drops his action figure Guy down a whole in the stairs, he imagines all the challenges he might be facing, including dragons and wild horses.

Sky-High Guy. New York: Holt, 2010. 32pp. ISBN 9780805087642. Sequel. `PreS-2`

Jack returns with his toy friend Guy, and this time the action is up in the air. Jack likes to play without being bothered by his brother Gus, but when Guy gets stuck in a tree, it's Gus who can rescue him.

de Sève, Randall.

The Toy Boat. See under "Boats" in chapter 8.

Freeman, Don.

*Corduroy. New York: Viking, 1968. 32pp. ISBN 9780670241330. `PreS-2` (SP)

When Corduroy, a stuffed bear wearing green overalls, learns that he is missing a button, he searches the department store, hoping to find the missing item, so that the little girl will take him home.

A Pocket for Corduroy. New York: Viking, 1978. 32pp. ISBN 9780670561728. Sequel. `PreS-2` (SP)

Now that he has a home with the African American girl who purchased him and she has fixed his button, Corduroy realizes that he does not have a pocket. While in the laundromat he looks high and low for one.

Gravett, Emily.

Monkey and Me. New York: Simon & Schuster, 2008. 24pp. ISBN 9781416954576. `PreS-1`

A little girl and her stuffed monkey visit the zoo and have fun pretending to be the animals they see.

Haseley, Dennis.

The Skywriter. Illustrated by Dennis Nolan. New York: Roaring Brook, 2008. Unpaged. ISBN 9781596432529. **Gr. K–3**

> Charles and his older sister play with toys that talk to them, but as they grow up, they stop conversing with their playthings. When they end up in the trash, Charles rescues them and saves them for his new baby brother.

Ichikawa, Satomi.

La La Rose. New York: Philomel, 2004. Unpaged. ISBN 9780399240294. **PreS–2**

> Clementine takes her beloved stuffed rabbit, La La Rose, with her everywhere. When she loses the rabbit in the Luxembourg Gardens in Paris, the rabbit has a variety of adventures before being reunited with Clementine. Lush watercolor illustrations highlight the uniqueness of the location as well as the emotions of the characters.

Come Fly with Me. New York: Philomel, 2008. Unpaged. ISBN 978-0399246791. **PreS–2**

> A toy wooden plane takes a stuffed dog for the ride of his life when they soar above the rooftops of Paris.

My Little Train. New York: Philomel, 2010. 40pp. ISBN 9780399254536. **PreS–2**

> When a toy train goes for a ride, he invites the stuffed animals along.

Long, Loren.

Drummer Boy. See under "Christmas" in chapter 6.

McAllister, Angela.

Brave Bitsy and the Bear. Illustrated by Tiphanie Beeke. New York: Clarion, 2006. 32pp. ISBN 9780618639946. **PreS–3**

> When Bitsy, a small stuffed bunny, gets lost in the woods, a friendly but sleepy bear helps her find her way home. She worries that he won't make it back to his cave to hibernate, so with the aid of other forest creatures, she builds him a shelter.

Meadows, Michelle.

Pilot Pups. Illustrated by Dan Andreasen. New York: Simon & Schuster, 2008. 29pp. ISBN 9781416924845. **T–K**

> As soon as their boy leaves the room, three toy pups zip into action. Two of them climb aboard two toys, a plane and a helicopter, and they zoom into adventure, flying around the house. They return to their room, just in time to be in place for the boy.

Pullen, Zachary.

Friday My Radio Flyer Flew. New York: Simon & Schuster, 2008. 30pp. ISBN 9781416939832. `PreS-2`

> When a boy finds his father's red wagon, he tinkers with it on each day of the week, and by Friday he soars into the sky, carried by the trusty wagon.

Rosen, Michael.

Red Ted and the Lost Things. Illustrated by Joel Stewart. Somerville, MA: Candlewick, 2009. 40pp. ISBN 9780763645373. `PreS-2`

> When a beloved teddy bear is accidentally left behind, he sets out on a journey to find his owner.

Schertle, Alice.

Adventures of Old Bo Bear. Illustrated by David Parkins. San Francisco: Chronicle, 2006. 32pp. ISBN 9780811834766. `PreS-1`

> A boy and his bear enjoy several adventures together, even after Mom tosses the bear in the washer and he emerges missing an ear.

Smith, Maggie.

Paisley. New York: Knopf, 2004. 40pp. ISBN 9780375821646. `PreS-2`

> When Paisley, a paisley-patterned stuffed elephant, accidently ends up in the trash, he embarks on a quest to find the Perfect Match. He discovers the laundromat, gets washed, and is then adopted by a girl dressed in paisley.

Watty, Piper.

The Little Engine That Could. Illustrated by Loren Long. New York: Philomel, 2005. 48pp. ISBN 9780399244674. `PreS-2`

> This classic story, first published in 1930, has been reissued in a larger format and with new, bold illustrations. A little blue engine pulls a load of toys and treats up an extremely tough mountain, with encouragement from the toys and the power of positive thinking. The new illustrations and format help the flow of the drama and are rich and delightful.

Wordless Picture Books

Wordless books engage the imaginations of children in a completely visual manner. Relating the story only through pictures allows them to imagine what is causing the action in the pictures. It is an important pre-reading activity that aids in the development of visual literacy. It also promotes verbal development and story comprehension, because children will often explain the story they see in the pictures.

Baker, Jeannie.

Home. New York: Greenwillow, 2004. 32pp. ISBN 9780066239354. `Gr. K-3`

Before the little girl was born, the neighborhood where her family lived was beautiful. Now her neighborhood shows its age as buildings get run down and crime becomes more prevalent. The girl comes back after she is grown up, and her neighborhood is beautiful once again.

Dematons, Charlotte.

The Yellow Balloon. Emeryville, CA: Front Street, 2004. 32pp. ISBN 9781932425017. `PreS-3`

When a yellow balloon escapes, it leads viewers on a seek-and-find expedition around the world. In addition to pouring over the pictures to locate the balloon, children will study them to uncover the mini stories depicted in the details.

Jay, Alison.

Welcome to the Zoo! New York: Dial, 2008. 32pp. ISBN 9780803731776. `PreS-2`

A family of four visits an unusual zoo, where the animals roam free and interact with their visitors.

Khing, T. T.

Where Is the Cake? New York: Abrams, 2007. 28pp. ISBN 9780810917989. `Gr. K-3`

When two rats steal a cake, they are chased through a variety of landscapes by monkeys, rabbits, and frogs, among others, who all have stories of their own. These vignettes and landscapes are portrayed in detailed watercolors that will keep children studying the pages, not simply to find the cake, but to follow the stories of the creatures following the cake.

Where Is the Cake Now? New York: Abrams, 2009. 26pp. ISBN 978-0810989269. Sequel. `Gr. K-3`

This time a cast of animal characters with stories of their own tote two cakes to a picnic, but when the cakes disappear, they must uncover the culprits and find the cakes.

Lee, Suzy.

Wave. San Francisco: Chronicle, 2008. 34pp. ISBN 9780811859240. `Gr. K-2`

Graceful acrylic-and-charcoal illustrations present a young girl enjoying a day at the beach.

Lehman, Barbara.

The Red Book. Boston: Houghton Mifflin, 2004. Unpaged. ISBN 978-0618428588. `Gr. K-3`

In this brilliant book of interconnected stories, a girl finds a red book in a snowy city and as she looks through the pages, she spots a boy on an island who is looking at a red book. When the boy looks at the pages in his book, he sees the girl, who finds an ingenious way to visit him.

Museum Trip. Boston: Houghton Mifflin, 2006. 40pp. ISBN 9780618581252. `Gr. K–3`

When a boy goes to visit a museum with his class, he gets separated from them and becomes intrigued by a special exhibit of maze drawings. He shrinks in size and enters the maze. The drawings transform into three dimensional mazes, and the boy must find his way through.

Rainstorm. **Boston: Houghton Mifflin, 2007. 30pp. ISBN 9780618756391.** `PreS–2`

On a rainy day, a lonely boy finds a key that leads him to unexpected places and friends.

Trainstop. **Boston: Houghton Mifflin, 2008. 32pp. ISBN 9780618756407.** `PreS–2`

A girl and her family board a train in the city, and it takes them on an unlooked-for adventure.

Pinkney, Jerry.

🏃*The Lion & the Mouse.* **New York: Little, Brown, 2009. 40pp. ISBN 978-0316013567.** `PreS–3`

Using only occasional animal sounds as text, Pinkney breathes life into the Aesop's fable in which a majestic lion lets a mouse go free and later the mouse repays his kindness by freeing him from hunters' nets. Pinkney's full-of-life watercolor and colored pencil illustrations superbly portray the African Serengeti setting, the action of the plot, and the wildness and emotion of the animals. A stunning work of art. (ALAN, Caldecott Medal)

Wiesner, David.

🏃*Sector 7.* New York: Clarion, 1999. Unpaged. ISBN 9780395746561. `Gr. K–3`

On a class trip to New York City's Empire State Building, a boy is whisked off the top of the observation deck by a friendly cloud. The cloud takes him to the Cloud Dispatch Center, where he witnesses the forming of all kinds of clouds, before his friend returns him to his class. Illustrated with masterful, misty yet detailed watercolors. (ALAN, Caldecott Honor)

🏃*Flotsam.* New York: Clarion, 2006. 39pp. ISBN 9780618194575. `Gr. K–3`

When a boy searches the shoreline for interesting items washed in by the tide, he discovers an old camera, whose pictures lead him on an imaginative adventure. The incredibly detailed watercolors are breathtaking. (ALAN, Caldecott Medal, New York Times Best Illustrated)

🏃*Free Fall.* **New York: HarperCollins, 2008. Unpaged. ISBN 9780061567414. Unpaged. ISBN 9780061567414.** `Gr. 2 & up`

In this reissue of the author's first book, a boy slumbers with an atlas in his hand. He dreams of adventures, from slaying dragons to being surrounded by Lilliputians, in this surrealistic presentation. (ALAN, Caldecott Honor)

Fantasy and Magic

These stories feature tales of magic, imaginary realms, witches, wizards, and mythical creatures. Included here are the newest editions of Hans Christian Andersen's fairy tales. These tales are so timeless that authors and illustrators periodically retell the stories and create new illustrations.

Addy, Sharon.

When Wishes Were Horses. **Illustrated by Brad Sneed. Boston: Houghton Mifflin, 2002. Unpaged. ISBN 9780618131662. PreS-1**

In this wishes-gone-awry story, young Jeb wishes for many things, including help hefting a heavy sack. This last wish occurs as a stranger wearing a white Stetson hat rides past. When he winks at Jeb, Jeb suddenly finds himself with a horse. In fact, every time he makes any kind of a wish, another horse appears. When he ends up amid a herd of horses, he finally wishes his wishes would just be wishes again, and his equine companions all disappear. An amusing anecdote with watercolor illustrations that set the story in a town of the Old West.

Andersen, Hans Christian (titles listed alphabetically rather than by publication date).

The Emperor's New Clothes. **Illustrated by Virginia Lee Burton. Boston: Houghton Mifflin, 2004. 44pp. ISBN 9780618344215. Gr. K-3**

Burton's illustrations add her inimitable sense of humor to the story of the boy who would not be fooled by the emperor's nonexistent clothes. Though these illustrations were created for the edition first released in 1949, here they have been newly photographed to enhance the colors and sharpness.

The Little Match Girl. **Illustrated by Rachel Isadora. New York: Putnam, 1987. 30pp. ISBN 9780399213366. Gr. 3 & up**

Isadora's poignant pictures beautifully capture the feel of a Victorian winter as they illustrate the tale of the poverty-stricken child who lights match after match to stay warm and is at last taken up into heaven by the spirit of her grandmother.

The Nightingale. **Retold and illustrated by Jerry Pinkney. New York: Phyllis Fogelman Books, 2002. 40pp. ISBN 9780803724648. Gr. K-3**

Pinkney vividly reimagines Andersen's tale of a nightingale whose melodious song enchants a kingdom until she is replaced by a mechanical bird. Pinkney sets the tale in Morocco and uses jewel tones in his gouache and watercolor illustrations, creating a unique retelling of a classic.

The Snow Queen. **Retold by Amy Ehrlich. Illustrated by Susan Jeffers. New York: Dutton, 2006. 40pp. ISBN 9780525476948. Gr. 2 & up**

With exquisite illustrations, Jeffers brings to life Andersen's tale of a brave sister who must find a way to rescue her brother from the evil Snow Queen, who has kidnapped him.

The Snow Queen. **Retold by Naomi Lewis. Illustrated by Christian Birmingham. Somerville, MA: Candlewick, 2008. 64pp. ISBN 9780763632298.** `Gr. 2 & up`

Birmingham's impressionist-style illustrations beautifully enhance this fluid retelling.

Thumbelina. **Retold by Brian Alderson. Illustrated by Bagram Ibatoulline. Somerville, MA: Candlewick, 2009. Unpaged. ISBN 9780763620790.** `Gr. 2 & up`

Ibatoulline employs a rich and dark palette in his illustrations of Thumbelina's adventures.

The Tinderbox. **Retold by Stephen Mitchell. Illustrated by Bagram Ibatoulline. Cambridge, MA: Candlewick, 2007. 48pp. ISBN 9780763620783.** `Gr. 3 & up`

In this dark tale, a soldier marching home from war encounters a witch, who helps him find money, but the ungrateful man murders her for her magic tinderbox. As he begins his new life in town, he discovers the secret of the tinderbox and woos the princess. When her parents grow displeased, he unleashes the witch's hounds to wreak murderous vengeance. Ibatoulline's illustrations, drawn in pen and ink, resemble etchings and illuminate the harshness of the tale.

The Ugly Duckling. **Illustrated by Rachel Isadora. New York: Putnam, 2009. 32pp. ISBN 9780399250293.** `Gr. 1–3`

Isadora softens the original Andersen tale of the young swan who believes himself an ugly duckling. Her characters show more kindness to the bird who does not fit in. Using jewel colors in both oil paints and her collages, Isadora successfully transplants the tale to Africa.

The Ugly Duckling. **Retold by Stephen Mitchell. Illustrated by Steve Johnson and Lou Fancher. Cambridge, MA: Candlewick, 2008. 40pp. ISBN 9780763621599.** `Gr. K–3`

The lacy and luminous art and tart retelling provide an entertaining version of the duckling who must find his place in the world.

The Ugly Duckling. **Illustrated by Robert Ingpen. New York: Minedition/Penguin, 2005. 40pp. ISBN 9780698400108.** `Gr. 1–3`

Here is the full original story of the now well-known duck, translated by Anthea Bell and elegantly illustrated by Ingpen.

🐦*The Ugly Duckling.* **Retold and illustrated by Jerry Pinkney. New York: Morrow, 1999. Unpaged. ISBN 9780688159320.** `Gr. K–3`

Pinkney's interpretation of Andersen's well-known tale of the experiences of the ugly duckling who finally learns he is a swan is a graceful, meticulous rendition that will mesmerize readers and listeners alike. (ALAN, Caldecott Honor)

The Wild Swans. **Retold by Amy Ehrlich, Amy. Illustrated by Susan Jeffers. New York: Dutton, 2008. 40pp. ISBN 9780525479147.** `Gr. 2 & up`

Noted illustrator Susan Jeffers's lush pictures bring Andersen's tale of eleven brothers turned into swans and the sister who will do anything to save them to vivid life in this handsome edition of a classic story.

Bernheimer, Kate.

The Girl in the Castle Inside the Museum. Illustrated by Nicoletta Ceccoli. New York: Schwartz & Wade, 2008. Unpaged. ISBN 9780375836060. **Gr. 1–3**

> A small girl who lives in a castle inside a museum is lonely until she is visited by children in reality and in her dreams. This ethereal story is illustrated with misty mixed-media paintings.

Bertrand, Lynne.

Granite Baby. Illustrated by Kevin Hawkes. New York: Farrar, Straus and Giroux, 2005. 40pp. ISBN 9780374327613. **Gr. K–3**

> In this rollicking original tall tale, five giant-sized sisters open a quarry on Umbagog Lake in New Hampshire and carve a town out of stone. When Beryl uses her chisel to chip a baby out of granite, it comes to life, and the sisters don't have a clue what to do to get the babe to stop crying. Everything they try fails, until young Nellie, a lass closer to normal size with a passel of brothers and sisters, shows them that a little lovin' goes a long way.

Bunting, Eve.

That's What Leprechauns Do. Illustrated by Emily Arnold McCully. New York: Clarion, 2005. 32pp. ISBN 9780618354108. **Gr. 1–3**

> A trio of mischievous leprechauns spy dark clouds looming in the sky and rush to dig up their pot of gold to place at the end of the rainbow, but they can't resist playing a few pranks along the way.

Cole, Brock.

🏵*Good Enough to Eat.* New York: Farrar Straus Giroux, 2007. 32pp. ISBN 9780374327378. **Gr. 1–3**

> When an ogre arrives at the town's gates and demands a bride, the townspeople offer up the outcast beggar they call Scraps-and-Smells. But the girl has more gumption than anyone imagined and handily outwits both the ogre and the townsfolk. (ALAN)

dePaola, Tomie.

The Knight and the Dragon. New York: Putnam, 1980. 29pp. ISBN 9780399207075. **PreS–1**

> In an amusing escapade, a novice knight prepares to fight an inexperienced dragon. They seek tips that could lead them to victory, but they are both in for a big surprise.

The Strega Nona Series. **Gr. K–3**

> Although the original *Strega Nona* is a folktale retelling, the rest of the books in the series are original tales, relating the adventures of the Italian "Grandma Witch" and her bumbling assistant, Big Anthony.

🏵*Strega Nona.* New York: Simon & Schuster, 1975. 32pp. ISBN 9780671662837. (Caldecott Honor)

🏵*Big Anthony and the Magic Ring.* New York: Harcourt Brace Jovanovich, 1979. 32pp. ISBN 9780152071240. (ALAN)

Strega Nona's Magic Lessons. New York: Harcourt Brace Jovanovich, 1982. 32pp. ISBN 9780152817855.

Merry Christmas, Strega Nona. San Diego: Harcourt Brace Jovanovich, 1986. 32pp. ISBN 9780152531843 (pb).

Strega Nona Meets Her Match. New York: Putnam, 1993. Unpaged. ISBN 9780399224218.

Strega Nona: Her Story. New York: Putnam, 1996. Unpaged. ISBN 9780399228186.

Big Anthony: His Story. New York: Putnam, 1998. Unpaged. ISBN 9780698118935 (pb).

Strega Nona Takes a Vacation. New York: Putnam, 2000. Unpaged. ISBN 9780399235627.

Strega Nona's Harvest. New York: Putnam, 2009. Unpaged. ISBN 9780399252914.

Demi.

The Boy Who Painted Dragons. **New York: Margaret K. McElderry Books, 2007. 40pp. ISBN 9781416924692.** `Gr. 1–3`

Demi's striking paintings illustrate the story of Ping, a boy who is afraid of dragons but loves to paint pictures of them. The Heavenly Dragons send him on a quest for pearls of wisdom to help him overcome his fear.

Donaldson, Julia.

Room on the Broom. **Illustrated by Axel Scheffler. New York: Dial, 2001. Unpaged. ISBN 9780803726574.** `Gr. K–3`

A witch and her cat soar through the night on her broomstick. Each time she loses something a helpful animal retrieves it and then finds "room on the broom" for a ride. When the broom breaks because of the extra weight, the witch lands at the feet of a hungry dragon, and it's up to her animal friends to rescue her.

Fox, Mem.

🏵*Possum Magic.* **Illustrated by Jules Vivas. San Diego: Harcourt Brace Jovanovich, 1983. 32pp. ISBN 9780152005726.** `PreS–2`

In Australia, Grandma Poss uses magic to turn Hush invisible, but when Hush decides that she would like to be visible once again, the two possums embark on a journey across the land, searching for the magic food that will restore her. (Ethel Turner Prize)

The Magic Hat. **Illustrated by Tricia Tusa. San Diego: Harcourt, 2002. Unpaged. ISBN 9780152010256.** `PreS-3`

> When a wizard's magic hat whirls into a park full of people, it lands on the heads of one grownup after another, transforming each into a different animal. The rhythmic cadence of this story begs for audience participation.

The Goblin and the Empty Chair. **Illustrated by Leo Dillon and Diane Dillon. New York: Beach Lane Books, 2009. 32pp. ISBN 9781416985853.** `Gr. 1-3`

> When a goblin helps a farming family that is going through a sad and difficult period, the family invites him into their home. The lyrical text is matched by the Dillons' signature watercolors.

Fraser, Mary Ann.

Mermaid Sister. **New York: Walker, 2008. 30pp. ISBN 9780802797469.** `Gr. K-2`

> Shelly wishes she had a sister instead of her pain of a little brother, so she advertises for one by slipping a message in a bottle. Coral, a mermaid, answers the ad and moves in with Shelly's family temporarily.

Funke, Cornelia.

The Princess Knight. **Illustrated by Kerstin Meyer. 32pp. New York: Scholastic, 2003. ISBN 9780439536301.** `Gr. K-3`

> Princess Violetta learns the knightly skills of jousting and sword fighting from her father, King Wilfred. When her brothers tease her for being smaller and weaker, she practices in secret and becomes an expert. On her sixteenth birthday, her father declares that the winner of the joust will win her hand in marriage. Outraged, she decides to enter the joust herself and take control of her own destiny.

Gaiman, Neil.

🌱*The Wolves in the Walls*. **Illustrated by Dave McKean. New York: HarperCollins, 2003. Unpaged. ISBN 9780380978274.** `Gr. 3 & up`

> When Lucy hears wolves in the walls, she tries to convince her family that they are real, but no one believes her until it's too late. The family flees, but Lucy convinces them they must return to evict the wolves. (New York Times Best Illustrated)

Gravett, Emily.

🌱*Wolves*. **New York: Simon & Schuster, 2006. 32pp. ISBN 9781416914914.** `Gr. 1-3`

> In a book told through the illustrations as much as the text, rabbit checks out a book about wolves from the local library. Absorbed in his reading, the rabbit doesn't notice a wolf emerging from the library book, until it's too late (or almost too late, depending on which ending the reader picks). (ALAN, Boston Globe Honor, Kate Greenaway Medal)

Spells. New York: Simon & Schuster, 2009. 32pp. ISBN 9781416982708. `PreS–2`

When a frog finds an old book of spells with torn pages, he searches it for just the right bit of magic, but discovers that mixing and matching spells isn't always the best idea. Split pages allow readers to play at making spells of their own.

Grey, Mini.

Ginger Bear. New York: Knopf, 2007. 32pp. ISBN 9780375842535. `PreS–2`

Horace's mum gives him his own bear-shaped cookie cutter, and he happily bakes his own ginger bear. Never getting a chance to eat his snack, he places it in a tin to save it until morning. At the stroke of midnight the cookie comes to life and makes his own batch of bears to keep him company. The bears are high-flying circus performers, until they are interrupted by Horace's dog, who spots his favorite treat cavorting before him.

Hakala, Marjorie Rose.

Mermaid Dance. See under "Seasons" in chapter 9.

Heide, Florence Parry.

Princess Hyacinth (The Surprising Tale of a Girl Who Floated). Illustrated by Lane Smith. New York: Schwartz & Wade, 2009. 40pp. ISBN 9780375845017. `PreS–2`

Princess Hyacinth floats wherever she goes, so her parents load her down with a heavy crown and other items to keep her from drifting away. She longs for the freedom of the great outdoors. When she finds a balloon, she can soar at last.

Larochelle, David.

The Best Pet of All. Illustrated by Hanako Wakiyama. New York: Dutton, 2004. Unpaged. ISBN 9780525471295. `PreS–2`

When a boy pesters his mother for permission to get a dog and she repeatedly refuses, he asks if he can have a dragon instead. His mother agrees to this, and much to her surprise, he not only finds one, but brings it home.

🎗 *The End.* Illustrated by Richard Egielski. New York: Arthur A. Levine, 2007. 40pp. ISBN 9780439640114. `Gr. K–3`

Beginning with the happily-ever-after ending, this tale winds backward through a story of the events linking a soggy knight, his princess, two giants, eleven rabbits, and a scaly green dragon. (Golden Kite Honor)

Manning, Jane.

Cat Nights. New York: Greenwillow, 2008. Unpaged. ISBN 9780061138881. `PreS–2`

Inspired by an Irish legend explaining why cats have nine lives, this story recounts the adventures of Felicity, a young witch who is about to grow into the magical ability to change into a cat. Once she has her new power, Felicity changes herself into a cat every night. She is delighted, but her cousins worry because if she changes more than seven times, the eighth change will be her last—she will remain a cat for the rest of her life.

Mayhew, James.

Who Wants a Dragon? Illustrated by Lindsey Gardiner. New York: Orchard, 2004. ISBN 32pp. 9780439672375. **PreS–1** (SP)

> A baby dragon wanders lost and alone, looking for someone to love him. Everyone from the knight, to the princess, even to the king and queen, shies away from him, until his mother soars into view and sweeps him up into her loving embrace. A perfect bedtime story.

The Knight Who Took All Day. New York: Chicken House, 2005. 32pp. ISBN 9780439748292. **Gr. K–2**

> An arrogant knight, wishing to woo a princess, decides to slay a dragon, but he takes so long to get ready that princess tames the dragon herself. The illustrations reveal a comic counterpoint to the straightforward text.

McGee, Marni.

Winston the Book Wolf. Illustrated by Ian Beck. New York: Walker, 2006. 32pp. ISBN 9780802795694. **PreS–2**

> Some wolves hunger for little pigs, some for grannies, but Winston craves words. After being banned from the library for literally sinking his teeth into the books, Rosie (who wears a red-hooded sweatshirt) tutors him in another way to devour books—reading.

Meddaugh, Susan.

The Witch's Walking Stick. Boston: Houghton Mifflin, 2005. 32pp. ISBN 9780618529483. **Gr. K–3**

> A wretched Margaret lives with her nasty brother and sister in a cottage in the woods. Fed up with their bullying, she decides to strike out on her own. As she strides through the forest she encounters an old woman, who offers her gold if she can retrieve her stick from the dog who has snatched it. Finding the stick, she discovers that it is a wishing stick and borrows it, for just a bit, to set things right.

Mora, Pat.

🖋*Doña Flor: A Tall Tale about a Giant Woman with a Great Big Heart.* Illustrated by Raul Colón. New York: Knopf, 2005. 40pp. ISBN 978-0375923371. **Gr. K–3**

> This original tall tale, set in the American Southwest and sprinkled with Spanish words and phrases, recounts the story of the giant Dona Flor. Shortly after she first moves into the pueblo, she is teased, but she soon wins the respect and affection of her neighbors. So when a giant puma begins lurking in the area, it is naturally Dona Flor who handles the situation. (ALAN, Golden Kite Award, Pura Belpre Award, Pura Belpre Honor)

Morales, Yuyi.

Just a Minute: A Trickster Tale and Counting Book. San Francisco: Chronicle Books, 2003. 36pp. ISBN 9780811837583. `Gr. 1–3`

> In this original trickster tale set in Mexico, Señor Calavera, a well-dressed skeleton who represents Death, pays a visit to Grandma Beetle. She forestalls him by explaining that she has chores to do before she can accompany him. Patiently, he counts each completed task in Spanish and English. He's delighted to see the preparations are for her birthday party, and he is an invited guest. He enjoys himself so much that he leaves without her, saying he looks forward to her party the following year.

Just in Case: A Trickster Tale and Spanish Alphabet Book. New York: Roaring Brook, 2008. Unpaged. ISBN 9781596433298. Sequel. `Gr. 1–3`

> Señor Calavera, the stylish skeleton, is on his way to Grandma Beetle's birthday party when he realizes that he doesn't have a gift for her. Indecisive, he gathers items representing each letter of the Spanish alphabet, to make sure he has the perfect gift.

Myers, Christopher.

🎖*Wings.* New York: Scholastic, 2000. 40pp. ISBN 9780590033770. `Gr. K–3`

> A shy girl narrates the story of a new boy attending her inner city school. When Ikarus Jackson arrives, his classmates make fun of him because of his wings, until the narrator scolds them and tells Ikarus how beautiful his flying is. The illustrations of cut-paper collage silhouettes make this a visually stunning picture book. (ALAN, Charlotte Zolotow Award)

O'Brien, John.

Poof! Honesdale, PA: Boyds Mills Press, 1999. Unpaged. ISBN 9781563978159. `PreS–2`

> A team of married wizards argue with each other over household responsibilities. When the baby begins to cry, Mrs. Wizard tells her husband it's his turn to change the baby. With a wave of his wand and a "Poof," he does indeed change the baby, into a cat. Now it's his wife's turn to feed the cat. She transforms him into a dog. The magic spells fly back and forth until the surprising but happy ending.

Palatini, Margie.

The Gritch the Witch Trilogy. Illustrated by Howard Fine. `Gr. K–3`

> This trio of tales describe the escapades of Gritch the Witch, who thinks she should always get exactly what she wants.

> 🎖*Piggie Pie.* New York: Clarion, 1995. Unpaged. ISBN 9780395716915.
>
> > Gritch the Witch knows just what she wants to eat, Piggie Pie. The trouble is, she needs eight plump piggies, and she has none. So she hops on her broomstick and zooms over to Old MacDonald's farm. But the piggies have spotted her and don a series of disguises so that even though she looks here and there and threatens the animals she finds with her most evil spell, she can't find any piggies. She is almost ready to give up when a rather battered wolf proposes a new plan. An amusing tale that is perfect for reading aloud. (ALAN)

Zoom Broom. New York: Hyperion, 1998. Unpaged. ISBN 9780786814671 (pb).

> This time, Gritch yearns for Rabbit Rye, but when she soars into the air on her trusty broom, it sputters and dies. After she picks herself up from her crash landing, Gritch heads over to Foxy's to negotiate for a new means of transportation.

Broom Mates. New York: Hyperion, 2003. 32pp. ISBN 9780786804184 (o.p.).

> Gritch is exhausted from all the preparations for her Howliday party, so she's not at all pleased to be woken up in the middle of the night by her sister, Mag the Hag, who has arrived a day early. The sisters bicker throughout the day, engaging in a spell-casting match and a cooking contest, until their "mummy" arrives and sets things to rights.

Gone with the Wand. **Illustrated by Brian Ahjar. New York: Orchard, 2009. 40pp. ISBN 9780439727686.** `Gr. K–3`

> Bernice Sparklestein was once the best fairy godmother in the business, but today she is having a very bad wand day. With every wave she creates chaos. In desperation she turns to her friend, Edith Molarnari, the tooth fairy, for help sorting out her magical messes.

Pearce, Philippa.

The Squirrel Wife. **Illustrated by Wayne Anderson. Cambridge, MA: Candlewick, 2007. 32pp. ISBN 9780763635510.** `Gr. 1–3`

> Jack, a pig-keeper, goes against his brother's wishes and ventures into the night-darkened forest when he hears a cry for help. His reward for aiding one of the "green people" is a ring that transforms a squirrel into a woman who is wise in the ways of the woods and who agrees to become Jack's wife. The couple is content until Jack's evil brother plots against them, and they must find a way to save each other.

Plourde, Lynn.

Grandpappy Snippy Snappies. See in chapter 14.

Ray, Jane.

The Apple-Pip Princess. **Cambridge, MA: Candlewick, 2008. 32pp. ISBN 9780763637477.** `Gr. 1–3`

> Shortly before her untimely death, the queen had each of her three daughters choose a magical treasure. Now, several years later, the kingdom is in desperate need of rejuvenation. The king gives the princesses a week to do something he can be proud of that will help him decide who will rule after him. Each daughter uses her treasure, but it is the youngest, who plants an apple-pip, who finds success. Gold-embellished illustrations add majesty to this lyrical, original fairy tale.

Reed, Neil.

The Midnight Unicorn. New York: Sterling, 2006. 36pp. ISBN 9781402732188. **Gr. K–2**

Millie, a young unicorn-lover, frequently visits a statue of a unicorn in the park. On one such visit, the statue comes to life and takes Millie for a glorious ride across the globe.

Root, Phyllis.

Lucia and the Light. Illustrated by Mary GrandPreì. Cambridge, MA: Candlewick, 2006. 40pp. ISBN 9780763622961. **Gr. 1–3**

In a little lonely cabin in the Far North live Lucia, her mother, and her baby brother. Outside the wind whips around, swirling the constantly falling snow. Inside the family is running out of food. Then comes the day when darkness dominates the winter sky. Lucia decides to brave the dastardly trolls who have hidden the sun and does everything in her power to restore light to the world.

Slater, Dashka.

The Sea Serpent and Me. Illustrated by Catia Chien. Boston: Houghton Mifflin, 2008. 38pp. ISBN 9780618723942. **PreS–2**

An imaginative and engaging story of friendship between a young girl and a baby sea monster who slips out of the faucet and into her bathtub one evening during bath time. The two frolic in the tub and become fast friends, but the sea serpent quickly outgrows the aquarium. When the girl learns that he longs to return to the ocean, they begin their trek to the shore together.

Smith, Linda.

🏵*Mrs. Biddlebox.* Illustrated by Marla Frazee. Orlando, FL: Harcourt, 2007. 28pp. ISBN 9780152063498. **Gr. 1–3**

Mrs. Biddlebox definitely wakes up on the wrong side of the bed, but she refuses to remain in a funk. She twirls all the ingredients of gloom around on her broomstick, adds a pinch of baking magic, and produces a sweet cake that turns a ho-hum day into a glorious night. (Golden Kite Award)

Sperring, Mark.

Wanda's First Day. Illustrated by Kate Pope and Liz Pope. New York: Scholastic, 2004. 32pp. ISBN 9780439627733. **PreS–1**

Wanda, a young witch, arrives atop her broomstick for her first day of school and realizes that something is not quite right. While she wears a black hat and dress, her winged classmates wear candy-colored dresses and use magic wands. She suggest to her teacher that as a witch in a group of fairies, she might be in the wrong class, but Miss Dewdrop assures her that as long as she is enjoying herself, she's in the right place.

Steig, William.

❦*Sylvester and the Magic Pebble*. New York: HarperCollins, 2005. 42pp. ISBN 9781416902065. Gr. K–3

This edition of the classic story has newly enhanced illustrations. Sylvester the donkey loves collecting pebbles. Just as he finds a magic pebble that grants wishes, he is scared by a lion and wishes to become a rock so that he will be safe. His wish comes true, but now he is no longer touching the magic pebble and must figure out a way to regain his true form. (Caldecott Medal)

The One and Only Shrek: Plus 5 Other Stories. New York: Square Fish/Farrar Straus & Giroux, 2007. 196pp. ISBN 9780312367138. Gr. K–3

Although the original single edition of *Shrek* is out of print, the story of the ogre seeking true love is featured in this collection along with "The Amazing Bone," "Brave Irene," "Spinky Sulks," "Doctor De Soto," and" Caleb & Kate," as well as an introduction by Eric Carle.

Thomas, Shelley Moore.

Take Care, Good Knight. Illustrated by Paul Meisel. New York: Dutton, 2006. 32pp. ISBN 9780525476955. Gr. K–3

The Good Knight and his dragon friends from the easy reader series are featured here in picture book format. The three dragons are watching the wizard's cats while he's away, but their inability to read means they make a mess of following the wizard's written instructions. Fortunately the Good Knight knows just what to do to set things to rights.

A Cold Winter's Knight. Illustrated by Jennifer Plecas. New York: Dutton, 2008. 32pp. ISBN 9780525479642. Sequel. Gr. K–3

The three young dragons sit shivering in their cave until the Good Knight comes to their rescue and brings them to the castle. He tells them they can come to the ball if they promise to behave. They promise quickly, but dragons will be dragons, and soon they need the Good Knight to rescue them once again.

Yarrow, Peter, and Lenny Lipton.

Puff, the Magic Dragon. Illustrated by Eric Puybaret. New York: Sterling, 2007. 24pp. ISBN 9781402747823. PreS–3

The lyrics of the famous Peter, Paul, and Mary song make a beautiful picture book. Puybaret's lush acrylic-on-linen paintings depict the magic dragon and little Jackie Paper on their various adventures and provide a happy ending to the story. A CD with Peter Yarrow and his daughter singing the title song and three others is included.

Yolen, Jane.

Come to the Fairies' Ball. Illustrated by Gary Lippincott. Honesdale, PA: Wordsong, 2009. Unpaged. ISBN 9781590784648. `Gr. K–3`

> All the fairies in the realm are excited by their invitations to the king's ball, except one young sprite that only has tattered garb to wear. With assistance from some good-willed ants and special attention from the prince, the fairy attends after all, in beautiful attire. Lavishly illustrated in sumptuous watercolors.

Magic and Fantasy: Easy Readers

Loehr, Mallory.

Dragon Egg. Illustrated by Hala Wittwer. New York: Random House, 2007. 32pp. ISBN 9780375943508 (lb). `Gr. K–1`

> When a dragon egg rolls away from its mother, one villager after another follows it until the baby dragon hatches. Suddenly, it's the dragon chasing the villagers until it soars home to Mama.

Roberts, Bethany.

May Belle and the Ogre. Illustrated by Marsha Winborn. New York: Dutton Children's Books, 2003. 47pp. ISBN 9780525468554 (o.p.). `Gr. K–2`

> May Belle is set to enjoy a summer day, when an ogre arrives. May Belle is afraid at first, but then she finds a way to befriend him.

Ogre Eats Everything. Illustrated by Marsha Winborn. New York: Dutton, 2004. 46pp. ISBN 9780525472919. Sequel. `Gr. K–2`

> When May Belle's friend Ogre gets hungry and bored, it's up to her to find ways to entertain him.

Thomas, Shelley Moore.

The Good Knight Series. Illustrated by Jennifer Plecas. `Gr. K–2`

> These stories about the adventures of a kindhearted knight and three young dragons are easy readers, but the two newest in the series are picture books.

Good Night, Good Knight. New York: Dutton, 2000. 47pp. ISBN 9780525463269.

> When the Good Knight hears a very loud roar, he mounts his trusty steed and rides out to investigate. He finds three young dragons who aren't quite ready for bed yet.

Get Well, Good Knight. New York: Dutton, 2002. 44pp. ISBN 9780525469148.

> The three dragons all have colds, so the Good Knight seeks a cure from a wizard, but in the end, nothing works as well as Mom's home remedy.

Happy Birthday, Good Knight. New York: Dutton, 2006. 48pp. ISBN 978-0525471844.

> It's the Good Knight's birthday, and his three dragon friends want to have a very special party for him, but nothing goes quite as planned.

Fractured Fairy Tales and Nursery Rhymes

The picture books in this section were inspired by well-known tales and characters, but the authors and illustrators have added a twist or two of their own to spin the stories in a new direction.

Ahlberg, Allan.

Previously. **Illustrated by Bruce Ingman. Cambridge, MA: Candlewick, 2007. 28pp. ISBN 9780763635428.** `PreS–2`

Ahlberg links a series of fairy tale and nursery rhyme characters through a story that follows events backward.

Auch, Mary Jane.

The Princess and the Pizza. **Illustrated by Herm Auch. New York: Holiday House, 2002. 32pp. ISBN 9780823416837.** `Gr. 1–3`

Princess Paulina enters a competition to win the hand of Prince Rupert in marriage. She passes the pea and glass-slipper tests without difficulty. There are only three ladies left by the time of the last trial. Whipping together a delicious pizza with some handy ingredients, Paulina wins the culinary phase and thus the competition, but instead of marrying the prince, she opens her own pizza parlor.

Chickerella. **Illustrated by Herm Auch. New York: Holiday House, 2005. 32pp. ISBN 9780823418046.** `Gr. 1–3`

Chickerella's life gets grim when a fox makes a meal of her mother and her stepmother moves into the hen house. Chickerella longs to attend the Fowl Ball because she is desperate to see all the lovely gowns. Her stepmother forbids it, but her Fairy Goosemother sends her along, to a happy ending that's perfect for Chickerella, though far from traditional in this fun-filled, eggstatic take on the tale.

Bar-El, Dan.

Such a Prince. **Illustrated by John Manders. New York: Clarion, 2007. 32pp. ISBN 9780618714681.** `Gr. K–3`

In this humorous variation of a French tale called "Three Perfect Peaches," fast-talking fairy Libby Gaborchik informs the ill Princess Vera that to recover she must eat three perfect peaches and marry within the week. Prospective grooms near and far gather their fruit and head toward the castle. Libby helps deter the less suitable candidates and lends her aid to the kind-hearted Marvin.

Bloom, Becky.

Wolf! **Illustrated by Pascal Biet. New York: Orchard, 1999. Unpaged. ISBN 9780531301555.** `PreS–2`

A weary wolf has no luck procuring a meal in the manner of traditional big bad wolves, for all of his intended targets—a duck, a pig, and a cow—are too engrossed in reading. But when wolf learns to read and begins reading aloud to the group, the animals become fast friends.

Buehner, Caralyn.

🎋*Fanny's Dream*. **Illustrated by Mark Buehner. New York: Dial, 1996. Unpaged. ISBN 9780803714960.** `Gr. K–3`

Fanny Agnes, a sturdy farm girl, dreams of marrying a prince and is convinced that her fairy godmother will work everything out. On the night of the mayor's ball, Fanny waits in the garden. No godmother, fairy or otherwise, arrives, but Heber Jensen does. He's plain but nice, and Fanny decides to give up on her fairy godmother and marry Heber.

Many years later, after the two have built a fulfilling life together, Fanny's fairy godmother finally arrives, bursting with apologies and offering Fanny a second chance. Fanny, realizing she has everything she ever wanted, turns her down. The ingenious and comic illustrations are a perfect match to the delightful text, and together they make this "Cinderella" variant a true treat. (ALAN, Boston Globe Honor)

Catalanotto, Peter.

Ivan the Terrier. **New York: Atheneum, 2007. 30pp. ISBN 9781416912477.** `PreS–1`

The narrator tries to tell four tradition tales, "The Three Billy Goats," "The Three Bears," "The Three Little Pigs" and "The Gingerbread Boy," and each time is interrupted by the energetic Ivan, a terrier who wants to have the central role in each story.

Christelow, Eileen.

Where's the Big Bad Wolf? **New York: Clarion Books, 2002. 33pp. ISBN 9780618181940.** `Gr. 1–3`

Three little pigs are having trouble keeping their houses upright. They keep getting blown down, until one finally builds a brick house. Detective Doggedly, a canine police officer, investigates, sure it's the BBW, but the Big Bad Wolf appears to be in the hospital. Instead there's a strange sheep named Esmeralda that might be the culprit. Pen-and-ink and gouache cartoons, along with dialogue balloons, add to the fun of this lively whodunit.

Edwards, Pamela Duncan.

Dinorella: A Prehistoric Fairytale. **Illustrated by Henry Cole. New York: Hyperion, 1997. Unpaged. ISBN 9780786803095.** `Gr. 1–3`

With an amazing amount of alliteration, Edwards delineates a dino Cinderella set in a cross between prehistory and the 1950s. Dinorella, a pink Apatosaurus, has two horrid sisters, but her life improves when her Fairydactyl sends her to the party at Duke Dudley's Den.

Egielski, Richard.

The Gingerbread Boy. New York: Laura Geringer Book, 1997. Unpaged. ISBN 9780060260309. `PreS–3`

> This gingerbread boy comes to life as he pops out of an oven somewhere in Lower Manhattan. As he flees from the little old woman and the little old man, he dashes around the streets of New York City and is followed by a rat, subway musicians, and other denizens of the Big Apple. He is finally outfoxed when he reaches a lake in Central Park. The detailed illustrations perfectly evoke the cityscape.

Ernst, Lisa Campbell.

The Gingerbread Girl. New York: Dutton, 2006. 32pp. ISBN 9780525476672. `PreS–2`

> The little old woman and little old man who baked the original gingerbread boy decide to try again, this time with a girl. They decorate her with colorful candies, including liquorish-whip hair. Much to their dismay, she runs away as well, and the traditional chase ensues, but when she needs a ride from the fox, the gingerbread girl is determined not to end up like her brother and proves that she is one smart cookie.

Grey, Mini.

🌷 *The Adventures of the Dish and the Spoon*. New York: Knopf, 2006. 32pp. ISBN 9780375836916. `Gr. 1–3`

> The Dish and the Spoon can't resist dancing when they hear their nursery rhyme and run away together to New York City, where they become instant stars. As time passes, their popularity wanes. They end up separated for twenty-five years, but when they're reunited in a junk shop, the possibilities seem endless. (ALAN, Kate Greenaway Medal)

Hale, Bruce.

Snoring Beauty. Illustrated by Howard Fine. Orlando, FL: Harcourt, 2008. 32pp. ISBN 9780152163143. `Gr. 2 & up`

> When the infant princess is doomed to death by pie wagon, a hard-of-hearing fairy modifies the curse so that at the age of sixteen she will turn into a dragon that can only be awakened by a quince. Although King Gluteus bans pie wagons of all kinds, the fateful day arrives, and when a pie wagon rolls over the princess's foot, she is transformed into a dragon, one who snores quite loudly, and only Prince Quince can restore her. Fine's double-page watercolor paintings contribute greatly to the hilarity of the tale.

Hughes, Shirley.

Ella's Big Chance: A Jazz-Age Cinderella. New York: Simon & Schuster, 2004. Unpaged. ISBN 9780689873997. `PreS–3`

> With glittering and stylish ink and gouache art, Hughes sets her "Cinderella" in the roaring twenties and clothes her characters in chic

flapper dresses. Ella Cinders and her father create these stylish garments and thoroughly enjoy each other's company. Everything changes when Mr. Cinders's second wife and her two daughters take over Ella's once happy home. Ella's cruel stepsisters make her dread each day, until her Fairy Godmother arrives, attires her appropriately, and whisks her away to the Duke's ball. Ella captures the Duke's affections, but Ella's heart leads her elsewhere, providing a surprise ending. (Kate Greenaway Award)

Isaacs, Anne.

Pancakes for Supper. **Illustrated by Mark Teague. New York: Scholastic Press, 2006. 40pp. ISBN 9780439644839.** PreS–3

Inspired by Helen Bannerman's *The Story of Little Black Sambo*, Isaacs uses the tone of an American tall tale to chronicle the adventures of a plucky New England girl who outwits a bevy of beasts who want to steal her fine clothing. The animals end up chasing each other around a tree so fast they turn to butter. The tree drinks it up and produces maple syrup so sweet that it's time for pancakes all around.

Krensky, Stephen.

Big Bad Wolves at School. **Illustrated by Brad Sneed. New York: Simon & Schuster, 2007. 29pp. ISBN 9780689837999.** Gr. K–3

Rufus, a young wolf, enjoys lounging in the meadow and howling at the moon. His parents are afraid that he'll never make it in the rough-and-tumble wolf world, so they send him to the Big Bad Wolf Academy. Rufus studies huffing and puffing, creating clever disguises, and how to speak sheep as a foreign language. Rufus would rather wander than prepare for his exams, so he's in exactly the right place to sound the alarm when hunters come to call.

Levine, Gail Carson.

*Betsy Who Cried Wolf. **Illustrated by Scott Nash. New York: HarperCollins, 2002. Unpaged. ISBN 9780060287641 (pb).** Gr. K–3

When Betsy finishes Shepherd School, she is determined to be the best shepherd ever. Zimmo, the only wolf left on the mountain, is hungry and crafty. He appears to Betsy and she blows her whistle, but he has disappeared by the time the villagers arrive. It's all part of his plan. By the third time, the villagers no longer come running, but Betsy will not abandon her charges. Realizing that Zimmo is hungry, she offers to share her lunch with him, beginning a long-lasting friendship between the two.

Betsy Red Hoodie. **Illustrated by Scott Nash. New York: HarperCollins, 2010. 40pp. ISBN 9780061468704. Sequel.** Gr. K–3

Betsy dons a red hoodie and invites her friend Zimmo the wolf to go with her with their flock of sheep to Grandma's, She has no idea of the surprise waiting for her.

Meddaugh, Susan.

Cinderella's Rat. **Boston: Houghton Mifflin, 1997. 32pp. ISBN 978-0395868331.** `Gr. K-3`

When the rat is turned into a coach boy, he delivers Cinderella to the ball and then makes his way to the kitchens, because food is scarce for rats. His sister, who is still a rat, follows her nose to him and is almost killed by the kitchen boy. The coach boy exclaims that the rat is his sister and the kitchen boy sends them to a wizard to have the spell taken off her. The wizard bungles the job, but gives the rat family an unusual happy ending.

Morgan, Mary.

Dragon Pizzeria. **New York: Knopf, 2008. Unpaged. ISBN 9780375823091.** `PreS-3`

Dragons BeBop and Spike decide their talents are uniquely suited for opening a pizzeria in Fairy Tale land. They cater to their magical clientele, creating special pies for each customer, such as a gingerbread pie for Hansel and Gretel and porridge pies for the three bears.

Osborne, Mary Pope.

The Brave Little Seamstress. **Illustrated by Giselle Potter. New York: Atheneum, 2002. Unpaged. ISBN 9780689844867.** `Gr. K-3`

When a clever seamstress kills seven flies in one blow, she embroiders the feat on her cloak and goes out in the world to seek her fortune. Although the phrase is repeatedly misunderstood, the seamstress outwits each adversary, even the king.

Palatini, Margie.

Earthquack. **Illustrated by Barry Moser. New York: Simon & Schuster, 2002. Unpaged. ISBN 9780689842801.** `PreS-1`

When Chucky Ducky feels the ground shaking beneath his feet, he races off to warn the skeptical animals on the farm of the purported impending earthquake.

The Three Silly Billies. **Illustrated by Barry Moser. New York: Simon & Schuster, 2005. Unpaged. ISBN 9780689858628.** `Gr. K-3`

This modern version of *The Three Billy Goats Gruff,* pits a hard-hatted, toll-collecting troll against three Billies and their friends, the Three Bears, Little Red Riding Hood, and Jack.

The Bad Boys Series. Illustrated by Henry Cole. `Gr. K-3`

Each hilarious tale in the series recounts the pun-filled adventures of a pair of wolves, Willy and Wally, who are trying their best to be Big and Bad.

Bad Boys. **New York: Katherine Tegen Books, 2003. Unpaged. ISBN 9780060001025.**

Wolves Wally and Willy are on the run from Little Red Riding Hood and the Three Little Pigs, so they decide to hide amid a herd of ewes, disguised as Willamina and Wallanda, Bo-Peep's lost sheep.

Bad Boys Get Cookie. New York: Katherine Tegen Books, 2006. 32pp. ISBN 9780060744366.

> Willy and Wally spot a runaway gingerbread cookie and decide they're in the mood for a treat, but when they can't outfox him, they try to lure him to his demise by dressing as Hansel and Gretel.

Bad Boys Get Henpecked! New York: Katherine Tegen Books, 2009. 32pp. ISBN 9780060744335.

> The Big Bad wolf pals return, plotting to catch a chicken dinner by disguising themselves as handymen for a hen house.

Root, Phyllis.

Paula Bunyan. **Illustrated by Kevin O'Malley. New York: Farrar, Straus & Giroux, 2009. 32pp. ISBN 9780374357597.** `Gr. 1-3`

> Paul Bunyan's younger sister Paula embarks on adventures of her own, including singing three-part harmony with wolves, using an angry bear as a foot warmer, and becoming a caretaker of the wild.

Scieszka, Jon.

❦*The True Story of the 3 Little Pigs.* **Illustrated by Lane Smith. New York: Viking, 1989. 32pp. ISBN 9780670827596.** `PreS-3`

> Alexander T. Wolf tells how he was just searching for a neighbor to lend him a cup of sugar for his dear old granny's birthday cake when he accidently blew down the houses of two little pigs and was caught banging on the door of the third little pig's brick house. Deliciously droll. (ALAN)

❦*The Frog Prince, Continued.* **Illustrated by Steve Johnson. New York: Viking, 1991. 32pp. ISBN 9780670834211.** `Gr. K-3`

> Despite the fact that his books say he and the princess lived happily ever after, the Frog Prince is not at all happy. When he gets the idea that turning back into a frog will solve his problems, he enters the enchanted forest in search of a witch to change him back. He meets one witch after another, until he decides maybe this wasn't the best idea after all. The dark illustrations are filled with clever clues as to which fairy tale the witches are from, and they add to the tongue-in-cheek humor. (ALAN)

❦*The Stinky Cheese Man and Other Fairly Stupid Tales.* **Illustrated by Lane Smith. New York: Viking, 1993. Unpaged. ISBN 9780670844876.** `Gr. 2 & up`

> A wisecracking Jack narrates nine fractured fairy tales with text and illustrations that are drenched with humor. (ALAN, BBYA, Caldecott Honor)

Stanley, Diane.

❦*Rumpelstiltskin's Daughter.* **New York: Morrow, 1997. Unpaged. ISBN 9780688143275.** `Gr. 2 & up`

> Here, the miller's daughter married Rumpelstiltskin instead of the king, and the two raised a beautiful daughter. They send her out into the world when she is sixteen. When she meets the same greedy king, he thinks she can also make gold. He

imprisons her as he did her mother, but this clever girl outwits the king and helps her country at the same time. (ALAN)

Goldie and the Three Bears. New York: HarperCollins, 2003. Unpaged. ISBN 9780060000080. **PresS–2**

9

Goldie likes to have everything just right, but she realizes that what's she's missing is a just right friend. All of that changes when she gets off the bus at the wrong stop and wanders into a house at the end of the path.

The Giant and the Beanstalk. New York: HarperCollins, 2004. Unpaged. ISBN 9780060000103. **Gr. 1–3**

10

Although his friends tease him for doing poorly in his curses and threats classes and for choosing a pet hen over a pet dragon, Otto continues to be a gentle giant. When the boy Jack steals his beloved hen, Otto overcomes his fear of heights to climb down the beanstalk to search for Jack. He finds many nursery rhyme Jacks and learns that the one he is looking for stole his hen so he could buy back his beloved cow. When he finally finds the right Jack, together they work out a way to get back their own pets.

11

The Trouble with Wishes. New York: HarperCollins, 2007. 32pp. ISBN 9780060554521 (pb). **Gr. 1–3**

Inspired by the Greek myth of Pygmalion, this version presents the sculptor Pyg, who falls in love with his masterpiece, a beautiful woman sculpted of marble. She comes to life and steps off her pedestal, but she turns out to be vain, shallow, and mean-spirited.

12

Stevens, Janet, and Susan Stevens Crummel.

Cook-a-Doodle-Doo. Illustrated by Janet Stevens. San Diego: Harcourt, 1999. Unpaged. ISBN 9780152019242. **PreS–2**

13

The Little Red Hen's great grandson, the Big Brown Rooster, yearns for something delicious to eat, so he and his barnyard friends concoct a strawberry shortcake.

🌹*And the Dish Ran Away with the Spoon.* Illustrated by Janet Stevens. San Diego: Harcourt, 2001. Unpaged. ISBN 9780152022983. **Gr. 1–3**

14

When the Dish and Spoon run away and don't return, their friends, the cat, the cow, and the dog, go out searching for them. (ALAN)

Wiesner, David.

🌹*The Three Pigs.* New York: Clarion, 2001. 32pp. ISBN 9780618007011. **Gr. K–3**

15

In this visually stunning masterpiece, the Three Little Pigs not only have their houses blown down by the Big Bad Wolf, they are blown right out of their traditional story and into the pages of a completely different book. (ALAN, Caldecott Medal)

Wilcox, Leah.

Falling for Rapunzel. **Illustrated by Lydia Monks. New York: Putnam, 2003. Unpaged. ISBN 9780399237942.** `Gr. K–3`

> In this spoof, Rapunzel is having a bad hair day, and when Prince Charming comes to save her, she keeps mishearing him. When he calls for her to let down her hair, she throws down some underwear. He keeps calling, and she keeps tossing down the wrong thing. When he at last asks for her braid, she sends down her maid. The prince and the maid fall madly in love and ride off happily ever after.

Waking Beauty. **Illustrated by Lydia Monks. New York: Putnam, 2008. 32pp. ISBN 9780399246159.** `Gr. K–3`

> Prince Charming wanders by a castle and hears a very strange sound. Assuming it's a wild animal of some kind, he burst into the room only to find a sleeping and snoring princess. He tries everything he can think of to wake her, including jumping on the bed and firing her out of a cannon, until the fairies finally inform him that what he has to do is wake her with a kiss.

Willey, Margaret.

The 3 Bears and Goldilocks. **Illustrated by Heather M. Solomon. New York: Atheneum, 2008. 40pp. ISBN 9781416924944.** `PreS–3`

> In this Goldilocks tale, set in the Far North, Goldilocks not only tries the bears' furniture and food, she also straightens up as she goes. The bears don't appreciate the way she has rearranged things, but they feel sorry for her because she has no fur, claws, or sharp teeth.

Folk and Fairy Tales

Folk and fairy tales are the most well-known of the magical stories shared with children. They are stories from the oral traditions of cultures across the globe. Many of them are archetypal, with versions of the same story occurring in different cultures. Originally they were stories told to adults. Many have been passed down through generations. Generally, a folktale is a story from oral tradition, centering around everyday people—folk. Usually something mysterious happens, although not necessarily something magical. Fairy tales often have fairies in them, although not always. They center around royalty and they often have magic in them. The Library of Congress also includes tall tales and legends in their broad number 398.2 for these kinds of stories. Authors and illustrators have been retelling and illustrating these tales for children for generations, and children still love to hear them and read them on their own. For purposes of clarity, we will follow the Library of Congress: if the reteller is listed as the author there, he or she will be listed so here. If the Library of Congress credits the original collector (e.g., the Brothers Grimm), then so will we. Generally the Library of Congress lists the reteller as author if it deems the text has been altered substantially.

Artell, Mike.

Petite Rouge: A Cajun Red Riding Hood. Illustrated by Jim Harris. New York: Dial, 2001. Unpaged. ISBN 9780803725140. **Gr. K–3**

> When Petite Rouge, a young duck, sets out across the Louisiana swamp with a basket of goodies for her grandmother, her mother warns her to be careful for "de swamp's fulla gators." Sure enough, instead of Grand-mere, Petite Rouge and her clever cat come across Ol' Claude the alligator. Together the duck and the cat must outwit the gator or they will be his next meal.

The Three Little Cajun Pigs. Illustrated by Jim Harris. New York: Dial, 2006. 32pp. ISBN 9780803728158. **Gr. K–3**

> In this Cajun version of the familiar tale, three pigs named Trosclair, Thibodeaux, and Ulysse match wits with their nemesis, Ol' Claude, the alligator.

Aylesworth, Jim.

🎄*The Gingerbread Man.* Illustrated by Barbara McClintock. New York: Scholastic, 1998. Unpaged. ISBN 9780590972192. **PresS–2**

> This is an excellent retelling of the rebellious cookie that gets his comeuppance in the end. Inspired by French illustrator Grandville, McClintock's illustrations give the story a nineteenth-century setting. (New York Times Best Illustrated)

Goldilocks and the Three Bears. Illustrated by Barbara McClintock. New York: Scholastic, 2003. 32pp. ISBN 9780439395458. **PreS–2**

> Aylesworth gives this traditional tale a folksy feel with his rhythmic retelling, concentrating on Goldilocks as a spunky heroine who is more curious than wicked as she investigates the bears' domain. McClintock's watercolor, sepia ink, and gouache illustrations bring the tale to life with humor and flourish.

Brett, Jan.

Goldilocks and the Three Bears. New York: Dodd, Mead, 1987. 32pp. ISBN 9780399220333. **PreS–3**

> Brett employs Eastern European motifs in the borders of her luxuriantly illustrated version of this classic tale. Giving her bears festive Bavarian garb, she adds many details in the artwork depicting the story of the intrepid Goldilocks.

Beauty and the Beast. New York: Clarion, 1989. 30pp. ISBN 9780899194974. **Gr. K–3**

> Brett's sumptuous retelling of the classic love story between a beautiful young woman and her beast is set in eighteenth-century France with luscious illustrations that make the book beautiful and the emotions of the characters real.

The Mitten: A Ukrainian Folktale. New York: Putnam, 1989. 32pp. ISBN 9780399219207. `PreS–2`

> When Nicki drops one of his beautiful white mittens, knitted for him by his grandmother, in the snow, a series of animals move in to stay warm. Gorgeously illustrated, with special pictures painted into the intricate borders.

The Town Mouse and the Country Mouse. New York: Putnam, 1994. Unpaged. ISBN 9780399226229. `PreS–2`

> A country mouse couple and their town counterparts meet on a picnic, each thinking they pine for the life of the other. They decide to switch places, but ultimately discover that there's really no place like home. Rich, detailed artwork adds depth and humor to this fable.

Gingerbread Baby. New York: Putnam, 1999. 32pp. ISBN 9780399234446. `PreS–2`

> Brett sets her version of "The Gingerbread Boy" in lush paintings with characters of warm tones against a snow-white background. This Gingerbread Baby leads everyone on a merry chase, except one smart young man named Matti, who lures the sweet treat to a different fate. The meticulous borders show readers what Matti is doing while the Gingerbread Baby races from one place to another.

The Three Snow Bears. New York: Putnam, 2007. 30pp. ISBN 9780399247927. `PreS–3`

> Aloo-ki, a young Inuit girl, becomes separated from her team of huskies while she is out fishing and stumbles onto the igloo of three snow bears. Like Goldilocks in the woods, she samples the food and belongings before falling asleep. Meanwhile, the bears rescue her huskies and enable the girl and her dogs to be reunited. Side panels depict the actions of the bears in the rich, detailed watercolor and gouache illustrations that are Brett's signature style.

Casanova, Mary.

🕮*The Hunter: A Chinese Folktale.* Illustrated by Ed Young. New York: Atheneum, 2000. Unpaged. ISBN 9780689829062. `Gr. 2 & up`

> When hunter Hai Li Bu saves the life of a pearly snake, he is rewarded by the Dragon King of the Sea with the gift of understanding all animal languages. The only condition is that he must not tell anyone the secret of how he obtained this gift, or he will turn to stone. Disaster strikes when the animals warn Hai Li Bu of a coming flood, but the villagers will not evacuate because they don't believe him. He knows the only way to save them is to tell his story. As he does so, he turns to stone. (ALAN)

Diakité, Baba Wagué.

🕮*The Hunterman and the Crocodile: A West African Folktale.* New York: Scholastic, 1997. Unpaged. ISBN 9780590898287. `PreS–2`

> Bamba the crocodile and his family need the help of Donso the hunter to return to the river. The crocodile promises not to harm Donso, but halfway through goes back on his word and clamps Donso's hand in his powerful jaws. The hunter begs the other animals for help, but finds that they are not willing to due to the way humans have treated them. Only rabbit is willing to pitch in, but his tricksy help is enough. (ALAN, Coretta Scott King Honor)

🍎*The Hatseller and the Monkeys: A West African Folktale.* **New York: Scholastic, 1999. Unpaged. ISBN 9780590960694.** `Gr. K–3`

> This is a West African tale similar to Slobodkina's *Caps for Sale*. Like his father and his grandfather before him, BaMusa makes and sells hats and is known far and wide for his enthusiasm. One day, while he is napping under a mango tree, a troop of monkeys capture his hats, and a groggy BaMusa has to figure out how to get them back. (ALAN)

9

The Magic Gourd. **New York: Scholastic, 2003. 32pp. ISBN 9780439439602.** `Gr. 1–3`

> In this Malian version of a "magic pot" folktale, Chameleon gives Dogo Zan the rabbit a magic gourd to thank him for his help. The gourd fills with whatever Dogo Zan wishes. When King Mansa Jugu learns of the treasure, he steals it, but the clever Dogo Zan wins it back and teaches the king a lesson at the same time.

10

Mee-An and the Magic Serpent. **Toronto: Groundwood, 2007. 32pp. ISBN 9780888997197.** `Gr. K–3`

> Mee-An only wants to marry someone who is perfect, and her sister believes she has found just such a man, but it turns out that he is a serpent in disguise. The serpent has dire plans for the sisters, and they must seek the help of a black heron to escape.

11

Bruchac, Joseph, and James Bruchac.

12

Turtle's Race with Beaver: A Traditional Seneca Story. **Illustrated by Jose Aruego and Ariane Dewey. New York: Dial, 2003. 32pp. ISBN 978-0803728523.** `PreS–3`

> Turtle is quite content in his pond until Beaver moves in and makes all kinds of changes. Turtle proposes discussing the best way to share the pond, but instead Beaver challenges him to a race. Beaver is confident that he will win easily, but Turtle has a plan.

13

Raccoon's Last Race: A Traditional Abenaki Story. **Illustrated by Jose Aruego and Ariane Dewey. New York: Dial, 2004. 32pp. ISBN 978-0803729773.** `PreS–2`

> Azban the Raccoon, a prominent figure in Abenaki trickster tales, used to be sleek and strong, with long legs. He was so strong and fast that he would win every race. He arrogantly challenges Big Rock to a race downhill. When Azban trips, Big Rock rolls right over him, squashing him flat and winning the contest. No one will help him return to his former shape except for the ants. Unfortunately, Raccoon breaks his promise to be their friend before they are finished, and they leave him in the short, squat form known today.

14

15

Climo, Shirley.

The Egyptian Cinderella. **Illustrated by Ruth Heller. New York: Crowell, 1989. 32pp. ISBN 9780690048223.** `PreS–3`

> Rhodopis, a Greek slave girl in ancient Egypt, is teased by the other slave girls, but when her kind master gives her leather slippers with toes of rose-red gold, she is able to attract the attention of the pharaoh and eventually become queen.

The Korean Cinderella. **Illustrated by Ruth Heller. New York: HarperCollins, 1993. Unpaged. ISBN 9780060204327.** `PreS-3`

Pear Blossom's cruel stepmother piles one impossible task after another on her until a magic fish-tail enables her to win the affection of the magistrate.

The Little Red Ant and the Great Big Crumb: A Mexican Fable. **Illustrated by Francisco X. Mora. New York: Clarion, 1995. 38pp. ISBN 9780395707326.** `PreS-2`

When a little red ant finds a cake crumb that is too big for her to get home, she seeks help from increasingly bigger and stronger animals, until she finally realizes that she can do it after all.

The Irish Cinderlad. **Illustrated by Loretta Krupinski. New York: HarperCollins, 1996. Unpaged. ISBN 9780064435772 (pb).** `Gr. K-3`

Little Becan is not treated well by his stepmother and stepsisters, but his fortunes change when a magic bull leaves him his tail. With it, Becan is able to save Princess Finola from a dragon and win her heart.

The Persian Cinderella. **Illustrated by Robert Florczak. New York: HarperCollins, 1999. Unpaged. ISBN 9780060267636.** `Gr. K-3`

Settareh and her less-than-loving stepsisters go to the local bazaar to purchase cloth to make gowns for the upcoming New Year's celebration at the Royal Palace. Instead of getting the material she needs, Settareh gives her money to a woman in need and buys an unusual blue jug. In the jug is a pari, a fairy, who grants Settareh's wish for a gown. She captures the interest of the prince. When their courtship leads to a wedding day, her jealous stepsisters plot against her, and her prince must stay true to save her.

Tuko and the Birds. **Illustrated by Francisco X. Mora. New York: Henry Holt, 2008. Unpaged. ISBN 9780805065596.** `Gr. K-3`

The birds on the island of Luzon sing every night, letting the villagers know when it is time to go to sleep, until Tuko, an arrogant gecko, storms into their hut and keeps them awake each night. The birds are too weary to serenade the people, and the people become confused about when to sleep. Nothing the birds try convinces Tuko to leave, until the eagle concocts a successful plan.

Coburn, Jewell Reinhart.

Jouanah: A Hmong Cinderella. **With Tzexa Cherta Lee. Illustrated by Anne Sibley O'Brien. Arcadia, CA: Shen's Books, 1996. Unpaged. ISBN 978-1885008015.** `Gr. 2 & up`

To aid her family, Jouanah's mother voluntarily turns into a cow. Her father marries again, but the woman and her daughter are cruel and mean-spirited. Jouanah's mother dies of grief, and her father soon follows her. Jouanah is miserable until her mother's spirit arranges for her to wear an exquisite dress to the New Year's celebration, where she meets and falls in love with the son of the village elder.

Domitila: A Cinderella Tale from the Mexican Tradition. **Illustrated by Connie McLennan. Auburn, CA: Shen's Books, 2000. Unpaged. ISBN 9781885008138.** `Gr. 2 & up` **(SP)**

Domitila is a talented cook and leather worker who must seek employment at the governor's mansion to help her family. The governor's son, Timoteo, falls in love with her culinary concoctions, so when she is called home, he goes searching for her. Although Domitila's new stepmother plots to wed Timoteo to her own daughter, Timoteo realizes that he loves Domitila.

Coleen, Salley.

<u>**Epossumondas Series**</u>. **Illustrated by Janet Stevens.** `Gr. K-3`

Epossumondas, a diaper-wearing possum, is a noodlehead character who never gets his mother's instructions right.

*Epossumondas. San Diego: Harcourt, 2002. 40pp. ISBN 9780152167486.

Epossumondas mixes everything up, with hilarious results. Here, he carries butter on his head because that is how he was supposed to carry cake. He wraps a puppy in green leaves and cools it in the brook because that is what he was supposed to do with the butter. The illustrations are as amusing as the text.

Why Epossumondas Has No Hair on His Tail. Orlando, FL: Harcourt, 2004. 40pp. ISBN 9780152049355.

When Epossumondas wonders why his tail looks the way it does, his mama tells the story of Papapossum, who loved eating persimmons just a little too much. He climbed up into Bear's tree and kept eating persimmons even though Bear warned him over and over again to stop. Bear finally caught him by his tail and pulled, stripping the hair off Papapossum's tail and stretching it to its long and slender length all possums have to this day.

Epossumondas Saves the Day. Orlando, FL: Harcourt, 2006. 48pp. ISBN 9780152057015.

Mama wants to make some light and fluffy biscuits for Epossumundas's birthday, but she is out of sody sallyraytus (baking soda). Everyone who goes to the store for her runs into trouble when they meet a great, big Louisiana snapping turtle, and it is up to Epossumondas to come up with a plan that will get Mama her sody sallyraytus.

Epossumondas Plays Possum. Orlando, FL: Harcourt, 2009. 32pp. ISBN 9780152064204.

Although his mama warns him to never go into the swamp because loup-garou could steal him away, Epossumondas wanders into the forbidden area anyway. He plays possum to avoid being eaten by a variety of predators, but when a buzzard wants to make a meal of him, he is too ticklish to hold still, which chases the bird away.

Craft, Charlotte.

King Midas and the Golden Touch. **Illustrated by Kinuko Y. Craft. New York: Morrow, 1999. 32pp. ISBN 9780688131654.** `Gr. K-3`

This version is inspired by Nathaniel Hawthorne's retelling of the Greek story of the king whose touch turned everything to gold, including his daughter. This mother and daughter duo has created a sumptuous edition with lavish oil-over-watercolor paintings that evoke the Middle Ages.

Craft, Kinuko Y.

Cinderella. **New York: SeaStar Books, 2000. Unpaged. ISBN 9781587170041.** `Gr. K-3`

Adapted from Arthur Rackham's and Andrew Lang's versions, this retelling begins with Cinderella in the woods nursing a bluebird back to health. Later the bluebird transforms into the fairy godmother, who helps Cinderella along to her happy ending. Craft's ornate illustrations are reminiscent of the opulent styles of seventeenth- and eighteenth-century France, depicting luxurious clothing, woods full of flora and fauna, and elegant ballrooms.

Craft, Mahlon F.

Sleeping Beauty. **Illustrated by Kinuko Y. Craft. New York: SeaStar Books, 2002. Unpaged. ISBN 9781587171208.** `Gr. 1-3`

Craft builds on the Grimm version of the tale of a princess cursed by a vengeful fairy. The exquisite illustrations are oil-on-watercolor paintings, which portray an elegant fifteenth-century Europe.

Cummings, Pat.

Ananse and the Lizard: A West African Tale. **New York: Holt, 2002. 40pp. ISBN 9780805064766.** `Gr. K-2`

This tale from Ghana features a reversal of fortunes as the famous trickster spider gets tricked himself. When the Chief announces that anyone who can guess his daughter's name will be rewarded with half the kingdom and his daughter's hand in marriage, there are many would-be suitors. Then the Chief announces that the punishment for a wrong guess is beheading. Those previously eager to win withdraw, but not Ananse, who has overheard the girl's name. He is confident that he has won, until Lizard tricks the secret from him.

Daly, Niki.

Pretty Salma: A Little Red Riding Hood Story from Africa. **New York: Clarion, 2007. 29. ISBN 9780618723454.** `Gr. K-3` **(SP)**

Daly sets this version of the classic story in urban Ghana. A red-bedecked Salma is sent to market on an errand for her grandmother, but a wily Mr. Dog tricks her out of her costume. Disguised as Salma, he heads off to fool Grandmother. Far from helpless, Salma enlists the aid of her grandfather, and together they foil Mr. Dog's plans.

Dasent, George Webbe.

East O' the Sun and West O' the Moon. **Illustrated by Patrick James Lynch. Cambridge, MA: Candlewick, 2005. 48pp. ISBN 9781564020499.** `Gr. 3 & up`

In this reissue, Dasent's translation of a Norwegian folktale relates the adventures of an impoverished girl who becomes the guest of a bear to save her family. She grows to love the bear, but when she sees him for the prince he truly is, she unwittingly condemns him to marry the troll queen. Appalled at the consequences of her actions, she resolves to save her beloved.

Demi.

The Empty Pot. **New York: Holt, 1990. Unpaged. ISBN 9780805012170.** `Gr. 1–3`

When the Emperor of China begins a search for a successor, he gives a seed to each child, including Ping, a boy who can usually make anything grow. Despite his best efforts, Ping cannot get the seed to sprout. In despair, he is the only one to present the emperor with an empty pot. But unbeknownst to Ping, the emperor has cooked the seeds, so he knows that Ping is the only honest one, the only one deserving to win. Amazingly delicate landscapes in round frames depict Chinese architecture, foliage, native birds, and clothing in a breathtaking way.

King Midas: The Golden Touch. **New York: Margaret.K. McElderry Books, 2002. ISBN 9780689832970.** `Gr. 2 & up`

Gold-leaf accents appropriately decorate the illustrations of this retelling of the Greek tale of Midas, who is so obtuse he wishes that everything he touches would turn to gold, without realizing the dire consequences.

The Hungry Coat: A Tale from Turkey. **New York: Margaret K. McElderry Books, 2004. Unpaged. ISBN 9780689846809.** `Gr. K–3`

Nasrettin Hoca was a renowned thirteenth-century Turkish philosopher, and there are many folktales about him. Here, Demi retells the story of Nasrettin stopping to help recapture a wandering goat. He doesn't have time to change his coat, which is now smelly as well as patched. He attends a banquet at friend's house, but no one will speak to him. He goes home and returns in a new outfit, but instead of eating, he stuffs the food into his coat, telling his fellow guests that it's clear it was his coat that was invited to dinner.

dePaola, Tomie.

The Legend of the Blue Bonnet. **New York: Putnam, 1983. 30pp. ISBN 9780399209376.** `Gr. 1–3`

The Caldecott-winning artist retells a Comanche legend about a young girl whose sacrifice brings blue bonnets to Texas.

The Legend of the Indian Paintbrush. **New York: Putnam, 1988. 40pp. ISBN 9780399215346.** `Gr. 1–3`

Little Gopher was much smaller than the other boys in his Plains tribe, and although he tried as hard as he could, he could not ride, run, wrestle, or shoot with bows the way the big boys did. In a dream vision, he is informed that his talents lie in other directions. He becomes a great artist, but his colors never match what he imagines until he finds natural brushes filled with color and creates his greatest work, the flowers called Indian paintbrush.

Edwards, Pamela Duncan.

The Leprechaun's Gold. **Illustrated by Henry Cole. New York: Katherine Tegen Books, 2004. 40pp. ISBN 9780066239743.** `Gr. K–3`

The king of Ireland calls for a contest to determine the best harpist in the land. Young Tom is convinced that he should win, and he does everything he can to keep Old Pat from entering. All seems lost for Pat until he aids a needy leprechaun, who rewards him handsomely.

Eilenberg, Max.

Beauty and the Beast. **Illustrated by Angela Barrett. Cambridge, MA: Candlewick, 2006. 64pp. ISBN 9780763631604.** `Gr. 2 & up`

Barrett's finely wrought paintings create a nineteenth-century setting that is both sumptuous and romantic for this retelling of the classic story of Beauty, who takes her father's place with the Beast and learns to love him.

Cinderella. **Illustrated by Niamh Sharkey. Cambridge, MA: Candlewick, 2008. 48pp. ISBN 9780763638566.** `Gr. K–3`

Shimmering illustrations of pinks, blues, and purples create a whimsical Cinderella.

Forest, Heather.

The Little Red Hen: An Old Fable. **Illustrated by Susan Gaber. Little Rock, AR: August House, 2006. 32pp. ISBN 9780874837957.** `PreS–2`

This rhyming version of the story gives the lazy friends who would not help the Little Red Hen a second chance t o help out.

The Contest Between the Sun and the Wind: An Aesop's Fable. **Illustrated by Susan Gaber. Little Rock, AR: August House, 2008. 28pp. ISBN 9780874838329.** `Gr. K–3`

This verse retelling of an Aesop fable recounts the course of the contest between the Sun and the Wind, who challenge each other to get a passerby to remove his coat.

Geras, Adele.

Sleeping Beauty. **Illustrated by Christian Birmingham New York: Orchard, 2004. 64pp. ISBN 9780439581806.** `Gr. 1–3`

Geras embroiders Perrault's classic tale, filling in details and dialogue, while Birmingham's romantic illustrations enhance the fantasy elements of the story.

Goble, Paul.

🏵 *The Girl Who Loved Wil d Horses*. Rev. ed. New York: Atheneum, 2001. ISBN 9780689845048. `Gr. 1–3`

This Native American tale features a young girl who loves horses so much she would rather be with them than her tribe. (ALAN, Caldecott Medal)

Mystic Horse. New York: HarperCollins, 2003. Unpaged. ISBN 978-0060298135. `Gr. K–3`

In this Pawnee legend, a young boy and his grandmother are so poor they do not have a horse and must walk behind the tribe. When they come across a lame horse, the boy cares for it and brings it back to health. In return the horse gives the boy advice that helps him gain status in the tribe.

Hamilton, Virginia.

The Girl Who Spun Gold. Illustrated by Leo Dillon and Diane Dillon. New York: Blue Sky Press, 2000. Unpaged. ISBN 9780590473781. `Gr. K–3`

This West Indian–based version of "Rumpelstiltskin" tells the story of Quashiba. Her mother bragged to Big King that Quashiba could spin a field full of gold cloth. The king was taken by her beauty and his own greed, so he married her, but after a year and a day he locks her in a room and demands she spin gold. Help arrives in the form of Lit'mahn, a troll-like creature who will spin the gold for her, but she must guess his name by the third night or he will turn her into a troll-like creature as well. Hamilton's elegant style and the Dillons' magical illustrations make this version a standout edition.

The People Could Fly: The Picture Book. Illustrated by Leo Dillon and Diane Dillon. New York: Atheneum, 2004. 40pp. ISBN 9780375824050. `Gr. 3 & up`

According to legend, folk in Africa could fly, but they shed their wings when they were carried away in the slave ships. When a mother and her child are brutally beaten, an aged slave revives the magic and helps her fly away. Dramatic illustrations and vivid storytelling make this book both powerful and moving.

Hennessy, B. G.

*The Boy Who Cried Wolf. Illustrated by Boris Kulikov. New York: Simon & Schuster, 2006. 32pp. ISBN 9780689874338. `PreS–2`

Hennessy and Kulikov bring the Aesop's fable to life with the addition of catchy refrains, amusing dialogue, and expressive watercolor-and-gouache paintings. They tell the age-old story of the boy who cried wolf one too many times.

Hodges, Margaret.

🏵 *Saint George and the Dragon: A Golden Legend*. Illustrated by Trina Schart Hyman. Boston: Little, Brown, 1984. 32pp. ISBN 9780316367899. `Gr. 3 & up`

Hodges adapts an episode from Spenser's *The Faerie Queene*, in which George, the Red Cross Knight, seeks out the dragon that has been plaguing the countryside, causing chaos and terror for all in the area. Confronting the dragon, he engages in an epic battle and ultimately defeats him. Illustrated with Hyman's stunning paintings. (ALAN, Caldecott Medal, New York Times Best Illustrated)

The Kitchen Knight: A Tale of King Arthur. **Illustrated by Trina Schart Hyman. New York: Holiday House, 1990. 32pp. ISBN 9780823407873.** `Gr. 3 & up`

The story is of Gareth of Orkney, Gawaine's brother. To earn his place in King Arthur's court, Gareth hides his identity and serves for a year in Arthur's kitchens. When he is sent on a quest, it is to rescue the fair Linesse, whose sister also disguises herself and accompanies him. Illustrated with Hyman's lush watercolor paintings.

Dick Whittington and His Cat. **Illustrated by Mélisande Potter. New York: Holiday House, 2006. 32pp. ISBN 9780823419876.** `Gr. K–3`

Using a spare yet dramatic text, Hodges retells a tale of the legendary Lord Mayor of London. Dick Whittington began life as a poor orphan boy who made his way to London to make his fortune. With the help of his cat, he was able to withstand misfortune and grew to become one of the city's most famous leaders.

Hyman, Trina Schart.

🌸*Little Red Riding Hood.* **New York: Holiday House, 1983. 32pp. ISBN 9780823404704.** `Gr. K–3`

Hyman presents a smooth retelling of the red-hooded lass who wonders off the path, and illustrates it with her superb, signature paintings. (ALAN, Caldecott Honor, Golden Kite Award)

Isadora, Rachel.

The Princess and the Pea. **New York: Putnam, 2007. 30pp. ISBN 9780399246111.** `PreS–3`

Isadora recasts Andersen's classic tale, as that of a prince who is traveling through Africa in search of a true princess. He meets princesses from Ethiopia, Somalia, and Kenya, but none is the right princess. He turns home and a woman turns up claiming she is a princess. The skeptical queen has her sleep on mattresses piled on top of a pea. When she feels it, she convinces all she is a true princess.

The Twelve Dancing Princesses. **New York: Putnam, 2007. 32pp. ISBN 9780399247446.** `Gr. K–3`

Isadora transplants the Grimms' tale to an African kingdom and depicts princesses whose skin tones vary from dark tan to deep ebony, using oil paints, printed paper, and palette paper, showing princesses who are compelled to dance.

The Fisherman and His Wife. **New York: Putnam, 2008. 32pp. ISBN 9780399247712.** `Gr. K–3`

Placing the tale in a generic Africa, Isadora creates illustrations comprised of collages of paint-striated paper in tropical colors, plus occasional scraps of fabric, to accompany the tale of the fisherman and his greedy wife.

Rapunzel. New York: Putnam, 2008. Unpaged. ISBN 9780399247729. `Gr. K-3`

Isadora sets this tale in Africa and retells the story, depicting a brown-skinned girl with dreadlocks as Rapunzel, using colorful, textured collages.

Hansel and Gretel. New York: Putnam, 2009. 32pp. ISBN 9780399250286. `Gr. K-3`

Following the style in text and art of her previous fairy tale retellings, Isadora again places her shortened story in Africa.

Jaffe, Nina.

🌺*The Golden Flower: A Taino Myth from Puerto Rico.* Illustrated by Enrique O. Saìnchez. Houston: Piñata Books, 2005. 32pp. ISBN 9781558854529. (SP) `Gr. K-3`

Bilingual storyteller and author Jaffe relates a tale of how Puerto Rico came to be surrounded by water. In the beginning, it was a mountain surrounded by desert. When a child plants seeds around the mountaintop, they grow into a luscious forest, with one especially stupendous blossom. An amazingly large melon grows from the blossom, and the people do not know that it contains the sea, until two men who are fighting break it and the sea bursts forth. Sánchez's jewel-tone pastel artwork beautifully illustrates the tale, giving it the flavor of pre-Columbian art. (Pura Belpre Honor)

The Way Meat Loves Salt: A Cinderella Tale from the Jewish Tradition. Illustrated by Louise August. New York: Holt, 1998. 32pp. 9780805043846. `Gr. 1-3`

In this Yiddish tale, when a rabbi asks his three daughters how much they love him, his first two daughters answer as much as diamonds, silver, and gold, but his third daughter tells him that she loves him as much as meat loves salt. Disappointed by her answer, he banishes her, until he comes to realize what her answer truly means.

Ketteman, Helen.

Waynetta and the Cornstalk: A Texas Fairy Tale. Illustrated by Diane Greenseid. Morton Grove, IL: Albert Whitman, 2007. 30pp. ISBN 978-0807586877. `Gr. K-3`

This Wild West version of "Jack and the Beanstalk" features the adventures of Waynetta, who lives on a ranch with her Ma. When an exceedingly dry summer forces them to trade their last longhorn for magic corn, Waynetta plants it, hoping it will bring the luck they need. A giant cornstalk grows, and the spunky Wyanetta climbs it to face the giant and reclaim the treasures he stole from her family long ago.

The Three Little Gators. Illustrated by Will Terry. Morton Grove, IL: Albert Whitman, 2009. 32pp. ISBN 9780807578247. `Gr. K-3`

The story of "The Three Little Pigs" gets a Texas twist here as three little gators leave home and seek to make their place in the world. They each build their own kind of house in the east Texas swamp, hoping that their homes will help them elude the Big-bottomed Boar.

Kimmel, Eric A.

Three Samurai Cats: A Story from Japan. **Illustrated by Gerstein Mordicai. New York: Holiday House, 2003. ISBN 9780823417421.** `Gr. 1-3`

Kimmel retells a Zen parable about a feudal lord in ancient Japan who begs the abbot of the nearest monastery to send help in ridding his castle of a large and clever rat. The first two samurai cats cannot defeat the rat, but the last, a ragged feline, uses nonviolent means to trick the rat into leaving on its own. Gerstein's upbeat cartoon illustrations add another dimension of humor to the story.

The Castle of the Cats. **Illustrated by Katya Krenina. New York: Holiday House, 2004. ISBN 9780823415656.** `Gr. K-3`

In this Latvian folktale set in Ukraine, Ivan, the youngest son of a farmer, and his two brothers each set out to accomplish three tasks assigned by their father. When Ivan comes upon the castle of the cats, he discovers the queen of cats. With her assistance he is assured his place as heir, but he gives the farm to his brothers because he would rather stay with his bride, the queen herself.

Fisherman and the Turtle. **Illustrated by Martha Aviles. New York: Marshall Cavendish, 2008. 32pp. ISBN 9780761453871.** `Gr. K-3`

In this Aztec version of "The Fisherman and His Wife," when a fisherman snares a green sea turtle in his net, he discovers that the turtle is one of the seven sons of Opochtli, god of the sea. He offers to grant a wish for the fisherman if he will set him free. The fisherman wishes for four fish, but his wife is dissatisfied with this. She sends him back repeatedly, until her husband at lasts asks for what he really wants, and the turtle grants it.

Anansi Tales. **Illustrated by Janet Stevens.** `Gr. 1-3`

Anansi the Spider is a trickster character featured in many tales from different countries in Africa. Kimmel uses rhythmic language and amusing details to retell many of the traditional tales. Stevens's bright watercolor illustrations add subtle slyness and bold humor to the presentations.

Anansi and the Moss-Covered Rock. New York: Holiday House, 1988. 30pp. ISBN 9780823406890.

Anansi Goes Fishing. New York: Holiday House, 1992. Unpaged. ISBN 9780823409181.

**Anansi and the Talking Melon.* New York: Holiday House, 1994. Unpaged. ISBN 9780823411047.

Anansi and the Magic Stick. New York: Holiday House, 2001. Unpaged. ISBN 9780823414437.

Anansi's Party Time. New York: Holiday House, 2008. Unpaged. ISBN 978-0823419227.

Lesser, Rika.

🎗*Hansel and Gretel*. **Illustrated by Paul O. Zelinsky. New York: Dutton, 1999. Unpaged. ISBN 9780525461524.** `Gr. K–3`

Zelinisky's rich and dark paintings add foreboding to this tale of the brother and sister who are left in the woods and lured into the gingerbread house. (ALAN, Caldecott Honor)

Lester, Julius.

🎗*John Henry*. **Illustrated by Jerry Pinkney. New York: Dial, 1994. Unpaged. ISBN 9780803716063.** `Gr. K–3`

Lester adds his own flourishes to this tall tale of a figure from African American folk ballads. He tells of John Henry's accomplishments, from his childhood of building a new wing for a house before lunch, through the tale of how he beat the steam drill with his sledgehammer. He concludes with his death, which left onlookers with the knowledge that it's how he lived that was important. Pinkney's detailed watercolors imbue the story with life. (ALAN, Boston Globe Honor, Caldecott Honor)

Louie, Ai-Ling.

🎗*Yeh Shen: A Cinderella Story from China*. **Illustrated by Ed Young. New York: Putnam, 1982. 31pp. ISBN 9780399209000.** `Gr. 1–3`

Luminescent watercolors illustrate this story of a young girl defeating the nefarious plots of her evil stepmother and stepsisters. It is based on Chinese manuscripts that predate the European versions of "Cinderella." (ALAN, Boston Globe Honor)

Lyons, Mary E.

Roy Makes a Car. **Illustrated by Terry Widener. New York: Atheneum, 2005. 32pp. ISBN 9780689846403.** `Gr. 1–3`

Inspired by a Zora Neale Hurston tale, Lyons spins a story about Roy Tyle, an African American folk hero, who was such an outstanding mechanic that he built a flying car and then sold it to God.

MacDonald, Margaret Read.

*Fat Cat: A Danish Folktale. **Illustrated by Julie Paschkis. Little Rock, AR: August House, 2001. 32pp. ISBN 9780874836165.** `Gr. K–3`

This fat Cat eats everything in sight, even her friend Mouse. However, clever Mouse has been swallowed with a sewing kit, which she uses to free all the animals, then to stitch Cat back together.

Conejito: A Folktale from Panama. **Illustrated by Geraldo Valério. Little Rock, AR: August House, 2006. 32pp. ISBN 9780874837797.** `Gr. K–3`

Using a mix of Spanish and English, McDonald recounts the adventures of Conejito (Little Bunny), who skips off to the mountains to visit his Tia Monica. Along the way he encounters three creatures who want to eat him, but he tells them all to wait until he comes back because he will be much fatter then. The animals believe him, unaware that his Tia Monica will help him engineer a successful escape.

Go to Sleep, Gecko!: A Balinese Folktale. **Illustrated by Geraldo Valério. Little Rock, AR: August House, 2006. 32pp. ISBN 9780874837803.** `PreS–2`

Gecko complains to Elephant that the blinking lights of the fireflies are keeping him awake. When Elephant investigates, one complaint leads to another, but in the end all life is connected, and Gecko really needs the fireflies.

The Squeaky Door. **Illustrated by Mary Newell DePalma. New York: HarperCollins, 2006. 40pp. ISBN 9780060283735.** `PreS–3`

In this cumulative folktale adapted from a Puerto Rican folk song, a little boy is staying overnight at Grandma's. He assures her that he's not scared, but he gets nervous when the door squeaks shut. Grandma brings in different animals from the house and barn to comfort him, but chaos ensues and the bed breaks. The next day Grandma fixes the bed and oils the hinges, enabling her grandson to get a good night's sleep.

*Teeny Weeny Bop. **Illustrated by Diane Greenseid. Morton Grove, IL: Albert Whitman, 2006. 32pp. ISBN 9780807579923.** `Gr. K–2`

Teeny Weeny Bop finds a coin and rushes off to purchase a pet, but each animal is more inappropriate than the last, in this silly story.

🐾*Tunjur! Tunjur! Tunjur!: A Palestinian Folktale.* **Illustrated by Alik Arzoumanian. Tarrytown, NY: Marshall Cavendish, 2006. 32pp. ISBN 9780761452256.** `PreS–2`

From a story originally collected by Ibrahim Muhawi and Sharif Kanaana, Mac-Donald tells the tale of a woman who prays for a child and instead receives an animated and naughty cooking pot. Little Pot successfully steals from people, despite reprimands from her mother, until the king and a rich man fill her with goat dung so that she will stay home until she has learned her lesson. (ALAN)

*Little Rooster's Diamond Button. **Illustrated by Will Terry. Morton Grove, IL: Albert Whitman, 2007. 32pp. ISBN 9780807546444.** `Gr. 1–3`

In this Hungarian folktale, Little Rooster finds a diamond button, but a greedy king snatches it and punishes Little Rooster every time he tries to get it back. What the king does not know is that Little Rooster has a magic stomach, which enables him to defeat the king and win back not only his own treasure but the king's as well.

Bat's Big Game. **Illustrated by Eugenia Nobati. Morton Grove, IL: Albert Whitman, 2008. 30pp. ISBN 9780807505878.** `Gr. K–3`

The Animals and the Birds are preparing for a soccer match, and Bat cannot decide which team to choose. First he plays for the Animals, because they appear bigger and stronger, but when the Birds start to take the lead, he switches sides. When the Birds fall behind, he tries to dump them, but this time neither team will take him, and he wanders off alone to contemplate the value of sticking with the team.

Martin, Rafe.

The Rough-Face Girl. **Illustrated by David Shannon. New York: Philomel, 1992. Unpaged. ISBN 9780399218590.** `Gr. 3 & up`

In this retelling of an Algonquin folktale, two cruel sisters force the youngest sister to tend the fire, where the sparks burn her skin and hair. They each long to wed the Invisible Being, but they must pass the test of seeing him first. Neither of them can, but their youngest sister sees him everywhere, and so she is the girl he marries.

Mayer, Marianna.

Twelve Dancing Princesses. **Illustrated by Kinuko Y. Craft. New York: Morrow, 1989. 40pp. ISBN 9780688080518.** `Gr. K-3`

With polished prose, Mayer tells the tale of the twelve princesses who disappear each night to dance until dawn, and the gardener, Peter, who breaks the spell and frees them. Craft's luminous illustrations bring exceptional beauty to the tale.

Baba Yaga and Vasilisa the Brave. **Illustrated by Kinuko Y. Craft. New York: Morrow, 1994. ISBN 9780688085001.** `Gr. 3 & up`

In this Russian variant of the "Cinderella" tale, Vasilia's cruel stepmother and stepsisters send her to the witch Baba Yaga, who makes her a servant and gives her three impossible tasks. Accomplishing the tasks with the help of her magical doll, a gift from her mother, Vasilia defeats her step-relations and moves in with Baba Yaga. She learns from her the craft of weaving and creates things of such beauty that she draws the attention of the tsar, who asks her to be his wife. Craft's illustrations, a mix of watercolor, gouache, and oils, give the feeling of Russian folk-art paintings on black-lacquered wood.

Pegasus. **Illustrated by Kinuko Y. Craft. New York: Morrow, 1998. Unpaged. ISBN 9780688133825.** `Gr. K-3`

Basing her retelling on standard collections of Greek mythology, Mayer presents a fluidly told rendition of the adventures of the winged horse and the young hero, Bellerophon. Craft provides oil-over-watercolor illustrations in the sweeping style of eighteenth-century classicism.

McClintock, Barbara.

Cinderella. **New York: Scholastic, 2005. 32pp. ISBN 9780439561457.** `Gr.1-3`

After visiting Paris, McClintock was inspired to create a version of "Cinderella" set in the lavish court of Louis XIV. She faithfully adapted the Perrault version and created intricate pen-and-ink and watercolor illustrations to bring this tale to life in a new era.

McDermott, Gerald.

🐾*Anansi the Spider: A Tale from the Ashanti*. New York: Holt, 1972. 41pp. ISBN 9780805003109. `Gr. K–3`

Hero and trickster, Anansi the Spider embarks on an arduous journey. Each time he gets into trouble, one of his sons saves him, leaving Anansi with the dilemma of deciding which son to reward. Illustrated with bold colors and Ashanti motifs. (Caldecott Honor)

🐾*Arrow to the Sun: A Pueblo Indian Tale*. New York: Viking, 1974. 42pp. ISBN 9780670133697. `Gr. K–3` (SP)

This pueblo folktale relates the journey of a young boy in search of his father. Because he is descended from the Lord Sun, the boy is transformed into an arrow so that he may traverse the distance between the earth and the sun. The illustrations are comprised of bright geometric shapes in the style of pueblo art, providing a moving visual experience. (Caldecott Medal)

Zomo the Rabbit: A Trickster Tale from Africa. San Diego: Harcourt, 1992. Unpaged. ISBN 9780152999674. `Gr. K–3`

Zomo the rabbit, a trickster character who originated in the folklore of Nigeria, pleads with the Sky God to grant him wisdom. The Sky God sets him three impossible tasks. Clever Zomo tricks three animals into giving him what he needs, but in the end the joke is on him, for the wisdom that the Sky God gives is that rabbit must run quickly from the animals he has fooled, who are now quite angry with him. Gouache illustrations in vivid shades of pink, green, orange, and yellow are reminiscent of West African textiles.

🐾*Raven: A Trickster Tale from the Pacific Northwest*. San Diego: Harcourt, 1993. Unpaged. ISBN 9780152656614. `Gr. K–3`

Raven, a trickster character from Native American mythology, arranges to be born as a baby to the Sky Chief's daughter in order to find the sun and bring light to the world. Painting with boldly hued watercolors, McDermott patterns his art on totem pole figures, enriching the tale with authentic details. (ALAN, Boston Globe Honor, Caldecott Honor)

🐾*Coyote: A Trickster Tale from the American Southwest*. San Diego: Harcourt, 1994. Unpaged. ISBN 9780152207243. `Gr. K–3` (SP)

Coyote, a boastful trickster from Native American folktales, is featured in this retelling of a Zuni story. Coyote longs to fly and convinces a flock of crows to lend him some feathers. He soars through the air, bragging that he is now the greatest Coyote of all, which annoys the crows, who take back their feathers. Coyote crashes to earth, his tail ablaze. To this day coyotes' tails are tipped with black. Master of folklore art, here McDermott uses brilliant desert colors and pueblo pottery designs. (ALAN)

Jabuti the Tortoise: A Trickster Tale from the Amazon Rain Forest. San Diego: Harcourt, 2001. Unpaged. ISBN 9780152004965. `Gr. K–3`

In this tale from South America, Jabuti the tortoise plays the flute so beautifully that all the birds gather to listen. When Jabuti wants to fly high so he can play for the King of Heaven, bitter Vulture, who cannot forgive tortoise for the tricks he has played in the past, volunteers to take him. Before their journey is completed,

Vulture drops Jabuti back to earth, shattering his shell. The King of Heaven bids the birds seek out the tortoise. They piece him back together, but his shell still looks cracked. As a reward, the birds are given songs of their own as well as beautiful plumage. All except for Vulture, whose punishment is to remain dull and songless. McDermott illustrates this with radiant colors and geometric images.

Pig-Boy: A Trickster Tale from Hawai'i. Orlando, FL: Harcourt, 2009. Unpaged. ISBN 9780152165901. **Gr. K–3**

Kamapua'a is a divine trickster shape-shifter who is frequently a figure in Hawaiian mythology. Here he takes the form of Pig-Boy, with a nurturing human grandmother. He is always hungry, and his appetite gets him into one scrape after another. The tropically hued watercolors brilliantly illustrate the tale.

Monkey: A Trickster Tale from India. Boston: Houghton Mifflin Harcourt, 2010. 32pp. ISBN 9780152165963. **Gr. K–3**

Monkey loves eating mangos and would eat them all day if he could, but first he has to find a way to outwit Crocodile, who wants to make a meal of him.

McGill, Alice.

🌂*Way up and over Everything*. Boston: Houghton, 2008. 32pp. ISBN 9780618387960. **Gr. 1–3**

Jane, a sixteen-year-old slave on Ol' Man Deboreaux's Georgia plantation, watches as five new slaves from Africa arrive. After the first day of back-breaking labor, the five slaves slip away. The master and overseer call out the dogs to sniff them out. Jane follows furtively and witnesses the five swirling into the air and disappearing. Jane is filled with hope that one day she may be able to escape as well, which she does with her own children. (ALAN)

Miller, Bobbi.

One Fine Trade. Illustrated by Will Hillenbrand. New York: Holiday House, 2009. Unpaged. ISBN 9780823418367. **Gr. 1–3**

Based on a Southern folk song, this rollicking story traces the movements of trader Georgy Piney Woods, who makes a series of unusual trades in order to get his daughter a wedding dress.

Mollel, Tololwa M.

Ananse's Feast: An Ashanti Tale. Illustrated by Andrew Glass. New York: Clarion, 1997. 31pp. ISBN 9780395674024. **Gr. K–3**

Ananse the Spider has managed to save up enough food for a feast despite the drought that has spread across the land. When his friend Akye the Turtle turns up just as he is about to eat, Ananse cannot turn him away, but he does send him to the river to wash before eating. Turtle returns to Ananse only to be sent back to the river as he is muddy again. After the third time, Turtle realizes Ananse's trickery and devises a scheme of his own.

Subira Subira. **Illustrated by Linda Saport. New York: Clarion, 2000. ISBN 9780395918098. 32pp.** `Gr. K-3`

Mollel sets this traditional African tale in contemporary Tanzania. Tatu and her younger brother Maulidi are still recovering from their mother's death. Father must go to work and it's up to Tatu to look after Maulidi. He fights her every step of the way. In desperation, Tatu searches for the wise woman of the forest, MaMzuka. She instructs Tatu to use patience and courage to obtain three whiskers from a lion. Full of fear but persevering, Tatu lulls the lion with a Swahili song, and after three nights she presents the whiskers to MaMzuka. It's not the whiskers that her guide is interested in, it's the character Tatu showed in succeeding. If Tatu shows the same patience and courage in dealings with her brother, their relationship will change.

Moses, Will.

Hansel and Gretel. **New York: Philomel, 2006. 40pp. ISBN 9780399242342.** `Gr. 1-3`

Folk artist Moses faithfully retells the tale from the Brothers Grimm of the abandoned siblings, illustrating it with his signature folk art, done in oil on fabriano paper. Moses's landscapes are full of details as small as mushrooms and as large as bears. The witch's house gleams with tempting candy on the outside and is chock full of all the comforts of home on the inside.

Nishizuka, Koko.

The Beckoning Cat: Based on a Japanese Folktale. **Illustrated by Rosanne Litzinger. New York: Holiday House, 2009. ISBN 9780823420513.** `PreS-3`

In this Japanese folktale, young Yohei, who lives by the sea with his sick father, survives by selling fish door-to-door. On a rainy night, a wet and bedraggled white cat appears at his door. He dries her off and shares his small supper. Unfortunately, his father becomes so ill he cannot be left alone, and Yohei despairs. He doesn't know how he will sell fish now, but suddenly villagers start coming to him, led to his door by a white cat.

Orgel, Doris.

Doctor All-Knowing: A Folk Tale from the Brothers Grimm. **Illustrated by Alexandra Boiger. New York: Atheneum, 2008. 30pp. ISBN 9781416912460.** `PreS-3`

Crayfish, the peasant, and his daughter are tired of watered down porridge night after night, so he takes a rich man's advice and sets himself up as "Doctor All-Knowing." When an even wealthier man engages him to discover who has been stealing from him, a series of twists and turns leads to a resolution where father and daughter eat sumptuously every night.

Palatini, Margie.

Lousy Rotten Stinkin' Grapes. **Illustrated by Barry Moser. New York: Simon & Schuster, 2009. 22pp. ISBN 9780689802461.** `PreS-3`

In this amusing retelling of Aesop's "Fox and the Grapes," Fox devises a number of plans to reach the tempting and luscious grapes, but none of them succeed. Other animals attempt to offer less silly strategies, but Fox will not listen to any of them, and in the end storms off without his treat. Moser's watercolor illustrations play up the humor of the fable.

Perrault, Charles.

🎖*Puss in Boots*. **Illustrated by Fred Marcellino. New York: Farrar Straus Giroux, 1990. 32pp. ISBN 9780374361600.** `Gr. K–3`

Striking paintings that often provide a cat's-eye view of the world bring to life the story of the cat who fools a king, outwits an ogre, and arranges for his master to marry the princess. (Caldecott Honor)

Cinderella. **Retold by Amy Ehrlich. Illustrated by Susan Jeffers. New York: Dutton, 2004. 32pp. ISBN 9780525473459.** `Gr. 1–3`

Ehrlich's dramatic retelling of the ashes to princess tale is illuminated by Jeffers's lush pen-and-ink and dye illustrations.

Pinkney, Jerry.

🎖*The Little Red Hen*. **New York: Dial, 2006. 32pp. ISBN 9780803729353.** `PreS–3`

The ever-talented Pinkney illustrates this traditional tale, of the barnyard fowl who gets no help from her fellow animals with planting wheat and baking bread, with sumptuous graphite, ink, and watercolor art. He adds five little chicks for the Little Red Hen and slips in a self-portrait as the miller who grinds the wheat. An outstanding edition. (ALAN, New York Times Best Illustrated)

🎖*Little Red Riding Hood*. **New York: Little, Brown, 2007. 40pp. ISBN 9780316013550.** `Gr. K–3`

Pinkney remains faithful to the Grimm version of the story, his watercolors casting a brown-skinned girl in the role of the child who strays from the path on the way to her grandmother's house in the woods.

Pullman, Philip.

Puss in Boots: The Adventures of That Most Enterprising Feline. **Illustrated by Ian Beck. New York: Knopf, 2001. Unpaged. ISBN 9780375813542.** `Gr. 2 & up`

Pullman reworks the Perrault tale and regales his readers with the many adventures of the orphaned miller's son and his remarkable cat.

Aladdin and the Enchanted Lamp. **Illustrated by Sophy Williams. New York: Arthur A. Levine, 2005. 70pp. ISBN 9780439692557.** `Gr. 3 & up`

This master of imaginary worlds and classic battles between good and evil retells the Arabian story, focusing on the adventures of Aladdin, whose life changes completely when he finds the magic lamp, and setting the tale in the original location, China.

Ryan, Pam Muñoz.

Nacho and Lolita. **Illustrated by Claudia Rueda. New York: Scholastic, 2005. 40pp. ISBN 9780439269681.** `Gr. 1–3`

> This retelling of a Mexican folktale is a love story extraordinaire. When Nacho, a pitacoche bird with brilliantly colored plumage, arrives in San Juan Capistrano, he forms a bond with all of the swallows who migrate there, but especially with Lolita. As the time nears for the flock to fly away, Nacho desperately wants to go with them, but he is too big to make the long journey. Lolita does not think she will ever come back, but Nacho sacrifices all of his colorful feathers, which turn to flowers. They transform the landscape from dull to lush. He hopes now that Lolita will be able to find her way back to him.

San Souci, Robert D.

The Talking Eggs: A Folktale from the American South. **Illustrated by Jerry Pinkney. New York: Dutton, 1989. 32pp. ISBN 9780803706194.** `Gr. K–3`

> In this Creole folktale, sisters Blanche and Rose live with their cruel mother. Kind Blanche tolerates a lot of abuse from her mother and her sister, but when she meets a mysterious old woman, she is rewarded for obedience with magic talking eggs. Pinkney's ever-vibrant paintings add depth of feeling and detail. (ALAN, Caldecott Honor, Coretta Scott King Honor)

Brave Margaret: An Irish Adventure. **Illustrated by Sally Wern Comport. New York: Simon & Schuster, 1999. Unpaged. ISBN 9780689810725.** `Gr. K–3`

> The copper-haired Margaret longs for a life beyond the farm she tends in ancient Ireland, and when swashbuckling Simon allows her to persuade him to let her join his crew, she embarks on seafaring adventures. Battles with sea serpents, giants, and a crafty sorceress ensue, leading to a traditional happy ending.

Cinderella Skeleton. **Illustrated by David Catrow. San Diego: Silver Whistle/ Harcourt, 2000. 32pp. ISBN 9780152020033.** `Gr. 3 & up`

> In this macabre edition of "Cinderella," Cinderella Skeleton lives in a mausoleum with her horrifying stepmother, Skreech, and stepsisters Gristlene and Bony-Jane. When the time comes for her to attend the Halloween Ball, a good witch of the woods gives her a gown and slippers and provides dragon steeds to pull her funeral wagon to the ball. All proceeds in traditional fashion, except when this Cinderella flees at sunrise, she leaves not only her slipper behind, but her foot as well.

Little Gold Star: A Spanish American Cinderella Tale. Illustrated by Sergio Martinez. New York: HarperCollins, 2000. Unpaged. ISBN 9780688147808. `Gr. 1-3`

This Southwest version of "Cinderella" combines elements from European fairy tales, Christian imagery, and Spanish folklore and is set in New Mexico. Teresa and her father Tomas the shepherd live a quiet life in the high hills, until Tomas marries a miserable woman with two daughters of her own. As Tomas spends more time with his sheep, Teresa's treatment worsens, until the Blessed Mother appears to her and asks her to care for an old man and a child for one night. Teresa complies and is rewarded for her kindness by the Virgin Mary's kiss, which appears as a gold star on Teresa's forehead. Although her stepmother puts obstacles in her way, Teresa ends up with her own true love, Don Miguel.

The Secret of the Stones: A Folktale. Illustrated by James Ransome. New York: Phyllis Fogelman Books, 2000. Unpaged. ISBN 9780803716407. `Gr. 2 & up`

Based on a tale found in both the Bantu and African American cultures, San Souci sets the story in nineteenth-century rural America and relates the experience of a hardworking farm couple, John and Clara. One day when they are returning from the fields they come across two white stones, which they bring home. The next day, when they arrive home, they find their house has been tidied up, their dinner is made, and a welcoming fire burns merrily on the hearth. A neighbor with supernatural sight tells them the stones are ensorcelled children, and they must find a way to outwit the conjuror to free them from their stone prisons.

Little Pierre: A Cajun Story from Louisiana. Illustrated by David Catrow. San Diego: Harcourt, 2003. 32pp. ISBN 9780152024826. `Gr. 1-3`

In this Cajun "Tom Thumb," Little Pierre is the smallest of his brothers, but also the smartest. When he hears them plotting to take on the Swamp Ogre and rescue Marie-Louise, Little Pierre follows them and is the one to save the day (and the girl).

The Well at the End of the World. Illustrated by Rebecca Walsh. San Francisco: Chronicle, 2004. 41pp. ISBN 9781587172120. `Gr. K-3`

In this tale based on the British "The King of Colchester's Daughters," Princess Rosamund, who is plain but of great help to her father the king, goes on a quest to find the healing waters her father needs after he becomes gravely ill.

As Luck Would Have It: From the Brothers Grimm. Illustrated by Daniel San Souci. Atlanta, GA: August House, 2008. Unpaged. ISBN 978-0874838336. `Gr. K-3`

In this noodlehead tale, twin bear cubs Jonas and Juniper try to run the family farm while their parents are away, but one mishap follows another, and soon chaos reigns.

Shepard, Aaron.

The King O' the Cats. **Illustrated by Kristin Sorra. New York: Atheneum, 2004. Unpaged. ISBN 9780689820823. `Gr. 1–3`**

In this spooky story from England, sexton Peter Black has a series of encounters with extraordinary cats, culminating in Father Allen's cat declaring that he is now the King 'o the Cats.

One-Eye! Two-Eyes! Three-Eyes! A Very Grimm Fairy Tale. **Illustrated by Gary Clement. New York: Atheneum, 2006. 32pp. ISBN 9780689867408. `Gr. K–3`**

Two-Eyes is teased by her older sisters, One-Eye and Three-Eyes, because having two eyes is so unusual. She's also the one who does all the housework, until a mysterious old woman introduces magic into her life, which eventually leads to riding off to her happily ever after with a knight in shining armor.

Sierra, Judy.

The Gift of the Crocodile: A Cinderella Story. **Illustrated by Reynold Ruffins. New York: Simon & Schuster, 2000. Unpaged. ISBN 9780689821882. `Gr. 1–3`**

Damura, an Indonesian Cinderella, is mistreated by her new stepmother and stepsister, but is helped by Grandmother Crocodile who not only provides beautiful sarongs for her but also saves her life from another hungry crocodile.

Spirin, Gennadii.

The Tale of the Firebird. **New York: Philomel, 2002. 32pp. ISBN 9780399235849. `Gr. 2 & up`**

Adapted from a Russian fairy tale. Spirin spins his own version of a young prince's quest for the magical firebird. Illustrated with exquisitely delicate and elaborate illustrations evoking the classic Russian lacquer ware. A visually sumptuous tale.

Goldilocks and the Three Bears. **New York: Marshall Cavendish, 2009. 32pp. ISBN 9780761455967. `PreS–3`**

Spirin illustrates this tale of trespassing with figures dressed in rich Renaissance costumes, detailed settings, and characters filled with personality.

Storace, Patricia.

Sugar Cane: A Caribbean Rapunzel. **Illustrated by Raúl Colón. New York: Jump at the Sun, 2007. 48pp. ISBN 9780786807918. `Gr. 1–3`**

With a lilting Caribbean rhythm, Storace provides an island version of the Grimm tale. A young couple who live by the sea are expecting a child. When his pregnant wife yearns for Sugar Cane, the husband sets out to find some. Unfortunately, he steals it from Madame Fate's garden. A powerful sorceress, she demands the life of the child as payment. When Sugar Cane is a year old, Madam Fate locks her in a tower, where she is tutored by musical spirits. When a young musician called King hears her singing, he searches for her and sets in motion events that eventually lead to a wedding and a reunion with Sugar Cane's parents.

Taback, Simms.

🌸*Joseph Had a Little Overcoat.* New York: Viking, 1999. Unpaged. ISBN 9780670878550. **PreS–2**

This adaptation of a Yiddish folk song conveys the steps Joseph goes through to transform his jacket into something new each time it needs repair. Impressive gouache, watercolor, and collage illustrations make use of die-cut holes to highlight aspects of each new garment. (ALAN, Caldecott Medal)

Tchana, Katrin.

Sense Pass King: A Story from Cameroon. Illustrated by Trina Schart Hyman. New York: Holiday House, 2002. 32pp. ISBN 9780823415779. **Gr. K–3**

At an early age, the child named Ma'antah demonstrates such cleverness that she earns the name Sense Pass King. Naturally the king, an indolent monarch, is not pleased with this. He brings Ma'antah to live in the palace and takes credit for her deeds. When the people grow annoyed past endurance with his dishonesty, they oust him from power and crown Sense Pass King queen. Hyman's striking acrylic paintings shine with beauty and emotion.

Wiesner, David, and Kim Kahng.

The Loathsome Dragon. Rev. ed. Illustrated by David Wiesner. New York: Clarion, 2005. 32pp. ISBN 9780618543595. **Gr. K–3**

Princess Margaret is turned into a loathsome dragon by her jealous stepmother, who is also an enchantress. She terrorizes the people, but instead of trying to kill her, they send for her brother, Prince Richard, the only one who can break the spell.

Willey, Margaret.

<u>**The Clever Beatrice Series.**</u> Illustrated by Heather Solomon. **PreS–2**

Clever Beatrice is a character from the folklore of Michigan's Upper Peninsula, an area with a strong French Canadian influence. She's a plucky heroine who proves that brains can definitely defeat brawn.

🌸*Clever Beatrice: An Upper Peninsula Conte.* New York: Atheneum, 2001. Unpaged. ISBN 9780689832543.

Young Beatrice is full of spirit, but her family is poor. When she asks her mother how she might get some money to help out the family, her mother tells her about a rich giant who loves to gamble. Beatrice sets off to find the giant and succeeds in winning away his fortune. (ALAN, Charlotte Zolotow Award)

Clever Beatrice and the Best Little Pony. New York: Atheneum, 2004. Unpaged. ISBN 9780689853395.

Every morning Beatrice finds her pony is exhausted and concludes someone is riding him at night. Her mother advises her to ask the baker for help, since he is an expert in things unseen. Although Beatrice does as her mother suggests, it is Beatrice herself who concocts a way to catch the lutin, a tiny elf-like creature, and stop him from tiring her pony.

A Clever Beatrice Christmas. New York: Atheneum, 2006. 40pp. ISBN 978-0689870170.

To convince her doubtful friends in the village that Pere Noel is real, Beatrice tricks him out of a button, a sleigh bell, and a curl from his beard. Or at least she thinks she does.

Young, Ed.

🕯*Lon Po Po: A Red-Riding Hood Story from China.* New York: Philomel, 1989. 32pp. ISBN 9780399216190. **Gr. 1–3**

When three sisters discover a wolf in their home pretending to be their grandmother, they trick him out of the house and lure him to his death. The astonishing watercolor and pastel pictures vividly portray a mystical Chinese landscape and a threatening wolf, juxtaposing the abstract and realistic in a way that heightens the emotion of the story. (ALAN, Boston Globe Award, Caldecott Medal)

🕯*Seven Blind Mice.* New York: Philomel, 1992. Unpaged. ISBN 9780399222610. **Gr. K–3**

In his reworking of a fable from India, "The Blind Men and the Elephant," Young presents the story of seven blind mice who encounter something unknown, one on each day of the week. The final mouse puts all the clues together and realizes the something is actually an elephant. Young creates a visual delight with boldly colored collages. (ALAN, Boston Globe Honor, Caldecott Honor)

What about Me? New York: Philomel, 2002. Unpaged. ISBN 9780399236242. **Gr. 1–3**

A cumulative teaching tale from the ancient Sufi tradition, relates a young boys quest for knowledge. He begins by asking a Grand Master for advice, who sends him off to find a carpet. The carpet maker sends him for thread, and so he continues, obtaining items from different people and being sent on to another, until he comes full circle with the carpet made and given to the Grand Master, where he learns that he has already gained what he has been seeking without even realizing it. Illustrated with Young's signature collages and watercolor paintings.

The Sons of the Dragon King: A Chinese Legend. New York: Simon & Schuster, 2004. Unpaged. ISBN 9780689851841. **Gr. 1–3**

When the Dragon King hears unsettling rumors about how his nine sons are frittering away their talents in useless pursuits, he finds each son and steers them into using his gifts wisely. Young balances his ink-and-brush illustrations with deft cut-paper pictures.

Zelinsky, Paul O.

🕯*Rumpelstiltskin.* New York: Dutton, 1986. 37pp. ISBN 9780525442653. **Gr. K–3**

Zelinsky smoothly retells the story of the miller's daughter and the king who wanted her to turn straw into gold. He includes details from a number of nineteenth-century Grimm versions and illustrates his medieval setting with rich colors that glow with beauty and life. This is a treat to read aloud and to display. (ALAN, Caldecott Honor)

🐾 *Rapunzel*. **New York: Dutton, 1997. Unpaged. ISBN 9780525456070.** `Gr. K-3` **9**

Zelinksy researched the pre-Grimm Brothers' origins of "Rapunzel" in French and Italian tales and here provides a version about the child who grows to womanhood locked in a tower, which includes a marriage ceremony with the prince who falls in love with her, and her resulting pregnancy. The magnificent illustrations richly depict the people, costumes, and architecture of the Italian Renaissance, with many allusions to the art of the fifteenth, sixteenth, and seventeenth centuries. A breathtaking achievement. (ALAN, Caldecott Medal) **10**

Science Fiction

Science fictions is often linked with fantasy because they are sister genres, occupying opposite ends of the speculative fiction continuum. Both genres spin stories around the answer to the "what if" musing. What if people could fly, what if unicorns existed, what if animals could talk? Fantasy answers the questions with magic and imaginary devices, and science fiction with scientific extrapolation. There is not as much science fiction published for picture book audiences, perhaps because the science requires a certain knowledge base that young readers and listeners have yet to develop. Nonetheless, aliens, robots, and interplanetary travel do appear in picture books to pique scientific curiosity. **11** **12**

Breathed, Berkeley.

Mars Needs Moms. **New York: Philomel, 2007. 38pp. ISBN 9780399247361.** `Gr. K-3` **13**

Milo doesn't think there is anything so special about moms, until his mother is kidnapped by Martians. Milo races after the culprits and sneaks aboard their rocket to rescue his mother, and along the way discovers the importance of mothers.

Gall, Chris.

There's Nothing to Do on Mars. **New York: Little, Brown, 2008. 29pp. ISBN 9780316166843.** `Gr. K-3` **14**

Davey is not happy that his family has moved to Mars. When he declares that he is bored, his father tells him to go out and play. With his robotic dog along, he explores the Martian landscape. Though he finds one amazing thing after another, nothing impresses him until he unwittingly locates a gushing water source. **15**

Hurd, Thatcher.

Moo Cow Kaboom! New York: HarperCollins, 2003. Unpaged. ISBN 978-0060505011. **PreS–2**

> When a loud Kaboom awakens Farmer George, he discovers that Moo Cow has been cownapped by the alien Zork. Zork whisks Moo Cow over the moon and to the planet 246 to become the star of their rodeo.

Jeffers, Oliver.

The Way Back Home. New York: Philomel, 2008. 32pp. ISBN 9780399250743. **PreS– 2** (SP)

> When a young boy finds an airplane in his closet, he decides to go for a flight. He gets stuck on the moon along with a Martian, and only by working together can they return home.

Landry, Leo.

Space Boy. Boston: Houghton Mifflin, 2007. 29pp. ISBN 9780618605682. **PreS–1**

> Nicholas is sleepy, but there is too much noise in his house, so he dons his space suit, boards his rocket ship, and soars to the moon. In blissful quiet, he munches on his snack and enjoys leaping in low gravity, until the beautiful blue planet calls him home again.

McCall, Bruce.

Marveltown. New York: Farrar, Straus & Giroux, 2008. Unpaged. ISBN 978-0374399252. **Gr. K–3**

> Marveltown is a future world in which a myriad of amazing inventions improve the life of its citizens, and even children are inventors. When the helping robots malfunction, though, it's the kids who fix the problem.

McClements, George.

Baron Von Baddie and the Ice Ray Incident. Orlando, FL: Harcourt, 2008. 32pp. ISBN 9780152061388. **PreS–2**

> Baron Von Baddie, a mad scientist who designs robots to wreak havoc, and his nemesis superhero, Captain Kapow, regularly battle each other until the day Baron Von Baddie invents a device that completely freezes Captain Kapow. Free to create chaos, Von Baddie works his evil wiles on a helpless world, until he realizes how boring it is. He develops a heat ray to thaw the Captain, and the two return to their respective roles in the war of good versus evil.

McNaughton, Colin.

We're Off to Look for Aliens. Cambridge, MA: Candlewick, 2008. 40pp. ISBN 9780763636364. **PreS–3**

> When Dad's new book arrives, he shows it to his family, but he can't handle waiting for their response, so he goes for a walk while they read the story of a man and his dog who journey to Mars and meet aliens. They befriend them and the man

marries an alien. When Dad returns home, his family wonders why anyone would want to read a true story.

O'Malley, Kevin.

Captain Raptor and the Moon Mystery. **Illustrated by Patrick O'Brien. New York: Walker, 2005. 32pp. ISBN 9780802789358. Gr. K–3**

A UFO lands on the moon Eon, and Captain Raptor and his crew of dinosaurs board their space ship and leave the Planet Jurassica to investigate. After braving a bevy of breathtaking adventures, they discover the aliens are humans and help the visitors return home. The boldly colored, graphic novel style illustrations heighten the action of the story.

Captain Raptor and the Space Pirates. **Illustrated by Patrick O'Brien. New York: Walker, 2007. 30pp. ISBN 9780802795717. Gr. K–3**

When space pirates steal Jurassica's most treasured jewels from the Imperial Palace, Captain Raptor and his faithful crew zoom into space to track down and confront the dastardly villains.

Reynolds, Aaron.

Snowbots. **Illustrated by David Barneda. New York: Knopf, 2010. 40pp. ISBN 9780375858734. PreS–2**

A variety of brightly colored robots have a glorious day enjoying their games in the freshly fallen snow.

Scieszka, Jon.

Robot Zot! **Illustrated by David Shannon. New York: Simon & Schuster, 2009. 48pp. ISBN 9781416963943. PreS–3**

When Robot Zot invades earth, he lands in a suburb and does battle with kitchen appliances in order to rescue the Queen of all Earth, a toy cell phone. Once the phone is safe, he zooms off to save more of those in need. Over-the-top humor and zany illustrations will make readers and listeners laugh out loud.

Favorites

The Magic Hat by Mem Fox

The Baby Beebee Bird by Diane Redfield Massie

Piggie Pie by Margie Palatini

The Lion & the Mouse by Jerry Pinkney

Robot Zot by Jon Scieszka

Where the Wild Things Are by Maurice Sendak

And to Think That I Saw It on Mulberry Street by Dr. Seuss

Good Night, Good Knight by Shelley Moore Thomas

Flotsam by David Wiesner

Rumpelstiltskin illustrated by Paul O. Zelinsky

Resources

Barr, Catherine, and John Thomas Gillespie. *Best Books for Children: Preschool Through Grade 6*. Westport, CT: Libraries Unlimited, 2006.

———. *Best Books for Children, Supplement to the 8th Edition: Preschool Through Grade 6*. Westport, CT: Libraries Unlimited, 2007.

Barstow, Barbara, Judith Riggle, and Leslie Molnar. *Beyond Picture Books: Subject Access to Best Books for Beginning Readers*. Westport, CT: Libraries Unlimited, 2008.

Freeman, Judy. *Books Kids Will Sit Still For 3: A Read-Aloud Guide*. Westport, CT: Libraries Unlimited, 2006.

———. *The Winners! Handbook: A Closer Look at Judy Freeman's Top-Rated Children's Books of 2007, Grades K–6*. Westport, CT: Libraries Unlimited, 2008.

———. *The Winners! Handbook: A Closer Look at Judy Freeman's Top-Rated Children's Books of 2008, Grades K–6*. Westport, CT: Libraries Unlimited, 2009.

Lima, Carolyn W., and John A. Lima. *A to Zoo: Subject Access to Children's Picture Books*. Westport, CT: Libraries Unlimited, 2008.

Pearl, Nancy. *Book Crush: For Kids and Teens—Recommended Reading for Every Mood, Moment, and Interest*. Seattle, WA: Sasquatch Books, 2007.

Silvey, Anita. *100 Best Books for Children*. Boston: Houghton Mifflin, 2004.

Author and Illustrator Index

Title Index

Subject Index

Specialty Stories Index

Awards Index